P9-EEF-310

Before you leave, you might want to give Mother Nature a call.

Remove card and see instructions on back.

Frommer's®
3 Free Minutes of Weather Information

THE WEATHER CHANNEL®

- Current conditions and forecasts for over 1,500 locations worldwide

- Severe-weather information, including winter storm advisories and tropical storm updates

- Wake-up call, complete with forecast for city of your choice

- Special-interest forecasts, featuring ski resort, boating and other outdoor conditions

Easy.
Convenient. Accurate.

During your free call, an automated operator will offer you an option to add $10, $20 or $30 to your phone card using any major credit card. Once a payment option is selected, five free minutes of long distance will be added to your phone card.

Use your card to:

• Save 20% on comprehensive weather information.

• Save up to 60% on long-distance calls to anywhere in the U.S., anytime.

• Save 20% on other helpful information, including lottery, sports and more.

THE WEATHER CHANNEL

Weather fans you're not alone.

Travel Discount Coupon

This coupon entitles you to special discounts when you book your trip through the

TRAVEL NETWORK®
RESERVATION SERVICE

Hotels ♦ Airlines ♦ Car Rentals ♦ Cruises
All Your Travel Needs

Here's what you get: *

♦ A discount of $50 USD on a booking of $1,000** or more for two or more people!

♦ A discount of $25 USD on a booking of $500** or more for one person!

♦ Free membership for three years, and 1,000 free miles on enrollment in the unique Travel Network Miles-to-Go® frequent-traveler program. Earn one mile for every dollar spent through the program. Redeem miles for free hotel stays starting at 5,000 miles. Earn free roundtrip airline tickets starting at 25,000 miles.

♦ Personal help in planning your own, customized trip.

♦ Fast, confirmed reservations at any property recommended in this guide, subject to availability.***

♦ Special discounts on bookings in the U.S. and around the world.

♦ Low-cost visa and passport service.

♦ Reduced-rate cruise packages and special car rental programs worldwide.

Visit our website at http://www.travelnetwork.com/Frommer or call us globally at 201-567-8500, ext. 55. In the U.S., call toll-free at 1-888-940-5000, or fax 201-567-1838. In Canada, call at 1-905-707-7222, or fax 905-707-8108. In Asia, call 60-3-7191044, or fax 60-3-7185415.

* To qualify for these travel discounts, at least a portion of your trip must include destinations covered in this guide. No more than one coupon discount may be used in any 12-month period, for destinations covered in this guide. Cannot be combined with any other discount or promotion.

**These are U.S. dollars spent on commissionable bookings.

***A $10 USD fee, plus fax and/or phone charges, will be added to the cost of bookings at each hotel not linked to the reservation service. Customers must approve these fees in advance. If only hotels of this kind are booked, the traveler(s) must also purchase roundtrip air tickets from Travel Network for the trip.

Valid until December 31, 1998. Terms and conditions of the Miles-to-Go® program are available on request by calling 201-567-8500, ext 55.

PAR234

Frommer's® 98

Paris

**by Darwin Porter
and Danforth Prince**

Macmillan • USA

ABOUT THE AUTHORS

Veteran travel writers **Darwin Porter** and **Danforth Prince** have written numerous best-selling Frommer guides, notably to England, France, the Caribbean, Italy, and Germany. Porter, a bureau chief for *The Miami Herald* at the age of 21, has lived in Paris periodically and written about the city for many years. Prince also has lived in the city for many years as a member of the Paris bureau for *The New York Times*.

MACMILLAN TRAVEL

A Simon & Schuster Macmillan Company
1633 Broadway
New York, NY 10019

Find us online at **www.frommers.com**
or on America Online at Keyword: **Frommers**.

ISBN 0-02-861650-2
ISSN 0899-3203

Editor: Dan Glover
Production Editor: Michael Thomas
Map Director: Douglas Stallings
Design by Michele Laseau
Digital Cartography by Ortelius Design and Peter Bogaty

SPECIAL SALES

Bulk purchases (10+ copies) of Frommer's and selected Macmillan travel guides are available to corporations, organizations, mail-order catalogs, institutions, and charities at special discounts, and can be customized to suit individual needs. For more information write to: Special Sales, Macmillan General Reference, 1633 Broadway, New York, NY 10019.

Manufactured in the United States of America

Contents

List of Maps

AN INVITATION TO THE READER

In researching this book, we discovered many wonderful places—hotels, restaurants, shops, and more. We're sure you'll find others. Please tell us about them, so we can share the information with your fellow travelers in upcoming editions. If you were disappointed with a recommendation, we'd love to know that, too. Please write to:

Darwin Porter and Danforth Prince
Frommer's Paris '98
Macmillan Travel
1633 Broadway
New York, NY 10019

AN ADDITIONAL NOTE

Please be advised that travel information is subject to change at any time—and this is especially true of prices. We therefore suggest that you write or call ahead for confirmation when making your travel plans. The authors, editors, and publisher cannot be held responsible for the experiences of readers while traveling. Your safety is important to us, however, so we encourage you to stay alert and be aware of your surroundings. Keep a close eye on cameras, purses, and wallets, all favorite targets of thieves and pickpockets.

WHAT THE SYMBOL MEANS

✪ Frommer's Favorites

Our favorite places and experiences—outstanding for quality, value, or both.

The following abbreviations are used for credit cards:

AE	American Express	DISC	Discover
CB	Carte Blanche	MC	MasterCard
DC	Diners Club	V	Visa

FIND FROMMER'S ONLINE

Arthur Frommer's Outspoken Encyclopedia of Travel (www.frommers.com) offers more than 6,000 pages of up-to-the-minute travel information—including the latest bargains and candid, personal articles updated daily by Arthur Frommer himself. No other Web site offers such comprehensive and timely coverage of the world of travel.

Paris at a Glance

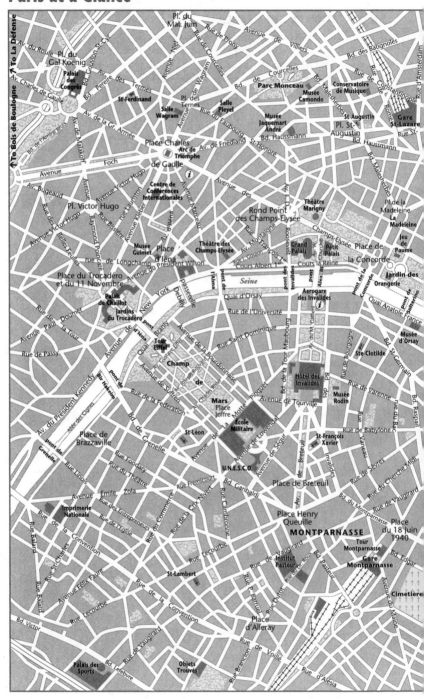

Paris by Arrondissement

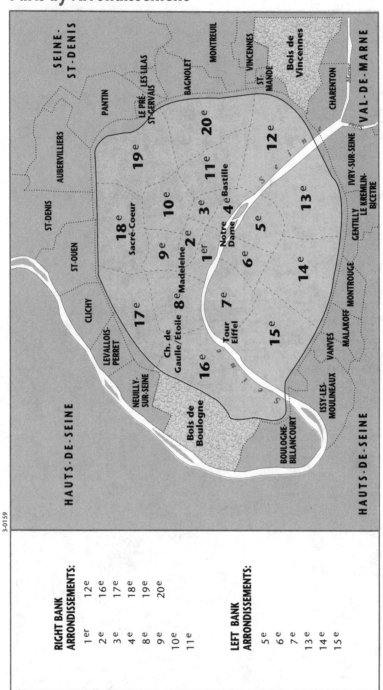

RIGHT BANK ARRONDISSEMENTS:

1er	12e
2e	16e
3e	17e
4e	18e
8e	19e
9e	20e
10e	
11e	

LEFT BANK ARRONDISSEMENTS:

5e
6e
7e
13e
14e
15e

3-0159

Introducing the City of Light

The government may be in shambles, the economy a disaster, the natives restless, but Paris has more *joie de vivre* as it faces the millennium than it did throughout the 1970s and 1980s. No one is proclaiming it is the most happening city in Europe: London, temporarily at least, has staked out that claim. But Paris is still queen of the continent. It's got more museums, more nighttime diversions, better hotels, more amusements, better shops, and the greatest brigade of talented chefs, both young and old, than it's ever had in its history.

If you're heading here for the first or the 50th time, the discovery of the City of Light and the experience of making it your own is and always has been the most compelling reason to visit. Neighborhoods such as Montmartre and Montparnasse, St-Germain and Le Marais, are waiting to be explored for the first time, or to be rediscovered by a returning visitor. In some ways, they remain the same, as if etched in stone, but after a second look it's obvious that they have changed. Everything is new and different—not always better, but always fresh and exciting.

The Seine has always flowed through Paris's culture and history, an inspiration for painters and lovers, sheltering in its gentle S-shaped curve that pair of islands, Ile de la Cité and Ile St-Louis, upon which the city was born.

Immediately, this river that divides the city geographically and culturally demands that you make a choice. Are you a Right Bank (Rive Droite) or a Left Bank (Rive Gauche) type of person?

All *quartiers* (quarters) are different, and since your experiences will likely be formed by where you choose to stay, so will your memory of Paris. Do you prefer a hotel deep in the heart of St-Germain, sleeping in a room where Jean-Paul Sartre and Simone de Beauvoir might have spent the night? Or do you identify with the Rive Droite, preferring to sleep in sumptuous quarters at the Crillon Hotel? Do you prefer looking for that special curio in a dusty shop on the Left Bank's rue Jacob, or inspecting the latest haute couture of Karl Lagerfeld, Jean Patou, or Guy Laroche in a Right Bank boutique along the avenue Montaigne?

If you're a first-timer, everything in Paris, of course, is new. But if you've been away for a long time, expect changes: Taxi drivers may no longer correct your fractured French, but address you in English—and that's tantamount to a revolution. More Parisians have a rudimentary knowledge of English, and the country, at least at first glance, seems less hysterically xenophobic than in past years. Part of this derives from Parisians' interest in music, videos, and films from foreign countries, and part from France's growing awareness of its role within a united Europe.

Yet France has never been more concerned about the loss of its unique identity within a landscape that has attracted an increasing number of immigrants from its former colonies. Many have expressed the legitimate concern that France will continue to lose the battle to keep its language strong, distinct, and unadulterated by foreign slang or catchwords. But as the country approaches the millennium, foreign tourists spending much-needed cash are no longer perceived as foes or antagonists. *Au contraire:* The rancor of France's collective xenophobia has been increasingly redirected toward the many immigrants seeking better lives in Paris, where the infrastructure has nearly been stretched to its limits.

Though Paris is clearly a city in flux culturally and socially, it still lures travelers for all the same reasons. Grand indestructible sights such as the Tour Eiffel are still here, as is the spruced-up Champs-Elysées—both are as crowded as ever. The beauty of Paris is still overwhelming, especially in the illumination of night. The City of Light, one of the premier tourist destinations in the world, always provides a memorable performance.

1 Frommer's Favorite Paris Experiences

- **A Walk along the Faubourg St-Honoré.** In the 1700s the wealthiest of Parisians resided in the Faubourg St-Honoré; today the quarter is home to the stores that cater to the rich. Even if you don't buy anything, it's great to window-shop the big names: Hermès, Larouche, Courrèges, Cardin, Saint-Laurent.
- **An Afternoon of Cafe-Sitting.** The cafe is integral to life in Paris. Whether you have one small coffee or the most expensive cognac in the house, nobody will hurry you.
- **Afternoon Tea at Angélina.** Drinking tea in London has its charm, but the Parisian *salon de thé* is unique. Skip over those cucumber-and-watercress sandwiches and delve into a rich, luscious dessert such as Mont Blanc, a creamy puree of sweetened chestnuts once beloved by the Aga Khan. Try the grandest Parisian tea salon of them all, **Angélina,** 226 rue de Rivoli, 1er (Métro: Concorde).
- **A Night at the Ballet.** Renoir may have detested the **Opéra Garnier,** at the place de l'Opéra, for an opulence he felt bordered on vulgarity, but since its opening it has been the center for ballet in Paris. An evening here takes you back to the Second Empire world of marble and gilt and grand staircases, all sheltered under a controversial ceiling by Chagall. Dress with pomp and circumstance.
- **A Day at the Races.** Paris has eight tracks for horse racing. The most famous and the classiest is **Longchamp,** in the Bois de Boulogne, 16e. It's the site of the Prix de l'Arc de Triomphe and the Grand Prix. These and other top races are major social events, so you'll have to dress up, of course. Take the Métro to Porte d'Auteuil, then a special bus from there to the track. *Paris Turf,* a racing newspaper, and other weekly entertainment magazines have details about racing times.
- **A Stroll along the Seine.** Painters such as Sisley, Turner, and Monet have fallen under the River Seine's spell. Lovers still walk hand in hand alongside it, and anglers still cast their lines here. *Clochards* still seek a home for the night under its bridges, and on its banks the *bouquinistes* still peddle their postcards, perhaps 100-year-old pornography, or a tattered edition of an old history of Indochina. Some

athletic visitors walk the full 7-mile stretch of the river through the city, but it is enough to confine your stroll to central Paris, passing the Louvre, Notre-Dame, and the Pont Neuf.

- **An Ice Cream at Bertillion.** A landmark on Ile St-Louis, Bertillion is said to offer the world's best selection of ice creams. Try rhubarb, fresh melon, kumquat, black currant, or any exotic fresh fruit in season—more than 50 flavors to choose from and nothing artificial. Parisians have flocked to this place in such numbers that *gendarmes* have been called out to direct the traffic of ice cream aficionados.

- **An Evening at the Folies-Bergère.** Though often attacked and denounced, this Parisian showcase has been pleasing audiences since 1868, even though classic acts like Chevalier, Mistinguett, and Josephine Baker, who performed her famous banana dance here, vanished long ago. The Tour Eiffel cancan is a bit corny, and the show has become less daring. But those ladies in their sequins, feathers, and pompoms still evoke an older Paris, immortalized on a Manet canvas, and the show, tacky or not, seems to go on forever.

- **An Evening of Opera.** The Opéra Bastille was inaugurated in July 1989 to compete with the grande dame of the Paris musical scene, the Opéra Garnier. With 2,700 seats in its main hall, the Bastille is the largest opera house in France, and features opera and symphony performances in four different concert halls. Wear your most elegant evening clothes and soak up the glorious music in an opulent atmosphere that is very, very cultured and very, very French.

- **Discovering Hidden Montmartre.** This district has earned a reputation as the most touristy part of Paris. It's true that buses swarm the area surrounding Sacré-Coeur; yet, far removed from here, another neighborhood unfolds—that of the true Montmartrois. To discover it, drift onto the back streets away from the souvenir shops. Many Parisian families have lived in the neighborhood for generations; actors, producers, journalists, and directors are restoring other homes. Arm yourself with a good map and seek out such streets as rue Lepic (refresh yourself at the Lux Bar at no. 12); rue Constance; rue Tholozé (with its view over the rooftops of Paris); the lively rue des Abbesses, or rue Germain-Pilon—none of these streets are famous or celebrated, but each has buildings whose detailing shows the pride and care that permeates Paris's architecture. Flank out from these, and discover dozens of other streets on your own.

- **Checking Out the Marchés.** A daily Parisian ritual is to amble through one of the open-air markets to purchase fresh food to be consumed that day—a ripe and properly creamy Camembert, or a pumpkin-gold cantaloupe to be consumed before sundown. Even if you're staying in a hotel room without a kitchen, you can partake of this time-honored French tradition and prepare for a picnic in one of the city's parks. Like artists, the vendors arrange their wares into a mosaic of vibrant colors. *Sanguine*, an Italian citrus whose juice is the color of a brilliant orange sunset; ruby-red peppers; golden yellow bananas from Martinique—all dazzle the eye. Our favorite market? The one on rue Montorgeuil, beginning at rue Rambuteau, 1er (Métro: Les Halles). On mornings at this grubby little cluster of food stalls, we've spotted some of France's finest chefs adding to their larders in anticipation of a day at their stoves.

- **Cocktails at Willi's.** Back in the early 1970s, the first-time visitor to Paris might arrive with a copy of Hemingway's *A Moveable Feast* and, taking the author's endorsement to heart, head first for Harry's Bar at *Sank roo doe Noo*. Harry's is still here and now draws an older, conservative clientele. Today's young, chic crowd heads for Willi's, currently in vogue; it's found at 13 rue des Petits-Champs, 1er

(Métro: Bourse, Louvre, or Palais-Royal). The young, long-haired bartenders are mostly English, as are the waitresses, dressed in Laura Ashley garb. The place, which gained popularity through word of mouth, is like an informal club for Brits, Australians, and Yanks, especially in the afternoon. Some 300 wines await your choice.

- **Calling on the Dead.** You don't have to be a ghoul to be thrilled by an afternoon at the most famous cemetery in Europe: Cimetière du Père-Lachaise. Chances are, one of your "favorites" will be resting here, and you can pay your respects to all the gang—Gertrude Stein and Alice B. Toklas, Jim Morrison, Oscar Wilde, and most definitely Edith Piaf and Isadora Duncan. It is not just the graves themselves that provide fascination, although Abélard and Héloïse, Chopin, Proust, and Delacroix lie here too; it is the tomb designs themselves that are eerie and intriguing. Laid out in 1803 on the slopes of a hill in Ménilmontant, the cemetery offers a surprise a minute in elaborate, often bizarre monuments, unexpected views, and ornate sculpture.

- **A Day at Fauchon.** "I'd much rather spend a day at Fauchon than a night at the Comédie-Française," a Frenchman confided to us. Perhaps he's right. An exotic world of food, Fauchon has a vast array of treasures. More than 20,000 products from the far corners of the globe are sold here. It's been called a "supermarket for millionaires," but it democratically maintains a reasonably priced self-service cafeteria for those who aren't. Whatever you've dreamed about in a foodstuff is here in aisle after aisle of coffees, spices, pastries, fruits, vegetables, and rare Armagnacs. Take your pick: Toganese mangoes, smoked Scottish salmon, preserved cocks' combs, rose petal jelly from Romania, blue-red pomegranates from India, golden brown dates from Tunisia (only from the most famous oasis, of course), larks stuffed with foie gras, dark morels from France's rich earth, reindeer's tongue from Finland, century-old eggs from China, and a Creole punch from Martinique that's reputed to be the best on earth.

- **Sneaking Away from It All.** When the glory and pomp of Paris overcome us, we slip away to **St-Germain-en-Laye,** 13 miles to the northwest. Take the RER (Réseau Express Régional) train, line A1. This suburb was once the residence of the kings of France, everybody from François I to Louis XIV ("The Sun King"), who was born here. Visitors often overlook this area, but Parisians adore it and often come here to escape the summer heat. You can visit the **Château Vieux** where Louis XIV lived, but mostly you'll want to wander around, inspecting the streets, parks, and gardens. A meal at the **Pavillon Henri IV,** a hotel with a restaurant, brings a summer day to perfection. It's named for the king who in the 1500s built a home on this site for his illegitimate children. Dumas wrote *The Three Musketeers* at the pavillon in 1843, and earlier, the Sun King romped (among other things) with Madame de Montespan. Whatever your main dish, you'll want to order it with béarnaise sauce, which is said to have been invented here.

2 The City Today

We need to recall Charles Dickens in his *Tale of Two Cities* to evoke the Paris of today: "It was the best of times; it was the worst of times." Of course, if he had looked at today's government only, he might skip the part about "the best of times." Still, despite its troubles, Paris has never looked better and has never been more accessible and international.

The entire world has arrived on the city's doorstep. Some come to visit and leave money behind. (Parisians especially like that kind of visitor.) Friction, however, has accompanied another kind of visitor: the one that has come to find a new life. A sizable number of Parisians have balked at this drain on their resources. Others are more welcoming, in the way they were to black artists like Josephine Baker in the 1920s or author James Baldwin in the 1960s, both of whom came to Paris to find an audience, acceptance, and honor.

Many Parisians view the immigrant population in positive terms, as a group that has diversified French society and had an important impact on the country's culture. The impact is evident in the vast array of new restaurants opening in Paris, with cuisines as diverse as Vietnamese, Senegalese, and Martinique Creole. The immigrants have also changed Paris's nightlife, bringing music from their own lands. In Paris today, you can find just as fine a salsa band as you can in Santo Domingo.

But conflicts are inevitable between the newly arriving citizens and those who find themselves living in already overcrowded Paris. This conflict boiled over in the summer of 1996 when nearly 300 African immigrants, slated for deportation, sought refuge in the Paris church of St. Bernard de la Chapelle, where they went on a hunger strike to protest. The police stormed the church, breaking down its doors with axes and whisking the immigrants away to detention centers. Many students and intellectuals claimed that this violent ratification of the 1994 immigration laws was nothing more than an attempt by the current administration to redirect blame for its inability to solve France's social and economic problems. Opposing them were French right-wingers who felt that such a crackdown against illegal immigration was long overdue.

Regardless of how Parisians were split on the issue, the government sent a message to the world that it is much less of a safe haven for the tired, the poor, the homeless, and the hungry from other lands. A new and tougher Parisian government dawned that summer in 1996, and it appears that the immigration issue will divide the city long past the millennium.

The year 1996 continued poorly for the rulers of Paris, this time in the form of terrorism, with bombs exploding and claiming lives in post offices and other government buildings. Paris's most violent enemies have promised more of the same. Some bombs were laid by Algerian militants upset with France's active support of Algeria's president Liamine Zeroual; others were detonated in response to then-Prime Minister Alain Juppé's hard-line approach toward separatist movements in the Basque regions of France and on the island of Corsica.

As strikes plagued and partially crippled Paris in 1997, everyone from civil servants to truck drivers joined to protest high unemployment rates because of budget cutbacks and layoffs. Malcontentment has entrenched itself like a cloud over Paris as President Jacques Chirac rules from his uneasy seat.

In spite of this economic withering and civic unrest, Paris and the rest of France remain the world's greatest tourist destination. Unless a strike or protest is called while you're visiting, you'll never encounter the turmoil going on behind the scenes. Although some of Paris's newer buildings are falling apart, the city looks more glamorous than ever, as a result of such monumental projects as the cleaning of the Louvre, the Opéra, and Notre Dame.

Lovers still walk arm in arm along the Seine as children scamper about in the Tuileries, and cafes fill with ripostes and laughter, and women dance the cancan at the Moulin Rouge—hardly the posture of a country on the brink.

The France of 1998 has more museums and attractions than ever before; it's never had as many star chefs earning Michelin stars (not just in Paris but also throughout the country); and more than ever the French are truly welcoming tourists. Since, as a traveler, you don't have to get up every day and face Chirac's woes, you can still come to France to enjoy *la douceur de vivre* (life's sweetness), which any chauvinistic French person will tell you is far more alluring than the Italian *la dolce vita*.

What hasn't changed is the Parisian emphasis on the primacy of French culture. While it may be true that the average Parisian of today prefers watching an old Jerry Lewis movie at home on TV to sitting in a cafe sipping an aperitif, the good things of life are still appreciated in the City of Light: food, sex, and fashion—entirely in that order.

Celebrities have always fascinated Parisians, and still do, as the stars of the past are succeeded by new talents who become cultural icons in their own right. While the intense aura of Bardot and Deneuve may have faded, actress Natascha McElhone now glows in the Parisian galaxy. In *Surviving Picasso*, she recently played Francoise Gilot, who met the artist when she was an art student. In the movie, she finds Picasso (actually Anthony Hopkins) on the Left Bank Café de Flore. The secret is that McElhone, although the embodiment of the natural elegance of Paris, is English.

McElhone shows you don't have to be French anymore to be an icon in Paris. To prove the point about the growing influence of immigrants, designer Christian Lacroix introduced tribal and "savage" African prints along with French boudoir lace into an audacious collection, worn by women all over the city in 1997. One reviewer found that Lacroix has run "the tom-tom beat of African color and pattern."

Director Eric Rohmer is reigning, however briefly, as a cinematic icon because of the release of his "Rendezvous in Paris," three graceful and elegant parables that earned him the title of Aesop of Amour. His movie, in the words of one critic, does for Paris something akin to what Woody Allen does for New York.

Lest we forget the icons of the past, Brigitte Bardot, who is now 62, made headlines by publishing her memoirs, *Initiales B.B.* France's once most famous export and sex kitten released a breathless "tell almost" book—a tale of fame, adulation, money, husbands (just four), lovers (too many to count), and animals, animals, animals. Just in case you don't read the book, here's some of the lowdown: Alain Delon is vain, Gunther Sachs (husband number three) a publicity seeker, Sophia Loren chilly, and Catherine Denevue a "cut-rate B.B." and a whiner. Her hero? Charles de Gaulle.

Since Matisse died in 1954, and France hasn't had a great painter since, there were no towering debuts of young artists in the cultural world. Instead it was yesterday's art that dominated the new. In spring 1997 the French government—embarrassed by charges that it still possesses artworks stolen by Nazi occupation forces and returned to France at the end of the war—revealed that it held nearly 1,000 paintings, sculptures, and drawings from this illegal seizure. The government announced these artworks have not been reclaimed by the families or estates of the former owners, most of whom were Jewish collectors.

Many of these works were already on the walls of the Musée d'Orsay, the Louvre, and the Pompidou Center. Paris gathered together some of these works and put on a major display, including works by Gauguin, Seurat, Renoir, Degas, and Monet. Among the works, it was noted by critics, are few masterpieces.

While still a dreamy, romantic city, Paris is on the brink of major change and upheaval. The city is the seat of a country facing a serious economic crisis and a great cultural decline, but most of these problems lurk beneath the surface.

One Frenchman recently told us, "Sure we have a few troubles. But it's merely because we are reinventing ourselves . . . becoming the new Paris for the 21st century. There will be some changes. But let's not be afraid of the future. Let's welcome its surprises."

3 History 101

In the Beginning   Paris emerged at the cross-roads of three major traffic arteries on the muddy island that today is known as the Ile de la Cité.

By around 2000 B.C. the island served as the fortified headquarters of the Parisii tribe, who referred to it as Lutetia. The pair of crude wooden bridges that connected the island to the left and right banks of the river were among the most strategically important in the region, and the settlement attracted the attention of the Roman empire. In his *Commentaries,* Julius Caesar described the Roman conquest of Lutetia, re-counting how its bridges were burned during the Gallic War of 52 B.C., and how the town on the island was pillaged, sacked, and transformed into a Roman-controlled stronghold.

Within a century, Lutetia had become a full-fledged Roman town, and some of the inhabit-ants abandoned the frequently flooded island in favor of higher ground on what is today the Left Bank. By A.D. 200, barbarian invasions increas-ingly threatened the stability of Roman Gaul, and the populace from the surrounding hills flocked to the fortified safety of the island.

Within about 50 years, a Christian commu-nity gained a tenuous foothold on the island. According to legend, St. Denis served as the city's first bishop (beginning around 250). Al-though the political power of the Roman Empire had begun to wane within the region by this time, the cultural and religious attachment of the community to the Christian bishops of Rome grew even stronger.

During the 400s, with the great decline of the Roman armies, Germanic tribes from the east (the Salian Franks) were able to successfully in-vade the island, founding a Frankish dynasty here, and prompting a Frankish-Latin cultural fusion in the growing town. The first of these Frankish kings, Clovis (466–511), founder of the Merovingian dynasty, embraced Christianity as his tribe's official religion, and spearheaded an explicit rejection of Roman cultural imperialism by encouraging the adoption of Parisii place names like "Paris," which came into common usage during this time.

The Merovingian dynasty was replaced by the Carolingians, whose heyday began with

Dateline

- **2000 B.C.** Paris (ancient Lutetia) thrives along a strategic crossing of the Seine, the fortified headquarters of the Parisii tribe.
- **52 B.C.** Julius Caesar conquers Paris during the Gallic Wars.
- **A.D.** 150 Lutetia flourishes as a Roman colony, expanding to Paris's Left Bank.
- **200** Barbarian Gauls force Romans to retreat to the fortifications on Ile de la Cité.
- **300** "Paris" officially named as such. Roman power weakens in northern France.
- **350** Beginnings of Paris's Christianization.
- **400s** Frankish invasions of Paris, with social transformation from Roman to Gallo-Roman culture.
- **466** Birth of Clovis, founder of the Merovingian dynasty, first non-Roman ruler of Paris since the Parisii.
- **800** Coronation of Charlemagne, founder of the Carolingian dynasty and first Holy Roman Emperor, who rules from Aachen in modern Germany.
- **987** Hugh Capet, founder of France's foremost early medieval dynasty, rises to power. He and his heirs rule from Paris.
- **1100** The Université de Paris attracts scholars from throughout Europe.
- **1200s** Paris's population and power grow, although frequently unsettled by plagues and feudal battles.
- **1422** England invades Paris during the Hundred Years' War.
- **1429** Joan of Arc tries unsuccessfully to regain Paris for the French. The Burgundians later capture and sell her to the English, who burn her at the stake in Rouen.
- **1500s** François I, considered first of the French Renaissance kings,

continues

- embellishes Paris but chooses to maintain court in the Loire Valley.
- **1549** Henri II rules France from Paris. Construction of public and private residences begins, many of them in the Marais neighborhood.
- **1564** Construction of Catherine de Médicis's Tuileries Palace. Building facades in Paris transform from half-timbered to more durable chiseled stonework.
- **1572** The Wars of Religion reach their climax with the massacre of Protestants on St. Bartholomew's Day.
- **1598** Henri IV, most eccentric and enlightened monarch of his era, endorses the Edict of Nantes, granting tolerance to Protestants, for which a crazed monk fatally stabs him 12 years later.
- **1615** Construction of the Luxembourg Palace by Henri IV's widow, Marie de Médicis.
- **1636** The Palais-Royal launched by Richelieu. Soon thereafter, two marshy islands in the Seine are interconnected and filled in to create the Ile St-Louis.
- **1643** Rise to power of Louis XIV, "the Sun King," the most powerful ruler since the Caesars. He moves his court to newly constructed Versailles.
- **1776** The American Declaration of Independence strikes a revolutionary chord in France.
- **1789** Outbreak of the French Revolution.
- **1793** Louis XVI and his Austrian-born queen, Marie Antoinette, are publicly guillotined.
- **1799** Napoléon Bonaparte crowns himself Master of France, and embellishes Paris further with neoclassical splendor.
- **1803** Napoléon abandons French overseas expansion and sells Louisiana to America.
- **1812** Defeat of Napoléon in the Russian winter campaign.

continues

the coronation of Charlemagne in 800. The Carolingian empire sprawled over western Germany and eastern France, but Paris was never its capital. The city did remain a commercial and religious center, sacred to the memory of St. Geneviève, who reputedly protected Paris when it was repeatedly attacked by the Huns in the final days of the Roman Empire.

The Carolingian dynasty came to an end in 987, when the empire fragmented because of the growing regional, political and linguistic divisions between what would eventually become modern France and modern Germany. Paris became the seat of a new dynasty, the Capetians, whose kings would rule France throughout the Middle Ages. Hugh Capet, the first of this line of kings, ruled as count of Paris and duke of France from 987 to 996.

The Middle Ages   Around 1100, Paris began to emerge as a great city, with a university established on what is today known as the Left Bank. It attracted scholars from all over Europe. Meanwhile, kings and bishops began building the towering Gothic cathedrals of France, one of the greatest of which became Paris's Notre-Dame, a soaring ecclesiastical monument rising from the beating heart of the city. Paris's population increased greatly, as did the city's mercantile activity. During the 1200s, a frenzy of building transformed the skyline with convents and churches (including the jewel-like Sainte-Chapelle, completed in 1249 after just two years of work). During the next century, the increasingly powerful French kings added dozens of monuments of their own.

As time passed, the fortunes of Paris became closely linked to the power struggles between the French monarchs in Paris and the various highly competitive feudal lords of the outlying provinces. Because of this tug-of-war, Paris was dogged by civil unrest, a series of plagues (including the famous Black Death), takeovers by one warring faction after another, and a dangerous alliance between the English and the powerful rulers of Burgundy during the Hundred Years' War. To the everlasting humiliation of the French monarchs, the city was invaded by the English army in 1422. Joan of Arc (ca. 1412–31) tried unsuccessfully to reconquer Paris in 1429, and two years later the English burned her at the stake in Rouen (Normandy). Paris was reduced to poverty and economic stagnation and its embittered and greatly reduced population turned to banditry and street crime to survive.

Despite Joan's ignominious end, the revolution she inspired continued in protracted form until Paris was finally taken from the English armies in 1436. During the several decades that followed, the English retreated to the Channel port of Calais, abandoning their once-mighty territories in France. France, under the leadership of Louis XI, witnessed an accelerating rate of change that included the transformation of a feudal and medieval social system into the nascent beginnings of a modern state.

Renaissance & Reformation   The first of the Renaissance monarchs, François I, began an extensive enlargement of Paris's Louvre (which had begun its life as a warehouse storing the archives of Philippe Auguste before being transformed into a gothic fortress by Louis IX in the 1100s) to make it suitable as a royal residence. Despite the building's embellishment, and the continued designation of Paris as the French capital, he spent much of his time at other châteaux amid the fertile hunting grounds of the Loire Valley. Many later monarchs would share his opinion that the narrow streets and teeming commercialism of Paris were unhealthy and upsetting and choose to reside elsewhere.

In 1549, however, Henri II triumphantly established his court in Paris and successfully ruled France from within the city's borders, solidifying Paris's role as the nation's undisputed capital. Responding to their ruler's initiative, fashionable aristocrats quickly began to build private residences on the Right Bank, within a marshy lowlying area known as *Le Marais* (the swamp).

Paris as the world knows it today came into existence during this period. The expansion of the Louvre continued, and Catherine de Médicis began building her Tuileries palace in 1564. From the shelter of dozens of elegant urban residences, the aristocracy of France imbued Paris with their sense of architectural and social style, as well as the mores and manners of the Renaissance. Stone quays were added to the banks of the Seine, defining their limits and preventing future flood damage, and royal decrees were passed establishing a series of building codes. To

- **1814** Aided by a military coalition of France's enemies, especially England, the Bourbon monarchy, under Louis XVIII, is restored.
- **1821** Death of Napoléon Bonaparte.
- **1824** Death of Louis XVIII; Charles X accedes.
- **1830** Charles X is deposed, the more liberal Louis-Philippe is elected king. Paris prospers as it industrializes.
- **1848** Violent working-class revolution deposes Louis-Philippe, who is replaced by autocratic Napoléon III. Baron Haussmann forcibly redesigns Paris's landscapes.
- **1860s** The Impressionist style emerges.
- **1870** Franco-Prussian War ends in the defeat of France; Paris is threatened with bombardment by Prussian cannons placed on the outskirts of the city. A revolution in the aftermath of this defeat destroys the Tuileries Palace and overthrows the government. Rise of the Third Republic and its elected president, Marshal MacMahon.
- **1878–1937** A series of international expositions adds many enduring monuments to the Paris skyline, including the Eiffel Tower.
- **1914–18** World War I.
- **1940** German troops invade Paris. The official French government, under Pétain, evacuates to Vichy, whereas the French Resistance under de Gaulle maintains symbolic headquarters in London.
- **1944** U.S. troops liberate Paris. De Gaulle returns from London in triumph.
- **1948** Revolt in French colony of Madagascar costs 80,000 French lives. France's empire continues to collapse in Southeast Asia and Equatorial Africa.

continues

- **1954–62** War begins in Algeria, eventuating in its loss. Refugees flood Paris, and the nation becomes bitterly divided over its North African policies.
- **1958** France's Fourth Republic collapses. General de Gaulle is called out of retirement to head the Fifth Republic.
- **1968** Paris's students and factory workers engage in a general revolt. The French government is overhauled in the aftermath.
- **1981** François Mitterrand is elected France's first socialist president since the 1940s. He is reelected in 1988.
- **1989** Paris celebrates the bicentennial of the French Revolution.
- **1992** Euro Disney opens on Paris's outskirts.
- **1994** François Mitterrand and Queen Elizabeth II take a ride together under the English Channel.
- **1995** Mitterrand dies; Chirac elected. Paris crippled by general strike. Terrorists bomb Paris.
- **1997** Authorities enforce strict immigration laws, causing strife for African and Arab immigrants and dividing the country. French voters rebuff Chirac, electing Socialist Lionel Jospin as his new prime minister.

an increasing degree, Paris adopted the planned perspectives and visual grace of the preferred residence of an absolute monarchy.

During the late 1500s and 1600s, Protestants were brutally persecuted by the French monarchs. Under Henry III the bloodletting reached a high point during the St. Bartholomew's Day massacre of 1572.

Henri III's tragic and eccentric successor, Henri IV, ended the Wars of Religion in 1598 by endorsing the Edict of Nantes, which offered religious freedom to the Protestants of France. Henry IV also laid out the lines for one of the memorable plazas of Paris: the place des Vosges. As a reward for his leniency, Henry IV was stabbed in 1610 by a deranged monk who was infuriated by the king's support of religious tolerance.

After Henri IV's death, his second wife, Marie de Médicis (acting as regent), planned the Luxembourg Palace (1615), whose gardens have functioned ever since as a rendezvous for Parisians. In 1636, Cardinal Richelieu, who virtually ruled France during the minority of Louis XIII (the period in which the boy king was still too young to rule), built the sprawling premises of the Palais-Royal.

Under Louis XIII (1601–43) two uninhabited islands in the Seine were joined together with landfill, connected to the Ile de la Cité and also to the mainland with bridges, and renamed the Ile St-Louis. Also laid out were the Jardin des Plantes, whose flowers and medicinal herbs were arranged according to their scientific and medical category.

The Sun King & the French Revolution   Louis XIV was crowned king of France when he was only 9 years old. Mazarin (1602–61), Louis's Sicilian-born chief minister, dominated the government in Paris during the Sun King's minority

This era marked the emergence of the French kings as absolute monarchs. As if to symbolize their power, the face of Paris was embellished with many of the monuments that still serve as symbols of the city. These included new alterations to the Louvre, and construction of the Pont-Royal, the quai Peletier, the place des Victoires, the place Vendôme, the Champs Elysées, and the Hôtel des Invalides. Meanwhile, Louis XIV absented himself from the city center, constructing, at staggering expense, the palace at Versailles, 13 miles southwest of Paris. Today, its echoing and sometimes tiresome splendor is the single most visible monument to the most flamboyant and ostentatious era of French history.

Meanwhile the rising power of England, particularly its navy, represented a serious threat to France, which was otherwise the most powerful nation in the world. One of the many theaters of the Anglo-French conflict was the American war for independence, during which the French kings supported American revolutionaries in their struggle against the Crown. To their dismay, within 15 years the fervor they had nurtured crossed the Atlantic and destroyed the French monarchy.

The spark that kindled the fire had come from Paris itself. For years before the outbreak of hostilities between the American revolutionaries and the British, the Enlightenment and its philosophers, usually formulating their views in the sophisticated salons of Paris, had fostered a new generation of thinkers who opposed absolutism, religious fanaticism, and superstition. Revolution had been brewing for almost 50 years, and after the French Revolution's explosive and world-shaking events, Europe was completely changed.

Though it began in 1789 with moderate aims, the Revolution had soon acquired the radical Jacobins as overlords, led by Robespierre.

On August 10, 1792, troops from Marseilles, aided by a Parisian mob, threw Louis XVI and his Austrian-born queen, Marie Antoinette, into prison. Several months later, after countless humiliations and a bogus trial, they were guillotined at the place de la Révolution (later renamed the place de la Concorde) on January 21, 1793. The Reign of Terror continued for another 18 months, with Parisians of all political persuasions fearing for their lives.

The Rise of Napoléon   It required the militaristic fervor of Napoléon to unite France once again. Considered then and today a strategic genius with almost limitless ambition, he restored to Paris and to France a national pride that had been diminished during the Revolution's horror. In 1799 at the age of 30, after many impressive political and military victories, he entered Paris and crowned himself "First Consul and Master of France."

A brilliant politician, Napoléon moderated the atheistic rigidity of the early adherents of the Revolution by establishing peace with the Vatican. Soon thereafter, the legendary love of Parisians for their amusements began to revive; the boulevard des Italiens became the rendezvous point of the fashionable, whereas the boulevard du Temple, which housed many of the capital's vaudeville and cabaret theaters, became the favorite watering hole of the working class. In his self-appointed role as a French Caesar, Napoléon continued to alter the face of Paris with the construction of the neoclassical arcades of the rue de Rivoli (1801), the triumphal arches of the Arc du Carrousel and the place de l'Etoile, and the neoclassical grandeur of the Church of the Madeleine. On a less grandiose scale, the city's slaughterhouses and cemeteries were sanitized and moved away from the center of town, and new industries began to crowd workers from the countryside into the cramped slums of a newly industrialized Paris.

Napoléon's victories had made him the envy of Europe, but his infamous retreat from Moscow during the winter of 1812 reduced his formerly invincible army to tatters as 400,000 Frenchmen lost their lives. After a complicated series of events that included his return from exile, Napoléon was defeated at Waterloo by the combined

---

Impressions

Paris (in each shape and gesture and avenue and cranny of her being) was continuously expressing the humanness of humanity. Everywhere I sensed a miraculous presence, not of mere children and women and men, but of living human beings.
—e.e. cummings

Paris is a sphinx. I will drag her secret from her.
—Mirabeau

armies of the English, the Dutch, and the Prussians. Exiled to the British-held island of St. Helena in the remote reaches of the South Atlantic, he died in 1821, probably the victim of an unknown poisoner. Some time later, his body was interred within a massive porphyry sarcophagus within Louis XIV's monument in Paris to the ailing and fallen warriors of France, Les Invalides.

In the power vacuum that followed the expulsion and death of Napoléon, Paris became the scene of intense lobbying concerning the future fate of France. The Bourbon monarchy was soon reestablished, but with reduced powers. In 1830 the regime was overthrown. Louis-Philippe, duke of Orléans and the son of a duke who had voted in 1793 for the death of Louis XVI, was elected king under a liberalized constitution. His calm, prosperous reign lasted for 18 years, during which England and France more or less collaborated on matters of foreign policy.

Paris reveled in its new prosperity, grateful for the funds and glamour that had elevated it to become one of the top cultural and commercial centers of the world. As a fringe benefit of France's campaigns in the Egyptian desert, Paris received the Luxor obelisk as a gift from the caliphs of Egypt. Transporting it across the Mediterranean and re-erecting it on a granite plinth in the place de la Concorde was a major triumph of engineering in 1836. Continuing to move into the modern age, Paris received its first railway line in 1837 (running from the center of town to a suburb near St-Germain), and shortly thereafter the first gas-fed streetlights. It was a time of wealth, grace, culture, and expansion for some French people, although the industrialization of certain working-class districts of Paris produced horrible poverty. The era also witnessed the development of French cuisine to the high form that still prevails, while a newly empowered *bourgeoisie* reveled in its attempts to create the good life.

The Second Empire   In 1848 a series of revolutions spread from one European capital to the next. The violent upheaval in Paris revealed the increasing dissatisfaction of many members of the working class. Fueled by a financial crash and scandals within the government, the revolt forced Louis-Philippe out of office. That year, on the dawn of the Second Republic, Emperor Napoléon's nephew, Napoléon III, was elected president by moderate and conservative elements. Appealing to the property-owning instinct of a nation that hadn't forgotten the violent revolution of less than a century before, he established a right-wing government and eventually assumed complete power as emperor in 1851.

In 1853, Napoléon III undertook the largest urban redevelopment project in the history of Europe. He commissioned Baron Haussmann (1809–91) to redesign the city of Paris. Haussmann created a vast network of boulevards interconnected with a series of squares (*places*) that cut across old neighborhoods. While this reorganization process greatly improved the capital and gave it the look for which it is famous today, screams of outrage sounded throughout the neighborhoods that construction split apart.

By 1866 the entrepreneurs of an increasingly industrialized Paris began to regard the Second Empire as a hindrance to its development. In 1870, during the Franco-Prussian War, the Prussians defeated Napoléon III at Sedan and held him prisoner along with 100,000 of his soldiers. Paris was threatened with bombardments from German cannons, by far the most advanced of their age, that were set up on the city's eastern periphery.

Although agitated diplomacy encouraged a Prussian withdrawal, international humiliation and perceived military incompetence sparked a revolt in Paris. One of the immediate effects of the revolt was the burning of one of Paris's historic palaces, the Tuileries. Today, only the sprawling gardens of this once-great palace remain. The tumultuous events of 1870 ushered in the Third Republic and its elected president, Marshal MacMahon, in 1873.

Under the Third Republic, peace and prosperity gradually returned and Paris regained its glamour. A series of Universal Expositions held in 1878, 1889, 1900, and 1937 was the catalyst for the construction of such enduring Paris monuments as the Trocadéro, the Palais de Chaillot, the Eiffel Tower, both the Grand and the Petit Palais des Champs-Elysées, and the neo-Byzantine church of Sacré-Coeur in Montmartre. Simultaneously, the *réseau métropolitain* (the Métro, or Paris subway) was constructed, providing a model for subsequent subway systems throughout Europe.

World War I   International rivalries and conflicting alliances led to World War I, which, after decisive German victories for two years, degenerated into the mud-slogged horror of trench warfare. Industrialization during and after the war transformed Paris and its outlying boroughs into one vast interconnected whole, by now one of the largest metropolitan areas in Europe and undisputed ever since as the center of France's intellectual and commercial life.

Immediately after the Allied victory, grave economic problems, coupled with a populace demoralized from years of fighting, encouraged the rise of socialism and the formation of a Communist party, movements which were centered in Paris. Also from Paris, the French government, led by the almost obsessively vindictive Clemenceau, occupied Germany's Ruhr Valley, then and now one of the most profitable and industrialized regions of Germany, and demanded every centime of reparations it could wring from its humiliated neighbor, a policy that contributed to the outbreak of World War II.

The 1920s—Americans in Paris   The so-called "Lost Generation," led by American expatriates Gertrude Stein and her longtime companion, Alice B. Toklas, led the list of celebrities that would "occupy" Paris after the war, ushering in one of its most glamorous eras, the 1920s. The living was cheap in Paris. For example, if you had a scholarship worth about $1,000, two people could manage for about a year, providing they could scrape up another $500 or so in extra earnings. Thus came the *littérateur*, the *bon viveur*, and the drifter, along with such writers as Henry Miller, Ernest Hemingway, and F. Scott Fitzgerald. Even Cole Porter arrived, living first at the Ritz, then later at 13 rue de Monsieur (7e). James Joyce, half blind and led around by Ezra Pound, arrived in Paris and went to the salon of Natalie Barney, leading exponent of Amazon Love. She became famous for pulling off such stunts as inviting Mata Hari to perform a Javanese dance, completely nude, at one of her parties, labeled "for women only, a lesbian orgy." Colette was barred, although she begged her husband to let her go. With the collapse of Wall Street, many Americans returned home, except some hard-core artists such as Henry Miller, who wandered around smoking Gauloise cigarettes and generating several pages a day of *Tropic of Cancer*, which would be banned in America for decades. "I have no money, no resources, no hopes. I am the happiest man alive," Miller said. Eventually, he met the narcissistic diary writer, Anaïs Nin, and they began to live a life that gave both of them material for their prose. Miller read Nin's diaries and proclaimed, "The whole thing is a bloody emission, the orgasm of a monster." But even such diehards as Miller and Nin eventually realized their Paris of the 1930s was collapsing as war clouds loomed. Gertrude and Alice remained in France, as other American expatriates fled to safer shores.

Paris Under Siege

Headlines around the world testify to the fact that a rip is tearing across Paris's cultural fabric. Parisians may soon preface recollections of many long-standing traditions with the words *il y avait un fois* ("once upon a time").

Gitanes. Gauloise. The mention of the names of these cigarettes—which in the minds of many are treasures the caliber of the Louvre or the Seine—conjures images of cluttered cafes filled with passionate talk and a thick blue-gray haze. Smokers are intrinsic to Paris, a city that rarely bows before the entreaties of nonsmokers.

So who would have ever thought of walking into a cafe, restaurant, or bistro and seeing a separate section for nonsmokers? Who would have believed that law suits would be brought against French tobacco companies? And, *sacre-bleu,* the stiff, strong tobacco of Gauloise and Gitanes is losing ground to the American brands with their weaker tobaccos and filters. Certainly there must be an internal conspiracy afoot.

Since 1991, France has had an antismoking law applicable to public places. It made headlines back then. But like a story in the tabloid press, no one ever really took it seriously—after all, this was France. Yet the law really was a law, and it is beginning to be more strictly enforced throughout the country, swaying French public opinion along with it. Even great photos from the past of such untouchable icons as Jean Cocteau, Jean-Paul Sartre, or Coco Chanel pursing their lips for the lens with their ever-present Gauloise glued in place are not safe from the legislation. Recently, a stamp was printed by the French post office commemorating André Malraux, French writer and adventurer and all-around provocateur. However, because of the 1991 antismoking law, it is also now illegal to have "any propaganda or publicity, direct or indirect, in favor of tobacco." So, the actual photo used for the stamp was doctored to delete Malraux's cigarette.

The Winds of War   Thanks to an array of alliances, France had no choice but to declare war on Germany in 1939 when Germany invaded France's ally, Poland. Within only a few months, on June 14, 1940, Nazi armies marched arrogantly down the Champs-Elysées. Newsreel cameras recorded the French openly weeping at the sight. The city suffered little from the war materially, but for four years it survived in a kind of half-life, cold, dull, and drab, fostering scattered pockets of fighters who resisted sometimes passively, and sometimes with active sabotage.

During the Nazi occupation of Paris, the French government, under Marshal Pétain (1856–1951), moved to the quiet and isolated resort of Vichy and cooperated (or actually collaborated, depending on your point of view) with the Nazis. Tremendous internal dissension, the memory of which still simmers today, pitted many factions against one another. The Free French Resistance fled for its own safety to London, where it was headed by Charles de Gaulle (1880–1970), who after the war became president of France's Fourth Republic.

Postwar Paris   Despite its gains in both prestige and prosperity after the end of World War II, Paris was rocked many times by internal dissent as domestic and international events embroiled the French government in dozens of controversies. In 1951 Paris forgot its cares by celebrating the 2,000th anniversary of the founding of the city, and poured much of its energy into rebuilding its image as a center of fashion, lifestyle, and glamour. Paris became internationally recognized as both a

Right on the heels of this antismoking travesty comes a threat to the Parisian's very staff of life: the baguette. How many of us went to French class and saw that famous poster hanging on the wall of a grandfather peddling his grandson on a bike complete with baguette tied to the back. This image is quintessentially French. After all, the baguette *is* France. Alas, the traditional baguette, with its light caramel-colored crust and airy white middle, is losing ground to the *retro,* or *retrodor,* a darker color bread made with rye flour and invented by Viron flour mills in Chartres. The retro is marketed under claims that it is a rustic baguette like those baked on farms in pre-1930s France. Here is the kicker, though, and much of the country is falling for it: a baguette (rustic or not) would never have been baked in the farm kitchens of long-ago France like the advertisements in Paris would like you to believe. The type of bread made then would have been a large round country loaf, the kind that would last several days, not a baguette that could be eaten at one sitting. A whole industry is capitalizing on a fabricated past to boost sales, and consequently, bread sales in Paris have been given a shot in the arm.

In what many are calling the most extreme scandal to the city, the English, those cross-channel fox-chasers and ale-tipplers, are reigning supreme in two Paris fashion houses. It's no wonder the French are reeling from a collective cultural nervous breakdown. Alexander McQueen has taken up residence with the house of Givenchy, and John Galliano has moved to the house of Dior. The fear of many Parisians is that the two quintessential haute-couture fashion houses, so famous for smart, traditional Parisian style, are now going to be creating a British sock-it-to-me-baby-let-it-all-hang-out, in-your-face, hard-edge, laborer style of fashion—one that may prove too *gauche* for the puritanical upper crust.

Is nothing sacred anymore?

touristic staple in the travel diets of many North Americans and as a beacon for art and artists.

The War of Algerian Independence (1954–58), in which Algeria sought to go from being a French *département* (an integral extension of the French nation) to an independent country, was an anguishing event, more devastating than the earlier loss of France's colonies. The population of France (and Paris in particular) ballooned immediately as French citizens fled Algeria and returned home with few possessions and much bitterness. In 1958, as a result of the enormous loss of lives, money, and prestige in the Algerian affair, France's Fourth Republic collapsed, and de Gaulle was called out of retirement to form a new government: The Fifth Republic.

In 1962 the Algerian war of liberation ended with victory for Algeria, as France's colonies in Central and Equatorial Africa became independent one by one. The sun had finally set on an empire that had transformed Paris into a mighty city.

In 1968 a general revolt by students in Paris, whose activism mirrored that of their counterparts in the United States, turned the capital into an armed camp, causing a near-collapse of the national government and the very real possibility of total civil war. Though the crisis was averted, for several weeks it seemed as if French society was tottering near the brink of anarchy.

Contemporary Paris   Paris today struggles with additional social unrest in Corsica and from Muslim fundamentalists residing both in and outside of France. In 1981

François Mitterrand (with a very close vote of 51%) was elected the first socialist president of France since World War II. The flight of massive amounts of capital held by French millionaires slowed somewhat after initial jitters, although many wealthy Parisians still prefer to invest their money elsewhere. Although much feared by the rich, Mitterrand was reelected in 1988 and (according to many of his critics) soon thereafter adopted a kind of demeanor better suited to a monarch than to a duly elected president.

In the mid-1990s, racial tensions continued to nag at France, as the debate over immigration raged. Many right-wing political parties have created a racial backlash against North Africans and against "corruptive foreign influences" in general. The government has recently tried to ban the use of Anglicisms in the French language. For his efforts, critics nicknamed culture minister Jacques Toubon "Mr. All-Good" (a rough but literal translation of his name into the dreaded English). The conflict in Bosnia and a ghastly rate of unemployment has continued to plague French politicians, but when Mitterrand and Queen Elizabeth II opened the Chunnel under the English Channel in 1994, it marked the first time since the Ice Age that France and England had been joined.

When former French president François Mitterrand died of cancer in 1995, France embarked upon a new era. Jacques Chirac won the presidential election in May of 1995 with 52% of the vote in his third attempt at the office, bringing the conservative Republic Party to power. The neo-Gaullist's popularity soon faded, however, in the wake of unrest caused by an 11.5% unemployment rate, an unpopular and seemingly nepotistic prime minister, a barrage of terrorist attacks by Algerian militants, and a threadbare economy struggling to meet European Monetary Union entry requirements.

Chirac was hard pressed to come up with answers to these crises. The former Mayor of Paris quickly became mired in his country's turmoil, chairing the government from a smoldering hot seat. Nicknamed "Bulldozer," Chirac proved the moniker apt, leveling his cabinet by ordering all 41 ministers to quit. French voters rebuffed him further in June 1997, ousting his Gaullist parliament and prime minister in favor of a coalition of Socialists, Communists, and Greens led by the rose-bearing Lionel Jospin, who promised a government that would pay less heed to the eurodollar, and more to France's chronically high level of joblessness.

Through the new year, terrorist scares continued to flood the borders of France, attacking the country on three fronts: extremist Algerians, Corsicans, and Basques. A highly visible armed police force, known as *Vigipirate,* was placed on the streets of Paris as part of the administration's program to protect citizens and visitors from terrorist acts. One of the unusual offshoots of the *Vigipirate* program involved the closing of the crypts of many of Paris's medieval churches to casual visitors, partly in fear of a terrorist bomb attack on national historic treasures.

4 Famous Parisians

Josephine Baker (1906–75)   Born in an African-American ghetto in St. Louis, this singer and cabaret entertainer became the toast of *tout Paris* with sensuously scintillating performances like her famous "Danse Sauvage." Dubbed "La Baker" by her adoring French public, she was granted French citizenship in 1937, and served her adopted country as a member of the French Resistance during World War II.

Charles Baudelaire (1821–67)   The work of this French impressionist poet was condemned by mainstream critics as obscene and decadent. One of the world's first

Impressions

I am the man who accompanied Jacqueline Kennedy to Paris, and I have enjoyed it.
—John F. Kennedy (1961)

modern poets, he ended his life in abject poverty, hopelessly addicted to opiates. His most famous work is *Les Fleurs du mal* (*Flowers of Evil,* 1857).

Simone de Beauvoir (1908–86)   A French essayist and novelist, she was the leading female writer of the existentialist movement and the on-again, off-again lover of Jean-Paul Sartre. Awarded the Prix Goncourt in 1945 for her novel *The Mandarins,* she was also one of the most articulate spokespersons for the postwar feminist movement. Her most influential feminist books are *The Second Sex* and *La Vieillesse* (Old Age). *Memoirs of a Dutiful Daughter* is her life story.

Gabrielle ("Coco") Chanel (1883–1971)   This French image-maker and designer created chic, simple women's clothing, the classic lines of which have endured longer than those of any other designer in the world. Establishing her career from a shop on the boardwalk of Deauville, she promoted small and pert hats to replace the garlands of fruit, swaths of veils, and masses of straw or linen that were fashionable during the Edwardian age. In the 1950s she introduced her famous "little black dress."

Jean Cocteau (1889–1963)   A multimedia French artist, Cocteau was a style-setter and enfant terrible. After experimenting in the surrealistic and avant-garde movements of the 1910s and 1920s, Cocteau wrote novels, poems, film scripts, essays, and scenarios for plays; painted church murals; designed restaurant menus; invented costumes; choreographed parties; and directed films. *Blood of a Poet, Beauty and the Beast,* and *Orphée* are three of his best-known films. His important writings include *Les Enfants terribles, Journal d'un unconnu,* and *La Difficulté d'être.* He was buried with full honors from the Académie Français.

Marie Curie (1867–1934)   A French physicist and chemist, born Marie Slodowska in Poland, she and her French-born husband, Pierre Curie, discovered radium and determined its radioactive properties in 1898. Winner of two Nobel prizes for her experimentation with the curative effects of radiation, she died in 1934, worn out and exhausted, from radium poisoning.

Georges Jacques Danton (1759–94)   A revolutionary and political philosopher, his policies of relative moderation evoked the rage of more radical factions, who had him guillotined. At his most powerful he served as minister of justice and president of the Committee of Public Safety shortly after the fall of Louis XVI.

Edith Piaf (1915–63)   The quintessential Parisian singer, who could move listeners to tears, was born Edith Gassion, the daughter of a circus acrobat. She was raised by her grandmother, who owned and operated a brothel. Piaf began singing in the streets at age 15 and later began appearing in cafes. Beautiful only when her plain features gave out into song, Piaf was nicknamed "The Little Sparrow" by her ardent admirers. Companion of pimps, thieves, prostitutes, and drug addicts, she led a life filled with tragedy, illness, despair, and lost love. Her best-loved songs include "Milord," "A quoi ça sert, l'amour," "La Foule," and "La Vie en Rose."

Cardinal Richelieu (Armand Jean du Plessis, duc de Richilieu; 1585–1642)   A French financier and prelate, Richelieu effectively controlled France after the death of

Americans Who Bombed in Paris

Carson McCullers, arriving with her husband, Reeves, in Paris in 1946, following success from *The Heart Is a Lonely Hunter* (1940), met the literary greats of the city: Gide, Colette, Simone de Beauvoir, André Malraux, and Albert Camus. Since she couldn't speak French, she nodded *oui, oui* to everything. To her horror one day, she discovered she'd agreed to speak at the Sorbonne on French literature. She knew nothing of the subject but appeared anyway and read one of her poems.

Café de la Rotonde, founded in 1911, included among its patrons Picasso, Max Jacob, and Apollinaire. In the spring of 1922, Edna St. Vincent Millay dined here almost daily with her mother. Writing home, she recorded her first impression of French food: "Mummie & I about live in this here kafe. We feed on *choucroute garnie,* which is fried sauerkraut trimmed with boiled potatoes, a large slice of ham & a fat hot dog,—yum, yum, werry excillint. Mummie & I come every day & eat the stinkin' stuff, & all our friends hold their noses & pass us by til we've finished."

Living in Paris in an apartment in 1925, Scott Fitzgerald owed $6,200 to his publisher, Scribner's. Even though *The Great Gatsby* had sold 20,000 copies (a huge total back then), the sales had disappointed the author. At the height of his fame and after having published his one masterpiece, Fitzgerald launched the year with "1,000 parties and no work." His drunken bouts sometimes lasted for a week. He'd show up at the *Chicago Tribune* office on rue Lamartine, staggering and shouting for reporters to get out "the goddamn paper." After getting evicted from the offices, he'd visit bars until he went into a coma. One couple reported taking him home only to hear Zelda yell down: "You bastard. Drunk again!"

Newspaper tycoon William Randolph Hearst visited Paris in September 1928, with his mistress, the actress Marion Davies. Upon his return to America, Hearst revealed a confidential memorandum exposing a Franco-British pact to increase the strength of their navies. When he returned again in 1930, along with Ms. Davies and a dozen of her girlfriends from Hollywood, a French official greeted him and asked him, "as an enemy of France," to leave the country at once. Hearst and his entourage hastened over to the Savoy in London. The yellow press baron later wrote that he could endure being persona non grata in France "without loss of sleep."

Louis XIII's mother, Marie de Médicis. Merciless in his hatred and persecution of Protestants, Richelieu starved and destroyed the Huguenot strongholds of France, most notably La Rochelle. He founded the Académie Française to impose linguistic and grammatical rules on the then loosely defined language that we now know as French.

Marquis de Sade (Donatien Alphonse Françoise, comte de Sade; 1740–1814)   Sade, a French soldier and libertine, wrote the sexually explicit novels *Justine* and *Juliette,* which so outraged the religious and political authorities of his era that he was thrown into prisons and mental asylums for most of his life. He was, in modern times, the first to advocate inflicting pain on others for the enhancement of one's own pleasure. Sade has the dubious distinction of having the psychological tendencies and the sexual acts that he encouraged (sadism) named after him. The painful techniques he pioneered included sexual experimentation with chains, whips, nails and knives, and other inventive devices.

5 La Ville des Beaux-Arts

Paris is arguably the premier artistic capital of Europe. For centuries, the city has produced, and been home to, countless artists and artistic movements, and it is still a hotbed of creativity and an important center for the international art world.

Paris's true artistic flowering began around 1150, when the city's active trade, growing population, and struggles for political and ecclesiastic power added dozens of new buildings to the city's skyline. Between 1200 and 1400, the city flowered in the Gothic style, generating among other buildings the city's everlasting architectural symbol, the Cathedral of Notre-Dame, as well as the Cathedral of St-Denis on the city's eastern outskirts. In these and other Gothic buildings, the medieval sculptures on the facades and inside the buildings depended less upon the structures they adorned and became more fully developed as freer artistic expressions. Secondary crafts, such as the manufacture and installation of stained glass (as represented by the windows in Paris's Sainte-Chapelle), became art forms in their own right, and French glass of this age attained an intensity of blues and reds that has never been duplicated.

Gothic painters became adept at the miniaturization of religious and secular scenes that art lovers (in an era without corrective lenses for myopia) could richly appreciate close at hand. The most famous of these, **Pol de Limbourg's** *Les très riches heures du duc de Berri* and **Fouquet's** *Heures d'Etienne Chevalier,* showed occasional scenes of medieval Paris in a charmingly idealized celebration of the changing of the seasons. Around 1360, Paris provided the setting for the painting of what is usually credited by art historians as the first (known) portrait, that of Jean le Bon (artist unknown), and the weaving of one of the most famous tapestries in history, the *Angers Apocalypse.*

The evolution of French art slowed during much of the 1400s. By the 1500s, however, Paris enjoyed a great artistic rebirth, thanks to a military campaign into Italy and a subsequent fascination with all things Italian. Two of that era's main sculptors, who embellished the facades and fountains of Paris, were **Jean Goujon** (1510–85), whose inspirations melded ancient Greek forms and Renaissance themes, and **Germain Pilon** (1535–90), whose carvings of the French kings at St-Denis kept to mostly religious, rather than neoclassical, themes. By the late 1500s, under the auspices of the Renaissance king François I, the royal château at Fontainebleau, 37 miles south of Paris, became a caldron of the arts, eventually producing a style of painting known later as the school of Fontainebleau.

The arts in and around Paris during the 1600s so permeated French culture that the century has been known ever since as *Le Grand Siècle* (the grand century). France's monarchy by now was so entrenched and society sufficiently stable and centralized that the arts flourished as Paris was embellished with hundreds of aristocratic mansions within Le Marais district. Important painters included **Philippe de Champaigne** (1602–74), famous for his severe portraits, **Charles le Brun** (1619–90), who painted the Galerie d'Apollon at the Louvre, and his rival **Pierre Mignard** (1610–95), painter of the interior of the cupola in the church of Val-de-Grâce. Simultaneously, the art of tapestry weaving was given a tremendous boost thanks to the establishment and royal patronage of the Manufacture Royale des Gobelins.

During the early 1700s, the taste for the grandiose in France was profoundly influenced by the personality of the Sun King, Louis XIV. His construction and furnishing of Versailles called for mind-boggling quantities of art and decoration, giving lavish commissions to sculptors and craftsmen of every kind. In furnishing the thousands of salons and apartments within the palace, the techniques of fine cabinetry reached their apogee under such cabinetmakers as **André-Charles Boulle**

(1642–1732). Boulle's writing tables, secretaries, and *bombé*-fronted chests, either eb-onized or inlaid with tortoiseshell, mother-of-pearl, and gilded bronze ornaments (ormolu), are today among the finest pieces of cabinetry in European history, and command appropriately stratospheric prices. Boulle was supplanted by Crescent and Oeben, under Louis XV, who were themselves replaced by such neoclassically inspired masters as Weisweiler and Kiesner during the reign of Louis XVI.

Painters from the era of Louis XIV and XV include Largilière and Rigaud and the skilled portraitists **La Tour** (1704–66) and **Perronneau** (1715–88), whose coloring techniques have been likened to those used by the Impressionists more than a century later. Also noteworthy, both as an artist and as a sociological phenomenon, was the female artist **Vigée-Lebrun** (1755–1842), whose lavish but natural style won her a position as Marie Antoinette's preferred painter. Especially famous paintings from this era are those of **Fragonard** (1732–1806) and **Boucher** (1703–70), whose canvases captured the sweetness and whimsy of aristocratic life during the *ancien régime*.

In sculpture, painting, and furniture, the 18th century in Paris began with an al-legiance to the baroque curve and a robustly sensual kind of voluptuousness, and ended with a return to the straight line and the more rigid motifs of the classical age. Especially indicative of this return to sobriety was **Houdon** (1741–1828), who is re-membered for his extraordinarily lifelike portrait busts such as that of Voltaire.

The French Revolution, whose first violence had erupted in 1789, brought a new politicization to the arts. Noteworthy was **David** (1748–1825), whose painting *Oath of the Horatii* has been credited as one of the most revolution-inducing catalysts in the history of Europe. To reward his zeal, David was appointed director of the Arts of the Revolution, an incentive that helped produce such richly idealized paintings as *The Murder of Marat*. Always in control of his own political destiny, David was later appointed court painter to Napoléon.

Meanwhile, as France grew wealthy from the fruits of the Industrial Revolution and the expansion of its colonial empire, Paris blossomed with the paintings of **Ingres** (1780–1867) and his bitter rival, **Delacroix** (1798–1863). Primary among their aca-demic disputes were allegiances to the beauty of line (Ingres) and the subtleties of color (Delacroix).

Between 1855 and 1869, the partial demolition of medieval Paris and its recon-struction into the series of panoramic plazas and monuments that the world today knows as the City of Light was engineered by Napoléon III's chief architect, Baron Haussmann.

The birth of Impressionism is commonly thought to have begun with the exhi-bition, in Paris in 1863, of the *Salon des Refusés*. Here, the works of painters such as **Manet,** rejected by the mainstream art establishment, were shown. One of the most memorable paintings seen there was Manet's then-scandalous and still-riveting *Déjeuner sur l'herbe*. Before that, the subtle colorings of the landscape artist **Corot** (1796–1875) had presaged Impressionism for several years. Soon after, such artists as Sisley, Pissarro, Degas, Renoir, and the immortal Monet painted in the open air, often evoking the everyday life and cityscapes of Paris and its surroundings.

Later, the best scenes ever painted of Paris would be credited to **Utrillo** (1883–1955) and, to a lesser degree, **Marquet** (1875–1947). Utrillo in particular concen-trated on the unpretentious, often working-class neighborhoods (especially Montmartre) rather than the city's more famous monumental zones. Marquet, whose work helped to establish the definition of the fauve school of painting, often executed his stylized and brightly colored works from the balcony of his Paris apartment.

Though many of them never made a career out of painting Paris itself, other 20th-century painters who for the most part made Paris their home included Vlaminck, Derain, Vuillard, Bonnard, Braque, Picasso, Dufy, and Matisse. Many of these artists used their canvasses as rebellions against the restrictions of "official" art as defined at the time by the aesthetic hierarchies of France. Several movements that emerged from this artistic rebellion have, since their origins, been classified among the most potent and evocative schools of art in the world. Included among them were Fauvism, a technique that employed vivid and arbitrary use of color in ways that paved the way for the nonfigurative perceptions of the movements that were to follow. Cubism, favorite style of early **Picasso** and **Braque**, developed as a means of breaking subject matter into a stylized version of their basic geometric forms. Dadaism, an elaboration of the avant-garde movements that developed out of Cubism and Fauvism, managed to permeate painting with some of the absurdist moral and political philosophies then pervasive in the arts scene of Paris. Most stylized of all was Surrealism, a movement that carried realism to boundaries never before explored, twisting everyday objects into bizarre, sometimes terrifying permutations that only a slightly mad genius, such as **Salvador Dalí**, could have perceived.

Among sculptors, Paris's greatest contribution to the art of the late 19th century was **Auguste Rodin** (1840–1917), whose figures added new dimensions to the human form. Especially famous was the raw power emanating from his rough-surfaced sculptures *The Thinker* and *The Kiss.*

French artists today struggle in the shadow of the great modernists who transformed the artistic perceptions of the world during the early decades of the 20th century. Although the *oeuvre* of these contemporary artists will doubtless not surpass the fame, notoriety, and price levels of, say, Matisse, Braque, or Monet, they are enjoying popularity and even energetic biddings whenever their works are presented at expositions. **Oliver DeBré** (born in Paris in 1920), for example, whose early studies in architecture and literature influenced his role as the most important abstract artist in France today, has garnered a significant reputation through a retrospective of his work at the Jeu de Paume. And there are many others.

Gérard Garouste (born in Paris in 1926), who does much of his painting in a studio in the Normandy countryside, is one of Europe's contemporary masters of the postmodern still-life.

Ernest Pignon-Ernest (born in Nice in 1942), on the other hand, has succeeded in taking contemporary art directly to the streets. Inspired by the canvasses of 17th-century Italian master Caravaggio, Pignon-Ernest executes "neo-Renaissance" serigraphs, produced cheaply and abundantly, which he then plasters over hundreds of buildings as an artistic statement. Although based in Paris throughout most of the year, his "decoration" of the walls of Naples was widely publicized in the art world and brought a new appreciation of Caravaggio even to Italy.

Pierre Soulages's detractors compare him to a Gallic version of Mark Rothko; his fans praise his all-black canvasses as "sumptuous" and claim that he can imbue shades of the color black with more meaning and subtlety than most artists can evoke with a full palette. He is the most controversial of France's contemporary artists, and possibly the most depressing.

Whatever the personal stylistic idiosyncrasies of this new generation of Paris artists, all of them are part of an artistic tradition that has endured in the City of Light for centuries. Art is, and has been, a vital and integral part of Parisian society since its humble beginnings, and Paris's current artistic sophistication is the product of centuries of development. The city's current art scene pays tribute to the legacy of all who came before, and is as diverse and volatile as ever. Whatever your artistic tastes, Paris offers something to suit them.

6 Architecture Through the Ages

Not only is Paris a world art capital, the city itself *is* art, an organic collection of beautifully designed and constructed buildings that represent diverse architectural styles and periods. Walking through Paris can be like excavating layers of sediment at an archaeological dig: each edifice bears the characteristic signatures of the period in which it was built. Paris's buildings are not only ornate and elegant, they tell the tale of the city's long and impressive architectural history.

Despite its role as an outpost of ancient Rome, the development of Paris into a bustling community of traders, merchants, and clerics didn't really come to pass until the 1100s. Historians cite the abandonment of **Romanesque** building techniques within the Ile de France at around 1150. Because of that, the city has surprisingly few Romanesque buildings, good examples of which are more common in such French provinces as Burgundy. Identified by their thick walls, barrel vaults, and groined vaults, small windows, and minimal carvings, the city's most important Romanesque buildings include the churches of St-Germain-des-Prés, St-Pierre-de-Montmartre, St-Martin des Champs, and, in the suburbs, the Church of Morienval.

The genius of Paris's architects, however, arrived during the **Gothic** age, which was signaled early in the 1200s with the construction of the cathedrals of St-Denis, in Paris's eastern suburbs; Chartres, 60 miles to the city's southwest; and Notre-Dame of Paris, situated on the Ile de la Cité. Before the mid-15th century, Gothic architecture would transform the skyline of Paris as dozens of new churches, chapels, and secular buildings outdid their neighbors in lavishness, beauty, and intricacy of design.

Although Gothic architecture was firmly rooted in the principles of the Romanesque, it differs from its predecessor in its penchant for complicated patterns of vaulting and columns, and walls that became increasingly thinner as the weight of ceilings and roofs were transferred onto newly developed systems of abutment piers (flying buttresses). Because of the thinner walls, larger openings became architecturally feasible. Churches became filled with light filtered through stained glass, and enormous rose windows awed their observers with the delicate tracery of their stonework.

During the **Renaissance**, beginning around 1500, influences from Italy rendered the Gothic style obsolete. In its place arose the yearning for a return to the aesthetics of ancient Greece and Rome. Massive arcades, often decorated with bas-relief sculpture of symbols of triumph, as well as Corinthian, Doric, and Ionic pediments, added grandeur to the Paris of the Renaissance kings. All links of royal residences to feudal fortresses vanished as the aristocrats of Paris competed with one another to construct elegant town houses and villas filled with sunlight, tapestries, paintings, music, and fine furniture.

During the early 17th century, many of Paris's distinctive Italianate baroque domes were created. Louis XIV employed such Italian-inspired architects as Le Vau, Perrault, both Mansarts, and Bruand for his buildings and Le Nôtre for the rigidly intelligent layouts of his gardens at Versailles. Paris and the surrounding region flourished with the construction of the lavishly expensive château of Vaux-le-Vicomte and the even more elaborate royal residence of Versailles. Meanwhile, wealthy entrepreneurs encouraged the development of new expressions of artistic and architectural beauty from the many salons sprouting up throughout the city.

By the early 19th century, a newly militaristic Paris, flushed with the titanic changes of the Revolution and the subsequent victories of Napoléon, returned to a restrained and dignified form of **classicism**. Modeling their urban landscape on an idealized interpretation of imperial Rome, buildings such as the Church of the Madeleine evoked the militaristic rigidity and grandeur of the classical age.

By 1850, enjoying a cosmopolitan kind of prosperity, Paris grew bored with things Greek and Roman. Despite a brief flirtation with **Egyptology** (based on Napoléon's campaign in the Egyptian desert and the unraveling of the secrets of the Rosetta stone) a new school of eclecticism added controversial but often elegant touches to the Paris landscape. Among them were the voluptuous lines of the **art nouveau** movement, whose aesthetic was inspired by the surging curves of the botanical world. Stone, cast iron, glass, and wood were carved or molded into forms resembling orchids, vines, laurel branches, and tree trunks, each richly lyrical and based on new building techniques made possible by the Industrial Age. Youthful and creative architects began to specialize in the use of iron as the structural support of bridges, viaducts, and buildings, such as the National Library (1860). These techniques opened the way for Gustave Eiffel to design and erect the most frequently slandered building of its day, the Eiffel Tower, for the Paris Exposition of 1889.

During the 1920s and 1930s, a newly simplified aesthetic was highly refined and greatly appreciated within Paris. **Art deco**, a style reflecting the newly developed materials and decorative techniques of the machine age, captured sophisticated sensibilities around the world. After Braque defined **Cubism**, the angular simplicity of the new artistic movement influenced architectural styles as well. Le Corbusier, a Swissborn architect who settled in Paris in 1917, eventually developed his jutting, gently curved planes of concrete, opening the doors for a new, but often less talented, school of modern French architects.

Critics haven't been kind to the rapidly rusting exposed structural elements of Paris's notorious Centre Pompidou. In the 1980s an obsolete railroad station beside the Seine was transformed into the truly exciting Musée d'Orsay and an expanse of dreary 19th-century slaughterhouses was refigured into a site of tourist worth by the addition of a hypermodern science museum. In the 1990s the Opéra Bastille brought new life to the decaying eastern edge of the Marais but, predictably, sparked a controversy regarding its iconoclastic design. And screams of outrage could be heard throughout France when I. M. Pei's glass pyramid was built as the postmodern centerpiece of one of the Louvre's most formal 17th-century courtyards.

Mitterrand inaugurated the Grande Arche de La Défense on France's bicentennial on July 14, 1989. This 35-story office complex shaped like a hollow cube is the endpoint of the *voie triomphale* (triumphal way) begun in 1664 at the Tuileries Gardens; its roof covers $2^{1}/_{2}$ acres (it's estimated that Notre-Dame could fit into its hollow core). One of the latest additions to the architectural scene (opened in 1995) is the Cité de la Musique, designed by architect Christian de Portzamparc as a complex of interconnected postcubist shapes.

Although the buildings of the Mitterrand presidency were "designed for eternity," critics are already sighting flaws in the late president's "chance for immortality," his $5.8 billion architectural spending spree. Many of the Mitterrand buildings are suffering defects and mishaps, including stone slabs falling from the Opera at Bastille, fragments of the Grand Arche flaking into a net, and rain gushing into the orchestra pit at the City of Music. Paris's futuristic National Library was scheduled to open when the builders realized that the light bathing the building was going to destroy the fragile paper of the rare books it was to house. After tinted glass and much tinkering, the building still has not been built. The pyramid at the Louvre remains trouble-free, so far.

The great French architect Paul Chametov said, "At the end of a decade [the 1980s] that was tipsy from competitions, drunk from media hype, and driven mad by the expectations of a real-estate boom, we inherit an architecture that is only new on the day it is inaugurated." Of course, the celebrated Pompidou Center, built in honor of former President George Pompidou, is in so much trouble that it has been shut and will host only jackhammers, leaky pipes, and time-whistles until the cusp of the millennium.

President Jacques Chirac can hardly match the cultural monuments of his predecessor, falling slabs of marble or not. In 1996, he announced his building plans: the creation of a major new museum for African, Oceanic, and pre-Columbian art. Assigned to the Passy Wing of the Palais de Chaillot in the Trocadero section of Paris, it will open, if plans go well, in late 2001, just months before the end of Chirac's 7-year term.

Planning a Trip to Paris

2

This chapter provides most of the nuts-and-bolts information you'll need before setting off for Paris. We've put everything from information sources to the major airlines at your fingertips.

1 Visitor Information & Entry Requirements

VISITOR INFORMATION

BEFORE YOU GO Your best source of information before you go is the French Government Tourist Office, which can be reached at the following addresses.

In the United States 444 Madison Ave., 16th floor, New York, NY 10022; 676 N. Michigan Ave., Suite 3360, Chicago, IL 60611-2819; or 9454 Wilshire Blvd., Suite 715, Beverly Hills, CA 90212-2967. To request information, call the "France on Call" hot line (☎ **900/990-0040**); each call costs 50¢ per minute.

In Canada Write or phone the **Maison de la France/French Government Tourist Office,** 1981 av. McGill College, Suite 490, Montréal, H3A 2W9 (☎ **514/288-4264**).

In the United Kingdom Write or phone the **Maison de la France/French Government Tourist Office,** 178 Piccadilly, London, W1V 0AL (☎ **0891/244-123;** fax 0171/493-6594).

In Australia Write or phone the **French Tourist Bureau,** 25 Bligh St., Sydney, NSW 2000, Australia (☎ **02/9231-5244;** fax 02/9221-8682).

In Ireland Write or phone the **Maison de la France/French Government Tourist Office,** 35 Lower Abbey St., Dublin 1, Ireland (☎ **01/703-4046**).

In New Zealand There's no representative in New Zealand, so citizens should contact the Australian representative.

In Paris You need never be totally alone in Paris. There's always someone who speaks your language standing ready to provide assistance, give information, and help solve problems. The **Office de Tourisme et des Congrès de Paris** (or Welcome Offices) in the city center will give you free maps, informative booklets, and "Paris Monthly Information," an English-language listing of all current shows, concerts, and theater. At 127 Champs-Elysées, 8e (☎ **01-49-52-53-54**), you can get information regarding both Paris and the provinces. The office is open daily except May 1 from 9am to 8pm. Métro: Charles-de-Gaulle–Etoile.

WEB SITES

- **French Government Tourist Office:** http://www.fgtousa.org
- **Maison de la France:** http://www.franceguide.com
- **The Paris Pages:** http://www.paris.org
- **FranceScape:** http://www.france.com/francescape

ENTRY REQUIREMENTS

PASSPORT   All foreign (non-French) nationals need a valid passport to enter France (check its expiration date).

VISA   The French government no longer requires visas for **U.S. citizens,** providing they're staying in France for less than 90 days. For longer stays, U.S. visitors must apply for a long-term visa, residence card, or temporary-stay visa. Each requires proof of income or a viable means of support in France and a legitimate purpose for remaining in the country. Applications are available from the Consulate Section of the French Embassy, 4101 Reservoir Rd. NW, Washington, DC 20007 (☎ **202/ 944-6000**), or from the visa section of the French Consulate at 10 E. 74th St., New York, NY 10021 (☎ **212/606-3689**). Visas are required for students planning to study in France even if the stay is for less than 90 days.

Visas are generally required for **citizens of other countries,** though Canadian, Swiss, and Japanese citizens and citizens of EU countries are exempt (but check with your nearest French consulate, as the situation can change overnight).

DRIVER'S LICENSE   U.S. and Canadian driver's licenses are valid in France, but if you're going to tour Europe by car you may want to invest in an **International Driver's License.** Apply at any branch of the American Automobile Association (AAA). You must be 18 years old and include two 2-by-2-inch photographs, a $12 fee, and your valid U.S. driver's license with the application. If AAA doesn't have a branch in your hometown, send a photograph of your driver's license (front and back) with the fee and photos to **AAA,** 1000 AAA Dr., M/S28, Heathrow, FL 32746-5063 (☎ **800/222-4357** or 407/444-4300; fax 407/444-4247). Always carry your original license with you to Europe, however.

In Canada, you can get the address of the **Canadian Automobile Club** closest to you by calling its national office at ☎ **613/226-7631.**

INTERNATIONAL INSURANCE CERTIFICATE   In Europe, you must have an international insurance certificate, called a green card (*carte verte*). The car-rental agency will provide one if you're renting.

CUSTOMS   Customs restrictions differ for citizens of the European Community (EC) and for citizens of non-EC countries. Non-EC nationals can bring in duty-free 200 cigarettes, 100 cigarillos, 50 cigars, or 250 grams of smoking tobacco. This amount is doubled if you live outside Europe. You can also bring in 2 liters of wine and either 1 liter of alcohol over 22 proof or 2 liters of wine under 22 proof. In addition you can bring in 60cc of perfume, $1/4$ liter of eau de toilette, 500 grams (1 pound) of coffee, and 200 grams ($1/2$ pound) of tea. Visitors 15 years of age and over may also bring in other goods totaling 300 F ($60), whereas the allowance for those 14 and under is 150 F ($30). (Customs officials tend to be lenient about general merchandise, realizing that the limits are unrealistically low.)

Visitors from European Union (EU) countries can bring in 300 cigarettes or 150 cigarillos or 75 cigars or 400 grams of smoking tobacco. You can also bring in 2 liters of wine and either 1 liter of alcohol over 38.80 proof or 2 liters of wine under 38.80 proof. In addition, visitors can bring in 75 grams of perfume, ³/₈ liter of toilet water, 1,000 grams of coffee, and 80 grams of tea. Passengers 15 and over can bring in 4,200F ($840) of merchandise duty-free; those 14 and under can bring in 1,000F ($200) worth.

2 Money

CURRENCY   French currency is based on the **franc (F)**, which consists of 100 centimes (c). Coins come in units of 5, 10, 20, and 50 centimes; and 1, 2, 5, and 10 francs. Notes come in denominations of 20, 50, 100, 200, 500, and 1,000 francs. The front of the new 200-franc note honors Gustave Eiffel, creator of the Eiffel Tower, father of experimental aerodynamics, and part-designer of New York's Statue of Liberty.

All banks are equipped for foreign exchange, and you will find exchange offices at the airports and airline terminals. Banks are open from 9am to noon and 2 to 4pm Monday through Friday. Major bank branches also open their exchange departments on Saturday between 9am and noon.

When converting your home currency into French francs, be aware that rates vary. Your hotel will probably offer the worst rate of exchange. In general, banks offer the best rate, but even banks charge a commission for the service, often $3, depending

The French Franc, the U.S. Dollar & the British Pound

For American Readers   At this writing, $1 = approximately 5F (or 1F = 20¢), and this was the rate of exchange used to calculate the dollar values given in this book.

For British Readers   At this writing, £1 = approximately 8.33F (or 1F = 12£), and that was the rate of exchange used to calculate the pound values in the table below.

Note: Because the exchange rate fluctuates from time to time, this table should be used only as a general guide

F	U.S.$	U.K.£	F	U.S.$	U.K.£
1	0.20	0.12	25	5.00	3.00
2	0.40	0.24	50	10.00	6.00
3	0.60	0.36	75	15.00	9.00
4	0.80	0.48	100	20.00	12.00
5	1.00	0.60	150	30.00	18.00
6	1.20	0.72	200	40.00	24.00
7	1.40	0.84	250	50.00	30.00
8	1.60	0.96	300	60.00	36.00
9	1.80	1.08	350	70.00	42.00
10	2.00	1.20	400	80.00	48.00
15	3.00	1.80	500	100.00	60.00
20	4.00	2.40	1000	200.00	120.00

What Things Cost in Paris	U.S. $
Taxi from Charles de Gaulle Airport to the city center	40.00
Taxi from Orly Airport to the city center	34.00
Public transportation for an average trip within the city from a Métro *carnet* (packet) of 10	.92
Local telephone call	.40
Double room at the Ritz (very expensive)	780.00
Double room at Lord Byron (moderate)	134.00
Double room at Hôtel Opal (budget)	90.00
Lunch for one, without wine, at Chez Georges (moderate)	40.00
Lunch for one, without wine, at Crémerie-Restaurant Polidor (inexpensive)	15.00
Dinner for one, without wine, at Le Grand Véfour (very expensive)	150.00
Dinner for one, without wine, at Rôtisserie du Beaujolais (moderate)	36.00
Dinner for one, without wine, at Aux Charpentiers (inexpensive)	31.60
Glass of wine	3.00
Coca-Cola	3.50
Cup of coffee	6.50
Roll of ASA 100 film, 36 exposures	8.00
Admission to the Louvre	9.00
Movie ticket	9.00
Theater ticket (at the Comédie-Française)	6.00–37.00

on the transaction. Whenever you can, stick to the big banks of Paris, like Crédit Lyonnais, which usually offer the best exchange rates and charge the least commission. Always make sure you have enough francs for the weekend.

If you need a check denominated in French francs before your trip, say, to pay a deposit on a hotel room, you can contact **Ruesch International,** 700 11th St. NW, 4th floor, Washington, DC 20001-4507 (☎ **800/424-2923**). Ruesch performs a wide variety of conversion-related services, usually for $3 per transaction. You can also inquire at a local bank.

ATM NETWORKS   Plus, Cirrus, and other networks connecting automated-teller machines (ATMs) operate in Paris. The exchange rate for ATM cards is very good, and the convenience is unbeatable. In fact, as long as the fees for such transactions remain low, obtaining cash this way is the best way to go. For Cirrus locations abroad, call ☎ **800/424-7787;** for Plus locations, call ☎ **800/843-7587.** And if your credit card has been programmed with a personal identification number (PIN), it is likely that you can use your card at Paris ATMs to withdraw money as a cash advance. Check to see if your PIN code must be reprogrammed for usage in Paris.

**TRAVELER'S CHECKS   ** Although it's now perfectly easy to find ATM machines in Paris and get cash as you would at home, some travelers still like the security of carrying traveler's checks so that they'll be able to get a refund in the event of theft.

Most large banks sell traveler's checks, charging fees that average between 1% and 2% of the value of the checks you buy. The American Automobile Association (AAA) does not charge its members a fee for traveler's checks.

Sometimes you can purchase traveler's checks in the currency of the country you're planning to visit, thereby avoiding a conversion fee, which could amount to as much as $5. Note, also, that you sometimes get a better rate if you cash traveler's checks at the institutions that issued them: VISA at a branch of Thomas Cook, American Express at American Express, and so forth.

For more information, contact the following companies: **American Express** (☎ **800/221-7282** in the U.S. and Canada); **Citicorp** (☎ **800/645-6556** in the U.S. and Canada, or 813/623-1709 collect from other parts of the world); or **Thomas Cook** (☎ **800/223-7373** in the U.S. and Canada).

CREDIT & CHARGE CARDS   Both American Express and Diners Club are widely recognized. The French equivalent for VISA is Carte Bleue. If you see the EuroCard sign on an establishment, it means it accepts MasterCard.

You may purchase something with a credit card thinking you will be charged at a certain exchange rate, only to find the dollar has declined by the time your bill arrives, and so you're actually paying more than you had bargained for, but those are the rules of the game. Of course, this principle works in your favor if the dollar rises after you make your purchase.

Some automated-teller machines in Paris accept U.S. bank cards such as VISA or MasterCard. The exchange rates are also good, and the convenience of obtaining cash on the road is without equal. Check with your credit-card company or bank before leaving home.

3 When to Go

In August, Parisians traditionally leave for their annual holiday and put the city on a skeleton staff to serve visitors. Now, July has also become a popular vacation month, with many a restaurateur shuttering up for a month-long respite.

Hotels, especially first-class and deluxe, are easy to come by in July and August when so many visitors are away. Budget hotels, on the other hand, are likely to be full in July and August, because those are the months of the greatest student invasion. You might also try to avoid the first two weeks in October when the annual auto show attracts thousands of automobile enthusiasts.

Paris is now a city of all seasons, as regards to hotels. However, if you're coming for the weather, it's more romantic in the spring and autumn.

THE CLIMATE   Balmy weather in Paris has prompted more popular songs and love ballads than weather conditions in any other city in the world. The city's weather is sometimes fickle and ever-changing. Rain is much more common than snow throughout the winter, prompting many longtime residents to complain about the occasional bone-chilling dampness.

In recent years, Paris has had only about 15 snow days a year, and there are only a few oppressively hot days (that is, over 86°F) in midsummer. What will most likely chill a Parisian heart, however, are blasts of rapidly moving air—wind tunnels sweep along the city's long boulevards, channeled by bordering buildings of uniform height. Other than the occasional winds and rain (which add an undeniable drama to many of the city's panoramas), Paris offers some of the most pleasant weather of any capital in Europe, with a highly tolerable average temperature of 53°F.

Paris's Average Daytime Temperature & Rainfall

	Jan	Feb	Mar	Apr	May	June	July	Aug	Sept	Oct	Nov	Dec
Temp (F)	38	39	46	51	58	64	66	66	61	53	54	40
Rain (inches)	3.2	2.9	2.7	3.2	3.5	3.3	3.7	3.3	3.3	3.0	3.5	3.1

HOLIDAYS   In France, holidays are known as *jours fériés*. Shops and banks are closed, as well as many (but not all) restaurants and museums. Major holidays include January 1, Easter, Ascension Day (40 days after Easter), Pentecost (seventh Sunday after Easter), May 1, May 8 (V-E Day), July 14 (Bastille Day), August 15 (Assumption of the Virgin Mary), November 1 (All Saints' Day), November 11 (Armistice Day), and December 25 (Christmas).

PARIS CALENDAR OF EVENTS

January

- **International Ready-to-Wear Fashion Shows** (Le Salon International de Prêt-à-Porter), Parc des Expositions, Porte de Versailles, Paris, 15e (☎ 01-44-94-70-00; Métro: Porte de Versailles). Hundreds of designers, from the giants to the virtually unknown, unveil their visions (some say hallucinations) about what the public should be wearing in six months. Technically, the event within the massive convention facilities of the Porte de Versailles is geared to wholesalers, retailers, buyers, writers, and industry professionals, but for the entrance fee of 130F ($26), the rules are usually bent to accommodate the merely fashion-conscious. Much more exclusive are the *défilés* (fashion shows) held around the same time at the headquarters of individual designers like Lanvin, Courrèges, and Valentino. Mid-January to mid-February.

February

- **Special Exhibitions, Special Concerts:** During Paris's grayest month, look for a splash of temporary expositions and concerts designed to perk up the city. Concerts and theaters spring up at such diverse sites as the **Salle Pleyel**, 252 faubourg St-Honoré, 8e (☎ 01-45-61-53-00; Métro: Ternes), **the Théâtre des Champs-Elysées,** 15 av. Montaigne, 8e (☎ 01-49-52-50-50; Métro: Alma-Marceau), and the **Maison Radio-France,** 116 av. du Président-Kennedy, 16e (☎ 01-42-30-15-16; Métro: Passy-Ranelagh). Also look for openings of new operas at the **Opéra National de Paris Bastille**, 2 place de la Bastille, 4e (☎ 01-44-73-13-00; Métro: Bastille); concerts beneath the most famous glass pyramid in Europe, **Pyramide du Louvre**, 1er (☎ 01-40-20-52-29; Métro: Musée du Louvre); and the **Salle Cortot**, 78 rue Cardinet, 17e (☎ 01-47-63-85-72; Métro: Malesherbes). A copy of *Pariscope*, or the listings in any French-language newspaper, are the best sources of information during a month in which much is happening, but not necessarily within the framework of any particular festival.

March

- **Foire du Trône,** on the lawns of the Pelouse de Reuilly, in the Bois de Vincennes, 12e (☎ 01-45-18-57-00 or 01-46-27-52-29; Métro: Porte Dorée). A mammoth amusement park that its fans promote as the largest country fair in France, the Foire du Trône's origins date from the year 957, when merchants met with farmers on a nearby site to exchange grain and wine. This high-tech continuation of that tradition incorporates a high-flying Ferris wheel, carrousels that go around and around, acrobats, jugglers, fire-eaters, and amusements and diversions that seem a Gallic version of Coney Island. It operates from the end of March until late May, daily from 2pm to midnight.

April

- **International Marathon of Paris.** Beginning at the Champs-Elysées at 9am, runners take over many of the boulevards of Paris in a televised race that brings in competitors from around the world. Depending on their speed and endurance, participants arrive at the finishing point on the Avenue Foch, 16e, beginning 2¹/₂ hours later. If you haven't felt like jogging lately, this event might inspire you to begin. First weekend in April. For more information, call ☎ 01-53-17-03-10.

May

- **End of World War II.** The celebration commemorating the capitulation of the Nazis on May 7, 1945, lasts from May 5 to 8 in Paris, with a parade along the Champs-Elysées and additional ceremonies in Reims. Pro-American sentiments are probably higher during this festival than at any other time of the Parisian calendar.

- **Les Grandes Eaux Musicales**. These musical events are intended to re-create the atmosphere of the *ancien régime* at Versailles. These are some of the rare occasions when the fountains of the parks around the palace are all turned on, with special emphasis on the Fountain of Neptune that sits squarely in front of the best view of the château. Visitors can promenade in the garden and listen to the drifting music of French-born composers (Couperin, Charpentier, Lully) and others (Mozart and Haydn) whose careers thrived in the years of the palace's construction. The music is generally recorded. Concerts take place every Sunday afternoon between 3:30 and 5:30pm from early May to early October.

- **French Open Tennis Championship,** Stade Roland-Garros, 16e (Métro: Porte d'Auteuil). The Open features 10 days of Grand Slam men's and women's tennis. European players traditionally dominate on the hot red slow dusty courts. Late May to mid-June.

June

- **Festival Juin.** Paris's well-heeled 16th arrondissement hosts a month of music, art exhibitions, and drama in its auditoriums, parks, and churches. For information, call ☎ 01-40-72-16-25.

- **Festival de Musique de St-Denis.** This series presents four days of artfully contrived music in the burial place of the French kings, a grim early Gothic monument in Paris's industrialized northern suburb of St-Denis. Call ☎ 01-48-12-06-07 for information; Métro: St-Denis-Basilique. June 1 through 4.

- **Le Prix du Jockey Club** (June 1 at 2pm) and the **Prix Diane-Hermès** (June 8 at 2pm), Hippodrome de Chantilly. Thoroughbreds from as far away as Kentucky and Brunei, as well as mounts sponsored by the old and new fortunes of Europe compete in a very civil format that's broadcast around France and talked about in horsey circles around the world. On race days, as many as 30 trains depart from Paris's Gare du Nord for Chantilly, where they are met with free shuttle buses to the track. Alternatively, buses depart on race days from Place de la République and Porte de St-Cloud, on a schedule that coincides with the beginning and end of the races. Call ☎ 01-49-10-20-30 for information on this and on all other equine events in this calendar.

- **Paris Air Show.** This is where the military-industrial complex of France shows off enough high-tech hardware to make anyone think twice about invading *La Patrie.*

Fans, competitors, and industrial spies mob the exhibition halls of Le Bourget Airport for a taste of what Gallic technocrats have wrought. Mid-June in alternate years only (next air show is 1999). For information, call ☎ **01-53-23-33-33.**

- **Festival Chopin.** Hear all you ever wanted to hear from the Polish exile who lived most of his life in Paris. Piano recitals take place in Versaille's Orangerie du Parc de Bagatelle. For information, call ☎ **01-45-00-69-75.** June 16 to July 14.

- **The Grand Steeplechase de Paris** and the **Grand Prix de Paris.** These are counterpoints to the earlier horse races conducted at Chantilly (see above). They take place at the Auteuil and Longchamp racetracks in the Bois de Boulogne in mid-June and late June, respectively. Métro: Porte d'Auteuil.

- **Gay Pride Parade.** A week of expositions and parties climaxes in a massive parade patterned after those in New York and San Francisco. It begins at place de l'Odéon and proceeds to place de la Bastille, and then is followed by the Grand Bal de Gay Pride at the Palais de Bercy, a major convention hall/sports arena. For more information, contact **Centre Gai et Lesbien,** 3 rue Keller, 75011 Paris (☎ **01-43-57-21-47**), or **L.G.P. (Lesbian and Gay Pride),** 27 rue du Faubourg-Montmartre, 75009 Paris (☎ **01-47-70-01-50**), for the exact date in 1998. Late June.

- **La Villette Jazz Festival.** One of the Paris region's most dynamic homages to the art of jazz incorporates 50 concerts in churches, auditoriums, and concert halls in all neighborhoods of the Paris suburb of La Villette. Past festivals have included Herbie Hancock, Shirley Horn, Michel Portal, and other artists from around Europe and the world. The festival runs from late June through the first week in July. For information, call ☎ **01-40-03-75-03.**

July

❂ **Bastille Day.** On July 14, the accepted birth date of modern-day France, festivities reach their peak in Paris with street fairs, pageants, fireworks, and feasts. The day begins with a parade down the Champs-Elysées and ends with fireworks at Montmartre. Wherever you are, before the end of the day you'll hear Piaf warbling "La Foule" (The Crowd), the song that celebrated her passion for the stranger whom she met and later lost in a crowd on Bastille Day. Get in the spirit by humming the "Marseillaise," outfitting yourself with a beret, a pack of Gauloises, and a bottle of cheap wine, and stamping around Paris madly.

- **Paris Quartier d'Été.** For a four-week period, the Arènes de Lutèce, or the "Cour d'Honneur" at the Sorbonne, both within the Latin Quarter, host pop orchestral concerts in a village green setting. The dozen or so concerts are usually grander than the outdoors setting would imply, and include performances by the Orchestre de Paris, the Orchestre National de France, and the Baroque Orchestra of the European Union. On the fringes one can find plays, jazz concerts, parades choreographed with the Tuileries Gardens for the pleasure of children and their guardians, and a scattering of jazz. For information, call ☎ **01-44-83-64-40** or fax 01-44-83-64-43. July 15 to August 15.

- **Le Grand Tour de France.** Europe's most visible, most highly contested, and most overabundantly televised bicycle race pits crews of wind-tunnel tested athletes along an itinerary that traces the six sides of the French "hexagon," and includes detours deep into the Massif Central and across the Alps of francophone Switzerland. The race is decided at a finish line drawn across the Champs-Elysées. July 5-27. For information, call ☎ **01-41-33-15-00.**

August

- **Musique au Carrousel du Louvre.** The ornate courtyards of the Louvre are the midsummer setting for concerts by Austrian, English, and French chamber orchestras. The series lasts five consecutive days and includes music by Schumann, Schubert, Britten, Janáček, and Stravinsky. For tickets and information, call ☎ 01-43-16-48-38. August 25 to 29.

- **Festival Musique en l'Ile.** A series of concerts, most dignified masses composed between the 17th and late 19th centuries, are given within medieval churches in the 4th, 5th, and 6th arrondissements. Sites include St-Louis-en-l'Ile, St-Severin, and St-Germain-des-Prés. Call ☎ 01-44-62-70-90 for more information. August to mid-September.

September

- **Festival d'Automne.** Paris welcomes the return of its residents from their August holidays with an ongoing, and eclectic, festival of modern music, ballet, theater, and modern art. Venues include art galleries, churches, concert halls, auditoriums, and parks throughout Paris. There's a great emphasis on experimental works, which the festival's promoters scatter judiciously between more traditional productions. Depending on the event, tickets cost from 100 to 300F ($20 to $60). For details, write to the Festival d'Automne, 156 rue de Rivoli, 75001 Paris (☎ 01-53-45-17-00; fax 01-53-45-17-01). Late September to mid-December.

- **International Ready-to-Wear Fashion Shows** (Le Salon International de Prêt-à-Porter), Parc des Expositions, Porte de Versailles, Paris, 15e (Métro: Porte de Versailles). More of what took place at the fashion shows in January, with a stress on what *le beau monde* will be wearing in six months. Late September.

October

- **Festival d'Automne.** Continues all month.

- ✪ **Paris Auto Show.** Glistening metal, glitzy attendees, lots of hype, and the latest models from world auto makers form a showcase for European car design. The auto show takes place at the Parc des Expositions, near the Porte de Versailles in western Paris, for a 10-day period in early October. In addition, a permanent exhibition on French auto design at the Cité des Sciences et de l'Industrie is upgraded and enriched during all of October. Call ☎ 08-36-68-29-30 for information on either venue.

- **Prix de l'Arc de Triomphe.** France's answer to England's Ascot is the country's most prestigious horse race, culminating the equine season in Europe. Hippodrome de Longchamp, 16e (☎ 01-49-10-20-30; Métro: Porte d'Auteuil). Early October.

November

- **Festival d'Automne.** Continues all month.

- **Armistice Day.** The signing of the controversial document that ended World War I is celebrated with a military parade from the Arc de Triomphe to the Hôtel des Invalides. November 11.

- **City of Paris Festival of Sacred Art.** A dignified series of classical concerts is held in five of the oldest and most recognizable churches of Paris. End of November through early December. For information, call ☎ 04-44-70-64-10.

December

- **Festival d'Automne.** Continues through mid-December.

- **The Boat Fair** (Le Salon International de la Navigation de Plaisance). Europe's most visible exposition of what's afloat and of interest to wholesalers, retailers, individual boat owners (or wannabes), and anyone involved in the business of waterborne holiday-making. Parc des Expositions, Porte de Versailles, Paris, 15e (☎ 01-41-90-47-47; fax 01-41-90-47-47; Métro: Porte de Versailles). The Fair lasts for 10 days in early December.

• **Fête de St-Sylvestre** (New Year's Eve). It's most boisterously celebrated in the *quartier latin* around the Sorbonne. At midnight, the city explodes. Strangers kiss strangers, and boulevard St-Michel becomes a virtual pedestrian mall, as does the Champs-Elysées. December 31.

4 Tips for Travelers with Special Needs

FOR TRAVELERS WITH DISABILITIES

Facilities in Paris for travelers with disabilities are certainly better than you'll find in most cities. Every year the French government does more and more to help ease life for persons with disabilities in the public facilities of the country.

Nearly all modern hotels in France now have rooms designed especially with persons with disabilities in mind. Older hotels, unless renovated, may not provide such important features as elevators, special toilet facilities, or ramps for wheelchair access. For a list of hotels in Paris offering facilities for persons with disabilities, contact the **APF Evasion (Association des Paralysés de France),** 17 bd. Auguste Blanqui, 75013 Paris (☎ **01-40-78-69-00**).

There are many agencies that provide advance data to help you plan your trip. One is the **Travel Information Service,** MossRehab Hospital, 1200 W. Tabor Rd., Philadelphia, PA 19141, which serves as a telephone resource for travelers with physical disabilities. Call ☎ **215/456-9600** (voice) or 215/456-9603 (TTY).

You may also want to consider joining a tour for travelers with disabilities. The names and addresses of such tour operators can be obtained from the **Society for the Advancement of Travel for the Handicapped,** 347 Fifth Ave., Suite 610, New York, NY 10016 (☎ **212/447-7284;** fax 212/725-8253). Yearly membership in this society which includes quarterly issues of *Open World* magazine is $45, $30 for senior citizens and students.

For the blind or visually impaired, the best source is the **American Foundation for the Blind,** 11 Penn Plaza, Suite 300, New York, NY 10001 (☎ **800/232-5463,** or 212/502-7600 to order information kits and supplies). The organization offers information on travel and various requirements for the transport and border formalities for seeing-eye dogs. It also issues identification cards to those who are legally blind.

In France, most high-speed trains can deal with wheelchairs. Guide dogs ride free. Older trains have special compartments built for wheelchair boarding. On the Paris Métro, persons with disabilities can sit in wider seats provided for their comfort. Some stations don't have escalators or elevators, however, and this may present problems.

In the United Kingdom, **RADAR (Royal Association for Disability and Rehabilitation),** Unit 12, City Forum, 250 City Rd., London ECIV 8AF (☎ **0171/250-3222**), publishes holiday "fact packs" (three in all), which sell for £2 each or a set of all three for £5. The first one provides general information, including planning and booking a holiday, insurance, finances, and useful organization and holiday providers. The second outlines transport and equipment, transportation available when going abroad, and equipment for rent. The third deals with specialized accommodations.

Another good resource is the **Holiday Care Service,** 2nd floor, Imperial Buildings, Victoria Road, Horley, Surrey RH6 7PZ, UK (☎ **01293/774-535;** fax 01293/784-647), a national charity that advises on accessible accommodations for elderly and persons with disabilities. Once a member, you can receive a newsletter and access to a free reservations network for hotels throughout Britain and, to a lesser degree, Europe and the rest of the world.

FOR GAY & LESBIAN TRAVELERS

"Gay Paree," with one of the world's largest homosexual populations, has dozens of gay clubs, restaurants, organizations, and services. Other than publications (see below), one of the best sources of information on gay and lesbian activities is **Centre Gai and Lesbien,** 3 rue Keller, 75011 (☎ **01-43-57-21-47; Métro: Bastille**). Well equipped to dispense information, and to coordinate the activities and meetings of gay people from virtually everywhere, it's open daily from 2 to 8pm. Sundays, they adopt a format known as *Le Café Positif,* and feature music, cabaret, and information about AIDS and the care for and prevention of sexually transmitted diseases.

SOS Écoute Gay (☎ **01-44-93-01-02**) is a gay hot line, theoretically designed as a way to creatively counsel persons with gay-related problems—the phone is answered by volunteers, some of whom are not as skilled and helpful as others. A phone counselor responds to calls Monday to Friday from 6 to 10pm. **SOS Homophobie** (☎ **01-48-06-42-41**) is a separate hot line specifically intended for victims of homophobia or gay-related discrimination; calls are received by a panel of French-trained lawyers and legal experts who offer advice every Monday to Friday from 8am to 10pm.

Another helpful source is **La Maison des Femmes,** 8 Cité Prost, 11e (☎ **01-43-48-24-91; Métro: Charonne**), offering information about Paris for lesbians and bisexual women and sometimes sponsoring informal dinners and get-togethers. Call any Wednesday or Friday from 4 to 7pm for further information.

Gai Pied's publication *Guide Gai* (revised annually) is the best source of information on gay and lesbian clubs, hotels, organizations, and services—even restaurants. Lesbian or bisexual women might also like to pick up a copy of *Lesbia,* if only to check out the ads. These publications and others are available at Paris's largest and best-stocked gay bookstore, **Les Mots à la Bouche,** 6 rue Ste-Croix-de-la-Bretonnerie, 4e (☎ **01-42-78-88-30**). Hours are Monday through Saturday from 11am to 11pm, Sunday from 3 to 8pm. Both French- and English-language publications are available.

France is one of the world's most tolerant countries toward gays and lesbians, and there are no special laws that discriminate against them. Technically, sexual relations are legal for consenting partners age 16 and over. However, one doesn't come of legal age in France until 18, so under the murkiness of French law, parents could bring a lawsuit claiming that their son or daughter was seduced or coerced into having sex, even though he or she in theory "consented." Therefore, sex with anyone 17 and under, consent or not, poses a certain legal danger. Paris, of course, is the center of gay life in France, although gay and lesbian establishments exist through the provinces as well.

The following information may be helpful before you leave home.

PUBLICATIONS   Before going to France, men can order *Spartacus,* the international gay guide ($32.95) or the new *Paris Scene* ($10.95), a guidebook published in London but available in the United States. Also helpful is *Odysseus, the International Gay Travel Planner* ($27). Both lesbians and gay men might want to pick up a copy of *Ferrari Travel Planner* ($16). *Gay Europe,* published by David Andrusia, a Perigee book (1995, $14), earned the praise of Michael Musto, a gay columnist for *The Village Voice.* It includes France in its Europe survey, but lacks details and specifics. These books and others are available from **Giovanni's Room,** 1145 Pine Street, Philadelphia, PA 19107 (☎ **215/923-2960;** fax 215/923-0813).

Our World, 1104 North Nova Rd., Suite 251, Daytona Beach, FL 32117 (☎ **904/441-5367;** fax 904/441-5604), is a magazine devoted to gay and lesbian travel worldwide. It costs $35 for 10 issues. *Out and About,* 8 W. 19th St., Suite 401, New York, NY 10011 (☎ **800/929-2268;** fax 800/929-2215), has been hailed for its "straight" reporting about gay travel. It profiles the best gay or gay-friendly hotels, gyms, clubs, and other places, with coverage ranging from Key West to Paris. It costs $49 a year for 10 information-packed issues. It's aimed at the more upscale gay traveler and has been praised by everybody from *Travel and Leisure* to *The New York Times.*

ORGANIZATIONS   **The International Gay Travel Association (IGTA),** P.O. Box 4974, Key West, FL 33041 (☎ **305/292-0217,** or voice mailbox 800/ 448-8550), is an international network of travel industry businesses and professionals who encourage gay/lesbian travel worldwide. With around 1,200 members, it offers quarterly newsletters, marketing mailings, and a membership directory that is updated four times a year. Membership often includes gay or lesbian businesses, but is open to individuals for $125 yearly, plus a $100 administration fee for new members. Members are kept informed of gay or gay-friendly hoteliers, tour operators, airline and cruise-line representatives, and also ancillary businesses such as the contacts at travel guide publishers and gay-related travel clubs.

TRAVEL AGENCIES   **Our Family Abroad,** 40 W. 57th St., Suite 430, New York, NY 10019 (☎ **800/999-5500** or 212/459-1800; fax 212/581-3756) operates escorted tours that include about a dozen itineraries through Europe.

In California, a leading option for gay travel arrangements is **Above and Beyond,** 300 Townsend St., Suite 107, San Francisco, CA 94107 (☎ **800/397-2681** or 415/ 284-1666; fax 415/284-1660).

5 Getting There

BY PLANE
FLYING FROM NORTH AMERICA

The flying time to Paris from New York is about 7 hours; from Chicago, 9 hours; from Los Angeles, 11 hours; from Atlanta, about 8 hours; and from Washington, D.C., about 7½ hours.

One of the best choices for passengers flying to Paris from both the southeastern United States and the Midwest is **Delta Airlines** (☎ **800/241-4141**), whose network greatly expanded after its acquisition of some of the former Pan Am routes. From such cities as New Orleans, Phoenix, Columbia (South Carolina), and Nashville, Delta flies to Atlanta, connecting every evening with a nonstop flight to Orly Airport in Paris. Delta also operates daily nonstop flights to Orly from Cincinnati and New York's JFK. All of these flights depart late enough in the day to permit easy transfers from much of Delta's vast North American network.

Another excellent choice for Paris-bound passengers is **United Airlines** (☎ **800/ 538-2929**), with nonstop flights from Chicago, Washington, D.C. (Dulles), and San Francisco to Paris's Charles de Gaulle Airport. United also offers discounted fares in the low and shoulder seasons to London's Heathrow from five major North American hubs. From London, it's an easy train and Hovercraft or Chunnel connection to Paris, a fact that tempts many passengers to spend a weekend in London either before or after their visit to Paris.

Another good option is **Continental Airlines** (☎ **800/231-0856**), which services the Northeast and much of the Southwest through its busy hubs in Newark and Houston. From both of those cities, Continental provides nonstop flights to Charles de Gaulle Airport. Flights from Newark depart daily, while flights from Houston depart between four and seven times a week, depending on the season.

La Gastronomie 101

In a nation devoted to the pursuit of gastronomic excellence, you'll find a wide array of chefs (skilled and otherwise) eager to impart a few of their culinary insights—for a fee. A knowledge of at least rudimentary French is a good idea before you enroll, although a visual demonstration of any culinary technique is often more valuable than reading or hearing about it. The cooking schools listed below will send you information in English or French if you write to them in advance; their courses might be attended by professional chefs and serious or competitive connoisseurs.

Ritz-Escoffier Ecole de Gastronomie Française, 15 place Vendôme, 75001 Paris (☎ **800/966-5758** in the U.S., or 01-43-16-30-50). Famed for his titanic rages in the kitchens of the French and English aristocrats who engaged him to prepare their banquets, and also for his well-publicized culinary codifications, Georges-Auguste Escoffier (1846–1935) taught the Edwardian Age how to eat. Today, the Ritz Hotel, site of many of Escoffier's meals, maintains a school that offers daily demonstration classes of the master's techniques. Ritz-Escoffier demonstrations are held Monday, Tuesday, and Thursday afternoons and cost 275F($55). Classes (taught in French or English) in specific techniques, such as baking, pastry, or French cooking, cost from 5,550F to 5,850F ($1,110 to $1,170) for one week to 63,000F ($12,600) for 12 weeks. The 12-week Ritz-Escoffier course is 71,000F ($14,200).

Le Cordon Bleu, 8 rue Léon Delhomme, 75015 Paris (☎ **800/457-CHEF** in the U.S., or 01-53-68-22-50). Originally established in 1895, this is the most famous French cooking school. Call for a brochure. Cordon Bleu's most famous courses last for 10 weeks, at the end of which certificates of competence are issued—highly desired within the restaurant world. Many gourmet enthusiasts prefer a less intense immersion into the rituals of French cuisine, and opt for either a 4-day workshop, or a 3-hour demonstration class. Enrollment in either of these is on a first-come, first-served basis; the cost is 220F ($44) for a demonstration, and 4,590F ($918) for the 4-day workshop. Also of interest to professional chefs (or wannabes) are the 2- and 5-week courses in catering; they're offered twice a year and attract avid business hopefuls. Any of these programs, even the 3-hour quickies, offer unexpected insights into the culinary subculture of Paris.

TWA (☎ **800/221-2000**) operates daily nonstop service to Charles de Gaulle Airport from New York's JFK, and in summer, several flights a week from Boston and Washington, D.C.'s Dulles airport. In summer, TWA also flies to Paris from St. Louis several times a week nonstop, and to Paris from Los Angeles three times a week which connect in St. Louis or New York's JFK. In winter, flights from Los Angeles and Washington, D.C., are suspended, and flights from St. Louis are routed with brief touchdowns en route to Paris in New York or Boston.

American Airlines (☎ **800/433-7300**) provides daily nonstop flights to Paris (Orly) from Dallas/Fort Worth, Chicago, Miami, Boston, and New York's JFK.

USAir (☎ **800/428-4322**) offers daily nonstop service from Philadelphia International Airport to Paris's Charles de Gaulle Airport.

The French flag carrier, **Air France** (☎ **800/237-2747**) offers daily or several-times-a-week flights between Paris's Charles de Gaulle and Newark, New Jersey; Washington, D.C.'s Dulles; Miami; Chicago; New York's JFK; Houston; San Francisco; Los Angeles; Montréal; Toronto; and Mexico City.

Canadians usually choose **Air Canada** (☎ 800/776-3000 from the U.S. and Canada) for flights to Paris from Toronto and Montréal. Nonstop flights from Montréal and Toronto depart every evening for Paris. Two of the nonstop flights from Toronto are shared with Air France, and feature Air France aircraft.

Some Good-Value Choices

Consolidators (known as "bucket shops") act as clearinghouses for blocks of tickets airlines discount and consign during normally slow periods of air travel. Tickets are usually priced 20% to 35% below the full fare. The terms of payment vary, from 45 days before departure to last-minute sales. You can purchase tickets through regular travel agents, who usually mark up the price 8% to 10%, maybe more, thereby greatly reducing your discount. But using such a ticket doesn't qualify you for an advance seat assignment, so you're likely to be assigned a "poor seat" at the last minute.

Most flyers estimate their savings at $200 per ticket off the regular price. Nearly a third of the passengers reported savings of up to $300 off the regular price. But, and here's the hitch, many people reported no savings at all, as the airlines sometimes match the consolidator ticket by announcing a promotional fare. The situation is a bit tricky and calls for some careful investigation to determine how much you're saving.

Bucket shops abound from coast to coast. Look for their ads in your local newspaper's travel section; they're usually very small and a single column in width. (*Note:* Since dealing with unknown bucket shops might be a little risky, it's wise to call the Better Business Bureau in your area to see if complaints have been filed against the company from which you plan to purchase a ticket.)

Here are some recommendations:

One of the biggest U.S. consolidators is **Travac,** 989 Sixth Ave., 16th Floor, New York, NY 10018 (☎ 800/TRAV-800 in the U.S., or 212/563-3303), which offers discounted seats from throughout the United States to most cities in Europe on airlines like TWA, United, and Delta. Another Travac office is at 2601 E. Jefferson St., Orlando, FL 32803 (☎ 407/896-0014).

In New York, try **TFI Tours International,** 34 W. 32nd St., 12th Floor, New York, NY 10001 (☎ 800/745-8000, or 212/736-1140 in New York). This tour company offers services to 177 cities worldwide.

From anywhere, explore the possibilities of **Travel Avenue,** 10 S. Riverside Plaza, Suite 1404, Chicago, IL 60606 (☎ 800/333-3335), a national agency. Its tickets are often cheaper than those at most shops, and it charges only a $25 fee on international tickets, rather than taking the usual 10% commission from an airline. Travel Avenue rebates most of that back to you—hence, the lower fares.

In Minnesota, a possibility is **Travel Management International (TMI),** 1129 E. Wayzata Blvd., Wayzata, MN 55391 (☎ 800/245-3672; fax 612/476-1480), which offers a wide variety of discounts, including youth fares, student fares, and access to other kinds of air-related discounts.

800-FLY-4-LESS is a nationwide airline reservation and ticketing service that specializes in finding the lowest fares. For information on available consolidator airline tickets for last-minute travel, call ☎ 800/359-4537. When fares are high and advance planning time low, such a service is invaluable.

FLYING FROM THE UNITED KINGDOM

From London, **Air France** (☎ 0181/742-6600) and **British Airways** (☎ 0345/222111 in the U.K. only) fly frequently to Paris with a trip time of only 1 hour.

These airlines alone operate up to 17 flights daily from Heathrow, one of the busiest air routes in Europe. Many commercial travelers also use regular flights originating from the London City Airport in the Docklands. Direct flights to Paris also exist from major cities such as Manchester, Edinburgh, and Southampton. Contact Air France, British Airways, **British Midland** (☎ **0181/754-7321**) or **Air UK** (☎ **0345/666777**) for details.

Flying from England to France is often quite expensive, even though the distance is short. That's why most Brits rely on a good travel agent to get them the lowest possible airfare. Good values are offered by a number of companies, including **Nouvelles Frontières**, 2-3 Woodstock St., London W1R 1HE (☎ **0171/ 629-7772**).

There are no hard-and-fast rules about getting the best deals for European flights, but do bear the following points in mind. Daily papers often carry advertisements for companies offering cheap flights. Highly recommended companies include **Trailfinders** (☎ **0171/937-5400**), which sells discounted fares, and **Avro Tours** (☎ **0181/715-0000**), which operates charters. In London, there are many ticket consolidators (who buy inventories of tickets from airlines and then resell them) in the neighborhood of Earl's Court and Victoria Station that offer cheap fares. For your own protection, make sure that the company you deal with is a member of the IATA, ABTA, or ATOL. **CEEFAX**, a British television information service (received by many private homes and hotels), presents details of package holidays and flights to Europe and beyond.

PARIS AIRPORTS

Paris has two major international airports: **Aéroport d'Orly** (☎ 01-49-75-15-15), 8½ miles south, and **Aéroport Roissy-Charles de Gaulle** (☎ 01-48-62-22-80), 14¼ miles northeast of the city. A shuttle operates between the two airports about every 30 minutes, taking 50 to 75 minutes to make the journey.

CHARLES DE GAULLE AIRPORT (ROISSY)   At Charles de Gaulle Airport, foreign carriers use Aérogare 1, and Air France uses Aérogare 2. From Aérogare 1, you take a moving walkway to the passport checkpoint and the Customs area. The two terminals are linked by a shuttle bus (*navette*).

The **free shuttle bus** connecting Aérogare 1 with Aérogare 2 also transports passengers to the Roissy rail station, from which fast RER trains leave every 15 minutes for such Métro stations as Gare du Nord, Châtelet, Luxembourg, Port-Royal, and Denfert-Rochereau. The train fare from Roissy to any point within central Paris is 45F ($9). You can also take an Air France shuttle bus to central Paris for 55F ($11). It stops at the Palais des Congrès (Port Maillot), then continues on to the place de l'Etoile, where underground lines can carry you further along to any other point within Paris. That ride, depending on traffic, takes between 45 and 55 minutes. The shuttle departs about every 12 minutes between 5:40am and 11pm.

Another option, the **Roissybus** (☎ 01-48-04-18-24), departs from a point near the corner of the rue Scribe and the place de l'Opéra every 15 minutes from 5:45am to 11pm. The cost for the 45- to 50-minute bus ride is 40F ($8).

Taxis from Roissy into the city will run about 200F ($40) on the meter. At night (from 8pm to 7am), fares are about 40% higher. Long queues of both taxis and passengers form outside each of the airport's terminals in a surprisingly orderly fashion.

ORLY AIRPORT   Orly has two terminals: Orly Sud (south) for international flights and Orly Ouest (west) for domestic flights. A free shuttle bus links them together.

Air France buses leave exit E of Orly Ouest, and from exit F, Platform 5 of Orly Sud, every 12 minutes between 5:45am and 11pm, heading for Gare des Invalides in central Paris. Other buses depart for the place Denfert-Rochereau in the south of Paris. Passage on any of these buses costs 65F ($13).

An alternative method for reaching central Paris involves taking a free shuttle bus that leaves both of Orly's terminals at intervals of approximately every 15 minutes for the nearby Métro and RER train station (Pont-de-Rungis/Aéroport-d'Orly), from which RER trains take 30 minutes for rides into the city center. A trip to Les Invalides, for example, costs 50F ($10).

A taxi from Orly to the center of Paris costs about 170F ($34) and is higher at night. Don't take a meterless taxi from Orly Sud or Orly Ouest—it's much safer (and usually cheaper) to hire a metered cab from the lines, which are under the scrutiny of a police officer.

Returning to the airport, buses to Orly Airport leave from the Invalides terminal to either Orly Sud or Orly Ouest every 15 minutes, taking about 30 minutes.

BY TRAIN

If you're already in Europe, you might decide to travel to Paris by train, especially if you have a Eurailpass. Even if you don't, the cost is relatively low. For example, the one-way fare from London to Paris by *Eurostar* is $199 in first class and $139 in second class. Rail passes as well as individual rail tickets within Europe are available at most travel agencies, at any office of **Rail Europe** (☎ 800/848-7245 in the U.S.), or at **BritRail Travel International** (☎ 800/677-8585; in New York City, call 212/575-2667). You might also want to stop in at the International Rail Centre, Victoria Station, London SW1V 1JY (☎ 0171/834-7066).

In London, an especially convenient place to buy railway tickets to virtually anywhere is just opposite Platform 2 in Victoria Station, London SW1V 1JZ, where **Wasteels, Ltd.** (☎ 0171/834-6744) provide railway-related services and discuss the pros and cons of various types of fares and rail passes. Occasionally, Wasteels charges a £5 fee for its services, but its information warrants the fee and the company's staff spends a generous amount of time planning itineraries with each client. Some of the most popular passes, including Inter-Rail and EuroYouth, are available only to those under 26 years of age for unlimited second-class travel in 26 European countries.

THE PARIS TRAIN STATIONS

There are six major train stations in Paris: **Gare d'Austerlitz**, 55 quai d'Austerlitz, 13e (serving the southwest, with trains to the Loire Valley, the Bordeaux country, and the Pyrénées); **Gare de l'Est**, place du 11 Novembre 1918, 10e (serving the east, with trains to Strasbourg, Nancy, Reims, and beyond to Zurich, Basel, Luxembourg, and Austria); **Gare de Lyon,** 20 bd. Diderot, 12e (serving the southeast with trains to the Côte d'Azur, Provence, and beyond to Geneva, Lausanne, and Italy); **Gare Montparnasse,** 17 bd. Vaugirard, 15e (serving the west, with trains to Brittany); **Gare du Nord,** 18 rue de Dunkerque, 15e (serving the north, with trains to Holland, Denmark, Belgium, and northern Germany); and **Gare St-Lazare**, 13 rue d'Amsterdam, 8e (serving the northwest, with trains to Normandy and London).

For general train information and to make reservations, call ☎ 01-45-82-50-50 from 7am to 8pm daily. Buses operate between rail stations. Each of these stations has a Métro stop, making the whole city easily accessible. Taxis are also available at every station at designated stands. Look for the sign that says "Tête de Station."

Note

The stations and the surrounding areas are usually seedy and frequented by pickpockets, hustlers, prostitutes, and drug addicts. Be alert, especially at night.

BY BUS

Bus travel to Paris is available from London as well as many other cities throughout the Continent. In the early 1990s, the French government established strong incentives for long-haul buses not to drive into the center of Paris. The arrival and departure point for Europe's largest bus operators, Eurolines France, is a 35-minute Métro ride from central Paris, at the terminus of Métro line 3 (Métro: Gallieni), in the eastern suburb of Bagnolet. Despite this inconvenience, many people prefer bus travel. **Eurolines France** is located at 28 av. du Général-de-Gaulle, 93541 Bagnolet (☎ **01-49-72-51-51**).

Long-haul buses are equipped with toilets and stop at mealtimes for rest and refreshment. The price of a round-trip ticket between Paris and London (a 7-hour trip) is 390F ($78) for passengers 26 or over, and 350F ($70) for passengers under 26.

A round-trip ticket from Rome to Paris (a trip time of $22\frac{1}{2}$ hours) costs 870F ($174) for passengers 26 or over, 780F ($156) for passengers under 26. The price of a round-trip ticket from Stockholm to Paris (a trip time of almost 28 hours) costs 1,290F ($258) for passengers 26 or over, 1,180F ($236) for passengers under 26.

Because Eurolines does not have a U.S.-based sales agent, most people wait until they reach Europe to buy their tickets. Any European travel agent can arrange these purchases. If you're traveling to Paris from London, you can contact **Eurolines (U.K.) Ltd.,** 52 Grosvenor Gardens, Victoria, London SW1 or call ☎ **0990/143219** for information or for credit-card sales.

Most buses arrive at **Gare Routière Internationale du Paris-Gallieni,** 28 av. du Général-de-Gaulle, Bagnolet (☎ **01-49-72-51-51;** Métro: Gallieni).

BY CAR

Driving in Paris is definitely not recommended unless you have lots of experience with European traffic patterns, nerves of steel, and lots of time and money. Parking is difficult, traffic is dense, and networks of one-way streets make navigation, even with the best of maps, a problem. If you do drive, remember that Paris is encircled by a ring road called the *périphérique.* Always obtain detailed directions to your destination, including the name of the exit you're looking for on the périphérique (exits are not numbered). Avoid rush hours.

Few hotels, except the luxury ones, have garages, but the staff will usually be able to direct you to one nearby.

The major highways into Paris are the A1 from the north (Great Britain and Benelux); the A13 from Rouen, Normandy, and other points of northwest France; the A10 from Bordeaux, the Pyrénées, France's southwest, and Spain; the A6 from Lyon, the French Alps, the Riviera, and Italy; and the A4 from Metz, Nancy, and Strasbourg in eastern France.

BY FERRY FROM ENGLAND

For many visitors, crossing the English Channel offers a highly evocative insight into European culture and history. If your plans call for water travel to France, there are three main carriers. The most frequently used are **SuperFerry** (conventional ferryboat service) and **Hoverspeed catamarans** (motorized catamarans, **Sealynx,** which skim along a few inches above the surface of the water). Despite the difference in speed (the catamarans are considerably faster), transportation with a car aboard either mode of transport costs the same: it costs $136 to $248 each way to transport a car with two to nine passengers. Cars with just a driver pay from $104 to $248 each way, depending on the service. Not all of the catamarans offer car service, and since those that do have only a limited capacity for vehicles, it's probable that your means of transport with a car will be aboard one of the conventional ferryboats. Foot passengers (travelers without cars) pay $36 each way on the SuperFerry, and $39 on the catamarans, regardless of which points of embarkation and disembarkation are involved.

The shortest and busiest route between London and Paris is the one from Dover to Calais. By ferryboat, the trip takes about 90 minutes, although a Sealynx can make the run in about 45 minutes. The Sealynx also crosses from Folkestone to Boulogne in about 60 minutes, but that route caters only to foot passengers.

Each crossing is carefully timed to coincide with the arrival and departure of trains from London and Paris, which disgorge passengers and their luggage a short walk from the piers. The U.S. sales agent for the above-mentioned lines is **Britrail** (☎ **800/677-8585** or 212/575-2667).

Another opportunity to travel by ferryboat from England to France is offered by **P&O Channel Lines** (☎ **01304/212121**). They operate car and passenger ferries between Portsmouth and Cherbourg, France (3 departures a day; 4 ¼ hours each way, 7 hours at night); between Portsmouth and Le Havre, France (3 a day; 5 ½ hours each way); between Dover and Calais, France (25 sailing a day; 75 minutes each way).

UNDER THE CHANNEL

Queen Elizabeth and the late French president François Mitterrand officially opened the Channel Tunnel in 1994, and the **Eurostar Express** now has twice-daily passenger service from London to both Paris and Brussels. The $15 billion tunnel, one of the great engineering feats of our time, is the first link between Britain and the continent since the Ice Age. The 31-mile journey takes 35 minutes, although the actual time spent in the Chunnel is only 19 minutes.

Eurostar tickets, for train service between London and Paris or Brussels, are available through **Rail Europe** (☎ **800/94-CHUNNEL** for information). A round-trip fare between London and Paris costs $278 to $298 in first class and $150 to $278 in second class. But you can cut costs to $140 with a nonrefundable second-class, 15-day advance purchase round-trip fare. In London, make reservations for Eurostar at ☎ **0345/303030** (accessible in the United Kingdom only); in Paris at ☎ 01-33-31-58-03, and in the United States, at ☎ 800/387-6782. Chunnel train traffic is roughly competitive with air travel, if you calculate door-to-door travel time. Trains leave from London's Waterloo Station and arrive in Paris at Gare du Nord.

The tunnel also accommodates passenger cars, charter buses, taxis, and motorcycles, transporting them under the English Channel from Folkestone, England, to Calais, France. It operates 24 hours a day, 365 days a year, running every 15 minutes during peak travel times, and at least once an hour at night. Tickets may be purchased at the toll booth at the tunnel's entrance. With "Le Shuttle," gone are the days of weather-related delays, seasickness, and advance reservations.

Before boarding Le Shuttle, motorists stop at a toll booth and then pass through British and French immigration services at the same time. They then drive onto a half-mile-long train and travel through an underground tunnel built beneath the seabed through a layer of impervious chalk marl and sealed with a reinforced-concrete lining. During the ride, motorists stay in bright, air-conditioned carriages, remaining inside their cars or stepping outside to stretch their legs. When the trip is completed, they simply drive off toward their destinations—in our case, Paris. Total travel time between the French and English highway systems is about one hour. Once on French soil, British drivers must remember to drive on the right-hand side of the road.

Stores selling duty-free goods, restaurants, and service stations are available to travelers on both sides of the Channel. A bilingual staff is on hand to assist travelers at both the French and British terminals.

PACKAGE TOURS

Booking a package can save a lot of money. Through volume purchases of hotel rooms, airlines and travel agents can arrange affordable visits to Paris (and elsewhere in Europe) that are geared to either first-timers or seasoned travelers. Tours can range from fully escorted excursions with trained guides, to independent and unsupervised trips (just booking air fare, transfers, and accommodations).

Delta Air Lines, for example, through its tour division (Delta Dream Vacations, ☎ 800/872-7786), offers a land package (without airfare) to the Ile de France that includes six nights at a good hotel in Paris, guided tours of the city's monuments, an excursion to Versailles, breakfasts, taxes, a 5-day pass for public transport in the city, and a 3-day museum pass. The cost begins at $679 per person, double occupancy, depending on the hotel you stay in. (Single occupancy for the same package costs $1,149.) Other packaged trips to the Riviera, Geneva, and the rest of Europe can save you a bundle compared to independently coordinated trips.

The French Experience, 370 Lexington Ave., New York, NY 10017 (☎ 212/986-1115; fax 212/986-3808), offers inexpensive airline tickets to Paris on most scheduled airlines. Several car-dependent tours use varied types and categories of country inns, hotels, private châteaux, and bed-and-breakfasts. They take reservations for about 30 small hotels in Paris, arrange short term apartment rentals in the city or farmhouse rentals in the countryside. They also offer all-inclusive packages in Paris as well as prearranged package tours of various regions of France. Any tour can be adapted to suit individual needs.

American Express Vacations (operated by Certified Vacations, Inc.), P.O. Box 1525, Fort Lauderdale, FL 33302 (☎ 800/446-6234 in the U.S. and Canada; fax 954/357-4682), is the most instantly recognizable tour operator in the world. Their offerings in France and the rest of Europe are more comprehensive than those of many other companies. More than 40 "go-any-day" city packages, 9 freelance vacations, and 18 escorted tours highlight an unparalleled variety.

3

Getting to Know Paris

Ernest Hemingway referred to the many splendors of Paris as a "moveable feast" and wrote, "There is never any ending to Paris, and the memory of each person who has lived in it differs from that of any other." It is this aura of personal discovery that has always been the most compelling reason to come to Paris. And perhaps that's why France has been called *le deuxième pays de tout le monde,* "everybody's second country."

The Seine not only divides Paris into a Right Bank and a Left Bank, but it also seems to split the city into two vastly different sections and ways of life. Depending on your time, interest, and budget, you may quickly decide which section of Paris suits you best.

1 Orientation

VISITOR INFORMATION

The main Paris **tourist information office** is at 127 av. des Champs-Elysées, 8e (☎ **01-49-52-53-69**), where you can find information about both Paris and the provinces. The office is open daily except May 1 from 9am to 8pm.

Welcome Offices, situated in each of the city's railway stations (except the Gare St-Lazare), will also give you free maps, brochures, and a copy of *Paris Selection,* a French-language listing of all current events and performances, which is published monthly.

CITY LAYOUT

Paris is surprisingly compact. Occupying 432 square miles (6 more than San Francisco), it is home to more than 10 million people. As mentioned, the River Seine divides Paris into the **Right Bank (Rive Droite)** to the north and the **Left Bank (Rive Gauche)** to the south. These designations make sense when you stand on a bridge and face downstream, watching the waters flow out toward the sea—to your right is the north bank, to your left the south. Thirty-two bridges link the banks of the **Seine,** some providing access to the two small islands at the heart of the city, **Ile de la Cité,** the city's birthplace and site of Notre-Dame, and **Ile St-Louis,** a moat-guarded oasis of sober 17th-century mansions. These islands can cause some confusion to walkers who think they've just crossed a bridge from one bank to the other, only to find themselves caught up in an almost medieval maze of narrow streets and old buildings.

MAIN ARTERIES & STREETS   Between 1860 and 1870 Baron Haussmann forever changed the look of Paris by creating the legendary boulevards: St-Michel, St-Germain, Haussmann, Malesherbes, Sébastopol, Magenta, Voltaire, and Strasbourg.

The "main street" on the Right Bank is, of course, the **Champs-Elysées**, beginning at the Arc de Triomphe and running to the place de la Concorde. Haussmann also created avenue de l'Opéra (as well as the Opéra), and the 12 avenues that radiate starlike from the Arc de Triomphe, giving it its original name, place de l'Etoile (renamed place Charles de Gaulle following the general's death). Today it is often referred to as place Charles de Gaulle–Etoile.

Haussmann also cleared Ile de la Cité of its medieval buildings, transforming it into a showcase for Notre-Dame. Finally, he laid out the two elegant parks on the western and southeastern fringes of the city: **Bois de Boulogne** and **Bois de Vincennes.**

FINDING AN ADDRESS   Paris is divided into 20 municipal wards called *arrondissements,* each with its own mayor, city hall, police station, and central post office. Some even have remnants of market squares. Most city maps are divided by arrondissement, and all addresses include the arrondissement number (written in Roman or Arabic numerals and followed by *e* or *er*). Paris also has its own version of a zip code. Thus, the proper mailing address for a hotel is written as, say, 75014 Paris. The last two digits, 14, indicate that the address is in the 14th arrondissement, in this case, Montparnasse.

Numbers on buildings running parallel to the River Seine usually follow the course of the river—that is, east to west. On perpendicular streets, numbers on buildings begin low closer to the river.

STREET MAPS   If you're staying more than 2 or 3 days, purchase an inexpensive, pocket-size book that includes the *plan de Paris* by arrondissement available at all major newsstands and bookshops. If you can find it, the little burgundy-colored *Paris Classique–L'indispensable* is a thorough, well-indexed, and accurate guide to the city and its suburbs. Most map guides provide you with a Métro map, a foldout map of the city, and indexed maps of each arrondissement, with all streets listed and keyed. And check out the free full-color foldout map in the back of this guide.

THE ARRONDISSEMENTS IN BRIEF

Each of Paris's 20 arrondissements possesses a unique style and flavor. You will want to decide which district appeals most to you and then find accommodations here. Later on, try to visit as many areas as you can.

Impressions

Paris is still monumental and handsome. Along the rivers where its splendours are, there's no denying its man-made beauty. The poor, pale little Seine runs rapidly north to the sea, the sky is pale, pale jade overhead, greenish and Parisian, the trees of black wire stand in rows, and flourish their black wire brushes against a low sky of jade-pale cobwebs, and the huge dark-grey palaces rear up their masses of stone and slope off towards the sky still with a massive, satisfying suggestion of pyramids. There is something noble and man-made about it all.

—D.H. Lawrence

Paris is the greatest temple ever built to material joys and the lust of the eyes.

—Henry James

1st Arr. (Musée du Louvre/Les Halles) "I never knew what a palace was until I had a glimpse of the Louvre," wrote Nathaniel Hawthorne. One of the world's finest art museums (some say the greatest), the **Louvre,** a former royal residence, still lures all visitors to Paris to the 1st arrondissement. Here are many of the elegant addresses of Paris, the rue de Rivoli, with the Jeu de Paume and Orangerie on raised terraces. Walk through its **Jardin des Tuileries,** the most formal garden of Paris (originally laid out by Le Nôtre, gardener to Louis XIV). Pause to take in the classic beauty of the **place Vendôme,** the opulent, wealthy home of the Ritz Hotel. Jewelers and art dealers are in plentiful supply, and the memories of Chopin are evoked on the square where he died. Zola's "the belly of Paris" (Les Halles) is no longer the food and meat market of Paris (traders moved to a new, more accessible suburb, Rungis), but is today **Forum des Halles,** a center of shopping, entertainment, and culture.

2nd Arr. (La Bourse) Home to the **Bourse** (stock exchange), this Right Bank district lies mainly between the Grands Boulevards and the rue Etienne Marcel. From Monday through Friday, the shouts of brokers—*J'ai!* (I have it!) or *Je prends!* (I'll take it!)—echo across the place de la Bourse until it's time to break for lunch, when the movers and shakers of French capitalism channel their hysteria into the restaurants of the district. Much of the eastern end of the arrondissement **(Le Sentier)** is devoted to wholesale outlets of the Paris garment district, where thousands of garments are sold (usually in bulk) to buyers from clothing stores throughout Europe. "Everything that exists elsewhere exists in Paris," wrote Victor Hugo in *Les Misérables,* and if you take on this district, you'll find ample evidence to support his claim. Dogged prospectors may find nuggets of beauty and value here amid an often overwhelming commercialism—none finer than the **Musée Cognacq-Jay,** 25 bd. des Capucines. Ernest Cognacq created the Samaritaine chain of stores, but also had time to collect some of the world's most exquisite art. His collection is a jewel box brimming with treasures, featuring work by every artist from Watteau to Fragonard.

3rd Arr. (Le Marais) This district embraces much of **Le Marais** (the swamp), one of the best loved of the old Right Bank neighborhoods. After decades of seedy decay, Le Marais recently made a comeback, although it may never again enjoy the prosperity of its aristocratic heyday during the 17th century. Over the centuries, kings have called Le Marais home, and its salons have resounded with the witty and devastating remarks of Racine, Voltaire, Molière, and Madame de Sévigné. One of the district's chief attractions today is **Musée Picasso,** a kind of pirate's ransom of painting and sculpture that the Picasso estate had to turn over to the French government in lieu of the artist's astronomical death duties. Forced donation or not, it's one of the world's great repositories of 20th-century art.

4th Arr. (Ile de la Cité/Ile St-Louis & Beaubourg) At times it seems as if the 4th has it all: not only Notre-Dame on **Ile de la Cité,** but **Ile St-Louis** and its aristocratic town houses, courtyards, and antique shops. Ile St-Louis, a former cow pasture and dueling ground, is home to dozens of 17th-century mansions and 6,000 lucky *louisiens,* its permanent residents. Voltaire found it "the second best" address in all the world, citing the straits of the Bosporus separating Europe from Asia as number one. Of course, the whole area is touristy and overrun. Forget the "I Love Paris" bumper stickers and seek out Ile de la Cité's two glorious Gothic churches, **La Sainte-Chapelle** and **Notre-Dame,** a majestic and dignified structure that, according to the poet e.e. cummings, doesn't budge an inch for all the idiocies of this world.

The heart of medieval Paris, the 4th evokes memories of Danton, Robespierre, and even of Charlotte Corday, who stabbed Marat in his bath. Here you not only get

France's finest bird and flower markets, but the nation's law courts. Balzac described the courts as a "cathedral of chicanery," and they do have a long tradition of dispensing justice, French-style: It was here that Marie Antoinette was sentenced to death in 1793. If all this weren't enough, the 4th is also home to the **Centre Georges Pompidou,** now one of the top three tourist attractions of France, partly because of its National Museum of Modern Art. (Sadly, Centre Pompidou will be closed for renovations until the tolling of the millennium on December 31, 1999.) Finally, after all this pomp and glory, you can retreat to the **place des Vosges,** a square of perfect harmony and beauty where Victor Hugo lived from 1832 to 1848 and penned many of his famous masterpieces.

5th Arr. (Latin Quarter)   The **Quartier Latin** is the intellectual heart and soul of Paris. Bookstores, schools, churches, smoky jazz clubs, student dives, Roman ruins, publishing houses, and, yes, expensive and chic boutiques, characterize the district. Discussions of Artaud or Molière over long cups of coffee aren't at all out of place here. Beginning with the founding of the **Sorbonne** in 1253, the *quartier* was called Latin because all students and professors spoke the scholarly language. As the traditional center of what was called "bohemian Paris," it formed the setting for Henri Murger's novel *Scènes de la vie de Bohème* (later the Puccini opera, *La Bohème*).

You'll follow in the footsteps of Descartes, Verlaine, Camus, Sartre, James Thurber, Elliot Paul, and Hemingway as you explore this historic district. For sure, the old Latin quarter is gone forever. Changing times have brought Greek, Moroccan, and Vietnamese immigrants, among others, hustling everything from couscous to fiery-hot spring rolls and souvlaki. The 5th also borders the Seine, and you'll want to stroll along **quai de Montebello**, inspecting the inventories of the *bouquinistes* who sell everything from antique Daumier prints to yellowing copies of Balzac's *Père Goriot* in the shadow of Notre-Dame. The 5th also stretches down to the **Panthéon,** which was constructed by a grateful Louis XV after he'd recovered from the gout and wanted to do something nice for Ste-Geneviève, Paris's patron saint. It's the dank, dark resting place of Rousseau, Gambetta, Emile Zola, Louis Braille, Victor Hugo, Voltaire, and Jean Moulin, the World War II Resistance leader whom the Gestapo tortured to death.

6th Arr. (St-Germain/Luxembourg)   This is the heartland of Paris publishing and, for some, the most colorful quarter of the Left Bank, where waves of earnest young artists still emerge from the famous **Ecole des Beaux-Arts.** To stroll the boulevards of the 6th, including St-Germain, has its own rewards, but the secret of the district lies in discovering its narrow streets and hidden squares as well as the Jardin du Luxembourg, a classic French garden overlooked by Marie de Médici's Italianate Palais du Luxembourg. Of course, to be really "authentic," you'll stroll these streets with an unwrapped loaf of country sourdough bread from the wood-fired ovens of **Poilâne,** the world's most famous baker, at 8 rue du Cherche-Midi. Everywhere you turn in the district, you encounter famous historical and literary associations, none more so than on rue Jacob. At 7 rue Jacob, Racine lived with his uncle as a teenager; Richard Wagner resided at 14 rue Jacob from 1841 to 1842; Ingres once lived at 27 rue Jacob (now it's the offices of the French publishing house Editions du Seuil); and Hemingway once occupied a tiny upstairs room at no. 44. Today's big name is likely to be filmmaker Spike Lee checking into his favorite, La Villa Hôtel, at 29 rue Jacob.

Delacroix (whom Baudelaire called "a volcanic crater artistically concealed beneath bouquets of flowers") kept his atelier in the 6th, and George Sand and her lover, Frédéric Chopin, used to visit him here to have their portraits done. His studio is now open to the public. **Rue Monsieur-le-Prince** has historically been a popular street for Paris's resident Americans, once frequented by Martin Luther King Jr., Richard Wright, James McNeill Whistler, Henry Wadsworth Longfellow, and even Oliver Wendell Holmes. The 6th takes in the **Luxembourg Gardens,** a 60-acre playground where Isadora Duncan went dancing in the predawn hours and a destitute writer, Ernest Hemingway, went looking for pigeons for lunch, carrying them in a baby carriage back to his humble flat for cooking.

7th Arr. (Eiffel Tower/Musée d'Orsay)   Paris's most famous symbol, the **Eiffel Tower**, dominates Paris and especially the 7th, a Left Bank district of respectable residences and government offices. Part of **the St-Germain neighborhood** is included here as well. The tower is now one of the most recognizable landmarks in the world, despite the fact that many Parisians (most notably some of its nearest neighbors) hated it when it was unveiled in 1889. Many of the most imposing monuments of Paris are in the 7th, including the **Hôtel des Invalides,** which contains both Napoléon's Tomb and the Musée de l'Armée. But there is much hidden charm here as well. Who has not walked these narrow streets before you? Your predecessors include Picasso, Manet, Ingres, Baudelaire, Wagner, Simone de Beauvoir, Sartre, even Truman Capote, Gore Vidal, and Tennessee Williams.

Rue du Bac was home to the swashbuckling heroes of Dumas's *The Three Musketeers,* and to James McNeill Whistler, who, after selling *Whistler's Mother,* moved to 110 rue du Bac, where he entertained the likes of Degas, Henry James, Manet, and Toulouse-Lautrec. Auguste Rodin lived at what is now the **Musée Rodin** at 77 rue de Varenne until his death in 1917.

Even visitors with no time to thoroughly explore the 7th at least rush to its second major attraction (after the Eiffel Tower), the **Musée d'Orsay**, the world's premier showcase of 19th-century French art and culture. The museum is housed in the old Gare d'Orsay, which Orson Welles used in 1962 as a setting for his film *The Trial,* based on the book by Franz Kafka.

8th Arr. (Champs-Elysée/Madeleine)   The prime showcase of the 8th is the **Champs-Elysées,** which stretches grandly from the **Arc de Triomphe** to the purloined Egyptian obelisk on **place de la Concorde.** Here you'll find the fashion houses, the most elegant hotels, expensive restaurants and shops, and the most fashionably attired Parisians. By the 1980s, this had become a garish strip, with too much traffic, too many fast-food joints, and too many panhandlers. In the 1990s, Jacques Chirac, then the Gaullist mayor of Paris, launched a massive cleanup, broadening sidewalks and planting new rows of trees. (The fast food places, here and in other arrondissements, are still breeding like rabbits.) The old glory? Perhaps it's gone forever, but what an improvement.

Whatever it is you're looking for, in the 8th it will be the city's "best, grandest, and most impressive": It has the best restaurant in Paris (Taillevent); the sexiest strip joint (Crazy Horse Saloon); the most splendid square in all of France (place de la Concorde); the best rooftop cafe (at La Samaritaine); the grandest hotel in France (The Crillon); the most impressive triumphal arch on the planet (L'Arc de Triomphe); the world's most expensive residential street (avenue Montaigne); the world's oldest Métro station (Franklin-D-Roosevelt); the most ancient monument in Paris (the Obelisk of Luxor, 3,300 years old). Also here is the Madeleine church, looking like a Greek temple. It stands at the junction of the boulevards at place de la Madeleine, reached from place de la Concorde by walking along rue Royale.

9th Arr. (Opéra Garnier/Pigalle)   Everything from the **Quartier de l'Opéra** to the strip and clip joints of **Pigalle** (the infamous "Pig Alley" for the GIs of World War II) falls within the 9th. When Balzac was writing his novels, the author considered the 9th's chaussée d'Antin as the most elite address for his socially ambitious characters. Radically altered by the 19th-century urban redevelopment projects of Baron Haussmann, the *grands boulevards* radiating through the district are among the most obvious of the baron's labors. Although the chaussée d'Antin is no longer particularly elegant, having been supplanted by some of Paris's largest department stores, the 9th endures, even if fickle fashion prefers other addresses. Over the decades, the 9th has been celebrated in literature and song for the music halls that brought gaiety to the city. The building at 17 bd. de la Madeleine was the death site of Marie Duplessis, who gained fame as the heroine Marguerite Gautier in Alexandre Dumas the younger's *La Dame aux camélias*. Greta Garbo later redoubled Marie's legend by playing her in the film *Camille*. Boulevard des Italiens is the site of the **Café de la Paix,** opened in 1856 and once the meeting place of a number of French Romantic poets, including Théophile Gautier and Alfred de Musset. Later, Charles de Gaulle, Marlene Dietrich, and two million Americans kept their seats warm.

At Place Pigalle, gone is the cafe La Nouvelle Athènes, where Degas, Pissarro, and Manet used to meet. Today, you're likely to encounter a few clubs where the action gets really down and dirty. Other major attractions include the **Folies Bergère,** where cancan dancers have been high-kicking it since 1868, and French entertainers such as Mistinguett, Edith Piaf, and Maurice Chevalier have appeared along with Josephine Baker, once hailed as "the toast of Paris." More than anything, it was the **Opéra Garnier** (Paris Opera House) that made the 9th the last hurrah of Second Empire opulence. Renoir hated it, but several generations later, Chagall did the ceilings. Pavlova danced *Swan Lake* here, and Nijinsky took the night off to go cruising.

10th Arr. (Gare du Nord/Gare de l'Est) **Gare du Nord** and **Gare de l'Est,** along with movie theaters, porno houses, and dreary commercial zones make the 10th one of the least desirable arrondissements for living, dining, and sightseeing in Paris. We always try to avoid the 10th, except for two longtime favorite restaurants, **Brasserie Flo** at 7 cour des Petites-Ecuries (go here for its *la formidable choucroute,* a heap of sauerkraut garnished with everything), and **Julien,** 16 rue du Faubourg St-Denis (called the poor man's Maxim's because of its belle epoque interiors and moderate prices).

11th Arr. (Opéra Bastille) For many years, this quarter seemed to sink lower and lower into poverty and decay, overcrowded by working-class immigrants from the far reaches of the former French Empire. The opening of the **Opéra Bastille,** however, has given the 11th new hope and new life. The facility, called the "people's opera house," stands on the landmark place de la Bastille, where on July 14, 1789, 633 Parisians stormed the fortress and seized the ammunition depot, as the French Revolution swept across the city. Over the years, the prison held Voltaire, the Marquis de Sade, and the mysterious "Man in the Iron Mask."

Even when the district wasn't fashionable, visitors flocked to **Bofinger,** at 5–7 rue de la Bastille, to sample its Alsatian *choucroute.* (Technically, although its fans have always associated it with the place de la Bastille, Bofinger lies in the 4th arrondissement.) Established around 1864, it is perhaps the most famous brasserie in Paris. The 11th has its charms, but they exist only for those who seek them out; *Le Marché* at place d'Aligre, for example, is surrounded by a Middle Eastern food market and is a good place to hunt for second-hand bargains: Everything is cheap, and although you must search hard for treasures, they often appear.

12th Arr. (Bois de Vincennes/Gare de Lyon) Very few out-of-towners came here until a French chef opened a restaurant called Au Trou Gascon. Then *tout le monde* started showing up at the door (see "Dining," chapter 5, for more details). In addition to this eatery, the 12th's major attraction remains the **Bois de Vincennes,** a sprawling park on the eastern periphery of Paris. It's been a longtime favorite of French families who enjoy its zoos and museums, its royal château and boating lakes, and most definitely, the Parc Floral de Paris, a celebrated flower garden whose springtime rhododendrons and autumn dahlias are among the major lures of the city. The dreary **Gare de Lyon** also lies in the 12th, but going here is worthwhile even if you don't have to take a train, because Le Train Bleu, a restaurant in the station, features ceiling frescoes and art nouveau decor that are classified as national artistic treasures. The food's good, too.

The 12th arrondissement, once a depressing urban wasteland, has been singled out for budgetary resuscitation, and is beginning to sport new housing, shops, gardens, and restaurants. Many of these new structures will occupy the site of the former Reuilly railroad tracks.

13th Arr. (Gare d'Austerlitz) Centered around the grimy **Gare d'Austerlitz,** the 13th might have its devotees, but we've yet to meet one. British snobs who flitted in and out of the train station were among the first of the district's foreign visitors, and in essence wrote the 13th off as a dreary working-class counterpart of London's East End. Certainly there are far more fashionable places, but there is at least one reason to visit the 13th: the **Manufacture des Gobelins** at 42 av. des Gobelins, the tapestry factory that made the word *Gobelins* internationally famous. Some 250 Flemish weavers, under the reign of Louis XIV, launched the industry to compete with the tapestries being produced in southern Belgium (Flanders), and in time they became the preferred suppliers of the French aristocracy—many of the walls of the Sun King's palace at Versailles were covered with Gobelins.

14th Arr. (Montparnasse) The northern end of this large arrondissement is devoted to **Montparnasse,** home of the "lost generation," and former stomping ground of Stein, Toklas, Hemingway, and other American expatriates who gathered here in the 1920s. After World War II, it ceased to be the center of intellectual life in Paris, but the memory lingers in its cafes. One of the monuments that sets the tone of the neighborhood is Rodin's statue of Balzac at the junction of boulevard Montparnasse and boulevard Raspail. At this corner are some of the world's most famous literary cafes, including **La Rotonde, Le Select, La Dôme,** and **La Coupole.** Though Gertrude Stein probably avoided this corner (she loathed cafes), all the other American expatriates, including Hemingway and Scott Fitzgerald, had no qualms about enjoying a drink here (or quite a few of them, for that matter). Henry Miller, plotting *Tropic of Cancer* and his newest seduction of Anaïs Nin, came to La Coupole for his morning porridge. So did Roman Polanski, Josephine Baker (with a lion cub on a leash), James Joyce, Man Ray, Matisse, Ionesco (ordering *café liègeois*), Jean-Paul Sartre, and even the famous Kiki as she worked on her memoirs. Though she shunned the cafes, Stein amused herself at home (27 rue de Fleurus) with Alice B. Toklas, collecting paintings, including those of Picasso, and entertaining the likes of Max Jacob, Apollinaire, T.S. Eliot, and Matisse. The southern end of the 14th arrondissement contains pleasant residential neighborhoods filled with well-designed apartment buildings, many constructed between 1910 and 1940.

15th Arr. (Gare Montparnasse/Institut Pasteur) A mostly residential district beginning at **Gare Montparnasse,** the 15th stretches all the way to the Seine. In size and population, it's the largest quarter of Paris, but it attracts few tourists and has few attractions, except for the **Parc des Expositions** and the **Institut Pasteur.** In the early 20th century, many artists—Chagall, Léger, and Modigliani—lived in this arrondissement in a shared atelier known as "The Beehive."

16th Arr. (Trocadéro/Bois de Boulogne)   Originally the village of Passy, where Benjamin Franklin lived during most of his time in Paris, this district is still reminiscent of Proust's world. Highlights include the **Bois de Boulogne;** the **Jardin du Trocadéro;** the **Musée de Balzac;** the **Musée Guimet** (famous for its Asian collections); and the **Cimetière de Passy,** resting place of Manet, Talleyrand, Giraudoux, and Debussy. One of the largest of the city's arrondissements, it's known today for its well-heeled bourgeoisie, its upscale rents, and some rather posh (and, according to its critics, rather smug) residential boulevards. Prosperous and suitably conservative addresses include the avenue d'Iéna and the avenue Victor Hugo. Also prestigious is the avenue Foch, the widest boulevard in Paris, with homes that at various periods were maintained by Onassis, the shah of Iran, the composer Achille-Claude Debussy, and Prince Rainier of Monaco. The arrondissement also includes the best place in Paris from which to view the Eiffel Tower; the **place du Trocadéro.**

17th Arr. (Parc Monceau/Place Clichy)   Flanking the northern periphery of Paris, the 17th incorporates neighborhoods of conservative bourgeois respectability (in its western end) and less affluent neighborhoods in its eastern end. Regardless of its levels of prosperity, most of the arrondissement is residential, and most of it, at least to habitués of glamour and glitter, is rather dull. Highlights include the **Palais des Congrès,** which is of interest only if you're attending a convention or special exhibit, and the **Porte Maillot Air Terminal,** no grand distinction. More exciting than either of those are two of the greatest restaurants of Paris, Guy Savoy and Michel Rostang (see chapter 5).

18th Arr. (Montmartre)   The 18th is the most famous outer quartier of Paris, containing **Montmartre,** the **Moulin Rouge,** the **Basilica of Sacré-Coeur,** and the **place du Tertre.** Utrillo was its native son, Renoir lived here, and Toulouse-Lautrec adopted the area as his own. The most famous enclave of artists in Paris's history, the Bateau-Lavoir, of Picasso fame, gathered here. Max Jacob, Matisse, and Braque were all frequent visitors. Today, place Blanche is known for its prostitutes, and Montmartre is filled with honky-tonks, too many souvenir shops, and terrible restaurants. Go to see the attractions and to glimpse at faded fame. The city's most famous flea market, **Marché aux Puces de Clignancourt,** is another landmark.

19th Arr. (La Villette)   Today, visitors come to what was once the village of La Villette to see the angular, much-publicized **Cité des Sciences et de l'Industrie,** a spectacular science museum and park built on a site that for years was devoted to the city's slaughterhouses. Mostly residential, and not at all upscale, the district is one of the most ethnically diverse in Paris, the home of people from all parts of the former French Empire. A highlight is **Les Buttes–Chaumont,** a park where kids can enjoy puppet shows and donkey rides.

20th Arr. (Père-Lachaise Cemetery)   The 20th's greatest landmark is **Père-Lachaise Cemetery,** the resting place of Edith Piaf, Marcel Proust, Oscar Wilde, Isadora Duncan, Sarah Bernhardt, Gertrude Stein, Colette, and many, many others. Otherwise, the 20th arrondissement is a dreary and sometimes volatile melting pot comprising residents from France's former colonies. Although nostalgia buffs sometimes head here to visit Piaf's former neighborhood, Ménilmontant-Belleville, it has been almost totally bulldozed and rebuilt since the bad old days when she grew up here. Parts of the 20th won't correspond to your vision of the legendary Paris in any way: The district contains many Muslims—you'll see turbaned men selling dates and grains on the street—and hundreds of deeply entrenched members of Paris's Sephardic community, many of whom fled their former homes in Algeria or Tunisia, fearing for their safety. The area can be grim, and is shunned by many upscale

Parisians. Sometimes there's a palpable sense of discontent here, but the 20th provides a vivid cultural contrast to some of Paris's other quartiers.

2 Getting Around

Paris is a city for strollers whose greatest joy in life is rambling through unexpected alleyways and squares. Given a choice of conveyance, use your own two feet whenever possible. Only when you're dead tired and can't walk another step, or are in a roaring hurry to reach a destination, should you consider using the swift and dull means of urban transport.

BY PUBLIC TRANSPORTATION

DISCOUNT PASSES   You can purchase a *Paris-Visite* pass, a tourist pass valid for 3 or 5 days on the public transportation system, including the Métro, city buses, even RER (Réseau Express Régional) trains. (The RER has both first- and second-class compartments, and the pass lets you travel in first class.) As a special bonus, the funicular ride to the top of Montmartre is also included. The cost is 110F ($22) for 3 days, or 170F ($34) for 5 days. The card is available at RATP (Régie Autonome des Transports Parisiens; ☎ 08-36-69-77-14), tourist offices, or at the main Métro stations; call ☎ 01-44-68-20-20 for information.

There are other discount passes as well, although most are available only to French residents with government ID cards and proof of taxpayer status. One, however, which is available to temporary visitors is *Formule 1,* which allows unlimited travel on all bus, subway, and RER lines of Paris during a 1-day period for a cost of 30F ($6). The pass can be purchased at RATP offices at 53 bis quai des Grands-Augustins, 6e (☎ 01-53-46-44-50; Métro: St-Michel), or at place de la Madeleine, 8e (☎ 01-40-06-71-45; Métro: Madeleine). For more information, call ☎ 04-43-46-14-14.

BY SUBWAY

The **Métro** (☎ 01-43-46-14-14 for information) is the most efficient means of transportation, and it's easy to use. Each line is numbered and the final destination of each is clearly marked on subway maps, on the trains themselves, and in the underground passageways. Most stations display a map of the system at the entrance; you'll find a copy of this map on the back cover of this book. Figure out the route from where you are to your destination, noting the stations where you will have to change. To make sure you catch the right train, find your destination, then visually follow the line it's on to the end of the route and note its name. This is the *direction* you follow in the stations and see on the train. Transfer stations are known as *correspondances.* (Note that some require long walks—Châtelet is the most notorious.)

Most trips will require only one transfer. Many of the larger stations have maps with push-button indicators that will help you plot your route more easily by lighting up automatically when you press the button for your destination. A ride on the urban lines costs 8F ($1.60) to any point within the 20 arrondissements of Paris, as well as to many of its near suburbs. A bulk purchase of 10 tickets (which are bound together into what the French refer to as a *carnet*) costs 46F ($9.20). Métro fares to far-flung, outlying suburbs on the Sceaux, the Noisy-St-Léger, and the St-Germain-en-Laye lines cost more, and are sold on an individual basis based on the distance you travel.

At the entrances to the Métro station, insert your ticket into the turnstile and pass through. At some exits, tickets and their validity are checked by uniformed police officers, so hold onto your ticket. There are occasional ticket checks on the trains, platforms, and passageways, too.

If you are changing trains, get out and determine which *direction* (final destination) on the next line you want, and follow the bright-orange "Correspondance" signs until you reach the proper platform. Don't follow a "Sortie" sign, which means "exit," or else you'll have to pay another fare to resume your journey.

The Métro starts running daily at 5:30am and closes around 1:15am. It's reasonably safe at any hour, but beware of pickpockets.

By Bus

Bus travel is much slower than the subway. Most buses run from 7am to 8:30pm (a few operate until 12:30am, and 10 operate during the early morning hours). Service is limited on Sunday and holidays. Bus and Métro fares are the same and you can use the same *carnet* tickets on both.

At certain bus stops, signs list the destinations and numbers of the buses serving that point. Destinations are usually listed north to south, and east to west. Most stops along the way are also posted on the sides of the buses. To catch a bus, wait in line at the bus stop. Signal the driver to stop the bus and board in order. During rush hours you may have to take a ticket from the dispensing machine, indicating your position in the line.

The same entity that maintains Paris's network of Métros and buses, the **RATP** (☎ 01-44-68-20-20), has initiated a motorized mode of transport designed exclusively as a means of appreciating the city's visual grandeur. Known as the **Balabus** (a word play on the French phrase *se ballader par bus*, or "to take a pleasure ride on a bus"), it's a program that unleashes a fleet of big-windowed orange-and-white motor coaches whose most visible drawback is their limited hours—they run only on Sundays and national holidays from noon to 9pm from April 15 to September 30.

The coaches journey in both directions between the Gare de Lyon and Grande Arche de La Défense, encompassing some of the city's most monumental vistas. The price will gladden the heart of any budgeteer—three Métro tickets (24F/$4.80) will carry you along the entire route. You'll recognize the bus and the route it follows by the *Bb* symbol emblazoned on each bus's side and on signs posted beside the route it follows.

If you intend to use the buses frequently, pick up a RATP bus map at the office on place de la Madeleine, 8e, or at the tourist offices at RATP headquarters, 55 quai des Grands-Augustins, 75006 Paris. For detailed information in English on bus and Métro routes, call ☎ **08-36-68-77-14.**

By Car

Don't even think about driving in Paris. The streets are narrow, with confusing one-way designations, and parking is next to impossible. Besides, most visitors don't have the ruthlessness required to survive in Parisian traffic.

If, at your peril, you ignore our advice, here are a few tips: Get an excellent street map and ride with a copilot because there's no time to think at intersections. Carry plenty of coins (1F, 5F, and 10F denominations) for parking meters. Depending on the neighborhood, the cost of an hour's parking beside a coin-operated meter can vary from 3F ($.60) to 10F ($2) an hour. Some out-of-the-way neighborhoods still rely on the increasingly old-fashioned "Blue Zones," where parking on weekdays and Saturdays requires a "parking disc" obtainable from garages, police stations, and hotels. Parking is unlimited in these zones Sundays and holidays. Attach the disc to your windshield, setting its clock to show the time of your arrival. Between 9am and noon and from 2:30 to 5pm you may park for one hour, from noon to 2:30pm for 2¹/₂ hours.

Watch for gendarmes, who lack patience and consistently countermand the lights. Horn-blowing is absolutely forbidden except in dire emergencies.

RENTALS   The major car-rental companies usually try to match one another's price schedules and rental conditions, although depending on circumstances, one or another sometimes offers rates that rival the cost of touring the French countryside by train. Of the major worldwide competitors, the cheapest weekly arrangements, as of this writing, were offered by **Budget,** followed in hot pursuit by **Avis, Hertz,** and **National.** These relative advantages change (sometimes radically) for luxury-category cars, but usually the best deal is a weekly rental with unlimited mileage and an advance reservation *made from North America,* between 2 days and 2 weeks in advance. Shop around at least 14 days before your departure, knowing that it pays to ask questions and make comparisons.

Renting a car in Paris (and France) is easy. All you need is a valid driver's license, a passport, and (unless the rate is prepaid in dollars in North America) a valid credit card. In some cases, the rental company will require that your driver's license has been valid for between 1 and 2 years before your rental, depending on the value of the car you want to rent. Usually it isn't obligatory, but small companies may require an international driver's license as well. The minimum age for renting cars is 21 at Hertz, 23 at Avis, and 25 at Budget.

Unless it's already factored into the rental agreement, an optional collision-damage waiver (CDW) carries an additional charge of between 80F and 95F ($16 to $19) a day for the least-expensive cars. Buying this additional insurance will usually eliminate all except 1,500F ($300) of your responsibility in the event of accidental damage to the car. Because most newcomers are not familiar with local driving customs and conditions, we highly recommend that you buy the CDW, although certain credit-card issuers will compensate a renter for any accident-related liability to a rented car if the imprint of their card appears on the original rental contract. At some of the companies (including Hertz) the CDW will not protect you against the theft of a car, so if this is the case, ask about buying additional theft protection, which costs around 37F ($7.40) extra per day.

Depending on the company and the season, prices may range from $176 to $195 per week, with unlimited mileage (but not including tax or CDW) included. Automatic transmission is regarded as a luxury in Europe, so if you want it, you'll have to pay dearly for it.

Budget Rent-a-Car (☎ **800/472-3325** in North America) maintains about 30 locations in Paris, including its largest branch at 81 av. Kléber, 16e (☎ 01-47-55-61-18; Métro: Trocadéro). For rentals of more than 7 days, cars can be picked up in one French city and dropped off in another for an additional charge. Drop-offs in cities within an easy drive of the French border (including Geneva and Frankfurt, for example) incur no secondary charges; drop-offs in other non-French cities can be arranged for a reasonable surcharge.

Hertz (☎ **800/654-3001** in North America) has about 15 locations in Paris, including the city's airports. The company's main office is at 27 rue St-Ferdinand, 17e (☎ 01-45-74-97-39; Métro: Argentine). Be sure to ask about any promotional discounts the company might offer.

Warning

All car-rental bills in France are subject to a 20.6% tax, one of the highest in Europe. In some cases, the tax will be factored into the rate quoted to you over the phone. Be sure to ask.

Avis (☎ **800/331-2112** in North America) has offices at both city airports, as well as an inner-city headquarters at 5 rue Bixio, 7e (☎ 01-44-18-10-50; Métro: Ecole Militaire), near the Eiffel Tower.

National Car Rental (☎ **800/227-3876** in North America) is represented in Paris by Europcar, whose largest office is at 145 av. Malakoff, 16e (☎ 01-45-00-08-06; Métro: Porte Maillot). It also has offices at both of the Paris airports and at about a dozen other locations throughout the city.

GASOLINE   Gasoline, or *essence,* as it's known in France, is extraordinarily expensive for the visitor who's used to North American prices. All but the least-expensive cars require an octane rating that the French classify as *essence super,* the most expensive variety. At press time, essence super sold for about 6.50F ($1.30) per liter, which works out to around 24.50F ($4.90) per North American gallon. Depending on your car, you'll need either unleaded gasoline (*sans plomb*) or, less frequently, leaded gasoline (*avec plomb*). What this means is that filling up the tank of a medium-sized car can cost between $45 and $65. Plan your finances accordingly.

DRIVING RULES   Everyone in the car, in both the front and the back seats, must wear seat belts. Children under 12 must ride in the back seat. Drivers are supposed to yield to the car on their right, except where signs indicate otherwise, for instance, at traffic circles. If you violate the speed limits, expect a large fine. **Speed limits** are usually 130 kmph (80 m.p.h.) on expressways, about 100 kmph (60 m.p.h.) on major national highways, and 90 kmph (56 m.p.h.) on small country roads. In towns, don't exceed 60 kmph (37 m.p.h.).

MAPS   Before setting out on a tour of Paris's environs, pick up a good regional map of the district you plan to explore. If you're visiting a town, ask at the local tourist office for a town plan. They are usually free.

For France as a whole, most motorists prefer the Michelin map 989. For regions, Michelin publishes a series of yellow maps that are quite good. Large travel bookstores in North America carry these maps, but they are commonly available in France at lower prices. One useful feature of the Michelin map is its designation of alternate *routes de dégagement,* which let you skirt big cities and avoid traffic-clogged highways.

BREAKDOWNS/ASSISTANCE   A breakdown is called *une panne* in France, and it is just as frustrating here as anywhere else. Call the police at ☎ 17, anywhere in France, and they will put you in touch with the nearest garage. Most local garages have towing services. If your breakdown should occur on an expressway, find the nearest roadside emergency phone box, pick up the phone, and put a call through. You'll be connected immediately to the nearest breakdown service facility.

BY TAXI

It's impossible to get a taxi at rush hour, so don't try. Taxi drivers are organized into an effective lobby to keep their number limited to 14,300.

Watch out for the common rip-offs. Always check the meter to make sure you're not paying the previous passenger's fare. Beware of cabs without meters, which often try to snare tipsy patrons outside nightclubs—always settle the tab in advance. Regular cabs can be hailed on the street when their signs read *libre.* Taxis are easier to find at the many stands near Métro stations.

The flag drops at 13F ($2.60), and from 7am to 7pm you pay 3.36F (65¢) per kilometer. From 7pm to 7am, expect to pay 5.45F ($1.10) per kilometer. On airport trips you're *not* required to pay for the driver's empty return ride.

You're allowed several small pieces of luggage free if they're transported inside and don't weigh more than 11 pounds (5kg). Heavier suitcases carried in the trunk cost

6F to 10F ($1.20 to $2) apiece. Tip 12% to 15%—the latter usually elicits a *merci*. For radio cabs, call ☎ 01-45-85-85-85, 01-42-70-41-41, or 01-42-70-00-42—note that you'll be charged from the point where the taxi leaves to pick you up.

BY BICYCLE

To ride a bicycle through the streets and parks of Paris, perhaps with a *baguette* tucked under your arm, might have been a fantasy of yours since you saw your first Maurice Chevalier film. If the idea appeals to you, you won't be alone: The city in recent years has added many miles of right-hand lanes specifically designated for cyclists, and hundreds of bike racks. (When these aren't available, many Parisians simply chain their bike to the nearest available fence or lamppost.) Cycling is especially popular in Paris's larger parks and gardens.

Paris-Vélos, 2 rue du Fer-à-Moulin, 5e (☎ **01-43-37-59-22;** Métro: Censier-Daubenton), rents by the day, weekend, or week, charging from 90F ($18) to 140F ($28) per day, from 160F ($32) to 220F ($44) Saturday and Sunday, and from 420F ($84) to 495F ($99) for a week. Deposits run from 1,000F ($200) to 2,000F ($400). The shop is open Monday through Saturday from 10am to 12:30pm and 2 to 7pm.

FAST FACTS: Paris

American Express   An office is at 11 rue Scribe, 9e (☎ **01-47-77-70-00**), which is close to the Opéra (also the Métro stop). Hours are from 9am to 6pm Monday to Friday. The bank window is open Saturday from 9am to 6pm, but you can't pick up mail until Monday. A less busy American Express office is at 38 av. de Wagram, 8e (☎ **01-42-27-58-80**; Métro: Ternes). It is open from 9am to 5:30pm on Monday through Friday.

Area Code   There isn't one. The previous area code for Paris and Ile-de-France, 1, ceased to exist in 1996. Instead, the prefix 01- should be added to all existing 8-digit numbers in France, which means callers no longer have to dial 16 to make a long distance call from Paris within France. The international access code from France will now be 00 replacing the former code 19.

Banks   American Express may be able to meet most of your banking needs. If not, banks in Paris are open from 9am to 4:30pm Monday through Friday. A few are open on Saturday. Ask at your hotel for the location of the bank nearest you. Shops and most hotels will cash your traveler's checks, but not at the advantageous rate a bank or foreign-exchange office will give you, so make sure you've allowed enough funds for the weekend.

Business Hours   Opening hours in France are erratic, as befits a nation of individualists. Most **museums** close one day a week (often Tuesday), and on national holidays; hours tend to be from 9:30am to 5pm. Some museums, particularly the smaller ones, close for lunch from noon to 2pm. Most French museums are open Saturday, but many close Sunday morning and reopen in the afternoon. (See chapter 6 for specific times.) Generally, **offices** are open Monday to Friday from 9am to 5pm, but don't count on it. Always call first. **Stores** are open from 9 or 9:30am (often 10am) to 6 or 7pm without a break for lunch. Some shops, particularly those operated by foreigners, open at 8am and close at 8 or 9pm. In some small stores the lunch break can last 3 hours, beginning at 1pm.

Car Rentals   See "Getting Around," above.

Climate   See "When to Go" in chapter 2.

Currency See "Visitor Information & Entry Requirements" in chapter 2.

Currency Exchange For the best exchange rate, cash your traveler's checks at banks or foreign-exchange offices, not at shops and hotels. Most post offices will also change traveler's checks or convert currency, and Paris's airports and train stations are also equipped with currency exchange desks. Every foreign exchange office seems to have its own rate, and the differences are dramatic. Some with a better exchange rate end up charging more because of a higher service fee. Obviously, the more you are cashing, the better it is to get a high rate and pay a single service fee. One conveniently positioned moneychanger considers its favorable rates an incentive for visitors to purchase its other products, which include an array of guided tours through Paris and nearby regions of France. **Paris Vision,** 214 rue de Rivoli, 1er (☎ **01-42-86-09-33;** Métro: Tuileries), a travel agency, also maintains a minibank that performs currency exchanges. It's open daily from 9am to 2:30pm and 3:30 to 6pm, and provides exchange rates that are only a fraction less favorable than those offered for very large blocks of money as listed by the Paris stock exchange.

Dentists For emergency dental service, call ☎ **01-43-37-51-00** Monday to Friday 8pm to midnight; Saturday and Sunday from 8am to midnight. You can also call or visit the **American Hospital,** 63 bd. Victor Hugo, Neuilly (☎ **01-46-41-25-41**). A 24-hour English/French dental clinic is on the premises. Métro: Pont de Levallois or Pont de Neuilly. Bus: 82.

Doctors See "Hospitals," below.

Documents Required See "Visitor Information & Entry Requirements" in chapter 2.

Driving Rules See "Getting Around," above.

Drugstores Go to the nearest *pharmacie.* If you need a prescription during off-hours, have your concierge get in touch with the nearest *commissariat de police.* An agent there will have the address of a nearby pharmacy open 24 hours a day. French law mandates that one pharmacy per neighborhood stays open 24 hours. You'll find the address posted on the doors or windows of all other drugstores. One of the most central all-nighters is **Pharmacie les Champs,** 84 av. des Champs-Elysées, 8e (☎ **01-45-62-02-41;** Métro: George V).

Electricity In general, expect 200 volts AC (60 cycles), although you'll encounter 110 and 115 volts in some older establishments. Adapters are needed to fit sockets. Many hotels have two-pin (in some cases, three-pin) sockets for electric razors. It's best to ask at your hotel before plugging in any electrical appliance.

Embassies/Consulates If you lose your passport or have a similar emergency, the consulate can usually handle your individual needs. An embassy is more often concerned with matters of state between France and the home country represented. Hours and offices of the various foreign embassies and consulates follow. **United States:** The **embassy** at 2 av. Gabriel, 75008 Paris (☎ **01-43-12-22-22**), is open Monday to Friday from 9am to 6pm. Passports are issued at its **consulate** at 2 rue St-Florentine (☎ **01-43-12-22-22;** Métro: Concorde), which is situated off the northeast section of place de la Concorde. To get a passport replaced costs about $65. In addition to its embassy and consulate in Paris, the United States also maintains the following consulates: 12 bd. Paul-Peytral, 13286 Marseille (☎ **04-91-54-92-00**); and 15 av. d'Alsace, 67082 Strasbourg (☎ **03-88-35-31-04**). **Canada:** The **embassy** is at 35 av. Montaigne, 75008 Paris (☎ **01-44-43-29-00;** Métro: F.D. Roosevelt or Alma-Marceau), open Monday to Friday from 9am to noon and

2 to 5pm. The Canadian consulate is located at the embassy. **Great Britain:** The **embassy** is at 35 rue du Faubourg St-Honoré, 75383 Paris (☎ 01-44-51-31-00; Métro: Concorde or Madeleine), open Monday to Friday from 9:30am to 1pm and 2:30 to 6pm. The **consulate** is at 16 rue d'Aujou, 75008 Paris (☎ 01-44-51-31-00; Métro: Concorde or Madeleine). Hours are Monday to Friday from 9:30am to 12:30pm and 2:30 to 5pm. **Ireland:** The **embassy/consulate** is at 12 ave. Foch, 16e, 75016 Paris (☎ 01-45-00-20-87; Métro: Argentine), open Monday to Friday 9:30am to noon. **Australia:** The **embassy/consulate** is at 4 rue Jean-Rey, 75015 Paris (☎ 01-45-59-33-00; Métro: Bir-Hakeim), open Monday to Friday from 9am to 1pm and 2:30 to 5:30pm. **New Zealand:** The **embassy/consulate** is at 7 rue Léonard-de-Vinci, 16e, 75016 Paris (☎ 01-45-00-24-11; Métro: Victor-Hugo), open Monday to Thursday from 9am to 1pm and 2 to 5:30pm, and Friday from 9am to 2pm.

Emergencies   For the **police,** call ☎ **17;** to report a **fire,** ☎ **18.** For an ambulance, call the **fire department** at ☎ **01-45-78-74-52;** a fire vehicle rushes patients to the nearest emergency room. For S.A.M.U., an independently operated, privately owned ambulance company, call ☎ **15.** For less urgent matters, you can reach the **police** at 9 bd. du Palais, 4e (☎ **01-53-71-53-71** or 01-53-73-53-73; Métro: Cité).

Holidays   See "When to Go" in chapter 2.

Hospitals   Central Médical Europe, 44 rue d'Amsterdam (☎ **01-42-81-80-00**), has practitioners in all fields under one roof. Appointments are recommended. Open Mon-Fri 8am to 7pm, Sat 8am to 6pm. Métro: Liège.

Centrally located general clinics include **Centre Figuier,** 2 rue du Figuier (☎ 01-42-78-55-53), open Mon-Fri 9am to 7pm, Sat 9 to 11am. Métro: St-Paul. Also, **Centre Médico-Social,** 3 rue Ridder (☎ 01-45-43-83-78), open Mon-Fri noon to 6:30pm, Sat 9:30am to noon. Métro: Plaisance.

Information   See "Visitor Information & Entry Requirements" in chapter 2.

Legal Aid   This may be hard to come by in Paris. The French government advises foreigners to consult their embassy or consulate (see "Embassies/Consulates," above) in case of a dire emergency, such as an arrest. Even if a consulate or embassy declines to offer financial or legal help, they will generally offer advice as to how you can obtain help locally. For example, they can furnish a list of attorneys who might represent you. Most visitor arrests are for illegal possession of drugs, and the U.S. embassy and consulate officials cannot interfere with the French judicial system in any way on your behalf. A consulate can only advise you of your rights.

Liquor Laws   Visitors will find it easier to get a drink—wine, beer, or other spirits—in France than in England or other countries. Supermarkets, grocery stores, and cafes all sell alcoholic beverages. The legal drinking age is 16, but persons under that age can be served an alcoholic drink in a bar or restaurant if accompanied by a parent or legal guardian. Wine and liquor are sold every day of the week, year-round.

Hours of cafes vary throughout the country and with local restrictions. Some open at 6am, serving drinks until 3am; others are open 24 hours a day. Bars and nightclubs may stay open as they wish.

The Breathalyzer test is in use in France, and a motorist is considered "legally intoxicated" with 0.8 grams of alcohol per liter of blood (the more liberal U.S. law is 1 gram per liter.) If convicted, a motorist faces a stiff fine and a possible prison term of 2 months to 2 years. If bodily injury results from a drunk-driving incident, the judge might sentence a convicted offender to 2, 5, 10 years, even life if he or she ran over five or six people while drunk.

Mail   Most post offices in Paris are open Monday to Friday from 8am to 7pm and Saturday from 8am to noon. Allow 5 to 8 days to send or receive mail from your home. To send an aerogram to the United States or Canada costs 4.30F (85¢). To send a letter weighing 40 grams (about an ounce) costs 7.90F ($1.60). A postcard to the United States or Canada is 4.30F (85¢). Letters to the United Kingdom cost 2.80F (55¢) for up to 20 grams.

If you don't have a hotel address in Paris, you can receive mail c/o American Express (see above). However, you may be asked to show an American Express card or traveler's check when you go to pick up your mail.

Another option is to send your mail *poste restante* (general delivery) in care of the major post office in whatever town you plan to visit. You'll need to produce a passport to pick up mail, and you may be charged a small fee for the service. You can also exchange money at post offices.

Many hotels sell stamps.

Maps   See "Getting Around," above.

Medical Emergencies   If you are ill and need medicine at night or on Sunday, the local commissariat de police will tell you the location of the nearest drugstore that's open or the address of the nearest doctor on duty. The police or fire department will also summon an ambulance if you need to be rushed to a hospital. Seek assistance first at your hotel desk if language is a problem. Also see "Hospitals," above.

Money   See "Money" in chapter 2.

Newspapers/Magazines   English-language newspapers are available at nearly every kiosk in Paris. Published Monday through Saturday, the *International Herald-Tribune* is the most popular paper with visiting Americans and Canadians; the *Guardian* provides a British point of view. For those who read in French, the leading domestic newspapers are *Le Monde, Le Figaro,* and *La Libération;* the top magazines are *L'Express, Le Point,* and *Le Nouvel Observateur.* Kiosks are generally open daily from 8am to 9pm.

Pets   If you have certificates from a vet and proof of antirabies vaccination, you can bring most house pets into France.

Police   Call ☎ 17 for emergencies. The principal Prefecture is at 9 boulevard du Palais, 4e (☎ **01-53-71-53-71;** Métro: Cité).

Post Office   The main post office (PTT) for Paris is **Bureau de Poste,** 52 rue du Louvre, 75001 Paris (☎ **01-40-28-20-00;** Métro: Louvre). Your mail can be sent here *poste restante* (general delivery) for a small fee. Take an ID, such as a passport, if you plan to pick up mail. It's open Monday to Friday from 8am to 7pm, and Saturday from 8am to noon for most services, 24 hours a day for telegrams, fax-mail, and phone calls. Stamps can also usually be purchased at your hotel reception desk and at *café-tabacs* (tobacconists).

Rest Rooms   If you are in dire need, duck into a cafe or brasserie to use the lavatory. It's customary to make some small purchase if you do so. In the street the domed self-cleaning lavatories are a decent option if you have small change; Métro stations and underground garages usually have public lavatories, but the degree of cleanliness varies.

Safety   In Paris, be especially aware of child pickpockets. They roam the French capital, preying on tourists around attractions such as the Louvre, Eiffel Tower, and Notre-Dame, and they also often strike in the Métro, sometimes blocking a victim from the escalator. A band of these young thieves can clean your pockets even while you try to fend them off. Their method is to get very close to a target, ask for a handout (sometimes), and deftly help themselves to your money or passport.

As in every world metropolis in the 1990s, public safety is more and more on people's minds, and the general perception in Paris is that urban life is increasingly dangerous. Although public safety concerns are not as prevalent in Paris as they are in such cities as Los Angeles and New York, concerns are growing. Robbery at gun- or knife-point is uncommon here, but definitely not unknown. Be careful.

Taxes Watch it: You could get burned. As a member of the European Community, France routinely imposes a **value-added tax (VAT)** on many goods and services. The standard VAT on merchandise is 20.6%, and is applied to clothing, appliances, liquor, leather goods, shoes, furs, jewelry, perfumes, cameras, and even caviar. Refunds on certain goods and merchandise are made, but not on services. The minimum purchase is 1,200F ($240) in the same store for nationals or residents of countries outside the European Union.

To get a refund, ask the store for a completed VAT form and a stamped, self-addressed envelope. They will ask you how you wish to be refunded: 1) in cash at the airport (international airports in France only, where the bank handling the refund is close to the customs desk); 2) by crediting your credit card; 3) by bank transfer; or 4) by check in French francs.

When exiting the country, for example at the airport, you must go to the Detaxe TVA/VAT refund counter with the merchandise you purchased to get the form stamped by a customs official. The customs officer can ask to see the merchandise as proof that you are taking it out of the country. After getting the stamp, one copy stays with customs, one is for you, and the third should be immediately mailed back to the store (there is a mailbox at the customs counter).

The store, after filing with the government, will then mail a check in francs to the buyer (unless a different method of payment was specified). If the store accepts credit cards, we recommend that you ask them to credit the refund to your card. Otherwise, ask the store to indicate that you wish to receive a cash refund at the airport—U.S. banks usually charge $10 to $15 to process a French check or bank transfer.

Taxis See "Getting Around," above.

Telegrams/Fax Telegrams may be sent from any Paris post office during the day (see "Post Office," above) and anytime from the 24-hour central post office. In telegrams to the United States, the address is counted in the price; there are no special rates for a certain number of words. If you're in Paris and wish to send a telegram in English to anywhere in France, call ☎ **3655.** For messages destined for outside the borders of France, dial ☎ **0800-33-44-11.** You can send faxes at the main post office in each arrondissement.

Telephone Public phone booths are found in cafes, restaurants, Métro stations, post offices, airports, train stations, and occasionally on the streets. Finding a coin-operated telephone in France may be an arduous task. A simpler and more widely accepted method of payment is the *télécarte,* a prepaid calling card. These debit cards are priced at 41F ($8.20) to 98F ($19.60) for 50 and 120 *unités* respectively. A local call costs one unité, which provides you with 6 to 18 minutes of conversation depending on the rate (and where you're calling). Télécartes are available at most post offices and Métro stations.

If possible, avoid making calls from your hotel, which might double or triple the charges.

When you're calling long distance within France, pick up the receiver, wait for the dial tone, and then dial the 10-digit number of the person or place you're calling. To call the United States or Canada, first dial 00, listen for the tone, then slowly dial 1, the area code, and the seven-digit number. To reach an AT&T operator from within France, for assistance in placing collect or credit-card calls back to North America, dial ☎ **00-CALL-ATT.**

When calling from outside France, all you need to dial is the international prefix (011), then the country code for France (33), and finally the last nine digits of the number, dropping the 0 (zero) from the regional prefix. Thus to call Notre-Dame (☎ 01-42-34-56-10) from overseas, you would need to dial ☎ 011-33-1-42-34-56-10.

For information, dial ☎ **12**.

Time   French summertime lasts from around April to September, and clocks are set 1 hour ahead of French winter time. Depending on the time of year, France is 6 or 7 hours ahead of eastern standard time in the United States.

Tipping   Tipping is practiced with flourish and style in France, and, as a visitor, you're expected to play the game. All bills, as required by law, show *service compris*, which means the tip is included; customary practices of additional gratuities are as follows:

Here are some general guidelines: For **hotel staff,** tip 6F to 10F ($1.20 to $2) for every item of baggage the porter carries on arrival and departure and 10F ($2) per day for the chambermaid. You're not obligated to tip the concierge (hall porter), doorman, or anyone else, unless you use his or her services. In cafes, **waiter** service is usually included. **Porters** have an official scale of charges; there is no real need to tip extra after their bill is presented, unless they have performed some special service. Tip **taxi drivers** 10% to 15% of the amount on the meter. In theaters and restaurants, give **cloakroom attendants** at least 5F ($1) per item. Give **rest room attendants** about 2F (40¢) in nightclubs and such places. Give **cinema and theater ushers** about 2F (40¢). Tip the **hairdresser** about 15%, and don't forget to tip the person who gives you a shampoo or a manicure 10F ($2). For **guides** for group visits to museums and monuments, 5F to 10F ($1 to $2) is a reasonable tip.

Transit Info   For information on the city's public transportation, stop in at **the Services Touristiques de la RATP,** at 53 bis quai des Grands-Augustins, 6e (Métro: St-Michel). For recorded information in French about stoppages, subway or bus breakdowns, or exceptionally heavy traffic on any particular bus or Métro line, call ☎ **01-43-46-14-14**.

Useful Telephone Numbers   Police, ☎ **17;** fire, ☎ **18;** emergency medical assistance, ☎ **15.**

Visas   See "Visitor Information & Entry Requirements" in chapter 2.

Water   Drinking water is generally safe, although it has been known to cause diarrhea in some unaccustomed stomachs. If you ask for water in a restaurant it will be bottled water (for which you'll pay) unless you specifically request tap water (*l'eau du robinet*).

Weather   Call ☎ **08-36-68-02-75.** The cost is 2.28F (45¢) per minute.

Yellow Pages   As in North America, the yellow pages are immensely useful. Your hotel will almost certainly have a copy, but you'll need the help of a French-speaking resident before tackling the French Telephone Company's (PTT's) yellow pages.

4 Accommodations

It was recently estimated that Paris had some 2,000 hotels—a total of about 80,000 bedrooms—spread across 20 arrondissements. They range from the Ritz down to dives so repellent that even George Orwell, author of *Down and Out in Paris and London,* wouldn't have considered checking in. (Of course, none of those are in this guide!)

The good news is that Paris is in a renovating mood. Hotels, and not just the palaces, are being rehabbed, redecorated, and rewired, and many of them needed it badly. Many little town house hotels, where the paint hadn't been freshened in 30 years, have felt increased competition, and are sprucing up.

With the French economy soured, businesspeople in Paris are looking to tourism as the answer to their woes. Since there are so many rooms in Paris, the competition is rough. Paint buckets and plumbers are seen all over town these days.

Though there are so many hotels in Paris, it isn't always easy to get a room. In fact, while there used to be a low season during the cold, rainy period from November through February, when tourism slowed and rooms were easy to find, hotels are now often packed in those months. If there's a low season for hotels at all, it might be in July and August, which normally is the peak season throughout most of Europe. Parisians are likely to be away on vacation, and trade fairs and conventions have fled southward. This leaves far more empty rooms waiting in the heat of a Paris summer.

Since hot weather never lasts long in Paris, most hotels, except the deluxe ones, don't provide air-conditioning. If you're trapped in a garret on a hot summer night, you'll have to sweat it out. You can open your window to get some cooler air, but open windows admit a major nuisance: noise pollution. To avoid this, you may wish to request a room in the back when making a reservation.

While in Paris, you may often be prompted to wonder, "When is a hotel not a hotel?" The answer is when it's another kind of building. The word *hôtel* in French has several meanings. It means a lodging, of course, but it also means a large mansion or town house, such as the Hôtel des Invalides, once a home for disabled soldiers, now the most important military museum in the world. Hôtel de Ville means town hall; Hôtel des Postes refers to the general post office; and Hôtel-Dieu is a hospital. So be warned.

It is important to remember that the last two numbers of the postal code indicate the arrondissement. For example, a postal code of 75008 Paris means that the hotel lies in the 8th arrondissement; 75005 indicates the hotel is in the 5th arrondissement. These can also be represented as 8e and 5e respectively.

Hotel breakfasts are fairly uniform and include your choice of coffee, tea, or hot chocolate, a freshly baked croissant and roll, plus limited quantities of butter and jam or jelly. It can be at your door moments after you call for it, and is served at almost any hour requested. (When we mention breakfast charges in our listings, we refer to continental breakfasts only.) Breakfasts with eggs, bacon, ham, or other items must be ordered from the à la carte menu. For a charge, larger hotels serve the full or "English" breakfast, but smaller hotels typically serve only the continental variety.

CHOOSING WHERE TO STAY

The first decision to make after choosing between lodgings in central Paris or an outlying district is simple: Right Bank or Left Bank?

If you desire chic surroundings, choose a Right Bank hotel. That puts you near all the most elegant shops—Dior, Cardin, Saint-Laurent—and within walking distance of important sights such as the Arc de Triomphe, the place de la Concorde, the Tuileries Gardens, and the Louvre. Afterwards, every glittering cafe along the Champs-Elysées is an oasis for a coffee during the day or for an apéritif at night.

The best Right Bank hotels are in the 8th arrondissement (home of the Arc de Triomphe), and many first-class lodgings cluster in the 16th (near the Trocadéro and Bois du Boulogne) and 17th arrondissements (near the Palais de Congrès). If you'd like to be near the place Vendôme, try for a hotel in the 1st arrondissement.

Other Right Bank hotel sections include the increasingly fashionable Marais and Bastille districts within the 3rd and 4th arrondissements, and Les Halles/Beaubourg, home of the Centre Pompidou and Les Halles shopping mall, which are stationed in the 3rd arrondissement.

If you want less formality and tiny bohemian streets, head for the Left Bank, where prices are traditionally lower. Hotels that cater to students are found in the 5th and 6th arrondissements, best known for the Sorbonne, cafe life, and bookstores. The 7th arrondissement provides a touch of avant-garde St-Germain.

A NOTE ON PRICE CATEGORIES

Classifying Paris hotels by price is a long day's journey into night. It's possible many times to find a moderately priced room in an otherwise "very expensive" hotel or an "expensive" room in an otherwise "inexpensive" property. That's because most hotel rooms, at least in the older properties, are not standard; therefore, the range of rooms goes from superdeluxe suites to the "maid's pantry," now converted into a small bedroom. At some hotels, in fact, you'll find rooms that are "moderate," "expensive," and "very expensive," all under one roof.

The following price categories are only for a quick general reference. When we've classified a hotel as "moderate," it means that the *average* room is moderately priced, not necessarily *all* the rooms. It should also be noted that Paris is one of the most expensive cities in the world for hotels. Therefore, what ranks as expensive in your hometown could be your wallet's salvation in Paris.

HOW TO READ GOVERNMENT RATINGS

The government of France grades hotels with a star system, ranging from one star for a simple inn to four stars for a deluxe hotel. Moderately priced hotels usually get two or three stars. This system is based on a complicated formula of room sizes, facilities, state of the plumbing, and dozens of other factors, including elevators, floor plans, dining options, and renovations. In a one-star hotel, bathrooms are often shared and facilities are extremely limited. Breakfast is often the only meal served. You may or may not have a phone in the room. In the two- or three-star hotels, there is usually a private bath in each room, a room phone, and even a private TV. You can also expect two- and three-star hotels to have elevators. In the four-star hotels you get "the works"—that is, all the amenities and the widest array of facilities and services, such as room service, a 24-hour concierge, elevators, perhaps a health club. The system is a bit misleading. For example, for tax reasons, a four-star hotel might deliberately elect to have a three-star rating, which, with the hotel's permission, is granted by the government. The government will not add a star where it's not merited, but with the hotel's request will remove a star.

1 Best Bets

- **Best for Business Travelers:** Corporate types from all over the world converge at the **Hôtel Balzac,** 6 rue Balzac, 8e (☎ **01-45-61-97-22**), a belle epoque town house with a good business center 2 blocks from many of the business offices along the Champs-Elysées. Its restaurant serves some of the best food in town and is suitable for entertaining clients.
- **Best for Families:** A good and affordable Left Bank choice is **Hôtel de Fleurie,** 32 rue Gregoire-de-Tours, 6e (☎ **01-43-29-59-81**), in the heart of St-Germain-des-Prés. Accommodations are thoughtfully appointed, and many are sold as family rooms, a pair of connecting rooms with two large beds. Children under 12 stay free with their parents.
- **Best Value:** Near the Champs-Elysées (but not that close), the **Résidence Lord Byron,** 5 rue de Chateaubriand, 8e (☎ **01-43-59-89-98**), is a classy little getaway that is far from opulent, but is clean, comfortable, and a good buy. Unlike so many of the grander places surrounding it in the 8th, it's totally lacking in pretension.
- **Best Location:** Le Pavillon de la Reine, 28 place des Vosges, 3e (☎ **01-40-29-19-19**), is a chic, elegant 17th-century mansion. It not only has a garden courtyard, but also opens onto the most harmonious and beautiful square of Paris, the place des Vosges, of Victor Hugo fame.
- **Best View:** In the small **Hôtel le Colbert,** 7 rue de L'Hôtel-Colbert, 5e (☎ **01-40-46-79-50**), a private home of the 18th century, you can take in the view of Notre-Dame while ordering breakfast in bed. Not the most luxurious accommodations in Paris, Le Colbert is still one of our favorite secrets.
- **Best for Nostalgia:** Offering the most panoramic views of the Seine and the Tuileries of any hotel in Paris, **Hôtel du Quai Voltaire,** 19 quai Voltaire, 7e (☎ **01-42-61-50-91**), is a venerable inn that the likes of Oscar Wilde, Richard Wagner, Jean Sibelius, and Charles-Pierre Baudelaire once frequented.
- **Best Stargazing:** Those California tycoons, legendary stars, and platinum mistresses of yesterday—Douglas Fairbanks and Mary Pickford, William Randolph Hearst and Marion Davies—knew where to stay back then. Tom Cruise and his ilk know it's still true today. **Hôtel de Crillon,** 10 Place de la Concorde, 8e (☎ **01-44-71-15-00**), is *the* address of Paris. If you want its grandest suite and have a discriminating taste for the macabre, ask for the Marie Antoinette Apartment; it exhibits classic Antoinette-style elegance, and its namesake was beheaded practically at the doorstep of this deluxe citadel.

- **Best for Opulence: Le Ritz,** 15 place Vendôme, 1er (☎ **01-43-16-30-30**), has dripped with wealth, luxury, and decadence since César Ritz opened it in 1898. Barbara Hutton, Coco Chanel, and Marcel Proust are just a few names inscribed in its glorious guest book. Join the parade of Saudi oil princes, Milanese divas, and movie legends.
- **Best-Kept Secret:** Constructed in 1913 and long in a seedy state, the fully restored **Terrass Hôtel,** 12-14 rue Joseph-de-Maistre, 18e (☎ **01-46-06-72-85**), is now the only four-star choice in Montmartre, an area not known for luxury accommodations. Its rooms take in far-ranging views: Tour Eiffel, Arc de Triomphe, the Paris Opéra.
- **Best Historic Hotel:** Inaugurated by Napoleon III in 1855, **Hôtel du Louvre,** Place André Malraux, 1e (☎ **01-44-58-38-38**), was once described by a French journalist as "a palace of the people, rising adjacent to the palace of kings." Today, the hotel offers luxurious accommodations and panoramic views down the avenue de l'Opéra.
- **Best for Romance:** Until the 1970s, **L'Hôtel,** 13 rue des Beaux-Arts, 6e (☎ **01-44-41-99-00**), was a fleabag filled with drunks and addicts. Millions of francs of renovations later, rooms that were cramped and claustrophobic are now ravishingly romantic, wrought like small jewel boxes of the decorator's art.
- **Best Trendy Hotel:** The **Hôtel Montalembert,** 3 rue de Montalembert, 7e (☎ **01-45-49-68-68**), has an impeccable pedigree: France's leading architectural designers enhanced an already illustrious frame into one of the most stylish hotel venues of Paris's Left Bank. Upscale and offbeat, it boasts rooms with individualized decors that vary from conservative French Empire style to Bauhaus and postmodern.
- **Best Deal:** Set in one of the most evocative neighborhoods of Old Paris, the Ile St. Louis, the **Hôtel de Lutèce,** 65 rue St-Louis-en-l'Ile, 4e (☎ **01-43-26-23-52**), resembles a Breton country house, and has flourished despite forever refusing to raise its prices. Its tasteful bedrooms, decorated with antiques and fine reproductions, provide the visitor affordable elegance.
- **Best Service:** Although no one can fault the Plaza Athénée, 23-27 av. Montaigne 8e (☎ **01-47-23-78-33**), for its flawless decor, the billionaires check in because they get the royal treatment from the jaded but indulgent and ever-so-polite staff. Nestled in an upscale neighborhood between the Seine and the Champs-Elysées, the Plaza Athénée offers service that is, quite simply, impeccable.

2 Right Bank

We'll begin with the most centrally located arrondissements on the Right Bank, then work our way through the more outlying neighborhoods.

1ST ARRONDISSEMENT (LOUVRE/LES HALLES)
VERY EXPENSIVE

Hôtel Lotti. 7-9 rue de Castiglione, 75001 Paris. ☎ **800/221-2626** in the U.S., 800/237-0319 in Canada, 800/282729 in the U.K., or 01-42-60-37-34. Fax 01-40-15-93-56. 127 rms, 6 suites. A/C MINIBAR TV TEL. 1,920–3,300F ($384–$660) double; 4,900F ($980) junior suite; 6,500F ($1,300) suite. AE, DC, MC, V. Parking 160F ($32). Métro: Opéra or Tuileries.

Despite a formidably grand reputation as a plush hotel with an impeccable pedigree, the Hôtel Lotti is among the most accessible of the second-tier grand hotels of Paris. The classic seven-story structure it occupies is a grand 19th-century building with

Right Bank Accommodations

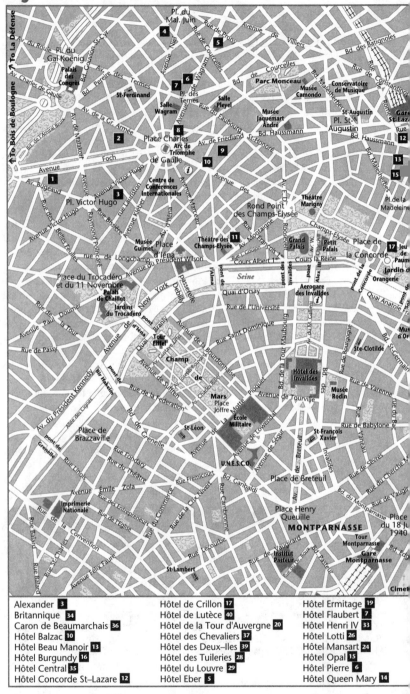

Alexander **3**	Hôtel de Crillon **17**	Hôtel Ermitage **19**
Britannique **34**	Hôtel de Lutèce **40**	Hôtel Flaubert **7**
Caron de Beaumarchais **36**	Hôtel de la Tour d'Auvergne **20**	Hôtel Henri IV **33**
Hôtel Balzac **10**	Hôtel des Chevaliers **37**	Hôtel Lotti **26**
Hôtel Beau Manoir **13**	Hôtel des Deux–Iles **39**	Hôtel Mansart **24**
Hôtel Burgundy **16**	Hôtel des Tuileries **28**	Hôtel Opal **15**
Hôtel Central **35**	Hôtel du Louvre **29**	Hôtel Pierre **6**
Hôtel Concorde St–Lazare **12**	Hôtel Eber **5**	Hôtel Queen Mary **14**

Hôtel Regent's Garden **4**
Hôtel Regina **27**
Hôtel Saint–Louis **41**
Hôtel Westminster **22**
Hôtel William's du Pré **21**
Le Pavillon Bastille **44**
Le Pavillon de la Reine **38**

Le Relais du Louvre **32**
Le Ritz **25**
Le Saint–Hubert **45**
Le Stendhal **23**
Les Trois Couronnes **8**
Libertel Croix de Malte **43**
Marmotel Étoile **2**

Nouvel Hôtel **46**
Plaza Athénée **11**
Résidence Alhambra **42**
Résidence Lord Byron **9**
St–James Club Paris **1**
Terrass Hôtel **18**
Timhôtel Bourse **30**
Timhôtel Louvre **31**

elegant trappings of marble, gilt, tapestries, and crystal. This hotel feels somewhat like a much smaller Ritz, lacking the pretension but not the grandeur. The staff is dignified and attentive. Accommodations have the ambience of a 19th-century Paris town house; they're outfitted with rosewood, mahogany, tambour desks, and damask. The top-story attics with sloping ceilings have a certain idiosyncratic charm and are kept for nonsmokers. Since the early 1980s, the Lotti has been administered by Jolly Hotels, a well-known chain based in Italy.

Dining/Entertainment: Le Lotti may not offer the most innovative cuisine, but the hotel restaurant is still one of the best in town. Its admirably accurate cooking features fragrant, feather-light sauces.

Services: Laundry, baby-sitting, room service (7am to midnight).

✪ **Le Ritz.** 15 place Vendôme, 75001 Paris. ☎ **800/223-6800** in the U.S. and Canada, or 01-43-16-30-30. Fax 01-43-16-31-78. 142 rms, 45 suites. A/C MINIBAR TV TEL. 3,400–3,900F ($680–$780) double; 4,700F ($940) junior suite; from 5,500F ($1,100) suite. AE, DC, MC, V. Parking 150F ($30). Métro: Opéra or Madeleine.

The Ritz is the greatest hotel in Europe. The Plaza Athénée and the Crillon have challenged it, but cannot measure up to this matchless hotel. This enduring symbol of elegance is located on one of the most beautiful and historic squares in Paris. César Ritz, the "little shepherd boy from Niederwald," converted the Lazun Mansion into this lavish hotel; it opened in 1898. César hired the legendary culinary master Escoffier to be the hotel's chef, and built the world's first shopping gallery into the premises. This house of luxury attracted some of the most celebrated people of the world, including Edward VII of England.

In 1979 the Ritz family sold the hotel to Egyptian businessman Mohamed al-Fayed, who has refurbished it and added a cooking school. All the hotel's drawing rooms, salons, three gardens, and courtyards were preserved. Museum-caliber antiques adorn the salons: gilt pieces, ornate mirrors, Louis XV and Louis XVI furnishings, and 10-foot-high candelabra. The bedrooms are impeccably French, with antique chests, desks with bronze trimmings, and crystal light fixtures.

The battle rages between the Ritz crowd and the Crillon crowd. Fans of the Ritz often call the Crillon "too American," whereas Crillon regulars retort that the Ritz has no soul. They misstate the case: The Ritz has an abundance of soul and manners recalling the *ancien régime.* Many guests arrive with bodyguards and in limos with bulletproof windows.

Dining/Entertainment: The Espadon is one of the finest restaurants in Paris. The Ritz Supper Club, which is open only to residents of the hotel and a handful of the Parisian elite, has a bar, a salon with a fireplace, and a dance floor. Live music begins at 11pm. The paneled Le Bar Vendôme is one of the world's most elegant places to have a drink or lunch in the resplendence of a garden view. Also in the hotel is the Hemingway Bar.

A Hotel Tale

During Paris's occupation, on August 25, 1944, Ernest Hemingway "liberated" the Ritz. Armed with machine guns, "Papa" and a group of Allied soldiers pulled up to the hotel in a Jeep, intent on capturing Nazis and freeing, if only symbolically, the landmark. After a sweep from the cellars to the roof, the group discovered that the Nazis had already fled. Hemingway led his team to the Ritz bar to order a round of dry martinis. In commemoration of the 50th anniversary of the liberation, the renovated Bar Hemingway reopened on August 25, 1994.

Services: Concierge, 24-hour room service, laundry, valet.

Facilities: Luxury health club with swimming pool, squash courts, and massage parlor; florist; shops.

EXPENSIVE

Hôtel Burgundy. 8 rue Duphot, 75001 Paris. ☎ **01-42-60-34-12.** Fax 01-47-03-95-20. 89 rms, 1 suite. MINIBAR TV TEL. 890F ($178) double; 1,300F ($260) suite. AE, DC, MC, V. Métro: Madeleine.

The Burgundy is one of the best values in an outrageously expensive neighborhood. This frequently renovated building stands in one of the city's most stylish business districts; it's a former run-down *pension* where Charles Baudelaire wrote some of his eerie poetry in the 1860s. What you'll see today was originally conceived as two side-by-side town houses from the 1830s. One of them flourished as a bordello before they were linked together by English-born hotel managers who insisted on referring to the Burgundy by its English-language name. This frequent nesting place for clients from the Americas was radically renovated in 1992, and now has very comfortable, conservatively decorated bedrooms.

Dining/Entertainment: Le Charles Baudelaire serves lunch and dinner between Monday and Friday. There's no bar on the premises, but drinks are served in the lobby during restaurant hours.

Services: Limited concierge services, room service 6:30am to 9:30pm, laundry/dry cleaning.

Facilities: Conference room.

Hôtel des Tuileries. 10 rue St-Hyacinthe, 75001 Paris. ☎ **01-42-61-04-17.** Fax 01-49-27-91-56. 26 rms. MINIBAR TV TEL. 790–1,200F ($158–$240) double. AE, DC, MC, V. Métro: Tuileries or Pyramides.

Set on a narrow and surprisingly quiet street in a neighborhood barely altered since the ancien régime, this hotel occupies a 17th-century town house. This was the minipalace that Marie Antoinette used whenever she left the palace at Versailles for an unofficial business or social visit to central Paris. Don't expect mementos of the queen, since her opponents long ago stripped away all the frippery of her era. But to honor her memory, the hotel's public areas and bedrooms are outfitted in slightly dowdy, but ever-so-comfortable, replicas of Louis XV furniture. The bathrooms have whirlpool tubs and a touch of marble.

Dining/Entertainment: None.

Services: Room service 7am to 11pm, newspaper delivery upon request.

✪ **Hôtel du Louvre.** Place André Malraux, 75001 Paris. ☎ **800/888-4747** in the U.S. and Canada, or 01-44-58-38-38. Fax 01-44-58-38-01. 178 rms, 22 suites. A/C MINIBAR TV TEL. 1,350–1,950F ($270–$390) double; 2,500F ($500) suite. Midwinter promotions available. AE, DC, MC, V. Métro: Palais-Royal.

When Napoléon III inaugurated this hotel in 1855, a French journalist described it as "a palace of the people, rising adjacent to the palace of kings." The people's palace now features soaring marble, bronze, and gilt decor. A member of the prestigious Concorde Hotel chain, of which the Crillon is the flagship, the hotel conducted a complete renovation of many of its smaller bedrooms during 1996. Accommodations are quintessentially Parisian—cozy and filled with souvenirs of *la belle époque.* Many bedrooms are soundproofed against the roar of traffic. Although the views of the inner courtyard have an understated charm, the sweeping panoramas down the avenue de l'Opéra are among the best cityscapes in the world.

This hotel presents formidable competition to all the other similarly priced hotels in the neighborhood, especially the Westminster and the declining Inter-Continental.

Dining/Entertainment: Le Bar "Defender" is a cozy, luxurious, and masculine hideaway with a pianist entertaining after dusk; it has overtones of Scotland and an impressive rack of single-malt whisky. The elegant Brasserie du Louvre is a bistro echoing the style of the French Empire. During fine weather, the Brasserie sets up tables on the terrace beneath the hotel's sandstone arcades.

Services: Concierge, 24-hour room service, baby-sitting, laundry/valet, filtered tap water.

Facilities: Business center.

Hôtel Regina. 2 place des Pyramides, 75001 Paris. ☎ **01-42-60-31-10.** Fax 01-40-15-95-16. 121 rms, 14 suites. A/C MINIBAR TV TEL. 1,900–2,200F ($380–$440) double; from 2,700F ($540) suite. AE, DC, MC, V. Métro: Pyramides or Tuileries.

Until a radical renovation restored its grandeur in 1995, the Regina slumbered in peaceful obscurity in a prime location in central Paris, adjacent to the rue de Rivoli's gilded equestrian statue of Joan of Arc. Built about a century ago, the hotel was known for its vaulted, richly paneled lobby, impeccably mannered staff, and antique-strewn rooms; some of its regular clients felt it had the charms of a dowdy but genteel London hotel.

All of that changed when the management poured funds into the site's recent renovation, retaining the patina and beeswax of the art nouveau interior, and adding hundreds of thousands of francs worth of historically appropriate flourishes. Scattered about the hotel are oriental carpets, Louis-style furniture from every period, 18th-century paintings and bowls of flowers; a flagstone-covered courtyard with fountains is another draw. Some of the rooms overlooking the Tuileries enjoy views as distant as the Eiffel Tower.

Dining/Entertainment: Le Pluvinel serves conservative French cuisine in a well-managed restaurant with an art deco ambience. Pluvinel is closed on weekends, forcing clients to satisfy themselves at a less appealing bistro-style snack bar.

Services: Concierge, 24-hour room service, twice-daily maid service, laundry/dry cleaning, valet parking, secretarial service, in-room massage.

Facilities: Conference room, visits to a nearby health club can be arranged upon request.

MODERATE

Britannique. 20 av. Victoria, 75001 Paris. ☎ **01-42-33-74-59.** Fax 01-42-33-82-65. 40 rms. MINIBAR TV TEL. 552–905F ($110–$181) double. AE, DC, MC, V. Parking 100F ($20). Métro: Châtelet.

After a complete renovation, the Britannique has attained three stars. It's near Les Halles, the Pompidou Centre, and Notre-Dame, in the heart of Paris. The rooms are small but spick-and-span, soundproof, and adequately equipped. The satellite receiver gets U.S. and U.K. TV shows. The Britannique has an elegant and cozy reading room that wouldn't be out of place in an Agatha Christie novel. The place is not only British in name, but has also cultivated an English graciousness in service.

✪ **Hôtel Mansart.** 5 rue des Capucines, 75001 Paris. ☎ **01-42-61-50-28.** Fax 01-49-27-97-44. 55 rms, 2 suites. 530–1,200F ($106–$240) double; 1,500F ($300) suite. AE, DC, MC, V. Métro: Opéra or Madeleine.

Originally designed by its namesake, 17th-century architect Jules Hardouin-Mansart, it takes part in the grand ensemble of the Place Vendôme, albeit in a corner building at the plaza's northern end. Operating as a glorious wreck for many decades (the Hôtel du Rhin, then the Hôtel de Calais since the mid–19th century), it

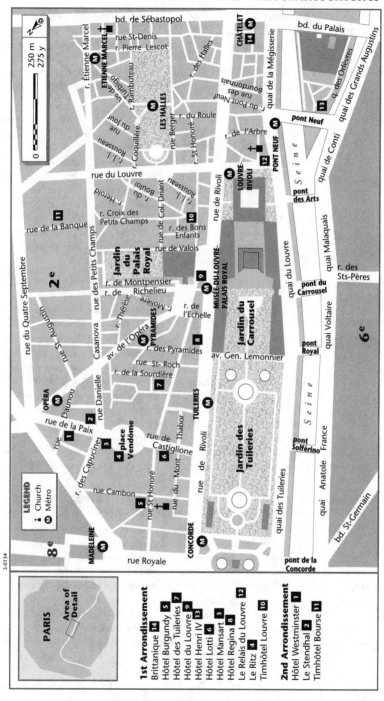

LEGEND
✝ Church
Ⓜ Métro

PARIS
Area of Detail

1st Arrondissement
Brittanique 14
Hôtel Burgundy 5
Hôtel des Tuileries 7
Hôtel du Louvre 9
Hôtel Henri IV 13
Hôtel Lotti 6
Hôtel Mansart 3
Hôtel Regina 8
Le Relais du Louvre 12
Le Ritz 4
Timhôtel Louvre 10

2nd Arrondissement
Hôtel Westminster 1
Le Stendhal 2
Timhôtel Bourse 11

3-0134

71

was radically renovated in 1991, and today offers some of the cheapest rates in this frightfully expensive neighborhood. Public areas contain Louis-inspired reproductions and startling floor-to-ceiling geometric designs inspired by the formal gardens and inlaid marble floors of the French Renaissance. Bedrooms are high-ceilinged, subtly formal, and comfortable, although only a half-dozen suites and expensive rooms actually overlook the famous square nearby. Breakfast, the only meal offered, is served one floor above lobby level.

Le Relais du Louvre. 19 rue des Preîtres, 75001 Paris. ☎ **01-40-41-96-42.** Fax 01-40-41-96-44. 18 rms, 2 suites. MINIBAR TV TEL. 820F ($164) double; 1,280–1,450F ($256–$290) suite. AE, DC, DISC, MC, V. Parking 70F ($14). Métro: Louvre-Rivoli or Pont-Neuf.

Opened in 1991, this hotel has what the French call *charme et caractère*. Many visitors from the provinces seek it out (it does suggest rural France) because it lies between the Louvre and Notre-Dame and within walking distance of the Pont Neuf in the historic heart of Paris. Nostalgia buffs are usually impressed with this building's history: Voltaire and Victor Hugo frequented the legendary Café Momus, which used to occupy the street level, where a pivotal scene of Puccini's *La Bohème* also takes place. Bright, strong hues enliven bedrooms containing reproductions of antique French furniture, soundproofed windows, and modern conveniences.

INEXPENSIVE

Hôtel Henri IV. 25 place Dauphine, 75001 Paris. ☎ **01-43-54-44-53.** 22 rms, 2 with shower. 155–200F ($31–$40) double without shower; 225–255F ($45–$51) double with shower. Rates include breakfast. No credit cards. Métro: Pont-Neuf.

Four hundred years ago, this narrow decrepit building housed the printing presses used for the edicts of Henri IV. Today one of the most famous, and one of the most consistently crowded, budget hotels in Europe sits in a dramatic location at the northernmost tip of the Ile de la Cîté, beside a formal and unexpected park lined with orderly rows of trees. The clientele is mostly bargain-conscious academics, journalists, and francophiles, many of whom reserve rooms as many as two months in advance. The low-ceilinged lobby, a flight above street level, is cramped and bleak; the creaky stairway leading to the bedrooms is almost impossibly narrow. Rooms are considered romantically threadbare by many, and run-down and substandard by others. Each contains a sink, but not even the two rooms with showers have toilets.

Timhôtel Louvre. 4 rue Croix des Petits Champs, 75001 Paris. ☎ **01-42-60-34-86.** Fax 01-42-60-10-39. 56 rms. A/C TV TEL. 550F ($110) double. Métro: Palais-Royal.

This hotel and its sibling, Timhôtel Bourse (see below), are mirror images of one another, at least from the inside; both are good examples of a new breed of two-star, business-oriented hotels cropping up around France. Both Timhôtels share the same manager and the same temperament, and although bedrooms at Timhôtel Bourse are larger than those at Timhôtel Louvre, the Louvre branch is so close to the museum as to be irresistible to anyone wishing to spend lots of time within its galleries. Both were conversions of venerable but decrepit older hotels (the Hôtel du Globe and the Hôtel de Normandie) that functioned for years as expatriate homes of writers, art lovers, and tourists. Today, the ambience is bland and standardized, but modern and comfortable, with wall-to-wall carpeting. Breakfasts are served rather anonymously from self-service cafeterias.

Timhôtel Bourse is located at 3 rue de la Banque, 75002 Paris (☎ **01-42-61-53-90;** fax 01-42-60-05-39), has 46 rooms, and charges the same price. Métro: Bourse.

2ND ARRONDISSEMENT (LA BOURSE)
VERY EXPENSIVE

Hôtel Westminster. 13 rue de la Paix, 75002 Paris. ☎ **800/203-3232** or 01-42-61-57-46. Fax 01-42-60-30-66. 84 rms, 18 suites. A/C MINIBAR TV TEL. 2,300–2,600F ($460–$520) double; from 3,000F ($600) suite. AE, DC, MC, V. Métro: Opéra.

Set within a desirably central neighborhood midway between the Opéra and the Place Vendôme, the Westminster was built during Baron Haussmann's redesigning of Paris in 1846, and incorporated a deconsecrated convent within its walls. Around 1900, it was bought by gilded-age entrepreneur, Monsieur Bruchon, who installed a famous collection of clocks. In 1996, the ownership painted the bedrooms and installed new fabrics, carpeting, air-conditioning, and telephone systems, while carefully maintaining its 19th-century design and allure. The Westminster is well groomed, but not as formidably elegant as some of its nearby competitors. It doesn't quite match the style of the nearby Lotti, but still has charm and character.

Dining/Entertainment: The hotel restaurant, le Céladon, is one of the finest hotel dining rooms in Paris. It's not only noted for its celadon porcelain on display but for serving light traditional dishes on an imaginative menu.

Services: Room service, laundry, valet.

EXPENSIVE

Le Stendhal. 22 rue Danielle Casanova, 75002 Paris. ☎ **01-44-58-52-52.** Fax 01-44-58-52-00. 17 rms, 3 suites. A/C MINIBAR TV TEL. 1,380–1,620F ($276–$324) double; from 1,800F ($360) suite. AE, DC, MC, V. Métro: Opéra.

Established in 1992, this hotel mixes a young and hip style with sense of tradition. Its location, close to the glamorous jewelry stores on the place Vendôme, couldn't be grander. Overall, the effect is that of a small, boutique-style *hôtel de luxe* that in some ways seems like an urban and very Parisian version of an upscale English B&B. Bedrooms, accessible via a tiny elevator, have vivid color schemes. The red-and-black Stendhal Suite pays homage to the most famous novel of the hotel's namesake, *Le Rouge et le Noir.* The author, who made this his private home for many years, died here in 1842.

Dining/Entertainment: Breakfast is served in a stone cellar with a vaulted ceiling. A small bar adjoins the lobby, but offers little in size or allure. Simple meals can be ordered and are served in the bedrooms or at the bar, 24 hours a day.

Services: A receptionist/concierge is able to arrange baby-sitting, massage, and car rentals.

3RD ARRONDISSEMENT (LE MARAIS)
VERY EXPENSIVE

✪ **Le Pavillon de la Reine.** 28 place des Vosges, 75003 Paris. ☎ **01-40-29-19-19.** Fax 01-40-29-19-20. 30 rms, 17 duplexes, 15 suites. A/C MINIBAR TV TEL. 1,800F ($360) double; 1,950–2,200F ($390–$440) duplex for 1 or 2; 2,800F ($560) suite. AE, DC, MC, V. Métro: Bastille or Chemin-Vert.

Lovers of Le Marais long lamented the absence of accommodations on this square where Victor Hugo lived, but the opening of this hotel in 1986 fulfilled their desire. You enter through an arcade leading under the northern side of the square. At the end of the arcade, flanked with vine-covered lattices and a small formal garden, is a cream-colored villa, a simple neoclassical facade that blends perfectly into the neighborhood. The building isn't as old or historic as the Place des Vosges, and although there's a small but well-planned garden in front, none of the public rooms or bedrooms looks over the place itself. Despite that, the hotel reigns supreme in the 3rd arrondissement. Its main competitor in classic tradition is the Relais Christine in the Latin Quarter, but the Pavillon de la Reine is more stylish. Romantics seeking a traditional French atmosphere that's not quaint and creaky come here, to the most beautiful square in Paris. The room furniture is either antique or a fool-the-eye reproduction.

Dining/Entertainment: The hotel has an "honesty bar" and a limited 24-hour room-service menu.

Services: A receptionist/concierge can arrange massage, and tickets for shows, concerts, and the theater.

MODERATE

Hotel des Chevaliers. 30 rue de Turenne, 75003 Paris. ☎ **01-42-72-73-47.** Fax 01-42-72-54-10. 24 rms. MINIBAR TV TEL. 590F ($118) double; 814F ($163) triple. Métro: Chemin-Vert or St-Paul.

Set within a half block from the northwestern edge of the Place des Vosges, this carefully renovated hotel occupies a starkly dramatic corner building whose l7th-century vestiges have been elevated into high dramatic art. These include the remnants of a stone-sided well in the cellar, a sweeping stone barrel vault that covers the breakfast area, artfully exposed half-timbering within the stairwell, and Louis XIII accessories that remind visitors of the hotel's antique origins. The bedrooms have simple, uncomplicated lines; each contains a safe and comfortable built-in furniture.

4TH ARRONDISSEMENT (ILE DE LA CITÉ/ ILE ST-LOUIS & BEAUBOURG)

EXPENSIVE

Hôtel des Deux-Iles. 59 rue St-Louis-en-l'Ile, 75004 Paris. ☎ **01-43-26-13-35.** Fax 01-43-29-60-25. 17 rms. A/C TV TEL. 840F ($168) double. AE, MC, V. Métro: Pont-Marie.

Set within a 17th-century town house, this much-restored building functioned as an inexpensive hotel until 1976, when owner/decorator Roland Buffat added an elaborate decor that included an abundance of bamboo and reed furniture and French provincial touches. The result is an unpretentious but charming hotel located on one of the most desirable islands in Europe. A flower garden off the lobby leads to a basement-level breakfast room whose blazing fireplace seems meant for a rustic tavern. Deux-Iles is comparable in price, decor, and setting to the nearby Hôtel de Lutèce, which shares the same owner. Whenever they're full, both hotels recommend each other to clients.

Services: Room service 7:30am to 8pm, laundry/dry cleaning.

MODERATE

✪ **Caron de Beaumarchais.** 12 rue Vieille-du-Temple, 75004 Paris. ☎ **01-42-72-34-12.** Fax 01-42-72-34-63. 19 rms. A/C MINIBAR TV TEL. 660–730F ($132–$146) double. AE, MC, V. Métro: St-Paul or Hôtel-de-Ville.

The 1993 renovation of this building was planned using documents that detailed its original construction in the 18th century. Consequently, you'll find floors of artfully worn gray stone, antique "Gustavien" reproductions with the pale-gray finish inspired by the 18th-century Swedish king Gustav, and fabrics whose elaborate designs are authentic duplicates of patterns popular during the heyday of the hotel's namesake, Caron de Beaumarchais. For what is Monsieur de B. best remembered? His authorship of the "Marriage of Figaro," from which Mozart adapted his opera, and the arms he provided to the fledgling American nation between 1776 and 1782. Most bedrooms still have their original ceiling beams, and while the rooms are compact, they are comfortable, soundproofed, and among the most evocative in the Marais.

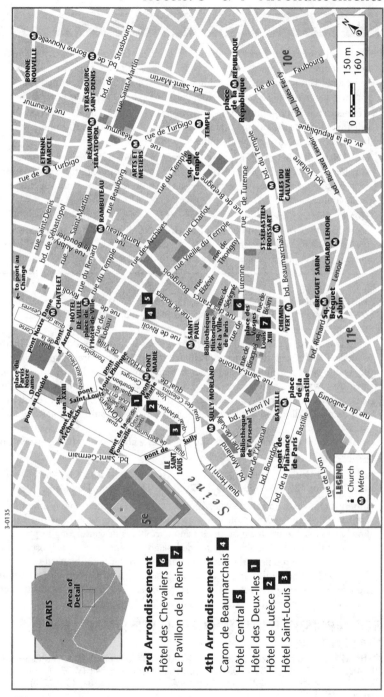

3rd Arrondissement

Hôtel des Chevaliers **6**

Le Pavillon de la Reine **7**

4th Arrondissement

Caron de Beaumarchais **4**

Hôtel Central **5**

Hôtel des Deux-Iles **1**

Hôtel de Lutèce **2**

Hôtel Saint-Louis **3**

☺ Family-Friendly Hotels

Timhôtel Louvre *(see page 72)* This is an especially convenient choice for families, as it offers some rooms with four beds. That's made even more appealing because a mother, father, and two children under 12 can stay in one of these rooms for the price of a double. And, of course, the location near the Louvre is irresistible.

Résidence Lord Byron *(see p. 80)* The Byron is not only a good value and a family-oriented place for the swanky 8th arrondissement, but is only a 10-minute walk from many of the city's major monuments.

Hôtel Saint-Louis *(see p. 76)* The family atmosphere cultivated by proprietor Guy Record and his wife, Andreé, is a precious commodity in Paris these days. This 17th-century town house is set fashionably on the historic Île Saint-Louis and priced with families in mind.

Hôtel de Fleurie *(see p. 94)* In the heart of St-Germain-des-Prés, this has long been a family favorite for those seeking a Left Bank ambience. The hotel is known for its *chambres familiales*—that is, two connecting rooms with a pair of large beds in each room. Children under 12 stay free with their parents.

✪ **Hôtel de Lutèce.** 65 rue St-Louis-en-l'Ile, 75004 Paris. ☎ **01-43-26-23-52.** Fax 01-43-29-60-25. 23 rms. A/C TV TEL. 830F ($166) double; 980F ($196) triple. AE, MC, V. Métro: Pont-Marie.

This hotel sparkles. It's located on the historic Ile St-Louis, where it seems everybody wants to live although there's just not enough room. You pass through glass entrance doors into what resembles the living room of a Breton country house. In the salon, inviting down-filled couches and armchairs huddle around a stone fireplace. All this is the creation of interior designer/hotelier Roland Buffat. The floors are done with *naïf* decorated tiles, and antiques and fine reproductions garnish the tasteful bedrooms.

The hotel is comparable in style and amenities with Deux-Iles (same ownership; see above).

✪ **Hôtel Saint-Louis.** 75 rue St-Louis-en-l'Ile, 75004 Paris. ☎ **01-46-34-04-80.** Fax 01-46-34-02-13. 21 rms. TEL. 695–785F ($139–$157) double. MC, V. Métro: Pont-Marie.

Proprietor Guy Record and his wife, Andrée, maintain a charming family atmosphere (which is becoming harder and harder to find in Paris) at this antique-filled small hotel in a 17th-century town house. It's an incredible value considering its prime location on the highly desirable but crowded island of Saint-Louis. The most charming and evocative rooms in the hotel lie on the uppermost floor. Flanked with *murs mansardés* (inclined walls) and old-fashioned moldings, each sports a tiny balcony from which sweeping views extend over the rooftops of Old Paris. The breakfast room is in the cellar, whose stone vaulting dates from the 17th century.

8TH ARRONDISSEMENT (CHAMPS-ELYSÉES/MADELEINE)
VERY EXPENSIVE

✪ **Hôtel Balzac.** 6 rue Balzac, 75008 Paris. ☎ **800/457-4000** in the U.S. and Canada, or 01-44-35-18-00. Fax 01-44-35-18-05. 56 rms, 14 suites. A/C MINIBAR TV TEL. 1,850–2,200F ($370–$440) double; from 3,200F ($640) suite. AE, DC, MC, V. Parking 150F ($30). Métro: George V. RER: Etoile.

If you consider the Crillon and the Ritz as Paris's versions of a Rolls-Royce, the Balzac could be likened to a Bentley. Elegant, discreet, and world-wise, it boasts a

Hotels: 8th Arrondissement

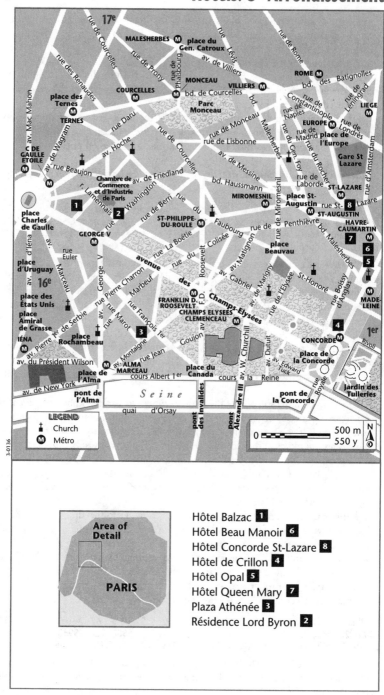

Hôtel Balzac **1**
Hôtel Beau Manoir **6**
Hôtel Concorde St-Lazare **8**
Hôtel de Crillon **4**
Hôtel Opal **5**
Hôtel Queen Mary **7**
Plaza Athénée **3**
Résidence Lord Byron **2**

well-trained and intensely formal staff, and comfortable accommodations that feature modern furniture. Motifs hint of Istanbul or colonial Beirut, and overall, the Balzac cloaks itself in a subtle opulence matched by few hotels within this lavish neighborhood near the upper end of the Champs-Elysées. The hotel opened in 1986 in a belle epoque mansion, then was redecorated in 1994 by the famed English designer Nina Campbell. Each room is soundproofed, easily muffling the exuberance of the nearby Champs-Elysées.

Dining/Entertainment: In November 1996, the hotel rented a prominent spot near the lobby to the Restaurant Pierre Gagnaire. Its namesake is a promising culinary newcomer to Paris whose three-star cuisine has impressed critics throughout France.

Services: 24-hour room service, dry cleaning, express laundry, "arrange anything" concierge.

✪ **Hôtel de Crillon.** 10 place de la Concorde, 75008 Paris. ☎ **800/241-3333** in the U.S. and Canada, or 01-44-71-15-00. Fax 01-44-71-15-02. 120 rms, 43 suites. A/C MINIBAR TV TEL. 3,200–4,100F ($640–$820) double; from 4,900F ($980) suite. AE, DC, MC, V. Parking 150F ($30). Métro: Concorde.

Only the Ritz can boast a classier address. The Crillon is superior to such frontrunners as Plaza Athénée and the Bristol, and this national monument is not only fit for a king but has actually housed a few. It offers the most dramatic setting in Paris, overlooking the place de la Concorde, where the guillotine claimed the lives of such celebrated victims as Louis XVI, Marie Antoinette, Madame du Barry, Madame Roland, and Charlotte Corday. This former home of the duke of Crillon was designed by the famed Jacques-Ange Gabriel, royal architect of France and enlarger of the Louvre, Fontainebleau, the Petit Trianon at Versailles, and the place de la Concorde. Although it is more than 200 years old, it has been a hotel only since 1909.

The restored hotel still evokes the 18th century in its parquet floors, crystal chandeliers, sculpture, 17th- and 18th-century tapestries, gilt moldings, antiques, and paneled walls. If you get a room at the front, you'll be treated to a view of one of the most beautiful plazas in the world. Don't expect all bedrooms to be spacious; many are a good size but hardly large. The styling, in the words of one critic, is Sonia Rykiel's "take on Louis XV." Soundproofing keeps out the street noise but not necessarily sounds from next door. All the bathrooms are fresh and well maintained, lined with travertine or pink marble.

Dining/Entertainment: Les Ambassadeurs is truly the formal dining room of ambassadors, with classic French food and superb service. Less formal is L'Obélisque, where the food isn't as grand (but at least it allows you to dine at the Crillon without going broke). The hotel encircles a large, formal 18th-century courtyard and garden, one of the ideal places in Paris for afternoon tea.

Services: 24-hour room service, secretarial and translation services.

Facilities: Meeting and conference rooms, elevators, shops.

✪ **Plaza Athénée.** 23-27 av. Montaigne, 75008 Paris. ☎ **01-53-67-66-65.** Fax 01-53-67-66-66. 205 rms, 42 suites. A/C MINIBAR TV TEL. 4,000–4,650F ($800–$930) double; from 6,500F ($1,300) suite. AE, DC, MC, V. Parking 150 ($30). Métro: F. D. Roosevelt.

The Plaza Athénée, though a slight tier below the Ritz and the Crillon, is a landmark of discretion, style, and elegance. The nine-story stone edifice is refurbished constantly over a 6-year cycle.

A palace of gilded luxury, the Plaza Athénée has been a celebrity haunt since the days when Mata Hari checked in. It is said that the hotel has two employees for each guest and spends more on flowers than on its electric bill. A citadel of the good life, it has arched windows and ornate balconies. The hotel's high style is exemplified by the Montaigne Salon's mellow wood-grain paneling and marble fireplace. The rooms have huge beds, fine antique mahogany pieces, elegant taffeta draperies, and exceptionally large marble bathrooms. Rooms facing Avenue Montaigne have a view of the Eiffel Tower rising up from the chestnut trees. Service is of the highest standard.

Dining/Entertainment: Meals are an occasion. The preferred choice for dining is La Régence, with its large curvy-topped windows opening onto the garden courtyard. It is known for its lobster soufflé. With its bright colors and decoration, the Grill Relais Plaza is the crossroads of *tout Paris* at lunch, drawing dress designers and personalities from publishing, cinema, and the arts. The Bar Anglais, in the cellar, is a favorite spot for a late-night drink (it's open until 1:30am).

Services: 24-hour room service, concierge, laundry, Reuters telex with international stock quotes.

Facilities: Conference rooms, beauty parlor and hairdresser, massage parlor.

EXPENSIVE

Hôtel Beau Manoir. 6 rue de l'Arcade, 75008 Paris. ☎ **800/528-1234** in the U.S. and Canada, or 01-42-66-03-07. Fax 01-42-68-03-00. 29 rms, 3 suites. A/C MINIBAR TV TEL. 1,155F ($231) double; 1,465F ($293) suite. Rates include breakfast. AE, DC, MC, V. Métro: Madeleine.

Open since 1994, this four-star hotel prides itself on 19th-century nostalgia and decorative zest. The lobby boasts the trappings of a private living room, with walnut reproductions of 18th- and 19th-century antiques, Aubusson tapestries, and fresh flowers. Breakfast is served beneath the chiseled vaults of a very old stone cellar, and the guest rooms are charming and very French. Each contains a safe for valuables, soundproofing, a marble bath, and the conveniences you'd expect. The suites often have exposed beams or sloping garret-style ceilings.

Dining/Entertainment: The hotel offers limited room service from 7am to 7pm, but does not have an attached restaurant or bar.

Services: A receptionist/concierge can arrange most things within reason.

Hôtel Concorde St-Lazare. 108 rue St-Lazare, 75008 Paris. ☎ **800/888-4747** in the U.S. and Canada; 212/752-3900 in New York State; 01-40-08-44-44; or 0171/630-1704 in London. Fax 01-42-93-01-20. 300 rms, 23 suites. A/C MINIBAR TV TEL. 1,200–2,500F ($240–$500) double; from 3,500F ($700) suite. AE, DC, MC, V. Parking 100F ($20). Métro: St-Lazare.

This is the best hotel in the Gare St-Lazare area. Though it's the kind of place where either a tourist or a traveling salesman would feel at home, it still bears lots of reminders of its grand origins. A careful restoration burnished its turn-of-the-century flair. Its granite-pillared lobby is a French national monument. St-Lazare was built in 1889 to accommodate the thousands of visitors who flocked to Paris for the Exposition Universelle. It's situated across from the Gare St-Lazare. A turn-of-the-century palace, it was inspired by British and Spanish models. The hotel's architects designed it to appeal to the tastes of France's emerging merchant class: Along with gilded-age details of bronze, white marble, mosaics, and mirrors, they combined Scottish granite, soaring ceilings, and the newfangled inventions of electricity and telephones.

All the bedrooms are soundproofed and elegantly decorated in floral fabrics of blue and yellow tones. The staff is proud and motivated.

Dining/Entertainment: Worthy of J.P. Morgan, a gilt-and-russet room is exclusively devoted to French billiards—it's the only room of its kind in Paris. An American bar, Le Golden Black, bears Sonia Rykiel's signature decor of black lacquer with touches of gold and amber. Café Terminus, accessible directly from the nearby railway station, bristles with turn-of-the-century accessories and daily brasserie service from noon to 11pm. The Bistro 108 offers provincial dishes along with great vintages, which can be ordered by the glass.

Services: 24-hour room service, baby-sitting, laundry/valet, concierge, currency exchange.

MODERATE

Hotel Queen Mary. 9 rue Greffulhe, 75008 Paris. ☎ **01-42-66-40-50.** Fax 01-42-66-94-92. 32 rms, 4 suites. A/C MINIBAR TV TEL. 725–895F ($145–$179) double; 1,200F ($240) suite. AE, DC, MC, V. Métro: Madeleine or Havre-Caumartin.

Meticulously renovated both inside and out in 1993, this hotel was built around the turn of the century by architects whose designs were optimistic and elegant. It's graced with an iron-and-glass canopy, ornately wrought iron, and the kind of detailing that you might expect of a much more expensive hotel. Public rooms have touches of greenery and reproductions of mid–19th-century antiques; behind bedroom doors are upholstered headboards, mahogany furnishings, well-balanced fabrics, and such English touches as a carafe of sherry set out for guests.

✪ **Résidence Lord Byron.** 5 rue de Chateaubriand, 75008 Paris. ☎ **01-43-59-89-98.** Fax 01-42-89-46-04. 25 rms, 6 suites. MINIBAR TV TEL. 670–920F ($134–$184) double; from 1,270F ($254) suite. AE, MC, V. Métro: George V. RER: Etoile.

Just off the Champs-Elysées on a curving street of handsome buildings, the Lord Byron may not be as grand as other hotels in the neighborhood, but it is affordable. Correct, unassuming, and a bit deliberately staid, it's exactly what its repeat clients want and expect: a sense of bourgeois luxury, solitude, and understatement. It remains a good value for the upscale 8th arrondissement, and is a fine choice for families. Some of the city's major monuments are only a 10-minute walk away. Lord Byron sports fine antique reproductions and framed prints of butterflies and of scenes in France. If you choose to have breakfast at the hotel, you can order it in the dining room or in a shaded inner garden.

INEXPENSIVE

Hôtel Opal. 19 rue Tronchet, 75008 Paris. ☎ **01-42-65-77-97.** Fax 01-49-24-06-58. 36 rms. MINIBAR TV TEL. 450–650F ($90–$130) double. Extra bed 100F ($20). AE, V. Métro: Madeleine.

In the heart of Paris, behind the Madeleine church and within an easy walk of the Opéra, this spruced-up hotel is a real find. Decorated with style and taste, it offers entirely renovated but small bedrooms, some with air-conditioning. Some people especially enjoy the closet-size bedrooms on the top floor, reached by a narrow staircase—these are really attic rooms. The Opal promises visitors a warm welcome and an intimate atmosphere.

9TH & 10TH ARRONDISSEMENTS (OPÉRA GARNIER/ GARE DU NORD)

INEXPENSIVE

Hôtel de la Tour d'Auvergne. 10 rue de la Tour d'Auvergne. 75009 Paris. ☎ **01-48-78-61-60.** Fax 01-49-95-99-00. 25 rms. TV TEL. 500F ($100) double. AE, MC, V. Métro: Cadet or Anvers.

You wouldn't know it from the exterior, but the building that contains this hotel was erected before Baron Haussmann reconfigured the avenues of Paris around 1870. Later, Modigliani rented a room here for 6 months, and the staff will tell you that both Victor Hugo and Rodin lived on this street for brief periods before moving on to greater glory, although no one is too sure of the details. The interior has long ago been modernized into a glossy internationalism, with touches of paneling and marble.

The comfortable bedrooms are meticulously coordinated, though the small decorative canopies over the headboards make the area look cluttered, particularly after you install all your luggage and travel gear. Views over the courtyard in back are uninspired, even gloomy, although some clients request a rear-view room for its relative quiet.

Hôtel William's du Pré. 3 rue Mayran, 75009 Paris. ☎ **01-48-78-68-35.** Fax 01-45-26-08-70. 30 rms. TV TEL. 490–515F ($98–$103) double. AE, MC, V. Métro: Cadet.

Front bedrooms overlook one of the arrondissement's largest public gardens, a verdant oasis within an otherwise highly congested and commercial neighborhood. Set behind a severely dignified six-story facade, this 19th-century building was bought by a citywide chain of unpretentious hotels and renovated in 1992. Bedrooms are simple, clean, and uncomplicated, although the decor is a bit cold and uninspired, despite the color schemes of either soft pink or pale blue. Rooms that open onto the fifth and second floors have small wrought-iron balconies. The hotel offers breakfast in a cellar room that shows vestiges of the original masonry.

11TH & 12TH ARRONDISSEMENTS (OPÉRA BASTILLE/ BOIS DE VINCENNES)
MODERATE

Le Pavillon Bastille. 65 rue de Lyon, 75012 Paris. ☎ **01-43-43-65-65.** Fax 01-43-43-96-52. 23 rms, 1 suite. A/C MINIBAR TV TEL. 650–955F ($130–$191) double; 1,200F ($240) suite. AE, DC, V. Métro: Bastille.

For those who want to stay in this increasingly fashionable district, this is the finest choice. This 1991-vintage town house hotel is situated across from the Bastille Opera House and about a block south of place de la Bastille. It's hardly your cozy little backstreet Paris digs; it's a bold, brassy, and innovative hotel with a clever color scheme. A 17th-century fountain graces the courtyard between the hotel and the street. The rooms provide twin or double beds, partially mirrored walls, and comfortable contemporary built-in furniture. The English-speaking staff is friendly and efficient, offering room service, baby-sitting, and laundry and valet service. Breakfast is served below the ceiling vaults of the cellar. Partly because of its location near Paris's hottest new classical music venue (l'Opéra de la Bastille) and partly because it emphasizes middle-bracket comfort and practicality, this hotel derives at least 70% of its business from foreign visitors, especially Americans, Australians, and Japanese.

Looking for a bargain? The cheapest rooms at 650F ($130) lie on the street level and although you'll probably opt to draw the blinds most of the day and night, they're the same size and configuration as the more expensive rooms upstairs. What to avoid? This hotel's *chambres privilegées,* priced at 955F ($191), are the same size and configuration as the others within the property. The extra costs derive from added amenities such as slippers, better cosmetics in the bathrooms, fruit baskets, and a complimentary bottle of wine that awaits your arrival. Nice extras, but not at that price.

INEXPENSIVE

Libertel Croix de Malte. 5 rue de Malte, 75011 Paris. ☎ **01-48-05-09-36.** Fax 01-43-57-02-54. 29 rms. TV TEL. 540F ($108) double. AE, MC, V. Métro: Oberkampf.

A member of a nationwide chain of mostly two-star hotels, this is a clean, well-maintained choice. Business here has been increasing thanks to a radical overhaul in 1992 and its proximity to both the Opéra de la Bastille and the Marais. The hotel consists of buildings of two and three floors, one of which is accessible through a shared breakfast room. There's a landscaped courtyard in back with access to a lobby bar, and a decor that includes paintings of tropical jungles richly stocked with exotic birds and flowers. The cozy bedrooms have brightly painted modern furniture accented with vivid patterns that flash back to the psychedelia of the 1960s.

Nouvel Hôtel. 24 av. du Bel-Air, 75012 Paris. ☎ **01-43-43-01-81.** Fax 01-43-44-64-13. 28 rms. TV TEL. 470–540F ($94–$108) double. Métro: Nation.

This hotel evokes the French provinces far more than the urban landscapes of Paris. Surrounded by greenery, and set within a neighborhood that's rarely visited by foreign tourists, the hotel conjures a calmer day, when parts of Paris still seemed like small country towns. The beauty of the place is most visible from the inside courtyard, site of warm-weather breakfasts, the only meal served here. In the court, thick masses of ivy climb weathered trellises favored by nesting birds, and a venerable tree and masses of shrubbery soften the masonry. Above, winding hallways lead to bedrooms that overlook either the courtyard, or (less appealingly) the street. Each contains flowered fabrics and old-fashioned furniture.

Résidence Alhambra. 11 bis, 13 rue de Malte, 75011 Paris. ☎ **01-47-00-35-52.** Fax 01-43-57-98-75. 58 rms. TEL. 320–350F ($64–$70) double; 450–490F ($90–$98) triple. MC, V. Métro: Oberkampf.

Named for the famous cabaret and vaudeville theater that once stood nearby, the Alhambra was built in the 1800s. A radical renovation in 1989 gave the hotel its comfortable contemporary format. The hotel rises five stories (10 rooms per floor); in the rear garden, its two-story chalet offers eight additional bedrooms. The thrifty and rather small accommodations are bland but comfortable, each outfitted in a monochromatic pastel scheme that differs from floor to floor. This hotel has been successful in marketing itself in the Netherlands, and not surprisingly, you'll find lots of Dutch people, and to a lesser extent, Americans, staying here. Other than breakfast, no meals are served on the premises, but a wide array of restaurants lies within the vicinity of the nearby Place de la République and the Place de la Bastille. About 60% of the rooms have TV sets.

16TH ARRONDISSEMENT (TROCADÉRO/BOIS DE BOULOGNE)
EXPENSIVE

Alexander. 102 av. Victor Hugo, 75016 Paris. ☎ **800/843-3311** in the U.S. and Canada, or 01-45-53-64-65. Fax 01-45-53-12-51. 60 rms, 2 suites. MINIBAR TV TEL. 1,210–1,320F ($242–$264) double; from 1,890F ($378) suite. AE, DC, MC, V. Parking 100F ($20) across the street. Métro: Victor Hugo.

Though it functioned as a simple pension throughout the 1950s, the hotel was radically upgraded in the 1970s, and became the four-star property you'll see today. Rich paneling in the reception hall immediately assures guests they will be met with luxury, and bedrooms cement the deal with fabric stretched over the walls for added ambience, warmth, and soundproofing. Half of the rooms face a well-planted, quiet courtyard.

Dining/Entertainment: There is a hotel bar open daily from 7am to 9:30pm which serves sandwiches and light snacks. Room service is available from 7am to 7pm.

Services: One-day laundry service is provided, and a receptionist/concierge can help meet most of your needs.

St-James Club Paris. 43 av. Bugeaud, 75016 Paris. ☎ **800/223-5652** in the U.S. and Canada, or 01-44-05-81-81. Fax 01-44-05-81-82. 14 rms, 34 suites. A/C MINIBAR TV TEL. 1,600–1,850 ($320–$370) double; from 2,000F ($400) suite. AE, DC, MC, V. Métro: Porte Dauphine. RER: Avenue Foch.

In an 1892 stone building inspired by a château in the French countryside, the St. James Club is as grand as any of the very expensive hotels within the more visible (and more central) neighborhoods of Paris. Set among the staid and aggressively luxurious residences of the 16th arrondissement, it was reconfigured in the 1980s by Peter de Savary, the British entrepreneur who had brought postmodern versions of semiprivate London clubs to sites in Antigua and Los Angeles. This one he sold to new owners around 1995. Though the St. James is a semiprivate club, its overnight accommodations are open to anyone who wants to check in. Residency, even for a night, permits access to facilities (including the otherwise private restaurant, bar, and fitness center), which you'll share with the aristocratic private members from around Paris. You're likely to find it intimate, discreet, and warm, even if exclusivity (and snobbery) are part of its image.

Dining/Entertainment: The hotel has a restaurant open daily for lunch serving classic French cuisine. The bar contains a polished-oak library with some 10,000 leather-bound books.

Services: 24-hour room service.

Facilities: Health club with Jacuzzi and sauna, billiard room.

17TH ARRONDISSEMENT (PARC MONCEAU)
MODERATE

Hôtel Eber. 18 rue Léon Jost, 75017 Paris. ☎ **01-46-22-60-70.** Fax 01-47-63-01-01. 15 rms, 3 suites. TV TEL 610–660F ($122–$132) double, 1,050–1,360F ($210–$272) suite. AE, DC, MC, V. Métro: Courcelles.

The public areas of this three-star hotel are the carefully decorated product of a decade of attention from its namesake, Jean-Marc Eber. It's set on a quiet side street off the busy Boulevard de Courcelles that has hidden away a turn-of-the-century building whose courtyard provides a quiet oasis for breakfast and afternoon tea. Inside, the hotel includes comfortably rustic touches of exposed stone and wood paneling, color schemes of yellow and white, paneled ceilings, and engravings of New York's Statue of Liberty. Bedrooms usually have an armchair for reading, and are done in coordinated fabrics; they're comfortable but not as appealing as those within the public areas.

Hôtel Regent's Garden. 6 rue Pierre Demours, 75017 Paris. ☎ **01-45-74-07-30.** Fax 01-40-55-01-42. 39 rms. MINIBAR TV TEL. 700–940F ($140–$188) double. AE, DC, MC, V. Parking 50F ($10). Métro: Ternes or Charles de Gaulle–Etoile.

The Regent's Garden has a proud heritage: Napoléon III built this stately château for his physician. It's near the convention center and minutes from the Arc de Triomphe. There are two gardens, one with ivy-covered walls and umbrella tables—a perfect place to meet other guests. The interior resembles a classically limned country house. Fluted columns mark the entryway, which leads to a casual mixture of comfortable furniture in the lobby. The rooms have flower prints on the walls, bedspreads, traditional French furniture, and tall soundproof windows with light, airy curtains.

INEXPENSIVE

Hôtel Flaubert. 19 rue Rennequin, 75017 Paris. ☎ **01-46-22-44-35.** 20 rms. MINIBAR TV TEL. 450–500F ($90–$100) double. AE, DC, MC, V. Métro: Ternes.

Rooms here are appealing, clean, and well maintained, and the staff grew accustomed long ago to handling whatever problems their international guests were able to create. The hotel's stars are the lush plantings that climb, creep, and cling to latticed rows, or drape gracefully from window boxes that line the balconies of the hotel's narrow interior courtyard. Though the horticulture overshadows the rooms, they are nonetheless comfortable and, particularly for those beneath the mansard's eaves, cozy. Outfitted in earth tones, they match the simple public areas, where terra-cotta tiles and bentwood furniture offers an efficient, if not lushly comfortable, setting for breakfasts.

Les Trois Couronnes. 30 rue de l'Arc de Triomphe, 75017 Paris. ☎ **01-43-80-46-81.** Fax 01-46-22-53-96. 20 rms. MINIBAR TV TEL. 465–530F ($93–$106) double. AE, DC, MC, V. Parking 80F ($16). Métro: Charles de Gaulle–Etoile.

This prestigious older hotel is located near the Etoile, where many important Paris streets intersect; Etoile is the business center of Paris and a hub of tourism, and affords easy access to the Métro and to many of the city's attractions. The hotel, with its blend of art deco and art nouveau, was radically redecorated and upgraded in 1995 and is under an enthusiastic new management. The cheerful rooms take in the surrounding area, and the hotel has a security system for protection, an elevator for convenience, and a small bar and a restaurant set adjacent to the lobby. Laundry service is available.

Marmotel Étoile. 34 av. de la Grande Armée, 75017 Paris. ☎ **01-47-63-57-26.** Fax 01-45-74-25-27. 22 rms. MINIBAR, TV, TEL. 440–460F ($88–$92) double. AE, MC, V. Métro: Argentine.

This hotel is set on a relatively inconvenient side of the Place de L'Etoile, and requires guests who want to walk along the nearby Champs-Elysées to ford a roaring river of traffic. Those who escape with their lives will find clean and simple rooms painted with coordinated shades of terra-cotta, blue, or parchment. Rooms that overlook the carefully landscaped, flagstone-covered courtyard benefit from an unexpected oasis of calm; those fronting the avenue's traffic are less peaceful.

18TH ARRONDISSEMENT (MONTMARTRE)
VERY EXPENSIVE

✪ **Terrass Hôtel.** 12-14 rue Joseph de Maistre, 75018 Paris. ☎ **800/344-1212** in the U.S. and Canada, or 01-46-06-72-85. Fax 01-42-52-29-11. 88 rms, 13 suites. MINIBAR TV TEL. 1,260–1,400F ($252–$280) double; 1,700F ($340) suite. Rates include breakfast. AE, DC, MC, V. Métro: Place de Clichy or Blanche.

Built in 1913, and richly renovated into a plush but traditional style in 1991, this is the only four-star hotel on the Butte Montmartre. In an area filled with some of the seediest hotels in Paris, this place is easily in a class of its own. Its main advantage is its location amid Montmartre's bohemian atmosphere (or what's left of it). Staffed with English-speaking employees and its owner-managers, it has a large, marble-floored lobby ringed with blond oak paneling and accented with 18th-century antiques and even older tapestries. The bedrooms are high-ceilinged, cozy, and well upholstered, and often have views.

   Dining/Entertainment: An elegant street-level restaurant, and a seventh-floor summer-only garden terrace with bar and food service and sweeping views of many of Paris's most important monuments. In colder weather, the hotel's Lobby Bar, with its own fireplace, offers live piano music.

   Services: Foreign exchange, car rentals, tour desk, laundry/dry cleaning.
   Facilities: Conference facilities.

INEXPENSIVE

Hôtel Ermitage. 24 rue Lamarck, 75018. ☎ **01-42-64-79-22.** Fax 01-42-64-10-33. 12 rms. TEL. 320–480F ($64–$96) double. No credit cards. Métro: Lamarck-Caulaincourt.

Erected in 1870 of chiseled limestone in the Napoléon III style, this hotel's facade might remind you of a perfectly proportioned, small-scale villa. It's set within a calm and quiet area where all the neighbors seem to have known each other for genera-tions. There's a verdant garden in the back courtyard, views that extend out over Paris, and a location that's a brief uphill stroll from the Basilica of Sacré-Coeur. Bed-rooms evoke an *auberge* in the French countryside because of their exposed ceiling beams, flowered wallpaper, and casement windows that open onto the garden or onto a street seemingly airlifted from the respectable provinces. No meals are served other than breakfast. Your hosts are Madame Maggy Canibel and her hardworking daugh-ter, Sophie.

3 Left Bank

We'll begin with the most centrally located arrondissements on the Left Bank, then work our way through the more outlying neighborhoods.

5TH ARRONDISSEMENT (LATIN QUARTER)
EXPENSIVE

✪ **Hôtel Le Colbert.** 7 rue de L'Hôtel-Colbert, 75005 Paris. ☎ **800/448-8355** in the U.S. and Canada, or 01-40-46-79-50. Fax 01-43-25-80-19. 34 rms, 2 suites. MINIBAR TV TEL. 1,010F ($202) double; from 1,630F ($326) suite. AE, DC, MC, V. Métro: Maubert-Mutualité or St-Michel.

How can you lose by staying at this little 18th-century inn? Not only is it on the Left Bank, just a minute's walk from the Seine, but many of its rooms have a fine view of Notre-Dame, too. Bordered by a wrought-iron fence, a small courtyard with evergreens sets the hotel apart from the narrow street and the bustle of Rive Gauche life.

Visitors who enter the hotel find themselves in a tastefully decorated lobby with marble floors and antiques. Gilt-accented furniture fills a sunny bar area. The guest rooms are well designed; most have comfortable chairs and a breakfast area. Those on the fifth floor, the uppermost *étage* (floor), seem like a handsome garret. The suites feature very old beams and inviting beds. Plenty of towels and efficient maid service are provided. Some rooms are suitable for persons with disabilities.

Services: Room service 7am to noon, newspaper delivery upon request.

MODERATE

Agora St-Germain. 42 rue des Bernardins, 75005 Paris. ☎ **01-46-34-13-00.** Fax 01-46-34-75-05. 39 rms. MINIBAR TV TEL. 680F ($136) double; 880F ($176) triple. AE, DC, MC, V. Park-ing 110F ($22). Métro: Maubert-Mutualité.

This is a good choice for travelers seeking that little St-Germain hotel of charm and character. It's the best of the many neighborhood hotels in its price range. Agora St-Germain was built in the early 1600s to house a group of guardsmen protecting the brother of the king at his lodgings in the nearby rue Monsieur-le-Prince. Despite its location in one of the oldest medieval neighborhoods in Paris, there's a distinct link to the United States; in fact, some of the staff members here are engaged to Cali-fornians on leave from their homes in Los Angeles. The recently renovated hotel has compact soundproofed rooms, each comfortably furnished and equipped with an alarm clock, hair dryer, and safety deposit box. Room service is provided every morning, from 7:30 to 10:30am.

Grand Hôtel St-Michel. 19 rue Cujas, 75005 Paris. ☎ **01-46-33-33-02.** Fax 01-40-46-96-33. 58 rms. MINIBAR TV TEL. 500–700F ($100–$140) double. AE, DC, MC, V. Métro: Cluny–La Sorbonne. RER: Luxembourg.

Built during the 19th century, this hotel is larger and more businesslike than many of the smaller town house–style inns that lie within the same neighborhood. It basks

Left Bank Accommodations

Agora St–Germain **33**
Best Western Hotel Derby Eiffel **3**
Delhy's Hotel **26**
Grand Hôtel de l'Univers **21**
Grand Hôtel St–Michel **36**
Hôtel Abbatial St–Germain **32**
Hôtel Charles Quinze **1**
Hôtel Clément **22**

Hôtel Danemark **43**
Hôtel de Beaune **10**
Hôtel de Fleurie **21**
Hôtel de l'Abbaye St–Germain **25**
Hôtel de l'Académie **14**
Hôtel de l'Université **13**
Hôtel Delavigne **30**
Hôtel de Nevers **8**

Hôtel des Arénes **37**
Hôtel des Deux Continents **19**
Hôtel des Grands Hommes **40**
Hôtel des Jardins
  de Luxembourg **41**
Hôtel des Saints–Pères **16**
Hôtel du Globe **28**
Hôtel du Lys **27**
Hôtel du Palais Bourbon **4**

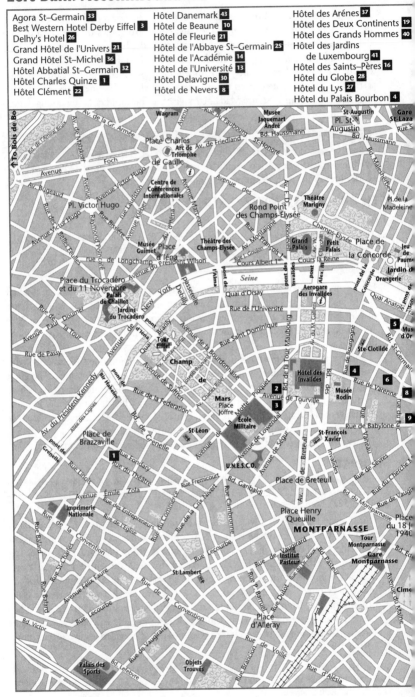

86

87

in the reflected glow of Brazilian dissident Georges Amado, whose 1996 memoirs recorded his 2-year literary sojourn in one of the bedrooms here. In 1997, the hotel completed a systematic, 2-year renovation of its bedrooms, bringing it from two- to three-star status. The architectural changes enlarged some of the rooms, lowered their ceilings, and added such modern amenities without displacing the old—they preserved details such as the wrought-iron fifth-floor balconies that overlook the surrounding neighborhood. Rooms on the sixth (uppermost) floor have interesting views over the surrounding rooftops. Overall, the hotel offers good value, cleanliness, and a central location in the Latin Quarter.

Hôtel Abbatial St. Germain. 46 bd. St-Germain. 75005 Paris. ☎ **01-46-34-02-12.** Fax 01-43-25-47-73. 43 rms. MINIBAR TV TEL. 580–750F ($116–$150) double. AE, MC, V. Métro: Maubert-Mutualité.

The origins of this hotel (known throughout the jazz age as the Grand Hotel de Lima) are so old that interior renovations have always revealed such 17th-century touches as dovecotes and massive oak beams. In the early 1990s, a radical restoration brought the six stories of bedrooms up to small, modern, and very comfortable standards. Furnishings are faux–Louis XVI, each with a different color scheme and many well-crafted decorative touches. The public areas are especially appealing in their postmodern blend of faux marble, elaborate cove moldings, and concealed lighting. All windows are double-glazed to keep out the bustle of the neighborhood, and many rooms on the fifth and sixth floors enjoy views over the cathedral of Notre-Dame. Fifth-floor rooms also have small balconies. The vaulted ceilings of the building's stone-sided cellar play host to breakfast.

Hôtel des Arènes. 51 rue Monge, 75005 Paris. ☎ **01-43-25-09-26.** Fax 01-43-25-79-56. 49 rms. MINIBAR TV TEL. 766F ($153) double. AE, MC, V. Parking: 120F ($24). Métro: Monge or Cardinal-Lemoine.

Set within a 19th-century structure whose chiseled stone facade evokes fine old traditions, this hotel offers well-maintained modern bedrooms. Many of those in back overlook the ruins of Paris's ancient Roman arena. Dotted with trees, and evocative of a public park with historic overtones, it was unearthed in 1865 during the construction of the surrounding labyrinth of streets. The only meal served on the premises is breakfast, an event that occurs in a simple, windowless room in the hotel's cellar. The staff is overworked and somewhat distracted, and the place a bit more anonymous than you might have preferred, but despite that, its location is appealing and its rooms are practical but comfortable.

Hôtel des Grands Hommes. 17 place du Panthéon, 75005 Paris. ☎ **01-46-34-19-60.** Fax 01-43-26-67-32. 32 rms. A/C MINIBAR TV TEL. 770–1,200F ($154–$240) double. AE, DC, MC, V. Métro: Cardinal-Lemoine.

Built in the 18th century and renovated inside and out during the early 1990s, this six-story hotel offers profile views over the most famous mausoleum (the Panthéon) in France. In fact, the hotel takes its name from the great men buried across the way: Voltaire, Mirabeau, Victor Hugo, and others. All but a handful of bedrooms contain exposed ceiling beams dating from the building's original construction, pleasantly old-fashioned furnishings that often include brass beds, and startlingly close views of either the Pantheon (from the front), or of a quiet courtyard in back. Rooms on the second and fifth floor have small balconies, those on the fifth and sixth floor have the best views, and those with the most space usually lie directly on the ground floor. The staff is discreet, charming, and English-speaking. There's a tiny bar on the premises, but virtually everyone here ignores it in favor of the wealth of bars and cafes nearby.

Hôtel des Jardins de Luxembourg. 5 impasse Royer-Collar, 75005 Paris. ☎ **01-40-46-08-88.** Fax 01-40-46-02-28. 25 rms. A/C MINIBAR TV. 750F ($150) double. AE, MC, V. Métro: Cluny–La Sorbonne. RER: Luxembourg.

Built during Baron Haussmann's 19th-century overhaul of the avenues of Paris, this hotel benefits from soundproofed walls, an imposing facade of honey-colored stone accented with ornate iron balconies, and a clientele that has included Sigmund Freud during a visit to Paris in 1885. The interior follows strong, unfussy lines, often with cozy groupings of vintage art deco furnishings from the 1930s. The well-maintained bedrooms have high ceilings, sometimes with provincial tiles, and ornate moldings. Best of all, their position overlooking a quiet "impasse" (dead-end alleyway) ensures relatively peaceful nights in this often turbulent neighborhood. Some rooms have balconies overlooking the surrounding rooftops.

Hôtel Moderne St-Germain. 33 rue des Ecoles, 75005 Paris. ☎ **01-43-54-37-78.** Fax 01-43-29-91-31. 45 rms. TV TEL. 600–750F ($120–$150) double; 700–900F ($140–$180) triple. Rates include breakfast. AE, DC, MC, V. Parking 170F ($34). Métro: Maubert-Mutualité.

Near Notre-Dame and the Panthéon, in the heart of the Latin Quarter, the Grand Hôtel Moderne was completely renovated in 1992. Its charming owner, Madame Gibon, welcomes guests warmly. The comfortably furnished bedrooms are spotlessly maintained. In the rooms fronting the rue des Ecoles, double-glazed aluminum windows hush the traffic. The hotel has a sauna and Jacuzzi along with an indoor swimming pool, a rarity for a hotel of this price range. Though the rooms are small, this is still one of the better three-star hotels in the neighborhood. Le Clos Bruneau, the hotel restaurant, serves traditional cuisine.

Hôtel Observatoire-Luxembourg. 107 bd. St-Michel. 75005 Paris. ☎ **01-46-34-10-12.** Fax 01-46-33-73-86. 37 rms. TV TEL. 700–810F ($140–$162) double. AE, DC, MC, V. Métro: Cluny–La Sorbonne.

The hotel's simple art nouveau facade—tall, narrow, and built around 1900—is something of an architectural oddity within this neighborhood. Many of its rooms, especially those on the fifth and sixth floors, overlook either the Luxembourg Gardens, which lie just across the street, or the nearby Church of St. Jacques. (Room 507, although not the largest, boasts the best view, encompassing both trees and medieval architecture.) Inside, a highly successful 1992 renovation upgraded public areas; they're streamlined and angular but softened by bright colors and an occasional Louis-Philippe reproduction and the bathrooms sport slabs of glossy marble. Breakfast is served in the cellar-level dining room.

Hôtel Résidence Saint-Christophe. 17 rue Lacépède, 75005 Paris. ☎ **01-43-31-81-54.** Fax 01-43-31-12-54. 30 rms. MINIBAR TV TEL. 650F ($130) double. AE, DC, MC, V. Parking 120F ($24). Métro: Monge.

In one of the most alluring but lesser-known parts of the *quartier Latin*, a short walk east of the Botanical Gardens, the Saint-Christophe was created in 1987 by combining a derelict hotel with an adjacent butcher shop. With millions spent on the restoration, the result is clean and warmly comfortable. Rooms have tall sunny windows, Louis XV style furniture, wall-to-wall carpeting, and marble baths. Only breakfast is served here; the gracious English-speaking staff offers good advice on neighborhood restaurants.

INEXPENSIVE

Familia-Hôtel. 11 rue des Ecoles, 75005. ☎ **01-43-54-55-27.** Fax 01-43-29-61-77. 30 rms (all with bath or shower). MINIBAR TV TEL. 370F ($64) single; 370–520F ($64–$90) double. Breakfast 30F ($5). AE, DC, MC, V. Métro: Jussieu.

As the name implies, this is a hotel that has been family run for decades. It is currently in the hands of the dynamic young Eric Gaucheron, who is justifiably proud of the many personal touches that make his place unique. The walls of 14 rooms are graced with finely executed sepia drawings of Parisian scenes, 8 rooms have restored stone walls, and 7 rooms have balconies with delightful views over the Latin Quarter. All of the rooms have cable TV (including CNN) and hair dryers, making the hotel more comfortable than most in this category.

Hôtel le Home Latin. 15-17 rue du Sommerard, 75005 Paris. ☎ **01-43-26-25-21.** Fax 01-43-29-87-04. 55 rms. TV TEL. 440F ($88) double. AE, MC, V. Métro: St-Michel or Maubert-Mutualité.

This is one of the most famous budget hotels of Paris, known since the 1970s for inexpensive, clean, uncomplicated lodgings. Countless numbers of foreign students have stayed here over the years. Home Latin originally consisted of two separate side-by-side buildings that management unified in the 1970s, retaining the original entrances. Renovations in 1992 transformed the bedrooms into blandly functional lodgings, some of which have small balconies overlooking the street. Bedrooms facing the courtyard are quieter than those fronting the street, and the elevator does not reach beyond the fifth floor. Guests in the sixth-floor *chambres mansardées* tend to appreciate their romantic location under the eaves, and the better views over the surrounding rooftops. Each room contains a hair dryer, plus a private bath.

Timhôtel Jardin des Plantes. 5 rue Linné, 75005 Paris. ☎ **01-47-07-06-20.** Fax 01-47-07-62-74. 33 rms. TV TEL. 450–620F ($90–$124) double. AE, DC, MC, V. Métro: Jussieu. Bus: 67 or 89.

Opened in 1986 and renovated in 1997, this two-star hotel lies near the Panthéon and across from the Jardin des Plantes, the botanical gardens created by order of Louis XIII's doctors in 1626 and first called the Jardin Royal des Plantes Médicinales. There are still some 15,000 medicinal herbs in the gardens. Some of the well-equipped bedrooms open onto flowered, sunny terraces. The hotel has a vaulted lounge in the basement, a sauna, and ironing facilities. Equipped with an elevator, the hotel has a small roof terrace and a brasserie and snack bar where breakfast is served.

6TH ARRONDISSEMENT (ST-GERMAIN/LUXEMBOURG)
Very Expensive

Relais Christine. 3 rue Christine, 75006 Paris. ☎ **01-43-26-71-80.** Fax 01-43-26-89-38. 38 rms, 13 duplex suites. A/C MINIBAR TV TEL. 1,700–1,800F ($340–$360) double; from 2,400F ($480) duplex or suite. AE, DC, MC, V. Métro: Odéon.

This hotel is one of the very best in the 6th, filled with style, atmosphere, and elegance. It's a chic address. We've only received one complaint about this hotel, from a woman who claimed her bedroom was "from hell," although we've yet to see that particular chamber. Rooms are fair-sized, a mix of rustic and traditional. The best accommodations open onto a central courtyard or a rear garden; at this writing, plans were in effect for an outdoor terrace that will eventually extend the bar and cafe areas. Relais Christine welcomes an international clientele into what was formerly a 16th-century Augustinian cloister. You enter from a narrow cobblestone street, first into a symmetrical courtyard and then an elegant reception area dotted with baroque sculpture, plushly upholstered chairs and sofas, and a scattering of Renaissance antiques.

Each bedroom is individually decorated with Louis XIII–style furnishings. Accents might include massively beamed ceilings, luxurious wall-to-wall carpeting, and marble bathrooms.

Hotels: 5th & 6th Arrondissements

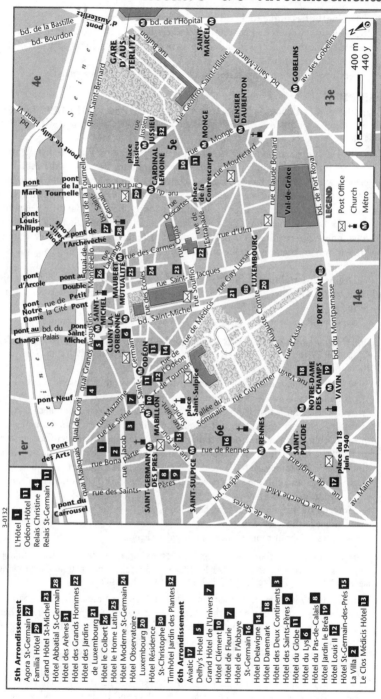

5th Arrondissement

- Agora St-Germain **27**
- Familia Hôtel **29**
- Grand Hôtel St-Michel **23**
- Hôtel Abbatial St-Germain **28**
- Hôtel des Arènes **31**
- Hôtel des Grands Hommes **22**
- Hôtel des Jardins de Luxembourg **21**
- Hôtel le Colbert **26**
- Hôtel le Home Latin **25**
- Hôtel Moderne St-Germain **24**
- Hôtel Observatoire - Luxembourg **20**
- Hôtel Residence St-Christophe **30**
- Timhôtel Jardin des Plantes **32**

6th Arrondissement

- Aviatic **17**
- Delhy's Hotel **5**
- Grand Hôtel de l'Univers **7**
- Hôtel Clément **10**
- Hôtel de Fleurie **7**
- Hôtel de l'Abbaye St-Germain **16**
- Hôtel Delavigne **14**
- Hôtel Danemark **18**
- Hôtel des Deux Continents **3**
- Hôtel des Saints-Pères **9**
- Hôtel du Globe **11**
- Hôtel du Lys **6**
- Hôtel du Pas-de-Calais **8**
- Hôtel Jardin le Bréa **19**
- Hôtel Louis II **12**
- Hôtel St-Germain-des-Prés **15**
- La Villa **2**
- Le Clos Médicis Hôtel **13**

L'Hôtel **1**
Odéon-Hôtel **11**
Relais Christine **4**
Relais St-Germain **11**

3-0132 **1**

91

Dining/Entertainment: There's a paneled sitting room and bar area ringed with 19th-century portraits and comfortable leather chairs. In the breakfast room in the vaulted cellar, the ancient well and the massive central stone column were part of the cloister's former kitchen.

Services: 24-hour room service, laundry, baby-sitting, private garage.

EXPENSIVE

Grand Hôtel de L'Univers. 6 rue Grégoire-de-Tours, 75006 Paris. ☎ **01-43-29-37-00.** Fax 01-40-51-06-45. 34 rms. A/C MINIBAR TV TEL. 850F ($170) double. AE, DC, MC, V. Métro: Odéon.

In the 1400s this was home to a family of the emergent bourgeoisie. The hotel's main competitor—on the same street near the Luxembourg Palace—is the Hôtel de Fleurie, which has a slight edge. But de l'Univers still exudes charm and tranquillity. Rooms are cramped but well maintained. Some of the pleasantly renovated rooms provide a panoramic view over the crooked rooftops of the surrounding neighborhood. La Bonbonnière (the Candy Box) is a red-and-white confection of a bedroom. All rooms have satellite TV reception, private safe, and a hair dryer. For reasons known only to them, Michelin consistently ignores this hotel even though it is a worthy choice.

Dining/Entertainment: Breakfast is served in the cellar beneath the 500-year-old stone vaults. There is also a small, not particularly impressive bar that serves residents of the hotel only.

Services: Room service 7am to 11pm, newspaper delivery upon request.

La Villa. 29 rue Jacob, 75006 Paris. ☎ **01-43-26-60-00.** Fax 01-46-34-63-63. 29 rms, 3 suites. A/C MINIBAR TV TEL. 900–1,800F ($180–$360) double; from 2,000F ($400) suite. AE, MC, V. Métro: St-Germain-des-Prés.

From the outside, the five-story facade of this hotel resembles those of many of the other buildings in the neighborhood. Inside, however, the decor is a stripped-down, ultramodern, minimalist 1989 creation that thoroughly rejected all tenets of traditional French aesthetics. The result is something like the Centre Pompidou of small hotels. Public areas and bedrooms contain furniture inspired by modernized versions of Bauhaus; angular lines in the lobby are somewhat softened with bouquets of leaves and flowers. Most unusual of all are the bathrooms, whose shimmering stainless steel, green marble, and chrome surfaces are either post-*Sputnik* or postmodern, depending on your frame of reference.

Entertainment: The cellar-level jazz club (same phone as hotel) offers live music every night of the week.

Services: 24-hour room service, laundry/dry cleaning.

✪ **L'Hôtel.** 13 rue des Beaux-Arts, 75006 Paris. ☎ **01-44-41-99-00.** Fax 01-43-25-64-81. 24 rms, 2 suites. A/C MINIBAR TV TEL. 800–2,500F ($160–$500) double; from 2,800F ($560) suite. AE, DC, MC, V. Parking 125F ($25). Métro: St-Germain-des-Prés.

During the 1980s, few other medium-sized hotels enjoyed the cachet and charm of this glamorous monument to the decorative arts and French style. Since then, L'Hôtel's cutting-edge style has faced serious challenge from other boutique hotels throughout Paris. With the death of its founder (actor Guy-Louis Duboucheron) in 1997, the place may need to coast for a while on some of its former glory. However, cyclical successes are nothing new to this place: During the 19th century, it was a deteriorating flophouse called the Hôtel d'Alsace, whose only real distinction was that Oscar Wilde died here in 1900, broke, self-exiled, and in despair. Today's guests aren't exactly on poverty row, at least not the fashion and show business personalities who march through the lobby. You may feel like a star yourself when you take a bath within a paradise of pink, green, or white Italian marble, with a single rose standing in a delicate vase next to the tub. Antiques are discretely placed throughout the hotel; the eclectic collection has pieces from the periods of Louis XV and Louis XVI, as well as Empire and Directoire styles. Rooms are small but impeccably maintained.

Dining/Entertainment: A winter garden provides the setting for breakfast. Le Bélier is the hotel bar.

Services: Concierge, room service from 6am to midnight, baby-sitting, laundry/valet.

Odéon-Hôtel. 3 rue de l'Odéon, 75006 Paris. ☎ **01-43-25-90-67.** Fax 01-43-25-55-98. 33 rms. AC TV TEL. 862–1,312F ($172–$262) double. AE, DC, MC, V. Métro: Odéon.

Conveniently located near both the Théâtre de l'Odéon and boulevard St-Germain, the Odéon stands on the first street in Paris to have pavements and gutters (it was first paved in 1779). By the turn of this century this area, which had drawn the bookshop Shakespeare and Company to no. 12 rue de l'Odéon, began attracting such writers as André Gide, Paul Valéry, James Joyce, T.S. Eliot, F. Scott Fitzgerald, Ernest Hemingway, and Gertrude Stein. Today the hotel feels like a modernized Norman country inn. Exposed beams, rough stone walls, high crooked ceilings, a battery of verdant plants, lots of exposed wood, and bouquets of flowers add considerably to the charm of this historic, and very hip hotel. Who books rooms at this place many months in advance? Anyone interested in Paris's spring fashion shows and autumn *salons du prêt-à-porter*. At that time, the place is awash with fashion types and their hangers-on.

Services: Limited concierge services, laundry/dry cleaning, newspaper delivery.

Relais Saint-Germain. 9 carrefour de l'Odéon, 75006 Paris. ☎ **01-43-29-12-05.** Fax 01-46-33-45-30. 18 rms, 4 suites. A/C MINIBAR TV TEL. 1,550–1,750F ($310–$350) double; 1,990F ($398) suite. Rates include breakfast. AE, DC, MC, V. Métro: Odéon.

Relais Saint-Germain is an oasis of charm and comfort whose devotees have kept a relative secret. Like the Relais Christine, its nearest rival, the Relais Saint-Germain was skillfully converted from a 17th-century edifice and is now one of the most charming of all Left Bank hostelries. Gilbert Laipsker, the well-known designer and owner, treated it as his opportunity to make a dramatic decorative statement. The interior, including the bedrooms, evokes a grand and charming country house. Bedrooms contain ultramodern plumbing and lighting, mingled with 18th- and 19th-century paintings and furniture and lots of fabric and idiosyncratic charm. Each is named after a French writer, and each contains all the necessary amenities tucked in under the beams, including soundproofing, a private safe, and a hair dryer. One of the suites is attached to a private terrace.

Dining/Entertainment: The hotel operates a small and unpretentious wine bar, the Comptoir du Relais. Outfitted in a 1930s art deco style, it serves some rather grand wines by the glass. The food is a foil to the wine: expect simple but flavorful dishes such as potted goose pâté, pork-and-pistachio sausage, or any number of sandwiches with roughly textured peasant bread, with fillings like "Rosette" sausage from Lyon or smoked salmon from Norway.

Services: Limited concierge services, dry cleaning/laundry, newspaper delivery upon request, twice-daily maid service.

MODERATE

Hôtel Danemark. 21 rue Vavin, 75006 Paris. ☎ **01-43-26-93-78.** Fax 01-46-34-66-06. 15 rms. TV TEL. 690–790F ($138–$158) double. AE, DC, MC, V. Métro: Notre-Dame-des-Champs.

Anyone who traveled in Paris during the 1960s might remember this place as a battered student hostel, but since it was taken over by a hardworking family in the mid-1980s, it has raised its standards to that of a three-star hotel. There is an overwhelming sense here that someone worked long and hard to transform its interior using magazine articles from home decor magazines. Overall, the effect is both economical and pleasing. Bedrooms are small but cozy, and sometimes have sloped ceilings. The staff is young and usually perky and well intentioned. The rooms have bathrooms trimmed in Italian marble, but be warned in advance that views from the bedrooms, when they exist at all, are of nearby walls. Some are windowless, illuminated only with small skylights, where you may feel trapped amid close, heavy walls. (Ask for a room with a view, even if it is of brick.)

✪ **Hôtel de Fleurie.** 32-34 rue Grégoire-de-Tours, 75006 Paris. ☎ **01-53-73-70-00.** Fax 01-53-73-70-20. 29 rms. A/C MINIBAR TV TEL. 850–1,200F ($170–$240) double; 1,400F–1,500F ($280–$300) family room. Children under 12 stay free in parents' room. AE, DC, MC, V. Métro: Odéon.

When de Fleurie opened it was one of the most exciting renovations in the neighborhood in years. So many hotels, such as the St-Germain-des-Prés, have opened to challenge de Fleurie that the excitement has dimmed. But de Fleurie is still going strong despite the competition. In the reception salon, stone walls peer through elaborate latticework, and beams support the ceiling. An elevator ascends to well-furnished, modern bedrooms and a spiral staircase descends to the breakfast room. Each room is equipped with safes and a modem plug. This has long been a Left Bank family favorite because of its *chambres familiales,* that is, connecting rooms with two large beds.

✪ **Hôtel de l'Abbaye St-Germain.** 10 rue Cassette, 75006 Paris. ☎ **01-45-44-38-11.** Fax 01-45-48-07-86. 42 rms, 4 suites. A/C TV TEL. 980–1,600F ($196–$320) double; from 1,950F ($390) suite. Rates include continental breakfast. AE, MC, V. Métro: St-Sulpice.

The hotel was conceived early in the 18th century as a convent for the nearby church of St-Germain, and later degenerated into a cheap youth hostel. Around 1985, teams of workmen transformed the site into a charming boutique hotel whose brightly colored, sophisticated bedrooms encase traditional furniture with lighthearted fabrics. There's a small garden in front of the hotel, and a verdant courtyard in back that features a fountain, raised flower beds, and masses of ivy and climbing vines that cling to rows of forest-green lattices. Public areas include a trio of salons, some with paneling, one with a working fireplace, and a charming little bar. If you don't mind the expense, ask for the room with its own terrace and an idyllic view of the upper floors of neighboring buildings in this very historic neighborhood.

Hôtel Delavigne. 1 rue Casimir Delavigne, 75006 Paris. ☎ **01-43-29-31-50.** Fax 01-43-29-78-56. 34 rms. TV TEL. 580–650F ($116–$130) double. MC, V. Métro: Odéon.

Despite the radical modernization of this hotel in 1994, the aura of its 18th-century origins remains. Public areas feature an attractively rustic chiseled stone, much of it recent, some original to the building. The vaulted bedrooms are distinct creations: Some have wooden furniture, others feature upholstered headboards, still others have Spanish-influenced wrought iron. Most are adorned with patterned or textured wallpaper in tones of blue, beige, brown, or pink. Only breakfast is served here.

Hôtel des Deux Continents. 25 rue Jacob, 75006 Paris. ☎ **01-43-26-72-46.** Fax 01-43-25-67-80. 41 rms. TV TEL. 695–815F ($139–$163) double; 1,020F ($204) triple. MC, V. Métro: St-Germain-des-Prés.

Built from three antique, interconnected buildings, each between three and six stories, this hotel is a solid and reliable choice permeated with a sense of Latin Quarter style. However, the staff doesn't offer much advice on venturing out. The carefully coordinated bedrooms range in size from small to medium, and include marble-trimmed bathrooms, reproductions of antique furnishings, and soundproofed upholstered walls. Which two continents are described in the hotel's name? Europe and North America, whose virtues are celebrated in the mural adorning the breakfast area.

Hôtel des Saints-Pères. 65 rue des Sts-Pères, 75006 Paris. ☎ **01-45-44-50-00.** Fax 01-45-44-90-83. 36 rms, 3 suites. MINIBAR TV TEL. 750–1,050F ($150–$210) double; 1,650F ($330) suite. AE, MC, V. Parking 170F ($34). Métro: St-Germain-des-Prés or Sèvres-Babylone.

This hotel just off boulevard St-Germain is comparable to the Odéon, attracting people who love Paris or, more specifically, love traditional Left Bank hotels. There is no better recommendation for this old favorite than the long list of guests who return again and again. The late Edna St. Vincent Millay enjoyed the camellia-trimmed garden. The hotel, designed in the 17th century by Louis XIV's architect Jacques Gabriel, is decorated in part with antique paintings, tapestries, and mirrors. Many of the bedrooms face a quiet courtyard accented in summer with potted plants. The most sought-after room is the *chambre à la fresque,* which has a 17th-century painted ceiling. The hotel has installed new plumbing and has replastered and repainted the rooms, half of which have air-conditioning. Breakfast is served in the courtyard, weather permitting.

Hôtel du Pas-de-Calais. 59 rue des Sts-Pères, 75006 Paris. ☎ **01-45-48-78-74.** Fax 01-45-44-94-57. 41 rms. A/C TV TEL. 700–810F ($140–$162) double. AE, DC, MC, V. Parking 150F ($30). Métro: St-Germain-des-Prés or Sèvres-Babylone.

The five-story Pas-de-Calais was built in the 17th century by the Lavalette family. Its elegant facade, complete with massive wooden doors, has been retained. The romantic novelist Chateaubriand lived here from 1811 to 1814. Its most famous guest of literary distinction was Jean-Paul Sartre, who struggled with the play *Les Mains Sales* (called *The Red Gloves* on Broadway) in room no. 41 during the hotel's prerestoration days. The hotel is a bit weak on style, but as one longtime guest confided, in spite of the updates and renovations, "we still stay here for the memories."

The guest rooms are modern with large baths. Inner rooms surround a modest courtyard with two garden tables and several trellises. All rooms have TVs, safety deposit boxes, and hair dryers. Off the lobby is a comfortable, carpeted sitting room.

Hôtel-Jardin Le Bréa. 14 rue Bréa. 75006 Paris. ☎ **01-43-25-44-41.** Fax 01-44-07-19-25. 23 rms. TV TEL. 640–750F ($128–$150) double; 750F ($150) triple. AE, MC, V. Métro: Vavin.

Although the building that contains this hotel originally had a garden in back, it was long ago covered with a roof and assimilated into the floor plan. Today, bright colors deck the public rooms, which lead to plain, small, efficiently decorated bedrooms that were partially renovated in 1997. To balance the lack of space, you can expect a polite welcome, and the neighborhood is convenient to the shops, cinemas, and the razzle-dazzle of Montparnasse.

Hôtel Louis II. 2 rue St-Sulpice, 75006 Paris. ☎ **01-46-33-13-80.** Fax 01-46-33-17-29. 22 rms. MINIBAR TV TEL. 550–770F ($110–$154) double; 920F ($184) triple. AE, DC, MC, V. Métro: Odéon.

Housed in a formerly neglected 18th-century building, this hotel has bedrooms decorated in rustic French tones. Afternoon drinks and morning coffee are served in the reception salon, where gilt-framed mirrors, fresh flowers, and well-oiled antiques radiate a provincial aura, as if we were at Proust's aunt's estate. Upstairs, soundproofed rooms with exposed beams and lace bedding complete the impression. Many visitors ask for the romantic attic rooms. TVs are available upon request.

Hôtel St-Germain-des-Prés. 36 rue Bonaparte, 75006 Paris. ☎ **01-43-26-00-19.** Fax 01-40-46-83-63. 28 rms, 2 suites. MINIBAR TV TEL. 750–950F ($150–$190) double; 1,600F ($320) suite. Rates include breakfast. AE, MC, V. Métro: St-Germain-des-Prés.

After an extensive renovation in 1994 embellished its graceful traditional interior, this hotel shot ahead of its nearby competitors. Much of this hotel's attractiveness comes from its enviable location in the Latin Quarter—near many shops and art galleries. Janet Flanner, a legendary correspondent for *The New Yorker* in the 1920s, lived at this hotel for a while. So did Henry Miller during his first stay in Paris. All of the bedrooms, capped with antique beams, are small but charming. The severely elegant public rooms have dentil moldings and Louis XIII furnishings, and throughout the building, evidence is exposed of its early 18th-century stonework. Most bedrooms have air-conditioning; every room has a safe and a trouser press.

Le Clos Médicis Hôtel. 56 rue Monsieur-le-Prince, 75006 Paris. ☎ **01-43-29-10-80.** Fax 01-43-54-26-90. 37 rms, 1 duplex. A/C MINIBAR TV TEL. 790–980F ($158–$196) double; from 1,200F ($240) duplex. AE, DC, MC, V. Métro: Cluny–La Sorbonne. RER: Luxembourg.

Built as a private home adjacent to the Luxembourg Gardens in 1860, then used as a bookstore and a run-down *hôtel de préfecture* (a polite term for a long-term dive for tramps and students), Le Clos Médicis opened in 1994 to become one of the Latin Quarter's most stylish small-scale hotels. If you want the charm and elegance of the Relais Christine or the Relais Saint-Germain at a more reasonable price, this hotel provides it. A multilingual staff runs the hotel. Throughout the public areas and bedrooms, the decoration sports the warm yellows, terra-cottas, and azure blues of Provence. Bedrooms are comfortable and stylish, but not overly large. Behind the hotel, a courtyard spills over into a small garden, where the staff serves a buffet-style breakfast (the only meal available) during clement weather; on less temperate days, look for it in the lobby.

INEXPENSIVE

Aviatic. 105 rue de Vaugirard, 75006 Paris. ☎ **01-45-44-38-21.** Fax 01-45-49-35-83. 43 rms. MINIBAR TV TEL. 520–720F ($104–$144) double. AE, DC, MC, V. Parking 120F ($24). Métro: Montparnasse-Bienvenue.

This is a bit of old Paris, with a modest inner courtyard and a vine-covered lattice on the walls. It has been a family-run hotel for a century. The reception lounge, with marble columns, brass chandeliers, antiques, and a small salon, provides an attractive traditional setting. It doesn't have the decorative flair of some of the other 6th-arrondissement hotels we've listed but does offer good comfort and a warm ambience. Completely remodeled, the hotel is in an interesting section of Montparnasse, surrounded by cafes frequented by artists, writers, and jazz musicians. The staff speaks English.

Delhy's Hotel. 22 rue de l'Hirondelle, 75006 Paris. ☎ **01-43-26-58-25.** Fax 01-43-26-51-06. 21 rms, 7 with shower only. TV TEL. 356F ($71) double without shower, 436F ($87) with shower; 576F ($115) triple with shower. Breakfast included. MC, V. Métro: St-Michel.

This urban six-story antique was built around 1400, and later was bought by François I as a home for one of his mistresses. It lies on a narrow, crooked alleyway, one end of which runs into a point adjacent to no. 6, place St-Michel, the densest and most frenetic part of the Latin Quarter. Don't expect Shangri-La, but look for certain charms that help compensate for the lack of an elevator. If you get a room without a shower, you'll have to voyage to the ground floor to use the public facilities. The building's staircase is listed as a French national relic, and most of the compact bedrooms still have the building's original, practically petrified, timbers and beams. The hotel has been owned for many years by Mme. Kenneche, who leaves the day-to-day management of the place to a hardworking North African staff.

Hôtel Clément. 6 rue Clément, 75006 Paris. ☎ **01-43-26-53-60.** Fax 01-44-07-06-83. 28 rms, 3 suites. TV TEL. 480–530F ($96–$106) double; 700F ($140) suite. AE, MC, V. Métro: Mabillon.

This hotel sits on a quiet, narrow street, within sight of the twin towers of the Église St-Sulpice. Built in the 1700s, the six-story structure that houses the Hotel Clément was stripped down and renovated several years ago into the bright, uncomplicated lodging you'll see today. Don't expect deluxe bedrooms; they're simple and small, in some cases not much bigger than the beds they contain. On the premises is a simple bistro where the specialties hail from the Auvergne.

✪ **Hôtel du Globe.** 15 rue des Quatre Vents, 75006 Paris. ☎ **01-46-33-62-69.** Fax 01-46-33-17-29. 15 rms, 14 with bath. 350–450F ($70–$90) double. No credit cards. Closed 3 weeks Aug. Métro: Odéon.

This 17th-century building occupies an evocative street in one of the oldest neighborhoods of Paris. Inside, you'll find most of the original stonework and dozens of timbers and beams that a team of craftspeople labored to restore. Each distinctly wrought bedroom has an old-fashioned style, a rarity in hotels this inexpensive. *A tip:* The rooms with a bath are almost twice the size as their counterparts with shower, so for the extra expense, you'll get a lot more than just an improvement in the plumbing. The facilities are what you'd expect in a 300-year-old building: You'll have to lug your suitcases up a narrow, inconvenient antique staircase, and eat breakfast in your room. The largest and most desirable rooms are 1, 12 (which has a baldaquin-canopied bed), 14, 15, and 16.

Hôtel du Lys. 23 rue Serpente, 75006 Paris. ☎ **01-43-26-97-57.** Fax 01-44-07-34-90. 22 rms. TV TEL. 480F ($96) double; 580F ($116) triple. Rates include breakfast. No credit cards. Métro: Cluny–La Sorbonne.

Built in the 17th century, with tall casement windows and high ceilings dating from its original construction, this establishment has functioned as a hotel since the turn of the century. Shortly after World War II, it was acquired by the Decharne family, who have spent the last 50 years restoring and upgrading it at frequent intervals. Today, you'll find a cozy, owner-maintained hotel where all rooms have different patterns of curtains and wallpaper. Don't expect attentive service, or much involvement in your comings and goings; this place is like an upscale dormitory, with residents pursuing a wide array of interests and activities in the surrounding Latin Quarter. Few of them spend any time within the hotel's limited public areas. There's no elevator, a fact that guarantees that you'll make frequent use of the historic 17th-century staircase during ascents that stretch as high as four floors above ground level. Breakfast, included in the price, can be served in your room if you so desire.

7TH ARRONDISSEMENT (EIFFEL TOWER/MUSÉE D'ORSAY)
VERY EXPENSIVE

✪ **Hôtel Montalembert.** 3 rue de Montalembert, 75007 Paris. ☎ **800/447-7462** in the U.S. and Canada, or 01-45-49-68-68. Fax 01-45-49-69-49. 51 rms, 5 suites. A/C MINIBAR TV TEL. 1,675–2,140F ($335–$428) double; 2,830F ($566) suite. AE, DC, MC, V. Parking 120F ($24). Métro: Rue-du-Bac.

The Montalembert's beaux-arts style (1926) made it the darling of France's intellectual crème de la crème and serious fashion types. There is no finer address in the

7th arrondissement. This is one of the most appealing small hotels of Paris, rivaled only in the 6th by Relais Christine and Relais Saint-Germain. In 1989, the Hong Kong–based Leo group bought the then-faltering hotel and hired one of France's premier architectural designers, Christian Liaigre, to direct a well-publicized overhaul. After millions of francs' worth of discreet improvements, they reopened the hotel in 1990. It was immediately hailed as one of the capital's most successful and imaginative restorations. In many ways, the Montalembert has become the quintessential hotel for trust-fund bohemians who want a traditional setting without leaving this amusing, hip, and relaxed neighborhood.

Unusually elegant for a Left Bank hotel, the public rooms—stippled in honey beiges, creams, and golds—borrow elements of Bauhaus design and postmodernism. Half of the bedrooms keep to a conservative French Empire style, and the rest are modern. Within, gray Portuguese marble ensheathes the bathrooms.

Dining/Entertainment: Le Montalembert is favored by area artists, writers, publishers, and antique dealers. The stylish dining room provides excellent service and exceptionally good food based on market-fresh ingredients. Dishes include traditional veal chops slathered with wild mushrooms, along with more inventive fare from the relatively young kitchen staff. Expect crowds for weekday lunches; it thins out at other times. In summer, dining is offered on the terrace. The hotel also has a full-fledged bar and 24-hour room service.

Services: The concierge can arrange for practically anything under the sun.

Facilities: All rooms contain VCRs and safes. Hotel clients receive privileges at a nearby health club.

EXPENSIVE

✪ **Hôtel de l'Université.** 22 rue de l'Université, 75007 Paris. ☎ **01-42-61-09-39.** Fax 01-42-60-40-84. 27 rms, baths only. A/C TV TEL. 850–1,300 F ($170–$260) double; 1,100–1,500 F ($220–$300) triple. AE, MC, V. Métro: St-Germain-des-Prés.

Long favored by the rich parents of North American students studying in Paris, this hotel enjoys an enviable location in a discreet upscale neighborhood. L'Université is the love child of Madame Bergmann, who has a flair for restoring old places and a collector's eye for assembling antiques. She has completely refurbished this 300-year-old town house and decorated it with unusually fine antiques. It long ago became the preferred little place to stay for those who want a St-Germain-de-Prés atmosphere (reservations are imperative). No. 54 is a favorite room, with a rattan bed, period pieces, and a marble bath. Opening onto a courtyard, no. 35 is another charmer, with a fireplace and a provincial armoire. The most expensive accommodation in the house has a small private terrace overlooking the surrounding rooftops. A bistro-style breakfast room opens onto a tiny courtyard with a fountain. Afternoon nappers, take note: There is a schoolyard close by the hotel, from which piping and exuberant voices have shipwrecked many a midday snooze.

Le Duc de Saint-Simon. 14 rue de St-Simon, 75007 Paris. ☎ **01-44-39-20-20.** Fax 01-45-48-68-25. 29 rms, 5 suites. TEL. 1,050–1,450F ($210–$290) double; from 1,825F ($365) suite. AE, MC, V. Métro: Rue-du-Bac.

Set on a quiet residential street on the Left Bank, this is the only hotel in the 7th arrondissement to seriously challenge the Montalembert. This small villa has a tiny front garden and an 1830s decor with *faux-marbre* trompe-l'oeil panels, a frescoed elevator, and climbing wisteria gracing the courtyard. The immortal cafes, Les Deux Magots and Le Flore, are a few steps away. Each bedroom is unique and sure to include at least one antique. The service reflects the owner's extensive training in the art of cosseting guests.

Hotels: 7th Arrondissement

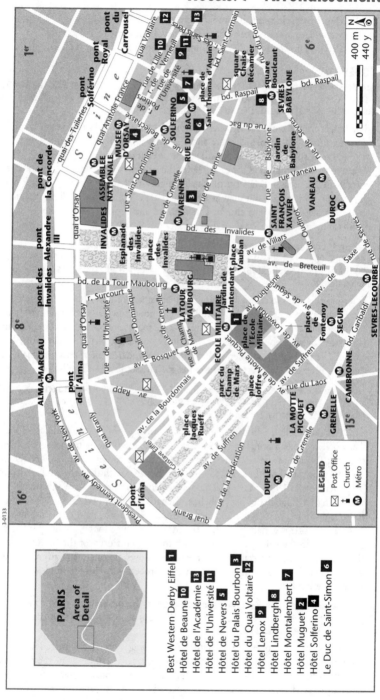

PARIS
Area of Detail

Best Western Derby Eiffel **1**
Hôtel de Beaune **10**
Hôtel de l'Académie **13**
Hôtel de l'Université **11**
Hôtel de Nevers **5**
Hôtel du Palais Bourbon **3**
Hôtel du Quai Voltaire **12**
Hôtel Lenox **9**
Hôtel Lindbergh **8**
Hôtel Montalembert **7**
Hôtel Muguet **2**
Hôtel Solferino **4**
Le Duc de Saint-Simon **6**

Dining/Entertainment: Room service is offered daily from 7am to 10:30pm.
Services: The concierge can arrange for just about anything, discreetly.
Facilities: The hotel supplies televisions for clients who request them.

MODERATE

Best Western Hotel Derby Eiffel. 5 av. Duquesne, 75007 Paris. ☎ **800/528-1234** or 01-47-05-12-05. Fax 01-47-03-43-43. 43 rms, 1 suite. MINIBAR TV TEL. 650–710F ($130–$142) double; 950F ($190) suite. AE, DC, MC, V. Métro: École Militaire.

The hotel's formal stone facade, shaped around 1910, overlooks the symmetry of the side entrance of the École Militaire and a sideshoot of expansive avenue Duquesne where an unusual (and perhaps fated) surplus of parking spots may be found. Converted to three-star status in the early 1990s, the six-story hotel contains airy and comfortable public areas, our favorite of which is a glass-roofed conservatory in back filled year-round with plants and used as a breakfast area. The soundproofed and conservatively modern bedrooms employ thick fabrics and soothing neutral colors. Most front-facing rooms offer views of the Eiffel Tower.

Hôtel de L'Académie. 32 rue des Sts-Pères, 75007 Paris. ☎ **800/246-0041** in the U.S., or 01-45-49-80-00. Fax 01-45-49-80-10. 29 rms, 5 suites. A/C MINIBAR TV TEL. 490–890F ($98–$178) double; from 990F ($198) suite. AE, DC, DISC, MC, V. Parking 150F ($30). Métro: St-Germain-des-Prés.

Exterior walls and old ceiling beams are all that remain of this 17th-century residence for the private guards of the duc de Rohan. The hotel now has an elegant marble and oak reception area. The comfortably up-to-date rooms are bathed in soft colors and have views over nearby 18th- and 19th-century buildings; they have Directoire beds and an "Ile de France" ambience. By American standards the rooms are small, but they're quite normal as Parisian bedrooms go. The staff speaks English.

✪ **Hôtel du Quai Voltaire.** 19 quai Voltaire, 75007 Paris. ☎ **01-42-61-50-91.** Fax 01-42-61-62-26. 32 rms. TV TEL. 620–690F ($124–$138) double; 800F ($160) triple. AE, DC, MC, V. Parking 110F ($22) nearby. Métro: Musée d'Orsay.

This is an inn with a rich past and one of the most panoramic views in all of Paris. The hotel occupies a prime site on the Left Bank quays of the Seine, halfway between the pont Royal and the gracefully arched pont du Carrousel. At least 29 of the traditional rooms had been renovated up to this writing, with the others scheduled for improvements in 1998. Many gaze across the Seine, toward the Louvre. Through the years, Charles Baudelaire, Jean Sibelius, Richard Wagner, and Oscar Wilde stayed here, and photos of Wagner and Baudelaire are enshrined in the small, plush sitting room inside the main door. Be warned, though: The rooms are not particularly imaginative in their decor. However, with the large majority of the rooms offering that river view through ceiling-high French windows, no one seems to mind. After all, inspiration's kiss blew through these very chambers—from these windows, Picasso painted Le Pont Royal.

Hôtel Lenox. 9 rue de l'Université, 75007 Paris. ☎ **01-42-96-10-95.** Fax 01-42-61-52-83. 32 rms, 2 duplex suites. TV TEL. 650–1,100F ($130–$220) double; 1,500F ($300) duplex suite. AE, DC, MC, V. Métro: Rue du Bac.

The Lenox has long been a favorite for those seeking a reasonably priced nest in St-Germain-des-Prés. T.S. Eliot spent the hot summer of 1910 here on "the old man's money." Once a rather basic little pension, this much-improved hotel has been radically upgraded over the years, most recently in 1996, when 3 million francs ($600,000) was spent on renovations that included adding white marble sheathing to the bathrooms. In the bedrooms, the chintzes and solid, traditional furniture of an English country house hold sway. Most have elaborate moldings on the ceiling and floral draperies, and many offer views over a quiet inner courtyard. Some guests ask for an attic duplex, which has a tiny balcony and a skylight. The lobby has a pair of marble fireplaces, and the staff is helpful. A bar off the main reception area is open daily from 5:30pm to 1:30am.

INEXPENSIVE

Hôtel de Beaune. 29 rue de Beaune, 75007 Paris. ☎ **01-42-61-24-89.** Fax 01-49-27-02-19. 17 rms. MINIBAR TV TEL. 430–445F ($86–$89) double. Métro: Rue du Bac.

This hotel is a stone's throw from several upscale antique stores. The white, seven-story, 19th-century building is undergoing a renovation that began in 1997 and should be completed sometime in 1998. Bedrooms are small and efficiently furnished, but lack imagination. The hotel is convenient to many nearby attractions, especially the Musée d'Orsay.

Hôtel de Nevers. 83 rue du Bac, 75007 Paris. ☎ **01-45-44-61-30.** Fax 01-42-22-29-47. 11 rms. MINIBAR TEL. 395–420F ($79–$84) double. No credit cards. Métro: Rue du Bac.

Named after a famous Romanesque town in Burgundy, this building is one of the most historic choices within a very old neighborhood. Between 1627 and 1790, it was a convent for the *Soeurs de la Recollettes* before the French Revolution forced them to abandon their way of life. (Look for the plaque on the stone wall opposite the reception desk.) The building, brought to its present level of modernization in 1983, is presently *classé,* which means that any restoration must respect the original architecture. Unfortunately, the nuns didn't have an elevator, so like them, you'll have to climb a never-ending but very beautiful white staircase. The rooms, cozy and pleasant, contain a mishmash of antique and reproduced furniture. Two rooms (nos. 10 and 11) are especially sought-after because of terraces that overlook either a corner of the rue du Bac or a rear courtyard. Each room contains a shower or tub and a toilet.

Hotel du Palais Bourbon. 49 rue de Bourgogne, 75007 Paris. ☎ **01-44-11-30-70.** Fax 01-45-55-20-21. 32 rms. MINIBAR TV TEL. 535F ($107) double; 654F ($130) triple. MC, V. Métro: Varenne.

The solid stone walls of this 18th-century, five-story building are not nearly as grand as many of the embassies and stately private homes that lie nearby. But don't be put off by the cramped entrance hall and rather dark hallways: During renovations in the mid-1990s, the owners outfitted bedrooms with carefully crafted built-in furniture, and the architects and decorators placed special emphasis on remaking the bathrooms in ultramodern style. Though bedrooms on the upper floors are larger, all rooms are comfortable and pleasantly decorated. The staff is well informed and can direct you to all the nearby monuments and attractions.

Hôtel Lindbergh. 5 rue Chomel, 75007 Paris. ☎ **01-45-48-35-53.** Fax 01-45-49-31-48. 26 rms. TV TEL. 490–600F ($98–$120) double; 550–700F ($110–$140) triple; 550–750F ($110–$150) quad. AE, DC, MC, V. Parking 170F ($34). Métro: Sèvres-Babylone.

Originally constructed between 1880 and 1881, this building was transformed into a hotel shortly after its namesake (Charles Lindbergh) electrified Paris with his solo flight across the Atlantic in 1927. Between then and the hotel's complete renovation in 1995, it looked as if they had left the dusting and repairs to the aviator himself. Today, however, the hotel sits behind a modern facade, has streamlined and simple but comfortable bedrooms, and lies a 3-minute walk from St-Germain-des-Prés. Breakfast is the only meal served, but the staff will point out good restaurants in the neighborhood.

Hôtel Muguet. 11 rue Chevert, 75007 Paris. ☎ **01-47-05-05-93.** Fax 01-45-50-25-37. 39 rms, 6 suites. TV TEL. 440–460F ($88–$92) double; 670F ($134) suite. AE, MC, V. Métro: École Militaire.

Solidly built as a private home during the belle epoque (around 1890), and exuding a good-natured bourgeois respectability, this building has functioned as a hotel since the dark days of 1942. It rises six stories above a small but verdant rear courtyard that its mother-daughter owners (Micheline and Catherine Pelletier) have planted with magnolias and an array of flowering shrubs. The conservative but modern bedrooms were each renovated in 1993 into coordinated arrangements of either pale green, beige, or soft pink. Every year around May 1, traditional flower arrangements containing lily of the valley (*muguet*), the hotel's namesake, are displayed throughout the hotel.

Hôtel Solferino. 91 rue de Lille, 75007 Paris. ☎ **01-47-05-85-54.** Fax 01-45-55-51-16. 33 rms (27 with bath). TV TEL. 532–702F ($106–$140) double with bath. MC, V. Métro: Solférino or Assemblée Nationale.

Built toward the end of the 1700s, this five-story brick building eventually became the home of Napoléon Bonaparte's surgeon. During the decades that followed, it survived a lengthy stint as a railway station hotel before the eventual closing of the nearby Gare d'Orsay; since the transformation of that monument into a noteworthy museum, the hotel has rallied with the times. Today, you'll find large, high-ceilinged rooms outfitted in omnipresent shades of cinnamon, golden-beige, and white. Furnishings in the public rooms are more opulent than most two-star properties.

13TH & 14TH ARRONDISSEMENTS (GARE D'AUSTERLITZ/ MONTPARNASSE)

INEXPENSIVE

Hôtel du Parc-Montsouris. 4 rue du Parc de Montsouris, 75014 Paris. ☎ **01-45-89-09-72.** Fax 01-45-80-92-72. 33 rms, 2 suites. TV TEL. 310–420F ($62–$84) double; 480F ($96) suite. AE, MC, V. Métro: Porte d'Orléans. RER: Cité Universitaire.

The staff is a bit absentminded, and the decor doesn't even pretend to be stylish, but because of that, prices are reasonable enough that this two-star hotel (a simple six-story structure built during the 1930s) attracts a loyal crowd of repeat clients. Your fellow guests might include parents of students studying at the nearby Cité Universitaire, or clothiers from the French provinces attending seasonal fashion shows at the nearby Porte de Versailles. The neighborhood is quiet, mostly residential, and far removed from the bustle of more central neighborhoods. Bedrooms are either blue or off-white, low-key and unpretentious, and quiet. There's nothing wildly exciting about this hotel, but it's configured in a way that many visitors find both appropriate and convenient.

Hôtel du Vert Galant. 41 rue Croulebarbe, 75013 Paris. ☎ **01-44-08-83-50.** Fax 01-44-08-83-69. 15 rms. MINIBAR TV TEL. 450–500F ($90–$100) double. Parking 30F ($6). AE, MC, V. Métro: Corvisart or Gobelins.

The name of this low-rise hotel, built in the late 1980s, derives from the patch of emerald-colored lawn encased within its wings and sunrooms. Verdant climbing plants and shrubs conspire to make this hotel seem like an *auberge* deep within the French countryside. Bedrooms have either tiled or carpeted floors, comfortable and unfussy furniture, enough space to stretch out in, and in most cases, green views of either the garden or the public park across the street. One of the best aspects of the place is its position adjacent to a well-known Basque inn, the Auberge Etchegorry, which shares the same management. Here, clients of both hotels receive a discount from the price paid by members of the public, enjoying set-price menus for 100F ($20) each.

Résidence les Gobelins. 9 rue des Gobelins, 75013 Paris. ☎ **01-47-07-26-90.** Fax 01-43-31-44-05. 32 rms. TV TEL. 395–425F ($79–$85) double; 515F ($103) triple; 595F ($119) quad. AE, MC, V. Métro: Gobelins.

There's nothing particularly glamorous about this hotel: Until the 1980s, it functioned as a cheap boardinghouse, and the location—far south of the Ile St-Louis and the Latin Quarter—rarely sees North American tourists. But thanks to ongoing renovations, the accommodations are clean, simple, and comfortable, and sell for much less than equivalent hotels within more central arrondissements. Rooms are plain, but with well-maintained accessories and furnishings. Though the staff isn't terribly helpful, if you're looking for a cheap room and plan to spend most of your days out and about Paris, it isn't a bad choice. There's an elevator on-site, TVs in the rooms have a cable hookup, and the breakfast room overlooks a small, plant-filled courtyard.

15TH ARRONDISSEMENT (GARE MONTPARNASSE/ INSTITUT PASTEUR)
INEXPENSIVE

Hôtel Charles Quinze. 37 rue St-Charles, 75015 Paris. ☎ **01-45-79-64-15.** Fax 01-45-77-21-11. 30 rms. MINIBAR TV TEL. 485–510F ($97–$102) double. AE, DC, MC, V. Métro: Dupleix or Charles Michels.

Why did the owners name this place after a king that only a handful of erudite scholars know anything about? Because it lies on the rue St-Charles, in the 15th arrondissement. Fortunately, its owners discovered that, indeed, there actually *was* a Charles XV, an obscure 19th-century Swedish monarch whose bloodlines extend in a labyrinthine skein to France. And the hotel? It's a modern, clean, and uncluttered place with no particular history, royal or otherwise, unless you count the pair of desirable antiques in the lobby. Built in 1988, the hotel scatters bedrooms over three upstairs floors, each with conservatively modern light-grained pinewood furnishings. Although you'll be able to crane your neck upward for views of the nearby Eiffel Tower from the street outside, the landmark isn't visible from any of the bedrooms. A small cafe serves breakfasts as well as snacks throughout the day.

4 Near the Airports

AT ORLY

Hilton International Orly. Aéroport Orly, 267 Orly Sud, 94544 Val-de-Marne. ☎ **800/ 445-8667** in the U.S. and Canada, or 01-45-12-45-12. Fax 01-45-12-45-00. 347 rms, 12 suites. A/C MINIBAR TV TEL. 1,070–1,270F ($214–$254) double; 1,500F ($300) suite. AE, DC, MC, V. Parking 90F ($18). Free shuttle bus between the hotel and both Orly terminals; 40-minute taxi ride from central Paris, except during rush hours.

Boxy and bland, this airport hotel betrays its 1960s design. Despite that, the Hilton International at Orly remains a solid and well-maintained, but not particularly imaginative, hotel that business travelers from around Europe and the world prefer for its convenience. Try as they might, incoming jets can't penetrate the bedrooms' sound barriers, guaranteeing a decent shot at a night's sleep. *Note:* Unlike the airport at Roissy, which accepts incoming flights 24 hours a day, Orly is closed to arriving flights between midnight and 6am.

Dining/Entertainment: The hotel has two restaurants, an upscale "gourmet" restaurant (La Terrasse) that's open Monday to Friday for lunch and dinner, and a less expensive bistro (Café du Marché) that serves lunch and dinner seven days a week.

Services: 24-hour room service, laundry.

Facilities: Exercise room and sauna, nearby tennis courts.

AT ROISSY/CHARLES DE GAULLE

Hôtel Sofitel Paris Aéroport CDG. Aéroport Charles de Gaulle, Zone Central, B.P. 20248, 95713 Roissy. ☎ **800/221-4542** in the U.S. and Canada, or 01-49-19-29-29. Fax 01-49-19-29-00. 344 rms, 8 suites. A/C MINIBAR TV TEL. 780–1,480F ($156–$296) double; from 1,700F ($340) suite. AE, DC, MC, V. Parking 50F ($10). Free shuttle bus service to and from the airport.

Many international travelers shuttle happily through this bustling but somewhat anonymous member of the nationwide French chain. It rises nine floors above a gray, industrial landscape, and employs a multilingual staff that's accustomed to accommodating constantly arriving and departing international business travelers. Travelers sleep in monochromatic, conservatively international bedrooms that are soundproofed havens against the all-night roar of jets.

Dining/Entertainment: International food with French overtones is served at a comfortable restaurant (L'Escale) and a bar (Le Debriefing) on the hotel's ground floor.

Services: 24-hour room service, a business center.

Facilities: Video movies in several different languages; swimming pool and sauna.

5 Gay-Friendly Hotels

Virtually any hotel receptionist in Paris will register a same-sex couple as a matter of course, and perform the required paperwork with the courtesy and nonchalance for which the French are famous. So, although any hotel recommended in this guidebook is considered at least tolerant of same-sex couples, the hotels that follow are especially welcoming of gay guests.

Hôtel Central. 33 rue Vieille-du-Temple, 75004 Paris. ☎ **01-48-87-99-33.** Fax 01-42-77-06-27. 7 rms (1 with bath). TEL. 485F ($97) double with shared bath. MC, V. Métro: Hôtel de Ville.

This is the most famous gay hotel in Paris. The bedrooms lie on the second, third, and fourth floors of an 18th-century building that contains Le Central, the leading gay bar in the Marais. If you arrive between 8:30am and 3pm, you'll find a registration staff one floor above street level; if you arrive anytime other than that, you'll have to retrieve your room keys and register at the street-level bar. Frankly, many visitors prefer Le Central's bar over its bedrooms, but if you want a hotel that will really put you smack in the middle of the gay scene, this is it. Bedrooms are simple and serviceable, but show evidence of much wear and tear. Women are welcome, but rare. The downstairs bar is open Sunday to Thursday from 2pm to 1am, Friday and Saturday from 2pm to 2am.

Hôtel Pierre. 25 rue Théodore-de-Banville, 75017 Paris. ☎ **01-47-63-76-69.** Fax 01-43-80-63-96. 50 rms. MINIBAR TV TEL. 870–950F ($174–$190) double. AE, DC, MC, V. Parking 80F ($16). Métro: Péreire.

The Pierre was named as a facetious counterpoint to a favorite North American hotel, the Pierre in New York City. To create it, the owners combined three five-story 19th-century buildings into a clean, modern hotel with art deco styling. Opened in 1986 and renovated in 1995, it sits at the end of a residential street a short walk from the Arc de Triomphe. The stylish accommodations each have a TV with video movies and a safe with a combination lock. Most are outfitted with conservative modern furnishings. There's no restaurant or bar, but room service is available from 7am till 10:30pm daily.

✪ **Le 55 Guest House.** 55 av. Reille, 75014 Paris. ☎ **01-45-89-91-82.** Fax 01-45-89-91-83. 2 suites. TV TEL. 900–1,200F ($180–$240) double. Rates include breakfast. No credit cards. Métro: Porte d'Orléans. RER: Cité Universitaire.

Its owners consider it the smallest luxury hotel in Paris, although it's better described as an upscale B&B with exceptionally tasteful furnishings. It's set on the southern periphery of Paris, between the trees of the Parc Montsouris and an expansive lawn, in a quiet and respectable residential neighborhood scattered with buildings from the 1920s. (Georges Braque lived in this house for a while, and Le Corbusier designed the house next door.) Jean-Marc Perry, a half-French, half-Irish linguist and former model of great charm who maintains the suites in good form, has owned the Le 55 since 1993. Breakfast is served either in your suite or on a flower-covered terrace, weather permitting. Oak paneling, monochromatic colors, and art deco furnishings accent the suites, each of which have cable TV and a telephone-answering machine, access to a fax, and a minibar stocked with complimentary soft drinks. Many guests are repeat visitors, often in Paris on business. The clientele is mixed.

Le Saint-Hubert. 27 rue Traversière, 75012 Paris. ☎ **01-43-43-39-16.** Fax 01-43-43-35-32. 15 rms. TEL TV. 290–335F ($58–$67) double. AE, MC, V. Métro: Gare de Lyon.

This hotel, renovated in 1996, occupies a five-story, 19th-century town house on a quiet but unremarkable residential street. The small but immaculately clean bedrooms have salmon-colored walls and simple accessories. Because there is no elevator, rooms on the fourth and fifth floors are cheaper than those closer to the street-level reception area and breakfast room. The eastern edge of the Marais is only a 10-minute westward walk.

5 Dining

Welcome to the city that prides itself on being the culinary capital of the world. Only in Paris can you turn onto the nearest side street, enter the first ramshackle hostelry you see, sit down at the bare and wobbly table, glance at an illegibly hand-scrawled menu, and get a memorable meal.

1 Today's Restaurant Scene

With the economy still sour, it is easier to get a reservation except at fabled places such as Ducasse or Taillevent, which are still booked up weeks in advance. *Le crise,* as the recession is known, seems to have arrived to stay. In the heady late 1980s, if you spoke only English or English-accented French, you might have been refused. But now, if you can afford $200 per meal, much of Paris's haute cuisine awaits you and your gold card.

Paris always has more restaurants than it can support. These temples of *haute gastronomie* include the legendary Alain Senderens or the reigning monarch, Alain Ducasse, although the legends of yesterday—Taillevent, Lasserre, and La Tour d'Argent—are still here, still dispensing ever-changing cuisines to the faithful. Only the faces in some of these places have changed: Franklin Roosevelt, Greta Garbo, the Aga Khan, Onassis (with either Jackie or Maria), and Cole Porter have given way to Tom Cruise, Madonna, Paul McCartney, or the latest computer billionaire.

What about belle epoque Maxim's, arguably the most famous restaurant in the world? Still going strong, it's as overrated and overpriced as ever. Colette and Cocteau no longer occupy its tables—more likely a Saudi prince with a blonde escort.

If your wallet tells you yes, have a memorable meal in one of the city's most renowned restaurants, perhaps chef-owner Bernard Pacaud's tiny, romantic L'Ambroisie on the patrician place des Vosges.

Savvy diners confine their trips to luxe establishments to special occasions. An array of other choices awaits, including simpler restaurants dispensing cuisines from every province of France and from former colonies such as Morocco and Algeria. Paris now has hundreds of restaurants serving exotic fare from all over the world, reflecting the changing complexion of Paris itself and the city's increasing appreciation for food from other cultures. Your most memorable meal in Paris may turn out to be Vietnamese or West African instead of French.

On a less expensive ground, hundreds of bistros and brasseries await you. Many bistros can be chic and elegant, but others dispense gutsy fare, including the pot-au-feu that the chef's *grand-mère* prepared for him as a kid. Brasseries are often open 24 hours, including Alsatian establishments that serve sauerkraut with an array of pork products. Cafes, too, are not just places for an apéritif, a cafe au lait, or a croissant; many serve rib-sticking fare as well, certainly entrecôte with pommes frites but often such classics as *blanquette* of veal.

More attention in the 1990s has focused on the wine bar. Originally, wine bars concentrated on their lists of wines, perhaps featuring many esoteric choices and ignoring the food except for some *charcuterie* (cold cuts) and cheeses. Today, you are likely to be offered various plats du jour as well, ranging from homemade foie gras to *boeuf à la mode.* (We list recommended wine bars beginning on page 283 in chapter 9.)

One often-asked question is, "Can you dine badly in Paris?" The answer is an emphatic yes, and increasingly so. Our mailbox fills with complaints from visitors who encountered haughty service and paid outrageous prices for what turned out to be swill.

Often these complaints are directed at restaurants that cater almost solely to tourists. To avoid them, survey our assessments, make new discoveries, and do as the Parisians do: Take your choice of a restaurant seriously. Considering the cost of a meal in Paris, view the culinary pursuit as an investment. While the tourists claw each other for a tacky table along the Champs-Elysées, you can enjoy finer fare at a distant well-recommended choice—truffle-studded foie gras served on Limoges china at Grand Véfour or the eponymous pig's feet at Pied de Cochon where the chefs follow a recipe unaltered since 1946.

Other changes have occurred. Today it's provincial to request *l'addition* (the bill). Chic Parisians ask for *la note.*

Although prices in cheap places seem extravagant to visitors from other parts of the world, there has been an emergence of informal, moderately priced restaurants here, and we'll recommend several of these.

In years gone by, no one thought of dining out, even at the neighborhood bistro, without a suit and a tie for men or a smart dress for a woman. That dress code is more relaxed now, except in first-class and luxe establishments. Relaxed doesn't mean sloppy jeans and jogging attire, however. Parisians still value style, even when dressing informally.

Establishments are still required by law to post menus outside, so review them carefully. The *prix-fixe menu* (fixed-price menu) still remains an admirable choice if you want a vague idea of what the bill will be when the waiter presents it.

A final trend that has hit the dining scene is the "baby bistro"—a reasonably priced spin-off from an ultradeluxe restaurant. We've covered the best of them.

WHAT'S NEW & HOT In the wake of the 1996 semiretirement of the brilliant chef Joël Robuchon, virtually everybody who ever worked in the kitchen of this culinary star has opened a restaurant of his own—some in faraway places like North Yorkshire. Of course, the up-and-coming chef may have been only a dishwasher, but the actual position is rarely mentioned. Robuchon now appears to be on his way to becoming today's Escoffier, and you'll find many dishes now throughout the world cooked "in the style of Robuchon." Robuchon remains a consultant at the **L'Astor,** 11 rue d'Astorg, 8e (☎ **01-53-05-05-20**).

The direct heir apparent to Robuchon is Benoit Guichard, who was the great chef's own chef de cuisine. The young Guichard has reopened **Jamin,** 32 rue de Longchamp, 16e (☎ **01-45-53-00-07**), where Robuchon rose to fame in the 1980s.

Tip

If these viands are far beyond your means, you can still get a peek into this celestial world of gastronomy by dropping into the bar at Alain Ducasse and ordering one of the best arrays of tapas in town. Of course, you'll have to put up with a lot of fashionable cigar smoke. Even Pierre Gagnaire features a highly touted plat du jour at lunch at his bar, costing 150F ($30).

Pierre Gagnaire, 6 rue Balzac, 8e (☎ **01-44-35-18-25**) arrives in Paris fresh from his disappointment in the town of St.-Étienne. There he rose to the Michelin three-star deity but was forced into receivership in 1996. At the Hotel Balzac, some of the most discriminating diners flock nightly to sample what has been called Gagnaire's "I dare you" approach to cuisine.

Overshadowing Guichard, however, is Alain Ducasse, who is now firmly entrenched at **Restaurant Alain Ducasse,** 59 av. Raymond Poincaré, 16e (☎ **01-47-27-12-27**). At this wunderkind's restaurant, you can order the finest meal in Paris today—if you can win a reservation. Actually, Ducasse isn't all that firmly entrenched in Paris. He's practically airborne at all times, flying between Paris and his palatial Louis XV in Monte Carlo, where he now enjoys two Michelin stars (down from last year's three).

Such excitement comes at a cost—a meal at one of the establishments of these hot, hot chefs will easily surpass $200 per person. If you go at all, it may be better to go for the cheaper lunch menus. In terms of tips, in simple bistros, the small change is left on the table; in luxe or first-class establishments, patrons often add another 5% to the bill.

Average visitors will head, as always, for the old-fashioned, family-run bistro, and we've ferreted out the best of these. In today's Paris, tradition and nostalgia, along with affordable prices, make these bistros busier than ever, especially since so many of them are being forced out of existence because of rising rents.

Although you'll still get grandmother's classic pot-au-feu and that nursery dish, blanquette de veau, many of the bistros are turning out innovative and exciting cuisine, sometimes heavily Mediterranean in style. Much of their food may still be familiar, but it's not trite. We'll lead you to the best value places.

In the addresses listed, such designations as "1er" and "12e," which follow the name of the street, refer (in French form) to the arrondissement (neighborhood) in which the establishment is located.

In France, lunch (as well as dinner) tends to be a full-course meal with meat, vegetables, salad, bread, cheese, dessert, wine, and coffee. It may be difficult to find a restaurant that serves the type of light lunch that North Americans usually eat. Cafes, however, offer sandwiches, soup, and salads in a relaxed setting.

Coffee, in France, is served after the meal and carries an extra charge. The French consider it barbaric to drink coffee during the meal, and, unless you specifically order it with milk (*au lait*), the coffee will be served black. In more conscientious establishments, it is prepared as the traditional *filtre*, a slow but rewarding java draw.

2 Best Bets

- **Best All-Around: Taillevent,** 15 rue Lamennais, 8e (☎ **01-45-63-39-94**), named for a chef of the 14th century who wrote one of the oldest known books on French cookery, is the most outstanding all-around restaurant in Paris.

- **Best Chef:** Can there be any doubt? **Alain Ducasse,** 59 av. Raymond Poincaré, 16e (☎ **01-47-27-12-27**), has overwhelmed Paris, assuming the throne of Joël Robuchon. He artfully combines produce from every region of the country in a cuisine that is contemporary but not quite new, embracing the Mediterranean without abandoning France.

- **Best Decor:** Declared a French national treasure, the belle epoque **Le Train Bleu** in the Gare de Lyon, 12e (☎ **01-43-43-09-06**), evokes the heyday of the gilded age. Completely restored, the restaurant is draped with heavy purple velvet hangings, boxes sprinkled with green plants, Napoléon III antiques, gleaming brass, and a glare of lighting fixtures made of bronze and Bohemia opaline-shaped glass cups—all in perfect harmony.

- **Best View:** La Tour d'Argent, 15-17 quai de la Tournelle, 5e (☎ **01-43-54-23-31**), is a penthouse restaurant owned by shrewd ex-playboy Claude Terrail, who pays part of Notre-Dame's electric bill to illuminate the cathedral at night for his diners' pleasure.

- **Best Unkept Secret:** In the fancy, expensive 8th, **Royal Madeleine,** 11 rue Richepance, 8e (☎ **01-42-60-14-36**), is an old-fashioned Paris bistro at its best. Established in the dark Nazi-occupied Paris of 1943, its invariably flavorful, well-prepared, and affordable French bistro standards like *blanquette de veau* and snails in garlic butter are eternal favorites.

- **Best Newcomer:** Although every escaped kitchen-scullion claims to be the "new Robuchon," you are likely to find his dead ringer at **L'Astor,** in the Hôtel Astor, 11 rue d'Astorg, 8e (☎ **01-53-05-05-20**), where Eric Lecerf enjoys suzerainty. As a kind of Richelieu to Lecerf's Louis XIII, Robuchon still drops in two to three times a week, and though some of his dishes are served, the menu has become Lecerf's.

- **Best Brasserie:** Head for the 10th arrondissement and the quintessentially Alsatian **Brasserie Flo,** 7 cour des Petites-Ecuries, 10e (☎ **01-47-70-13-59**), where time stands so still you expect to see Proust at the bar taking notes for *A Remembrance of Things Past* and washing down sauerkraut with a frisky Riesling.

- **Best Baby Bistro:** Near place de l'Étoile, **La Rôtisserie d'Armaillé,** 6 rue d'Armaillé, 17e (☎ **01-42-27-19-20**), is a sideshow created by one of France's grandest chefs, Jacques Cagna. Unlike his citadel devoted to haute cuisine, the food here is democratically priced. Cagna, along with other great French chefs, realized that the average visitor can't afford haute cuisine, so they created these baby bistros to serve "food like our mothers fed us." If that claim was sincere, we suspect Cagna must have been a fat, happy baby.

- **Best Underappreciated Restaurant:** Once hailed as the best restaurant in Paris by some critics, **Le Vivarois,** 192-194 av. Victor Hugo, 16e (☎ **01-45-04-04-31**), the domain of eccentric chef-patron Claude Peyrot, no longer enjoys such acclaim. Yet we think his cuisine is better than ever. He's not flashy, inventive, or pretentious, but a classic chef that Escoffier would have blessed.

- **Best Seafood:** The fattest lobsters and prawns in the Rungis market emerge on platters at **Gourmard-Prunier,** 9 rue Duphot, 1er (☎ **01-42-60-36-07**), which is so chic that even the toilets are classified as a historical monument by the French government. Nothing is allowed to interfere with the taste of the sea here: You'll have to fly to the Riviera to find a better bouillabaisse.

- **Best Cuisine Bourgeoise:** If today Joyce, Verlaine, Valéry, and Hemingway rose from the grave and strode into the **Crémerie-Restaurant Polidor,** 41 rue

Monsieur-le-Prince, 6e (☎ 01-43-26-95-34), they wouldn't notice any difference, not even on the menu, but would calmly ask for their napkins locked in a cabinet in back with their names on them.

- **Best Atmosphere:** A favorite of Colette and Cocteau, the world-famous **Grand Véfour,** 17 rue de Beaujolais, 1er (☎ 01-42-96-56-27), at the Palais-Royal has an interior that's classified as a historical monument. It serves some of the most refined cuisine in Paris.

- **Best Opulence:** Although "Pierre Cardin's place," as it is called, has an ever-growing list of detractors, **Maxim's,** 3 rue Royale, 8e (☎ 01-46-65-27-94), is still the ultimate choice in art nouveau grandeur, just as it was decades ago when Leslie Caron dined here in *Gigi*.

- **Best Kosher Food:** If corned beef, pastrami, schmaltz herring, and dill pickles thrill you, then head out to rue des Rosiers in the 4th arrondissement (Métro: St-Paul). This street is in one most of the colorful neighborhoods of Paris where the blue-and-white Star of David is prominently displayed. John Russel wrote that rue des Rosiers is the "last sanctuary of certain ways of life; what you see there in miniature is Warsaw before the ghetto was razed." North African overtones also reflect the arrival, long ago, of Jews from Morocco, Tunisia, and especially Algeria. The best time to go is Sunday morning, when many parts of Paris are still sleeping. You can wander the streets eating as you go—apple strudel, Jewish rye bread, pickled lemons, smoked salmon, and *merguez,* a spicy smoked sausage from Algeria. Many spots offer proper sit-down meals, including **Chez Jo Goldenberg,** 7 rue des Rosiers, 4e (☎ 01-48-87-20-16), where the *carpe farcie* (stuffed carp) is outstanding, but the beef goulash is also good.

- **Best American Cuisine: Joe Allen,** 30 rue Pierre-Lescot, 1er (☎ 01-43-36-70-13), is a Yankee outpost in Les Halles. The burgers are the finest in the city. Desserts include real New York cheesecake, pecan pie with fresh pecans imported from the United States, and the inspired cultural fusion of American brownies made with French chocolate.

- **Best Vegetarian Cuisine: Aquarius,** 54 rue Ste-Croix-de-la-Bretonnerie, 4e (☎ 01-48-87-48-71), is one of the best-known veggie restaurants in the Marais. Choose from their array of soups and salads, or have a galette of wheat served with crudités, or a mushroom tart. In this rustic 17th-century setting you can expect flavorful, wholesome, and generous meals.

- **Best Wine Cellar:** At the elegant **Lasserre,** 17 av. Franklin D. Roosevelt, 8e (☎ 01-43-59-53-43), you'll find one of the great wine cellars of France—some 180,000 bottles. This remarkable collection was amassed by René Lasserre, who decants his treasures into silver pitchers or ornate crystal.

- **Best Cheese:** Cheese is king at **Androuët,** 6 rue Arsène Houssaye, 8e (☎ 01-48-74-26-93). Many cheese lovers opt for a bottle of wine, a green salad, and all-you-can-eat choices from the most sophisticated *dégustation de fromages* in the world.

- **Best on the Champs-Elysées:** The specialties of Denmark are served with flair at the **Copenhague/Flora Danica,** 142 av. des Champs-Elysées, 8e (☎ 01-44-13-86-26). In summer you can dine on the terrace of this "Maison du Danemark."

- **Best Late-Night Dining:** Where else in Paris can you be assured of getting a good meal at 3am than at **Au Pied de Cochon,** 6 rue Coquillière, 1er (☎ 01-40-13-77-00)? Although everyone lauds its grilled pig's feet served with béarnaise sauce, few have noticed that you can also purchase some of the freshest oysters in town here.

- **Best Wine Bar: Willi's Wine Bar,** 13 rue des Petit-Champs, 1er (☎ 01-42-61-05-09; Métro: Porte Maillot), named after owner Mark Williamson, is as close as Paris gets to a typical London wine bar. Excellent quality wines are available by the glass. Meet that strange creature here, the tweedy Frenchman.
- **Best Breakfast:** At the **Restaurant des Ambassadeurs,** 10 place de la Concorde, 8e (☎ 01-44-71-15-00; Métro: Concorde), you can enjoy breakfast along with the diplomatic elite amid the marble and crystal of the Hôtel de Crillon.
- **Best Brunch:** The **Hôtel Méridien Étoile,** 81 bd. Gouvion-St-Cyr, 17e (☎ 01-40-68-34-34; Métro: Porte Maillot), hosts "Le Sunday Jazz Brunch," where jazz artists play as you gorge yourself on smoked salmon and succulent roasts.
- **Best Tea:** Try **Angélina,** 226 rue de Rivoli, 1er (☎ 01-42-60-82-00), for a view of haute couture's lionesses having their tea. The house specialty, which goes exquisitely with a cup of tea, is the Mont Blanc, a combination of chestnut cream and meringue and much favored as the signature sweet.
- **Best Picnic Fare:** For the most elegant picnic fixings in town, go to **Fauchon,** 26 place de la Madeleine, 8e (☎ 01-47-42-60-11; Métro: Madeleine). Here you'll find a complete charcuterie and famous pastry shop. It's said to offer 20,000 kinds of imported fruits, vegetables, and other exotic delicacies, snacks, salads, and canapés, all packed to take out. (See "Food" in Chapter 8 for full details.)
- **Best Place to Experiment:** Tripe is a delicacy at **Pharamond,** 24 rue de la Grande-Truanderie, 1er (☎ 01-42-33-06-72). If you're at all experimental, you'll find no better introduction to it than here in Les Halles.
- **Best Champagne Julep:** While you wait for a table at the **Closerie des Lilas,** 171 bd. du Montparnasse, 6e (☎ 01-43-26-70-50), savor the best champagne julep in the world at the bar.
- **Best Ice Cream:** Try **Bertillion,** 31 rue St-Louis-en-l'Ile, 4e (☎ 01-43-54-31-61; Métro: Pont-Marie), a *salon de thé* that after three dozen years in the business still sells 30 of the most delectable ice cream flavors ever concocted. It's open Wednesday through Sunday from 10am to 8pm.
- **Best Pizza:** The **Chicago Pizza Pie Factory,** 5 rue de Berri, 8e (☎ 01-45-62-50-23), is devoted to the almighty pizza pie. The chef creates endless delicious variations of eight different themes.
- **Best People-Watching:** Spend an afternoon on the terrace of **Café de la Paix,** place de l'Opéra, 9e (☎ 01-40-07-30-20), and watch the world go by. See and be seen or settle into anonymity while enjoying the vast variety of faces in this international mingling joint.

3 Restaurants by Cuisine

ALGERIAN

Au Clair de Lune (2e, *I*)

ALSATIAN

Bofinger (4e, *M*)
Brasserie de l'Ile St-Louis (4e, *I*)
Brasserie Flo (10e, *M*)

AMERICAN

Chicago Pizza Pie Factory (8e, *I*)
Hard Rock Café (9e, *I*)

Joe Allen (1er, *I*)
Planet Hollywood (8e, *I*)

AUVERGNAT

Auberge des Deux Signes (5e, *M*)
L'Ambassade d'Auvergne (3e, *I*)
Restaurant Bleu (14e, *M*)

BASQUE

Auberge Etchegorry (13e, *M*)
Chez l'Ami Jean (7e, *I*)

Key to abbreviations: *E* = Expensive; *I* = Inexpensive; *M* = Moderate; *VE* = Very Expensive

BRETON

Chez Michel (10e, *I*)

BURGUNDIAN

Chez Pauline (1er, *M*)

CAFES

Brasserie Lipp (6e, *M*)
Café Beaubourg (4e, *I*)
Café de Flore (6e, *M*)
Café de la Paix (9e, *I*)
Café de l'Industrie (11e, *I*)
Café des Hauteurs (7e, *I*)
Café Marly (1er, *M*)
Fouquet's (8e, *M*)
La Coupole (14e, *M*)
La Rotonde (6e, *M*)
Le Café Zephyr (9e, *I*)
Le Gutenberg (1er, *I*)
Le Rouquet (7e, *I*)
Les Deux-Magots (6e, *I*)
The Lizard Lounge (4e, *I*)

CENTRAL EUROPEAN

Chez Jo Goldenberg (4e, *I*)

CHINESE

Le Canton (6e, *I*)

CREOLE

Babylone (2e, *I*)
La Théière dans les Nuages (4e, *I*)

DANISH

Copenhague/Flora Danica (8e, *E*)

FRENCH

Alain Ducasse (16e, *VE*)
Androuët (8e, *M*)
Astier (11e, *I*)
Auberge des Deux Signes (5e, *M*)
Au Clair de Lune (2e, *I*)
Au Gourmet de l'Ile (4e, *I*)
Au Pactole (5e, *M*)
Au Pied de Cochon (1er, *I*)
Au Pied de Fouet (7e, *I*)
Au Rendezvous des Camionneurs
  (1er, *I*)
Aux Charpentiers (6e, *I*)
Berrys (8e, *I*)
Bistro de la Grille (6e, *I*)
Bistro Mazarin (6e, *I*)
Bofinger (4e, *M*)

Brasserie Balzar (5e, *M*)
Brasserie de l'Ile St-Louis (4e, *I*)
Café le Départ-St-Michel (5e, *I*)
Carré des Feuillants (1er, *VE*)
Chartier (9e, *I*)
Chez Clément (8e, *I*)
Chez Diane (6e, *I*)
Chez Dumonet (Chez Josephine)
  (6e, *I*)
Chez Edgard (8e, *M*)
Chez Georges (17e, *M*)
Chez Georges (2e, *M*)
Chez Pauline (1er, *M*)
Chez René (5e, *I*)
Closerie de Lilas (6e, *E*)
Crémerie-Restaurant Polidor (6e, *I*)
Dame Tartine (4e, *I*)
Faugeron (16e, *VE*)
Guy Savoy (17e, *VE*)
Jacques Cagna (6e, *VE*)
Jamin (16e, *VE*)
Julien (10e, *M*)
La Butte Chaillot (16e, *M*)
L'Affriolé (7e, *M*)
La Fontaine de Mars (7e, *I*)
La Grille (10e, *I*)
L'Amazonial (1er, *I*)
L'Ambassade d'Auvergne (3e, *M*)
L'Ambroisie (4e, *E*)
L'Ami Louis (3e, *E*)
La Petite Chaise (7e, *M*)
La Petite Hostellerie (5e, *I*)
La Rose de France (1er, *I*)
La Rôtisserie d'Armaillé (17e, *M*)
La Rôtisserie d'en Face (6e, *I*)
L'Arpège (7e, *VE*)
Lasserre (8e, *VE*)
L'Astor (8e, *VE*)
La Tour d'Argent (5e, *VE*)
La Tour de Monthléry (Chez Denise)
  (1er, *I*)
L'Ébauchoir (12e, *I*)
Le Bistro d'à Côté (17e, *M*)
Le 30 (Chez Fauchon) (8e, *M*)
Le Bistro de l'Étoile (16e, *I*)
Le Brise-Miche (4e, *I*)
Le Clementine (2e, *I*)
Le Grand Véfour (1er, *VE*)
Le Grand Zinc (9e, *I*)
Le Petit Vatel (6e, *I*)
Le Poule au Pot (1er, *I*)

Le Procope (6e, *I*)
Lescure (1er, *I*)
Les Gourmets des Ternes (17e, *I*)
Le Train Bleu (12e, *M*)
Le Vaudeville (2e, *I*)
Le Vieux Bistro (4e, *I*)
Le Violin d'Ingres (7e, *E*)
Le Vivarois (16e, *E*)
L'Imprimerie (3e, *I*)
Lucas-Carton (Alain Senderens)
   (8e, *VE*)
Marc-Annibal de Coconnas (4e, *M*)
Marie-Louise (18e, *I*)
Maxim's (8e, *VE*)
Michel Rostang (17e, *VE*)
Perraudin (5e, *I*)
Pharamond (1er, *M*)
Pierre Gagnaire (8e, *VE*)
Pub Saint-Germain-des-Prés (6e, *I*)
Restaurant d'Eric Frechon
   (19e, *M*)
Restaurant des Beaux-Arts (6e, *I*)
Restaurant Opéra (9e, *E*)
Rôtisserie du Beaujolais (5e, *M*)
Royal Madeleine (8e, *I*)
Taillevent (8e, *VE*)
Trumilou (4e, *I*)

GASCONY
Au Trou Gascon (12e, *E*)

INDIAN
Yugaraj (6e, *E*)

INDOCHINESE
Café Indochine (8e, *I*)

JEWISH
Chez Jo Goldenberg (4e, *I*)

KOREAN
Shing-Jung (8e, *I*)

LANDES
Chez Dumonet (Chez Josephine)
   (6e, *I*)
Restaurant du Marché (14e, *M*)

LIGHT FARE
Angélina (1er, *I*)

LOIRE VALLEY (ANJOU)
Au Petit Riche (9e, *M*)

MEDITERRANEAN
Alain Ducasse (16e, *VE*)

MIDDLE OF THE NIGHT
Au Pied de Cochon (1er, *I*)
Babylone (2e, *I*)
Café le Départ-St-Michel (5e, *I*)
La Tour de Monthléry (Chez Denise)
   (1er, *I*)
Le Poule au Pot (1er, *I*)
Le Vaudeville (2e, *I*)
Pub Saint-Germain-des-Prés (6e, *I*)

NORMAND
Chez Michel (10e, *I*)

NORTHERN FRENCH
Le Bambouche (7e, *M*)

PIZZA
Chicago Pizza Pie Factory (8e, *I*)

PROVENÇAL
Campagne et Provence (5e, *I*)
Chez Janou (3e, *I*)
La Bastide Odéon (6e, *I*)

PYRENÉE
Chez Lulu (L'Assiette) (14e, *M*)

SEAFOOD
Goumard-Prunier (1er, *VE*)
Keryado (13e, *I*)
La Grille (10e, *I*)
Paul Minchelli (7e, *E*)

SENEGALESE
Le Dogon (10e, *I*)
Paris-Dakar (10e, *I*)

SOUTH AMERICAN
L'Amazonial (1er, *I*)

SOUTHWESTERN FRENCH
Chez l'Ami Jean (7e, *I*)
La Fermette du Sud-Ouest (1er, *I*)
La Régalade (14e, *M*)

SPIT-ROASTED
Rôtisserie du Beaujolais (5e, *M*)

TEA
Angélina (1er, *I*)

VEGETARIAN

Aquarius (4e, *I*)
Le Grain de Folie (17e, *I*)

VIETNAMESE

Le Canton (6e, *I*)
La P'tite Tonkinoise (10e, *I*)

4 Right Bank

We'll begin with the most centrally located arrondissements on the Right Bank, then work our way through the more outlying neighborhoods.

1st ARRONDISSEMENT (MUSÉE DU LOUVRE/LES HALLES)
VERY EXPENSIVE

✪ **Carré des Feuillants.** 14 rue de Castiglione, 1er. ☎ 01-42-86-82-82. Reservations required. Main courses 205–285F ($41–$57); fixed-price lunch 330F ($66); fixed-price dinner 600–850F ($120–$170). AE, DC, MC, V. Mon–Fri noon–2:30pm; Mon–Sat 7:30–10:30pm. Closed Aug. Métro: Tuileries, Concorde, Opéra, or Madeleine. FRENCH.

Alain Dutournier, one of France's leading chefs, established his reputation as a leading chef de cuisine at Au Trou Gascon, now run by his wife, Nicole. His current showcase is this restaurant in a beautifully restored 17th-century convent, near the place Vendôme and the Tuileries. The interior is like a turn-of-the-century bourgeois house, with several small salons that have *faux-bois* painted walls. The salons open onto an inviting skylit interior courtyard, across which you can view the glass-walled kitchen (no secrets here).

Dutournier used to call his brand of French cooking *cuisine du moment,* the product of an imaginative mind. He feels the term is now a bit dated, but hasn't come up with a replacement. He prefers a light, healthful cuisine built on fresh produce. His beef comes from one of France's oldest cattle breeds, the race *bazadaise,* and his lamb is raised in Pauillac. He garners rave reviews for his chestnut soup with white truffles, a jarret of suckling veal served with a blanquette of wild mushrooms, an exotic species of red snapper roasted on a fondue of lettuce, a gâteau of Jerusalem artichokes with foie gras and truffles, and the signature dessert, almond pistachio cream cake served with pistachio ice cream and a confit of mandarin oranges. The wine list includes several exciting little-known wines and a fabulous collection of Armagnacs.

✪ **Goumard-Prunier.** 9 rue Duphot, 1er. ☎ 01-42-60-36-07. Reservations recommended. Main courses 210–380F ($42–$76); fixed-price lunch 295F ($59); *menu gastronomique* 780F ($156). AE, DC, MC, V. Tues–Sat 12:30–2pm and 7:30–10:30pm. Closed 2 weeks in Aug; Mon (Oct–Mar). Métro: Madeleine or Concorde. SEAFOOD.

Goumard-Prunier, done in tones of green and warm gold, is the forerunner of the 16th arrondissement's staid, bourgeois Prunier. An unusual collection of Lalique crystal fish is displayed in "aquariums" lining the walls. (Even more unusual are the men's and women's toilets, designed by the art nouveau master cabinetmaker Majorelle and classified as a *monument historique* by the French government.) Some of Paris's freshest and best seafood (usually flown in from Brittany) is served here. Examples are Breton lobster with a herbed *beurre-blanc* (white butter) sauce, line-caught turbot cooked whole (the bones add extra flavor), and grilled seawolf with basil-soaked vegetables. The best seafood pasta in town is served here and is justifiably the pride of the house—prepared very simply with a concasse of tomatoes, herbs, olive oil, and lavish use of shellfish. Nothing is allowed to interfere with the natural flavor of the sea. The staff will help translate menu items for you.

✪ **Le Grand Véfour.** 17 rue de Beaujolais, 1er. ☎ 01-42-96-56-27. Reservations required. Main courses 230–380F ($46–$76); fixed-price lunch 335–750F ($67–$150); fixed-price dinner

750F ($150). AE, DC, MC, V. Mon–Fri 12:30–2:15pm and 7:30–10:15pm. Métro: Louvre. FRENCH.

Lodged within the arcades of the Palais-Royal, Le Grand Véfour has been a restaurant since the reign of Louis XV, and, like most institutions, has had its ups and downs. Although the exact date of its opening as the Café de Chartres is not precisely known, it is more than 200 years old and is classified as a historical treasure. Its present name dates from 1812, when Jean Véfour, former chef to a member of the royal family, owned it. Since that time it has attracted such notables as Napoléon, Danton, and a host of writers and artists, such as Victor Hugo, Colette, and Jean Cocteau (who designed the menu cover in 1953).

Jean Taittinger, of the Taittinger Champagne family, and the Concorde hotel group purchased the restaurant, and it has now recaptured, perhaps even surpassed, its former glories. At Le Grand Véfour, you eat from elegant Limoges china at a table bearing a brass plaque with the name of a famous former occupant.

The chef, Guy Martin, a native of the Savoy region, is able to please even the most discriminating palates, bringing originality to French classics in a near perfect blend of classical tradition and the robust flavors of his childhood. Try his noisettes of lamb with star anise or the Breton lobster. Another favorite is pigeon in the style of Rainier III of Monaco. The chef also brings in *omble chevalier,* a troutlike fish from Lake Geneva, which he feels is so delectable that he prepares it simply, merely sautéing it and serving it meunière.

MODERATE

Chez Pauline. 5 rue Villedo, 1er. ☎ **01-42-96-20-70.** Reservations recommended. Main courses 120–155F ($24–$31); set menu 220F ($44). AE, DC, MC, V. Mon–Fri 12:15–2:30pm; Mon–Sat 7:30–10:30pm. Métro: Pyramides. BURGUNDIAN/FRENCH.

Many of its loyal fans compare it to a less expensive, less majestic version of Grand Véfour (see above), which lies nearby and whose 19th-century decor contains some similarities. The setting is grand enough to impress a business client, and fun and lighthearted enough to have attracted an impressive roster of VIPs (Very Important Parisians). You'll be ushered to a table on one of two different levels, amid polished mirrors, red leather banquettes, and the memorabilia of old Paris. The emphasis is on the cuisine of central France, especially Burgundy, as shown by the liberal focus on wines that appear within such time-honored favorites as foie gras, hot oysters, stews swimming with savory herbs and morsels of duck, wild boar, and venison; stuffed cabbage, and a dish that's the celebrated favorite of every red-blooded Burgundian, *boeuf bourguignon.* Looking for a way to inseparably combine wine with your food? Sample the terrine of wild hare congealed within an aspic of Pouilly.

Pharamond. 24 rue de la Grande-Truanderie, 1er. ☎ **01-42-33-06-72.** Reservations required. Main courses 88–170F ($18–$34); fixed-price lunch 200F ($40); fixed-price dinner 310F ($62), both including wine. AE, DC, MC, V. Tues–Sat noon–2:30pm; Mon–Sat 7:30–10:45pm. Métro: Les Halles or Châtelet. FRENCH.

On a street in Les Halles, Norman-born Alexandre Pharamond founded this restaurant in 1832 and it's been a legend ever since, occupying a building more evocative of Rouen than Paris. For an appetizer, work your way through half a dozen Breton oysters (available between October and April). Next, the main dish to order here is *tripes à la mode de Caen,* served in charcoal-fired brass braziers. Tripe is a delicacy, and if you're at all experimental you'll find no better introduction anywhere. If you're not up to tripe, try the *coquilles St-Jacques au cidre* (scallops in cider), available from mid-October through April. Other main-dish specialties include *grillade au feu de bois* (meat grilled over fire wood), as well as *filets de sole normande.*

Right Bank Restaurants

Alain Ducasse ◆2	Café Beaubourg ◆70	Copenhague/Flora Danica ◆14
Androuët ◆16	Café Bernardaud ◆32	Dalloyau ◆23
Angélina ◆35	Café de la Paix ◆36	Dame Tartine ◆77 ◆29
Aquarius ◆79	Café de l'Industrie ◆93	Fauchon (Le 30) ◆29
Astier ◆61	Café Indochine ◆21	Faugeron ◆3
Au Clair de Lune ◆65	Café Marly ◆50	Fouquet's
Au Gourmet de l'Ile ◆87	Carré des Feuillants ◆34	Goumard–Prunier ◆30
Au Petit Riche ◆39	Chartier ◆43	Guy Savoy ◆9
Au Pied de Cochon ◆68	Chez Clement ◆15	Hard Rock Café ◆40
Au Rendezvous des Camionneurs ◆74	Chez Edgard ◆20	Jamin ◆5
Au Trou Gascon ◆96	Chez Georges (rue de Mail) ◆46	Joe Allen ◆69
Babylone ◆64	Chez Georges (blvd. Pereire) ◆6	Julien ◆58
Berrys ◆24	Chez Janou ◆90	Lasserre ◆22
Bertillion ◆86	Chez Jo Goldenberg ◆33	Lescure ◆33
Bofinger ◆92	Chez Michel ◆51	L'Amazonail ◆76
Brasserie de l'Ile St–Louis ◆85	Chez Pauline ◆47	L'Ambassade d'Auvergne ◆66
Brasserie Flo ◆56	Chicago Pizza Pie Factory ◆17	L'Ambroisie ◆89

'Ami Louis 60
'Astor 25
'Ebauchoir 95
'Imprimerie 80
a Butte Chaillot 4
a Fermette du Sud–Ouest 67
a Grille 53
a P'tite Tonkonoise 55
a Rose de France 75
a Rôtisserie d'Armaillé 8
a Théière dans les Nuages 82
a Tour de Monthléry (Chez Denise) 73
e Bistro d'à Côté 11
e Bistro de l'Étoile 7
e Brise–Miche
e Café Zephyr 41
e Carrousel 49

Le Clementine 42
Le Dogon 59
Le Grain de Folie 37
Le Grand Véfour 48
Le Grand Zinc 65
Le Gutenberg 62
Le Poule au Pot 72
Le 30 (Chez Fauchon) 29
Le Train Bleu 94
Le Vaudeville 44
Le Vieux Bistro 84
Le Vivarois 1
Les Gourmets des Ternes 12
Lizard Lounge 81
Lucas–Carton (Alain Senderens) 27
Marc–Annibal de Coconnas 91
Marie–Louise 38

Maxim's 31
Michel Rostang 10
Paris–Dakar 54
Pharamond 71
Pierre Gagnaire 13
Restaurant d'Eric Frechon 52
Restaurant Opéra 25
Royal Madeleine 28
Shing–Jung 26
Stohrer 63
Taillevent 18
Trumilou 88

0   450 m
     500 yds

N

INEXPENSIVE

☼ Angélina. 226 rue de Rivoli, 1er. ☎ **01-42-60-82-00.** Reservations accepted for lunch, but not for teatime. Pot of tea for one 35F ($7); sandwiches and salads 35–58F ($7–$12); plats du jour 85–95F ($17–$19). AE, MC, V. Daily 9am–7pm. Métro: Tuileries. TEA/LIGHT FARE.

In the high-rent district near the Inter-Continental Hotel, this *salon de thé* has an ambience that manages to combine glitter, bourgeois respectability, and frantic hysteria all at the same time. The ceilings are high, and the gilded interior has been worn to just the right patina. In contrast, the carpets, tables, and chairs, by well-known designer Jean-Michel Wilmotte and computer-generated artwork by Francis Giacobetti, are deliberately modern. For a view of the lionesses of haute couture having their tea and delicate sandwiches, the place is without equal. Bearing silver trays, overwrought waitresses serve light platters, pastries, coffee, drinks, and tea at tiny marble-topped tables. The claustrophobic charm here seems a part of the commercial whirl of central Paris. Lunches usually consist of a salad and a plat du jour, such as chicken salad, sole meunière, fillet of barbue (brill) on a bed of braised fennel, and poached salmon. The house specialty, designed to go well with tea, is Mont Blanc. Priced at 36F ($7), it's a combination of chestnut cream and meringue and is much favored as the signature sweet of the tea room. There are two drawbacks, however: This neighborhood is not as nice as it used to be, and the service here can be a bit snooty.

☼ Au Pied de Cochon. 6 rue Coquillière, 1er. ☎ **01-40-13-77-00.** Reservations recommended for conventional lunch and dinner hours. Main courses 78–150F ($16–$30); fixed-price menu 178F ($36). AE, DC, MC, V. 24 hours. Daily. Métro: Les Halles. FRENCH/MIDDLE OF THE NIGHT.

Although the great market that used to surround this restaurant has moved to Rungis, by the distant expanses of Orly, traditions die hard. Au Pied de Cochon's famous onion soup still lures visitors, and besides, where else in Paris can you be assured of getting a good meal at 3am? The house specialty is the restaurant's namesake: pig's feet grilled and served with béarnaise sauce. Both dishes are as good—or, in the view of some, as bad—as they always were. Try the suckling pig St-Eustache or another well-known specialty, *andouillette* (chitterling sausage) with béarnaise sauce.

On the street outside, you can buy some of the freshest oysters in town. The attendants will give you slices of lemons to accompany them, and you can down them on the spot.

Au Rendezvous des Camionneurs. 72 quai des Orfèvres, 1er. ☎ **01-43-54-88-74.** Reservations recommended on weekends. Main courses 88–98F ($18–$20); fixed-price menu 78–128F ($16–$26). AE, MC, V. Daily noon–2:30pm and 7–11:30pm (last order). Métro: Pont-Neuf. FRENCH.

Set adjacent to the Pont-Neuf on the Ile de la Cité, this restaurant has the look, feel, and service of a traditional Lyonnais bistro. It was founded in 1870, and many of its original mirrors and banquettes remain, even the burgundy, olive, and khaki color scheme. Its traditional fare is reasonably priced and well prepared. Dishes include terrine of rabbit, *crottin de chavignol* (a traditional appetizer layered with goat's cheese), snails with garlic cream sauce, a ragout of mussels and shrimp with a fondée of leeks, and the blanquette de veau (veal in white sauce). The staff is intelligent and charming, and the majority of the regular dinner crowd is gay.

☼ Joe Allen. 30 rue Pierre-Lescot, 1er. ☎ **01-42-36-70-13.** Reservations recommended for dinner. Main courses 75–140F ($15–$28). AE, MC, V. Daily noon–2am. Métro: Etienne-Marcel. AMERICAN.

Restaurants: 1st Arrondissement

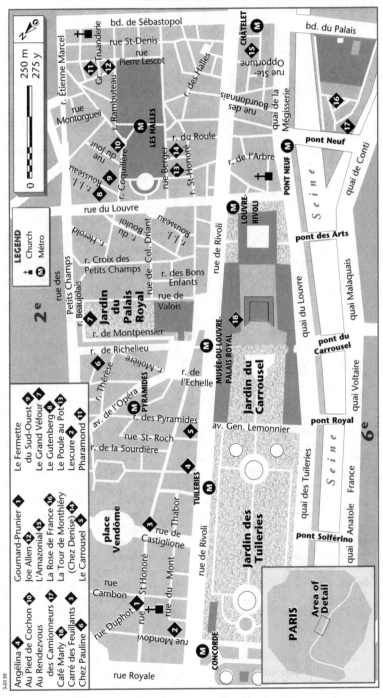

LEGEND
✝ Church
Ⓜ Métro

Angélina **4**
Au Pied de Cochon **10**
Au Rendezvous
des Camionneurs **17**
Café Marly **18**
Carré des Feuillants **3**
Chez Pauline **6**

Goumard-Prunier **1**
Joe Allen **12**
L'Amazonial **15**
La Rose de France **16**
La Tour de Monthléry
(Chez Denise) **14**
Le Carrousel **5**

Le Fermette
du Sud-Ouest **9**
Le Grand Véfour **7**
Le Gutenberg **8**
Le Poule au Pot **13**
Lescure **2**
Pharamond **11**

3-0139

In Pursuit of the Perfect Parisian Pastry

Could it be true, as rumor has it, that more eggs, sugar, cream, and butter per capita are consumed in Paris than any other city in the world, with the possible exception of Vienna? From the modern-day Proust sampling the madeleine to the child munching into a *pain au chocolat* (a chocolate-filled croissant), everybody in Paris seems to be in pursuit of two things: the perfect lover and the perfect pastry, not necessarily in that order. As a Parisian food critic once said, "A day without a pastry is a day in hell!"

Who would think of beginning a morning in Paris without a croissant—not those made with leadlike dough and prepackaged, but flaky and freshly baked, light as a feather in texture and made with real butter, preferably from Norman cows.

The Greeks may have invented pastry-making, at least according to Bourdeau's *Histoire de l'Alimentation,* but the French pastry cook perfected it. They were first called *oubleyeurs,* named for a wafer cooked in an iron which was their main source of income. Rabelais in his *Fourth Book of Pantagruel* celebrates the pastries in vogue during his day, ranging from *caillebotte* (curd cakes) to *poupelins* (baby dolls). In time, the "Twelfth Night Cake" (a decorated cake with a bean or silver coin baked inside) even aroused the wrath of the Revolutionaries. The person who got the Twelfth Night Cake, a kind of fortune cookie, was accepted as a king for the occasion. The Revolutionaries of 1794 saw liberticide tendencies in this mock-royal custom. They claimed that any pastry cook baking such a cake was trying to destroy liberty in France.

By the 19th century, the era of the great pâtissiers had arrived, and Leblanc, Jacquet, Rouget, Lesage, and Félix have gone down in culinary lore. Many cakes and pastries created in that heady time are still around today and sold in Paris's pastry shops in one form or the other. These include *trois frères* created by a trio of brothers who molded this pastry with rice flour and candied angelica flavored with a glass of maraschino.

Spiced with rum or kirsch, the yeasty Savarin cake was tasted by Parisians for the first time in the 1800s. The fabled Gorenflot, a sweet made of baba dough baked in a hexagonal mold, was named in memory of the hero of Alexandre Dumas's play, *La Dame de Monsoreau.* Saint-Honoré is still a specialty of Parisian pastry cooks—named in memory of St. Honoré, plump patron saint of pastry cooks and bakers. Made of two kinds of pastry dough, this delectable pastry has a cream filling.

Of all French pastries, some have made a greater impact on the world than others, namely the already mentioned croissant. But brioche, a sweet, yeasty breakfast bread, is also baked around the world today, as is the fabled *éclair au chocolate,* a cream-filled choux pastry. The other pastry that you should sample in Paris on home turf (and that you can never get right in your own kitchen) is the "Napolitain," which was not created in Naples. Made with cake flour and almonds, the layers of this pastry are spread with a different fruit puree. The term *Neapolitan* is also used today, indicating sweets and cakes made with layers of two or more colors, each

---

The last place in the world you'd expect to find Joe Allen is Les Halles, that once-legendary Paris market. But the New York restaurateur long ago invaded Paris with an American hamburger that's easily the finest in the city.

Joe Allen's "little bit of New York" is complete with a saloon's brick walls and oak floors, imported red-checked tablecloths, a green awning over the entrance, and

layer being flavored differently. The most common pastry for morning or after-noon snacking is a *financier* or little almond cake. It's named a financier because it resembles a solid gold brick. A pastry very much in vogue in Paris is *mille-feuille,* or "a thousand leaves," made by arranging thin layers of flaky pastry one on top of the other, along with layers of cream or some other filling such as thick fruit purées or jams.

In today's Paris, names of pastries mean little. Each pastry chef is increasingly inventive today, concocting new flavors and varying combinations and naming these goodies after their girl- or boyfriend, perhaps a favorite maiden aunt. Apparently pastry cooks took this anonymous advice seriously: "Make your pastry; when it is ready and you have added whatever you please, give it whatever shape and name you consider suitable."

A world of delectable, freshly baked pastries awaits you in Paris. To get you go-ing, here are some of our favorites. **Stohrer,** 51 rue Montorgueil, 2e (☎ 01-42-33-38-20), was opened by the pastry chef of Louis XV in 1730, and is still going strong. You can always order an 18th-century specialty, *une pithivier* (a.k.a. *une galette des rois*) that resembles a crown, but it will take a least a day in advance to prepare. Available at any time is one of the most succulent desserts in Paris, a *baba au rhum,* or its even richer cousin, *un Ali Baba* that also incorporates cream-based rum and raisin filling. Stohrer boasts an interior decor that's classified as a national historic treasure, with frescoes of damsels in 18th-century costume bearing flowers and, what else, pastries.

In business since Napoléon was in power, **Dalloyau,** 101 rue Faubourg Saint-Honoré, 8e (☎ 01-42-99-90-00; Métro: Saint-Philippe-du-Roule), has a name instantly recognizable throughout Paris, feeding pastries even to the Elysée Palace and many Rothschild mansions rising nearby. Its specialties include Le Dalloyau, a praline cake filled with almond meringue that's marvelously light-textured, the famous Mogador (chocolate cake, chocolate mousse, and a fine layer of raspberry jam), and Le Régale, fashioned from a particularly unctuous version of bitter choco-late. Unlike Stohrer, Dalloyau has a tea room (open seven days a week from 8:30am to 7:30pm) one floor above street level, where ladies who lunch can drop in for a slice of pastry that Dalloyau admits is "too fragile to transport, or to mail, over long distances."

The best way to end your pastry tour of Paris is to sample a madeleine, a tea cake shaped like tiny scallop shells, at **Lerch,** 4 rue Cardinal-Lemoine, 5e (☎ 01-43-26-15-80; Métro: Cardinal-Lemoine). Founded in 1971 by the Alsatian-born Lerch family, this pastry shop sells goods to such luminaries as Martha Stewart, who pops in for a sample when she's in Paris, and dozens of Proust fans who come here for the madeleine hoping it will "invade the senses with exquisite pleasure," as it did for Proust himself, launching him into his *Remembrance of Things Past.* Ideally the madeleine is dipped into tea, preferable the slightly lime-flavored *tilleul.*

waiters who speak English. It was made possible by "grants" from such fans as Lauren Bacall, whose poster adorns one of the movie-still–studded walls. A blackboard lists such menu items as black-bean soup, chili, and apple pie. A spinach salad makes a good beginning, although some food critics have claimed this popular dish is "not serious." The barbecued ribs are succulent as well, but Joe Allen is getting more sophisticated in its menu, catering to modern tastes with such dishes as grilled lamb chops with ratatouille and polenta.

Joe Allen's also claims that it is the only place in Paris where you can have real New York cheesecake or authentic key lime pie. Praise be to French chocolate: It permits Joe to make "better brownies than in the States."

La Fermette du Sud-Ouest. 31 rue Coquillière, 1er. ☎ **01-42-36-73-55.** Reservations recommended. Main courses 70–130F ($14–$26). Set menu (served at lunch and before 9pm at dinner) 90F ($18). MC, V. Mon–Sat noon–2:30pm and 7:30–10:30pm. Métro: Les Halles. SOUTHWESTERN FRENCH.

Set in the heart of one of the most ancient neighborhoods of Paris, a stone's throw from the Church of Ste-Eustache, this restaurant occupies the site of what was built as a convent during the 1500s. After the French Revolution, the convent was converted into a coaching inn that preserved the original's stonework and massive beams. La Fermette prepares rich, savory stews and *confits* that celebrate agrarian France, and serves them on the ground floor and on a mezzanine resembling a medieval choir loft. Menu items include an age-old but ever-popular version of *magret* of duckling with flap mushrooms; *andouillettes* (chitterling sausages); a sometimes startling array of *cochonailles* (pork products and by-products) that you probably need to be French to appreciate, and quail stuffed with foie gras and Armagnac.

L'Amazonial. 3 rue Ste-Opportune, 1er. ☎ **01-42-33-53-13.** Reservations recommended. Main courses 65–118F ($13–$24); fixed-price menus 83–129F ($17–$26). AE, MC, V. Daily noon–3pm and 7pm–1am (last order). Métro: Châtelet. SOUTH AMERICAN/FRENCH.

Established a decade ago in the heart of the Marais, this is one of Paris's busiest and most popular gay restaurants, with an estimated 80% gay clientele (male and female). Set within a 19th-century building that features a flowered terrace extending out onto the pavement outside, L'Amazonial incorporates elements from ancient Egypt, ancient Greece, and the Amazon basin into one large dining room. Menu items include codfish cooked in coconut milk, prawns grilled in the style of Barbados, ostrich steak with exotic mushrooms, Bahia (Brazil)-style lamb curry, tacos, guacamole, and Brazilian-style feijoida.

La Rose de France. 24 place Dauphine, 1er. ☎ **01-43-54-10-12.** Reservations recommended. Main courses 78–99F ($16–$20); menu du jour 138F ($28); *menu gastronomique* 315F ($63). MC, V. Mon–Fri noon–2pm and 7–10pm. Closed last 3 weeks in Aug and 15 days at end of Dec. Métro: Cité or Pont-Neuf. FRENCH.

This restaurant is located in the old section of Ile de la Cité near Notre-Dame, just around the corner from the old Pont-Neuf. You'll dine with a crowd of young Parisians who know that they can expect a good meal at reasonable prices. In warm weather the sidewalk tables overlooking the Palais de Justice are most popular.

Main dishes include sweetbreads, veal cutlet flambéed with calvados (French apple brandy), fillet of beef *en croûte,* and lamb chops seasoned with the herbs of Provence and served with gratin of potatoes. For dessert, try the fruit tart of the day, a sorbet, or iced melon (in summer only). Founded more than 30 years ago by its present owner, Mr. Cointepas, this place can be relied on for fresh food at affordable prices served in a warm and friendly atmosphere.

La Tour de Monthléry (Chez Denise). 5 rue des Prouvaires, 1er. ☎ **01-42-36-21-82.** Reservations not necessary. Main courses 90–130F ($18–$26). V. Open continuously from Mon at 7am to Sat at 7am. Métro: Louvre or Les Halles. FRENCH/MIDDLE OF THE NIGHT.

This restaurant manages to be both workaday and stylish at the same time, no small feat considering the fact that its gregarious owner, Denise Bénariac, has maintained her reign over this place for more than 30 years. The name derives from the establishment's position at the end of one of France's first rail spurs. Produce and passengers from Monthléry, near Lyons, were carried to a point near this restaurant for generations before the line's eventual shutdown. Amid a decor little changed since 1900 (note the long nickel-plated bar near the entrance), you can order hearty, unfussy cuisine. The food tastes best late at night after a long night of carousing. Menu items include grilled pig's trotters, grilled pork sausage served with mustard and vegetables, mutton stew, steaks with peppercorns, stuffed cabbage, and a golden-velvety pâté of chicken livers. Wine goes with this kind of food beautifully, and the restaurant complies by recommending several worthy but unpretentious vintages.

Le Poule au Pot. 9 rue Vauvilliers, 1er. ☎ **01-42-36-32-96.** Reservations recommended before 10pm, otherwise, not necessary. Main courses 100–130F ($20–$26); set-price menus 160F ($32). Daily 7pm–6am. Métro: Louvre or Les Halles. FRENCH/MIDDLE OF THE NIGHT.

More than most of its competitors, this all-night bistro welcomes a clientele of late-night carousers, show-biz personalities looking for a meal after one of their appearances, and anyone on his or her way to nocturnal assignations of virtually any type. Established in 1932, it continues a tradition established long ago of late-night revelers wandering through Les Halles with very adult priorities on their minds. The decor is flawlessly authentic art deco, the ambience nurturing, permissive, and warm-hearted, thanks to the humor and zest of its long-time owner, Paul Racat, who often is on hand to welcome his old regulars. Amid polished copper, burnished hardwoods, and columns accented with glass mosaics, you follow the steps of such former clients as Frank Sinatra, the Rolling Stones, Pink Floyd, and The Police. Menu items are time-tested and savory, and especially flavorful whenever cold and fog descend onto Les Halles; examples include a salad of warm goat cheese on toast; burgundy-style snails; country pâté on a bed of onion marmalade; *confit* of duckling; fillet of salmon trout in champagne sauce, and a particularly succulent version of the restaurant's namesake, chicken served in a pot with slices of pâté and fresh vegetables. Despite the presence of other restaurants bearing the same name, including a well-known outfit in the 7th arrondissement, this is the older, more authentic Poule au Pot.

Lescure. 7 rue de Mondovi, 1er. ☎ **01-42-60-18-91.** Reservations not accepted. Main courses 26–84F ($5–$17); four-course fixed-price menu 100F ($20). MC, V. Mon–Fri noon–2:15pm and 7–10:15pm. Closed 2 weeks in Aug. Métro: Concorde. FRENCH.

Lescure is a small, inexpensive restaurant in the high-priced district surrounding place de la Concorde. Right off rue de Rivoli, the restaurant has been serving simple French bourgeoise cuisine since 1919. In fair weather, a few sidewalk tables are placed outside; inside, an exposed kitchen highlights rustic decor. Duckling pâté is a fine preface to main courses that include a hearty fillet of duckling in a green pepper sauce and cabbage stuffed with salmon. The beef bourguignon seems to have been served here since the beginning of time. Small wars have broken out over the chef's fruit tarts, our favorite dessert. This place is animated, fun, slightly irreverent, and very appealing. You'll get your fill of food and atmosphere for your franc.

2nd ARRONDISSEMENT (LA BOURSE)
MODERATE

Chez Georges. 1 rue du Mail, 2e. ☎ **01-42-60-07-11.** Reservations required. Main courses 100–165F ($20–$33). AE, MC, V. Mon–Sat noon–2pm and 7–9:30pm. Closed 3 weeks in Aug. Métro: Bourse. FRENCH.

This bistro, which has thrived since 1964, is a local landmark, and the food critics (ourselves included) always claim the atmosphere is more interesting than the cuisine.

At lunch it's packed with Parisian stockbrokers (the stock exchange is about a block away), who come to enjoy the food and fun with the Broillet family, who have run the restaurant for three generations. The owner serves what he calls "food from our grandmother in the provinces." Waiters bring around bowls of appetizers, such as celery rémoulade, to get you started. Then you can follow with such favorites as fillet of duckling with flap mushrooms, sweetbreads with morels, veal kidneys in the style of Henri IV (with béarnaise sauce), and fillet of sole with a crème fraîche (fresh thick cream) sauce made with Pouilly wine. You can also enjoy a classic cassoulet (the famed meat, poultry, and white bean stew of Gascony). Beaujolais goes well with this hearty food.

INEXPENSIVE

Au Clair de Lune. 27 rue Tiquetonne, 2e. ☎ **01-42-33-59-10.** Main courses 55–70F ($11–$14); set-price menu 62F ($12). MC, V. Daily noon–2:30pm and 7:30–11pm. Métro: Étienne Marcel or Sentier. ALGERIAN/FRENCH.

This well-entrenched place has flourished from within the heart of Paris's wholesale garment district since the 1930s, when Algeria was a distinct part of the French-speaking world. Today, you'll dine within a long and narrow room hung with colorful Berber carpets and filled with shop workers from the district's clothiers. The Algerian staple of couscous is always on the menu, as are an array of oft-changing daily specials like *blanquette de veau* (veal stew), shoulder or rack of lamb, grilled or panfried fish, and roasted chicken, complemented by French and North African wines. Portions are large enough to gorge a lion.

Babylone. 34 rue Tiquetonne, 2e. ☎ **01-42-33-48-35.** Main courses 70–120F ($14–$24). V. Daily 8pm–8am. Métro: Étienne Marcel or Sentier. CREOLE/MIDDLE OF THE NIGHT.

The theme at this place honors the French Caribbean island of Guadeloupe, with culinary specialties of *accras* of codfish and Creole *boudin* (blood sausage) that usually prefaces such main courses as fricassee of shrimp or chicken, or a *colombo* (stew) of baby goat. Look for African masks, touches of zebra skin, nostalgia for warmer climes, and photos of the divas and celebrities, who have dined here. Some (Diana Ross, Marvin Gaye, Jesse Jackson) you might know, others represent a medley of sports stars and models better known in France than abroad. Don't think of coming before dark to this purely nocturnal place, which focuses on reggae, jazz, and cocktails after 2am.

Le Clementine. 5 rue St-Marc, 2e. ☎ **01-42-36-91-72.** Reservations required. Main courses 80–90F ($16–$18). Fixed-price menu 135F ($27). AE, MC, V. Mon–Fri noon–2:30pm and 8–10:30pm. Métro: Bourse or Rue Montmartre. FRENCH.

Set within an antique building adjacent to the Musée Grévin, this is a well-managed bistro serving time-honored food that occasionally exhibits an individualistic flair. Among turn-of-the-century panels, polished brass, and mirrors, you can order *steak au poivre,* such fish dishes as sole meunière or a codfish steak studded with lard; veal braised in the oven and served in its own juices; and an unusual preparation of chicken breast with goat cheese. We're convinced the *fondant au chocolat* is an assiduously guarded, long-cherished family recipe. Since the site includes room for barely 25 diners, advance reservations are important.

Le Vaudeville. 29 rue Vivienne, 2e. ☎ **01-40-20-04-62.** Reservations recommended in the evenings. Main courses 85–175F ($17–$35); fixed-price lunch 123F ($25); fixed-price dinner 129–169F ($26–$34). AE, DC, MC, V. Daily 11:30am–3pm and 7pm–4am. Métro: Bourse. FRENCH/MIDDLE OF THE NIGHT.

Restaurants: 2nd Arrondissement

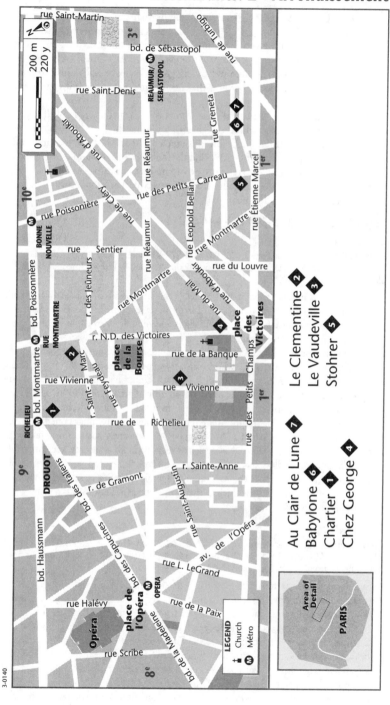

Le Clementine 2
Le Vaudeville 3
Stohrer 5

Au Clair de Lune 7
Babylone 6
Chartier 1
Chez George 4

Adjacent to the stock exchange (La Bourse), this bistro has retained its original marble walls and art deco carvings since 1918. It has the same nostalgic atmosphere as the fabled La Coupole on the Left Bank, but is smaller and more convivial. In summer, tables stud a terrace in front, amid banks of geraniums. Any time of year, the place is boisterous and informal, often welcoming groups of six or eight diners at a time to its closely spaced tables. A bar near the entrance provides a perch if your reservation is delayed.

The bountiful roster of platters includes snails in garlic butter, smoked salmon, steak au poivre, sauerkraut, and several kinds of grilled meats. Two dishes in particular reign as enduring favorites: the fresh codfish served with mashed potatoes and truffle juice, reasonably priced at 139F ($28), and the fresh escalope of warm foie gras served with grapes. Le Vaudeville serves the type of fare French bistro-goers have come to expect, but its food is rarely innovative, and not every dish is inspirational—the main value here is the fixed-price menu.

3rd ARRONDISSEMENT (LE MARAIS)
EXPENSIVE

L'Ami Louis. 32 rue de Vertbois, 3e. ☎ **01-48-87-77-48.** Reservations required. Main courses 195–275F ($39–$55). AE, DC, MC, V. Wed–Sun noon–2pm and 8–11pm. Closed July 10 to Aug 25. Métro: Temple. FRENCH.

L'Ami Louis is in one of the least fashionable neighborhoods of Paris, and its facade has seen better days. Nonetheless, this bistro preserves something magical from the prewar years. It's always luring in politicians and moguls, who could be accused of slumming if it were any cheaper.

The bistro was established in 1924 by someone named Louis, who sold it in the 1930s to "Monsieur Antoine," who became a legend for intimidating (and at times, deliberately insulting) the grandest of his guests. Under his direction, L'Ami Louis became one of the most famous brasseries in all of Paris, thanks to excellent food served in copious portions, and its ostentatiously old-fashioned decor. Though the Master died in 1987, his traditions are fervently (but politely) maintained by a new generation of directors. Amid a "brown gravy" decor—the walls retain a smoky patina established in the 1920s—dishes such as suckling lamb, pheasant, venison, confit of duckling, and endless slices of foie gras may commune atop your marble table. Though some whisper that the restaurant's ingredients aren't as select as they were in its heyday, its sauces are as thick as they were between the wars. Don't save room for dessert, which isn't very good.

INEXPENSIVE

Chez Janou. 2 rue Roger-Verlomme, 3e. ☎ **01-42-72-28-41.** Reservations recommended. Main courses 55–90F ($11–$18). No credit cards. Mon–Fri noon–3pm and Mon–Sat 8pm–midnight. Métro: Chemin-Vert. PROVENÇAL.

Set on one of the narrow 17th-century streets behind the Place des Vosges, this unpretentious bistro operates from a pair of cramped but cozy dining rooms outfitted with memorabilia from faraway Provence. It retains hints of its earliest function, a butcher-shop and cafe, and includes a terrace that the owners hope to transform into a venue for weekend brunches in 1998. The somewhat brusque and hectic service brings food steeped in the herbs and aromas of southern France, including such dishes as *gambas* (large shrimp) with pastis sauce; a *brouillade des pleurotes* (baked eggs with oyster mushrooms); a velouté of frog's legs; a fondue of ratatouille; lamb cutlets; and a simple, savory *daube Provençale,* a dish that's sometimes compared to pot roast.

L'Ambassade d'Auvergne. 22 rue de Grenier-St-Lazare, 3e. ☎ **01-42-72-31-22.** Reservations recommended. Main courses 88–120F ($18–$24). AE, MC, V. Daily noon–2pm and 7:30–10pm. Métro: Rambuteau. AUVERGNAT.

Located in an obscure cranny of Paris, this rustic tavern serves the hearty *cuisine bourgeoise* of Auvergne, the heartland of France. You enter through a busy bar decorated with ceramic plates and hams and sausages hung from heavy oak beams. Rough wheat bread is stacked in baskets, and rush-seated ladderback chairs are placed at brightly covered tables, each bearing stem glassware, mills to grind your own salt and pepper, and a jug of mustard.

More than any other restaurant in Paris, this well-established favorite showcases the culinary generosity and old-fashioned zest of France's most isolated district, where change drips slower than honey. If the agrarian region intrigues you, consider ordering the 300F ($60) *grand menu dégustation d'Auvergne,* where a copious medley of the region's traditional dishes is presented in a way that you might only see at a wedding celebration or family fete. Both red and white wines from the region are included, along with a collection of *cochonailles* (pork by-products, including sausages and cured hams) and a savory *pot-au-feu* (beef simmered with vegetables) in the antique style. The potato, garlic, and cheese medley known as *aligot* is made with a young Cantal cheese; it is less pungent and more appealing to those not used to strong French cheeses. Desserts such as verveine-flavored ice creams and flaky pastries complement the hearty meals.

L'Imprimerie. 101 rue Vieille du Temple, 3e. ☎ **01-42-77-93-80.** Reservations recommended. Main courses 77–93F ($15–$19); fixed-price menus 97–139F ($19–$28). AE, MC, V. Mon–Sat noon–3pm and 8–11:30pm (last order). Métro: Filles-du-Calvaire. FRENCH.

Set within a building that in the 19th century functioned as a printing press (*imprimerie*) for the National Archives (which lie a few steps away), this restaurant welcomes a largely gay clientele from the arts community of the Marais. The setting reminds some newcomers of a brick-lined bistro in New York's Greenwich Village, particularly because of the changing array of paintings that decorate the walls. (Some are for sale.) The menu features conservative French-inspired dishes that include an *effeullantine* of avocado with shrimp and fresh basil, a ravioli of goat cheese, magret of duckling with a honey-coriander sauce and braised cabbage, and Norwegian salmon which is prepared with recipes that vary according to the season.

4th ARRONDISSEMENT (ILE DE LA CITÉ/ ILE ST-LOUIS & BEAUBOURG)
EXPENSIVE
✪ **L'Ambroisie.** 9 place des Vosges, 4e. ☎ **01-42-78-51-45.** Reservations required. Main courses 290–500F ($58–$100). AE, MC, V. Tues–Sat noon–1:30pm and 8–9:30pm. Métro: St-Paul. FRENCH.

Bernard Pacaud is one of the most talented chefs in Paris, and his cuisine has drawn world attention with his strikingly vivid flavors and expert culinary skill. He trained at the prestigious Vivarois before striking out on his own, first on the Left Bank and now at this early 17th-century town house in Le Marais, a former goldsmith's shop converted into two high-ceilinged salons with a decor that vaguely recalls an Italian *palazzo.* In summer, there's outdoor seating as well.

Pacaud's tables are nearly always filled with satisfied diners, who come back again and again to see where his imagination will take him next. His cooking has a certain elegant and harmonious simplicity.

The dishes change with the seasons. From time to time they'll include a fricassee of Breton lobster with a civet/red wine sauce served with a puree of peas; or a fillet of turbot braised with celery and celeriac, served with a julienne of black truffles; or one of our favorite dishes in all of Paris, *poulard de Bresse demi-deuil hommage à la Mère Brazier*, chicken roasted with black truffles and truffled vegetables in a style invented by a Lyonnais matron (La Mère Brazier) after World War II. An award-winning dessert is a *tarte fine sablée* served with bitter chocolate and mocha-flavored ice cream.

MODERATE

✪ **Bofinger.** 5-7 rue de la Bastille, 4e. ☎ **01-42-72-87-82.** Reservations recommended. Main courses 76–144F ($15–$29); fixed-price menu 169F ($34). AE, DC, MC, V. Daily noon–3pm and 6:30pm–1am. Métro: Bastille. ALSATIAN.

Bofinger was founded in the 1860s and is the oldest Alsatian brasserie in town and certainly one of the best. It's actually a belle epoque dining palace, resplendent with shiny brass and stained glass. If you prefer, you can dine on an outdoor terrace, weather permitting.

In 1996, the restaurant was acquired by one of the largest restaurant management groups in Paris (Les Restaurants de Jean Bucher), losing its independent status but gaining a new lease on life thanks to bulk purchases of its raw ingredients. Affiliated today with la Coupole, Julien, and the Brasserie Flo, it updated its menu, retaining only the most popular of the dishes for which it earned its reputation (such as sauerkraut and a well-prepared version of sole meunière). Recent additions have included such stylish platters as roasted leg of lamb with a *fondant* of artichoke hearts and a puree of parsley; grilled turbot served with a *brandade* of fennel; and fillet of stingray with chives and a burnt butter sauce. Shellfish, including an abundance of fresh oysters and lobster, are almost always available when they're in season.

Marc-Annibal de Coconnas. 2 bis place des Vosges, 4e. ☎ **01-42-78-58-16.** Reservations required. Main dishes 90–150F ($18–$30); fixed-price 170F ($34). AE, DC, MC, V. Wed–Sun noon–2pm and 7:45–10:45pm. Métro: Bastille or St-Paul. FRENCH.

Chef Claude Terrail (owner of La Tour d'Argent) serves superb cuisine in this restaurant located in the district where Henri II was mortally wounded, and where Victor Hugo once lived.

Named after the legendary rake whose peccadilloes involving members of the royal family scandalized the place des Vosges, the restaurant features a Louis XIII decor of high-backed chairs and elegantly rustic accessories. Menu items change frequently but might include a soup of scallops with anise; a *pastillade* of crayfish; a rack of veal *en papillote* (in parchment) with crème fraîche, white wine, and mushrooms; and turbot poached in an essence of almonds and served on a bed of fennel. None of these items sets off fireworks, but the ingredients are fresh and harmonious.

INEXPENSIVE

✪ **Aquarius.** 54 rue Ste-Croix-de-la-Bretonnerie, 4e. ☎ **01-48-87-48-71.** Reservations not required. Main courses 20–55F ($4–$11); fixed-price lunch 55F ($11); fixed-price dinner 84F ($17). MC, V. Mon–Sat noon–9:45pm. Closed 2 weeks in Aug. Métro: Hôtel-de-Ville. RER: Châtelet–Les Halles. VEGETARIAN.

In a 17th-century building whose original stonework forms part of the rustic, earthy decor, this is one of the best-known vegetarian restaurants of the Marais. The owners serve neither wine nor spirits, and shoo away smokers. Their flavorful meals are healthfully prepared and come in generous portions. Choose from an array of soups

Restaurants: 3rd & 4th Arrondissements

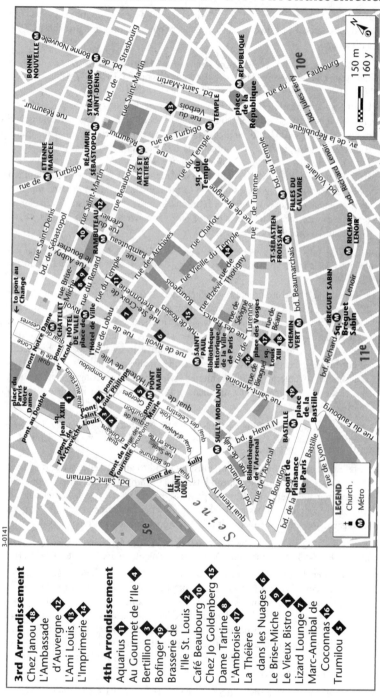

3rd Arrondissement

Chez Janou 18
L'Ambassade d'Auvergne 12
L'Ami Louis 13
L'Imprimerie 14

4th Arrondissement

Aquarius 11
Au Gourmet de l'Ile 4
Bertillion 3
Bofinger 19
Brasserie de l'Ile St. Louis 2
Café Beaubourg 10
Chez Jo Goldenberg 15
Dame Tartine 8
L'Ambroisie 17
La Théière 16
dans les Nuages 6
Le Brise-Miche 9
Le Vieux Bistro 1
Lizard Lounge 7
Marc-Annibal de Coconnas 16
Trumilou 5

129

and salads; a galette of wheat served with crudités and mushroom tarts; or a country plate composed of fried mushrooms and potatoes, garlic, and goat cheese, served with a salad.

✪ **Au Gourmet de l'Ile.** 42 rue St-Louis-en-l'Ile, 4e. ☎ **01-43-26-79-27.** Reservations required. Main courses 70–95F ($14–$19); fixed-price menus 85–130F ($17–$26). AE, MC, V. Wed–Sun noon–2pm and 7–10pm. Métro: Pont-Marie. FRENCH.

Local regulars swear by the cuisine at Au Gourmet de l'Ile. Its fixed-price meals are among the best bargains in Paris. The setting is beautiful, with a beamed ceiling, walls dating from the 1400s, and candlelit tables. Many Parisian restaurants have attained this level of decor, but they cannot approach the food on this "Gourmet Island."

In the window you'll see a sign emblazoned with five A's, which, roughly translated, stands for the Amiable Association of Amateurs of the Authentic Andouillette. These chitterling sausages are soul food to the French. Popular and tasty, too, are *la charbonnée de l'Ile,* a savory pork with onions, and the stuffed mussels in shallot butter. Fixed-price menus include a choice of 15 appetizers, 15 main courses, salad or cheese, and a choice of 15 desserts.

Brasserie de l'Ile St-Louis. 55 quai de Bourbon, 4e. ☎ **01-43-54-02-59.** Reservations recommended. Main courses 85–110F ($17–$22). MC, V. Thurs–Tues noon–midnight. Métro: Pont-Marie. ALSATIAN.

It's the kind of retro-chic brasserie where fading stars such as Mitterrand, Bardot, Elizabeth Taylor, Grace Jones, and filmmaker John Frankenheimer have always scheduled informal meals and rendezvous. Little about the establishment's patina and paneled decor has changed since the 1880s, giving it an aura more modern competitors would love to have. The menu is conservative and well prepared, but heedless of cutting-edge fads and trends. Plates include an always-popular version of Alsatian sauerkraut; cassoulet in the old-fashioned style of Toulouse; stingray with a nut and butter sauce; calf's liver; and a succulent version of *jarret* of pork with a warm apple marmalade.

✪ **Chez Jo Goldenberg.** 7 rue des Rosiers, 4e. ☎ **01-48-87-20-16.** Reservations recommended. Main courses 70–90F ($14–$18). AE, DC, MC, V. Daily noon–1am. Métro: St-Paul. JEWISH/CENTRAL EUROPEAN.

Interesting paintings and strolling musicians add to an ambience set by a collection of samovars and Central European kitsch. *Carpe farcie* (stuffed carp) is our favorite choice, but the beef goulash is also good. We also like the eggplant moussaka, and the highly sought-after pastrami. The menu offers Israeli wines, but as the proprietor Monsieur Joseph Goldenberg admits, they're not as good as French labels.

Dame Tartine. 2 rue Brise-Miche, 4e. ☎ **01-42-77-32-22.** Reservations not necessary. Platters 37–40F ($7–$8). No credit cards. Daily noon–midnight. Métro: Rambuteau. FRENCH.

The ambience at this place is like a busy cafe, except that clients ingest something more substantial than a lump of sugar with their cafe. Don't expect either intimacy or haute gastronomy: This place is hectic with streams of clients on their way to and from the nearby Centre Pompidou and students counting their francs. You can expect simple but generous platters that include salads, chicken with curries or cinnamon sauce, ham steak, and fried fillet of fish with tartar sauce. Most are served with bread, with the expectation that you'll create your own made-to-order open-faced sandwich from the ingredients on your platter.

La Théière dans les Nuages. 14 rue du Cloche-Percé, 4e. ☎ **01-42-71-96-11.** Reservations recommended. Main courses 54–95F ($11–$19). Set-price lunches 45–108F ($9–$22); set-price dinner 108F ($22). MC, V. Mon–Sat noon–2pm and 7:30–11pm. Métro: Hotel de Ville or St-Paul. CREOLE.

Cramped and crowded with Parisians who are happy to recollect holidays on Martinique or Guadeloupe, this restaurant showcases paintings whose colors reproduce lush Caribbean greens. The menu follows recipes Creole *mères-cuisinières* have taught their daughters ever since the island was colonized. Items include spicy blood sausage, a fricassee of conch, octopus in Creole sauce, goat-meat stew, and savory Creole-style chicken in a sauce that someone is likely to warn you is "*piquante.*" Also available is a West African dish, *maffé,* concocted with chicken, peanuts, herbs, and rice, that goes well with any of the restaurant's long list of tropical fruit drinks and herbal teas.

Le Brise-Miche. 10 rue Brise-Miche, 4e. ☎ **01-42-78-44-11.** Reservations recommended. Main courses 65–105F ($13–$21); set menu 74F ($15) until 9pm. AE, DC, MC, V. Daily 8am–midnight (full menu available daily noon–midnight). Métro: Rambuteau, Hôtel-de-Ville, or Châtelet-Les Halles. FRENCH.

Whimsical and sometimes chaotic, this appealing restaurant shares something of the avant-garde aesthetic of its neighbor, the Centre Pompidou. Named after the bread rations (*les brise-miches*) that were issued here during World War II, it occupies an enviable location beside the medieval church of St-Merri and the neighborhood's most charming fountain. In fair weather, tables and chairs overlook a dozen spinning, spitting, and bobbing fountains, which were beautifully sculpted by Jean Tingueley and Niki de Saint-Phalle. Each table receives a round loaf of bread, crayons, and paper place mats for doodlings (if your impromptu artwork is good enough, it will be framed and displayed as part of the restaurant's permanent decor).

You might begin with a beef carpaccio with green salad (or else a shark carpaccio), then follow with a noisette of lamb flavored with whisky and fresh thyme, or perhaps a fricassee of poultry with morels. Finish with an orange and kiwi salad in a vanilla-flavored wine sauce.

Le Vieux Bistro. 14 rue du Cloître-Notre-Dame, 4e. ☎ **01-43-54-18-95.** Main courses 80–165F ($16–$33). MC, V. Daily noon–2pm and 7:30–11pm. Métro: Cité. FRENCH

Few other restaurants in Paris offer so close-up, and so forbidding, a view of the massive and somber walls of Paris's cathedral, visible through lacy curtains from the windows of the front dining room. To reach it, you'll bypass a dozen flanking souvenir stands, and then settle into one of two old-time dining rooms for a flavorful meal of standard French staples. Within a pair of rooms flanked with mirrors and a jutting zinc-plated bar, you can order snails with garlic butter, filet mignon roasted in a bag and served with marrow sauce, fillets of veal, and a dessert that every French child is exposed to early in life, a *tarte-Tatin* (Auntie's tart) studded with apples and sugar, drenched with Calvados, and capped with fresh cream.

Trumilou. 84 quai de l'Hôtel-de-Ville, 4e. ☎ **01-42-77-63-98.** Reservations recommended on Sat–Sun. Fixed-price menus 65–102F ($13–$20). MC, V. Daily noon–3pm and 7–11pm. Métro: Hôtel-de-Ville. FRENCH.

This is one of the most popular of the many restaurants surrounding Paris's Town Hall (Hôtel-de-Ville), and, as such, has welcomed most of France's politicians, including George Pompidou, who came here frequently before he was elected President of France. ("As soon as they become president they opt for grander restaurants," say the good-natured owners, the Drumond family.) The name comes from the hamlet in Auvergne where the Drumonds were born, Trumilou, a *lieu-dit* with no more than three houses that this restaurant has made famous. The countrified decor includes a collection of farm implements and family memorabilia, amidst a clutch of tables.

Most diners remain on the street level, although additional seating is available in the cellar. The menu rarely changes, nor does it need to, regardless of whomever rules France. Examples include chicken Provençale, sweetbreads *grand-mére,* duckling with plums, stuffed cabbage, and the inevitable *blanquette de veau,* or veal in white sauce.

8th ARRONDISSEMENT (CHAMPS-ELYSÉES/MADELEINE)
VERY EXPENSIVE

✪ **Lasserre.** 17 av. Franklin D. Roosevelt, 8e. ☎ **01-43-59-53-43.** Reservations required. 140–160F ($28–$32) lunch main courses, 240–280F ($48–$56) dinner main courses. AE, MC, V. Tues–Sat 12:30–2:30pm; Mon–Sat 7:30–10:30pm. Closed Aug. Métro: F.D. Roosevelt. FRENCH.

This elegant restaurant was a simple bistro before World War II, a "rendezvous for chauffeurs." Then along came René Lasserre, who bought the dilapidated building and set out to create his dream. He succeeded in creating a legend that now attracts gourmets from around the world.

Two white-painted front doors lead to the dining rooms and a reception lounge with Louis XVI–style furnishings and brocaded walls. The main salon stretches two stories high; on each side is a mezzanine. Tall arched windows draped with silk open onto a street that sees tables set with fine porcelain, crystal glasses edged in gold, a silver candelabrum, and even a silver bird and ceramic dove. You study the menu sitting on a Louis XV–style salon chair.

Overhead, the ceiling is painted with lamb-white clouds and a cerulean sky, but in fair weather the staff slides back the roof to reveal the real sky, letting moonlight or sunshine pour into the room.

The food is a combination of classicism and originality. The presentation of dishes is one of the most winning and imaginative aspects of Lasserre. Always count on high drama. Michelin only awards this restaurant two stars, as opposed to three for Lucas-Carton or Taillevent, but we've never understood why it's not at the very top.

The appetizers are among the finest in Paris, including a salad of truffles, a three-meat terrine, or Belon oysters flavored with Chablis. The signature main course is fillets of sole Club de la Casserole (poached fillets served in puff pastry with asparagus tips and asparagus-flavored cream sauce). When you taste the meat and poultry dishes, such as veal kidneys flambé or pigeon André Malraux, you'd swear Escoffier were still alive. The spectacular desserts include a soufflé Grand Marnier or a selection of three freshly made sorbets of the season. The cellar, with some 180,000 bottles of wine, is among the most remarkable in Paris; red wines are decanted into silver pitchers or ornate crystal.

✪ **L'Astor.** In the Hotel Astor, 11 rue d'Astorg, 8e. ☎ **01-53-05-05-20.** Reservations recommended. Main courses 100–500F ($20–$100). AE, DC, MC, V. Mon–Fri noon–2pm and 7:30–10pm. Métro: St-Augustin. FRENCH.

What happens to great French chefs after they retire? If they're lucky enough, they maintain their role by defining themselves as "culinary consultants" and dropping in to keep an eye on what's happening two or three times a week. That's what happened when guru Joël Robuchon retired from his citadel on avenue Raymond Poincaré in favor of a quieter life. His replacement is well-respected Eric Lecerf, a formidable chef who knows better than anyone else alive how to match the tours-de-force of the master. The setting, established early in 1996, is a gray-and-white enclave sheltered by a stained-glass art deco ceiling with discreetly luxurious touches inspired by the 1930s and 1940s.

Restaurants: 8th Arrondissement

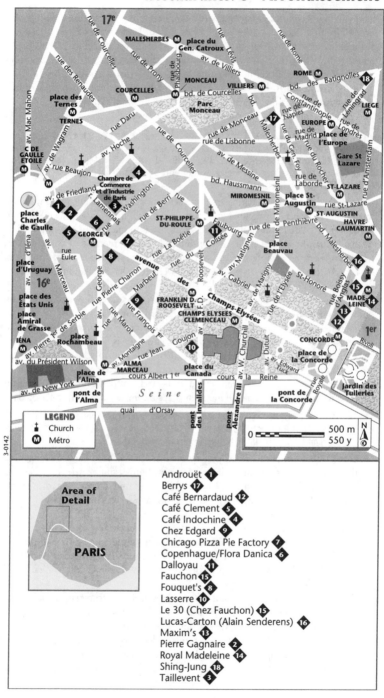

LEGEND
✝ Church
Ⓜ Métro

3-0142

Area of Detail

PARIS

Androuët ❶
Berrys ❶⑦
Café Bernardaud ⑫
Café Clement ❺
Café Indochine ❹
Chez Edgard ❾
Chicago Pizza Pie Factory ❼
Copenhague/Flora Danica ❻
Dalloyau ⑪
Fauchon ⑮
Fouquet's ❽
Lasserre ❿
Le 30 (Chez Fauchon) ⑮
Lucas-Carton (Alain Senderens) ⑯
Maxim's ⑬
Pierre Gagnaire ❷
Royal Madeleine ⑭
Shing-Jung ⑱
Taillevent ❸

133

If you dine here, expect a menu with a double-tiered price structure: Those items created by Eric Lecerf (roasted and braised rack of lamb, a galette of scallops with sea urchins) cost from 100F to 180F ($20 to $36). Those invented by, and forever associated with, Robuchon (truffle tarte, Bresse chicken with truffles and macaroni; a gelée of caviar with cauliflower cream sauce) are dearer at 250F to 500F ($50 to $100). Do the old Robuchon standbys withstand time's cruel hand? Certainly, although to an increasing degree, they're viewed as one would vintage Chanel or Dior, and priced at rates that are correspondingly expensive.

Lucas-Carton (Alain Senderens). 9 place de la Madeleine, 8e. ☎ **01-42-65-22-90.** Reservations required several days ahead for lunch and several weeks ahead for dinner. Main courses 240–700F ($48–$140); fixed-price lunch 395F ($79). AE, DC, MC, V. Mon–Fri noon–2:30pm; Mon–Sat 8–10:15pm. Closed 3 weeks in Aug and 3 weeks in Dec (dates vary). Métro: Madeleine. FRENCH.

This landmark restaurant, dating from the belle epoque, was designed by an Englishman named Lucas and a talented French chef, Francis Carton. When Alain Senderens took over, he added some welcome modern touches to the historic restaurant, along with a brilliantly realized culinary repertoire. The dining rooms downstairs and private rooms upstairs are decorated with mirrors, fragrant bouquets of flowers, and wood paneling that has been polished every week since its installation in 1900.

Every dish here is influenced by the creative flair of Senderens. Menu items change with the seasons: Examples include *ravioli aux truffes* (ravioli with truffles), foie gras with cabbage, duckling *Apicius* (roasted with honey and spices), a *pastillade* of rabbit, and sweetbreads with acidified carrot juice. The puree of chestnuts is a perfect choice to end the meal. However, Senderens is constantly creating and experimenting, so, by the time you visit, there will probably be a fresh addition to his innovative menu. His latest sensation is *poularde demi-deuil*, which is a Bresse hen whose flesh has been scored with black truffles. He says the resulting black-and-white flesh is "in partial mourning." It's accompanied by saffron-flavored rice.

✪ **Maxim's.** 3 rue Royale, 8e. ☎ **01-42-65-27-94.** Reservations required. Main courses 225–300F ($45–$60) for lunch, 265–460F ($53–$92) for dinner. AE, DC, MC, V. Mon–Sat 12:30–2:30pm and 7:30–10:30pm. Métro: Concorde. FRENCH.

Maxim's is the world's most legendary restaurant. The Michelin guide no longer even bothers to recommend it, much less give it stars, but Maxim's carries on in its overpriced way. It even has clones in New York, Beijing, and Tokyo. Maxim's has preserved its belle epoque decor; during that era, it was a favorite dining spot of Edward VII, then the Prince of Wales.

The restaurant was the setting for *The Merry Widow*, where John Gilbert dipped and swayed with Mae Murray. You can always be sure the orchestra will play that tune at least once per evening. Much later in film history, Louis Jourdan, at that time considered "the handsomest man in the world," took Leslie Caron to dine here in the musical *Gigi*.

Today, rich tourists from around the world are likely to occupy fabled tables where Onassis wooed Callas. Clothing-industry giant Pierre Cardin took over the restaurant in 1981. Although not always available, billiby soup—made with mussels, white wine, cream (of course), chopped onions, celery, parsley, and coarsely ground pepper—is a classic opener. Another favorite, the sole Albert, named after the late maître d'hôtel, is flavored with chopped herbs and bread crumbs, plus a large glass of vermouth. For dessert, try the tarte Tatin.

✪ **Pierre Gagnaire.** 6 rue Balzac, 8e. ☎ **01-44-35-18-25.** Fax 01-44-35-18-37. Reservations are imperative and difficult to make. Set lunches 270–360F ($54–$72), set dinners 360F ($72). AE, DC, MC, V. Mon–Fri 12:30–2:15pm and Sun–Thurs 7–10pm. Métro: George V. FRENCH.

In the town of St-Étienne, Pierre Gagnaire rose to culinary greatness and won the coveted Michelin three-star fame. However, in spite of the acclaim, his restaurant there fell into receivership. When he popped up on the premises of the Hotel Balzac, all of Paris tried to make its way to Gagnaire's closely guarded door. The chef is hot, hot, hot, but this shy, reclusive man, who prefers to remain in the kitchen rattling his pots and pans instead of appearing on TV, is hard to reach. In many cases, his reception doesn't even answer the phone from eager clients demanding a reservation. They are often told by an answering machine to fax a "request" for a table. Although their PR may be the worst in Paris, if you do get through, it's worth the effort.

Gagnaire's flame burns brightly in Paris against the backdrop of a sumptuous environment. Menus are seasonally adjusted to take advantage of France's rich bounty. The chef blends flavors and textures in ways that are dazzling. Every dish is cooked to order, and Gagnaire demands perfection before the plate is served. One critic wrote, "Picasso stretched the limits of painting; Gagnaire does it with cooking." Try *anything,* especially turbot wrapped in herb leaves and served with a side dish of celeriac lasagne, and most definitely his bundles of rolled farm chicken roasted in goose fat and braised in an aromatic medley of spices, onions, and carrots. Anyone who ever ate at St-Étienne is eager to arrive here, hoping some of the dishes that made him famous will appear in Paris, as they often do. We're talking about the likes of smoked bacon in a casserole with pan-roasted rabbit kidneys and sea snails, served with a bean puree flavored with Chinese peppercorns. It's hard to match that.

✪ **Taillevent.** 15 rue Lamennais, 8e. ☎ **01-44-95-15-01.** Reservations required weeks, even months, in advance for both lunch and dinner. Main courses 295–500F ($59–$100). AE, DC, MC, V. Mon–Fri noon–2:30pm and 7–10pm. Closed Aug. Métro: George V. FRENCH.

Taillevent dates from 1946, and it has climbed steadily in the ranks of excellence since then. Today it's recognized as the most outstanding all-around restaurant in Paris. In the highly competitive 8th arrondissement, with its temples of haute cuisine, Taillevent surfaces at the top, challenged only by Lucas-Carton and Lassere.

The setting is a grand 19th-century town house off the Champs-Elysées, once inhabited by the duc de Morny. The rooms are paneled and have crystal chandeliers. The restaurant is named after a famous chef of the 14th century (Guillaume Tirel Taillevent) who wrote one of the oldest known books on French cookery. The place is small, as the owner wishes, since it permits him to give personal attention to every facet of the operation and maintain a discreet club atmosphere. You might begin with a *boudin* (sausage) of Breton lobster *à la nage* (cooked in court bouillon and flavored with herbs); red snapper with black olives; duck liver with spice bread and ginger; red mullet with basil sauce; and Scottish salmon cooked in sea salt with a sauce of olive oil and lemons. Dessert might be a nougatine glacé with pears. The wine list is among the best in Paris.

Although Monsieur Vrinat likes Americans, it isn't always easy for visitors from the States and other countries to book a table, since the owner prefers for about 60% of his clients to be French.

EXPENSIVE

✪ **Copenhague/Flora Danica.** 142 av. des Champs-Elysées, 8e. ☎ **01-44-13-86-26.** Reservations recommended. Main dishes 70–180F ($14–$36); fixed-price menu 165–240F ($33–$48). AE, DC, MC, V. Restaurant Copenhague Mon–Fri noon–2pm, Mon–Sat 7:15–10:30pm (closed Aug and Jan 1–7). Flora Danica daily noon–2pm and 7:15–11pm. Métro: George V. DANISH.

The specialties of Denmark are served with flair at the "Maison du Danemark," which functions as a quasi-official Danish goodwill ambassador. In many ways, it's the best restaurant along the Champs-Elysées, with an outside terrace for midsummer dining.

There are two dining areas to choose from: the Flora Danica, on the street level, and the somewhat more formal Restaurant Copenhague, upstairs.

To be thoroughly Danish, order an apéritif of aquavit and ignore the wine list in favor of Carlsberg. Menu items include a terrine of reindeer, foie gras, smoked salmon, fresh shrimp, or any of an elegant array of open-face sandwiches. The house specialty is a platter of *délices Scandinaves,* composed of the many seafood and dairy specialties that the Danes prepare exceptionally well. Our preferred dish here is grilled Norwegian salmon cooked on one side only. The cookery is forever competent here, not "forever boring," as one critic suggested.

MODERATE

Chez Edgard. 4 rue Marbeuf, 8e. ☎ **01-47-20-51-15.** Reservations recommended. Main courses 90–180F ($18–$36). AE, DC, MC, V. Mon–Sat noon–3pm and 7pm–12:30am. Métro: F.D. Roosevelt. FRENCH.

A chic crowd of neighborhood residents regard this belle epoque restaurant as their favorite local spot, and ebullient owner Paul Benmussa makes a special point of welcoming them on their frequent visits as if they were family members. Customers include politicians (Jacques Chirac dined here before becoming president of France), journalists, and show-business personalities such as Roman Polanski and Sydney Pollack. The noise level sometimes reaches quite a din.

Specialties include breast of duckling; red mullet with basil in puff pastry; and scallops served either simply, with lemon, or with a *beurre Nantais* (whipped butter, at times flavored with shallots and wine). Also offered is a range of reliably delicious meat dishes, seafood and oysters shipped from Brittany in winter, and delectable ice-cream sundaes. There's a small outdoor terrace, but most guests prefer to eat inside on one of the semiprivate banquettes.

Le 30 (Chez Fauchon). 30 place de la Madeleine, 8e. ☎ **01-47-42-56-58.** Reservations recommended, especially for lunch. Main courses 125–220F ($25–$44). AE, DC, MC, V. Mon–Sat 12:15–2:30pm and 7:30–10:30pm. Métro: Madeleine. FRENCH.

In 1990, Fauchon, one of Europe's most legendary delicatessens (see "Food," chapter 8), transformed one of its upper rooms into an airy pastel-colored showplace dotted with neo-Grecian columns and accessories. It caught on immediately as a lunch spot for local bankers, stockbrokers, and merchants. Menu selections employ the freshest ingredients available downstairs, and might include crayfish tails roasted with sweet spices, escalope of warm foie gras garnished with apples and Calvados, panfried lobster perfumed with orange and essence of lemon, sea bass garnished with Sevruga caviar, and a *navarin* of lamb with pasta and fresh basil.

Le 30 is our personal favorite of the four restaurants that Fauchon operates along the place de la Madeleine. Other choices include **La Trattoria,** 26 place de la Madeleine, for upscale Italian food, and **Le Bistro du Caviar,** 30 place de la Madeleine, where a *chariot de caviar* dispenses epicurean samples of foie gras and smoked salmon, as well as every imaginable type of caviar. Fauchon also operates a seafood bistro, **Bistro de la Mer,** at 6 place de la Madeleine. The Bistro de la Mer shares a phone with Le 30. The other two restaurants can be reached by calling ☎ **01-47-42-60-11.**

INEXPENSIVE

Berrys. 46 rue de Naples, 8e. ☎ **01-40-75-01-56.** Reservations recommended. Main courses 45–92F ($9–$18); set menus 100F ($20). MC, V. Mon–Fri noon–2:30pm and Mon–Sat 7pm–1am. Métro: Villiers. FRENCH.

This restaurant was conceived as an inexpensive bistro to complement one of the district's grandest restaurants, Le Grenadin. Its platters emerge from the same kitchen and are infused with the same kind of zeal as those presented next door for three times the price. Don't expect the cutting-edge experimentation you're likely to find next door, but do look for honest dishes from France's agrarian heartland (the *Berry* district, site that produces such wines as Sancerre), and a refreshing lack of pretension. The hearty, unfussy dishes are listed on a chalkboard within a setting whose artwork celebrates the traditions and stars of the game of rugby. Items include a fricassee of chicken prepared with white wine; braised rack of pork; thin-sliced smoked ham from Sancerre; raw pike with cabbage; and a traditional *Berry* pear tart.

Café Indochine. 195 rue du Faubourg St-Honoré, 8e. ☎ **01-53-75-15-63.** Reservations recommended. Main courses 70–105F ($14–$21); set menu 160F ($32). AE, MC, V. Mon–Fri noon–2:30pm and Mon–Sat 7–11:30pm. Métro: Étoile or Ternes. INDOCHINESE.

The setting evokes the French colonial empire at the peak of its involvement in the Vietnamese hostilities, and includes art objects from Laos, Cambodia, and Thailand, artfully outdated maps, and photographs of the region and its people. Within any of the street-level dining rooms, you can enjoy a cross-section of the cuisines of at least four different nations. Caramelized pork or chicken, cooked with coconut milk, accents an array of shrimp, scallops, and beef dishes that are prepared with red or green curry, and fiery-hot soups that the waiters will warn you are "*très, très pimenté.*" Equally appealing are the grilled meats, seared over flames and served with a spicy sauce that goes especially well with wine or, even better, any of the restaurant's medley of international beers.

Chez Clément. 123 av. des Champs-Elysées, 8e. ☎ **01-40-73-87-00.** Reservations recommended. Main courses 45–120F ($9–$24). MC, V. Daily 11am–1am. Métro: George V. FRENCH.

This restaurant's low prices and generous portions are especially impressive considering the staggeringly expensive rent the owners are forced to pay for its heartbeat location. Scattered over two floors sheathed mostly with varnished paneling, the place prides itself on well-prepared platters of standardized French food. Presentation and flavor rarely varies, despite the fact that three dozen daily specials might be made within the span of a single busy afternoon. The staff long ago grew accustomed to clients with different appetites and degrees of hunger, and offer everything from a platter of cheeses, which makes a minimeal when accompanied with a salad, to a generously proportioned mixed grill (they call it *une grande rotisserie*) that combines grilled versions of steak, chicken, and pork with mashed potatoes on the same oversized platter.

✪ Chicago Pizza Pie Factory. 5 rue de Berri, 8e. ☎ **01-45-62-50-23.** Reservations accepted only on weekdays for groups of eight or more. Pizza for two, 86–189F ($17–$38); pizza for four, 129–195F ($26–$39); fixed-price lunch 51–71F ($10–$14); fixed-price dinner 100F ($20). AE, DC, MC, V. Daily noon–1am. Métro: Champs-Elysées–Clemenceau. AMERICAN/PIZZA.

On a side-street of the Champs-Elysées, you'll find a busy tribute to the city of Chicago in a former garage. The bar is outfitted with anything and everything to do with Chicago: photos, sports banners, kitsch. The dining room is as large and raucous as the Windy City itself. Although they serve rather dull platters of chicken parmesan, chili, and salads, you come here for pizza, prepared in endless variations on eight basic themes. It's the best in Paris. They also offer cheesecake, mud pie, and marvelous-tasting high-fat brownies. The management proudly refuses, except under dire circumstances, to serve burgers of any kind. No one will mind if you bypass the food

Le Grand Fromage

Cheese is king at **Androuët,** 6 rue Arsène Houssaye, 8e (☎ 01-48-74-26-93). True, it's a novelty restaurant, but if you're devoted to cheese, there is nothing like it in Europe. Established in 1909 by M. Androuet, who frequently asked friends over to sample cheese and wine, the restaurant is now more than chic; it's an institution. To accommodate its continued and growing popularity, it moved to new headquarters in spring 1997. Most of the dishes here are concocted with a cheese base. A savory and impressive array of wines, well-prepared green salads, and ultrafresh bread is available to accompany whatever you order. Examples include a fondue of three cheeses, a *filet de boeuf contentin* (beef fillet with Roquefort sauce flambéed with calvados), grilled chateaubriand, and *magret de canard* (duckling). Many cheese lovers, however, opt for just a bottle of wine, a green salad, and all-you-can-eat choices from the most sophisticated *dégustation de fromages* in the world. Six platters, each loaded with a different category of cheese (one with goat cheeses, another with *triple crèmes,* and so on) are brought to your table, allowing you to select random samples. Reservations are required. Main courses are 100F to 140F ($20 to $28); set-price meals are 95F to 280F ($19 to $56); and the *dégustation des fromages* is 250F ($50). AE, DC, MC, V are accepted. Androuët is open Monday to Saturday from noon to 3pm and 7:30 to 10pm. Métro: Étoile.

altogether in favor of a drink at the bar. Happy hour in the restaurant is from 4 to 7pm, and at the bar from 6 to 8pm. During these times some drinks (but not beer) are reduced in price.

Planet Hollywood. 78 av. des Champs-Elysées, 8e. ☎ 01-83-83-78-27. Reservations not accepted. Burgers 69–80F ($14–$16); salads 50–85F ($10–$17); main courses 75–105F ($15–$21). AE, DC, MC, V. Daily 11am–1am. Métro: George V or F.D. Roosevelt. AMERICAN.

It would have been a distressing gaffe to deny Paris one of the nearly 50 Planet Hollywoods in the world, so in 1995, Hollywood's grit-and-glitter *kulturmeisters* (Bruce and Demi, Sly and Arnold, plus two less visible partners) opened a branch smack bang in the heart of the Champs-Elysées. Your experience here will be overwhelmingly American, with dishes such as boeuf bourguignon set uncomfortably next to fajitas, pizza, and the burger with a thousand disguises, both meat and vegetarian. No one here even thinks of accepting reservations, so your journey into blockbuster consciousness begins the moment you line up at the bar to wait for a table. (Enjoy such high-octane libations as a Beetle Juice, an Indecent Proposal, or a Terminator, or such alcohol-free substitutes as a Home Alone while you wait.) Don't worry that you'll lack for entertainment: The sound system is better than at many discos, and a vast and endlessly perky gift shop does a hot trade in American trinkets destined for garage sales the world over. Eventually you'll be ushered to the cellar-level restaurant to continue your immersion in everything you might have left home to forget, albeit with worthy service from a battalion of youthful staff members from a united Europe, as well as the Americas, the Balkans, and virtually everywhere else.

✪ Royal Madeleine. 11 rue Richepance, 8e. ☎ 01-42-60-14-36. Main courses 90–105F ($18–$21); set menus 120–150F ($24–$30). AE, DC, MC, V. Mon–Fri noon–3pm and 6:30–10pm. Métro: Madeleine or Concorde. FRENCH.

Very little about the decor of this place has changed since it was established by the present owner's parents in 1943. You'll find the same nickel-covered bar, the same sepia-colored walls, and many of the same artifacts, looking a lot like a possible screen site for a remake of *Casablanca*. Many of the clients have made it their haunt for the past 50 years; others include youngish office workers from the nearby American Embassy. The food is as solid and predictable as the seasons, but invariably flavorful and well prepared. Examples include scallops, either grilled on brochettes or prepared with tomatoes, garlic, and onions in the Provençal style; roasted salmon in a salt crust and served with fresh spinach; *confit de canard* (duckling) in a style probably unchanged since the days of Charles de Gaulle; and an even more traditional *blanquette de veau* (veal in white sauce). Salmon with anise, snails in garlic butter, or sliced magret of duckling make worthy starters. The Eche family is your congenial host.

Shing-Jung. 7 rue Clapeyron, 8e. ☎ **01-45-22-21-06.** Reservations recommended for dinner. Main courses 80–110F ($16–$22); fixed-price lunch 65–75F ($13–$15); fixed-price dinner 100–120F ($20–$24). Daily noon–2:30pm and 7–10:30pm. Métro: Rome. KOREAN.

Of the 30 or so Korean restaurants in all of Paris, Shing-Jung is known for its low prices and generous portions. Its sashimi is comparable to versions served in Japanese restaurants, although the portions of the fresh tuna, salmon, or *duarade* tend to be more generous. A specialty is the Korean barbecue called *bulgoogi*, which seems more authentic thanks to a clever decor that juxtaposes Korean chests and paintings.

9th ARRONDISSEMENT (OPÉRA GARNIER/PIGALLE)
EXPENSIVE

Restaurant Opéra. In Le Grand Hôtel Inter-Continental, place de l'Opéra, 9e. ☎ **01-40-07-30-10.** Reservations recommended. Main courses 140–295F ($28–$59); fixed-price menu 240–345F ($48–$69). AE, DC, MC, V. Mon–Fri noon–2pm and 7:30–10:30pm. Métro: Opéra. FRENCH.

This elegant and prestigious restaurant is situated in the historic Grand Hôtel Inter-Continental. We no longer recommend the hotel for accommodations, but there's no denying that it's played an important role in Parisian history since its construction in 1860. If you dine here, you'll join the roll of patrons such as Salvador Dalí, Harry Truman, Josephine Baker, Marlene Dietrich, Maurice Chevalier, Maria Callas, and Marc Chagall, who often came here while working on the famous ceiling of the nearby Opéra. On August 25, 1944, Charles de Gaulle placed this famous restaurant's first food order in a newly freed Paris: a cold plate to go. One of the best things about this place is the way that, despite a formidable elegance, the staff doesn't take itself too seriously. The bons vivants who dined here long ago established a still-strong sense of fun.

Today you can enjoy an apéritif in a lavishly ornate bar before heading for a table in the gilded jewel box of a dining room. Menu choices change with the seasons. The menu is not a prisoner of the past, but is fairly inventive and, in its repertoire, reaches out to the provinces of France and to the world. Start with a sautéed veal head and foot ravioli. Follow with the perfectly prepared fillet of John Dory (a delicately fleshed fish not unlike turbot or sole in flavor) with celery, or else a thick rack of veal for two. *Tout chocolat* is just that; it is the perfect dessert for die-hard chocoholics.

MODERATE

Au Petit Riche. 25 rue Le Peletier, 9e. ☎ **01-47-70-68-68.** Reservations recommended. Main courses 90–140F ($18–$28); set-price lunches 160F ($32); set-price dinners 135–175F ($27–$35). AE, MC, V. Mon–Sat noon–2:15pm and 7pm–midnight. Métro: Le Peletier or Richelieu-Drouot. LOIRE VALLEY (ANJOU).

When it opened in 1865, this bistro was conceived as the food outlet for a grandly ornate cafe (Café Riche) that stood next door. Today, all that remains is yesterday's grandeur and simple, well-prepared food. You'll be ushered to one of five different areas, each crafted for maximum intimacy, with red velour banquettes, ceilings limned with allegorical themes, and accents of brass and frosted glass. The wine list favors Loire Valley vintages that go well with such dishes as *rillettes* and *rillons* (potted fish or meat, especially pork) in an aspic of Vouvray wine; a platter of poached fish served with a buttery white wine sauce; seasonal game dishes that include a *civet* of rabbit; roasted pork with lentils; and duck breast roasted with green peppercorns.

INEXPENSIVE

Chartier. 7 rue de Faubourg Montmartre, 2e. ☎ **01-47-70-86-29.** Main courses 37–57F ($7–$11). MC, V. Daily 11am–3pm and 6–9:30pm. Métro: Rue Montmartre. FRENCH.

Established in 1896, this unpretentious fin de siècle restaurant lies near the Montmartre and is now an official monument. Chartier has long been a favorite budget place offering good value in authentic French surroundings. The focal point is a whimsical mural with trees, a flowering staircase, and an early depiction of an airplane. It was painted in 1929 by a penniless artist who executed his work in exchange for food. Menu items follow conservative brasserie-style traditions, using recipes that haven't changed very much since the mural's commission. They include dishes few foreigners dare to eat (including boiled veal's head, tripe, tongue, sweetbreads, and lamb's brains) as well as some old-time tempters that never lose their popularity. The waiter will advise you, and you'll do well with beef bourguignon, pot-au-feu (one of the best-sellers, combining beef, turnips, cabbage, and carrots into a savory platter), *pavé* of rumpsteak, and at least five kinds of fish. There are also daily specials such as *petit salé* (salted, roasted pork) with lentils. Prices are low enough that three courses are easy on the budget, a fact that as many as 320 diners appreciate at a time.

Hard Rock Café. 14 bd. Montmartre, 9e. ☎ **01-42-46-10-00.** Sandwiches, salads, and platters 62–99F ($12–$20). AE, MC, V. Daily 11:30am–2am. Métro: Rue Montmartre or Richelieu-Drouot. AMERICAN.

Like its counterparts, which now stretch from Hong Kong to Reykjavik, the Hard Rock Café offers a collection of musical memorabilia as well as musical selections from 35 years of rock 'n' roll classics. You'll be able to identify the place by the vintage Cadillac suspended over the sidewalk and the music pouring out into the street (at fairly reasonable levels during lunch and fairly unreasonable levels in the evening). The crowd appreciates the juicy steaks, hamburgers, veggie burgers, salads, and heaping platters of informal, French-inspired food. As you dine, scan the high-ceilinged room for such venerated objects as the stage tuxedo worn by Buddy Holly, Jim Morrison's leather jacket, Jimi Hendrix's psychedelic vest, or the black-and-gold bustier sported by Madonna during one of her concerts in Paris.

✪ **Le Grand Zinc.** 5 Faubourg Montmartre, 9e. ☎ **01-47-70-88-64.** Reservations not required. Main courses 54–138F ($11–$28); fixed-price menu 99F ($20). AE, DC, MC, V. Mon–Sat noon–midnight. Métro: Rue Montmartre. FRENCH.

1880s Paris lives on in the spirit lamps hanging here. You make your way into the restaurant past baskets of *bélons* (brown-fleshed oysters) from Brittany, a year-round favorite. The specialties of the house are *coq au vin* (chicken in white wine) and savory, old-fashioned staples like rack of lamb and rump steak. Nothing ever changes—certainly not the time-tested recipes.

10th ARRONDISSEMENT (GARE DU NORD/GARE DE L'EST)
MODERATE

Brasserie Flo. 7 cour des Petites-Ecuries, 10e. ☎ **01-47-70-13-59.** Reservations recommended. Main courses 70–140F ($14–$28); fixed-price lunch 123F ($25); fixed-price dinner

189F ($38); fixed-price late-night supper (served only after 10pm) 128F ($26). AE, DC, MC, V. Daily noon–3pm and 7pm–1:30am. Métro: Château-d'Eau or Strasbourg–St-Denis. ALSATIAN.

Brasserie Flo is a remembrance of things past. You walk through an area of passageways, stumbling over garbage littering the streets, then come upon this sepia world of turn-of-the-century Paris: old mahogany, leather banquettes, and brass-studded chairs.

The thing to order, of course, is the delicious *la formidable choucroute paysanne* (sauerkraut), but don't expect just a heap of sauerkraut: The mound is surrounded by ham, bacon, and sausages. It's bountiful in the best Alsatian tradition. The onion soup is always good, as is the guinea hen with lentils. Look for the plats du jour, ranging from roast pigeon to fricassee of veal with sorrel.

Julien. 16 rue du Faubourg St-Denis, 10e. ☎ **01-47-70-12-06.** Reservations required. Main courses 80–130F ($16–$26); fixed-price lunch (and after 10pm) 128F ($26). AE, DC, MC, V. Daily noon–3pm and 7pm–1:30am. Métro: Strasbourg–St-Denis. FRENCH.

"The poor man's Maxim's," Julien offers an opportunity to dine in one of the most sumptuous belle epoque interiors in Paris. Located near Les Halles, it began life at the turn of the century as an elegant and acclaimed restaurant but became tawdry, grimy, and unappreciated after World War II. But more recently, an apt renovation returned Julien to its former elegance. The dirt has vanished, vivifying the magnificent dining room. Of special interest are four murals representing the four seasons, and a sometimes very fashionable clientele.

The food served here is in the style of *cuisine bourgeoise,* but without the heavy sauces formerly used. The sumptuous dishes include eggplant caviar and wild mushroom salad. Among the main courses are a Gascony cassoulet, fresh salmon with sorrel, and chateaubriand béarnaise. The wine list is extensive and reasonably priced.

INEXPENSIVE

✪ **Chez Michel.** 10 rue de Belzunce, 10e. ☎ **01-44-53-06-20.** Reservations recommended. Set-price menu 160F ($32). Tues–Sat 12:30–2pm and 7:30–11pm. AE, MC, V. Métro: Gare du Nord. BRETON/NORMAND.

Consciously adapting itself to the tastes and income level of a loyal crowd, this restaurant near the Gare du Nord serves well-prepared Normand and Breton dishes in generous portions. At least part of this derives from the northwestern origins of the owner and chef Thierry Breton. (The name never lies.) Within a pair of dining rooms accented in exposed wood, you'll enjoy the fruits of the fields and seacoast. Dishes are savory, densely flavored, and traditional, and include veal chops fried in butter, served with gratin of potatoes enriched with bits of calves' foot gelatin; codfish fillets served on beds of tomatoes and onions and a *tapenade* of black olives—even lobster served in puff pastry with a lobster sauce. The appropriate conclusion to a meal here is a snifter of Calvados, the apple-based brandy of the northern French coast, a potent pick-me-up that sometimes sneaks its way into everything from apple tarts to roasted loins of pork.

La Grille. 80 rue du Faubourg-Poissonière, 10e. ☎ **01-47-70-89-73.** Reservations required. Main courses 96–160F ($19.20–$32). AE, DC, MC, V. Mon–Fri noon–2:30pm and 7:15–10pm. Métro: Poissonière. FRENCH/SEAFOOD.

Few other restaurants within this price category are as hotly pursued by Parisians as this nine-table holdover from another age. When patrons from grander neighborhoods show up, it's usually because of a particular dish that has been perfected since its development three decades ago by the site's congenial owner, Mme. Geneviève Cullerre. The holy grail, at least in the case of La Grille, is an entire turbot, cooked whole, and prepared at tableside with a slightly foamy emulsified white butter sauce. If you opt for a meal here, you won't be the first: For at least a century after the French Revolution, fishermen from the coastal town of Dieppe used the site as a springboard for carousing and cabaret-watching after delivering their cartloads of fish to the food markets at Les Halles. If the turbot doesn't appeal to you, consider other dishes such as seafood terrine; old-fashioned beef bourguignon; fried scallops in a white-wine butter sauce; marinated sardine fillets, and such high-calorie, high-satisfaction desserts as chocolate mousse or vanilla custard. Incidentally, don't think that this establishment's name derives from a grill used for cooking. The 200-year-old wrought-iron grills that protect the street-level windows from break-ins are classified as national treasures, among the best examples of their kind in Paris. Inside, velvet banquettes covered with lace antimacassars complete the allegiance to an older France.

La P'tite Tonkinoise. 56 rue du Faubourg-Poissonière, 10e. ☎ **01-42-46-85-98.** Reservations recommended. Main courses 85–140F ($17–$28); fixed-price lunch 133F ($26.60). DC, MC, V. Mon–Fri noon–2pm; Mon–Sat 7:30–10:15pm. Métro: Poissonière or Bonne Nouvelle. VIETNAMESE.

Paris has hundreds of Vietnamese restaurants, and this is our favorite. Named after the old, diminutive matriarch of the family that has run this restaurant since 1972, La P'tite Tonkinoise provides an exceptional opportunity to learn more about Tonkin (the 19th-century Asian province later renamed North Vietnam), its culture, and its cuisine. The decor mimics a Vietnamese hut, with walls almost completely sheathed in bamboo. Since the dining room can only accommodate about 30 diners at a time, it's a good idea to reserve in advance. Menu items, usually based on seafood, chicken, or pork, are milder than the norm. A perennial favorite served only on Friday and Saturday is *my sao,* a medley of stir-fried vegetables on a crispy rice cake and garnished with shrimp. Few tourists venture into this neighborhood, but you'll be rewarded if you do.

Le Dogon. 30 rue René Boulanger, 10e. ☎ **01-42-41-95-85.** Reservations recommended. Main courses 95–110F ($19–$22). AE, MC, V. Mon–Fri noon–3pm and daily 6:30–1am. Métro: République. SENEGALESE.

Amid animal pelts and carved masks from Mali, the place offers well-seasoned exotica that the curious French view as culinary oddities but nonetheless return to from time to time. Examples include *maffé,* a spicy concoction that mixes peanuts with chicken, herbs, and rice; grilled fish with cumin and rice; vegetarian platters seasoned with lots of onions and lemons; and a North African version of couscous. You can opt for conventional wines or beers, but truly adventurous diners sometimes ask for either date-palm wine or fermented coconut juice.

Paris-Dakar. 95 rue du Faubourg St-Martin, 10e. ☎ **01-42-08-16-64.** Reservations recommended. Lunch plats du jour 36F ($7); lunch prix-fixe 59–149F ($12–$30); prix-fixe dinner 99–149F ($20–$30). MC, V. Tues–Sun noon–3pm and 7pm–midnight. Métro: Gare de l'Est. SENEGALESE.

Named after the famous rally that carries vehicles across the toughest race terrains in the world, this restaurant celebrates the culinary traditions of France's former colonies in West Africa. Amid a genuine welcome and decorative carved masks and textiles, you'll have the option of sampling such Senegalese dishes as *yassa* (chicken braised with limes and onions); *maffé* (beef fried with peanuts, onions, and spice); and *tiep bou dieone* (fish sautéed with rice, fresh vegetables, and dollops of fiery-hot chile peppers). The owners offer attractively priced luncheons and an insight into a cuisine that you might not have automatically thought of before arriving in this congested neighborhood.

11th & 12th ARRONDISSEMENTS (OPÉRA BASTILLE/ BOIS DE VINCENNES)

EXPENSIVE

✪ **Au Trou Gascon.** 40 rue Taine, 12e. ☎ **01-43-44-34-26.** Reservations required. Main courses 158–168F ($32–$34); fixed-price lunch 190F ($38); fixed-price dinner 285F ($57). AE, DC, MC, V. Mon–Fri noon–2pm; Mon–Sat 7:30–10pm. Closed Aug. Métro: Daumesnil. GASCONY.

One of the most acclaimed chefs in Paris today, Alain Dutournier launched his cooking career in the Gascony region of southwest France. His parents mortgaged their own inn to allow Dutournier to open a turn-of-the-century bistro in an unfashionable part of the 12th arrondissement. At first he got little business, but word soon spread of a savant in the kitchen who knew and practiced authentic *cuisine moderne*. He has lately opened another restaurant in Paris, and he has shared his secret recipes with his kitchen staff. His wife, Nicole, is the welcoming hostess, and the wine steward has distinguished himself for his exciting *cave* containing several little-known wines along with a fabulous collection of Armagnacs. It is estimated that the wine cellar has some 800 varieties.

Here you can enjoy the true and authentic cuisine of Gascony. Start with fresh duck foie gras cooked in a terrine, or Gascony cured ham cut from the bone. The best *cassoulet* in town (a local white bean stew with traditional preserved duck, lamb, pork, and homemade sausage) is served here. Tip: Order the chicken from the Chalosse region of Landes, which Dutournier roasts and serves in its own drippings. We'd compare these hens to the finest birds of Bresse for good quality and flavor.

MODERATE

✪ **Le Train Bleu.** In the Gare de Lyon, 12e. ☎ **01-43-43-09-06.** Reservations recommended. Main courses 95–165F ($19–$33); fixed-price menu 250F ($50), including wine. AE, DC, MC, V. Daily 11:30am–3pm and 7–11pm. Métro: Gare de Lyon. FRENCH.

To reach this restaurant, climb the ornate double staircase that faces the grimy platforms of the Gare de Lyon. Both restaurant and station were built simultaneously with the Grand Palais, the Pont Alexandre III, and the Petit Palais, as part of the World Exhibition of 1900. As a fitting end to a traveler's long trip, the station's architects designed a restaurant whose decor is classified as a national artistic treasure. Inaugurated by the French president in 1901 and renovated and cleaned at great expense in 1992, the restaurant displays an army of bronze statues, a lavishly frescoed ceiling, mosaics, mirrors, old-fashioned banquettes, and 41 belle epoque murals. Each of these celebrates the distant corners of the French-speaking world, which join Paris via its rail network.

Service is fast, attentive and efficient, in case you're about to catch a train. A formally dressed staff will bring steaming platters of soufflé of brill, escargots in Chablis sauce, steak tartare, loin of lamb Provençal, veal kidneys in mustard sauce, rib of beef for two, and rum baba (rum cake with raisins). Although the cuisine is well prepared in a classic French Escoffier manner, the grand setting competes with the food.

INEXPENSIVE

Astier. 44 rue Jean-Pierre-Timbaud, 11e. ☎ **01-43-57-16-35.** Reservations recommended. Set menu 135F ($27). V. Mon–Fri noon–3pm and 8–11pm. Métro: Oberkampf. FRENCH.

🍴 Family-Friendly Restaurants

Meals at the grand restaurants of Paris are rarely suitable for young children. Nevertheless, many parents drag their children along, often to the annoyance of other diners. If you want to dine at a fancy restaurant, consider leaving the kids with a baby-sitter. However, if you prefer to dine with your children, then you may have to make some compromises, such as dining earlier than most Parisians. **Hotel dining rooms** can be another good choice for family dining. They usually have children's menus, or at least one or two *plats du jour* cooked for children, such as spaghetti with meat sauce.

If you take your child to a moderate or inexpensive restaurant, ask if the restaurant will serve a child's plate. If not, order a plat du jour or *plat garni,* which will be suitable for most children, particularly if a dessert is to follow.

Most **cafes** welcome children throughout the day and early evening. At a cafe, children always seem to like the sandwiches (try a croque-monsieur), the omelettes, and especially the *pommes frites* (crispy french fries). Although this chapter lists a number of cafes (see "The Best Cafes," below), one that particularly appeals to children is **La Samaritaine,** 75 rue de Rivoli (☎ **01-40-41-20-20;** Métro: Pont-Neuf). The snack bar down below doesn't have a panoramic view, but the restaurant on the fifth floor does. You can take children to the top and order ice cream for them at tea time daily from 3:15 to 6pm.

Les Drug Stores (149 bd. St-Germain-des-Prés, 6e, and at Publicis Champs-Elysées, 133 av. des Champs-Elysées, 8e) also welcome children, especially in the early evening, as do most **tearooms,** and you can tide the kids over with pastries and ice cream if dinner will be late. Try a **picnic** in the park. Also, there are lots of fast-food chains, such as **Pizza Hut** and **McDonald's,** all over the city.

Le Brise-Miche *(see p. 131)*   The ideal choice when visiting Beaubourg. Diners receive crayons for doodling on the place mats as they watch the gamboling fountains.

Chicago Pizza Pie Factory *(see p. 137)*   There are no frogs' legs or snails to gross out little minds and stomachs at Chicago Pizza Pie Factory, but there is the City of Light's best pizza followed by a kid-pleasing cheesecake.

Androuët *(see p. 138)*   If your kids love cheese, they'll get the fill of a lifetime here, where cheese enters all the dishes—especially delectable is the ravioli stuffed with goat cheese.

Joe Allen *(see p. 118)*   This American restaurant in Les Halles delivers everything from chili to chocolate mousse pie to the best hamburgers in Paris.

Crémerie-Restaurant Polidor *(see p. 158)*   One of the most popular restaurants on the Left Bank, this reasonably priced dining room is so family-friendly it calls its food cuisine familiale. This might be the best place to introduce your child to bistro food.

Since it was established "sometime during the administration of Charles de Gaulle," no one has tried to make this place glamorous, understanding that hearty, well-prepared food has its own allure. Indeed this philosophy has attracted patrons from all over Paris: Some walk from the relatively nearby Opéra de la Bastille; others come from throughout Paris's northeastern quadrant, primarily because the set menu (the only offering available) represents an honest and worthwhile value. At least 10 different choices are available for each of four courses. Examples include roasted rabbit with mustard sauce; variations on tripe; shellfish; *racasse* (scorpionfish) with fresh spinach; grilled steaks and chops of all kinds; brochettes of monkfish wrapped in bacon; and breast of duckling served with a foie-gras cream sauce. Access to a superbly varied cheese platter, as well as desserts such as crème caramel or chocolate mousse, is included in the cost.

L'Ébauchoir. 43 rue de Cîteaux, 12e. ☎ **01-43-42-49-31.** Reservations recommended for dinner. Main courses 75–95F ($15–$19); fixed-price lunch 66F ($13). MC, V. Mon–Sat noon–2:30pm and 6:30–10:30pm. Métro: Faidherbe-Chaligny. FRENCH.

Tucked into a neighborhood rarely visited by foreign tourists, and decorated with a 1950s decor that, to the surprise of its staff, has suddenly become fashionable again, this bistro attracts neighborhood carpenters, plumbers, and electricians, as well as an occasional journalist and screenwriter. Framed with buffed aluminum trim, and plaster and stucco walls tinted dark yellow and green, the place might remind you of a canteen in an automobile factory. You can order generous, surprisingly well-prepared versions of stuffed sardines, crabmeat soup, grilled tuna steak served with orange-flavored butter, fried calf's liver with coriander and honey, and a dish that combines rack of lamb with saddle of lamb on the same platter.

16th ARRONDISSEMENT (TROCADÉRO/BOIS DE BOULOGNE)
VERY EXPENSIVE

✪ **Alain Ducasse.** 59 av. Raymond Poincaré, 16e. ☎ **01-47-27-12-27.** Reservations 6 weeks in advance. Main courses 325–490F ($65–$98); set lunch 490F ($98); set dinner 890–1,450F ($178–$290). AE, DC, MC, V. Métro: Trocadéro. FRENCH/MEDITERRANEAN.

The celebrated Monte Carlo chef has taken Paris by storm since taking over the reins from the great Joël Robuchon (now semiretired). This three-star Michelin chef divides his time between Paris and Monaco, although he insists that he does not repeat himself in the Paris restaurant. Ducasse has a wizard's larder: In this restored four-story mansion he seeds his dishes with produce from every region of France. The nation seems within his armspan: He serves rare local vegetables and fish from the country's ocean-torn coasts. Like an incantation, recipes incorporate cardoons, turnips, celery, turbot, cuttlefish, and Bresse fowl. His French cuisine is contemporary and Mediterranean, though not new. Although many dishes are light, Ducasse isn't afraid of lard, as he proves by his thick, fatty, oozing slabs of pork grilled to a crisp. Ducasse has kept a single Robuchon dish on the menu as a tribute: the famed jellied creation, the caviar in aspic with cauliflower cream. The food remains sober in presentation: it is true, precise, and authentic.

The wine list is based on the fine cellar left by Robuchon and noted for its classic composition, extensiveness, and high quality. Ducasse has added many new acquisitions from France's vineyards, but he has also opened his cellar doors to young wine growers of his generation, including those from Germany, Switzerland, Spain, and Italy. His bar seals the spell with rare brandies and fine cigars. As Ducasse told us, "The tasting of a dish must leave a remembrance. If nothing remains in the memory of a single guest, I have fooled myself."

✪ **Faugeron.** 52 rue de Longchamp, 16e. ☎ **01-47-04-24-53.** Reservations required. Main courses 185–260F ($37–$52); fixed-price lunch 295–650F ($59–$130); fixed-price dinner 550–650F ($110–$130). AE, MC, V. Mon–Fri 11:30am–2pm and 7:30–10pm (Oct–Apr only, dinner Sat 7:30–10pm). Closed Aug. Métro: Trocadéro. FRENCH.

Henri Faugeron is an inspired chef who many years ago established this restaurant as an elegant yet unobtrusive backdrop for his superb cuisine, which he calls "revolutionary." The interior of this turn-of-the-century building now glitters with discreet touches of gilt and has a sun motif emblazoned on the ceiling. Even so, the food outshines its surroundings. Much of the zesty cuisine depends on the season and the market, since Faugeron only chooses the freshest ingredients. In winter your taste for truffles can be indulged by one of the many dishes expertly prepared in the bustling kitchen. Examples include a brunoise of truffles with asparagus and olive oil and ravioli stuffed with truffles and foie gras. Milk-fed veal and lamb and crispy-skinned quail are also succulent choices.

✪ **Jamin.** 32 rue de Longchamp, 16e. ☎ **01-45-53-00-07.** Reservations imperative. Main courses 105–165F ($21–$33); set menus 280–375F ($56–$75) at lunch; 375F ($75) at dinner. AE, DC, MC, V. Mon–Fri 12:30–2pm and 7:30–10pm. Métro: Trocadéro. FRENCH.

In the 1980s Joël Robuchon, the great French chef, became a sensation at this very spot, and all Paris made its way to his door. Nowadays, Benoit Guichard, long-time second in command, is in charge. He's clearly inspired by his master, but is an imaginative and inventive chef in his own right. Guichard has chosen pale green panels and pink banquettes—referred to as "Italo-New Yorkaise"—for a soothing backdrop to his brief but well-chosen menu. Lunches can be relatively simple affairs, although each dish, such as a beautifully seasoned salmon tartare, is done to perfection. Classic technique and a homage to tradition characterize the cuisine, which is filled with such offerings as a panfried veal flank steak with drop-dead potatoes laced with Cantal cheese. His beef shoulder was so tender it had obviously been braising for hours. Many begin with ocean-fresh Brittany lobster married to spaghetti-sized strips of ginger-laced squid. In a spartan manner, this grand chef makes delectable what is normally thrown away. His earthy "sonnet to the sow" blends the robust cheeks and tail of the animal with golden panfried potatoes. His wife, Majorie, is on hand, as is his dream team of chefs. Finish yourself off with an apple tarte tatin.

EXPENSIVE

✪ **Le Vivarois.** 192-194 av. Victor Hugo, 16e. ☎ **01-45-04-04-31.** Reservations required. Main courses 240–300F ($48–$60); fixed-price lunch 345F ($69). AE, DC, MC, V. Mon–Fri noon–2pm and 8–10pm. Closed Aug and Sat–Sun. Métro: Pompe. FRENCH.

Food critics have called Le Vivarois "a revelation." *Gourmet* magazine once hailed it as "a restaurant of our time . . . the most exciting, audacious, and important restaurant in Paris today." Le Vivarois still maintains its standards, but it no longer occupies such a lofty position.

Le Vivarois is the child of its supremely talented owner and chef, Claude Peyrot. The tasteful modern decor is accented by slabs of marble and polished cherrywood, and the food is equally impressive. Peyrot's menu is constantly changing. One food critic once said, and quite accurately, "the menu changes with the marketing and his genius." He does a most recommendable lobster ravioli and *coquilles St-Jacques* (scallops). To many his most winning dish is *rognons de veau* (veal kidneys).

Madame Peyrot is one of the finest maîtres d'hôtel in Paris. She'll guide you through wine selections to the right complement to her husband's superlative cuisine.

MODERATE

La Butte Chaillot. 110 bis av. Kleber. 16e. ☎ **01-47-27-88-88.** Reservations recommended. Main courses 98–125F ($20–$25). AE, MC, V. Daily noon–2:30pm and 7pm–midnight. Métro: Trocadéro. FRENCH.

First conceived as the headquarters for a bank, this site was converted into a baby bistro for the showcasing of culinary high priest Guy Savoy. As such, it draws a busy clientele deriving from the affluent neighborhood's many corporate headquarters. Diners congregate within posh but congested areas tinted in salmon and dark yellow. Menu items change weekly (and sometimes daily), depending on what is in season, and betray a strange sense of mass production not unlike that found in a luxury cruise line's dining room. Examples include a sophisticated medley of terrines; a salad of snails and herbed potatoes; grilled fillet of *rascasse* (scorpion fish) with ginger and lemon; a succulent rack of lamb, and a form of ravioli that's likely to crop up on other Guy Savoy menus around Paris, *raviolis du Royans aux herbes fines* (cheese ravioli with herbs). A starkly contemporary stainless steel staircase leads to supplemental seating in the cellar.

INEXPENSIVE

Le Bistro de l'Étoile. 19 rue Lauriston, 16e. ☎ **01-40-67-11-16.** Reservations recommended. Main courses 89–105F ($18–$21). AE, MC, V. Mon–Fri noon–2:30pm, Mon–Sat 7pm–midnight. AE, MC, V. Métro: Étoile. FRENCH.

This is the most interesting of three separate baby bistros, each with the same name, that are clustered around place de l'Étoile, within one of Paris's more predictably prosperous neighborhoods. Each benefits from sponsorship by superstar Guy Savoy, who inspired affordable versions of the very grand cuisine featured in his nearby temple of French gastronomy. The setting is a warmly contemporary dining room outfitted in shades of butterscotch and caramel. Menu items include a *mijotée* of cheeks of pork with sage, and codfish studded with dabs of lard and prepared with a coconut-lime sauce. A particularly interesting sampler involves three of Savoy's creations on a platter, including a cup of lentil cream soup, a fondant of celery, and a panfried slice of foie gras. Expect some odd terms on the dessert menu, which only a professional chef can fully describe. An example is spice bread baked in the fashion of *pain perdu* (lost bread) garnished with banana sorbet and pineapple sauce.

17th & 18th ARRONDISSEMENT (PARC MONCEAU/ MONTMARTRE)
VERY EXPENSIVE

✪ **Guy Savoy.** 18 rue Troyon, 17e. ☎ **01-43-80-40-61.** Reservations required, 1 week in advance. Main courses 250–300F ($50–$60); *menu dégustation* 900F ($180). AE, MC, V. Mon–Fri noon–2pm; Mon–Sat 7:30–10:30pm. Métro: Charles de Gaulle–Étoile. FRENCH.

Guy Savoy serves the kind of food that he himself likes to eat, and it is prepared with consummate skill. When the five or six hottest chefs in Europe are named today, his name is on the list, and deservedly so. His nearest rival is Michel Rostang (see below), over whom we think he has a very slight edge. Both have earned two stars from Michelin. Though the food is superb and meals comprise as many as nine courses, the portions are small; you won't necessarily be satiated before the meal has run its course.

The menu changes with the seasons, but might, at the time of your visit, include a light cream soup of lentils and crayfish, foie gras of duckling with aspic and gray salt, and red snapper with a liver and spinach sauce served with crusty potatoes. If you visit in the right season, you may have a chance to order such masterfully prepared game as mallard or venison. Savoy is fascinated with the *champignon* in its many varieties, and has been known to serve a dozen different types of mushrooms, especially in the autumn.

✪ **Michel Rostang.** 20 rue Rennequin, 17e. ☎ **01-47-63-40-77.** Reservations required. Main courses 235–320F ($47–$64); fixed-price lunch 298–740F ($60–$148); dinner 540–740F ($108–$148). AE, MC, V. Mon–Fri 12:30–2:30pm; Mon–Sat 8–10:30pm. Closed 2 weeks in Aug. Métro: Ternes. FRENCH.

Monsieur Rostang is one of the most creative chefs in Paris. He's the fifth generation of one of the most distinguished French "cooking families," who have been connected with the famed Bonne Auberge at Antibes on the French Riviera.

The restaurant is composed of four different dining rooms, each paneled in mahogany, cherry, or pearwood, and in some cases, accented with frosted panels of Lalique crystal. One contains collages of broken musical instruments crafted by the contemporary French artist Arman. Another features a collection of 19th-century liqueur bottles (*Robj*) crafted in the shape of famous figures from French history, and a glassed-in view of the kitchen where Mr. Rostang or his assistants can be observed preparing their highly nuanced cuisine.

The menu changes every two months, and features modern improvements on France's *cuisine bourgeoise*. In midwinter, truffles are the dish of choice; in spring, you'll find racks of suckling lamb from the salt marshes of France's western seacoasts; and in game season, look for sophisticated preparations of pheasant and venison. Also delicious are artichokes with fresh truffles and foie gras of duckling, served in a rich cream sauce reduced and flavored with vinegar. Three year-round staples include quail eggs with a *coque* of sea urchins, a fricassee of sole, or a young chicken from Bresse (the finest in France) served with a chervil sauce.

MODERATE

Chez Georges. 273 bd. Pereire, 17e. ☎ **01-45-74-31-00.** Reservations recommended. Main courses 100–150F ($20–$30). AE, MC, V. Daily noon–2:30pm and 7–11:30pm. Closed: August. Métro: Porte-Maillot. FRENCH.

Not to be confused with a bistro with the same name in the 2nd arrondissement, this worthy choice has flourished since 1926, despite an obscure location. The setting has changed little—cheerfully harassed waiters barge through the lace and mirror-sheathed dining room laden with trays, and savory odors emerge from an hysterically busy kitchen. Two enduring specialties are the leg of lamb with white kidney beans, and roast beef served with herbs (especially thyme) in its own juices. Preceding these are Baltic herring in cream sauce, cabbage soup, or a wide selection of sausages and pork products that taste best when consumed with bread, butter, and sour pickles. Common daily specials include mutton stew with green beans, and stew swimming with portions of braised beef ribs. The adventurous French love the calf's head and the braised veal trotters, both served cold, in vinaigrette.

۞ La Rôtisserie d'Armaillé. 6 rue d'Armaillé, 17e. ☎ **01-42-27-19-20.** Reservations recommended. Set menu 198F ($40). AE, MC, V. Daily noon–2:30pm and 7:30–11pm. Métro: Étoile. FRENCH.

The impresario behind this attractive baby bistro is Jacques Cagna, who established his role as a gastronomic star long ago from headquarters in the Latin Quarter. This chic bistro bristles with business lunches and dinners, as well as well-shod residents and shoppers from the inner recesses of a very grand neighborhood surrounding the place d'Étoile. It's ringed with light-colored wood paneling and banquettes with patterns of pink and green. You'll have only one option at both lunch and dinner, a set-price, three-course medley with many choices within each category. Examples include a flan of wild mushrooms with a red wine sauce; a terrine of foie gras; a salad of sweetbreads and crayfish; *rascasse* (scorpion fish) *en papillote;* and a rack of lamb accented with parsley and sage. The artwork features bucolic depictions of the cows, pigs, and lambs that are likely to figure among the grilled steaks and chops featured on the menu.

Le Bistro d'à Côté. 10 rue Flaubert, 17e. ☎ **01-42-67-05-81.** Reservations recommended. Main courses 140-180F ($28–$36). AE, MC, V. Daily 12:30-2pm and 7:30-11pm. Métro: Ternes. FRENCH.

In case you want to see the world.

At American Express, we're here to make your journey a smooth one. So we have over 1,700 travel service locations in over 120 countries ready to help. What else would you expect from the world's largest travel agency?

do more.

Travel

http://www.americanexpress.com/travel

In case you want to be welcomed there.

We're here to see that you're always welcomed at establishments everywhere. That's why millions of people carry the American Express® Card – for peace of mind, confidence, and security, around the world or just around the corner.

do more

Cards

In case you're running low.

We're here to help with more than 118,000 Express Cash locations around the world. In order to enroll, just call American Express before you start your vacation.

do more

Express Cash

And just in case.

We're here with American Express® Travelers Cheques and Cheques *for Two*® They're the safest way to carry money on your vacation and the surest way to get a refund, practically anywhere, anytime.

Another way we help you...

do more

Travelers Cheques

This is one of four branches of Michel Rostang's baby bistro, each of which feature a pared-down version of his haute gastronomy. You'll enter a nostalgically decorated dining area ringed with unusual porcelain and antique copies of Michelin guides, some of which date from around 1900. The venue is breezy, stylishly informal, and chic, with a simple menu enhanced by daily specials written on a blackboard. Tantalizing items include ravioli stuffed with pulverized lobster; roasted Bresse chicken accompanied with a salad of chicken thighs and herbs; and a *rable de lievre* (rabbit stew) *en cocotte.* We feel this branch, above all the others, is the most interesting because of its proximity (that is, next door) to the restaurant where Rostang reigns as culinary king.

INEXPENSIVE

Le Grain de Folie. 24 rue de la Vieuville, 18e. ☎ **01-42-58-15-57.** Reservations recommended. Main courses 45–65F ($9–$13); fixed-price menus 50–100F ($10–$20). No credit cards. Daily noon–2:30pm and 7–11pm, Sat–Sun 11am–midnight. Métro: Abbesses. VEGETARIAN.

Simple, wholesome, and unpretentious, the cuisine at this vegetarian restaurant has been inspired by France, Greece, California, and India. The menu includes an array of salads, cereals, tarts, terrines, and casseroles. Dessert selections might include an old-fashioned tart or a fruit salad. The decor includes potted plants, exposed stone, and a gathering of masks from around the world. You can choose one of an array of wines or a frothy glass of vegetable juice to accompany your meal.

Les Gourmets des Ternes. 87 bd. de Courcelles, 17e. ☎ **01-42-27-43-04.** Main courses 70–140F ($14–$28). AE, MC, V. Mon–Fri noon–2:30pm and 7–10pm. Métro: Ternes. FRENCH.

It's brusque in a way that betrays symptoms of a bistro's success, catering as it does to hordes of clients who appreciate affordable prices and lack of pretension. Satisfied clients have included the mayor of Atlanta, who wrote a thank-you letter for a worthwhile meal here, as well as hundreds of ordinary folks from the decorous confines of this residential neighborhood. Thriving in this spot since it was established in 1892, the place retains a turn-of-the-century paneled decor, with some additions from the 1950s, including Bordeaux-colored banquettes, mirrors, wooden panels, touches of brass, and paper tablecloths. Its finely grilled signature dishes include rib steak with marrow sauce and french fries; medallions of pork; country pâtés and sausages; sole, turbot, and monkfish; and simple, satisfying desserts that include peach Melba and *baba au Rhum* (rum cake with raisins).

Marie-Louise. 52 rue Championnet, 18e. ☎ **01-46-06-86-55.** Reservations recommended. Main courses 85–120F ($17–$24). DC, MC, V. Wed–Sat noon–2pm and 7:30–10pm. Closed: Aug. Métro: Simplon or Porte-de-Clignancourt. FRENCH.

Established in a decidedly unfashionable neighborhood in 1957, and named after the matriarch who first owned it, this bistro offers views of Paris rarely experienced by visitors who gravitate toward the low Seine. The decor evokes old-time France with allusions to the establishment's birth in the age of *Sputnik.* Staff members will be less effusive and smooth than at, say, the Hard Rock Café, but that tendency should appeal to anyone looking to be far away from the usual places. Opt for a table on the busy main floor, or on the quieter floor above street level. The item that long-time fans of this place order again and again is *boeuf à la ficelle* (poached fillet of beef tied together with string and served in its natural juices). The staff also proffers large and unpretentious platters of veal kidneys in mustard or Madeira sauce; sautéed monkfish with pasta; chicken "Marie-Louise" (with rice and a paprika-cream sauce); and grilled sirloin steak with pepper or béarnaise sauce.

19th ARRONDISSEMENT (BUTTES CHAUMONT)
MODERATE

Restaurant d'Eric Frechon. 10 rue Géneral Brunet, 19e. ☎ **01-40-40-03-30.** Reservations required. Set menu 190F ($38). MC, V. Tues–Sat noon–2:30 and 7–11pm. Métro: Botzaris. FRENCH.

With perfect justification, this place calls itself a "bistro gastronomique," and as such, attracts a remarkably stylish crowd to the city's calm and rarely visited northern periphery within the Buttes Chaumont district. Frechon learned his craft at some of the grandest restaurants of Paris, including the spectacularly expensive restaurants within the Hotel de Crillon. Don't expect an impressive decor; ideas of that were eliminated in favor of a monochromatically brown-and-beige decor that the staff refers to as "1970s-retro."

Menu items include roasted chicken stuffed with foie gras, celery, and artichoke hearts; a seasoned tartare of salmon and oysters floating on a bed of creamy horseradish sauce; and a bouillon of pot-au-feu garnished with ravioli stuffed with foie gras. Note that if you're hoping for a table here on a Friday or Saturday, it's wise to reserve several days in advance.

5 Left Bank

We'll begin with the most centrally located arrondissements on the Left Bank and then survey the outlying neighborhoods.

5th ARRONDISSEMENT (LATIN QUARTER)
VERY EXPENSIVE

✪ **La Tour d'Argent.** 15–17 quai de la Tournelle, 5e. ☎ **01-43-54-23-31.** Reservations required. Main courses 200–400F ($40–$80); fixed-price lunch 395F ($79). AE, DC, MC, V. Tues–Sun noon–2:30pm and 8–10:30pm. Métro: Maubert-Mutualité or Pont-Marie. FRENCH.

La Tour d'Argent is a national institution. From this penthouse restaurant, the view over the Seine and of the apse of Notre-Dame is panoramic. Although this restaurant's long-established reputation as "the best" in Paris has been eclipsed by Taillevent and Alain Ducasse, to dine here remains unsurpassed as a theatrical event.

La Tour d'Argent traces its history back to 1582, when a restaurant of some sort stood on this site. Madame de Sévigné refers to the cafe in her celebrated letters, and Dumas set part of one of his novels here. The fame of La Tour d'Argent spread during its ownership by Frédéric Delair, who bought the fabled wine cellar of Café Anglais to supply his restaurant. It was Delair who started the practice of issuing certificates to diners who ordered the house specialty: *caneton* (pressed duckling). The birds, incidentally, are numbered, and the first one was served to Edward VII in 1890. As of January 18, 1997, La Tour d'Argent had served 856,468 canetons, and they're still counting.

Under the sharp eye of its current owner, Claude Terrail, the cooking is superb, and the service impeccable. Limoges china adorns each table. Although part of the menu is devoted to the various ways you can order duck, we assure you that the kitchen *does* know how to prepare other dishes. We especially recommend the ravioli with foie gras, salmon and turbot à la Sully, and, to begin your meal, the pheasant consommé.

MODERATE

Auberge des Deux Signes. 46 rue Galande, 5e. ☎ **01-43-25-46-56.** Reservations required for dinner. Main courses 136–192F ($27–$38); fixed-price lunch 150F ($30); fixed-price dinner

230F ($46). AE, DC, DISC, MC, V. Mon–Fri 12:30–2pm; Mon–Sat 7:30–10:30pm. Closed Aug.
Métro: Maubert-Mutualité or St-Michel. AUVERGNAT.

This restaurant was once the chapel of St-Blaise. In the evening you'll enjoy the view
of floodlit Notre-Dame (without having to pay the prices charged by Tour d'Argent)
and the Church of St-Julien-le-Pauvre. Try to get a table upstairs with a garden view,
but be prepared for a wait.

The kitchen draws its inspiration from the ancient province of Auvergne. The food
is packed with robust flavor and is well crafted into delectable combinations. Choices
are wisely limited to keep everything fresh. Try the potted goose with *cépes* (flap
mushrooms) or the slices of veal sweetbreads au gratin. And the sole soufflé with crayfish tails is well worth a trip across Paris.

Au Pactole. 44 bd. St-Germain, 5e. ☎ **01-46-33-31-31.** Reservations recommended. Main
courses 159–279F ($32–$56); fixed-price menu 80–300F ($16–$60). AE, MC, V. Sun–Fri
11:30am–3pm; daily 7–10:45pm. Métro: Maubert-Mutualité. FRENCH.

The late Mitterrand no longer drops in for dinner (he once brought German chan-
cellor Helmut Kohl here), and Jacques Chirac doesn't send them flowers anymore,
but Au Pactole has survived without the big names. It consistently remains one of
the best restaurants (and best values) of the 5th arrondissement. Roland Magne,
whose gracious wife, Noëlle, is Au Pactole's hostess, is not as celebrated as some Paris
chefs, but his is an award-winning cuisine nonetheless. His ravioli stuffed with snails
is exceptional, and he also prepares the best beef ribs in the 5th, roasted in a crust
of salt. His *cabillaud* (a large Northern Atlantic cod) is excellent: The flesh is white
and flaky, and seasoned with green olive oil and herbs. Another popular dish is the
rack of lamb prepared with herbs and red wine sauce.

Brasserie Balzar. 49 rue des Ecoles, 5e. ☎ **01-43-54-13-67.** Reservations strongly recommended. Main courses 90–115F ($18–$23). AE, MC, V. Daily noon–midnight. Métro: Odeon
or Cluny–La Sorbonne. FRENCH.

Established in 1898, the Brasserie Balzar is battered but cheerful, with some of the
friendliest waiters in Paris. The menu makes almost no concessions to nouvelle cuisine, and includes *steak au poivre* (pepper steak), sole meunière, sauerkraut garnished
with ham and sausage, pigs' feet, and calves' liver fried and served without garnish.
The food is decently prepared, and it's clear these dishes still keep people happy. Be
warned that if you just want coffee or a drink, you probably won't get a table during meal hours. But the staff will be happy to serve you if you want to have a full
dinner in the midafternoon, accustomed as they are to the odd hours of their many
clients.

If you select this place, you'll be in good company: Former patrons have included
both Sartre and Camus (who often got in arguments), William Shirer, Elliot Paul,
James Thurber, countless professors from the nearby Sorbonne, and a bevy of
English and American journalists.

✪ **Rôtisserie du Beaujolais.** 19 Quai de la Tournelle, 5e. ☎ **01-43-54-17-47.** Reservations
recommended. Main courses 85–135F ($17–$27). MC, V. Tues–Sun noon–2:30pm and 7:30–
10:30pm. Métro: Pont-Marie. FRENCH/SPIT-ROASTED.

You may be surprised to learn that this place, with its no-nonsense cuisine and reasonable prices, was founded by the owner of the heartbreakingly expensive Tour
d'Argent, which occupies the top floor of a building across the street. Set at the edge
of the Seine, overlooking the Ile St-Louis, the Rôtisserie contains a stone, zinc, and
wood-inlaid antique bar imported from the Beaujolais region of France. Comfortable banquettes and a deliberately unpretentious design evoke a brasserie in the

Left Bank Restaurants

Au Pactole 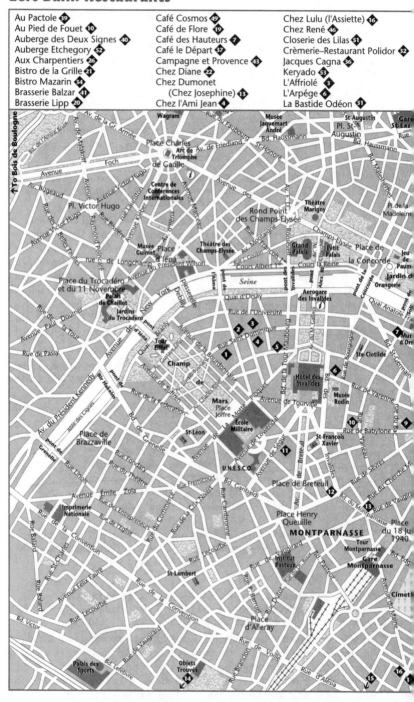 39
Au Pied de Fouet 10
Auberge des Deux Signes 40
Auberge Etchegory 52
Aux Charpentiers 26
Bistro de la Grille 21
Bistro Mazarin 34
Brasserie Balzar 41
Brasserie Lipp 20

Café Cosmos 49
Café de Flore 19
Café des Hauteurs 7
Café le Départ 37
Campagne et Provence 43
Chez Diane 22
Chez Dumonet
  (Chez Josephine) 13
Chez l'Ami Jean 4

Chez Lulu (l'Assiette) 16
Chez René 46
Closerie des Lilas 51
Crèmerie–Restaurant Polidor 32
Jacques Cagna 36
Keryado 53
L'Affriolé 3
L'Arpège 6
La Bastide Odéon 31

a Coupole **50**
a Fontaine de Mars **2**
a Petite Chaise **8**
a Petite Hostellerie **38**
a Régalade **17**
a Rotonde **49**
a Tour d'Argent **45**
e Bambouche **9**
e Canton **25**

Le Petit Vatel **30**
Le Procope **29**
Le Rouquet **18**
Le Violin d'Ingres **1**
Lerch **47**
Les Deux Magots **24**
Les Olivades **11**
Paul Minchelli **5**
Peltier **12**

Perraudin **42**
Pub Saint–Germain–des–Prés **28**
Restaurant Bleu **15**
Restaurant des Beaux–Arts **23**
Restaurant du Marché **14**
Rôtisserie d'en Face **35**
Rôtisserie du Beaujolais **44**
Yugaraj **33**

French provinces. Appetizers include a fricassee of wild mushrooms, a gâteau of chicken livers, and salads. Main courses are usually roasted on spits in the kitchen, and arrive savory and steaming with a garnish of mashed potatoes in the old-fashioned style. Examples include spit-roasted chicken, duck, quail, or pigeon, as well as nonspit dishes such as *coq au vin* (chicken in wine) or a side of beef prepared for two. The wine list is prudently selected, with many different vintages from Beaujolais.

INEXPENSIVE

Café le Départ-St-Michel. 1 place St-Michel, 5e. ☎ **01-43-54-24-55.** Reservations not accepted. Platters 28–72F ($6–$14); sandwiches 18–45F ($4–$9); crêpes 18–50F ($4–$10). AE, DC, MC, V. Daily 24 hours. Métro: St-Michel. FRENCH/MIDDLE OF THE NIGHT.

One of the most popular cafes on the Left Bank, Le Départ is open 24 hours a day. On the banks of the Seine, it has a view of both the steeple of the Sainte-Chapelle and the dragon statue of place St-Michel. The decor is warmly modern, with etched mirrors. The menu offers warm and cold snacks, including sandwiches. The most popular late-night order is a grilled steak with french fries, and eating it at 3am is a Parisian tradition.

Campagne et Provence. 25 quai de la Tournelle, 5e. ☎ **01-43-54-05-17.** Reservations recommended. Fixed-price lunch 120F ($24); two-course fixed-price dinner 180F ($36); three-course fixed-price dinner 215F ($43). AE, MC, V. Tues–Fri 12:30–2pm; Mon–Sat 7:30–11pm. Métro: Maubert-Mutualité. PROVENÇAL.

This modestly priced restaurant rests across from the Ile de la Cité beside a quay. Bouquets of dried flowers garnish pale blue walls under which the upholstery hints of Provence's blue sky. The waiters are likely to speak with the modulated accents of southern France. The savory foods served here include a salad of wild Provençal mesclun garnished with Parmesan; aioli of codfish; a *pissaladière* (Provençal tart) flavored with onions or a combination of sardines and red mullet; and grilled fish served with risotto. A particularly tasty dessert is the anise-flavored crème brûlée.

Chez René. 14 bd. St-Germain, 5e. ☎ **01-43-54-30-23.** Reservations recommended. Main courses 76–170F ($15–$34); fixed-price lunch 153F ($31). MC, V. Mon–Fri 12:15–2:15pm; Mon–Sat 7:45–11pm. Métro: Maubert-Mutualité. FRENCH.

Restaurants like this used to be widespread, particularly on the Left Bank, but many became pizzerias. Established in 1957, Chez René maintains its allegiance to the tenets of French cuisine. The staff is often harassed, and the seating is cramped as only a bistro can be. The dining room isn't fancy, but its clients return loyally, often several nights a week, for the steady and reliable stream of food and the frequently changing plats du jour.

For an appetizer, try fresh wild mushrooms laced with butter and garlic or a platter of country-style sausages. You'll find such reliable old-time French fare as beef bourguignon and a dish of the day that might be pot-au-feu or blanquette de veau. Enjoy it all with a bottle of Beaujolais.

La Petite Hostellerie. 35 rue de la Harpe (just east of bd. St-Michel), 5e. ☎ **01-43-54-47-12.** Fixed-price menu 59F ($12) at lunch, 89F ($18) at dinner. AE, DC, MC, V. Métro: St-Michel or Cluny–La Sorbonne. FRENCH.

This place has two dining rooms: a usually crowded ground-floor one and a larger (seating 100) upstairs one with attractive 18th-century woodwork. People come for the cozy ambience and decor, decent French country cooking, polite service, and excellent prices. The fixed-price dinner menu might feature favorites like *coq au vin* (chicken in wine), *canard* (duckling) *à l'orange*, or *entrecôte à la moutarde* (steak with mustard sauce). Start with onion soup or stuffed mussels and finish with cheese or salad and *pêches Melba* (peach Melba) or *tarte aux pommes* (apple tart). Rue de la Harpe is a side street running north of boulevard St-Germain.

Perraudin. 157 rue Saint-Jacques, 5e. ☎ **01-46-33-15-75.** Reservations not accepted. Main courses 59F ($12); set-price lunch 63F ($13). No credit cards. Tues–Fri noon–2:15pm and Mon–Sat 7:30–10:15pm. Métro: Cluny–La Sorbonne. RER: Luxembourg. FRENCH.

Everything about this place—decor, cuisine, price, and service rituals—attempts to duplicate the bustling allure of the turn-of-the-century bistro. This one was built in 1870 as an outlet for coal and wine. (Because of its ownership by an Auvergnat—resident of an agrarian district in central France—it was known as a "*Boujnat,*" where both coal and wine were sold as remedies against the cold.) Eventually, the site evolved into the old-fashioned, wood-paneled bistro you'll see today, where very little has changed since Émile Zola was buried nearby in the Pantheon. Walls look like they've been marinated in tea for about a year; the marble-topped tables, old mirrors, and posters of Parisian vaudeville likely have been here forever.

Reservations aren't made in advance: Instead, clients usually drink a glass of kir at the zinc-topped bar as they wait. (Tables turn over quickly at this amazingly reasonable bistro.) Marie-Christine K'vella and her brother offer old-fashioned, completely standard dishes that include roast leg of lamb served with *dauphinois* potatoes; boeuf bourguignon; grilled salmon with sage sauce; or blanquette of veal. An onion tart, pumpkin soup, snails, or any of several pâtés and terrines precede the main course.

6th ARRONDISSEMENT (ST-GERMAIN/LUXEMBOURG)
VERY EXPENSIVE

✪ **Jacques Cagna.** 14 rue des Grands-Augustins, 6e. ☎ **01-43-26-49-39.** Reservations required. Main courses 230–389F ($46–$78); fixed-price lunch 270F ($54); fixed-price dinner 490F ($98). AE, DC, MC, V. Mon–Fri noon–2pm; Mon–Sat 7:30–10:30pm. Closed 3 weeks in Aug. Métro: St-Michel. FRENCH.

St. Germain knows no finer dining than at Jacques Cagna, a sophisticated restaurant set in a 17th-century town house that bears massive timbers and has an interior swaddled in soft red colors and studded with 17th-century Dutch paintings. The main dining room is located a flight above street level.

Jacques Cagna is one of the best classically trained chefs in Paris, yet has become a half-apostle to the cuisine moderne. This is evident in his delectable carpaccio of pearly sea bream with a caviar-lavished *céleric rémoulade* (celery root in a mayonnaise sauce tinged with capers, parsley, gherkins, spring onions, chervil, chopped tarragon, and anchovy essence). Other dishes, such as rack of veal with ginger and lime sauce, and fried scallops served with celery and potatoes in a truffle sauce, are equally sublime. The menu is forever changing, according to the season and momentary inspirations, but if you're lucky, he'll offer his line-caught sea bass served with caviar in a potato shell when you visit.

EXPENSIVE

✪ **Closerie des Lilas.** 171 bd. du Montparnasse, 6e. ☎ **01-40-51-34-50.** Reservations required. Main courses 190–250F ($38–$50). Brasserie main courses 90–130F ($18–$26). AE, DC, MC, V. Restaurant daily noon–3pm and 7:30pm–midnight. Brasserie daily 11:30am–1am. Métro: Port-Royal or Vavin. FRENCH.

The famous people who have sat in the Closerie watching the leaves blow along the streets are almost countless: Gertrude Stein, Ingres, Henry James, Chateaubriand, Picasso, Hemingway, Apollinaire, Lenin and Trotsky (at the chess board), and Whistler, who would expound on the "gentle art" of making enemies. Established in 1847, "the Pleasure Garden of the Lilacs" has ever since been a social and culinary monument to the avant-garde. Today the crowd is likely to include a sprinkling of stars and the starstruck.

It's tough to get a seat in what is called the *bateau* section of the restaurant, but you can make the wait a lot more enjoyable by ordering the best champagne julep in the world at the bar. What does it matter that the fickle guidebooks, including Michelin, have turned elsewhere? The food here is better than it was when the place was highly touted. By pushing open the door to Closerie you breath in a century and a half of French history as well as the aroma of classic good food. Try the veal kidneys with mustard or ribs of veal in a cider sauce.

Yugaraj. 14 rue Dauphine, 6e. ☎ **01-43-26-44-91.** Reservations recommended. Main courses 98–115F ($20–$23); fixed-price lunch 130–220F ($26–$44); fixed-price dinner 170–220F ($34–$44). AE, DC, MC, V. Tues–Sun noon–2:15pm, daily 7–11pm. Métro: Odeon. INDIAN.

Set within two floors of an old building in the Latin Quarter, this restaurant serves flavorful, moderately priced food based on the recipes of northern and, to a lesser degree, southern India. In rooms outfitted in vivid shades of "Indian pink," with formally dressed staff and lots of intricately carved Kashmiri panels and statues, you can sample the spicy, aromatic tandoori dishes that are becoming all the rage in France. Seafood specialties are usually concocted from warm-water fish imported to Rungis from the Seychelles, including species such as *thiof, capitaine,* and *bourgeois,* prepared as they would be in Calcutta, with tomatoes, onions, cumin, coriander, ginger, and garlic. Flavors are spicy and earthy, rich with mint and, sometimes, touches of yogurt.

INEXPENSIVE

Aux Charpentiers. 10 rue Mabillon, 6e. ☎ **01-43-26-30-05.** Reservations required. Main courses 71–185F ($14–$37); fixed-price menu 120F ($24) at lunch, 153F ($31) at dinner. AE, DC, MC, V. Daily noon–3pm and 7:30–11:30pm. Métro: Mabillon. FRENCH.

This bistro, established more than 130 years ago, was once the rendezvous of the master carpenters, whose guild was next door. Nowadays it's where the young men of St-Germain-des-Prés take their dates. Although the food is not especially imaginative, it is well prepared in the best tradition of *cuisine bourgeoise:* hearty but not refined. Appetizers include pâté of duck and rabbit terrine. Especially recommended as a main course is the roast duck with olives. The plats du jour recall French home cooking: salt pork with lentils, pot-au-feu, or stuffed cabbage. The wine list has a large selection of Bordeaux wines direct from the châteaus, including Château Gaussens.

Bistro de la Grille. 14 rue Mabillon, 6e. ☎ **01-43-54-16-87.** Reservations recommended. Main courses 70–110F ($14–$22); set lunch 95F ($19); set dinner 165F ($33). V. Daily noon–3:30pm and 7pm–12:30am. Limited menu available 3:30–7pm. Métro: Mabillon. FRENCH.

Many of your fellow diners at this arts-conscious bistro are likely to own, or work in, nearby fashionable boutiques. The bistro's popularity has survived since the French Revolution, when plots and counterplots were hatched among its clients, many of whom eventually ended up on the guillotine themselves. If you're alone, you might opt to dine at the bar near the entrance, surrounded by photos of film stars from the early years of the French-based Pathé cinema. There are tables on the bustling street level, as well as marginally more sedate ones set upstairs. Menu items arrive in generous portions, but are rarely daring. Examples include platters of fresh shellfish, as well as traditional versions of bone marrow spread over roughly textured bread, pot-au-feu, sautéed salmon with wild mushrooms, grilled steaks with french fries, and the old-fashioned but ever-popular (at least within France) veals' head with capers and a mayonnaise and mustard sauce. Desserts include traditional favorites (*tarte tatin, mousse au chocolat*) that most patrons remember from their childhood.

Restaurants: 5th & 6th Arrondissements

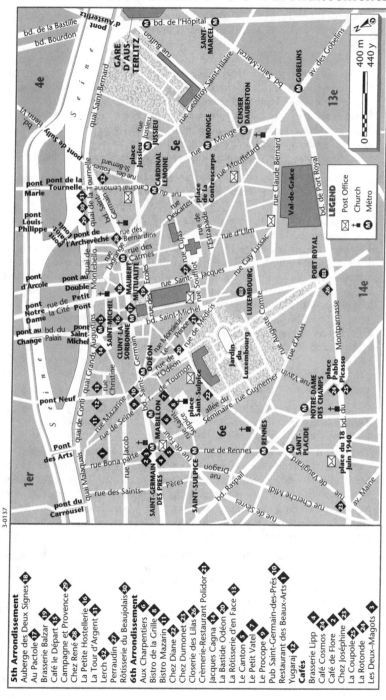

5th Arrondissement
Auberge des Deux Signes 18
Au Pactole 17
Brasserie Balzar 19
Café le Départ 15
Campagne et Provence 29
Chez René 28
La Petite Hostellerie 16
La Tour d'Argent 31
Lerch 27
Perraudin 32
Rôtisserie du Beaujolais 30

6th Arrondissement
Aux Charpentiers 6
Bistro de la Grille 8
Bistro Mazarin 11
Chez Diane 22
Chez Dumonet 23
Closerie des Lilas 26
Crémerie-Restaurant Polidor 21
Jacques Cagna 14
La Bastide Odéon 20
La Rôtisserie d'en Face 13
Le Canton 5
Le Petit Vatel 7
Le Procope 9
Pub Saint-Germain-des-Prés 10
Restaurant des Beaux-Arts 1
Yugaraj 12

Cafés
Brasserie Lipp 4
Café Cosmos 24
Café de Flore 2
Chez Joséphine 23
La Coupole 25
La Rotonde 24
Les Deux-Magots 3

3-0137

157

Bistro Mazarin. 42 rue Mazarine, 6e. ☎ **01-43-29-99-01.** Reservations recommended. Main courses 55–65F ($11–$13). AE, MC, V. Daily noon–3pm and 7:30pm–midnight. Métro: Odeon. FRENCH.

It bustles, it vibrates, and just about everyone inside associates with the shops or universities of the historic and highly commercial neighborhood around it. Within dining rooms whose wood paneling has been congenially battered throughout the years, you can order from a spectrum of dishes unaltered since France's collective childhood. Examples include a *petit salé* of pork, prepared like a stew, and beef bourguignon. Other good choices are veal chops sautéed with butter and lemon juice and an earthily satisfying combination of lentils with roughly textured *charcuterie* and herbs. Don't expect exaggerated pomp—this place is down-home, with a very Gallic flavor.

✪ **Chez Diane.** 25 rue Servandoni, 6e. ☎ **01-46-33-12-06.** Reservations recommended for groups of four or more. Main courses 90–130F ($18–$26); set menu 150F ($30). V. Mon–Fri noon–2pm and Mon–Sat 8–11:30pm. Métro: St-Sulpice. FRENCH.

Although its prices resemble a simple bistro's, its cuisine is closer to that of a fashionable restaurant. This is a function of the care and dedication displayed by the (relatively) new owners Didier and Diane Derrieux. Designed to accommodate only 40 diners at a time, the site is illuminated with Venetian glass chandeliers and paved with old-fashioned floor tiles manufactured near Aix-en-Provence. Inside, deep ochres and terra-cottas are redolent of the landscapes and villas of Provence. Chez Diane's offerings sway with the seasons, perishable ingredients, and their owners' inspirations. Recently we enjoyed a Toulouse-inspired cassoulet of fish with emulsified butter sauce; minced salmon prepared as a terrine with green peppercorns; and a modern, light-textured adaptation of a dish every French-born diner remembers from the kitchens of his or her grandmother, *hachis Parmentier,* an elegant meat loaf lightened with parsley, chopped onions, and herbs. Fish dishes are likely to include turbot with béarnaise sauce or stingray with a caper-flavored butter sauce.

Chez Dumonet (Chez Josephine). 117 rue du Cherche-Midi, 6e. ☎ **01-45-48-52-40.** Reservations recommended. Main courses 80–130F ($16–$26). AE, MC, V. Mon–Fri noon–2:30pm and 7:15–10:30pm. Closed: Aug. Métro: Duroc. LANDES.

Very little about this warm, intimate bistro has changed since it was established in the 1930s. The leather banquettes and rich patinas have never left, nor has the emphasis on classic and flavorful dishes that have withstood many hundreds of satisfied local residents. Opt for any of the specialties of Landes, on south-central France's Atlantic seaboard, which include beef bourguignon; foie gras, confit of duck, roasted pigeon in puff pastry, a flavorful roast saddle of lamb with artichokes, and roasted turbot with béarnaise sauce.

✪ **Crémerie-Restaurant Polidor.** 41 rue Monsieur-le-Prince, 6e. ☎ **01-43-26-95-34.** Reservations not accepted. Main courses 40–69F ($8–$14); fixed-price lunch (Mon–Fri) 55F ($11); fixed-price dinner 100F ($20). No credit cards. Daily noon–2:30pm; Mon–Sat 7pm–12:30am, Sun 7–11pm. Métro: Odeon. FRENCH.

Crémerie Polidor is the most traditional bistro in the Odeon area, serving the *cuisine familiale.* Its name dates from the early part of this century, when the restaurant specialized in frosted cream desserts, but the restaurant itself can trace its history back to 1845.

The Crémerie is one of the Left Bank's oldest and most established literary bistros. It was André Gide's favorite, and Hemingway, Valéry, Artaud, Joyce, and Kerouac also dined here. The place is still frequented largely by students and artists, who head for the rear.

Peer beyond the lace curtains and polished brass hat racks to see drawers in the back where repeat customers lock up their cloth napkins. Smiling overworked waitresses with frilly aprons and T-shirts bearing the likeness of old mère Polidor serve a 19th-century cuisine. Try the old-fashioned pumpkin soup followed by hearty portions of beef bourguignon or veal in white sauce. Equally satisfying is the *poulet basquaise* (Basque-style chicken). For dessert, get a chocolate, raspberry, or lemon tart—the best ones in all of Paris.

La Bastide Odeon. 7 rue Corneille, 6e. ☎ **01-43-26-03-65.** Reservations recommended. Set menus 139–180F ($28–$36). MC, V. Tues–Sat noon–3pm and 7:30–10:30pm. Métro: Odeon. RER: Luxembourg. PROVENÇAL.

Those who can't afford to rush off to southern France can alleviate some of their yearnings with a visit to a brasserie that's become a star amid the city's inexpensive restaurants. The sunny climes of Provence come through in pale yellow walls, heavy oaken tables, and artfully arranged bouquets of wheat and dried roses. Chef Gilles Ajuelos, formerly employed in some very grand Parisian restaurants, prepares a market-based Provençal cuisine that varies according to the freshness and availability of ingredients. His simplest first courses are the most satisfying, including a platter of sardines and seared sweet peppers with olive oil and pine nuts; grilled eggplant layered with herbs and oil; and roasted rabbit stuffed with eggplant and served with olive toast and balsamic vinegar. Main courses include wild duckling with pepper sauce, stuffed suckling pig with a gratin of polenta and Parmesan, and such exotica as lamb's feet and giblets prepared in the immemorial style of Provence. A recurrent winner among desserts is warm almond pie served with prune and Armagnac ice cream.

La Rôtisserie d'en Face. 2 rue Christine, 6e. ☎ **01-43-26-40-98.** Reservations recommended. Fixed-price menu 198F ($40). AE, MC, V. Mon–Fri noon–2:30pm; Mon–Sat 7–11pm. Métro: St-Michel. FRENCH.

This is the most frequented "chef–baby bistro" in Paris. It's operated by Jacques Cagna, whose vastly more expensive restaurant, which bears his name (see page 155), is across the street. The food, although simply prepared, is very good, using high quality ingredients. The place features a postmodern decor with high-tech lighting and black lacquer chairs; it's informal, and often very, very busy. Menu items include several types of ravioli, a pâté of duckling *en croûte* with foie gras, a *friture d'éperlans* (tiny fried freshwater fish), smoked Scottish salmon with spinach, and several varieties of fresh fish and grilled meats. Recently Monsieur Cagna has added pork cheeks to the menu; it's based on an old-fashioned recipe his mother passed down. His Barbary duckling in red wine sauce is incomparable.

Le Canton. 5 rue Goizlin, 6e. ☎ **01-43-26-51-86.** Set lunches 55–69F ($11–$14); set dinners 75–90F ($15–$18). Main courses 40–59F ($8–$12). MC, V. Mon–Sat noon–2:30pm and 7–11pm. Métro: St-Germain-des-Prés. CHINESE/VIETNAMESE.

The cuisine is exotic, especially the Vietnamese dishes, and the setting is relaxing and evocative of faraway Asia. Best of all, the food is as affordable as virtually anything else within the district, and a lot more savory than what you'll find at the fast-food joints that lie nearby. Begin a meal with any of several versions of *nem* (Vietnamese ravioli) stuffed with shrimp and vegetables. Delicate dim sum are available, as well as such main courses as "salt and pepper shrimp," Szechuan-style chicken, and one of the best-selling dishes in the house, the "Yorkson shrimp" quick-fried with garlic, peppers, and onions. Soups here are succulent and tasty, and throughout the repertoire, the chefs rely on ample use of basil, the smell of which permeates the establishment's two dining rooms.

Le Petit Vatel. 5 rue Lobineau, 6e. ☎ **01-43-54-28-49.** Main courses 45–55F ($9–$11); two-course fixed-price lunch 70F ($14). MC, V. Tues–Sat noon–3pm and 7pm–midnight. Closed Dec 25 to Jan 1. Métro: Mabilion (then walk up rue Mabilion and turn left unto rue Lobineu) or Odeon. FRENCH.

One of Paris's best buys, Le Petit Vatel has 22 seats (plus a few more on the sidewalk in the summer) in a pocket-sized dining room where tables and chairs jostle each other for position. Marie Bosquet is the amusing and hardworking owner. Until 1990, she prepared most of her meals in the dining room on a pink-sided cookstove made in 1914. (Not-so-nostalgic fire marshals ordered her to remove it; framed photos commemorate the good old days.) The daily specials may be stuffed cabbage, rice sautéed with seafood, moussaka, or roast chicken; all come with a vegetable or salad. A local favorite is pamboli, a Catalan specialty with grilled bread, olive oil, tomato sauce, cured ham, and mountain cheese. The two-course lunch consists of a choice of an appetizer, cheese or dessert, and a choice of the daily special or a *plat garni*. A candlelit meal here is something you'll remember for a long time.

Le Procope. 13 rue de l'Ancienne-Comédie, 6e. ☎ **01-40-46-79-00.** Reservations recommended. Main courses 82–148F ($16–$30); fixed-price menu 115F ($23) 11:30am–8pm; 175F ($35) all day; 125F ($25) after 11pm. AE, DC, MC, V. Daily 11:30am–1am. Métro: Odeon. FRENCH.

Le Procope, opened in 1686 by a Sicilian named Francesco Procopio dei Coltelli, is the oldest cafe in Paris. Now more restaurant than cafe, it is sumptuously decorated with gilt-framed mirrors, antique portraits of former illustrious clients, crystal chandeliers, banquettes of Bordeaux-colored leather, and marble-topped tables.

Voltaire, Benjamin Franklin, Rousseau, Anatole France, Robespierre, Danton, Marat, a youthful Bonaparte, Balzac (who drank endless cups of very strong coffee), and Verlaine (who preferred absinthe, now illegal) all dropped by in their day. There are two levels for dining: two rooms downstairs, five rooms upstairs. Fresh oysters and shellfish are served from a chilled display. A well-chosen selection of classic French dishes is presented, including baby duckling with spices and "green coffee," fillet of beef with peppercorns, and "drunken chicken." The food is typical brasserie fare, but few places have the nostalgia of this old and venerated cafe. Its major drawback is that it's too famous—everybody wants to venerate it at once.

Pub Saint-Germain-des-Prés. 17 rue de l'Ancienne-Comédie, 6e. ☎ **01-43-29-38-70.** Reservations not required. Bottle of beer 28–75F ($6–$15); meals 48–150F ($10–$30). AE, DC, MC, V. 24 hours. Métro: Odeon. FRENCH/MIDDLE OF THE NIGHT.

For late-night drinking and snacking, this is one of the most popular spots on the Left Bank. The pub offers one of the best beer selections in France, with 26 varieties on tap and 500 international beers by the bottle. There are nine different rooms and 600 seats, making it the largest pub in France. Sit in one of the leather booths and enjoy a great late-night snack. Rock and variety bands play every night from 10:30pm to at least 3:30am.

Restaurant des Beaux-Arts. 11 rue Bonaparte, 6e. ☎ **01-43-26-92-64.** Reservations recommended. Fixed-price menu 75F ($15), including wine. No credit cards. Daily noon–2:30pm and 7–10:45pm. Métro: St-Germain-des-Prés. FRENCH.

Located across from Paris's École Nationale Supererieure des Beaux-Arts (School of Fine Arts), this is the most famous budget restaurant in Paris. Does it please everyone? Hardly. Are there complaints about bad food and service? Some. Is it packed everyday with hungry patrons? Inevitably. That means it must please thousands of diners every year, drawn to its cheap prices, large portions, and stick-to-the-ribs dishes, all featured on a set menu. The place still captivates the starving students of the Latin Quarter.

The best tables are upstairs, but if you can get a place on the main floor you can see the steaming pots in the open kitchen. This is what a provincial French family might cook at home—*bourguignon navarin d'agneau* (lamb chops cooked with carrots, onions, and tomatoes); *lapin sauce moutarde* (rabbit leg with mustard sauce); codfish fillet with garlic sauce; and a French staple that doesn't always appeal to foreigners, blanquette de veau.

7th ARRONDISSEMENT (EIFFEL TOWER/MUSÉE D'ORSAY)
VERY EXPENSIVE

L'Arpège. 84 rue de Varenne, 7e. ☎ **01-47-05-09-06.** Reservations required. Main courses 240–320F ($48–$64); fixed-price lunch 320F ($64); *menu dégustation* 690F ($138). AE, DC, MC, V. Mon–Fri noon–2pm and 7:30–10pm; Fri–Sun 7:30-9:45pm. Métro: Varenne. FRENCH.

One of the least expensive of Paris's three-star restaurants, L'Arpège is where chef Alain Passard prepares adventurous and divine culinary specialties. No restaurant in the 7th serves better food. The restaurant is in a prosperous residential neighborhood, across from the Rodin Museum on the site of what for years was the world-famous l'Archestrate, where Passard worked in the kitchens.

Amid an intensely cultivated modern decor of etched glass, burnished steel, monochromatic oil paintings, and pearwood paneling, you can enjoy specialties that some have heralded as being among the most innovative to emerge in recent culinary history. Some of his latest creations include Breton lobster in a sweet-and-sour rosemary sauce, scallops prepared with cauliflower and a lime-flavored grape sauce, and panfried duck with juniper and lime sauce, followed by the signature dessert, a candied tomato stuffed with 12 kinds of dried and fresh fruit and served with anise-flavored ice cream.

EXPENSIVE

✪ **Le Violin d'Ingres.** 135 rue St-Dominique, 7e. ☎ **01-45-55-15-05.** Reservations required. Main courses 80–130F ($16–$26); fixed-price menu 240F ($48) at lunch, 290F ($58) at dinner. AE, MC, V. Mon–Fri noon–2:30pm and 7:15–10:30pm. Métro: École Militaire. FRENCH.

This is it, the restaurant that is quickly becoming Paris's *pièce de résistance.* For a chance to experience chef/owner Christian Constant's gastronomic masterpieces, you have to reserve a table a minimum of three to four days in advance. There is talk that Monsieur Constant will be "the new Robuchon," although many Parisian chefs are vying for that lofty position. Those who are fortunate enough to dine here in the Violin's warm atmosphere of rose-colored wood, soft cream walls, and elegant chintz fabrics patterned with old English tea roses always rave about the cleverly artistic dishes. They range from a starter of panfried foie gras with gingerbread and spinach salad to more elegant main courses such as lobster ravioli with crushed vine-ripened tomatoes, roasted veal in a light and creamy milk sauce served with tender spring vegetables, or even a selection from the popular rôtisserie, like leg of lamb rubbed with fresh garlic and thyme. Even his familiar dishes seem new at each tasting. Chef Constant keeps a copious and well-chosen selection of wine to accompany any of his overwhelmingly satisfying meals. The service is charming and discreet.

Paul Minchelli. 54 bd. de la Tour-Maubourg, 7e. ☎ **01-47-05-89-86.** Reservations required. Main courses 160–350F ($32–$70). MC, V. Tues–Sat noon–3pm and 8–11pm. Métro: La Tour Maubourg. SEAFOOD.

This restaurant had an immediate and powerful impact on the Paris dining scene upon its arrival in 1994. The chef is said to have reinvented fish (or at least the way we cook it) by stripping away extra sauces and conflicting flavors to reveal a true "taste of the sea." Much of this restaurant's appeal derives from its deliberate earthiness, its refusal to indulge in the gratuitously pretentious rituals of some of its competitors. Its founder is Marseille-born Paul Minchelli, whose cuisine is described even by his financial backers as "marginal," having breached this city's culinary conventions for an old-fashioned Provençal technique he learned over the bouillabaisse pots of his childhood. Some of the shellfish is so fresh it might have been scooped from an aquarium just moments before it was cooked.

In a dining room lined with Norwegian birchwood that's been stained to a distinctive tone of yellow and outfitted with modern furniture and round seascapes evocative of the portholes on a ship, you can order such dishes as raw saltwater fish served only with olive oil, salt, and pepper; an old-fashioned recipe known as *merlan Colbert;* grilled John Dory; and fillet of sea bass steamed in seaweed. Other popular dishes include lobster cooked with honey and spices and one of the best versions of herring salad in Paris. Be warned: There aren't many alternatives for those who dislike fish.

MODERATE

L'Affriolé. 17 rue Malar, 7e. ☎ **01-44-18-31-33.** Reservations required. Set menu 180F ($36). MC, V. Mon–Sat noon–2:30pm and 7:30–11:30pm. Closed 3 weeks in Aug. Métro: Invalides. FRENCH.

Fine food, reasonable prices, and simplicity have guaranteed this upscale bistro's burgeoning business. The prices apply to some remarkably sophisticated (and normally expensive) raw ingredients because, as owners Véronique and Alain Atibard say, "One has to know how to buy." Consequently they make early-morning bulk purchases three times a week at Rungis, the wholesale food suppliers north of Paris and watch loyal clients line up by the dozen for a table within a long and narrow, deliberately old-fashioned Art Deco dining room. The house staple is the fixed-price menu—they refer to it as a "menu-carte." It includes an "amuse-bouche," a starter (often concocted with some derivation of foie gras), a main course (worthy choices include a jarret of glazed and roasted pork or scallops with lime juice), a cheese, a "pre-dessert" (pear tarte, caramelized banana), and a dessert (crêpes stuffed with quince marmalade, chocolate soup, or clafoutis with grapes were all available during our recent visit). In most of these stages, seven options are available, each of which changes at frequent intervals. If you're not feeling particularly hungry, you can order a two-course menu (starter and main course) for 140 ($28), although here, the vast majority opt for the six-course medley.

Le Bambouche. 15 rue de Babylone, 7e. ☎ **01-45-49-14-40.** Reservations recommended. Main courses 100–150F ($20–$30). Set menu 190F ($38). AE, MC, V. Mon–Fri noon–2:30pm and 8–11pm. Métro: Sèvres-Babylone. NORTHERN FRENCH.

The fact that it's relatively new, and still struggling to gain a niche, contributes to prices that are more reasonable than you'd expect for cuisine with this degree of finesse. Established in 1995 by a denizen of Lille, David van Laer, it offers a gastronomic focus presented within a cozy dining room whose colors of dark ocher and burnt orange were inspired by the excavations of ancient Pompeii. Menu items change with the season: Examples include raw crayfish served with rémoulade sauce and a galette of Parmesan; a papillotte of scallops and foie gras served with a confit of turnips; and young guineau fowl prepared with pears and fresh truffles. Dessert might consist of a hot chocolate soufflé, which guests should order at the beginning of the meal.

La Petite Chaise. 36–38 rue de Grenelle, 7e. ☎ **01-42-22-13-35.** Reservations required. Fixed-price menu 150–180F ($30–$36). AE, MC, V. Daily noon–2:15pm and 7–11pm. Métro: Sèvres-Babylone. FRENCH.

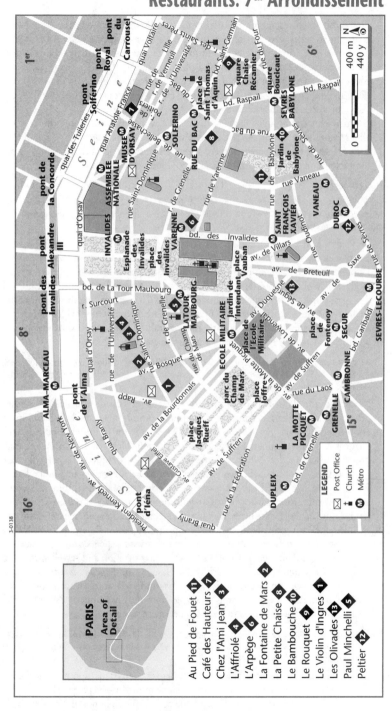

Restaurants: 7th Arrondissement

Au Pied de Fouet **11**
Café des Hauteurs **7**
Chez l'Ami Jean **3**
L'Affriolé **4**
L'Arpège **6**
La Fontaine de Mars **2**
La Petite Chaise **8**
Le Bambouche **10**
Le Rouquet **9**
Le Violin d'Ingres **1**
Les Olivades **13**
Paul Minchelli **5**
Peltier **12**

163

This is the oldest restaurant in Paris, established by the Baron de la Chaise in 1680 as an inn at the edge of what at the time was a large hunting preserve. (According to popular lore, the baron used the upstairs bedrooms for midafternoon dalliances, which he conducted between fox and pheasant hunts.) Very Parisian, the "Little Chair" invites you into a world of cramped but attractive tables, very old wood paneling, and ornate wall sconces. Guests choose from a four-course set menu with a large choice of dishes within each category.

A new chef has brought renewed taste and flavor to this longtime favorite. Samplings from the menu might include salad with strips of duck breast on a bed of fresh lettuce; fillet of beef prepared with green peppercorns; and poached fish with steamed vegetables served in a sauce of fish and vegetable stock and cream.

INEXPENSIVE

Au Pied de Fouet. 45 rue de Babylone, 7e. ☎ **01-47-05-12-27.** Reservations not necessary. Main courses 45–65F ($9–$13). No credit cards. Mon–Sat noon–2:30pm and Mon–Fri 7–9:30pm. Métro: Vaneau. FRENCH.

Au Pied de Fouet is one of the smallest restaurants in the neighborhood, and preserves one of its longest histories and some of its most reasonable prices. In the 1700s it was a stopover for carriages en route to Paris from other parts of Europe, offering wine, food, and stabling. Don't expect a leisurely or attentive meal: Food and drink will disappear quickly from your table, under the gaze of others waiting their turn. Dishes are solid and unpretentious, and include blanquette of veal (veal in white sauce), *petit salé* (a savory stew made from pork and vegetables), and such fish dishes as sole meunière, a cliché of French cuisine but always good.

Chez l'Ami Jean. 27 rue Malar, 7e. ☎ **01-47-05-86-89.** Reservations recommended. Main courses 75–95F ($15–$19). V. Mon–Sat noon–3pm and 7–10:30pm. Métro: Invalides. BASQUE/SOUTHWESTERN FRENCH.

Its ardent fans claim that its presentation of Basque cuisine and Basque cultural preoccupations is the most authentic and uncompromising on the Left Bank. It was established by a Basque nationalist in 1931, and is today maintained by Pierre Pagueguy, who remembers his Basque hometown of Hasparren in intimate detail. You'll dine amid a decor that's as close to an authentic Basque *auberge* (inn) as any other in Paris. Wood panels, memorabilia from *pelote* (a Basque game much like *jai alai*) and soccer, and red and white woven tablecloths like the ones sold in Bayonne are the norm, along with a bent bar-goer or two sporting the Basque nation's headwarmer of choice, the beret. Menu items include cured Bayonne ham; earthy and herb-laden Béarn-influenced vegetable soups; marinated anchovies and fresh duck liver; a succulent omelette (*piperade basque*) laden with peppers, tomatoes, and onions; *chipirons à la Basquaise* (squid) stewed in their own ink and served with tomatoes and herbs; and the poultry dish of the Basque world, *poulet basquaise,* cooked with spicy sausage, onions, peppers, and very strong red wine. In springtime, look for a truly esoteric specialty rarely available from nearby competitors: saumon de l'Adour (Adour river salmon) served with béarnaise sauce.

La Fontaine de Mars. 129 rue Saint-Dominique, 7e. ☎ **01-47-05-46-44.** Reservations recommended. Main courses 65–130F ($13–$26). AE, MC, V. Mon–Sat noon–2:30pm and 7:30–11pm. Métro: École-Militaire. FRENCH.

Don't think that the name of this restaurant derives from its location near the Champ de Mars. Instead, its namesake is an ornate stone fountain—its plaque shows Hygeia offering a drink to Mars—carved during the early 1800s in honor of Napoléon's victories, that sits on a tree-lined terrace. By the fountain, an additional 70 or so seats become available whenever weather permits. On the street level, you'll find an animated, sometimes boisterous dining room, plus two cozier and calmer upstairs rooms whose round tables and wooden floors seem to belong to a private home. Much of the cuisine here derives from the Pyrénées and southwestern France, bearing rich heady flavors that go well with robust red wines. Examples include a confit of duckling with parsley potatoes; veal chops with morels; fillets of red mullet or monkfish with herb-flavored butter; and other examples from a list of food traditionally associated with traditional bistros in Paris. Our favorite dessert is a thin tart filled with a sugared purée of apples, capped with more apple, and garnished with calvados and cream.

13th ARRONDISSEMENT (GOBELINS/PORTE D'IVRY)
MODERATE

Auberge Etchegorry. 41 rue Croulebarbe, 13e. ☎ **01-44-08-83-50.** Reservations recommended. Set-price menus 140–215F ($28–$43). AE, MC, V. Mon–Sat noon–2:30pm and 7:30–10:30pm. Métro: Gobelins or Censier. BASQUE.

Its windows overlook a verdant patch of lawn that's so green you might for a moment imagine that you've entered a rustic inn deep within the countryside. Dark paneling, deep colors, hanging hams and pigtails of garlic, and lacy curtains emulate the Basque country, the corner of southwestern France adjacent to Spain, that gastronomes prize for succulent cuisine. The only drawback involves cramped tables, although in this atmosphere, constricted seems to matter less. The menu includes a standardized roster of Basque or southwestern French specialties, including cassoulet, magret of duckling, fillet of beef with peppercorns, the peppery omelettes known as *piperades, cocottes* of mussels, and foie gras configured both as terrines or as panfried slices. If you opt to dine here, you won't be alone—Victor Hugo and Chateaubriand ate at this auberge in centuries past. There's a comfortable and unpretentious three-star hotel associated with the restaurant.

INEXPENSIVE

Keryado. 32 rue de Regnault, 13e. ☎ **01-45-83-87-58.** Reservations recommended. Main courses 80–180F ($16–$36); set-price menus 110–150F ($22–$30). MC, V. Mon–Sat noon–2:30pm and Tues–Sat 7:30–10:30pm. Métro: Porte d'Ivry. SEAFOOD.

Since it was taken over by a sophisticated management in 1992, this all-blue-and-white seafood bistro has made a name for itself because of its preparation of a dish that only the most dedicated or arrogant chef would presume to make in his or her own kitchen: bouillabaisse. Priced at the relatively modest figure of 170F ($34) per person, much less than at grander restaurants, making bouillabaisse has led to more lost reputations, crack-ups, and suicides than any other dish in the storied history of French cuisine. Fortunately, the version at Keryado is as rich, as savory, and as satisfying as those served in some of the best restaurants of Provence. If bouillabaisse isn't your cup of soup, consider such other fish dishes as a *chaudrée* (stewpot) *de poissons aïoli,* composed of fillets from six different types of fish and laced with a rich garlicky broth. Slightly more experimental is a *profiterolle* of stingray with endive and curry.

14th & 15th ARRONDISSEMENT (GARE MONTPARNASSE/ DENFERT-ROCHEREAU)
MODERATE

Chez Lulu (L'Assiette). 181 rue du Château, 14e. ☎ **01-43-22-64-86.** Reservations recommended. Main courses 100–180F ($20–$36). AE, MC, V. Wed–Sun noon–2pm and 8–10:30pm. Closed: Aug. Métro: Pernety. PYRENEE.

⭐ A Few of Our Dining Favorites

- **Peltier,** 66 rue de Sevrès, 7e. ☎ **01-47-34-06-62.** The best *tarte au chocolat* in Paris. Métro: Vaneau/Duroc.

- **Le Carrousel,** 194 rue de Rivoli, 1er. ☎ **01-42-60-63-28.** We think its *croque-monsieur* is the most authentic in Paris. Métro: Palais-Royal.

- **Chez Joséphine,** 117 rue du Cherche-Midi, 6e. ☎ **01-45-48-52-40.** A 19th-century bistro with an *omelette aux truffes* (omelette with truffles) worth crossing town to eat. Métro: Croix-Rouge.

- **Café Cosmos,** 101 bd. du Montparnasse, 6e. ☎ **01-43-26-74-36.** Does today's generation have a cafe to equal the Lost Generation's Select or Coupole? Perhaps it's the ultramodern Cosmos. Today you might rub elbows with a French film star or executive ("no one writes novels anymore"). The cafe features black tables, black leather chairs, and black clothing in winter—just the backdrop for smoked salmon with toast. Métro: Vavin.

- **Les Olivades,** 41 av. de Ségur, 7e. ☎ **01-47-83-70-09.** Puts to shame restaurants that play at cooking Provençal. Nimes-born Flore Mikula is the real thing, inviting you into her cozy world evoking memories of the land of the Mistral. Near the Champs de Mars, Les Olivades is filled with the zest and authenticity of Provence—from delicate goat cheese and meaty black olives bathed in a rich tomato sauce to batter-fried zucchini blossoms drizzled with an herb-flavored vinaigrette. Métro: St-Fr.-Xavier.

Everything about this place seems to appeal to a clientele that seeks nostalgia in tandem with down-to-earth prices and flavorful food. Mitterrand used to drop in here, along with political cronies, for his favorite platters of oysters, crayfish, sea urchins, and clams. The setting was conceived as a *charcuterie* (pork butcher's shop) in the 1930s, and today maintains some old accessories. You'll recognize it behind a Bordeaux-colored facade with windows accented with potted plants. Menu items are unashamedly inspired by Paris's long tradition of bistro cuisine, along with a handful of twists added by the *patronne* and sometimes chef, Lulu Rousseau. Examples include a salad of chanterelle mushrooms; rabbit pâté with sausage; *rillettes* (a roughly textured pâté) of mackerel; sea bass with a butter and red wine sauce; roasted guinea fowl; and desserts made on the premises, including a crumbly version of apple cake served with fresh North African figs.

La Régalade. 49 av. Jean-Moulin, 14e. ☎ **01-45-45-68-58.** Reservations recommended. Set menu 170F ($34). Mon–Fri noon–2:15pm and Mon–Sat 7pm–midnight. Closed: Mid-July to mid-Aug. Métro: Alésia. SOUTHWESTERN FRENCH.

The setting is that of a crowded, convivial bistro with banquettes the color of aged Bordeaux wine, congenially harassed service, and unexpectedly good food. Priced at an unchanging rate, the obligatory set menu presents a choice of at least 10 starters, 10 main courses, and either one of about a dozen freshly made desserts or selections from a cheese tray. The inspiration is Yves Camdeborde's, known for his training at the frighteningly posh Hotel de Crillon. The menu changes with the seasons, but is likely to include fillet of *marcassin* (wild boar) prepared with red wine sauce; exotic mushrooms simmered with basil; a savory mixture of potatoes with blood sausage; and an always-popular platter of fried goose liver served on toasted slices of spice bread.

Restaurant Bleu. 46 rue Didot, 14e. ☎ **01-45-43-70-56.** Reservations recommended. Set menus 100–160F ($20–$32). MC, V. Mon–Fri noon–2:30pm; Mon–Sat 7:30–10:15. Closed: Aug. Métro: Alésia. AUVERGNAT.

Why is this restaurant named blue? The answer is no secret—it's in honor of the blue eyes of the chef and owner, Elie Bousquet, and the blue skies of his native Auvergne, the rocky, agrarian region of south-central France known for rich flavors and succulent pork dishes. Even the decor will remind you of a market town's inn—dark paneling, farm implements, paintings of barnyard animals (especially sheep), and souvenirs of another time. The hostess, who speaks English, recommends a house specialty (*truffade des bergers*) to anyone who doesn't know a *saucisson* from a *saucisse*. Made with potatoes, goose fat, Auvergnat cheese, and parsley, it's a worthy opener for such main courses as grilled Charolais beefsteak served with a sauce made from the heady red wine of Cahors; grilled *boudin* (blood sausage); confit of duckling; stuffed cabbage; and braised shoulder of pork. Prune tarts make a flavorful ending. There are only about 40 places here, so advance reservations are important.

Restaurant du Marché. 57–59 rue de Dantzig, 15e. ☎ **01-48-28-31-55.** Reservations recommended. Main courses 140–170F ($28–$34). Set menu 190F ($38). AE, DC, MC, V. Mon–Fri noon–2:30pm and Mon–Sat 7:30–11pm. Métro: Porte-de-Versailles. LANDES.

Very little about the decor of this place has changed since the 1930s, although you'll get the feeling that the wood panels are waxed and shined, and bouquets of fresh flowers are brought in at frequent intervals. Very little has changed with the classic French cuisine, either. Menu items derive from dishes popular in and around Bordeaux, and include an impressive roster of wines from that region to accompany the heaping platters of traditional foie gras, *daube* of beef; *cassoulet* in the style of Toulouse prepared with goose meat and white beans; deboned hare stuffed with foie gras and braised in red wine and brandy; and hen stewed with vegetables and Armagnac. Incidentally, the restaurant's name derives from the fact that many of its fresh, unusual ingredients are supplied directly by producers in the Landes district, near Bordeaux.

6 The Best Cafes

Parisians use cafes as combination club/tavern/snack bars, almost as extensions of their living rooms. They are spots where you can read your newspaper or meet a friend, do your homework or write your memoirs, nibble at a hard-boiled egg or drink yourself into oblivion. At cafes you meet your dates to go on to a show or to stay and talk. Above all, cafes are for people-watching.

Their single common denominator is the encouragement of leisurely sitting. Regardless of whether you have one small coffee or the most expensive cognac in the house, nobody badgers, pressures, or hurries you. If you wish to sit here until the place closes, that's your affair. For the cafe is one of the few truly democratic institutions—a solitary soda buys you the same view and sedentary pleasure as an oyster dinner.

Coffee, of course, is the chief drink. It comes black in a small cup, unless you specifically order it *au lait* (with milk). Tea (*thé*, pronounced *tay*) is also fairly popular, but is generally not of a high quality.

If you prefer beer, we advise you to pay a bit more for the imported German, Dutch, or Danish brands, which are much better than the local brew. If you insist on a French beer, at least order it *à pression* (draft), which is superior. There is also a vast variety of fruit drinks, as well as Coca-Cola, which is far more expensive in Paris than in North America.

French chocolate drinks—either hot or iced—are absolutely superb and on par with the finest Dutch brands. They're made from ground chocolate, not a chemical compound.

Cafes keep flexible hours, depending on the season, the traffic, and the part of town they're in. Nearly all of them stay open until 1 or 2am, and a few are open all night.

Now just a few words on cafe etiquette. You don't pay when you get your order—only when you intend to leave. Payment indicates that you've had all you want. *Service compris* means the tip is included in your bill, so it really isn't necessary to tip extra; still, feel free to leave an extra franc or so if the service has been attentive.

You'll hear the locals call the *garçon*, but as a foreigner it would be more polite to say *monsieur*. *All* waitresses, on the other hand, are addressed as *mademoiselle*, regardless of age or marital status.

In the smaller cafes, you may have to share your table. In that case, even if you haven't exchanged a word with your table companion, when you leave it is customary to bid them good-bye with a perfunctory *messieurs et dames*.

Brasserie Lipp. 151 bd. St-Germain, 6e. ☎ **01-45-48-53-91.** Full meals average 220F ($44); café au lait 18F ($3.60). Daily 9am–1am; restaurant service noon–2:30am. Métro: St-Germain-des-Prés.

On the day of Paris's liberation in 1944, former owner Roger Cazes (now deceased) spotted Hemingway, the first man to drop in for a drink. Then as now, famous people often drop by the Lipp for its beer, wine, and conversation. Cazes's nephew, Michel-Jacques Perrochon, now runs this quintessential Parisian brasserie. The food is secondary, yet quite good, providing you can get a seat (an hour and a half waiting time is customary if you're not familiar to the management). The specialty is *choucroute garni,* the best sauerkraut in Paris. You not only get sauerkraut, but a thick layer of ham and braised pork as well. It can be downed with the house Riesling or beer. You may also enjoy the gigot of lamb or the beef cooked in a salt shell. You can perch on a banquette, admiring your face reflected in the "hall of mirrors" while taking in the activity at this stylish nerve center in the neighborhood around St. Germain. The Lipp was opened in 1870–71, following the Franco-Prussian War, when its founder, Léonard Lipp, fled German-occupied territory for Paris. It's been a Parisian tradition ever since, with a staff known for its temperamental ways. Even if you don't go inside for a drink, you can sit at a sidewalk cafe table to enjoy a cognac and people-watch.

Café Beaubourg. 100 rue St-Martin, 4e. ☎ **01-48-87-63-96.** Glass of wine 22–35F ($4–$7), beer 26–45F ($5–$9), American breakfast 110F ($22), sandwiches and platters 30–120F ($6–$24). Sun–Thurs 8am–1am, Sat–Sun from 8am–2am. Métro: Rambuteau or Hôtel-de-Ville.

Located across the all-pedestrian plaza from the Centre Pompidou, this is an avant-garde cafe with soaring concrete columns and a minimalist decor designed by the noted architect Christian de Portzamparc. Many of the regulars work in the neighborhood's eclectic shops and galleries. In warm weather, tables are set up on the sprawling outdoor terrace, providing a great place to watch the young and the restless go by.

Café de Flore. 172 bd. St-Germain, 6e. ☎ **01-45-48-55-26.** Café espresso 24F ($5), glass of beer 42F ($8). Daily from 7am to 1:30am. Métro: St-Germain-des-Prés.

Sartre, the granddaddy of existentialism, a key figure in the Resistance movement, and a renowned cafe-sitter, often came here during World War II. Wearing a leather jacket and beret, he sat at his table and wrote his trilogy, *Les Chemins de la Liberté* (*The Roads to Freedom*). In *A Memoir in the Form of a Novel* (*Two Sisters*), Gore Vidal introduces his two main characters with, "I first saw them at the Café de Flore in the summer of 1948. They were seated side by side at the center of the first row of sidewalk tables, quite outshining Sartre and de Beauvoir, who were holding court nearby." Camus, Picasso, and Apollinaire also frequented the Flore. The cafe is still going strong, although the famous ones have moved on, and tourists have taken up all the tables.

Café de l'Industrie. 16 rue St-Sabin, 11e. ☎ **01-47-00-13-53.** Reservations not accepted. Glasses of wine 16–26F ($3–$5). Main courses 48–65F ($10–$13). MC, V. Sun–Fri 11am–2am. Métro: Bastille or Breguier-Sabin.

Founded just before the outbreak of World War II, this cafe received a vital new lease on life, and new floods of business, after the nearby opening of the Opéra de la Bastille. Today, amid three dining rooms and a decor that manages to evoke aspects of both the tropics and faux-baroque Europe, it combines generous platters of food with green plants and lots of original oil paintings by long-term clients. If you opt to drop in for just a glass of wine, you won't be alone: Known for decanting obscure vintages from the Touraine and the region around Beaujolais, it appeals to photographers and lesser-known characters within French-speaking show biz. If you're hungry, consider any of the plats du jour, which arrive in generous portions that are based on long-term staples of the French *brasserie* tradition. Examples include leeks steeped in vinaigrette; creamed fillets of codfish; boeuf bourguignon, fried haddock, and such pasta dishes as tagliatelle flavored with salmon, chives, and cream sauce.

Café de la Paix. Place de l'Opéra, 9e. ☎ **01-40-07-30-20.** Café espresso 19F ($4); fixed-price menu 119F ($24) for two course, 159F ($32) for three courses; daily specials 90F ($18). Daily from 10am–1am; meals 11am–1am. Métro: Opéra.

This hub of the tourist world rules the place de l'Opéra, and the legend goes that if you sit here long enough, you'll see someone you know passing by. Huge, grandiose, frighteningly fashionable, and sometimes brusque and anonymous, it harbors not only Parisians, but, at one time or another, nearly every visiting American—a tradition dating from the end of World War I. Once Émile Zola sat on the terrace; later, Hemingway and Fitzgerald frequented it. The best news for tourists who stop in for a bite is that prices have recently been lowered because of stiffer competition in the area.

Café des Hauteurs. In the Musée d'Orsay, 1 rue de Bellechasse, 7e. ☎ **01-40-49-48-14.** Reservations not accepted. "Suggestions du Jour" 30–45F ($6–$9). AE, MC, V. Tues–Wed and Fri–Sun 10am–5pm, Thurs 10am–9pm. Métro: Solférino. RER: Musée d'Orsay. FRENCH.

The designers of the Musée d'Orsay recognized the crushing fatigue that can sometimes accompany an attentive tour of their monument. Consequently, if you ascend to the museum's fifth floor, you're likely to find yourself in something midway between a short-term rest home and a bar. Here, before a sweeping view that stretches as far as Notre-Dame and Sacré-Coeur, and looks over the glass-encased mechanism of a clock that resembles London's Big Ben, you can recuperate. In addition to the usual doses of caffeine and alcohol, you can order platters that somehow are more substantial than a snack, but less filling than the main course of a conventional meal. Examples include terrine of roebuck, or a platter of assorted cheeses.

Café Marly. Cour Napoléon du Louvre, 93 rue de Rivoli, 1er. ☎ **01-49-26-06-60.** Reservations recommended. Main courses 90–140F ($18–$28). AE, DC, MC, V. Daily 8am–2am; meals noon–3pm and 8–11pm. Métro: Palais-Royal or Musée-du-Louvre.

In 1994, the French government gave the green light for a cafe and restaurant to open in one of the most historic courtyards of the Louvre. It's accessible only from a point close to the famous glass pyramid that rises above the Cour Marly, and has become a favorite refuge for Parisians trying to escape the roar of traffic. Anyone is welcome to sit down for a café au lait (anytime between 8am and 2am daily, whenever meals are not being served), which costs 32F ($6). More substantial fare is the norm here, served in one of three different dining rooms, each outfitted in tones of burgundy, black, and gilt. Even if you don't understand the nuances between Louis-Philippe and Napoléon III decorative styles, the setting is very grand and appropriate to its position overlooking the Cour Marly of the Louvre. Menu items include club sandwiches, fresh oysters and shellfish, *steak au poivre* (pepper steak), sole meunière, and an array of upscale, bistro-inspired food. In summer, outdoor tables overlook views of one of the most celebrated courtyards in Europe.

Café/Restaurant/Salon de Thé Bernardaud. 11 rue Royale, 8e. ☎ **01-42-66-22-55.** Reservations recommended at lunch, not necessary for breakfast or afternoon tea. Continental breakfast 60F ($12); lunch main courses 80–120F ($16–$24); cup of afternoon tea with a pastry 70F ($14). DC, MC, V. Mon–Sat 8–10:30am, noon–3pm, and 3:30–7pm. Métro: Concorde. FRENCH.

Few other cafes and tearooms in Paris mingle salesmanship with culinary pizzazz as effectively as this one. It was established in 1995 by a venerable, Limoges-based manufacturer of porcelain, Bernardaud, S.A.R.L., a name known to the prosperous *bourgeoisie* of France since 1863. Set squarely within some of the most expensive commercial real estate in Europe, it occupies a medium-green, aggressively upscale art deco–style space revolving around the establishment's staggeringly beautiful porcelain. Lunchtime is flooded with employees of the nearby offices, and no one minds if you opt just for a salad or something more substantial, such as a *panaché de poisson* (medley of fresh fish in herb sauce with vegetables). Afternoon teas add a new, not terribly discreet commercial twist: A staff member will present a choice of five different porcelain patterns in which your tea will be served, and if you finish your Earl Grey with an absolute fixation on the particular pattern you've chosen, you'll be directed into the adjacent showroom to place your order.

Fouquet's. 99 av. des Champs-Elysées, 8e. ☎ **01-47-23-70-60.** Glass of wine from 42F ($8); sandwiches 42–65F ($8–$13); fixed-price lunch 265F ($53); main courses 160–260F ($32–$52). Daily 9am–2am. Restaurant noon–3pm and 8pm–1am, bar 9am–2am. Métro: George V.

Fouquet's has been collecting anecdotes and a patina since it was founded in 1901. A celebrity favorite, it has attracted Chaplin, Chevalier, Dietrich, Churchill, Roosevelt, and Jackie O. The premier cafe on the Champs-Elysées sits behind a barricade of potted flowers at the edge of the sidewalk. You can choose a table in the sunshine or retreat to the glassed-in elegance of the leather banquettes and rattan furniture of the street-level grill room. Although Fouquet's is a full-fledged restaurant, with a beautiful, very formal dining room on the second floor, most visitors come by just for a glass of wine, coffee, or a sandwich.

La Coupole. 102 bd. du Montparnasse, 14e. ☎ **01-43-20-14-20.** Breakfast buffet 82F ($16); main courses 67–178F ($13–$36); fixed-price lunch 123F ($25); set menu 128F ($26) every night after 10pm. Breakfast buffet Mon–Fri 7:30–10:30am. Daily from 7:30am–2am. Métro: Vavin.

Once a leading center of artistic life, La Coupole is now a bastion of the grand Paris brasserie style in Montparnasse. It was born in 1927 at the height of the city's jazz age. This big, attractive cafe has grown more cosmopolitan through the years, attracting fewer locals and art-school waifs. But some of the city's most interesting foreigners show up. Former patrons included Josephine Baker, Henry Miller, Dalí, Calder,

Hemingway, Dos Passos, Fitzgerald, and Picasso. Today you might see Gérard Depardieu.

The sweeping outdoor terrace is among the finest in Paris. At one of its sidewalk tables, you can sit and watch the passing scene and order a coffee or a cognac VSOP. The food is quite good, despite the fact that the dining room resembles an enormous railway station waiting room. Try, for example, such main dishes as sole meunière, curry *d'agneau* (lamb), cassoulet, and some of the best steak au poivre in Paris. The fresh oysters and shellfish are especially popular.

La Rotonde. 105 bd. du Montparnasse, 6e. ☎ **01-43-26-68-84.** Glass of wine 20F ($4); fixed-price menus 72.50F ($14.50) at lunch, 144–180F ($29–$36) at dinner. Métro: Vavin.

Once patronized by Hemingway, the original Rotonde faded into history but is immortalized in the pages of *The Sun Also Rises,* in which Papa wrote, "No matter what cafe in Montparnasse you ask a taxi driver to bring you to from the right bank of the river, they always take you to the Rotonde." Lavishly upgraded, its reincarnation has a paneled art deco elegance, and shares the once-hallowed site with a motion-picture theater. If you stand at the bar, prices are lower.

Le Café Zephyr. 12 bd. Montmartre, 9e. ☎ **01-47-70-80-14.** Reservations not accepted. Café au lait 22F ($4), plats du jour 60–72F ($12–$14). MC, V. Mon–Sat 8am–2am, Sun 8am–10pm. Métro: Rue Montmartre.

The patrons of this cafe like it for the quiet refuge it provides in the midst of a bustling, heavily commercialized neighborhood. Understated and sedate, it holds firmly to its French roots in an area of Paris that is becoming increasingly modern and international. Stop by here for a leisurely café au lait or a light snack, but don't expect any culinary masterpieces—you're more likely to enjoy the atmosphere than the food.

Le Gutenberg. 64 rue Jean-Jacques Rousseau, 1er. ☎ **01-42-36-14-90.** Reservations not accepted. Café au lait 10F ($2); sandwiches 14F ($3); plat du jour 45F ($9). No credit cards. Daily 7am–7pm. Métro: Louvre-Rivoli.

Set behind the largest post office in France, and named in honor of the printing presses that used to operate nearby, this is the most evocative and authentic of the cafes close to the Louvre. There's a zinc-topped bar, and two inner rooms loaded with antique mirrors and uniformed staff members. The staff adores debating whether it's 150 or 225 years old, but never really reaches a conclusion.

Le Rouquet. 188 bd. Saint-Germain, 7e. ☎ **01-45-48-06-93.** Reservations not accepted. Café au lait 12–24F ($2–$5). Plats du jour 50–60F ($10–$12). MC, V. Mon–Sat 7am–9pm. Métro: St-Germain-des-Prés.

Its platters of food are conventionally modeled on old-fashioned recipes (boeuf bourguignon, roasted loin of pork, grilled steak with french fries) and because of its position in a hyper-desirable neighborhood (less than 60 yards from the Church of St-Germain), its prices aren't particularly competitive. Despite that, Le Rouquet enjoys an enviable cachet and sense of chic, partly because it competes on a less flamboyant scale with the nearby *Café de Flore* and *Deux Magots,* and partly because the decor hasn't changed since a remodeling in 1954. Within a pair of dining rooms, enhanced with a sidewalk terrace, you can sit for as long as you want, watching a clientele composed of stylish Italians and Americans performing shopping and people-watching rituals barely altered since Le Roquet's founding in 1922.

Les Deux-Magots. 6 place St-Germain-des-Prés, 6e. ☎ **01-45-48-55-25.** Café au lait 25F ($5); whisky soda 65F ($13); cold platters 50–195F ($10–$39). Daily from 7:30am to 1:30am. Métro: St-Germain-des-Prés.

This legendary cafe is still the hangout for the sophisticated residents of St-Germain-des-Prés; it becomes a tourist favorite in summer and never was as chic as Café de Flore. Visitors virtually monopolize the few sidewalk tables as waiters rush about, seemingly oblivious to anyone's needs. Regulars from around the neighborhood reclaim it in the off-season.

The Deux-Magots was once a gathering place of the intellectual elite, including Sartre, Simone de Beauvoir, and Jean Giraudoux. Inside are two large Asian statues that give the cafe its name. The crystal chandeliers are too brightly lit, but the regulars seem to be accustomed to the glare. After all, some of them even read their daily newspapers here.

The Lizard Lounge. 18 rue du Bourg-Tibourg, 4e. ☎ **01-42-72-81-34.** Reservations not accepted. Cocktails 32–48F ($6–$10); sandwiches, salads, and plats du jour 25–76F ($5–$15), Sun brunch 45–95F ($9–$19). Bar service daily 11:30am–2am; food service daily noon–10:30pm. Sun brunch noon–4pm. MC, V. Métro: Hôtel de Ville.

Founded by Los Angeles escapee Phil Morgan in 1994, it resembles an Amsterdam or New York City cocktail lounge, an indulgently heterosexual enclave within an increasingly gay neighborhood. A rectangular space with a high ceiling, wood paneling, and bars on three different levels, it doubles as a restaurant. Looking to strike up a friendship? Order one of the margaritas, the house beer (a Dutch brew known as "Cheap Blond"), or the drink nobody can seem to get enough of, a cream-and-Kahlúa–based "Screaming Orgasm." Hungry for more? Try a New York–style deli sandwich (turkey with bacon is the best seller), a Lizard Salad garnished with Cheddar cheese and tikka slow-cooked chicken, or any of the French-inspired plats du jour. Sunday brunch features an all-you-can-eat vegetarian buffet whose offerings are augmented with such garnishes as omelettes with Canadian bacon or American-style ham and sausage.

Exploring Paris 6

Paris is one of those cities where taking in the street life should claim as much of your time as sightseeing in churches or museums. A gourmet picnic in the Bois de Boulogne, a sunrise pilgrimage to the Seine, an afternoon of bartering at the flea market—Paris bewitches you with these kinds of experiences. For all the Louvre's beauty, you'll probably remember the Latin Quarter's crooked alleyways better than the 370th oil painting of your visit.

SUGGESTED ITINERARIES FOR THE FIRST-TIMER

These itineraries are obviously intended for the first-time visitor, but even those making their 30th trip to Paris will want to revisit such attractions as the Louvre, which you could roam every day of your life, and always see something you'd missed before. Use these tips as a guide, but not a bible. Paris rewards travelers with guts and independence of mind, those who will pull open the doors to a chapel or an antiquarian's shop not because they're listed on a souvenir map, but because they look intrinsically interesting. In Paris, they usually are.

If You Have 1 Day

Far too little time, but you'll have to make the most of it. Get up early and begin walking the streets in the neighborhood of your hotel. The streets of Paris are live theater. Find a little cafe; chances are there will be one on every block. Go in and order a typical Parisian breakfast of coffee and croissants. If you're a museum and monument junkie, and you don't dare returning home without seeing what guidebooks for years have called the "must" sights, know that the two most popular museums are the **Louvre** and the **Musée d'Orsay.** The three most enduring monuments are the **Eiffel Tower,** the **Arc de Triomphe,** and **Notre-Dame** (which can be seen later in the day). If it's a toss-up between the Louvre and the d'Orsay, we'd make it the Louvre if you're a first-timer, because it holds a greater variety of works. If you feel the need to choose between monuments, we'd make it the Eiffel Tower just for the panoramic view of the city. If you feel your day is too short to visit museums or wait in lines for the Tower, we'd suggest that instead you spend most of your time strolling the streets of Paris. The most impressive venue is the **Ile St-Louis,** which we believe is the most elegant place for a walk in Paris. After exploring this island and its mansions, wander at will through such Left Bank districts as **St-Germain-des-Prés** or the area around **place St-Michel,** the heart of the student quarter. As the sun sets over Paris, head for Notre-Dame, which stands majestically along the banks of the Seine. This is a good place to watch shadows fall over Paris as the lights come on for the night. Afterward, walk along the banks of the Seine, where vendors sell books and souvenir prints. Promise yourself a return visit and have dinner in the Left Bank bistro of your choice.

If You Have 2 Days

Since you've paid so much attention to the Left Bank on your first day, spend most of this day taking in the glories of the Right Bank. Begin at the Arc de Triomphe and stroll down the **Champs-Elysées,** the main boulevard of Paris, until you reach the Egyptian obelisk at the **place de la Concorde.** This grand promenade is one of the most famous walks in the world. The place de la Concorde affords terrific views of the **Madeleine,** the **Palais-Bourbon,** the Arc de Triomphe, and the Louvre. This is where some of France's most notable figures lost their heads at the guillotine. A nearby square, **place Vendôme,** is worth a walk, too, as it represents the Right Bank at its most elegant, with such addresses as the Ritz, and Paris's top jewelry stores. After all this walking, we'd suggest a rest stop in the **Jardin de Tuileries,** directly west and adjacent to the Louvre. After a long lunch in a Right Bank bistro, and in total contrast to the heart of monumental Paris, go for a walk on the seedy side. Our favorite is a stroll along the rue des Rosiers in the **Marais,** a narrow street that's the heart of the Jewish community. After a rest at your hotel, select one of the restaurants down in **Montparnasse,** following in Hemingway's footsteps. The area is far livelier at night. We'd suggest **La Coupole** for both dinner and drinks.

If You Have 3 Days

Spend days 1 and 2 as above. As you've already gotten a look at the Left Bank and the Right Bank, this day should be about following your special interests. If you're a Monet fan, you might head for the **Musée Marmottan-Claude Monet.** Or perhaps you'd rather wander around the sculpture garden of the **Musée National Auguste-Rodin.** If it's the **Picasso Museum** you select, you can use part of the morning to explore a few of the art galleries of the Marais. Following in the trail of Descartes and Madame de Sévigné, select a cafe or restaurant here for lunch. Reserve the afternoon for **Ile de la Cité,** where you can not only get to see Notre-Dame again, but can visit the **Conciergerie** where Marie Antoinette and others were held captive before they were beheaded. See also the stunning stained glass of **Sainte-Chapelle** in the Palais de Justice. For dinner that night, we'd suggest a Right Bank bistro in Le Marais. Afterward, if your energy persists, you can sample Paris's nightlife—whatever you fancy, the dancers at the **Lido** or the **Folies Bergère** or a smoky Left Bank jazz club. If you'd just like to sit and have a drink, Paris has some of the most elegant hotel bars in the world at such places as the **Hôtel Crillon** or **Plaza-Athenée.**

If You Have 4 Days

For your first three days, follow the itinerary above. On your fourth day, head to **Versailles,** 13 miles south of Paris, and the greatest attraction in the Ile de France. When Louis XIV decided to move to the suburbs, he created a spectacle unlike anything the world had ever known. The good news is that most of the palace remains ⁻act with its opulence and glitter. A full day here is really too little time. After you ⁻n to Paris for the night, take a good rest and spend the evening wandering around the Left Bank's **Latin Quarter,** enjoying the student cafes and bars and selecting your bistro of choice for the evening. Some of the livelier streets for wandering include rue de la Huchette and rue Monsieur-le-Prince.

If You Have 5 Days

Spend days 1 through 4 as recommended above. On your fifth day, devote at least a morning to an area heretofore neglected, **Montmartre,** the community formerly known for its artists perched atop the highest of Paris's seven hills. It's like a village encircled by sprawling Paris. Although the starving artists who made it the embodiment of *la vie de bohème* have long since departed, there is much to charm and enchant you, especially if you wander the back streets. Here, away from the tacky shops and sleazy clubs, you'll see the picture-postcard lanes known to Picasso, Toulouse-Lautrec, and Utrillo. Of course, it's virtually mandatory to visit the **Basilica of Sacré-Coeur,** for the view if nothing else. Since it's your last night in Paris, let your own interests take over here. Lovers traditionally spend it clasping hands in a farewell along the Seine; less goggle-eyed visitors can still find a full agenda. We'd suggest a final evening at **Willi's Wine Bar** (see chapter 9), with more than 250 vintages and good food to go along with it. For a nightcap, we always head for the **Hemingway Bar** at the Ritz, where Garbo, Noel Coward, and F. Scott Fitzgerald once lifted their glasses. If that's too elegant, head for **Closerie des Lilas** in the 6th arrondissement, where you can rub shoulders with the movers and shakers of the film industry and fashion's "playthings." Even if you've been saving money up to now, our final suggestion is that you go all out for one really grand French meal at a fabulous restaurant. It's a memory you might treasure long after you've recovered from paying the tab.

1 The Top Museums

Paris museums fit into three categories: city museums, national museums, and those run by private organizations. The municipal and national museums have fairly standard hours. They are often closed on Tuesday and national holidays. Fees vary, but half-price tickets are usually provided to students, children ages 3 to 7, and extra-large families or groups. If you want to museum-hop in earnest, the best day is Sunday, when most museums let you in for half price.

Whatever time of the year you come, Paris seems to be hosting an outstanding exhibition—keep your eyes open for huge, colorful posters hanging from lampposts. In the halls and museum rooms across the city, at least 15 special shows are on during any given week, events such as a Chagall retrospective, a special exhibition of Giacometti sculptures, a show on Art of the Workers' Movement, or a description of the public life of Napoléon. The fees charged depend on the exhibit.

To find out what's showing while you're in town, stop at the **Welcome Office,** 127 av. des Champs-Elysées (☎ **01-49-52-53-54;** Métro: Charles de Gaulle–Etoile). Here you can pick up a free copy of the English-language booklet *Paris Weekly Information,* published by the Paris Convention and Visitors' Bureau; open daily from 9am to 8pm except May 1.

You can buy **Le Carte Musées et Monuments** at any of the museums that honor it, or at any branch of the Paris Tourist office. It offers free entrance to the permanent collections of 65 monuments and museums in Paris and the Ile-de-France. A 1-day pass is 70F ($14); a 3-day pass is 140F ($28); a 5-day pass is 200F ($40).

✪ **Musée du Louvre.** 34-36 quai du Louvre. ☎ **01-40-20-53-17** (01-40-20-51-51 recorded message, 01-49-87-54-54 advance credit card sales). Admission 45F ($9) before 3pm, 26F ($5.20) after 3pm and on Sun. Ages 17 and under free. Free first Sun of every month. Mon and

A Timesaving Tip

Museums require that you check shopping bags and book bags, and sometimes lines for these can be longer than the ticket/admission lines. Visitors who value their time should leave their bags behind: Some coat lines in Paris can take 30 minutes. Ask if a museum has more than one coat line, and if so, avoid the main one and go to the less frequented ones.

Wed 9am–9:45pm (Mon, short tour only), Thurs–Sun 9am–6pm. 1½-hour English-language tours leave Mon and Wed–Sat various times of the day for 33F ($6.60) adults, 22F ($4.40) ages 13–18; 12 and under free with museum ticket. Métro: Palais-Royal or Musée-du-Louvre.

From far and wide they come—from North Dakota to Pakistan, from Nova Scotia to Japan—all bent on seeing the legendary Louvre. People on one of those "Paris-in-a-day" tours try to break track records to get a glimpse of the two most famous ladies of the Louvre: the *Mona Lisa* and the armless *Venus de Milo.* (The scene in front of the *Mona Lisa* is best described as a circus. Viewers push and shove in front of the lady's bulletproof glass as the staff looks idly on, and flashbulbs, which are forbidden, go off like popcorn on a hot stove. In all this fracas, it's hard to contemplate (or share in) her inimitable smile.) The herd then dashes on a five-minute stampede in pursuit of *Winged Victory,* that headless statue discovered at Samothrace and dating from about 200 B.C. In preference to the assembly-line theory of art, we head instead for David's *Portrait of Madame Récamier,* depicting Napoléon's opponent at age 23. On her comfortable sofa, she reclines agelessly in the style of classical antiquity.

Then a big question looms: Which of the rest of the 30,000 works on display would you like to see?

The Louvre suffers from an embarrassment of riches. Here, the casual visitor often passes masterpieces blindly, simply because there are too many to behold. The Louvre is the world's largest palace and the world's largest museum (some say the greatest). As a palace, it leaves us cold, except for its old section, the Cour Carrée. As a museum, it's one of the greatest art collections in the world.

Between the Seine and the rue de Rivoli (Métro to Palais-Royal or Louvre, the latter the most elegant subway stop in the world), the Palace of the Louvre stretches for almost half a mile. In the days of Charles V it was a fortress, but François I, a patron of Leonardo da Vinci, had it torn down and rebuilt as a royal residence. Less than a month after Marie Antoinette's head and body parted company, the Revolutionary Committee decided that the king's collection of paintings and sculpture would be opened to the public. At the lowest point in its history, in the 18th century, the Louvre was home for anybody who wanted to set up housekeeping. Laundry hung out the windows, corners were literally pig pens, and each family built a fire somewhere to cook a meal during the long winter. Napoléon ended that, chasing out squatters and restoring the palace. In fact, he chose the Louvre for the site of his wedding to Marie-Louise.

So where did all these paintings come from? The kings of France, notably François I and Louis XIV, acquired many of them. Others have been willed to or purchased by the state. Many that Napoléon contributed were taken from reluctant donors like the church, an especially heavy and unwilling giver. Much of Napoléon's plunder had to be returned, although France hasn't seen its way clear to giving back all the booty.

To enter the Louvre, you'll pass through a controversial 71-foot-high glass pyramid in the courtyard. Commissioned by French president François Mitterrand and completed in 1989, it has received mixed reviews. Designed by I.M. Pei to allow

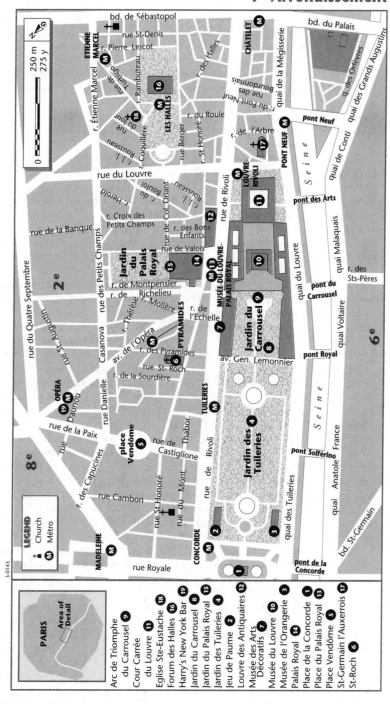

1st Arrondissement

bd. de Sébastopol

bd. du Palais

CHÂTELET

rue St-Denis

ETIENNE MARCEL

r. Pierre Lescot

r. Etienne Marcel

rue Rambuteau

rue Turbigo

rue des Halles

16

LES HALLES

18

r. du Roule

r. Berger · r. St-Honoré

r. de l'Arbre

17

quai de la Mégisserie

q. des Orfèvres

quai des Grands Augustins

PONT NEUF

pont Neuf

r. du Pont Neuf · rue des Bourdonnais

rue du Louvre

rue de Rivoli

LOUVRE-RIVOLI

Seine

quai de Conti

pont des Arts

11

12

r. Hérold

r. du Boul.

r. Rousseau

r. Croix des Petits Champs

rue de la Banque

r. de Col. Driant

r. des Bons Enfants

rue de Valois

Jardin du Palais Royal

15

14

13

MUSÉE-DU-LOUVRE-PALAIS ROYAL

10

quai du Louvre

quai Malaquais

r. des Sts-Pères

6e

2e

r. de Montpensier

r. de Richelieu

r. Molière

rue des Petits Champs

r. de Thérèse

Casanova

av. de l'Opéra

PYRAMIDES

r. de l'Echelle

7

9

Jardin du Carrousel

8

pont du Carrousel

quai Voltaire

rue du Quatre Septembre

rue St-Augustin

Daunou

r. des Pyramides

6

rue St-Roch

r. de la Sourdière

av. Gen. Lemonnier

pont Royal

OPÉRA

19

rue de la Paix

rue Danielle

place Vendôme

5

rue de Castiglione

TUILERIES

Jardin des Tuileries

4

Seine

quai Anatole France

8e

rue

rue de la Paix

Thabor

rue de Rivoli

pont Solférino

rue Cambon

r. St-Honoré

r. du Mont-Thabor

quai des Tuileries

bd. St-Germain

r. de Capucines

MADELEINE

CONCORDE

pont de la Concorde

rue Royale

1

PARIS

Area of Detail

3-0143

sunlight to shine on an underground reception area, it shelters a complex of shops and restaurants. Automatic ticket machines help relieve the long lines of yesteryear.

The collections are divided into seven departments: Egyptian, Asian, Greek, Etruscan, and Roman antiquities; sculpture; painting; prints and drawings; and art objects. In 1997, a number of new galleries were opened as part of a metamorphosis that will end in 1998. New galleries are devoted to Italian paintings, Roman glass and bronzes, Oriental antiquities, and Egyptian antiquities. If you don't have to "do" Paris in a day, perhaps you can return here several times, concentrating on different collections or schools of painting. Those with little time should go on one of the guided tours (in English), which last about 1¹/₂ hours.

Da Vinci's much-traveled *La Gioconda* (*Mona Lisa*) was acquired by François I to hang above his bath. Note the guard and bulletproof glass: The world's most famous painting was stolen in the summer of 1911 and found in Florence in the winter of 1913. At first, both Guillaume Apollinaire, the poet, and Picasso were suspected as the thieves, but it was discovered in the possession of a former Louvre employee, who had apparently carried it out of the museum under his overcoat. The *Mona Lisa* has been the source of legend and lore for centuries. Less well known (but to us even more enchanting) are Da Vinci's *Virgin and Child with St. Anne* and the *Virgin of the Rocks*.

After paying your respects to the enigmatically "Smiling One," which the French call La Joconde, allow time to see some French works stretching from the Richelieu wing through the entire Sully wing and even overflowing into part of the Denon wing. It's all here: Antoine Watteau's *Gilles* with the mysterious boy in a clown suit staring back at you; Jean-Honoré Fragonard's and François Boucher's rococo renderings of the aristocracy; and the greatest masterpieces of Jacques-Louis David, including his stellar 1785 work, *The Oath of the Horatii,* and the vast and vivid *Coronation of Napoléon.* Only the Uffizi in Florence rivals the Denon wing for its Italian Renaissance collection—everything from Raphael's *Portrait of Balthazar Castiglione* to Titian's *Man with a Glove.* Paolo Veronese's gigantic *Wedding Feast at Cana* occupies an entire wall. This painting is a delight: a romp of high Viennese society of the 1500s. (That's Paolo himself playing the cello.)

Of the Greek and Roman antiquities, the most notable collections, aside from the *Venus de Milo* and *Winged Victory,* are fragments of the frieze from the Parthenon (located in the Denon wing). In Renaissance sculpture, you'll see two slaves by Michelangelo, originally intended for the tomb of Julius II but sold into other bondage. The Denon wing houses the masterpieces: Ingres's *The Turkish Bath;* the Botticelli frescoes from the Villa Lemmi; Raphael's *La Belle Jardinière,* and Titian's *Open Air Concert.* The Sully wing is also filled with wise old masters, including Boucher's *Diana Resting after Her Bath* and Fragonard's *Bathers.*

The Richelieu wing, inaugurated in 1993, houses the museum's collection of northern European and French paintings, along with decorative arts, French sculpture, Oriental antiquities (a rich collection of Islamic art), and the salons of Napoléon III. First built from 1852 to 1857, the Richelieu wing was expanded to add some 230,000 square feet of exhibition space, and now shelters 12,000 works of art in 165 rooms and three covered courtyards. One of its galleries displays 21 works Rubens painted in a space of only 2 years for Marie de Médicis's Luxembourg Palace. This wing stacks masterpiece upon masterpiece: Dürer's self-portrait, Anthony Van Dyck's portrait of Charles I of England, and Holbein the Younger's *Portrait of Erasmus of Rotterdam,* with a wealth of art surrounding that includes Sumerian and Babylonian treasures, Assyrian winged bulls, and Persian friezes.

When you tire, consider a pick-me-up at Café Marly in the Richelieu wing. In three grandiose rooms with high ceilings and lavish adornments, the cafe overlooks

The Louvre

The Pyramid

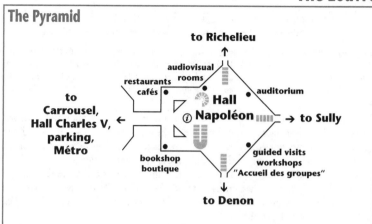

to Richelieu

audiovisual rooms

restaurants cafés

auditorium

Hall Napoléon

to Carrousel, Hall Charles V, parking, Métro

→ to Sully

bookshop boutique

guided visits workshops "Accueil des groupes"

to Denon

The Levels

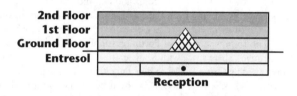

2nd Floor
1st Floor
Ground Floor
Entresol

Reception

The Wings

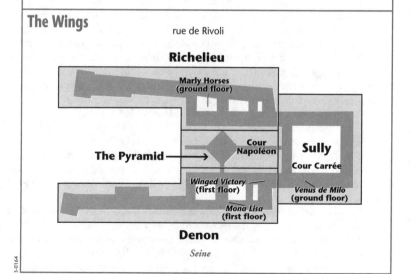

rue de Rivoli

Richelieu

Marly Horses (ground floor)

Cour Napoléon

Sully
Cour Carrée

The Pyramid →

Winged Victory (first floor)

Venus de Milo (ground floor)

Mona Lisa (first floor)

Denon

Seine

3-0164

the museum's glass pyramid and offers a selection of coffees, pastries (by Paris's most legendary pastry-maker, Lenôtre), salads, sandwiches, and simple platters.

✪ **Musée d'Orsay.** 1 rue de Bellechasse or 62 rue de Lille, 7e. ☎ **01-40-49-48-14.** Admission 36F ($7.20) adults, 24F ($4.80) ages 18–24 and over 60; children 17 and under free, reduced admission on Sundays. Tues–Wed and Fri–Sat 10am–6pm, Sun 9am–6pm, Thurs 10am–9:45pm. June 20 to Sept 20, museum opens at 9am. Métro: Solférino. RER: Musée d'Orsay.

In the middle of Paris, architects have transformed a defunct rail station, the handsome neoclassical Gare d'Orsay, into one of the greatest museums in the world. Don't skip the Louvre, but come here even if you have to skip all the other art museums of Paris. It contains one of the world's most important collections devoted to the watershed years between 1848 and 1914. Standing across the Seine from the Louvre and the Tuileries, it has a treasure trove of Van Gogh, Manet, Monet, Degas, and Renoir, but of all the less known groups as well: the Symbolists, Pointillistes, Nabis, Realists, and late Romantics.

Musée d'Orsay houses thousands of pieces of sculpture and painting spread across 80 different galleries. It also displays belle epoque furniture, photographs, objets d'art, and architectural models; it even contains a cinema that shows classic films.

A monument to the Industrial Revolution, the Orsay station, once called "the elephant," is covered by an arching glass roof, flooding the museum with light. The museum displays works ranging from the creations of academic and historic painters such as Ingres to Romanticists such as Delacroix, to neo-Realists such as Courbet and Daumier. The Impressionists and Postimpressionists, including Cézanne, Van Gogh, and the Fauves, share space with Matisse, the Cubists, and the Expressionists in a setting once used by Orson Welles to film a nightmarish scene in *The Trial*, based on a Kafka work. Where else than heaven could lie Millet's sunny wheat fields, Barbizon landscapes, the mists of Corot, and parti-colored Tahitian Gauguins, all in the same hall?

But for all these painters, it's the Impressionists who keep the crowds lining up. When the Louvre tripped over its traditional toes and chose not to display their works, it gave birth to a great rival. Led by Manet, Renoir, and the blessedly myopic Monet, the Impressionists shunned ecclesiastical and mythological set-pieces for a light-bathed Seine, faint figures strolling in the Tuileries, pale-faced women in hazy bars, even vulgar rail stations such as the Gare St-Lazare. The Impressionists were the first to paint the most characteristic feature of Parisian life: the sidewalk cafe, especially in the artists' quarter of Montmartre.

The most famous painting from this era is Manet's 1863 painting of *Picnic on the Grass*, which sent shock waves through respectable society when it was first exhibited. (It depicts a forest setting with a nude woman and two fully clothed men.) Two years later, his *Olympia*, also here, created another scandal. It depicts a woman lounging on her bed and wearing nothing but a flower in her hair and high-heeled shoes; she is attended by an African maid in the background. Zola called Manet "a man among eunuchs."

One of Renoir's brightest, most joyous paintings is also here: the *Moulin de la Galette*, painted in 1876. Degas is represented by his paintings of racehorses and dancers; his 1876 cafe scene, *Absinthe*, also here, remains one of his most reproduced works. Paris-born Claude Monet was fascinated by the effect changing light had on Rouen Cathedral, and in a series of five paintings displayed here, its stone bubbles to life.

One of the most celebrated works at the Orsay is by an American, Whistler's *Arrangement in Gray and Black: Portrait of the Painter's Mother*, perhaps better known

Closed!

What has been called "the most avant-garde building in the world" and, alternately, "a Utopian oil refinery," the **Centre Pompidou** closed on September 29, 1997, for extensive renovations. The dream of former president Georges Pompidou, this center for 20th-century art (designed by Renzo Piano) opened in 1977 and immediately became the focus of loud controversy: A bold exoskeletal architecture and Day-Glo pipes and ducts crisscrossing the transparent facade were considered jarring in the old Beaubourg neighborhood. Perhaps the detractors were right all along—within 20 years the building began to deteriorate so badly that a major restoration was deemed necessary. Though authorities planned to keep stages of the building open as work progressed, insurance companies intervened to spoil the fun. Centre Pompidou will reopen as bells ring in the millennium on December 31, 1999. In the meantime, expect parts of its modern art collection to appear in other area museums, and for its library and music institute to operate in the proximity of plateau Beaubourg. Call ☎ **01-44-78-12-33** for more information.

as *Whistler's Mother.* It is said that this painting heralded the advent of modern art, although many critics denounced it at the time as "Whistler's Dead Mother" because of its funereal overtones. Today the painting has been hailed as a "veritable icon of our consciousness." Whistler was content to claim he made "Mummy just as nice as possible."

✪ **Musée Picasso.** Hôtel Salé, 5 rue de Thorigny, 3e. ☎ **01-42-71-25-21.** Admission 30F ($6) adults; 18F ($3.60) ages 18–25 and over 60; children under 18 free. Apr–Sept Wed–Mon 9:30am–5:30pm; off-season Wed–Mon 9:30am–5:30pm. Métro: St-Paul, Filles-du-Calvaire, or Chemin-Vert.

When it opened at the beautifully restored Hôtel Salé (Salty Mansion), a state-owned property in Le Marais, the press hailed it as a "museum for Picasso's Picassos." And that's what it is. Almost overnight the museum became, and continues to be, one of the most popular attractions in Paris.

The state acquired the greatest Picasso collection in the world in lieu of a $50 million levy in inheritance taxes. The tax man claimed 203 paintings, 158 sculptures, 16 collages, 19 bas-reliefs, 88 ceramics, and more than 1,500 sketches and 1,600 engravings, along with 30 notebooks. These works span some 75 years of his life and ever-changing style.

The range of paintings includes a remarkable self-portrait from 1901 and the masterpiece *Le Baiser* (*The Kiss*), painted at Mougins on the Riviera in 1969. The museum also acquired another masterpiece he did a year later at the same place on the Riviera: It's called *Reclining Nude and the Man with a Guitar.* It's easy to stroll through the handsome museum seeking your own favorite work—perhaps a wicked one: *Jeune Garçon à la Langouste,* "young man with a lobster," painted in Paris in 1941. The Paris museum owns several intriguing studies for *Les Demoiselles d'Avignon,* the painting that shocked the establishment and launched Cubism in 1907.

Salacious Scrawls

Some visitors go here just to view the ribald paintings Picasso turned out in his later years—perhaps just for his erotic amusement.

Many of the major masterpieces, such as *The Crucifixion* and *Nude in a Red Armchair,* should remain on permanent view. However, because the collection is so vast, temporary exhibitions featuring such items as his studies of the Minotaur, will be held for the public at the rate of two each year.

In addition to Picasso's own treasure trove of art, his private collection of other masters' works is also displayed, including the contributions of such world-class artists as Cézanne, Rousseau, Braque, André Derain, and Miró. Picasso was fascinated with African masks, and many of these are on view as well.

2 Ile de la Cité: Where Paris Was Born

Medieval Paris, that blend of grotesquerie and Gothic beauty, bloomed on this island in the Seine. Ile de la Cité, which the Seine protects like a surrounding moat, has been known as "the cradle" of Paris ever since. As Sauval once observed, "The Island of the City is shaped like a great ship, sunk in the mud, lengthwise in the stream, in about the middle of the Seine."

Few have written more movingly about 15th-century Paris than Victor Hugo, who invited the reader "to observe the fantastic display of lights against the darkness of that gloomy labyrinth of buildings; cast upon it a ray of moonlight, showing the city in glimmering vagueness, with its towers lifting their great heads from that foggy sea."

Medieval Paris was not only a city of legends and lovers, but also of blood-curdling tortures and brutalities. No story illustrates this better than the affair of Abélard and his charge Héloïse, whose jealous and unsettled uncle hired ruffians to emasculate her lover. (The success of the attack predictably quelled their ardor, and he became a monk, she an abbess.) Explore as much of the island as you can, but even if you're in a hurry, don't miss Notre-Dame, the Sainte-Chapelle, and the Conciergerie.

✪ **Cathédrale de Notre-Dame.** 6 place du parvis Notre-Dame, 4e. ☎ **01-42-34-56-10.** Cathedral free; towers, treasury, or crypt 28F ($5.60), 18F ($3.60) ages 18–24 and over 60, 15F ($3) children 12–17; free for children 11 and under. Cathedral daily 8am–7pm (closed Sat from 12:30–2pm); towers, daily 9:30am–5pm; museum Wed and Sat–Sun 2:30–6pm; treasury and crypt Mon–Sat 9:30am–5:30pm. Six masses are celebrated on Sun, four on weekdays, and one on Sat. Métro: Cité or St-Michel. RER: St-Michel.

Notre-Dame is the heart of Paris, even of France; distances from Paris to all parts of France are calculated from its center.

Although many disagree, Notre-Dame is, in our opinion, more interesting outside than in. You'll want to walk around the entire structure to fully appreciate this "vast symphony of stone." Better yet, cross over the bridge to the Left Bank and view it from the quay.

Its setting on the banks of the Seine has always been memorable. Founded in the 12th century by Maurice de Sully, bishop of Paris, Notre-Dame grew and grew. Over the years the cathedral has changed as Paris has, often falling victim to whims of decorative taste. Its famous flying buttresses (the external side-supports, which give the massive interior a sense of weightlessness) were rebuilt in 1330.

The history of Paris and that of Notre-Dame are inseparable. Many prayed here before going off to lose their lives in the Crusades. "Our Lady of Paris" was not spared by the revolutionaries, who destroyed the Galerie des Rois and converted the building into a secular temple. Later, Napoléon was crowned emperor in Notre-Dame, yanking the crown out of Pius VII's hands and placing it on his own head. But carelessness, vandalism, embellishments, and wars of religion had already demolished much of the previously existing structure.

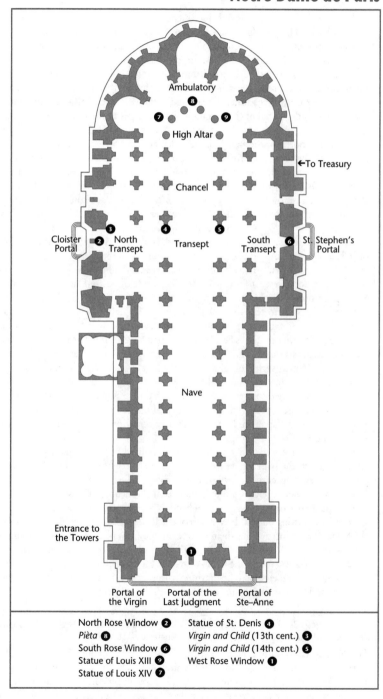

Notre-Dame de Paris

Ambulatory

High Altar

←To Treasury

Chancel

Cloister Portal

North Transept

Transept

South Transept

St. Stephen's Portal

Nave

Entrance to the Towers

Portal of the Virgin

Portal of the Last Judgment

Portal of Ste–Anne

North Rose Window ②	Statue of St. Denis ④
Pièta ⑧	*Virgin and Child* (13th cent.) ③
South Rose Window ⑥	*Virgin and Child* (14th cent.) ⑤
Statue of Louis XIII ⑨	West Rose Window ①
Statue of Louis XIV ⑦	

The cathedral was once scheduled for demolition, but, partly because of the popularity of Victor Hugo's *Hunchback of Notre Dame* and the revival of interest in the Gothic, a movement mushroomed to restore the cathedral to its original glory. The task was completed under Viollet-le-Duc, an architectural genius.

Once the houses of old Paris crowded in on Notre-Dame, but Haussmann ordered them torn down to show the cathedral to its best advantage from the square known as *parvis*. This is the best vantage for seeing the three sculpted 13th-century portals.

On the left, the portal of the Virgin depicts the signs of the zodiac and the coronation of the Virgin, an association found in dozens of medieval churches. The restored central portal of the Last Judgment depicts three levels: the first shows Vices and Virtues; the second, Christ and his Apostles; and above that, Christ in triumph after the Resurrection. The portal is a close illustration of the Gospel according to Matthew. Over this portal is a remarkable rose window, 31 feet wide, forming a showcase for a statue of the *Virgin and Child.* On the far right is the portal of St. Anne, depicting such scenes as the Virgin enthroned with Child. It is the best preserved and the most perfect piece of sculpture in Notre-Dame.

Equally interesting (although often missed by the scurrying visitor) is the portal of the cloisters (around on the left), with its dour-faced 13th-century Virgin, a survivor of the many that originally adorned the facade. (Unfortunately, the Child she is holding is decapitated.) Finally, on the Seine side of Notre-Dame, the portal of St. Stephen traces that saint's martyrdom.

If possible, come to see Notre-Dame at sunset. Inside, of the three giant medallions that warm the austere cathedral, the north rose window in the transept, dating from the mid–13th century, is best. The main body of the church is typically Gothic, with slender, graceful columns. In the choir, a stone-carved screen from the early 14th century depicts such biblical scenes as the Last Supper. Near the altar stands the 14th-century Virgin and Child, highly venerated among Paris's faithful.

In the treasury are displayed vestments and gold objects, including crowns. Exhibited are a cross presented to Haile Selassie, the former emperor of Ethiopia, and a reliquary given by Napoléon. Notre-Dame is especially proud of its relic of the True Cross and the Crown of Thorns.

Finally, to visit those grimy gargoyles immortalized by Hugo, you have to scale steps leading to the twin square towers that rise to a height of 225 feet. Once here, you can closely inspect those devils (some giving you the raspberry), hobgoblins, and birds of prey. Look carefully, and you may see the hunchback Quasimodo.

Approached through a garden behind Notre-Dame is Le Memorial de la Déportation, jutting out on the very tip of the Ile de la Cité. There, birds chirp and the Seine flows gently by, but the memories are far from pleasant. It commemorates French martyrs of World War II, who were deported to such camps as Auschwitz and Buchenwald. Carved into stone in blood red are the words (in French): "Forgive, but don't forget." The memorial is open Monday through Friday 8:30am to 9:45pm, and Saturday and Sunday from 9am to 9:45pm. Admission is free.

Conciergerie. 1 quai de l'Horloge, 1er. ☎ **01-53-73-78-50.** Admission 28F ($5.60) adults, 18F ($3.60) ages 12–18 and over 60, 15F ($3) children under 12. Apr–Sept daily 9:30am–6:30pm; Oct–Mar daily 10am–5pm. Métro: Cité, Châtelet, or St-Michel. RER: St-Michel.

London has its Tower of London, Paris its Conciergerie. Although it had a long and regal history before the Revolution, it is visited today chiefly by those wishing to relive the Reign of Terror and other horrors. The Conciergerie lives on as an infamous symbol, recalling the days when carts pulled up daily to haul off the fresh supply of victims to the guillotine.

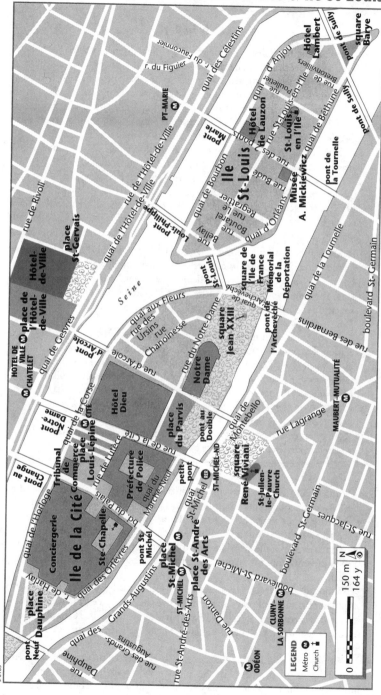

LEGEND
Métro **M**
Church **†**

150 m
164 y
0

3-0165

185

Only in Paris

- **A stroll along the Seine** is for many visitors the most memorable and romantic way to experience Paris. The riverbanks afford breathtaking views of the city's most important monuments. You may also stumble across the next Matisse in the clusters of young artists peddling their canvases. For a spectacular view of the Louvre, cross the Pont des Arts. The first iron bridge in the city, it is one of only four pedestrian bridges in Paris. As you continue your stroll, you encounter the Pont Neuf, the oldest and most famous bridge in Paris. (In the Middle Ages, Parisians came here to have their teeth pulled.) From here you have an excellent view of the Palais de Justice and Sainte-Chapelle on Ile de la Cité.

   A fine finish to any day spent meandering with the river would include a stroll through *marché aux fleurs,* the city's flower market. Here you can purchase rare flowers, the gems of the French Riveria, bouquets that have inspired artists throughout the centuries. From here, enter the famed *marché aux oiseaux* (bird market), where you can examine or purchase rare birds from around the world.

- If there's a literary bone in your body, you'll feel a vicarious thrill on finding the haunts of the famous writers and artists who have lived, worked, and played in Paris. Take the Métro to place St-Michel to begin your tour. As you wander away from the Seine, you encounter **Rue de la Huchette,** one of the most famous streets on the Left Bank. Its inhabitants were immortalized in Eliot Paul's *The Last Time I Saw Paris.*

   As you continue into the Left Bank, you enter the territory of the Beat Generation. This area is home to the Café Gentilhomme, described by Jack Kerouac in *Satori in Paris.* Allen Ginsberg's favorite, the **Hôtel du Vieux-Paris,** still attracts those in search of the Beats. You must also include a stroll down **rue Monsieur-le-Prince,** the "Yankee alleyway," where Richard Wright, James McNeill Whistler, Henry Wadsworth Longfellow, and Oliver Wendell Holmes lived at one time or another.

   A perfect end to your literary tour is a drink at the famed **Hôtel de Crillon,** where heroine Brett Ashley broke her promise to rendezvous with Jake Barnes

On the Seine, the Conciergerie is approached through its landmark twin towers, the Tour d'Argent and the Tour de César. The vaulted 14th-century Guard Room, which dates from when the Capets made the Palace of the Cité a royal residence, is the actual entrance to the building. Also dating from the 14th century, and even more interesting, is the vast, dark, and foreboding Gothic *Salle des Gens d'Armes* (People at Arms), utterly changed from the days when the king used it as a banqueting hall.

Architecture, however, plays a secondary role to the list of famous prisoners who spent their last miserable days on earth at the Conciergerie. Few in its history endured tortures as severe as Ravaillac's, who assassinated Henry IV in 1610. He got the full treatment—pincers in the flesh, and hot lead and boiling oil poured on him like bath water.

During the revolution the Conciergerie became more than a symbol of terror to the nobility or the enemies of the State. Just a short walk from the prison, the Revolutionary Tribunal dispensed a skewed, hurried justice to the beat of the guillotine. If it's any consolation, the jurists of the Revolution did not believe in torturing their victims, only in decapitating them.

in Hemingway's *The Sun Also Rises*. Zelda and F. Scott Fitzgerald lifted their glasses here as well.

- **Free concerts** are one of the joys of Paris. In the summer, they're held all over the city, in parks and churches. Pick up an entertainment weekly for details.

  Some of the best concerts are held at the **American Church in Paris,** 65 quai d'Orsay (☎ **01-40-62-05-00;** Métro: Alma-Marceau; RER: Pont de l'Alma). **Eglise St-Merri,** 76 rue de la Verrerie, 4e (☎ **01-42-71-40-75;** Métro: Châtelet), is also known for its free concerts, which are regularly featured during September and July at 9pm on Saturday and 4pm on Sunday. **Sainte-Chapelle,** 4 bd. du Palais, 1er (☎ **01-42-77-65-65;** Métro: Cité), also stages concerts most nights in summer, but these concerts charge an admission ranging from 120F to 150F ($24 to $30). Call the box office for more details (daily from 11am to 6pm).

- The **Place des Vosges,** Paris's oldest square, is best enjoyed on a balmy spring evening. From the center of the square a glance in any direction will conjure up ancient Paris. First called the Palais Royale, the square was constructed as the royal residence for Henri IV, though an assassin took his life before he could take up lodgings. Once the setting of jousts and duels, this placid square boasts some of the finest architecture in Europe. Walk here at night under the square's spacious arcades, which allowed shopping in fair or inclement weather, a luxury in ancient Paris.

  Although strict architectural limits have preserved the square, each facade bears different windows and balconies. The most famous resident was Victor Hugo, who lived here for 16 years before fleeing to Guernsey in 1848. His home is now the site of the Musée Victor Hugo.

- Even if you have only 24 hours in Paris and can't explore most of the sights recommended in this chapter, try to make it to the **Basilique du Sacré-Coeur** at Place St-Pierre in Montmartre at dusk. Here, as you sit on the top steps with the church at your back and the square Willette in front of you, nighttime Paris begins to come alive. First a twinkle like a firefly—then all the lights go on like magic.

In failing health and shocked beyond grief, Marie Antoinette was brought here to await her trial. Only a small screen (and sometimes not even that) protected her modesty from the gaze of guards stationed in her cell. The Affair of the Carnation failed in its attempt to abduct her and secure her freedom. (By accounts of that day, she was shy and stupid, although the evidence is that upon her death she displayed the nobility of a true queen. Furthermore, it seems unlikely that she really uttered the famous quotation attributed to her, "Let them eat cake," when told the peasants had no bread.) It was shortly before noon on the morning of October 16, 1793, when her executioners came for her, grabbing her and cutting her hair, as was the custom for victims marked for the guillotine.

Later the Conciergerie housed yet more noted prisoners, including Madame Elizabeth; Madame du Barry, mistress of Louis XV; Madame Roland ("O Liberty! Liberty! What crimes are committed in thy name!"); and Charlotte Corday, who killed Marat with a kitchen knife while he was taking a sulfur bath. In time the revolution consumed its own leaders, such as Danton and Robespierre. Finally, even one of the most hated men in Paris, the public prosecutor Fouquier-Tinville, faced the same guillotine to which he'd sent so many others.

Among the few interned here who lived to tell the tale was America's Thomas Paine, who reminisced about his chats in English with Danton.

✪ **Sainte-Chapelle.** Palais de Justice, 4 bd. du Palais, 1er. ☎ **01-43-54-30-09.** Admission 32F ($6.40) adults, 21F ($4.20) students and ages 12–17, 15F ($3) ages 12–17; ages 11 and under free. Apr–Sept daily 9:30am–6:30pm; Oct–Mar daily 10am–5pm. Métro: Cité, St-Michel, or Châtelet–Les Halles. RER: St-Michel.

Countless travel writers have called this tiny chapel a jewel box. That hardly suffices. Nor will it do to call it "a light show." Go when the sun is shining, and you'll need no one else's words to describe the remarkable effects of natural light on Sainte-Chapelle.

The church is approached through the Cour de la Sainte Chapelle of the Palais de Justice. If it weren't for the chapel's 247-foot spire, the law courts here would almost swallow it up.

Built in only 5 to 7 years, beginning in 1246, the chapel has two levels. It was constructed to house relics of the True Cross, including the Crown of Thorns acquired by St. Louis (the Crusader king, Louis IX) from the emperor of Constantinople. (In those days, cathedrals throughout Europe were busy acquiring relics for their treasuries, regardless of their authenticity. It was a seller's, perhaps a sucker's, market.) Louis IX is said to have paid heavily for his relics, raising the money through unscrupulous means. He died of the plague on a crusade and was canonized in 1297.

You enter through the lower chapel, supported by flying buttresses and ornamented with fleur-de-lis designs. The lower chapel was used by the servants of the palace, the upper chamber by the king and his courtiers. The latter is reached by ascending narrow spiral stairs.

Viewed on a bright day, the 15 stained-glass windows seem to glow with Chartres blue, and reds that have inspired the Parisian saying, "Wine the color of Sainte-Chapelle's windows." The walls consist almost entirely of the glass, which had to be removed for safekeeping during the Revolution and again during both world wars. In their biblical designs are embodied the hopes and dreams—and the pretensions—of the kings who ordered their construction.

PONT NEUF

After leaving the Conciergerie, turn left and stroll along the Seine past medieval towers till you reach the Pont Neuf or "New Bridge." The span isn't new, of course; actually it's the oldest bridge in Paris, erected in 1604. In its day the bridge had two unique features: It was not flanked with houses and shops, and it was paved.

At the Hôtel Carnavalet, a museum in the Marais section (see below), a painting called *Spectacle of Buffons* shows what the bridge was like between 1665 and 1669. Duels were fought on the bridge; the nobility's great coaches crossed it; peddlers sold their wares on it; and as public facilities were lacking, the bridge became an outhouse as well. With these crowds, entertainers such as Tabarin came here to seek a few coins from the gawkers on this corbeled grotesquerie.

SQUARE DU VERT GALANT

Finally, continue on to the "prow" of the island, the Square du Vert Galant, pausing first to look at the equestrian statue of the beloved Henri IV, who was killed by an assassin. A true king of his people, Henry was also (to judge from accounts) regal in the boudoir. Hence the nickname "Vert Galant," or gay old spark. Gabrielle d'Estrées and Henriette d'Entragues were his best-known mistresses, but they had to share him with countless others, some of whom would casually catch his eye as he was riding along the streets of Paris.

In fond memory of the king, the little triangular park continues to attract lovers. If at first it appears to be a sunken garden, that's because it remains at its natural level; the rest of the Cité has been built up during the centuries.

ANOTHER ISLAND IN THE STREAM: ILE ST-LOUIS

As you walk across the little iron footbridge from the rear of Notre-Dame toward the Ile St-Louis, you'll enter a world of tree-shaded quays, aristocratic town houses with courtyards, restaurants, and antique shops. (You can also take the Métro to Sully-Morland or Pont-Marie.) The twin island of Ile de la Cité, it's primarily residential, and plaques on the facades of houses identify the former residences of the famous. Marie Curie lived at 36 quai de Béthune, near Pont de la Tournelle.

The most exciting mansion is the **Hôtel de Lauzun,** at 17 quai d'Anjou, which can be viewed only from the outside. It was the home of the duc de Lauzun, a favorite of Louis XIV, until his secret marriage angered the king, who had him tossed into the Bastille. Baudelaire lived here in the 19th century, squandering his family fortune and penning poetry that would be banned in France until 1949.

Voltaire lived with his mistress in the **Hôtel Lambert,** at 2 quai d'Anjou, where their quarrels were legendary. The mansion also housed the Polish royal family for over a century.

Farther along, at no. 9 quai d'Anjou, stands the house where Honoré Daumier, the painter, sculptor, and lithographer, lived between 1846 and 1863. Here he produced hundreds of lithographs satirizing the bourgeoisie and attacking government corruption. His caricature of Louis-Philippe landed him in jail for 6 months.

3 The Champs-Elysées: The Grand Promenade of Paris

In 1891 that "Innocent Abroad," Mark Twain, called the Champs-Elysées "the liveliest street in the world." It was designed for that favored pastime of Parisians, promenading. (It's *too* innocent to rank walking as Parisians' number-one pastime, but surely it comes in second or third.) Nowadays, tourists follow the old Parisian tradition; Americans who would normally drive half a block to the drugstore are seen doing the sprint from place Charles-de-Gaulle (Etoile) to place de la Concorde. That walk is surely a grand promenade, and you won't know Paris until you've done it. (And it's even lovelier at night.) In late 1995, after two hard, dusty, and hyperexpensive years of construction, Paris's most prominent triumphal promenade was reinaugurated with several important improvements. The contre-allées (constantly clogged side lanes) were removed, new lighting was added, pedestrian sidewalks widened, new trees planted, and underground parking garages built to rid the neighborhood of its curse: too many parked cars. The Grand Promenade is grand once again.

We'll start at the Tuileries and the place de la Concorde and take the Champs-Elysées toward the Arc de Triomphe. Part of the boulevard is a drive through a chestnut-lined park; the other section is a commercial avenue of sidewalk cafes, automobile showrooms, airline offices, cinemas, lingerie stores, and hamburger joints. The dividing point between the park and the commercial sections is Rond-Point des Champs-Elysées. Close to that is a philatelist's delight, the best-known open-air stamp market in Europe, held Sunday and Thursday. To chronicle the people who have walked this broad avenue would be to tell the history of Paris through the last few centuries. Ever since the days of Thomas Jefferson and Benjamin Franklin, Americans have gravitated here, and even if the avenue has lost some of its turn-of-the-century elegance, it still hums like a hive.

The Grand Promenade

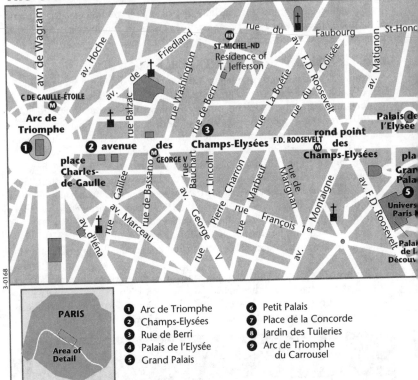

PARIS
Area of Detail

1. Arc de Triomphe
2. Champs-Elysées
3. Rue de Berri
4. Palais de l'Elysée
5. Grand Palais
6. Petit Palais
7. Place de la Concorde
8. Jardin des Tuileries
9. Arc de Triomphe du Carrousel

✪ **Jardin de Tuileries.** Place de la Concorde, 1er. ☎ 01-44-50-75-01. Métro: Tuileries.

Behind the Louvre and bordering the place de la Concorde, the Tuileries are as much a part of Paris as the Seine. These statue-studded gardens were designed by Le Nôtre, the gardener to Louis XIV, who planned the grounds of Versailles.

About 100 years before that, a palace was ordered to be built by Catherine de Médicis. Connected to the Louvre, it was occupied by Louis XVI after he left Versailles; after the Revolution, Napoléon I called it home. Twice attacked by the people of Paris, it was burnt to the ground in 1871 and never rebuilt. The gardens, however, remain. In the orderly French manner, the trees are arranged according to designs and the paths are arrow-straight. To break this sense of order and formality there are bubbling fountains.

The neoclassic statuary is sometimes insipid and from time to time, rebellious "art critics" have desecrated it. Seemingly half of Paris is found in the Tuileries on a warm spring day, listening to the birds and watching the daffodils and red tulips bloom. Fountains gurgle, and mothers roll carriages over the grounds where 18th-century revolutionaries killed the king's Swiss guards.

Also here, 2 miles from place Charles-de-Gaulle (Etoile), stands the Arc de Triomphe du Carrousel, at the Cour du Carrousel. Pierced with three walkways and supported by marble columns, the monument celebrates Napoléon and the Grand Armée's victory at Austerlitz on December 5, 1805. Surmounting the arch are statuary, a chariot, and four bronze horses. "Paris needs more monuments," Napoléon once shouted. He got his wish.

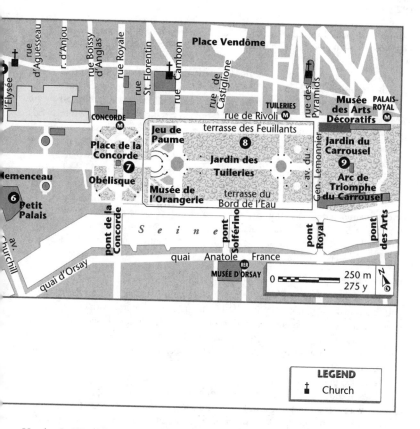

Musée de l'Orangerie des Tuileries. Jardin des Tuileries, place de la Concorde, 1er. ☎ **01-42-97-48-16.** Admission 30F ($6) adults, 20F ($4) ages 18–24, and on Sun; children under 18 free. Wed–Mon 9:45am–5pm. Métro: Concorde.

In the Tuileries stands this gem among galleries. By all means, visit the Louvre and the Musée d'Orsay first, but if you have a spare hour and a half, here is a good place to spend it. It has an outstanding collection of art and one acclaimed masterwork: Claude Monet's exquisite *Nymphéas* (1915–27), in which water lilies float amorphously on the canvas. The work blankets the walls of two oval rooms on the ground floor; the artist himself supervised the installation.

Creating his effects with hundreds and hundreds of minute strokes of his brush (one irate 19th-century critic called them "tongue lickings"), Monet achieved the unity and harmony of his Rouen Cathedral series and his haystacks. Artists with lesser talent might have stirred up "soup." But Monet was a genius. See his lilies and evoke for yourself the melancholy he experienced so many years ago. Monet continued to paint his water landscapes until his death in 1926, although he was greatly hampered by failing eyesight.

The renovated building also shelters the Walter-Guillaume collection, which includes more than 24 Renoirs, including *Young Girl at a Piano.* Cézanne is represented by 14 works, notably *The Red Rock,* and Matisse by 11 paintings. The highlight of Rousseau's 9 works displayed here is *The Wedding,* and the dozen paintings by Picasso reach the pinnacle of their brilliance in *The Female Bathers.* Other outstanding paintings are by Utrillo (10 works in all), Soutine (22), and Derain (28).

Galerie Nationale du Jeu de Paume. Jardin des Tuileries/place de la Concorde, 1er. ☎ **01-42-60-69-69.** Admission 38F ($7.60) adults, 28F ($5.60) students; ages 12 and under free. Tues noon–9:30pm; Wed–Fri noon–7pm; Sat–Sun 10am–7pm. Métro: Concorde.

For years the national gallery in the Jeu de Paume, in the northeast corner of the Tuileries gardens, was one of the treasures of Paris, displaying some of the finest works of the Impressionists. To the regret of many, that collection was hauled off to the Musée d'Orsay in 1986. Following a $12.6 million facelift, this Second Empire building has been transformed into a state-of-the-art gallery with a video screening room. No permanent collection is housed here, but every two or three months a new show is mounted. Sometimes the works of little-known contemporary artists are on display; at other times, an exhibit will feature unexplored aspects of established artists.

Originally, in this part of the gardens, Napoléon III built a ball court on which *jeu de paume,* an antecedent of tennis, was played—hence the museum's name. The most infamous period in the national gallery's history came during the Nazi occupation, when it served as an "evaluation center" for works of modern art. Paintings from all over France were shipped to the Jeu de Paume; art condemned by the Nazis as "degenerate" was burned.

Place de la Concorde. 1er. Métro: Concorde.

In the east, the Champs-Elysées begins at place de la Concorde, an octagonal traffic hub built in 1757 to honor Louis XV. The statue of the king was torn down in 1792 and the name of the square changed to place de la Révolution. Floodlit at night, it is dominated nowadays by an **Egyptian obelisk** from Luxor, the oldest man-made object in Paris. It was carved circa 1200 B.C. and spirited out of French-dominated Egypt in 1829.

In the Reign of Terror, the dreaded guillotine was erected on this spot, and claimed the lives of thousands, everybody from Louis XVI, who died bravely, to Madame du Barry, who went screaming and kicking all the way. Before leering crowds, Marie Antoinette, Robespierre, Danton, Mme Roland, and Charlotte Corday were executed. (You can still lose your life on the place de la Concorde; all you have to do is chance the traffic and cross over.)

For a spectacular sight, look down the Champs-Elysées—the Marly horses frame the view. On the opposite side, the winged horses of Coysevox flank the gateway to the Tuileries. On each side of the obelisk are two fountains with bronze-tailed mermaids and bare-breasted sea nymphs. Gray-beige statues ring the square, honoring the cities of France. To symbolize the city's fall to Germany in 1871, the statue of Strasbourg was covered with a black drape that wasn't lifted until the end of World War I. Two of the palaces on the place de la Concorde are today the Ministry of the Marine and the deluxe Crillon Hotel, both designed in the 1760s by Ange-Jacques Gabriel.

✪ **Arc de Triomphe.** Place Charles-de-Gaulle–Etoile, 16e. ☎ **01-43-80-31-31.** Admission 35F ($7) adults, 23F ($4.60) ages 12–25; free for children 11 and under. Apr–Sept Tues–Sat 9:30am–10pm; Sun–Mon 9:30am–6:30pm; Oct–Mar Tues–Sat 10am–10:30pm, Sun–Mon 10am–6pm. Métro: Charles de Gaulle or Etoile.

At the western end of the Champs-Elysées, the Arc de Triomphe suggests one of those ancient Roman arches, only it's larger. Actually, it's the biggest triumphal arch in the world, about 163 feet high and 147 feet wide. To reach it, don't try to cross the square, the busiest traffic hub in Paris (death is certain!). Take the underground passage and live a little longer. With one dozen streets radiating from the "Star," the roundabout was called by one writer "vehicular roulette with more balls than numbers."

After the death of Charles de Gaulle, the French government—despite protests from anti-Gaullists—voted to change the name of this site from place de l'Etoile to place Charles-de-Gaulle.

The arch has witnessed some of France's proudest moments, and some of its more shameful and humiliating defeats, notably those of 1871 and 1940. The memory of German troops marching under the arch that had come to symbolize France's glory and prestige is still painful to the French. Who could ever forget the 1940 newsreel of the Frenchman standing on the Champs-Elysées openly weeping as the Nazi storm troopers goose-stepped through Paris?

Commissioned by Napoléon in 1806 to commemorate his victories, the arch wasn't ready for the entrance of his new empress, Marie-Louise, in 1810. It served its ceremonial purpose anyway, and in fact, wasn't completed until 1836, under the reign of Louis-Philippe. Four years later the remains of Napoléon, brought from his grave at St. Helena, passed under the arch on the journey to his tomb at the Invalides. Since that time it has become the focal point for state funerals. It is also the site of the permanent tomb of the unknown soldier, in whose honor an eternal flame is kept burning.

The greatest state funeral was that of Victor Hugo in 1885; his coffin was placed under the center of the arch, and much of Paris turned out to pay tribute to the author. Another notable funeral was that of Ferdinand Foch, the supreme commander of the Allied forces in World War I who died in 1929. Perhaps the Arc's happiest moment occurred in 1944, when the liberation of Paris parade passed through. That same year, Eisenhower paid a visit to the tomb of France's unknown soldier, a new tradition among leaders of state and important figures.

Of the sculptures on the monument, the best-known is Rude's *Marseillaise,* also called *The Departure of the Volunteers. The Triumph of Napoléon in 1810,* by J. P. Cortot, and the *Resistance of 1814* and the *Peace of 1815,* both by Etex, also adorn the facade. The monument is engraved with the names of hundreds of generals (those underlined died in battle) who commanded French troops in Napoleonic victories.

You can take an elevator or climb the stairway to the top, where there is an exhibition hall with lithographs and photos depicting the arch throughout its history. From the observation deck, you have the finest view of the Champs-Elysées and of such landmarks as the Louvre, the Eiffel Tower, Sacré-Coeur, and the new district of La Défense.

OTHER SIGHTS NEARBY

Palais de l'Elysée. Rue du Faubourg St-Honoré, 8e. Métro: Miromesnil.

A slight detour from the Champs-Elysées along the avenue de Marigny takes you to France's presidential palace, which occupies a block along fashionable Faubourg St-Honoré. It is now occupied by the president of France and cannot be visited by the public without an invitation.

Built in 1718 for the Count d'Evreux, the palace had many owners before it was purchased by the Republic in 1873. One owner was Madame de Pompadour, who, when she "had the supreme delicacy to die discreetly at the age of 43," bequeathed it to the king. The world première of Voltaire's play *The Chinese Orphan* was presented here. After her divorce from Napoléon, Josephine lived here, as did Napoléon III when he was president, beginning in 1848. When he became emperor in 1852, he moved to the Tuileries. Such celebrated English visitors as Queen Victoria and Wellington have spent nights here as well.

Among the palace's works of art are tapestries made at Beauvais in the 18th century, Raphael and Leonardo da Vinci paintings, and Louis XVI furnishings. A grand dining hall was built for Napoléon III, as well as an orangery for the Duchess du Berry (now converted to a winter garden).

Palais Royal. Place du Palais-Royal/rue St-Honoré, 1er. Métro: Louvre.

At the demolished Café Foy in the Palais Royal, Camille Desmoulins jumped up on a table and shouted for the mob "to fight to the death." The date was July 13, 1789. The French Revolution had begun. But the renown of the Palais Royal goes back much further. Facing the Louvre, the gardens were planted in 1634 for Cardinal Richelieu, who presented them to Louis XIII. As a child, Louis XIV played around the fountain, and once nearly drowned in it. Despite his close call so long ago, children frolic here to this day. Sculptor Daniel Buren's prison-striped columns, which were added to the garden in 1986, are controversial. Note, too, Pol Bury's steel-ball sculptures decorating the fountains.

In time the property became the residence of the dukes of Orléans. Philippe-Egalité, a cousin of Louis XVI, built his apartments on the grounds, and subsequently rented them to prostitutes. By this century those same apartments were rented by such artists as Colette and Cocteau. Of the gardens Colette wrote, "It is as though I were living in the provinces under the shadow of the parish church! I go into the temple en passant." (A plaque at 9 rue Beaujolais marks the entrance to her apartment, which she inhabited until her death in 1954.) Today the Palais Royal contains apartments, some discreet shops, and a few great restaurants (like Le Grand Véfour; see chapter 5). New York–born American actor and playwright John Howard Payne wrote *Home, Sweet Home* while living in one of the apartments.

Turning back the clock again: As an 18-year-old lieutenant, Napoléon Bonaparte met his first prostitute in the Palais Royal. Robespierre and Danton dined here. An actress, Mlle Montansier, "knew" many of them, including the Corsican. Charlotte Corday came this way, looking for a dagger with which to kill Marat. During the Directoire, gambling dens flourished at the Palais Royal, and foreigners reported seeing Frenchmen leaving the salons absent their silk breeches—they had literally lost their trousers at the tables!

Today a sleepy provincial air predominates, and it's hard to imagine the palace's former life. From the place Colette, you enter the Court of Honor, with colonnades on three sides. The palace is now the headquarters of the Councils of State, and the Court of Honor is a parking lot by day. In the center of the Palais Royal is the Galerie d'Orléans, with two fountains and many colonnades. You can stroll through the gardens or down the Galerie Montpensier, which is filled with little shops.

Place Vendôme. 1er. Métro: Opéra.

Always aristocratic, sometimes royal, place Vendôme enjoyed its golden age in the heyday of the Second Empire. Dress designers—the great ones, such as Worth—introduced the crinoline here. Louis Napoléon lived here, wooing his future empress, Eugénie de Montijo, at the Hôtel du Rhin. In halcyon days Strauss waltzes echoed across the plaza, to be in time replaced by cannon fire.

Today Place Vendôme's most prestigious tenant is the Ritz, around which banks and offices abound. Yet for some reason, the Paris of Louis XIV doesn't seem far distant.

A column crowned by Napoléon dominates the plaza. (The plaza was originally planned by Mansart to honor Louis XIV—so it's a good thing he died earlier.) There was a statue of the Sun King here until the Revolution, when it was replaced briefly by "Liberty."

Then came Napoléon, who ordered that a sort of Trajan's Column be erected in honor of the victor at Austerlitz. That Napoléon himself won the battle was

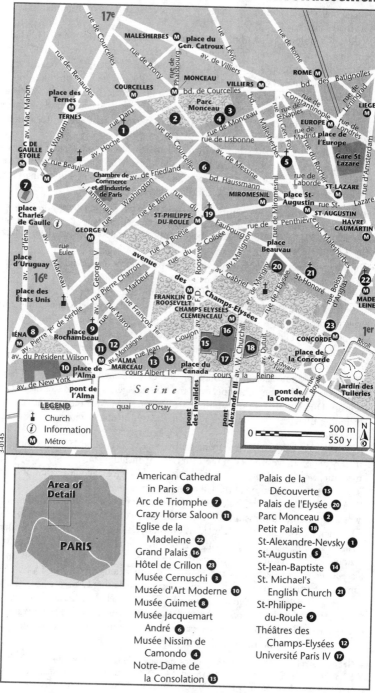

LEGEND
† Church
ⓘ Information
Ⓜ Métro

0 — 500 m
0 — 550 y
N

3-0145

Area of Detail

PARIS

American Cathedral in Paris ❾
Arc de Triomphe ❼
Crazy Horse Saloon ⓫
Eglise de la Madeleine ㉒
Grand Palais ⓰
Hôtel de Crillon ㉓
Musée Cernuschi ❸
Musée d'Art Moderne ❿
Musée Guimet ❽
Musée Jacquemart André ❻
Musée Nissim de Camondo ❹
Notre-Dame de la Consolation ⓭

Palais de la Découverte ⓯
Palais de l'Elysée ⓴
Parc Monceau ❷
Petit Palais ⓲
St-Alexandre-Nevsky ❶
St-Augustin ❺
St-Jean-Baptiste ⓮
St. Michael's English Church ㉑
St-Philippe-du-Roule ❾
Théâtres des Champs-Elysées ⓬
Université Paris IV ⓱

195

"incidental." The column was made of bronze melted from captured Russian and Austrian cannons.

After Napoléon's downfall the statue was replaced with one of Henri IV, everybody's favorite king and every woman's favorite man. Later Napoléon surmounted it once again, this time in uniform and without the pose of a Caesar.

The Communards of 1871, who detested royalty and its false promises, pulled down the statue, led by the artist Courbet. For his part in the drama, he was jailed and fined the cost of restoring the statue. He couldn't pay it, of course, and was forced into exile in Switzerland. Eventually, Napoléon, wrapped in a Roman toga, finally won out.

The plaza is one of the best known in Paris. It has attracted such tenants as Chopin, who lived at no. 12 until his death in 1849. Who was Vendôme, you ask? He was the son (delicate writers refer to him as "the natural son") of roving Henri IV and his best-known mistress, Gabrielle d'Estrées.

Petit Palais. Petit Palais, av. Winston-Churchill, 8e. ☎ **01-42-65-12-73.** Admission 27F ($5.40) adults, 14.50F ($2.90) ages 18–25, free 17 and under and over 60, free on Sun. Special exhibitions 30–40F ($6–$8) adults, as above for discounted rates. Tues–Sun 10am–5:40pm. Métro: Champs-Elysées.

Built by architect Charles Girault, this small palace faces the Grand Palais (housing special exhibitions); both were erected for the 1900 exhibition.

The Petit Palais contains works of art belonging to the city of Paris. As such, it is a hodgepodge, and mainly interests the serious viewer of art who has more than a few days to spend in Paris. Most visitors come here for the temporary exhibitions, not the permanent collections. Of the latter, the most prominent are the Dutuit and Tuck collections. In the Dutuit collection are Egyptian, Greek, and Roman bronzes, rare ivory statues (the most prominent of which is of a Roman actor), and a series of ancient Greek porcelains. The collection also boasts enamels, sculpture, and hand-lettered and -painted manuscripts from the Middle Ages. A good collection of 17th-century Dutch and Flemish paintings are also on view, with representative artists including Breughel the Younger (*Wedding Pageant*), Rubens, Hobbema, Ruysdaël, and others.

Edward Tuck donated the museum's other major collection in 1930. It's composed mainly of decorative artwork of the 18th century, including tapestries, heavily gilded furniture, wood-paneled salons, and porcelains, which give a good overview of French aesthetic sense at the time of the fall of the *ancien régime*.

A number of rooms are dedicated to 19th-century French painting, including a few works by major Impressionists. The collection contains canvases by Courbet, Daumier, Corot, Delacroix, Manet, Sisley, Mary Cassatt (*Le Bain*), Maurice Denis, Odilon Redon, a series of portraits (one of Sarah Bernhardt by Clairin), and art by Edouard Vuillard and Pierre Bonnard. The museum has a strong emphasis on the "academic school," especially the enormous compositions of Gustave Doré. Other important artists come from the symbolist school, including Osbert, whose *Soir Antique* is a cherished item. Notable paintings displayed include *The Death of Seneca* by David, the *Portrait of Lalande* by Fragonard, and the *Young Shepherd Holding a Flower* by Greuze. The museum also has sculptures by Rodin, Bourdelle, Maillol, and Carpeaux, and glassworks by Galle and Lalique.

La Grande Arche de La Défense. 1 place du parvis de La Défense, 18e. ☎ **01-49-07-27-57.** Admission 40F ($8) adults, 30F ($6) ages 4–18; 3 and under free. Summer, daily 10am–6pm; off-season, Mon and Wed–Fri 11am–6pm, Sat–Sun 10am–6pm. RER: La Défense.

Designed as the architectural centerpiece of the sprawling and futuristic satellite suburb of La Défense, this massive steel-and-masonry arch rises 35 stories from the pavement. Built with the blessing of the late Pres. François Mitterrand, the deliberately overscaled archway is the latest landmark to dot the Paris skyline. Though it is removed from the sights listed above, it extends that magnificently engineered straight line that links the Louvre, the Arc du Carroussel, the Champs-Elysées, the Arc de Triomphe, the avenue de la Grande Armée, and the place du Porte Maillot. The arch is ringed with a circular avenue (*périphérique*), patterned after the one that winds around the more famous Arc de Triomphe. The monument is tall enough to shelter the Cathedral of Notre-Dame below its heavily trussed canopy. An elevator carries visitors to an observation platform, where they get a view of the carefully planned geometry of the surrounding streets. See something strange rigged along the structure of the Grande Arche? They're nets: Pieces of Mitterrand's grand project started falling to the ground, and thus a mesh was erected to catch fragments before they hit people on the head. Would this were true for all politicians' follies.

4 The Eiffel Tower & Environs

Everyone visits the landmark that has become the symbol of Paris. To see it best, however, don't sprint—approach it gradually.

Take the Métro to place du Trocadéro, dominated by a statue of Marshal Foch. Once you've surfaced, you'll be at the gateway to the Palais de Chaillot. Replacing the 1878 Palais du Trocadéro, the new palace was built in 1937 for the International Exhibition. If you have time, try to visit at least two of the three important museums lodged in the building: one a maritime showcase, another a gallery of reproductions of many of the monuments of France, a third devoted to civilizations and cultures from prehistoric times until today—everything from a Sicilian peasant cart to a totem pole from British Columbia.

From the palace terrace (one writer called it "Mussolinian"), you have a panoramic view across the Seine to the Eiffel Tower. In back, the fountain-filled Jardins du Palais de Chaillot sweep down to the Seine. From April to October the gardens are a hodgepodge of international tongues.

✪ **La Tour Eiffel.** Champ-de-Mars, 7e. ☎ **01-44-11-23-23.** First landing 20F ($4), second landing 42F ($8.40), third landing 57F ($11.40). Stairs to second floor 14F ($2.80). Sept–May daily 9:30am–11pm; June–Aug daily 9am–midnight. In fall and winter the stairs are open only until 6:30pm. Métro: Trocadéro, Ecole-Militaire, or Bir-Hakeim. RER: Champ-de-Mars–Tour Eiffel.

Except for the Leaning Tower of Pisa, this is the single most recognizable structure in the world. Weighing 7,000 tons but exerting about the same pressure on the ground as an average-size person sitting in a chair, the tower was never meant to be permanent. It was built for the Exhibition of 1889 by Gustave Alexandre Eiffel, the French engineer whose fame rested mainly on his iron bridges. (Incidentally, he also designed the framework for the Statue of Liberty.)

The tower, including its 55-foot television antenna, is 1,056 feet high. On a clear day you can see it some 40 miles away. An open-framework construction, the tower unlocked the almost unlimited possibilities of steel construction, paving the way for the skyscrapers of the 20th century. Skeptics said it couldn't be built, and Eiffel actually wanted to make it soar higher than it did. For years it remained the tallest man-made structure on earth, until such skyscrapers as the Empire State Building usurped it.

We could fill an entire page of this guide with Eiffel Tower statistics. Its plans spanned 6,000 square yards of paper, and it weighs 7,000 tons and contains $2^{1}/_{2}$ million rivets. But forget the numbers. Just stand underneath the tower and look straight up. It's like a rocket of steel lacework shooting into the sky.

Initially, artists and writers vehemently denounced it, although later generations sang its praise. People were fond of calling it names: "a giraffe," "the world's greatest lamppost," "the iron monster." Others suggested, "Let's keep art nouveau grounded." Nature lovers feared it would interfere with the flights of birds over Paris.

In the early 1890s the tower escaped destruction because it found a new practical use: The French government installed antennae on the tower, thus enabling wireless communications throughout the city.

You can visit the tower in three stages. Taking the elevator to the first landing, you have a view over the rooftops of Paris. On the first level, a cinema museum that shows films can be visited, and restaurants and a bar are open year-round. The second landing provides a panoramic look at the city. The third and final stage gives the most spectacular view, allowing you to identify monuments and buildings that are visible. On the ground level, in the eastern and western pillars, you can visit the 1899 lift machinery when the tower is open. Eiffel's office has been re-created on the fourth level; wax figures depict the engineer receiving Thomas Edison.

Of course, it's the view that most people come for, and this extends for 42 miles, theoretically. In practice, weather conditions tend to limit it. Nevertheless, it's fabulous, and the best time for visibility is about an hour before sunset.

Champ-de-Mars and École Militaire. 7e. Métro: Trocadéro, École-Militaire, or Bir-Hakeim.

Leave some time to explore the Champ-de-Mars, the gardens between the Eiffel Tower and the Military School. Laid out around 1770, these gardens were the World's Fair grounds of Paris and the scene of many military parades.

Thanks in part to one of France's best-known mistresses, Madame de Pompadour, who persuaded the king to finance the project, the Ecole Militaire (Military School) was established; the plans were drawn up by A.J. Gabriel. This classical school was founded in 1751 for about 500 young men who wanted a military career.

Napoléon entered in 1784, the year his father died of cancer. He graduated a year later as a lieutenant, aged 16. According to accounts, he wasn't popular with his classmates, many of whom openly made fun of him. One wrote, "All boots, no man." Pity those creatures when their names came up for promotions years later. Another French general, Charles de Gaulle, also studied at the school. The Military School normally only grants special permission to enter to military bodies; apply in writing to the Général Commandant Militaire, Ecole Militaire, 13 place Joffre.

Hôtel des Invalides (Napoléon's Tomb). Place des Invalides, 7e. ☎ 01-44-42-37-72. Admission 37F ($7.40) adults, 27F ($5.40) children 12–18 and people over 60; children 11 and under free. The ticket covers admission to the Musée de l'Armée, Napoléon's Tomb, and the Musée des Plans-Reliefs. Oct–Mar, daily 10am–5pm; Apr–Sept, daily 10am–6pm. The tomb of Napoléon is open until 7pm June–Sept. Closed Jan 1, May 1, Nov 1, Dec 25. Métro: Latour-Maubourg, Varenne, or Invalides.

It was the Sun King who decided to build the "hotel" to house soldiers who'd been disabled. It wasn't entirely a benevolent gesture, since these veterans had been injured, crippled, or blinded while fighting his battles. Louvois was ordered in 1670 to launch this massive building program. When it was completed—and Louis XIV was long dead—the corridors stretched for miles. Eventually the building was crowned by a gilded dome designed by Jules Hardouin-Mansart.

It is best to approach the Invalides by crossing over the Right Bank via the turn-of-the-century Alexander III Bridge. In the building's cobblestone forecourt, a display of massive cannons makes for a formidable welcome.

Before rushing on to Napoléon's tomb, you may want to take the time to visit the greatest military museum in the world, the **Musée de l'Armée**. In 1794 a French

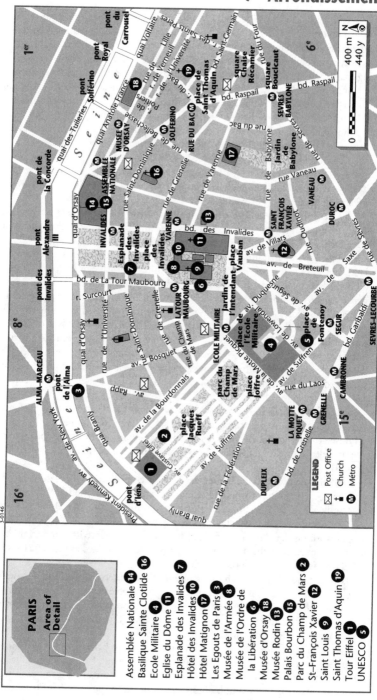

7th Arrondissement

LEGEND

- ⊠ Post Office
- ✚ Church
- Ⓜ Métro

PARIS
Area of Detail

Assemblée Nationale **14**
Basilique Sainte Clotilde **16**
Ecole Militaire **4**
Eglise du Dôme **11**
Esplanade des Invalides **7**
Hôtel des Invalides **10**
Hôtel Matignon **17**
Les Egouts de Paris **3**
Musée de l'Armée **8**
Musée de l'Ordre de
   la Libération **6**
Musée d'Orsay **18**
Musée Rodin **13**
Palais Bourbon **15**
Parc du Champ de Mars **2**
St-François Xavier **12**
Saint Louis **9**
Saint Thomas d'Aquin **19**
Tour Eiffel **1**
UNESCO **5**

199

3-0146

inspector started collecting weapons, uniforms, and equipment, and with the continued accumulation of war material over the centuries, the museum has become a horrifying documentary of man's self-destruction. Viking swords, Burgundian bacinets, blunderbusses from the 14th century, Balkan khandjars, American Browning machine guns, war pitchforks, salamander-engraved Renaissance serpentines, "Haute Epoque" armor, a 1528 Griffon, musketoons, grenadiers . . . if it can kill, it's enshrined here. As a sardonic touch, there's even the wooden leg of General Daumesnil. Oblivious to these ironies, the Germans looted the place in 1940.

Among the outstanding acquisitions are **suits of armor** worn by the kings and dignitaries of France, including Louis XIV, the best of which lie in the new Arsenal. The most famous one, the "armor suit of the lion," was made for François I. Henri II ordered his suit engraved with the monogram of his mistress, Diane de Poitiers, and (perhaps reluctantly) that of his wife, Catherine de Médicis. The showcases of swords are among the finest in the world.

The mementos of **World War I,** including those of American and Canadian soldiers, are especially interesting. Included is the Armistice Bugle, which sounded the cease-fire on November 7, 1918, before the general cease-fire on November 11, 1918.

And then there's that little Corsican general who became France's greatest soldier. Here you can see the plaster death mask Antommarchi made of him, as well as an oil by Delaroche, painted at the time of Napoléon's first banishment (April 1814), which depicted him as he probably looked, paunch and all. The First Empire exhibit displays Napoléon's field bed with his tent. In the room devoted to the Restoration, the 100 Days, and Waterloo, you can see Napoléon's reconstituted bedroom at the time of his death at St. Helena. On the more personal side, you can view Vizir, a horse he owned (stuffed), as well as a saddle he used mainly for state ceremonies. The Turenne Salon contains other souvenirs, including the hat Napoléon wore at Eylau, his sword from his victory at Austerlitz, and his "Flag of Farewell," which he kissed before departing for Elba.

The Salle Orientale in the west wing shows arms of the Eastern world, including Asia and the Muslim countries of the Mideast, from the 16th to the 19th centuries. Turkish armor (look for Bajazet's helmet) and weaponry, and Chinese and Japanese armor and swords, are on display. The west wing also houses exhibits on World Wars I and II.

You can gain access to the **Musée des Plans-Reliefs** through the west wing. This collection shows French towns and monuments done in scale models.

A walk across the Court of Honor delivers you to the **Eglise du Dôme (Church of the Dome),** designed by Hardouin-Mansart for Louis XIV. The great architect began work on the church in 1677, although he died before its completion. The dome is the second-tallest monument in Paris. The hearse used at the emperor's funeral on May 9, 1821, is in the Napoléon Chapel.

To accommodate the **Tomb of Napoléon,** the architect Visconti had to redesign the high altar in 1842. First buried at St. Helena, Napoléon's remains were returned to Paris in 1840, as Louis-Philippe had demanded of England. The triumphal funeral procession passed under the Arc de Triomphe, down the Champs-Elysées, en route to the Invalides, as snow swirled through the air.

The tomb is made of red Finnish porphyry, the base from green granite. Napoléon's remains were locked inside six coffins. Legends have abounded that not all of Napoléon was buried with Napoléon, but that some of his body parts went missing, notably his penis and his heart. According to Napoleonic scholars, the two doctors who dissected the emperor placed all his body parts in an urn positioned between his legs. Scholars deny the truth of these legends about the missing parts, although one wealthy gentleman in Connecticut frequently exhibits a penis preserved in alcohol, claiming it was once attached to the emperor. Surrounding the tomb are a dozen amazonlike figures representing his victories. Almost lampooning the smallness of the man, everything is done on a gargantuan scale. You'd think a real giant was buried here, not a symbolic one. In his coronation robes, the statue of Napoléon stands 8¹/₂ feet high. The grave of Napoléon's son, "the King of Rome," lies at his feet.

Napoléon's tomb is surrounded by those of his brother, Joseph Bonaparte; the great Vauban; Foch, the Allied commander in World War I; Turenne; and La Tour d'Auvergne, the first grenadier of the republic (actually, only his heart is entombed here).

Palais Bourbon. 33 Quai d'Orsay, 7e. ☎ **01-40-63-64-08.** Admission free. Hours vary. Métro: Chambre-des-Députés.

The lower house of the French parliament, the Chamber of Deputies, meets at this 1722 mansion built by the Duchess of Bourbon, a daughter of Louis XIV. Reservations for one of two types of visits to the Palais must be made up to four months in advance. Tours that emphasize the art and architecture of the building and explain basic French government processes are given Mondays, Fridays, and Saturdays. However, the tours are given only in French. Guests may also observe sessions of the Assemblée, which are held Tuesday afternoons and all day Wednesday and Thursday beginning at 9:30am. Do remember that this is a working government building and therefore all visitors are subject to rigorous security checks.

5 Montparnasse

For the "lost generation," life centered around the literary cafes of Montparnasse. Hangouts such as Dôme, Coupole, Rotonde, and Sélect became legendary. Artists, especially American expatriates, turned their backs on Montmartre, dismissing it as too touristy.

Picasso, Modigliani, and Man Ray came this way, and Hemingway was also a popular figure. So was Fitzgerald when he was poor (when he was in the chips, you'd find him at the Ritz). William Faulkner, Archibald MacLeish, Isadora Duncan, Miró, James Joyce, Ford Madox Ford, even Trotsky—all were here.

All, that is, except for Gertrude Stein, who never frequented the cafes. To see her, you would have to wait for an invitation to her salon at 27 rue de Fleurus. She bestowed this favor on Sherwood Anderson, Elliot Paul, Ezra Pound, and, for a time, Hemingway. However, Pound launched himself into a beloved chair and broke it, incurring Stein's wrath; Hemingway decided there wasn't "much future in men being friends with great women."

When not receiving guests, Stein was busy buying the paintings of Cézanne, Renoir, Matisse, and Picasso. One writer said that her salon was engaged in an international conspiracy to promote modern art. At her Saturday-evening gatherings you might have met Braque.

Aside from the literary legends, one of the most notable characters of the sector was Kiki de Montparnasse. Actually she was an artist's model and prostitute named Alice Prin. She sang at Le Jockey at 127 boulevard du Montparnasse, which no longer exists, although Hemingway called it the best night club "that ever was." Her songs were suggestive, as were her gestures. In her black hose and garters against milk-white thighs, she captivated dozens of men, among them Frederick Kohner, who called his own memoirs, *Kiki of Montparnasse.* However, Kiki would later write her own memoirs, with an introduction by Hemingway. Papa called her "a Queen," noting that was "very different from being a lady."

The Mother of the Lost Generation

"So Paris was the place that suited those of us that were to create the twentieth century art and literature, naturally enough." Gertrude Stein, who made this pronouncement, wasn't known for her modesty.

In the 1920s she and her lover, Alice B. Toklas, became the most famous expatriates in Paris. To get an invitation to call on Lovey and Pussy (nicknames for Gertrude and Alice) at 27 rue de Fleurus, in the heart of Montparnasse, was to be invited into the innermost circle of expatriate Paris. Although their former residence is in private hands and you can't go inside, literary fans flock to this fabled address to stare at the facade that once housed literature's two most celebrated female companions.

Though Gertrude didn't achieve popular success until the 1933 publication of her *Autobiography of Alice B. Toklas,* she was known and adored by many members of the Lost Generation—all except Ernest Hemingway, who later tarred her in his posthumous memoir, *A Moveable Feast.*

But to the young sensitive men, arriving from America in the 1920s, La Stein was "The Mother of Us All." These young fans hung onto her every word, while Alice baked her notorious hash brownies in the kitchen.

At rue de Fleurus, Gertrude and Alice surrounded themselves with modern paintings, including a nude by Vallotton, and pieces by Toulouse-Lautrec, Picasso, Gauguin, and Matisse. Gertrude paid $1,000 for her first Matisse, $30 for her first Picasso. Matisse, in fact, first met Picasso here. The Saturday-night soirées became a Montparnasse legend.

Not all visitors came to worship. Gertrude was denounced by many, including avant-garde magazines of the time, which called her a "fraud, egomaniac, and publicity seeking." Braque called her claim to influence art in Paris "nonsense."

In spite of the attacks, the jokes, and the lurid speculation, Stein, at least in public, kept her ego intact. Bernard Fay once told her he'd met three people in his life who ranked as geniuses: Gide, Picasso, and Stein herself.

"Why include Gide?" Stein asked.

The life of Montparnasse still centers around its cafes and exotic nightclubs, many only a shadow of what they used to be. Its heart is at the crossroads of the boulevard Raspail and the boulevard du Montparnasse, one of the settings of *The Sun Also Rises.* Hemingway wrote that "the boulevard Raspail always made dull riding." Rodin's controversial statue of Balzac swathed in a large cape stands guard over the prostitutes who cluster around the pedestal. Balzac seems to be the only one in Montparnasse who doesn't feel time's weight.

6 The Latin Quarter

The University of Paris (the Sorbonne) lies on the Left Bank in the 5th arrondissement. This is where students meet and fall in love over *café-crème* and croissants. Rabelais called it the *Quartier Latin,* because of the students and professors who spoke Latin in the classroom and on the streets. The neighborhood teems with belly dancers, exotic restaurants (from Vietnamese to Balkan), sidewalk cafes, bookstalls, *caveaux* (basement nightclubs), and gamin boys and girls.

Musée National du Moyen Age/Thermes de Cluny (Musée de Cluny). 6 place Paul-Painlevé, 5e. ☎ **01-53-73-78-00.** Admission 30F ($6) adults, 20F ($4) ages 18–25; ages 17 and under free. Wed–Mon 9:15am–5:45pm. Métro: Cluny-Sorbonne.

You stand in the cobblestoned Court of Honor, admiring the flamboyant Gothic building with its clinging vines, turreted walls, gargoyles, and dormers with seashell motifs. Along with the Hôtel de Sens in Le Marais, the Hôtel de Cluny is all that remains of domestic medieval architecture in Paris. Originally the Cluny was the mansion of a rich 15th-century abbot; it was built over and beside the ruins of a Roman bath. By 1515 it was the residence of Mary Tudor, teenage widow of Louis XII and daughter of Henry VII of England and Elizabeth of York.

Seized during the revolution, the Cluny was rented in 1833 to Alexandre du Sommerard, who adorned it with his collection of medieval works of art. Upon his death in 1842, both the building and the collection were bought back by the government.

The present-day collection of arts and crafts of the Middle Ages is the finest in the world. Most people come primarily to see the **Unicorn Tapestries,** the most acclaimed tapestries in the world. A beautiful princess and her handmaiden, beasts of prey, and just plain pets—all the romance of the age of chivalry lives on in these remarkable yet mysterious tapestries discovered only a century ago in Limousin's Château de Boussac. Five seem to deal with the five senses (one, for example, depicts a unicorn looking into a mirror held up by a dour-faced maiden). The sixth shows a woman under an elaborate tent with jewels, her pet dog resting on an embroidered cushion beside her, with the lovable unicorn and his friendly companion, a lion, holding back the flaps. The background in red and green forms a rich carpet of spring flowers, fruit-laden trees, birds, rabbits, donkeys, dogs, goats, lambs, and monkeys.

The other exhibitions range widely, including several Flemish retables; a 14th-century Sienese (life-size) John the Baptist and other Italian sculptures; statues from Sainte Chapelle, dating from 1243 to 1248; 12th- and 13th-century crosses, studded with gems; golden chalices, manuscripts, ivory carvings, vestments, leatherwork, jewelry, coins; a 13th-century Adam; and recently discovered heads and fragments of statues from Notre-Dame de Paris. In the fan-vaulted medieval chapel hang tapestries depicting scenes from the life of St. Stephen.

Downstairs are the ruins of the Roman baths, dating from around A.D. 200, among which rests a votive pillar as old as Tiberius.

The Panthéon. place du Panthéon, 5e. ☎ **01-43-54-34-51.** Admission 35F ($7) adults, 23F ($4.60) ages 12–25, ages 11 and under free. Apr–Sept, Tues–Sat 9:30am–11pm, Sun–Mon 9:30am–6:30pm; Oct–Mar, Tues–Sat 10am–10:30pm, Sun–Mon 10am–6pm. (Last entrance is 30 minutes before closing.) Métro: Cardinal-Lemoine or Maubert-Mutualité.

Some of the most famous men in the history of France (Victor Hugo, for one) are buried here in austere grandeur, on the crest of the mount of St. Geneviève. In 1744 Louis XV made a vow that if he recovered from a mysterious illness, he would build a church to replace the decayed Abbey of St. Geneviève.

Well, he recovered. In 1764, Madame de Pompadour's brother hired Soufflot to design a church in the form of a Greek cross with a dome reminiscent of St. Paul's Cathedral in London. When Soufflot died, his pupil Rondelet carried out the work, completing the structure nine years after his master's death.

After the revolution the church was converted into a "Temple of Fame"—ultimately a pantheon for the great men of France. The body of Mirabeau was buried here, although his remains were later removed. Likewise, Marat was only a temporary tenant. However, Voltaire's body was exhumed and placed here—and allowed to remain.

In the 19th century the building changed roles so many times—first a church, then a pantheon, then a church—that it was hard to keep its function straight. After Victor Hugo was buried here, it became a pantheon once again. Other notable men entombed within include Jean-Jacques Rousseau, Soufflot, Emile Zola, and Louis Braille.

Most recently, the ashes of André Malrux were transferred here because "you lived your dreams and made them live in us," at least according to President Jacques Chirac. As Charles De Gaulle's culture minister, he decreed that the arts should be part of the lives of all French people, not just Paris's elite.

The finest frescoes, the Puvis de Chavannes, line the end of the left wall before you enter the crypt. One illustrates St. Geneviève relieving victims of famine with supplies. The most outstanding of these depicts her white-draped head looking out over medieval Paris, the city whose patron she became.

Arènes de Lutèce. Rues Monge and Navarre, 5e. No phone. Free admission. May–Sept daily 10am–8:30pm; Oct–Apr daily 10am–5:30pm. Métro: Jussieu.

Discovered and partially destroyed in 1869, this Roman amphitheater is Paris's second most important Roman ruin (after the Roman Baths). Today the site is home to a small arena, not so grand as the original, and pleasant gardens. You may feel as if you've discovered a private spot in the heart of the city, but don't be fooled. Your solitude is sure to be interrupted, if not by groups of students playing football then at least by parents pushing strollers down the walking paths. This is an ideal spot for a picnic. Bring a bottle of wine and fresh baguettes to enjoy in this vestige of the ancient city of Lutetia.

Mosquée de Paris. place du Puits-de-l'Ermite, 5e. ☎ **01-45-35-97-33.** 15F ($3) adults, 10F ($2) students and children. Sat–Thurs 9am–noon and 2–6pm. Métro: Monge.

Located near the Jardin des Plantes, this Muslim place of worship is considered by many of its devotees to be one of the most beautiful structures of its kind in the world. The pink marble mosque was constructed in 1922 to honor the countries of North Africa who had given aid to France during World War I. Today, North Africans living in Paris gather on Fridays, the Muslim holy day, or during Ramadan to pray to Allah. Short tours are given of the building, its central courtyard, and Moorish garden; guides present a brief history of the Islamic faith. However, you may just want to wander on your own, then join the students from nearby universities for couscous and sweet mint tea at the popular Muslim restaurant that adjoins the grounds.

7 Les Halles

In the 19th century Zola called it "the underbelly of Paris." For eight centuries Les Halles was the major wholesale fruit, meat, and vegetable market of the city. The smock-clad vendors, the carcasses of beef, the baskets of the best fresh vegetables in the world—all belong to the past. Today the action has moved to a steel-and-glass edifice at Rungis, a suburb near Orly Airport. The original market, Baltard's old zinc-roofed Second Empire "iron umbrellas," has been torn down.

Replacing these so-called umbrellas is **Les Forum des Halles,** 1er, which opened in 1979 (Métro: Les Halles; RER: Châtelet–Les Halles). This large complex, much of it underground, contains dozens of shops, plus several restaurants and movie theaters. Many of these shops aren't attractive, but others contain a wide display of merchandise that has made the complex popular with both residents and visitors alike.

For many tourists a night on the town still ends in the wee hours with a bowl of onion soup at Les Halles, usually at Au Pied de Cochon ("Pig's Foot") or at Au Chien

5th & 6th Arrondissements

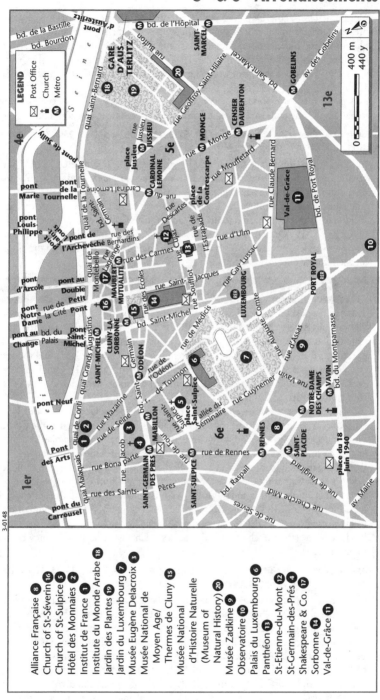

Alliance Française 8
Church of St-Séverin 16
Church of St-Sulpice 5
Hôtel des Monnaies 2
Institut de France 1
Institute du Monde Arabe 18
Jardin des Plantes 19
Jardin du Luxembourg 7
Musée Eugène Delacroix 3
Musée National de
Moyen Age/
Thermes de Cluny 15
Musée National
d'Histoire Naturelle
(Museum of
Natural History) 20
Musée Zadkine 9
Observatoire 10
Palais du Luxembourg 6
Panthéon 13
St-Etienne-du-Mont 12
St-Germain-des-Prés 4
Shakespeare & Co. 17
Sorbonne 14
Val-de-Grâce 11

3-0148

Qui Fume ("Smoking Dog"). One of the most classic scenes of Paris was elegantly dressed Parisians (many fresh from Maxim's) standing at a bar drinking cognac with blood-smeared butchers. Some writers have suggested that one Gérard de Nerval introduced the custom of frequenting Les Halles at such an unearthly hour. (De Nerval was a 19th-century poet whose life was considered "irregular." He hanged himself in 1855.)

A newspaper correspondent described today's scene this way: "Les Halles is trying to stay alive as one of the few places in Paris where one can eat at any hour of the night."

Church of St-Eustache. 2 rue du Jour, 1er. ☎ **01-42-36-31-05.** Daily 9am–7:30pm, Sun, mass 11am, organ recitals 5:30pm. Métro: Les Halles.

In our opinion, this mixed Gothic and Renaissance church completed in 1637 is rivaled only by Notre-Dame. It took nearly a century to build. Madame de Pompadour and Richelieu were baptized here, and Molière's funeral was held here in 1673. The church has been known for organ recitals ever since Liszt played here in 1866. Inside rests the black-marble tomb of Jean-Baptiste Colbert, the minister of state under Louis XIV. On top of his tomb is his marble effigy flanked by statues of *Abundance* by Coysevox and *Fidelity* by J.B. Tuby. There's a side entrance to the church on rue Rambuteau.

8 St-Germain-des-Prés

This was the postwar home of existentialism, associated with Jean-Paul Sartre, Simone de Beauvoir, Albert Camus, and an intellectual, bohemian crowd that gathered at the Café de Flore, the Brasserie Lipp, and Les Deux-Magots. Among them, the black-clad poet Juliette Greco was known as *la muse de St-Germain-des-Prés,* and to Sartre she was the woman who had "millions of poems in her throat." Her long hair, black slacks, black sweater, and black sandals launched a fashion trend adopted by young women from Paris to California.

In the 1950s new names appeared like Françoise Sagan, Gore Vidal, and James Baldwin, but by the 1960s the tourists were just as firmly entrenched at the Café de Flore and Deux-Magots. Today St-Germain-des-Prés retains a bohemian and intellectually stimulating street life, full of many interesting bookshops, art galleries, *cave* (basement) nightclubs, and bistros and coffeehouses, as well as two historic churches.

Just a short walk from the Delacroix museum, **rue Visconti** was designed for push-carts and is worth visiting today. At no. 17 is the maison where Balzac established his printing press in 1825. (The venture ended in bankruptcy, forcing the author back to his writing desk.) In the 17th century the French dramatist Jean-Baptiste Racine lived across the street. Such celebrated actresses as Champmeslé and Clairon were also in residence.

Eglise St-Germain-des-Prés. 3 place St-Germain-des-Prés, 6e. ☎ **01-43-25-41-71.** Daily 9am–7:30pm. Métro: St-Germain-des-Prés.

Outside it's an early 17th-century town house, and handsome at that. But inside it's one of the oldest churches in Paris, dating from the 6th century when a Benedictine abbey was founded on the site by Childebert, son of Clovis, the "creator of France." Unfortunately, the marble columns in the triforium are all that remains from that period. At one time the abbey was a pantheon for Merovingian kings. Restoration of St. Symphorien Chapel, which is the site of the Merovingian tombs, at the entrance of the church, began in 1981. During that work, unknown Romanesque paintings were discovered on the chapel's triumphal arch, making it one of the most interesting places of old Christian Paris.

Gregorians Unplugged

St-Sulpice stages the most wonderful concerts on the Left Bank; it has fantastic acoustics and a marvelous medieval atmosphere. The church was built to accommodate an age without microphones, and the sound effects will thrill you. For more information, call ☎ **01-42-50-70-72.** Arrive about 45 minutes before the performance if you'd like a front-row seat.

The Romanesque tower, topped by a 19th-century spire, is the most enduring landmark in the village of St-Germain-des-Prés. Its church bells, however, are hardly noticed by the patrons of Deux-Magots across the way.

The Normans nearly destroyed the abbey at least four times. The present building, the work of four centuries, has a Romanesque nave and a Gothic choir with fine capitals. Among the people interred at the church are Descartes, his heart at least, and Jean-Casimir, the king of Poland who abdicated his throne.

When you leave St-Germain-des-Prés Church, turn right on rue de l'Abbaye and have a look at the 17th-century Palais Abbatial, a pink palace.

Eglise St-Sulpice. rue St-Sulpice, 6e. ☎ **01-46-33-21-78.** Daily 7:30am–7:30pm. Métro: St-Sulpice.

Pause first outside quiet St-Sulpice. The 1844 fountain by Visconti displays the sculpted likenesses of four bishops of the Louis XIV era: Fenelon, Massillon, Bossuet, and Flechier. Work on the church itself, at one time Paris's largest, began in 1646 as part of the Catholic revival then occurring in France. Although laborers built the body of the church by 1745, work on the bell towers continued until 1780 when one was finished, and the other left incomplete. One of the most priceless treasures inside is Servandoni's rococo Chapel of the Madonna, which contains a Pigalle statue of the Virgin. The church has one of the world's largest organs; it comprises 6,700 pipes and has been played by such musicians as Charles-Mari Widor and Marcel Dupre.

But the real reason to come to St-Sulpice is to see the Delacroix frescoes in the Chapel of the Angels (the first on your right as you enter). Seek out his muscular Jacob wrestling (or is he dancing?) with an effete angel. On the ceiling St. Michael is having some troubles with the Devil, and yet another mural depicts Heliodorus being driven from the temple. Painted in the final years of his life, the frescoes were a high point in the baffling career of Delacroix. If these impress you, you can pay the painter tribute by visiting the Delacroix museum reviewed below.

Musée National Eugène Delacroix. 6 place de Furstenberg, 6e. ☎ **01-44-41-86-50.** Admission 22F ($4.40) adults, 15F ($3) ages 18–25 and over 60, ages 17 and under free. Wed–Mon 9:45am–5pm. Closed holidays. Métro: St-Germain-des-Prés.

This museum is only for serious Delacroix groupies, among which we include ourselves. If you admire this artist and want to see where he lived and worked, then follow in the footsteps of his friends, George Sand and Baudelaire, and head here for a unique insight. It's worth at least an hour of your time. To art historians, Delacroix (1798–1863) is something of an enigma. Even his parentage is a mystery. Many believed that Talleyrand had the privilege of fathering him. A Frank Anderson Trapp biography saw him "as an isolated and atypical individualist—one who respected traditional values, yet emerged as the embodiment of Romantic revolt." The poet Baudelaire saw him as "a volcanic crater artistically concealed beneath bouquets of flowers."

❓ Did You Know?

- The world's oldest "grocery store," Les Halles moved in 1969, its first relocation in eight centuries.
- Place Denfert-Rochereau, an old burial ground, was once called place d'Enfer, or "Hell Square"—it was stacked with millions of bones from old charnel houses to conserve space in 1785.
- On the narrow Seine island Allée des Cygnes stands a tiny Statue of Liberty.
- At the end of the 18th century, the place de Charles-de-Gaulle–Étoile was the world's first organized traffic circle.
- Pont-Neuf (New Bridge) isn't so new. Dating from 1607, it's the oldest and most famous bridge in Paris.
- The Sorbonne began in 1253 as modest lodgings for 16 theology students who pursued their education on the site of the present-day University of Paris.
- In 1938 workmen discovered 3,350 22-karat gold coins weighing 1.3 grams each while digging at 51 rue Mouffetard. An accompanying note said they belonged to Louis Nivelle, royal counselor to Louis XV, who mysteriously disappeared in 1757.

By visiting his atelier, you will see one of the most charming squares on the Left Bank and also the museum's romantic garden. A large arch on a stone courtyard leads to the studio.

Delacroix died in this apartment on August 13, 1863. This is no poor artist's studio, but the tasteful creation of a solidly established man. Sketches, lithographs, watercolors, and oils are hung throughout, and a few mementos remain, including a lovely mahogany paint box.

9 Le Marais

When Paris began to overflow the confines of Ile de la Cité in the 13th century, the citizenry settled in Le Marais, the marsh that used to be flooded regularly by the high-rising Seine. By the 17th century the Marais had become fashion's pinnacle and the center of aristocratic Paris. At that time, some of its great mansions, many now restored or still being spruced up today, were built by the finest craftsmen in France.

In the 18th and 19th centuries, fashion deserted the Marais for the expanding Faubourg St-Germain and Faubourg St-Honoré. Industry eventually took over, and once-elegant hotels deteriorated into tenements. There was talk of demolishing this blighted neighborhood, but in 1962 an alarmed Comité de Sauvegarde du Marais banded together and saved the historic district.

Today the 17th-century mansions are fashionable once again. The *Herald-Tribune* called this area the latest refuge of the Paris artisan fleeing from the tourist-trampled St-Germain-des-Prés. The "marsh" sprawls across the 3rd and 4th arrondissements bounded by the grands boulevards, the rue du Temple, the place des Vosges, and the Seine.

The neighborhood has become the center of gay life in Paris, and is a great place for window-shopping in unconventional boutiques, up-and-coming galleries, and more. (See the Marais walking tour in chapter 7 for a few of these.)

Tip

To see the work that earned Delacroix his niche in art history, go to the Louvre for such passionate paintings as his *Liberty Leading the People on the Barricades,* or to the nearby Church of St-Sulpice (Métro: Mabillon) for the famed fresco *Jacob Wrestling with the Angel,* among others.

Maison de Victor Hugo. 6 place des Vosges, 3e. ☎ **01-42-72-10-16.** Admission 17.50F ($3.50) adults, 9F ($1.80) children 8–18; children 7 and under free. Tues–Sun 10am–5:40pm. Closed national holidays. Métro: St-Paul, Bastille, or Chemin-Vert.

Today theater-goers who saw *Les Misérables,* even those who haven't read anything by Paris's great 19th-century novelist, come to place des Vosges to see where he lived and wrote. Some thought Hugo a genius, but Cocteau called him a madman, and an American composer discovered that in the folly of his dotage he carved furniture, with his teeth! From 1832 to 1848 the novelist and poet lived on the second floor of the old Hôtel Rohan Guéménée, built in 1610 on what was then the place Royale. The museum owns some of Hugo's furniture as well as pieces that once belonged to Juliette Drouet, the mistress with whom he lived in exile on Guernsey, one of the Channel Islands.

Worth the visit are Hugo's drawings, more than 450, illustrating scenes from his own works. Mementos of the great writer abound: samples of his handwriting, his inkwell, and first editions of his works. A painting of his funeral procession at the Arc de Triomphe in 1885 is on display, as are plentiful portraits and souvenirs of Hugo's family. Of the furnishings, a chinoiserie salon stands out. The collection even contains Daumier caricatures and a bust of Hugo by David d'Angers, which, compared to Rodin's, looks saccharine.

Grand Carnavalet. 23 rue de Sévigné, 3e. ☎ **01-42-72-21-13.** Admission 27F ($5.40) adults, 14.50F ($2.90) 18–25 and over 60; 17 and under free. Tues–Sun 10am–5:40pm. Métro: St-Paul or Chemin-Vert.

If you like history but history books bore you, spend 2 hours here and shine some light on Paris's past. The comprehensive and lifelike exhibits are great for kids too.

At the Grand Carnavalet (now also referred to as the Musée Carnavalet), the history of Paris comes alive in intimate detail, right down to the chessmen Louis XVI used to distract his mind while waiting to go to the guillotine. A renowned Renaissance palace, it was built in 1544 by Pierre Lescot and Jean Goujon and later acquired by Madame de Carnavalet. The great François Mansart transformed it between the years 1655 and 1661.

But it's probably best known because one of history's most famous letter writers, Madame de Sévigné, moved here in 1677. Fanatically devoted to her daughter (she ended up moving in with her because she couldn't bear their separation), she poured out nearly every detail of her life in letters, virtually ignoring her son. A native of the Marais district, she died at her daughter's château in 1696. It wasn't until 1866 that the city of Paris acquired the mansion, eventually turning it into a museum.

Many salons depict events related to the Revolution, such as a bust of Marat, a portrait of Danton, and a model replica of the Bastille (one painting shows its demolition). Another salon tells the story of the captivity of the royal family at the Temple, including the bed in which Madame Elizabeth slept. The exercise book of the dauphin is there—the pathetic legacy he left the world before his mysterious disappearance.

There is much to see: the Bouvier collection on the first floor, facades of old apothecary shops, extensive wrought-iron works, a bust of Napoléon by Charles-Louis Corbet, a Cazals portrait of Paul Verlaine that makes him look like Lenin, Jean Beraud's parade of 19th-century opulence, and Baron François Gérard's painting of Madame Récamier, lounging, of course.

One room is crammed with signposts from the 17th and 18th centuries, each bearing designs that remind us a greater portion of the world was illiterate then—instead of words, a tree indicates a carpenter's workshop and a pig was the symbol for a butcher's shop. An entire jewelry shop designed by Mucha in 1900 is installed here.

Exhibits continue at the Hôtel le Pelletier de St-Fargeau, across the courtyard. On display is furniture from the Louis XIV period to the early 20th century. Here, too, is a replica of Marcel Proust's cork-lined bedroom with his actual furniture, including his brass bed.

Musée de la Chasse (Hunting Museum). 60 rue des Archives, 3e. ☎ **01-42-72-86-43.** Admission 25F ($5) adults, 12.50F ($2.50) students and seniors, 5F ($1) children (5–16), free 4 and under. Wed–Mon 10am–12:30pm and 1:30–5:30pm. Métro: Rambuteau or Hôtel-de-Ville.

Near the Hôtel Carnavalet, the Hôtel Guénégaud, also built by François Mansart, has been restored and turned into the Musée de la Chasse by the Sommer Foundation. This museum, classified as one of the "eccentricities" of Paris, is obviously for the specialist—that is, those who like to hunt like Hemingway for sport. If that is your game, you'll find no better exhibition in all of Europe.

Mounted heads are plentiful, ranging from the antelope to the elephant, from the bushbuck to the waterbuck, from the moose to the bush pig. Rembrandt's sketch of a lion is here, along with a collection of wild-animal portraits by Desportes (1661–1743). The hunt tapestries are outstanding and often amusing—one a cannibalistic romp, another showing a helmeted man standing eye to eye with a bear he is stabbing to death. The rifles, some inlaid with pearls, others engraved with ivory, are exceptional, many dating from the 17th century. The museum displays other historical weapons and a remarkable collection of paintings, including works by Rubens, Breughel, Oudry, Chardin, and Corot.

Musée de l'Histoire de France. 60 rue des Francs-Bourgeois, 3e. ☎ **01-40-27-61-78.** Admission 15F ($3) adults, 10F ($2) children and seniors. Mon and Wed–Fri noon–5:45pm, Sat–Sun 1:45–5:45pm. Métro: Hôtel-de-Ville or Rambuteau.

A short walk from the hunting museum brings you to this landmark steeped in French history. If you found Musée Carnavalet's exhibits intriguing, expand your knowledge to include the entire history of France, brilliantly showcased here in realistic exhibits that range from King Dagobert to World War II and the occupation of Paris.

On Napoléon's orders, the Palais Soubise was made the official records depository of France. But the building, designed by the much underrated Delamair, is as fascinating as—or even more so than—the exhibits contained within. Apartments that once belonged to the Prince and Princess de Soubise have been turned into the Musée de l'Histoire de France.

You enter through the colonnaded Court of Honor. Before going inside, walk around the corner to 58 rue des Archives to the medieval turreted gateway to the original Clisson mansion. (The Clisson mansion gave way to the residence of the dukes of Guise, who owned the property until it was purchased by the Soubise family. The Princess Soubise was once the mistress of Louis XIV, and apparently the Sun King was very generous, giving her the funds to remodel and redesign the palace.)

3rd & 4th Arrondissements

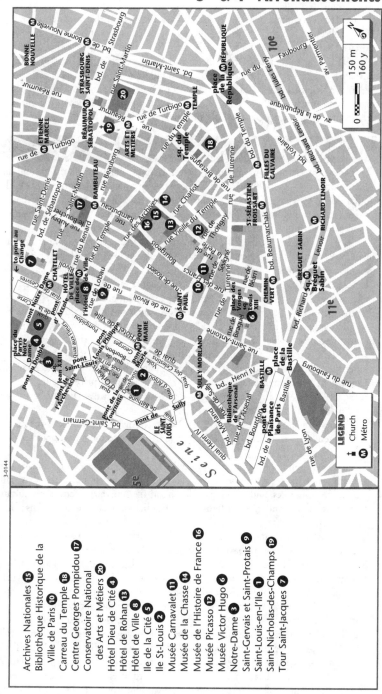

Archives Nationales 15
Bibliothèque Historique de la
   Ville de Paris 10
Carreau du Temple 18
Centre Georges Pompidou 17
Conservatoire National
   des Arts et Métiers 20
Hôtel Dieu de Cité 4
Hôtel de Rohan 13
Hôtel de Ville 8
Ile de la Cité 5
Ile St-Louis 2
Musée Carnavalet 11
Musée de la Chasse 14
Musée de l'Histoire de France 16
Musée Picasso 12
Musée Victor Hugo 6
Notre-Dame 3
Saint-Gervais et Saint-Protais 9
Saint-Louis-en-l'Ile 1
Saint-Nicholas-des-Champs 19
Tour Saint-Jacques 7

The archives contain documents that go back even farther than Charlemagne. The letter collection is highly valued, exhibiting the penmanship of Marie Antoinette (a farewell letter), Louis XVI (his will), Danton, Robespierre, Napoléon I, and Joan of Arc. The museum possesses the only known living sketch of the maid of Orléans. Even the jailer's keys to the old Bastille are found here.

In 1735 Germain Boffrand designed a Salon Ovale, with *parfaites* (faultless) *expressions,* for a much later Princess de Soubise. Adding to the lush décor, the gilt, and the crystal are paintings by Van Loo, Boucher, and Natoire.

10 Montmartre

Soft white three-story houses, slender, barren trees sticking up from the ground like giant toothpicks—that's how Utrillo, befogged by absinthe, saw Montmartre. On the other side of the canvas, Toulouse-Lautrec brush-stroked it into a district of cabarets, circus freaks, and prostitutes. Today Montmartre remains truer to the dwarfish artist's conception than it does to that of Utrillo.

Before its discovery by the chic, Montmartre was a sleepy farming community with windmills dotting the landscape. The name has always been the subject of disagreement, some maintaining that it originated from the "mount of Mars," a Roman temple that crowned the hill, others asserting that it means "mount of martyrs," a reference to the martyrdom of St. Denis, the patron saint of Paris, who was beheaded on the mountain along with his fellow saints Rusticus and Eleutherius.

The name Montmartre has spread chaos and confusion in many an unwary tourist's agenda. So just to make things clear, there are three of them.

The first is boulevard Montmartre, a busy commercial street nowhere near the mountain. The second is the tawdry, expensive, wanna-be-naughty, and utterly phony amusement belt along boulevard de Clichy, culminating at place Pigalle (the "Pig Alley" of World War II GIs). The third—the Montmartre we're talking about—lies on the slopes and the top of the actual hill.

The best way to get here is to take the Métro to Anvers, then walk to the nearby rue de Steinkerque, and ride the curious little **funicular** to the top. It operates daily between 6am and 11pm.

The center point of Montmartre, **place du Tertre,** looks like a village square, particularly when the local band is blowing and puffing oompah music on tubas, sousaphones, trombones, and trumpets. All around the square run terrace restaurants with dance floors and colored lights. The Basilica of Sacré-Coeur gleams white through the trees.

Behind the church and clinging to the hillside below are steep and crooked little streets that almost seem to have survived the relentless march of progress. Rue des Saules has a cabaret and Montmartre's last vineyard. Rue Lepic almost looks the way Renoir, van Gogh, and the unfortunate genius Toulouse-Lautrec saw it, nearly making up for the blitz of portraitists and souvenir stores and postcard vendors on top.

The traditional way to explore Montmartre is on foot, but many visitors who are not in tip-top physical shape find the uphill climb to Paris's highest elevation arduous. Those who prefer to ride can take a white-sided, diesel-powered train, which rolls on rubber tires along the steep streets, on a 35-minute guided tour. **Le Petit Train de Montmartre** carries 55 passengers who can listen to an English commentary as they pass by major landmarks. You may board at either the place du Tertre (beside the Church of St-Pierre) or near the Moulin Rouge in the place Blanche. Trains run throughout the year, beginning at 10am and continuing until midnight between June and September, and until 6pm the rest of the year. Depending on the

love 0-800-99-0011

n the springtime.

Every country has its own AT&T Access Number which makes calling from France and other countries really easy. Just dial the AT&T Access Number for the country you're calling from and we'll take it from there. And be sure to charge your calls on your AT&T Calling Card. It'll help you avoid outrageous phone charges on your hotel bill and save you up to 60%.* 0-800-99-0011 is a great place to visit any time of year, especially if you've got these two cards. So please take the attached wallet card of worldwide AT&T Access Numbers.

All you need for the
fastest, clearest connections home.

www.att.com/traveler

plete list of AT&T Access Numbers and other helpful services, call 1-800-446-8399.
d clearest connections from countries with voice prompts, compared to major U.S. carriers on calls to
clearest based on customer preference testing. *Compared to certain hotel telephone charges based on
e U.S. in October 1995. Actual savings may be higher or lower depending upon your billing method,
ay, length of call, fees charged by hotel and the country from which you are calling. "I Love Paris"
er) © 1952 Chappel & Co. (ASCAP). © 1997 AT&T

season, departures are scheduled every 30 to 45 minutes. The cost is 30F ($6) for adults, half price for children. For information, call **Promotrain,** 131 rue de Clignancourt, 18e (☎ **01-42-62-24-00**).

For a more detailed look at Montmartre, see the walking tour in chapter 7.

✪ **Basilique du Sacré-Coeur.** Place St-Pierre, 18e. ☎ **01-42-51-17-02.** Basilica free; dome 15F ($3) adults, 8F ($1.60) students 6–25; crypt 15F ($3) adults, 5F ($1), children 6–25. Ticket to both 25F ($5). Basilica daily 6:45am–11pm. Dome and crypt Apr–Sept daily 9:15am–7pm; Oct–Mar daily 9:15am–6pm. Métro: Abbesses. Take the elevator to the surface and follow the signs to the funiculaire, which takes you up to the church for the price of one Métro ticket.

After the Eiffel Tower, Sacré-Coeur is the most characteristic landmark of the Parisian scene. Like the tower, it has always been, and still is, the subject of much controversy. One Parisian called it "a lunatic's confectionery dream." An offended Zola declared it "the basilica of the ridiculous." Sacré-Coeur has had warm supporters as well, including the poet Max Jacob and the artist Maurice Utrillo. Utrillo never tired of drawing and painting it, and he and Jacob came here regularly to pray.

Its gleaming white domes and *campanile* (bell tower) tower over Paris like a Byzantine church of the 12th century. But it's not that old. After France's defeat by the Prussians in 1870, the basilica was planned as a votive offering to cure France's misfortunes. Rich and poor alike contributed money to build it. Construction was begun on the church in 1876 and it was not consecrated until 1919, but perpetual prayers of adoration have been made here day and night since 1885. The interior of the basilica is brilliantly decorated with mosaics. The stained-glass windows were shattered during the struggle for Paris in 1944, but have been well replaced. Look for the striking mosaic of Christ on the ceiling, and also the mural of his Passion at the back of the altar. The crypt contains a relic of what some of the devout believe is Christ's sacred heart—hence the name of the church.

On a clear day you can see for 35 miles from the dome. You can also walk around the inner dome of the church, peering down like a pigeon (one is likely to be keeping you company).

11 Belleville & Ménilmontant

The 20th arrondissement of Paris is often overlooked by sightseers who scurry to the most famous sights of the city and fail to explore its ethnic backwaters. This area, between the Père-Lachaise cemetery to the south and the rue de Belleville to the north, is comprised of two districts, each with its own personality and allure. Belleville and Ménilmontant (in the northern and southern parts of the arrondissement, respectively) began as pretty country villages but quickly became slums when Haussmann expelled many of Paris's workers from the city during his rebuilding projects.

Belleville was the sight of some of the heaviest fighting during the uprising of the Paris Commune; today new battles are being waged. The present fight centers on the explosion of urban renewal that has taken Paris by storm. Residents have formed a group known as the "Bellevilleuse," that is working to gain promises from developers that restoration, not demolition, will be the way to give the area new life. The aim is to spruce up Belleville without sacrificing its international, working-class atmosphere—no chi-chi boutiques or polenta bars here. Merchants are more likely to offer specialties from countries such as Greece, China, North Africa, and Eastern Europe.

The hill in the center of Belleville is a good place to start a tour. Narrow alleyways emerge to panoramic views near the top of the hill and cheap ethnic restaurants and fun shops at the base. You can also look out over Paris from the **Jardin de Belleville,** although development has seriously lessened the garden's tranquility.

The **Parc des Buttes-Chaumont,** created by Baron Haussmann's designers, is one of the area's most appealing attractions. It has a small classical temple that provides a view westward toward Montmartre from its perch in the center of a small lake. Provincial houses and gardens line streets in the park's eastern range and seem a bit out of place in such a quickly expanding city.

In contrast to these quaint remnants from days gone by is the **Parc de Villette,** an ultramodern science park that surrounds some of the newest housing developments in Paris. Playgrounds, fountains, and sculptures are all innovative creations of more modern city planners. Here, you'll also find La Géode, a geodesic dome that houses a cinema, in the midst of colorful gardens and several surprising additions, including a real submarine.

Ménilmontant is even more ethnically diverse than its sibling district in the 20th arrondissement. A perpetual influx of immigrants, including Russian Jews, Spanish Republicans, Poles, Armenians, North Africans, and Asians, keeps the area constantly changing. The big attraction of this part of the arrondissement is **Père-Lachaise Cemetery** (see page 226 for more details). Famous for the many celebrities interred within its walls, the cemetery is also the sight of the Paris Commune's last stand against the French government. Here 147 Fédérés were lined up and shot against its eastern wall in revenge for the murder of the Archbishop of Paris. A much less violent attraction is the **Musée Edith Piaf,** located at 5 rue Crespin-du-Gast (☎ **01-43-55-52-72;** Métro: Ménilmontant), open Monday through Thursday from 1 to 6pm. The daughter of an acrobat, the great Piaf grew up in this neighborhood, and her songs, in time, including *"La Vie en Rose"* and *"Non, je ne regrette rien,"* would be heard around the world. Born as Giovanna Gassion, she assumed the name of Piaf or "little sparrow." This privately run museum is filled with Piaf memorabilia and is a tribute to this songbird whose memory lives on in the heart of the French.

Nearby is the **Villa Calte,** a beautiful example of the fine architecture that many residents of the arrondissement are trying to save. The house is fronted by an intricate wrought-iron fence and has a pleasant garden where parts of Truffaut's *Jules et Jim* was filmed.

12 More Museums

Below is a partial listing of the balance of the city's museums. Be sure to refer back to Section 1, "The Top Museums," for details on where to get information.

Cité des Sciences et de L'Industrie. La Villette, 30 av. Corentine-Cariou, 19e. ☎ **08-36-68-29-30.** Cité Pass (entrance to all exhibits), 50F ($10) adults, 35F ($7) on Saturday, 17 and under free; Géode 57F ($11.40). Tues–Sat 10am–6pm, Sun 10am–7pm. Métro: Porte de la Villette.

A city of science and industry has risen here from most unlikely ashes. When a slaughterhouse was built on the site in the 1960s, it was touted as the most modern of its kind in the world. When the site was abandoned as a failure in 1974, its echoing vastness and unlikely location on the northern edge of the city presented the French government with a problem. In 1986 the converted premises opened as the world's most expensive ($642 million) science complex designed to "modernize mentalities" as a step in the process of modernizing society.

The place is so vast, and has so many exhibits, that a single visit gives only an idea of the scope of the Cité. It's like a futuristic airplane hangar. Busts of Plato,

Hippocrates, and a double-faced Janus gaze silently at a tube-filled, space-age riot of high-tech girders, glass, and lights—something akin to what a layperson might think of the interior of an atomic generator.

The sheer dimensions of the place are awesome, a challenge to the curators of its constantly changing exhibits. Some exhibits are couched in Gallic humor—imagine using the comic-strip adventures of a jungle explorer to explain seismographic activity. The Cité contains the silver-skinned geodesic dome (called the Géode) that projects the closest thing to a 3-D cinema in Europe on the inner surfaces of its curved walls; it is a 112-foot-high sphere with a 370-seat theater.

Explora, a permanent exhibit, spreads over the three upper levels of the building; its displays examine four themes: the universe, life, matter, and communication. The Cité also has a multimedia library, a planetarium, and an "inventorium" for children.

The Cité is in **La Villette** park, the city's largest, with 136 acres of greenery, twice the size of the Tuileries. Here you'll find a belvedere, a video workshop for children, and information about exhibitions and events, along with a cafe and restaurant.

Institut du Monde Arabe. 1 rue des Fossés-St-Bernard, 5e. ☎ **01-40-51-38-38.** Admission to permanent collections 25F ($5); to special exhibitions 30F ($6). Tues–Sun 10am–6pm. Métro: Jussieu.

In a glass and aluminum structure built with funds from the French and 20 Arab governments, Institut du Monde Arabe is much more than a museum. The building, which many consider to be one of the finest modern structures in Paris, houses a multimedia cultural center whose aim is to promote relations between France and the Arab world. The institute features art, some of which dates from the 3rd century, from three Arab regions. There is also a massive library with literary works and periodicals in Arabic, French, and English, and an auditorium where Arab movies and plays are presented. If nothing else, come here to enjoy coffee or a light lunch at the center's 9th-floor restaurant/cafe while taking in the panoramic view of the city from the terrace that hangs out over the Seine.

Manufacture Royale des Gobelins. 42 av. des Gobelins, 13e. ☎ 01-44-08-53-32. Tours given in French (with English pamphlets) Tues–Thurs 2 and 2:15pm for 45F ($9) adults, 36F ($7.20) ages 7–24 and 65 or older; children under 7 free. Métro: Les Gobelins.

This is a museum for tapestry-lovers, and need not occupy much time for those not devoted to the subject. Sick of mass production? Take heart—a single tapestry can take well past 3 or 4 years to complete, employing as many as three or five full-time weavers. The founding father of this dynasty, Jehan Gobelin, came from a family of dyers and cloth-makers. In the 15th century he discovered a scarlet dye that was to make him famous. By 1601 Henry IV had become interested, bringing up 200 weavers from Flanders whose full-time occupation was to make tapestries (many of which are now scattered across various museums and residences). Oddly enough, until this endeavor the Gobelin family had not made any tapestries, although the name would become synonymous with that art form.

Colbert, the minister of Louis XIV, purchased the works, and under royal patronage the craftsmen set about executing designs by Le Brun. After the revolution, the industry was reactivated by Napoléon.

Les Gobelins is still going strong and you can visit the studios of the craftspeople, called *ateliers.* Some of the ancient high-warp looms are still in use. Weavers sit behind huge screens of thread, patiently inserting stitch after stitch.

Manufacture Nationale de Sèvres. 4 Grande rue, Sèvres. ☎ **01-45-34-34-00.** Free admission. Wed–Mon 10am–5:30pm, salesroom Mon–Sat 10am–5:30pm. Métro: Pont-de-Sèvres, then walk across the Seine to the Right Bank.

Madame de Pompadour loved Sèvres porcelain. She urged Louis XV to order as much as possible, thus ensuring its favor among the chic people of the 18th century. Two centuries later, it's still fashionable. A warning: If porcelain's your thing, you'll find plate after plate to study and stand in awe of its beauty; but if you'd rather see pork chops on your plate than a design, you'll find far more intriguing diversions in Paris.

The state of France has owned the Sèvres factory for more than 2 centuries. It was founded originally in Vincennes, and moved to Sèvres, a riverside suburb on the western edge of Paris, in 1756. The factory's commercial service sells porcelain to the public Monday through Saturday (it's closed on holidays).

Next door, the **Musée National de Céramique de Sèvres** (☎ 01-41-14-04-20) boasts one of the finest collections of faience and porcelain in the world, some of which belonged to Madame du Barry, Pompadour's hand-picked successor. On view, for example, is the "Pompadour rose" (which the English insisted on calling the "rose du Barry"), a style much in vogue in the 1750s and 1760s. The painter Boucher made some of the designs used by the factory, as did the sculptor Pajou (he created the bas-reliefs for the Opéra at Versailles). The factory pioneered what became known in porcelain as the *Louis Seize* (Louis XVI) style—it's all here, plus lots more, including works from Sèvres's archrival, Meissen. This museum is open Wednesday to Monday from 10am to 5pm. Admission is 18F ($3.60) adults, 12F ($2.40) ages 19 to 25 and over 65; free for 17 and under.

Musée Cernuschi. 7 av. Velasquez, 8e. ☎ **01-45-63-50-75.** Admission 17.50F ($3.50) adults, 9F ($1.80) students and seniors; free 17 and under. Tues–Sun 10am–5:40pm. Métro: Monceau or Villiers. Bus: 30 or 94.

Bordering the Parc Monceau, this small museum is devoted to the arts of China. If you share a love of art objects of the Far East, as did the original collector, Henri Cernuschi (1820–96), then by all means head here, at least for a cursory visit. The museum has a number of treasures, even a 3-ton bronze Japanese Buddha, although the treasure trove is no match for the Guimet, of course. The building is another one of those mansions whose owners stuffed them with art objects, then bequeathed them to the city of Paris. The address was quite an exclusive one when the town was built in 1885.

Inside, there is, of course, a bust of Cernuschi, a self-perpetuating memorial to a man whose generosity and interest in the East was legend in his day. Now the collections include a fine assortment of Neolithic potteries, as well as bronzes from the 14th century B.C., the most famous being the tiger-shaped vase. The jades, ceramics, and funereal figures are exceptional, as are the pieces of Buddhist sculpture. Most admirable is a Bodhisattva originating from Yun-kang (6th century). Rounding out the exhibits are some ancient paintings, the best known of which is *Horses with Grooms,* attributed to Han Kan (8th century, Tang dynasty). The museum also houses a good collection of contemporary Chinese paintings.

Musée d'Art Moderne de la Ville de Paris. 11-13 av. du Président Wilson, 16e. ☎ **01-53-67-40-00.** Admission 50F ($10) adults, 40F ($8) ages 18–24 and over 60; ages 17 and under free. Tues, Wed, Fri 10am–5:30pm, Thurs, Sat, Sun 10am–7:45pm. Métro: Iéna or Alma-Marceau.

Right next door to the Palais de Tokyo, this museum displays a permanent collection of paintings and sculpture owned by the city of Paris. Come here only if repeated visits to the Musée d'Orsay and the Louvre have not satiated your need to see fine art in Paris. In addition, the M.A.M. section of the city's modern art museum presents ever-changing exhibitions on individual artists from all over the world or on trends in international art. Bordering the Seine, the salons display works by such

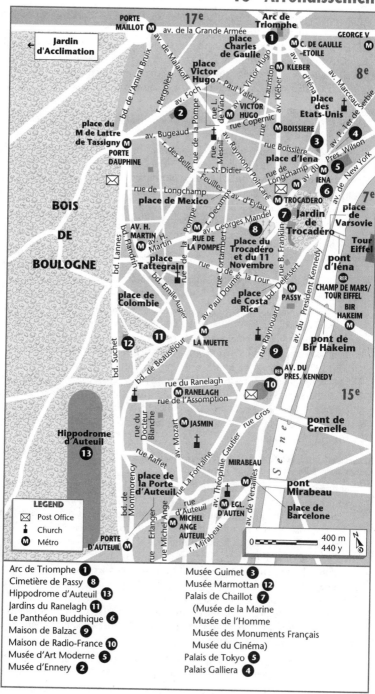

LEGEND

⊠ Post Office
† Church
Ⓜ Métro

0 ———— 400 m
440 y

Arc de Triomphe ❶
Cimetière de Passy ❽
Hippodrome d'Auteuil ⓭
Jardins du Ranelagh ⓫
Le Panthéon Buddhique ❻
Maison de Balzac ❾
Maison de Radio-France ❿
Musée d'Art Moderne ❺
Musée d'Ennery ❷

Musée Guimet ❸
Musée Marmottan ⓬
Palais de Chaillot ❼
  (Musée de la Marine
  Musée de l'Homme
  Musée des Monuments Français
  Musée du Cinéma)
Palais de Tokyo ❺
Palais Galliera ❹

artists as Chagall, Matisse, Léger, Braque, Picasso, Dufy, Utrillo, Delaunay, Rouault, and Modigliani.

See, in particular, Pierre Tal Coat's *Portrait of Gertrude Stein.* Picasso wasn't the only artist to tackle this difficult subject. Other sections in the museum are ARC, which shows work of young artists and new trends in contemporary art, and the Musée des Enfants, which has exhibitions and shows for children.

Musée de Baccarat. 30 bis rue de Paradis, 10e. ☎ **01-47-70-64-30.** Admission 10F ($2) adults, 5F ($1) under 17 and over 60. Mon–Sat 10am–6pm. Métro: Poissonnière or Château d'Eau.

This museum, attracting only people mad about Baccarat crystal, resembles an ice palace, filled with crystal of all shapes and sizes. It's found in a Directoire building from the late 18th century, which houses the crystal maker's headquarters. The museum contains some of the most impressive pieces produced by this crystal company through the years. Czars, royalty, and oil-rich sheiks have numbered among the best patrons of this prestigious name in crystal, established in 1764. At the entrance to the museum stands "Lady Baccarat," a chandelier in the form and size of a woman.

Musée des Arts Décoratifs. In the Palais du Louvre, 107 rue de Rivoli, 1er. ☎ **01-44-55-57-50.** Admission 25F ($5) adults, 16F ($3.20) ages 5–24, free for children 4 and under. Wed–Sat 12:30–6pm, Sun noon–6pm. Métro: Palais-Royal or Tuileries.

In the northwest wing of the Louvre's Pavillon de Marsan, this museum holds a treasury of furnishings, fabrics, wallpaper, *objets d'art,* and other items displaying living styles from the Middle Ages to the present. A visit here is recommended only if you have an abiding interest in the decorative arts of France, and take the kids only if one of them has expressed an interest in becoming a decorator. Notable on the first floor are the 1920s Art Deco boudoir, bath, and bedroom done for couturier Jeanne Lanvin by designer Rateau. Decorative art from the Middle Ages to the Renaissance is on the second floor, whereas rich collections from the 17th, 18th, and 19th centuries occupy the third and fourth floors. The fifth has specialized centers, such as wallpaper and drawings, and documentary centers detailing fashion, textiles, toys, crafts, and glass trends.

Musée National des Arts Asiatiques-Guimet. 6 place d'Iéna, 16e. ☎ **01-45-05-00-98.** Closed until 1999. Métro: Iéna or Alma-Marceau.

Comprised of three museums devoted to the art and archaeology of the vast Asian region from Afghanistan to Japan, this museum was named after its founder, the wealthy industrialist Emile Guimet, and established originally at Lyon. Later, in 1889, the Guimet was transferred to Paris. In 1931, it received the collections of the Musée Indochinois du Trocadéro and, after World War II, the Asian collections of the Louvre. Today it's one of the world's richest museums of its genre. The most interesting exhibits encompass Buddhas, heads of serpentine monsters, funeral figurines, and antiquities from the temple of Angkor Wat. The Jacques Bacot gallery is devoted to Tibetan art: fascinating scenes of the Grand Lamas entwined with serpents and demons. However, this main museum is currently undergoing extensive renovations and will be closed until 1999. But two ancillary buildings with similar exhibitions remain open to the public during this time.

Le Panthéon Bouddhique. 19 av. d'Iéna, 16e. ☎ **01-40-73-88-11.** Admission 16F ($3.20) for adults, and children under 18 are admitted free. Open Wed–Mon 9:45am–6pm. Métro: Iéna.

This museum retraces the religious pasts of China and Japan from the 4th to the 19th centuries. Approximately 250 Japanese works of art represent different Buddhist traditions and, along with 33 Chinese masterpieces, show the evolution of Buddhism as it passed from India to China and migrated to Japan, where it was embraced around A.D. 1000. Many of the pieces were acquired by Emile Guimet on his 1876 voyage to Japan. His booty included a large number of sculptures from the Kamakura period (1192–1333) and the Muromachi-Momoyama period (14th–16th centuries). The museum's peaceful seasonally changing Japanese garden is an ideal place to meditate. The gift shop sells textiles, porcelain, jewelry, and reproductions of Buddhas and other divinities.

Musée Bourdelle. 16 rue Antoine-Bourdelle, 15e. ☎ **01-45-48-67-27.** Admission 18F ($3.60) for adults and 9F ($1.80) for students and children. Tues–Sun 10am–5:30pm. Métro: Falguière.

Here you can see works by the prime student of Rodin, Antoine Bourdelle (1861–1929), who became a celebrated artist in his own right. The museum displays the artist's drawings, paintings, and sculptures, and lets you wander at will through his studio, garden, and the house where he lived. The most notable exhibits are the 21 different studies he did of Beethoven alone. The original plaster casts of some of his greatest works are also on display. Although some of the exhibits are badly captioned, the impact of Bourdelle's genius is still felt here.

Musée de la Musique. 221 av. Jean-Jaurès, 19e. ☎ **01-44-84-45-00.** Admission 35F ($7) adults, 24F ($4.80) students and seniors 60 and over, 10F ($2) children 17 and under. Visits with commentary, 59F ($11.80) adults, 48F ($9.60) students and seniors 60 and over, 20F ($4) children 17 and under. Tues–Sat noon–6pm (to 9:30pm Fri), Sun 10am–6pm. Métro: Porte-de-Pantin.

Situated within the $120 million, stone-and-glass Cité de la Musique, the museum serves as a tribute and testament to the rich musical tradition that has been passed down through the many ages and cultures of the world. Visitors can view 4,500 instruments primarily from the 17th century to the present as well as paintings, engravings, and sculptures that all relate to musical history. One especially appealing section of mandolins, lutes, and zithers evokes music from 400 years ago. It's all here: cornets disguised as snakes, antique music boxes, even a postwar electric guitar that Elvis might have collected. As part of the museum's permanent collection, models of the world's great concert halls and interactive display areas give visitors a chance to hear and better understand the art and technology of musical heritage.

Musée d'Ennery. 59 av. Foch, 16e. ☎ **01-45-53-57-96.** Admission free. Thurs and Sat 2–6pm. Métro: Porte Dauphine.

This is the result of the fierce passion and determination of Madame Clémence d'Ennergy, who in 1876 began assembling more than 7,000 Japanese *objets d'art*, many of which she found in antiques shops and boutiques around Paris. Some of her more compelling finds include the Kyoto ceramics from the 18th and 19th centuries; Namban art objects, a style resulting from the collision of Japanese and Portuguese cultures from 1543 to 1630; as well as Chinese furniture from the 17th to 19th centuries.

Musée d'Arts d'Afrique et d'Oceanie. 293 av. Daumesnil, 12e. ☎ **01-44-74-84-80.** Admission 38F ($7.60) for adults, free for children under 18. Mon and Wed–Fri 10am–5:30pm; Sat–Sun 10am–6pm. Métro: Porte-Dorée.

In a building put up for the Colonial Exhibition of 1931, you'll find an extensive collection of ethnic art, from Aboriginal bark paintings to Benin bronzes. The display of North African Islamic art is the best in Europe. One of the finest tropical aquariums in Europe, complete with its own crocodile pit, is situated in the basement.

Musée Jacquemart-André. 158 bd. Hausmann, 8e. % 01-42-89-04-91. Admission 45F ($9). Daily 10am–6pm. Métro: Miromesnil or St-Philippe-du-Roule.

It's the finest museum of its type in Paris, an inspired 19th-century blend of taste and money, the treasure trove of a married couple that was devoted to 18th-century French paintings and furnishings, 17th-century Dutch and Flemish paintings, and works from the Italian Renaissance. In other words, it's what Jackie O could have acquired if Kennedy and Onassis hadn't been so tight. The collection used to belong to the André family, a prominent family of French Protestants who made a fortune in banking and industry in the 19th century. The family's last scion, Edouard André, spent most of his life as an officer in the French army stationed abroad, returning later in his life to marry a well-known portraitist of French governmental figures and members of the aristocracy, Nélie Jacquemart. Together, they compiled a collection of rare French 18th-century decorative art and European paintings within an 1850s town house that was continually upgraded and redecorated according to the fashions of their time.

In 1912, Mme Jacquemart willed the house and its collection to the Institut de France, which paid for an extensive renovation and enlargement that was completed in 1996. The pride of the collection are works by Bellini, Carpaccio, and Uccelo, which are complemented by Houdon busts, Gobelins tapestries, Savonnerie carpets, della Robbia terra-cottas, an awesome collection of antiques, and works by Rembrandt (*The Pilgrim of Emmaus*), Van Dyck, Tiepolo, Rubens, Watteau, Fragonard, Boucher, and Mantegna. Salons drip with gilt and the ultimate in fin de siècle style.

Take a break from all this gilded age opulence with a cup of tea in Mme Jacquemart's high-ceilinged dining room, where 18th-century tapestries adorn a tea-room well suited to light lunches. Salads, tartes and *tourtes* (a round pastry filled with meat or fruit), and an assortment of Viennese pastries are served throughout the opening hours of the museum, and are eminently suited for a light lunch or a pick-me-up.

Musée Marmottan-Claude Monet. 2 rue Louis-Boilly, 16e. ☎ **01-42-24-07-02.** Admission 35F ($7) adults, 15F ($3) children ages 8–18 and over 60; children 7 and under free. Tues–Sun 10am–5:30pm. Métro: La Muette.

Occasionally a lone art historian would venture here on the edge of the Bois de Boulogne to see what Paul Marmottan donated to the Académie des Beaux-Arts. Hardly anybody else did, until 1966, when Michel Monet, son of Claude Monet, died in a car crash, leaving a bequest of his father's art, valued at the time at $10 million, to the little museum. The Académie des Beaux-Arts suddenly became heir to more than 130 paintings, watercolors, pastels, drawings, and a whole lot of Monet lovers, who can now trace the evolution of the great man's work in a single museum.

The gallery owns more than 30 paintings of his house at Giverny, and many of water lilies, his everlasting fancy. The bequest included *Willow* (1918), *House of Parliament* (1905), even a portrait Renoir painted of the 32-year-old Monet. The collection has been hailed as "one of the great art treasures of the world," and that it is. Ironically, the museum had always owned Monet's *Impression*, from which the movement got its name.

Paul Marmottan's original collection includes fig-leafed nudes, First Empire antiques, assorted objets d'art, bucolic paintings, and crystal chandeliers. Many tapestries date from the Renaissance, and you can also see an extensive collection of miniatures donated by Daniel Waldenstein.

Musée Rodin. In the Hôtel Biron, 77 rue de Varenne, 7e. ☎ **01-44-18-61-10.** Admission 28F ($5.60) adults, 18F ($3.60) ages 18–25; ages 17 and under free. Apr–Sept Tues–Sun 9:30am–5:45pm; Oct–Mar Tues–Sun 9:30am–4:45pm. Métro: Varenne.

Insider's View

The little alley behind the mansion housing the Musée Rodin winds its way down to a pond with fountains and flower beds, even sandpits for children. It's one of the most idyllic hidden spots of Paris.

These days Rodin is acclaimed as the father of modern sculpture, but in a different era his work was labeled obscene. The world's artistic taste changed, and in due course the government of France purchased the gray-stone 18th-century luxury residence in Faubourg St-Germain. The mansion was the Rodin's studio from 1910 until his death in 1917. After the government bought the studio, it restored the rose gardens to their 18th-century splendor, making them a perfect setting for Rodin's most memorable works.

In the courtyard are three world-famous creations: *The Gate of Hell, The Thinker,* and *The Burghers of Calais.* Rodin's first major public commission, *The Burghers* commemorated the heroism of six burghers of Calais who, in 1347, offered themselves as a ransom to Edward III in return for ending his siege of their port. Perhaps the single best-known work, *The Thinker,* in Rodin's own words, "thinks with every muscle of his arms, back, and legs, with his clenched fist and gripping toes." Not yet completed when Rodin died, *The Gate of Hell,* as he put it, is "where I lived for a whole year in Dante's Inferno."

Inside the building, the sculpture, plaster casts, reproductions, originals, and sketches reveal the freshness and vitality of that remarkable man. Many of his works appear to be emerging from marble into life. Everybody is attracted to *The Kiss* (of which one critic wrote, "the passion is timeless"). Upstairs are two different versions of the celebrated and condemned nude of Balzac, his bulky torso rising from a tree trunk (Albert E. Elsen commented on the "glorious bulging" stomach). Included are many versions of his *Monument to Balzac* (a large one stands in the garden), which was Rodin's last major work and which caused a furor when it was first exhibited.

Other significant sculpture includes Rodin's soaring *Prodigal Son, The Crouching Woman* (called the "embodiment of despair"), and *The Age of Bronze,* an 1876 study of a nude man, modeled by a Belgian soldier. (Rodin was falsely accused of making a cast from a living model.)

Generally overlooked is a room devoted to Camille Claudel, Rodin's mistress and a towering artist in her own right. She had been his pupil, model, and lover, and created such works as *Maturity, Clotho,* and the recently donated *The Waltz* and *The Gossips.*

Musée Nissim de Camondo. 63 rue de Monceau, 8e. ☎ **01-45-63-26-32.** Admission 27F ($5.40) adults, 18F ($3.60) under 18 and over 60. Wed–Mon 10am–5pm. Closed: Christmas and New Year's Day. Métro: Villiers.

This museum is a jewel box of elegance and refinement, evoking the days of Louis XVI and Marie Antoinette. Visit here if you'd like a keen insight into the decorative arts of the 18th century, all in a town house setting that brings these elements more alive than in most museums. The pre–World War I town house was donated to the Museum of Decorative Arts by Comte Moïse de Camondo (1860-1935) in memory of his son, Nissim, a French aviator killed in combat during World War I.

Entered through a courtyard, the museum is like the private home of an aristocrat of 2 centuries ago—richly furnished with needlepoint chairs, tapestries (many from Beauvais or Aubusson), antiques, paintings (inevitable Francesco Guardi scenes of Venice), bas-reliefs, silver, Chinese vases, crystal chandeliers, Sèvres porcelain, and Savonnerie carpets. And, of course, a Houdon bust (in an upstairs bedroom). The

Blue Salon, overlooking the Parc Monceau, is impressive. You can wander unimpaired through the gilt and oyster-gray salons.

Musée Zadkine. 100 bis rue d'Assas, 6e. ☎ **01-43-26-91-90.** Admission 27F ($5.40) adults, 19F ($3.80) children. Tues–Sun 10am–5:30pm. Métro: Notre-Dame des Champs.

This museum near the Luxembourg Gardens and boulevard St-Michel was once the private residence of Ossip Zadkine (1890–1967), the sculptor. Now this famous artist's collection has been turned over to the city of Paris for public viewing. Included are some 300 pieces of sculpture, displayed both within the museum and in the garden, bringing a little rural charm to the city's heart. Some drawings and tapestries are also exhibited. Chances are you won't be visiting here unless you've already seen some of Zadkine's works and want to know more about him and his work. At these headquarters where he worked from 1928 until his death, you can see how he moved from "left wing" Cubism extremism to a renewed appreciation of the classic era. You can visit his garden for free even if you don't want to go into the museum. In fact, it's one of the finest places to relax in Paris on a sunny day, sitting on a bench taking in Zadkine's two-faced *Woman with the Bird.*

Paristoric. 11 bis rue Scribe, 9e. ☎ **01-42-66-62-06.** Admission 50F ($10) adults, 30F ($6) students and children under 18. Daily 9am–6pm (open until 9pm in summer). Métro: Opéra. RER: Auber.

This unique multimedia show retraces the history of Paris for visitors in a state-of-the-art theater located in the heart of the city. The 2,000 years since Paris's birth unroll chronologically to the music of such varied musicians as Wagner and Edith Piaf. Maps, portraits, and scenes from dramatic times in the city's history are projected on the large screen as a running commentary (heard through headphones in one of 10 languages) gives details about the art, architecture, and events in the city's past. Many visitors come here first for a preview of what they want to see, others stop in for a more in-depth look at what they've already visited. Although the show is sometimes hard to follow and a bit expensive for some, it's worth the 45 minutes it takes to view it.

13 More Churches

St-Etienne-du-Mont. Place Ste-Geneviève, 5e. ☎ **01-43-54-11-79.** Mon–Sat 8:30am–noon and 2–7pm, Sun 8:30–noon and 3–7:15pm. Closed Mon in July–Aug. Métro: Cardinal-Lemoine or Luxembourg.

Once there was an abbey on this site, founded by Clovis and later dedicated to St. Geneviève, the patroness of Paris. Such was the fame of this popular saint that the abbey proved too small to accommodate the pilgrimage crowds. Now part of the Lycée Henri IV, the Tower of Clovis is all that remains of the ancient abbey (you can see the Tower from rue Clovis).

Today the task of keeping alive her cult has fallen on the Church of St-Etienne-du-Mont, on place St. Geneviève, practically adjoining the Panthéon. The interior is Gothic, an unusual style for a 16th-century church. Construction on the present building began in 1492 and was plagued by delays until the structure was finished, 134 years later, in 1626.

Besides the patroness of Paris, such men as Pascal and Racine were entombed in the church. Though St. Geneviève's tomb was destroyed during the Revolution, the stone on which her coffin rested was discovered later, and her relics were gathered for a place of honor at St. Etienne.

The church possesses a remarkable rood screen, built in the first part of the 16th century. Crossing the nave, it is unique in Paris—called spurious by some uncharitable souls, and a masterpiece by others. Another treasure is a wood-carved pulpit, held up by a seminude Samson who clutches a bone in one hand, having slain a lion at his feet. The fourth chapel on the right (when entering) contains impressive stained glass dating from the 16th century.

St-Germain l'Auxerrois. 2 place du Louvre, 1er. ☎ **01-42-60-13-96.** Daily 8am–8pm. Métro: Louvre.

Once it was the church for the Palace of the Louvre, drawing an assortment of courtesans, men of art and of law, local artisans, even royalty. Sharing the place du Louvre with Perrault's colonnade, the church contains only the foundation stones of its original belfry built in the 11th century. It was greatly enlarged in the 14th century by the addition of side aisles. The little primitive chapel that had stood on the spot eventually gave way to a great and beautiful church, with 260 feet of stained glass, including some rose windows from the Renaissance.

The saddest moment in its history was on August 24, 1572, the evening of the St. Bartholomew Massacre. On that night, the bells rang in the tower, signaling the supporters of Catherine de Médicis, Marguerite of Guise, Charles IX, and the future Henri III to launch a slaughter of thousands of Huguenots, who had been invited to celebrate the marriage of Henri of Navarre to his cousin, Marguerite of Valois. There is little evidence of the bloodbath now, of course. The intricately carved church-wardens' pews are outstanding, based on designs by Le Brun in the 17th century. Behind the pew is a 15th-century triptych and Flemish retable (so badly lit you can hardly appreciate it). The organ was originally ordered by Louis XVI for the Sainte Chapelle. In that architectural mélange, many famous men were entombed, including the sculptor Coysevox and Le Vau, the architect. Around the chancel is an intricate 18th-century grille.

Val-de-Grâce. 1 place Alphonse-Laveran, 5e. ☎ **01-40-51-40-00.** Free admission. Mon–Sat 9am–noon and 2–5pm. Touring prohibited during services. Métro: Port-Royal.

According to an old proverb, to understand the French you must like Camembert cheese, the Pont-Neuf, and the dome of Val-de-Grâce.

After 23 years of a childless marriage to Louis XIII, Anne of Austria gave birth to a boy who would one day be known as the Sun King. In those days, if monarchs wanted to express gratitude, they built a church or monastery. On April 1, 1645, 7 years after his birth, the future Louis XIV laid the first stone of the church. At that time, Mansart was the architect. To him we owe the facade in the Jesuit style. Le Duc, however, designed the dome, and the painter Mignard decorated it with frescoes. Le Mercier and Le Muet also had a hand in the church's fashioning.

Val-de-Grâce's origins go back even further, to 1050, when a Benedictine monastery was established on the grounds. In 1619 Marguerite Veni d'Arbouze was appointed abbess by Louis XIII. She petitioned Anne of Austria for a new monastery because the original one was decaying. Then came Louis XIV's church, which in 1793 was turned into a military hospital and in 1850 an army school. As of this writing, you must admire the church and take in its controversial dome from the outside only, as the interior remains closed because of a fear of a terrorist bomb, possibly due to the presence of a new military hospital nearby.

14 Gardens & Parks

See section 3, "The Champs-Elysées: The Grand Promenade of Paris," for details on the **Tuileries,** the most famous gardens in Paris.

Hemingway told a friend that the ✪ **Jardin du Luxembourg,** 6e; (Métro: Odéon, RER: Luxembourg) "kept us from starvation." He related that in his poverty-stricken days in Paris, he wheeled a baby carriage (the vehicle was considered luxurious) and child through the gardens because it was known "for the classiness of its pigeons." When the *gendarme* went across the street for a glass of wine, the writer would eye his victim, preferably a plump one, then lure him with corn and ". . . snatch him, wring his neck," then flip him under Bumby's blanket. "We got a little tired of pigeon that year," he confessed, "but they filled many a void."

Before it became a feeding ground for famished artists of the 1920s, Luxembourg knew greater days. Leon Daudet claimed, "There is nothing more charming, which invites one more enticingly to idleness, reverie, and young love, than a soft spring morning or a beautiful summer dusk at the Jardin du Luxembourg." But it's always been associated with artists, although students from the Sorbonne and children predominate nowadays. Watteau came this way, as did Verlaine. Balzac, however, didn't like the gardens at all. In 1905 Gertrude Stein would cross the gardens to catch the Batignolles-Clichy-Odéon omnibus pulled by three gray mares across Paris, to meet Picasso in his studio at Montmartre, where she sat while he painted her portrait.

The gardens are the best on the Left Bank (some say in all of Paris). Marie de Médicis, the much-neglected wife and later widow of the roving Henri IV, ordered a palace built on the site in 1612. She planned to live here with her "witch" friend, Leonora Galigal. A Florentine by birth, the regent wanted to create another Pitti Palace, or so she ordered the architect, Salomon de Brossee. She wasn't entirely successful, although the overall effect is most often described as Italianate.

The queen didn't get to enjoy the palace for very long after it was finished. She was forced into exile by her son, Louis XIII, after it was discovered that she was plotting to overthrow him. Reportedly, she died in Cologne in poverty, quite a step down from the luxury she had once known in the Luxembourg. Incidentally, the 21 paintings she commissioned from Rubens that glorified her life were intended for her palace, but are now in the Louvre. You can visit the palace the first Sunday of each month at 10:15am, for 45F ($9). However, you must call ☎ **01-44-33-99-83** to make a reservation. There is no information number to call for the park itself.

But you don't come to the Luxembourg to visit the palace—not really. The gardens are the attraction. For the most part, they are in the classic French tradition: well groomed and formally laid out, the trees planted in designs. A large water basin in the center is encircled with urns and statuary on pedestals, one honoring Paris's patroness St. Geneviève, who has pigtails reaching to her thighs. Another memorial is dedicated to Stendhal.

Come here to soak in the atmosphere, and bring the kids if you have any. You can sail a toy boat, ride a pony, or attend a grand guignol puppet show on occasion. Best of all, play boules with a group of elderly men who aren't ashamed to wear black berets and have Gauloises dangling from the corner of their mouths.

Crowds throng the park on May Day, when Parisians carry their traditional lilies of the valley. Birds sing, and all of Paris (those who didn't go to the country) celebrates the rebirth of spring.

One of the most spectacular parks in Europe is the ✪ **Bois de Boulogne,** Porte Dauphine, 16e (☎ **01-40-67-90-82;** Métro: Les-Sablons, Porte-Maillot, or Porte-Dauphine). The Bois is often called the "main lung" of Paris. Horse-drawn carriages traverse it, but you can also take your car through. Many of its hidden pathways,

Warning

Beware of muggers and knife-carrying prostitutes at night in the Bois de Boulogne.

however, must be discovered by walking. If you had a week to spare, you could spend it all in the Bois de Boulogne and still not see everything.

Porte Dauphine is the main entrance, although you can take the Métro to Porte Maillot as well. West of Paris, the park was once a forest kept for royal hunts. In the late 19th century it was in vogue: Along the avenue Foch carriages containing elegantly attired and coiffured Parisian damsels would rumble along with their foppish escorts. Nowadays, it's more likely to attract picnickers from the middle class. (And at night, hookers and muggers are prominent, so be duly warned.)

When Emperor Napoléon III gave the grounds to the city of Paris in 1852, they were developed by Baron Haussmann. Separating Lac Inférieur from Lac Supérieur is the Carrefour des Cascades (you can stroll under its waterfall). The Lower Lake contains two islands connected by a footbridge. From the east bank, you can take a boat to these idyllically situated grounds, perhaps stopping off at the cafe-restaurant on one of them.

Restaurants in the Bois are numerous, elegant, and expensive. The Pré-Catelan contains a deluxe restaurant of the same name and a Shakespearean theater in a garden said to have been planted with trees mentioned in the bard's plays.

The **Jardin d'Acclimation** at the northern edge of the Bois de Boulogne is for children, with a small zoo, an amusement park, and a narrow-gauge railway. (See "Especially for Kids," below, for more details.)

Two **racetracks,** Longchamp and the Auteuil, are in the park. The annual Grand Prix is run in June at Longchamp (the site of a medieval abbey). The most fashionable people of Paris turn out, the women gowned in their finest haute couture. Directly to the north of Longchamp is Grand Cascade, the artificial waterfall of the Bois de Boulogne.

In the 60-acre **Bagatelle Park,** the Comte d'Artois (later Charles X), brother-in-law of Marie Antoinette, made a wager with her that he could erect a small palace in less than 3 months. He hired nearly 1,000 craftsmen and irritated the local populace by requisitioning all shipments of stone and plaster arriving through the west gates of Paris. He hired cabinetmakers, painters, and the Scottish landscape architect Thomas Blaikie—and he won his bet. If you're in Paris in late April, go to the Bagatelle to look at the tulips, if for no other reason. In late May one of the finest and best-known rose collections in all of Europe is in full bloom. For some reason, as the head gardener confides to us, "This is the major rendezvous point in Paris for illicit couples." If you can, visit also in September, when the light is less harsh than summer or even in February, when stripped of much of its greenery, the park's true shape can be seen.

Much of the **Parc Monceau,** 8e (☎ **01-42-27-39-56;** Métro: Monceau or Villiers), is ringed with 18th- and 19th-century mansions, some evoking Proust's *Remembrance of Things Past*. The park was opened to the public in the days of Napoléon III's Second Empire. It was built in 1778 by the duke of Orléans, or Philippe-Egalité, as he became known. Carmontelle designed the park for the duke, who was at the time the richest man in France. "Philip Equality" was noted for his debauchery and pursuit of pleasure. No ordinary park would do.

Monceau was laid out with an Egyptian-style obelisk, a dungeon of the Middle Ages, a thatched alpine farmhouse, a Chinese pagoda, a Roman temple, an enchanted grotto, various chinoiseries, and of course a waterfall. These fairy-tale touches have largely disappeared except for a pyramid and an oval *naumachie* fringed by a colonnade. Many of the former fantasies have been replaced with solid statuary and monuments, one honoring Chopin. In spring, the red tulips and magnolias are worth the air ticket to Paris.

15 Cemeteries

The cemeteries of Paris are often viewed by sightseers as being somewhat like parks, suitable places for strolling. The graves of celebrities past also lure the sightseers. Père-Lachaise, for example, is a major sightseeing goal in Paris; the other cemeteries are of lesser importance. Some of the burial sites, such as de Montrouge and Saint-Pierre, are only of very minor interest.

✪ **Cimetière du Père-Lachaise.** 16 rue du Repos, 20e. ☎ **01-43-70-70-33.** Mon–Fri 8am– 6pm, Sat 8:30am–6pm, Sun 9am–6pm; closes at 5:30pm from early Nov to early Mar. Métro: Père-Lachaise.

When it comes to name-dropping, this cemetery knows no peer; it's been called the "grandest address in Paris." Everybody from Madame Bernhardt to Oscar Wilde (his tomb by Epstein) was buried here. So were Balzac, Delacroix, and Bizet. The body of Colette was taken here in 1954, and in time the little sparrow, Piaf, would follow. The lover of George Sand, Alfred de Musset, the poet, was buried here under a weeping willow. Napoléon's marshals, Ney and Masséna, lie here, as do Chopin and Molière. Marcel Proust's black tombstone rarely lacks a tiny bunch of violets. Colette's black granite slab always sports flowers, and legend has it that the cats replenish the red roses.

Some tombs are sentimental favorites: Lovetorn graffiti radiates a half mile from the tomb of singer Jim Morrison. The great dancer Isadora Duncan came to rest in a "pigeon hole" in the columbarium where bodies have been cremated and then "filed." If you search hard enough, you can find the tombs of that star-crossed pair Abélard and Héloïse, the ill-fated lovers of the 12th century. At Père-Lachaise they have found peace at last. Other famous lovers also rest here: A stone is marked Alice B. Toklas on one side, Gertrude Stein on the other.

Spreading over more than 110 acres, Père-Lachaise was acquired by the city of Paris in 1804. Nineteenth-century sculpture abounds, each family trying to outdo the other in ornamentation and cherubic ostentation. Some French Socialists still pay tribute at the Mur des Fédérés, the anonymous grave site of the Communards who were executed on May 28, 1871. Frenchmen who died in the Resistance or in Nazi concentration camps are also honored by several monuments. It was among the graves of the cemetery that these last-ditch fighters of the Paris Commune, the world's first anarchist republic, made their final desperate stand against the troops of the French government; overwhelmed, they were stood up against this wall and shot in batches. All died except a handful who had hidden in vaults and lived for years in the cemetery like wild animals, venturing into Paris at night to forage for food.

Note: A free map is available at the newsstand across from the main entrance. It will help you find the tombs.

Cimetière du Montparnasse. 3 bd. Edgar-Quinet, 14e. ☎ **01-44-10-86-50.** Free admission. Mon–Fri 8am–6pm, Sat 8:30am–6pm, Sun 9am–6pm; closes at 5:30pm Nov–Mar. Métro: Edgar-Quinet.

In the shadow of the Tour Montparnasse, this debris-littered and badly maintained cemetery is a burial ground of *célébrités* of yesterday. A map (available to the left of the main gateway) will direct you to its most famous couple, the shared grave site of Simone de Beauvoir and Jean-Paul Sartre. Others resting here include Samuel Beckett, Guy de Maupassant, editor Pierre Larousse (famous for his dictionary), and Alfred Dreyfus. The auto tycoon André Citroën is also interred here, as are sculptor Ossip Zadkine; composer Camille Saint-Saëns; Man Ray, the famous surrealist photographer and familiar figure in the cafes of Montparnasse; and Charles Baudelaire, who had already written about "plunging into the abyss, Heaven or Hell."

Cimetière St-Vincent. 6 rue Lucien-Gaulard, 19e. ☎ **01-46-06-29-78.** Free admission. Mar 15–Nov 5 daily 8:30am–5:30pm; off-season daily 8:30am–5pm. Métro: Lamarck-Caulaincourt.

Along this street lies the modest burial ground of St-Vincent, with a view of Sacré-Coeur on the hill. Because of the artists and writers who have their final resting place here, it is sometimes called "the most intellectual cemetery of Paris," but that epithet seems more apt for other graveyards. The artists Maurice Utrillo (1883–1955) and Théopile-Alexandre Steinien (1859–1923) were buried here, as was the musician Arthur Honegger. The writer Marcel Aymé came to rest here, too. In theory, the cemetery is open all day, but it would be foolish to disturb the caretaker's lunch any time from noon to 2pm—you'll regret it.

Cimetière de Passy. 2 rue du Comandant-Schloesing, 16e. ☎ **01-47-27-51-42.** Free admission. Daily 8:30am–5:30pm. Métro: Trocadéro.

This cemetery runs along the old northern walls of Paris, south and southwest of Trocadéro. It's a small graveyard, sheltered by a bower of chestnut trees, but it contains many grave sites of the famous. A concierge at the gate will provide directions to some of the stellar locations. The painter Edouard Manet was buried here, as was Claude Debussy. Many great literary figures since 1850 were interred here, including Tristan Bernard, Giraudoux, and Croisset. Also resting here are composer Gabriel Fauré, aviator Henry Farman, and actor Fernandel.

Cimetière de Montmartre. 20 av. Rachel, 18e. ☎ **01-43-87-64-24.** Free admission. Mon–Fri 8am–6pm, Sat 8:30am–6pm, Sun 8am–7pm. Closes at 5:30pm in winter. Métro: La Fourche.

This cemetery, which opened in 1795, lies west of the Butte and north of the boulevard de Clichy. The Russian dancer Nijinsky and novelist Alexandre Dumas the Younger are interred here. The great Stendhal was buried here, as were lesser literary lights, including novelists Edmond and Jules de Goncourt. The composer Hector Berlioz rests here, as does the poet and writer Heinrich Heine. The impressionist painter Edgar Degas still has fans who show up at his grave site, as does the composer Offenbach. Alfred de Vigny, the poet and dramatist, is among the buried here; a more recent tombstone honors François Truffaut, the film director of the *nouvelle vague.* We like to pay our respects at the tomb of Alphonsine Plessis, the heroine of *La dame aux camélias,* and Madame Récamier, who taught the world how to lounge. Originally, Emile Zola was interred here, but his corpse was exhumed and hauled off to the Panthéon in 1908. In the tragic year of 1871, the cemetery became the site of the mass burials of victims of the Siege and the Commune.

16 Especially for Kids

Boasting playgrounds with tiny merry-go-rounds and gondola-style swings, the large parks of Paris are always a treat for kids.

If you're staying on the Right Bank, take the children for a stroll through the **Tuileries** (see section 3 of this chapter), where there are donkey rides, ice-cream stands, and a marionette show; at the circular pond, you can rent a toy sailboat. On the Left Bank, similar delights exist in the **Jardin du Luxembourg** (see section 14). After a visit to the **Eiffel Tower**, you can take the kids for a donkey ride in the nearby gardens of the **Champ-de-Mars** (see section 4 of this chapter).

A great Paris tradition, **puppet shows** are worth seeing for their enthusiastic, colorful productions—they're a genuine French child's experience. At the Jardin du

The Père-Lachaise Cemetery

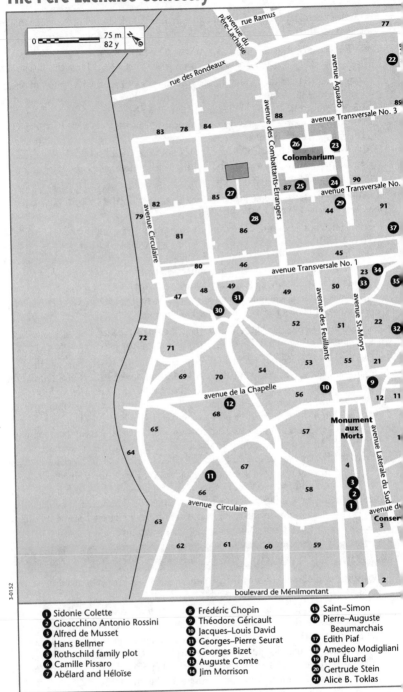

1. Sidonie Colette
2. Gioacchino Antonio Rossini
3. Alfred de Musset
4. Hans Bellmer
5. Rothschild family plot
6. Camille Pissaro
7. Abélard and Héloïse
8. Frédéric Chopin
9. Théodore Géricault
10. Jacques–Louis David
11. Georges–Pierre Seurat
12. Georges Bizet
13. Auguste Comte
14. Jim Morrison
15. Saint–Simon
16. Pierre–Auguste Beaumarchais
17. Edith Piaf
18. Amedeo Modigliani
19. Paul Éluard
20. Gertrude Stein
21. Alice B. Toklas

3-0152

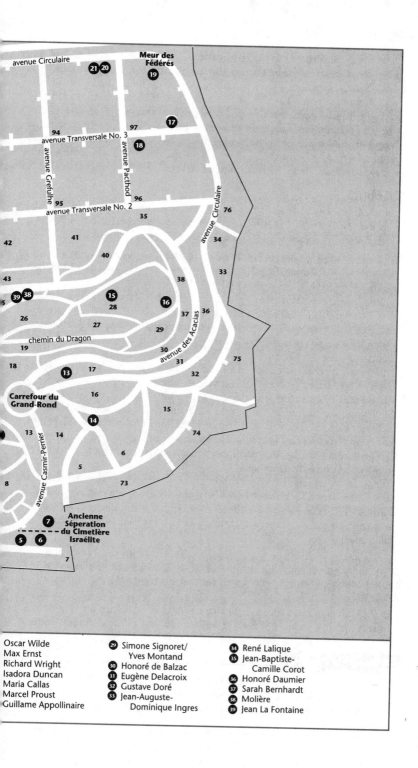

avenue Circulaire

**Meur des
Fédérés**

21 20

19

94   avenue Transversale No. 3   97

17

18

avenue Greffulhe

avenue Pacthod

95   avenue Transversale No. 2   96

76

35

42

41

40

avenue Circulaire

34

33

43

38

39 38

15

28

16

26

27

29

36

37

chemin du Dragon

19

30

avenue des Acacias

18

13

17

31

75

Carrefour du
Grand-Rond

16

32

14

15

avenue Casmir-Perrier

13   14

74

5

6

73

8

**Ancienne
Séperation
du Cimetière
israélite**

7

5   6

7

Oscar Wilde	29 Simone Signoret/ Yves Montand
Max Ernst	30 Honoré de Balzac
Richard Wright	31 Eugène Delacroix
Isadora Duncan	32 Gustave Doré
Maria Callas	33 Jean-Auguste- Dominique Ingres
Marcel Proust	
Guillame Appollinaire	

34 René Lalique
35 Jean-Baptiste-
      Camille Corot
36 Honoré Daumier
37 Sarah Bernhardt
38 Molière
39 Jean La Fontaine

Luxembourg, puppets reenact sinister plots set in Gothic castles and Oriental palaces; many young critics say the best puppet shows are held in the Champ-de-Mars.

On Sunday afternoons, French families head up to the Butte Montmartre to bask in the fiesta atmosphere. You can join in the fun: Take the Métro to Anvers and walk to the Funiculaire de Montmartre (the silver cable car that carries you up to Sacré-Coeur). Once up top, follow the crowds to place du Tertre, where a Sergeant Pepper–style band will usually be blasting off-key and where you can have the kids' picture sketched by local artists. You can take in the views of Paris from the various vantage points and treat your children to ice cream.

MUSEUMS

Set within the city's largest park and with special areas dedicated to children, the **Cité des Sciences et de l'Industrie** is one of the best museums for kids in Paris; for a full description, see section 12, "More Museums," earlier in this chapter.

Musée Grévin. 10 bd. Montmartre, 9e. ☎ **01-47-70-85-05.** Admission 50F ($10) adults, 36F ($7.20) children 14 and under. Daily 1–7pm; during French school holidays daily 10am–7pm. Ticket office closes at 6pm. Métro: rue Montmartre or Richelieu-Drouot.

The desire to compare this place to Madame Tussaud's of London is almost irresistible. Grévin is the number-one waxworks of Paris. It isn't all blood and gore, and doesn't shock some as Tussaud's might. Presenting a panorama of French history from Charlemagne to the mistress-collecting Napoléon III, it shows memorable moments in a series of tableaux.

Depicted are the consecration of Charles VII in 1429 in the Cathedral of Reims (Joan of Arc, dressed in armor and carrying her standard, stands behind the king); Marguerite de Valois, first wife of Henri IV, meeting on a secret stairway with La Molle, who was soon to be decapitated; Catherine de Médicis with the Florentine alchemist Ruggieri; Louis XV and Mozart at the home of the marquise de Pompadour; and Napoléon on a rock at St. Helena, reviewing his victories and defeats.

There are also displays of contemporary sports and political figures, as well as 50 of the world's best-loved film stars.

Two shows are staged frequently throughout the day. The first, called the *Palais des Mirages,* starts off as a sort of Temple of Brahma, and through magically distorting mirrors, changes into an enchanted forest, then a fete at the Alhambra at Granada. A magician is the star of the second show, "Le Cabinet Fantastique"; he entertains children of all ages.

Musée National d'Histoire Naturelle (Museum of Natural History). 57 rue Cuvier, 5e. ☎ **01-40-79-30-00.** Admission 40F ($8) adults, 10F ($2) ages 4–17; 3 and under free. Wed–Fri 10am–5pm (Thurs until 10pm), Sat–Sun 11am–6pm. Métro: Jussieu or Gare d'Austerlitz.

In the Jardin des Plants, this museum has a wide range of science and nature exhibits that draw the children of Paris. It was founded in 1635 as a scientific research

A Note for Parents

Most exhibits in Paris museums have only French explanations, so unless you fondly recollect your high school French lessons, or have some expertise on the display's subject matter, or are a seasoned exaggerator, you aren't going to distinguish yourself with wise explanations.

center by Guy de la Brosse, physician to Louis XIII. The museum's Grande Gallery of Evolution recently received a $90 million restoration. At the entrance, an 85-foot-long skeleton of a whale greets visitors. One display containing the skeletons of dinosaurs and mastodons is dedicated to endangered and vanished species. The museum also houses galleries that specialize in the fields of paleontology, anatomy, mineralogy, and botany. Within the museum's grounds are tropical hothouses containing thousands of species of unusual plant life and a menagerie with small animal life in simulated natural habitats.

Musée de la Marine. In the Palais de Chaillot, place du Trocadéro, 16e. ☎ **01-45-53-31-70.** Admission 38F ($7.60) adults, 25F ($5) ages 5–25 and over 65; children 4 and under free. Wed–Mon 10am–6pm. Métro: Trocadéro.

If your children have saltwater in their veins, you may want to take them to this museum.

A lot here is pomp: gilded galleys and busts of stiff-necked admirals. There's a great number of old ship models, including, for instance, the big galley *La Réale,* the *Royal-Louis,* the rich ivory model *Ville de Dieppe,* the gorgeous *Valmy,* and a barge constructed in 1811 for Napoléon I, which was used to carry another Napoléon (the Third) and his empress, Eugénie, on their first visit to the port of Brest in about 1858. Winged cherubs hold up the imperial crown.

There are many documents and artifacts concerning merchant fishing and pleasure fleets, oceanography, hydrography, with films illustrating the subjects. Thematic exhibits explain ancient wooden shipbuilding, the development of scientific instruments, merchant navy, fishing, steam, and sea traditions, and show some souvenirs of explorer Laperouse's wreck on Vanikoro Island in 1788. Important paintings include Joseph Vernet's *The Ports of France* during the 18th century.

AN AMUSEMENT PARK

Jardin d'Acclimation. Bois de Boulogne, 16e. ☎ **01-40-67-90-82.** Admission 12F ($2.40); 3 and under free. Daily 10am–6pm. Métro: A suitable itinerary, covering most of the park's sights, would involve arriving at Métro Sablons, walking across the park, and exiting at the far end (a distance of about ¹/₂ mile), and then returning to central Paris from the Métro Porte de Neuilly.

The definitive children's park in Paris is the Jardin d'Acclimation, a 25-acre amusement park on the northern side of the Bois de Boulogne. This is the kind of place that satisfies tykes and adults alike, but makes teenagers shudder in horror. The visit starts with a ride from Porte Maillot to the Jardin entrance, through a stretch of wooded park, on a jaunty green-and-yellow narrow-gauge train. Inside the gate is an easy-to-follow layout map. The park is circular—follow the road in either direction and it will take you all the way around and bring you back to the train at the end. (The train operates only on Wednesday, Saturday, and Sunday from 1:30pm until the park closes. A one-way fare costs 6F ($1.20). En route you will discover a house of mirrors, an archery range, a miniature-golf course, zoo animals, an American-style bowling alley, a puppet theater (performances are only on Thursday, Saturday, Sunday, and holidays), a playground, a hurdle-racing course, and a whole conglomerate of junior-scale rides, shooting galleries, and waffle stalls.

You can trot the kids off on a pony or join them in a boat on a mill-stirred lagoon. Also fun to watch (and a superb idea for American cities to copy) is *La Prévention Routière,* a miniature roadway operated by the Paris police. The youngsters drive through in small cars equipped to start and stop and are required by two genuine Parisian gendarmes to obey all street signs and light changes.

A ZOO

Parc Zoologique de Paris. Bois de Vincennes, 53 av. de St-Maurice, 12e. ☎ **01-44-75-20-00.** Admission 40F ($8) adults; 30F ($6) ages 4–16, students 16–25, and over 60; ages 3 and under free. Daily 9am–6pm. Métro: Porte Dorée or Château de Vincennes.

There's a modest zoo in the Jardin des Plantes, near the natural history museum, but without a doubt, the best zoo this city has to offer is in the Bois de Vincennes on the outskirts of Paris, quickly reached by Métro. Many of this modern zoo's animals live in settings similar to their natural habitat, hemmed in by rock barriers, not bars or cages. Here you'll never hunch up about the shoulders by empathizing with a leopard in a cage too small for stalking. The lion has an entire veldt to himself, and you can lock eyes comfortably across a deep protective moat. On a cement mountain reminiscent of Disneyland's Matterhorn, exotic breeds of mountain goats and sheep leap from ledge to ledge or pose gracefully for hours watching the penguins in their pools at the mountain's foot. The animals seem happy here and are consequently playful. Keep well back from the bear pools or you might get wet.

17 Literary Landmarks

Countless Left Bank streets have tales to tell, so our list will be necessarily incomplete. There's **rue Monsieur-le-Prince,** 6e, in the Odéon section (Métro: Odéon). During a famous visit in 1959, Martin Luther King, Jr. came to call on Richard Wright, the Mississippi-born African-American novelist famous for *Native Son.* King climbed to the third-floor apartment at no. 14, only to find that Wright's opinions on the civil rights movement conflicted with his own. Whistler rented a studio at no. 22, and, in 1826, Longfellow lived for a short time at no. 49. Oliver Wendell Holmes, Sr. lived at no. 55. After strolling along this street, you can dine at the former haunts of such figures as Kerouac and Hemingway. (See our recommendation of **Crémerie-Restaurant Polidor,** 41 rue Monsieur-le-Prince, 6e, in chapter 5.)

See also the listing for Victor Hugo's home in section 9 of this chapter, "Le Marais."

Deux-Magots. 170 bd. St-Germain, 6e. ☎ **01-45-48-55-25.** Métro: St-Germain-des-Prés.

This long-established watering hole of St-Germain-des-Prés is where Jake Barnes meets Lady Brett in Hemingway's *The Sun Also Rises.*

Harry's New York Bar. 5 rue Daunou, 2e. ☎ **01-42-61-71-14.** Métro: Opéra or Pyramides.

F. Scott Fitzgerald and Ernest Hemingway went on frequent benders here, Gloria Swanson gossiped about her affair with Joseph Kennedy, and even Gertrude Stein deigned to show herself from time to time. The place is still going strong (see chapter 9).

La Rotonde. 105 bd. Montparnasse, 6e. ☎ **01-43-26-68-84.** Métro: Raspail.

When they had money, Americans tended to drink on the Right Bank, notably in the Ritz Bar. When they didn't, they headed for one of the cafes of Montparnasse, which, according to Hemingway, usually meant La Rotonde.

Maison de Balzac. 47 rue Raynouard, 16e. ☎ **01-42-24-56-38.** Admission 17.50F ($3.50) adults, 9F ($1.80) children and people over 60. Tues–Sun 10am–5:45pm. Métro: Pasay or La Muette.

In the residential district of Passy, near the Bois de Boulogne, sits a modest house. Here the great Balzac lived for 7 years beginning in 1840. Fleeing here after his possessions and furnishings were seized, Balzac cloaked himself in secrecy (to see him, you had to know a password). If a creditor knocked on the Raynouard door, Balzac was able to escape through the rue Berton exit.

The museum's most notable memento is the Limoges coffee pot (the novelist's initials are in mulberry pink) that his "screech-owl" kept hot throughout the night as he wrote *La comédie humaine* to forestall creditors. Also enshrined here are Balzac's writing desk and chair, and a library of special interest to scholars.

The little house is filled with reproduced caricatures of Balzac. (A French biographer once wrote: "With his bulky baboon silhouette, his blue suit with gold buttons, his famous cane like a golden crowbar, and his abundant, disheveled hair, Balzac was a sight for caricature.")

The house is built on the slope of a hill, with a small courtyard and garden.

Shakespeare and Company. 37 rue de la Bûcherie, 5e. ☎ **01-43-26-96-50.** Daily 11am–midnight. Métro: St-Michel.

The most famous bookstore on the Left Bank was Shakespeare and Company, on rue de l'Odéon, home to the legendary Sylvia Beach, "mother confessor to the Lost Generation." Hemingway, Fitzgerald, and Gertrude Stein were all frequent patrons. Anaïs Nin, the diarist noted for her description of struggling American artists in 1930s Paris, also stopped in often. At one point she helped her companion, Henry Miller, publish *Tropic of Cancer,* a book so notorious in its day that returning Americans trying to slip a copy through Customs often had it confiscated as pornography. (When times were hard, Nin herself wrote pornography for a dollar a page.)

Long ago, the shop moved to rue de la Bûcherie, where expatriates swap books and literary gossip.

Le Procope. 13 rue l'Ancienne-Comédie, 6e. ☎ **01-40-46-79-00.** Métro: Odéon.

Dating from 1686, this is the oldest cafe in Paris. It's located in St-Germain-des-Prés and was the restaurant of choice for such historical figures as Franklin and Jefferson. Writers from Diderot, Voltaire, George Sand, Victor Hugo, and Oscar Wilde all stopped by in their day as well. (See chapter 5.)

18 Paris Underground

Les Catacombs. 1 place Denfert-Rochereau, 14e. ☎ **01-43-22-47-63.** Admission 27F ($5.40) adults, 19F ($3.80) ages 7–18 and over 60; 6 and under free. Tues–Fri 2–4pm, Sat–Sun 9–11am and 2–4pm. Métro: Denfert-Rochereau.

Every year an estimated 50,000 tourists explore some 1,000 yards of tunnel in these dank Catacombs to look at six million ghoulishly arranged skull-and-crossbones skeletons. First opened to the public in 1810, this "empire of the dead" is now illuminated with overhead electric lights over its entire length.

In the Middle Ages the Catacombs were originally quarries, but in 1785 city officials decided to use them as a burial ground. The bones of several million persons were moved here from their previous resting places, since the overcrowded cemeteries were considered health menaces. In 1830 the prefect of Paris closed the Catacombs to the viewing public, considering them obscene and indecent. He maintained that he could not understand the morbid curiosity of civilized people who wanted to gaze upon the bones of the dead. Later, in World War II, the Catacombs were the headquarters of the French Resistance.

The Sewers of Paris (Les Egouts). Pont de l'Alma, 7e. ☎ **01-47-05-10-29.** Admission 25F ($5) adults, 20F ($4) students; under 10 and over 60 free. May–Oct Sat–Wed 11am–5pm; winter Sat–Wed 11am–4pm. Closed 3 weeks in Jan for maintenance. Métro: Alma-Marceau. RER: Pont de l'Alma.

The sophistication of a society can be judged by the way it disposes of waste, some sociologists assert. If that's the criteria, Paris receives good marks for its mostly invisible network of sewers. Victor Hugo is credited with making these sewers famous in *Les Misérables*. "All dripping with slime, his soul filled with a strange light," Jean Valjean in his desperate flight through the sewers of Paris is one of the heroes of narrative drama. Hugo also wrote, "Paris has beneath it another Paris, a Paris of sewers, which has its own streets, squares, lanes, arteries, and circulation."

In the early Middle Ages, drinking water was taken directly from the Seine, and wastewater was poured onto fields or thrown onto the then-unpaved streets, transforming the urban landscape into a sea of rather smelly mud.

Around 1200, the streets of Paris were paved with cobblestones, with open sewers running down the center of each. These open sewers helped spread the Black Death, which devastated the city. In 1370, a vaulted sewer was built in the rue Montmartre, draining effluents directly into a tributary of the Seine. During the reign of Louis XIV improvements were made, but the state of waste disposal in Paris remained deplorable.

During the early 1800s, under the reign of Napoléon I, 18 1/2 miles of underground sewer were added beneath the Parisian landscape. By 1850, as the Industrial Revolution made the manufacture of iron pipe and steam-digging equipment more practical, Baron Haussmann developed a system that used separate underground channels for both drinking water and sewage. By 1878, it was 360 miles long. Beginning in 1894, under the guidance of Belgrand, the network was enlarged, and new laws required that discharge of all waste and storm water runoff be funneled into the sewers. Between 1914 and 1977, an additional 600 miles of sewers were added beneath the pavements of a burgeoning Paris.

Today, the city known for its gastronomy boasts some memorable statistics regarding waste disposal: The network of sewers, one of the world's best, is 1,300 miles long. Within its cavities, it contains freshwater mains, compressed air pipes, telephone cables, and pneumatic tubes. Every day, 1.2 million cubic meters of wastewater are collected and processed by a plant in the Parisian suburb of Achères. One of the largest in Europe, it's capable of treating more than two million cubic meters of sewage per day.

The *égouts* of the city, as well as telephone and telegraph pneumatic tubes, are constructed around four principal tunnels, one 18 feet wide and 15 feet high. It's like an underground city, with the street names clearly labeled. Further, each branch pipe bears the number of the building to which it is connected. These underground passages are truly mammoth, containing pipes bringing in drinking water and compressed air as well as telephone and telegraph lines.

Tours of the sewers begin at Pont de l'Alma on the Left Bank. A stairway here leads into the bowels of the city. However, you often have to wait in line as much as half an hour. Visiting times might change when there is bad weather, as a storm can make the sewers dangerous. The tour consists of seeing a movie on sewer history, visiting a small museum, and then a short trip through the maze.

19 Organized Tours

ORIENTATION TOURS

The most popular way to get acquainted with Paris is on a 2-hour double-decker bus tour that takes you past the major attractions. No time is allotted to stop at any of the points of interest, but you'll get a panoramic view out of the large windows. Seats are comfortable, and individual earphones are distributed with a recorded commentary in 10 different languages. Contact **Cityrama,** 147–149 rue Saint-Honoré, 1er (☎ **01-44-55-61-30**). A 2-hour "orientation tour" of Paris costs 150F ($30). A morning tour with interior visits to Notre Dame and the Louvre sells for 290F ($58). Tours to Versailles and Chartres are also offered. Métro: Palais-Royal or Musée-du-Louvre.

A separate tour of the nighttime illuminations leaves daily at 10pm in summer and 9pm in winter. The cost is 150F ($30).

CRUISES ON THE SEINE

The river that winds through the heart of Paris is the third longest of the four great rivers of France, yet its role in French history is greater than that of the other three waterways combined. Sailing along its banks, with the architecture of the most beautiful city in the world passing on either side of you, is one of the most rewarding experiences in France. **Bateaux-Mouches** cruises depart frequently from the Pont de l'Alma on the Right Bank. Some boats have open sun decks, bars, and restaurants. All provide commentaries in six languages, including English. Tours depart daily every 30 minutes from 10am to 11:30pm; in good weather, boats leave every 15 minutes. Fares are 40F ($8) for adults and 20F ($4) for children for a ride lasting about 1¹/₂ hours; luncheon cruises cost 300F ($60) Monday through Saturday; a deluxe dinner cruise costs 500F to 650F ($100 to $130). Call ☎ **01-42-25-96-10** for information and reservations. Métro: Alma-Marceau.

Some visitors, however, prefer longer excursions along the river that gave rise to the French nation. **Paris Canal** (☎ **01-42-40-96-97**) requires advance reservations for 3-hour waterborne tours that begin either at the quays in front of the Musée d'Orsay (Métro: Solférino) or in front of the Musée des Sciences et de l'Industrie at Parc de la Villette (Métro: Porte de la Villette). Excursions negotiate the waterways and canals of Paris, including the Seine, an underground tunnel below the place de la Bastille, and the Canal St-Martin. The cost is 95F ($19) for adults, and free for children under 4. With the exception of excursions on Sunday and holidays, prices are usually reduced to 70F ($14) for passengers from 12 to 25 and over 60, and to 55F ($11) for passengers aged 4 to 11. Tours are offered daily, from March through November; on Sundays after November 11.

20 Special & Free Events in Paris

It won't cost you a franc to explore the streets of Paris. Walk along the quays of the Seine, browse through the shops and stalls; each street opens onto a new vista.

If you're an early riser, a walk through Paris at dawn can be memorable; you'll see the city come to life. Shop fronts are washed clean for the new day, cafes open, and vegetable vendors arrange their produce.

The spacious forecourt of the Centre Georges Pompidou, place Georges Pompidou, is a free "entertainment center" featuring mimes, fire-eaters, would-be circus performers, and sometimes first-rate musicians. Métro: Rambuteau or Hôtel-de-Ville.

In the corridors of the Métro, classical music students (often from the Conservatoire National) perform; a hat or violin case is passed for donations.

If you're in Paris during one of the major festivals, you can join in the fun on the streets for free. On **Summer Solstice (June 21),** clowns, fire-eaters, and other performers roam the streets. On **Bastille Day (July 14),** the French traditionally drink wine and dance in the streets—fireworks are displayed, free concerts are given, and a parade of tanks heads down the Champs-Elysées.

Many cultural events (such as concerts, films, and lectures) in Paris are free; foreign nations often sponsor these events.

For free Sunday-afternoon organ concerts in the city's old churches, check *Pariscope,* the guide to entertainment events.

Concerts featuring jazz, classical, and contemporary music from the Netherlands are held at the **Institut Neerlandais,** 121 rue de Lille, 7e (☎ **01-53-59-12-40;** Métro: Assemblée-Nationale). Concerts cost 50F ($10).

The **American Church,** 65 quai d'Orsay, 7e (☎ **01-47-05-07-99;** Métro: Invalides), presents free chamber-music concerts most every Sunday at 6pm.

21 A Day at the Races

Paris boasts an army of avid horse-racing fans who get to the city's eight racetracks whenever possible. Information on current races is available in such newspapers and magazines as *Tierce, Paris-Turf, France-Soir,* or *L'Equipe,* all sold at kiosks throughout the city.

The bastion of Paris horse-racing is the **Hippodrome de Longchamp,** Bois de Boulogne (☎ **01-44-30-75-00**). Established in 1855, during the autocratic but pleasure-loving reign of Napoléon III, it has the most prestige, boasts the greatest number of promising Thoroughbreds, and awards the largest purse in France. The most important racing months at Longchamp are late June (Le Grand Prix de Paris) and early October (Prix de l'Arc de Triomphe). Métro: Auteuil, then take one of the shuttle buses that operate on race days.

Another horse-racing venue is the **Hippodrome d'Auteuil,** also in the Bois de Boulogne (☎ **01-40-71-47-47**). Known for its steeplechases and obstacle courses, it sometimes attracts more than 50,000 Parisians at a time. These spectators appreciate the park's open-air promenades as much as they do the equestrian events. Established in 1870, the event is scattered over a sprawling 30 acres of parkland. It's designed to show to maximum advantage the skill and agility of both horses and riders. Métro: Auteuil.

Also popular, though rough around the edges, is the **Hippodrome de Vincennes,** 2 route de la Ferme, Bois de Vincennes, 12e (☎ **01-49-77-17-17**). It holds most of its racing events under floodlights during evening hours in midwinter. Métro: Château de Vincennes.

Strolling Around Paris

The best way to discover Paris is on foot, using your own shoe leather. This chapter highlights the attractions of Montmartre, the Latin Quarter, the Grand Promenade, and the Marais.

WALKING TOUR 1
Montmartre

Start: Place Pigalle.
Finish: Place Pigalle.
Time: Five hours—more if you break for lunch. It's a 3-mile trek.
Best Time: Any day that it isn't raining. Set out by 10am at the latest.
Worst Time: After dark.

The traditional way to explore Montmartre is on foot. (We also tell you how to do it by funicular or train in chapter 6.) Take the Métro to place Pigalle. Turn right after leaving the station and proceed down boulevard de Clichy, turn left at the Cirque Medrano, and begin the climb up rue des Martyrs. Upon reaching rue des Abbesses, turn left and walk along this street, crossing the place des Abbesses. Walk uphill along rue Ravignan, which leads directly to place Emile-Goudeau, a tree-studded square in the middle of rue Ravignan. At no. 13, across from the Timhotel, stood:

1. **Bateau-Lavoir** (Boat Washhouse), called the cradle of Cubism. Although gutted by fire in 1970, it has been reconstructed by the city of Paris. Picasso once lived here and, in the winter of 1905–06, painted one of the world's most famous portraits, *The Third Rose* (Gertrude Stein). Other residents have included Kees van Dongen and Juan Gris. Modigliani had his studio nearby, as did Rousseau and Braque.

Rue Ravignan ends at place Jean-Baptiste-Clément. Go to the end of the street and cross it onto rue Norvins (which will be on your right). Here rues Norvins, St-Rustique, and des Saules collide in a scene famously painted by Utrillo. Turn right and head down rue Poulbot. At no. 11 you'll come to the:

2. **Espace Montmartre Dalí** (☎ 01-42-64-40-10). This phantasmagorical world of Dalí features 300 original works by the artist,

including his famous 1956 lithograph of *Don Quixote*. It is open daily from 10am to 6pm, charging 35F ($7) for adults, 25F ($5) for children.

The rue Poulbot crosses the tiny:

3. Place du Calvaire, which offers a panoramic view of Paris. On this square (a plaque marks the house) lived artist, painter, and lithographer Maurice Neumont (1868–1930). From here, follow the sounds of an oompah band to:

4. Place du Tertre, the old town square of Montmartre. Its cafes are overflowing, and its indoor and outdoor art galleries are always overcrowded. Some of the artists still wear berets, and the cafes bear such names as La Bohème. Everything is so loaded with local color, applied as heavily as on a Seurat canvas, as to get somewhat gaudy and inauthentic.

☕ **TAKE A BREAK**   Chances are, you'll be in Montmartre for lunch. Many restaurants, especially those around place du Tertre, are unabashed tourist traps. You'll be asked eight times if you want your portrait sketched in charcoal. The exception is **La Crémaillère 1900,** 15 place du Tertre, 18e (☎ 01-46-06-58-59), a short distance from Sacré-Coeur. As its name suggests, this is a belle epoque dining room, still retaining much of its original look, including paintings by Mucha. A terrace opens onto the square, or else you can retreat to the internal courtyard garden. A full menu is served throughout the day, including a standard array of French dishes—all the classics from sole meunière to mussels marinière. Go any time daily from 11am to 12:30am.

Right off the square fronting rue du Mont-Cenis is the:

5. Church of St-Pierre. Originally a Benedictine abbey, it has played many roles—Temple of Reason during the French Revolution, food depot, clothing store, even a munitions factory. These days are calmer: one of the oldest churches in Paris is back to being a church. Though the church was consecrated in 1147, even older parts are in evidence: Two of the columns in the choir stall are the remains of a Roman temple. Among the sculptured works is a nun with the head of a pig, a symbol of sensual vice. At the entrance of the church are three bronze doors sculpted by Gismondi in 1980, of which the middle door depicts the life of St. Peter; the left door is dedicated to St. Denis, first bishop of Paris; and the right door honors the Holy Virgin.

Facing St-Pierre, turn right and follow rue Azaïs to:

6. Sacré-Coeur, overlooking square Willette, whose raindrop domes and bell tower loom above Paris, and present a wide vista on sunny days. (For a complete description, see "Montmartre," chapter 6.) Facing the basilica, take the street on the left (rue du Cardinal Guibert), then go left onto rue du Chevalier-de-la-Barre and when you reach rue du Mont-Cenis, take a right. Continue on this street to rue Cortot, then turn left. At no. 12 is the:

7. Musée de Vieux Montmartre (☎ 01-46-06-61-11), with a wide collection of mementos of *vieux Montmartre.* Luminaries such as Dufy, van Gogh, and Renoir occupied this famous 17th-century house. Suzanne Valadon and her son, Utrillo, also lived here. It's open Tuesday through Sunday from 11am to 6pm. Admission is 25F ($5) for adults, 20F ($4) for students; free for children 11 and under.

From the museum, turn right heading up rue des Saules past a winery, a reminder of the days when Montmartre was a farming village on the outskirts of Paris. A grape-harvesting festival is held here every October.

The intersection of rue des Saules and rue St-Vincent is one of the most visited and photographed corners of the Butte. Here, on one corner, sits the famous old:

Montmartre

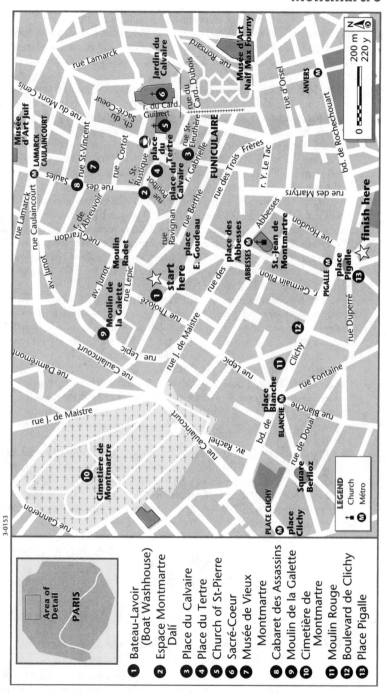

LEGEND
- ✝ Church
- Ⓜ Métro

1. Bateau-Lavoir (Boat Washhouse)
2. Espace Montmartre Dalí
3. Place du Calvaire
4. Place du Tertre
5. Church of St-Pierre
6. Sacré-Coeur
7. Musée de Vieux Montmartre
8. Cabaret des Assassins
9. Moulin de la Galette
10. Cimetière de Montmartre
11. Moulin Rouge
12. Boulevard de Clichy
13. Place Pigalle

Area of Detail
PARIS

3-0153

8. **Cabaret des Assassins,** long ago renamed Au Lapin Agile (see chapter 9 for details). Picasso and Utrillo once patronized this little cottage which numerous artists have patronized and painted. On any given afternoon French folk tunes, love ballads, army songs, sea chanteys, and music-hall ditties will stream out of the cafe and onto the street.

Turn left on rue St-Vincent, passing the Cimetière St-Vincent on your right. Utrillo is just one of the many famous artists buried here. Take a left onto rue Girardon and climb the stairs. In a minute or two, you'll spot on your right two of the windmills (*moulins*) that used to dot the Butte. One of these:

9. **Moulin de la Galette** (entrance at 1 av. Junot), was immortalized by Renoir.

Turn right onto rue Lepic and walk past no. 54. In 1886, van Gogh lived here with Guillaumin. Take a right turn onto rue Joseph-de-Maistre, then left again on rue Caulaincourt until you reach the:

10. **Cimetière de Montmartre,** second in fame only to Père-Lachaise and haunt of the mad Nijinsky, Dumas the younger, Stendhal, Degas, and Truffaut, among many of the sacred dead. The burial ground (Métro: Clichy) lies west of the Butte, north of boulevard de Clichy. See "Cemeteries" in chapter 6 for more information.

From the cemetery, take avenue Rachel, turn left onto boulevard de Clichy, and go to place Blanche, where an even better-known windmill than the one in Renoir's painting stands, the:

11. **Moulin Rouge,** one of the most talked-about nightclubs in the world. It was immortalized by Toulouse-Lautrec, but now exists in a much different form. The windmill is still here and so is the cancan. But the rest has become a superslick, outrageously expensive, gimmick-ridden variety show with a heavy emphasis on the undraped female form. (See chapter 9 for a full account.)

From place Blanche, you can begin a descent down:

12. **Boulevard de Clichy,** fighting off the pornographers and hustlers trying to lure you into tawdry sex joints. With some rare exceptions, notably the citadels of the *chansonniers* (songwriters), boulevard de Clichy is one gigantic tourist trap. But everyone who comes to Paris invariably winds up here. The boulevard strips and peels its way down to:

13. **Place Pigalle,** center of nudity in Paris. The square is named after a French sculptor, Pigalle, whose closest association with nudity was a depiction of Voltaire in the buff. Place Pigalle, of course, was the notorious "Pig Alley" of World War II. Toulouse-Lautrec had his studio right off Pigalle at 5 av. Frochot. When she was lonely and hungry, Edith Piaf sang in the alleyways, hoping to earn a few francs for the night.

WALKING TOUR 2
The Latin Quarter

Start: Place St-Michel.
Finish: The Panthéon.
Time: Three hours, not counting stops.
Best Time: Any school day, Monday through Friday, from 9am to 4pm.
Worst Time: Sunday morning, when everybody is asleep.

This is the precinct of the Université de Paris (known for its most famous constituent, the Sorbonne), where students meet and fall in love over *café-crème* and croissants. Rabelais named it the *quartier latin* after the students and the professors who spoke Latin in the classroom and on the streets. The sector teems with belly dancers, exotic restaurants, sidewalk cafes, bookstalls, basement nightclubs, *clochards* (bums), and *chiffonniers* (ragpickers). A good starting point for your tour is:

1. **Place St-Michel** (Métro: Pont St-Michel), where Balzac used to draw water from the fountain when he was a youth. This was the scene of frequent skirmishes between the Germans and the Resistance in the summer of 1944.

☕ **TAKE A BREAK** Open 24 hours a day, **Café le Départ St-Michel,** 1 place St-Michel (☎ 01-43-54-24-55), lies on the banks of the Seine, within view of both the steeple of Sainte-Chapelle and the dragon statue of place St-Michel. The decor is warmly modern, with etched mirrors reflecting the faces of a diversified clientele, often Left Bank students. If you're hungry, opt for one of the warm or cold snacks, including sandwiches. Many patrons come here for a grilled *entrecôte* (steak) with french fries.

The quarter centers around:

2. **Boulevard St-Michel** to the south, which the students call "boul Mich." From place St-Michel, with your back to the Seine, turn left down:

3. **Rue de la Huchette,** the setting of Elliot Paul's *The Last Time I Saw Paris.* Paul first wandered into this typical street "on a soft summer evening, and entirely by chance," in 1923. Although much has changed since his time, some of the buildings are so old that they have to be propped up by timbers. Paul captured the spirit of the street more evocatively than anyone, writing of "the delivery wagons, makeshift vehicles propelled by pedaling boys, pushcarts of itinerant vendors, knife-grinders, umbrella menders, a herd of milk goats, and the neighborhood pedestrians." (The local bordello has closed, however.)

Branching off from this street to your left is:

4. **Rue du Chat-qui-Pêche** (Street of the Cat Who Fishes), said to be the shortest, narrowest street in the world, containing not one door and only a handful of windows. It's usually filled with garbage or lovers, or both.

Now, retrace your steps toward place St-Michel and turn left at the intersection with rue de la Harpe, which leads to rue St-Séverin. At the intersection, take a left to see the:

5. **Church of St-Séverin.** This flamboyant Gothic church, named for a 6th-century recluse, lies just a short walk from the Seine. It was built from 1210 to 1230, and reconstructed in 1458, over the years adopting many of the features of Notre-Dame, located across the river. The tower was completed in 1487, the chapels between 1498 and 1520. Hardouin-Mansart designed the Chapel of the Communion in 1673 when he was 27 years old.

Before entering, walk around the church to examine the gargoyles, birds of prey, and reptilian monsters projecting from its roof. To the right, facing the church, is the 15th-century "garden of ossuaries." Inside St-Séverin, the stained glass is a stunning adornment.

After visiting this flamboyant Gothic church, go back to rue St-Séverin and follow it to rue Galande. Stay on rue Galande until you reach the:

6. **Church of St-Julien-le-Pauvre.** First stand at the gateway and look at the beginning of rue Galande, especially the old houses with the steeples of St-Séverin rising across the way—one of the most characteristic and most frequently painted scenes on the Left Bank. Enter the courtyard and you'll be in medieval Paris. The garden to the left of the entrance offers the best view of Notre-Dame.

Walking Tour—The Latin Quarter

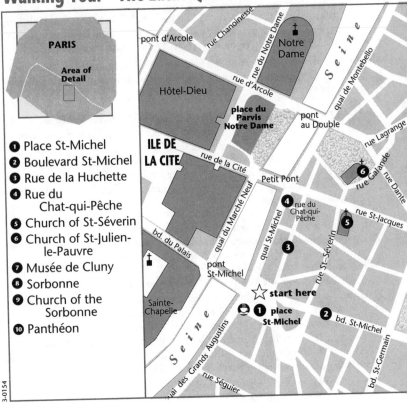

PARIS

Area of Detail

1. Place St-Michel
2. Boulevard St-Michel
3. Rue de la Huchette
4. Rue du Chat-qui-Pêche
5. Church of St-Séverin
6. Church of St-Julien-le-Pauvre
7. Musée de Cluny
8. Sorbonne
9. Church of the Sorbonne
10. Panthéon

3-0154

Everyone from Rabelais to Thomas Aquinas has passed through the doors of this church. Before the 6th century, a chapel stood on this spot. The present structure goes back to the Longpont monks, who began work on it in 1170 (making it the oldest existing church in Paris). In 1655 it was given to the Hôtel Dieu, and in time it became a small warehouse for salt. In 1889 it was presented to the followers of the Melchite Greek rite, a branch of the Byzantine church.

Return to rue Galande. Turn left at the intersection with rue St-Séverin. Continue on until you reach rue St-Jacques, then turn left and follow it to boulevard St-Germain. Turn right onto this boulevard and follow it until you reach rue de Cluny. Turn left and follow the street to the entrance to the:

7. **Musée de Cluny** (see chapter 6 for details). Even if you're rushed, take time out to see *The Lady and the Unicorn* tapestry. After your visit to the Cluny Museum, exit onto boulevard St-Michel, but instead of heading back to place St-Michel, turn left, and walk down to place de la Sorbonne and the:

8. **Sorbonne,** a constituent of the Université de Paris, one of the most famous academic institutions in the world. Founded in the 13th century, it had become the most prestigious university in the West by the 14th century, attracting such professors as Thomas-Aquinas; subsequently, it was reorganized by Napoléon in 1806.

At first glance from place de la Sorbonne, the Sorbonne seems architecturally undistinguished. In truth, it was rather indiscriminately reconstructed at the turn of the century. A better fate lay in store for the:

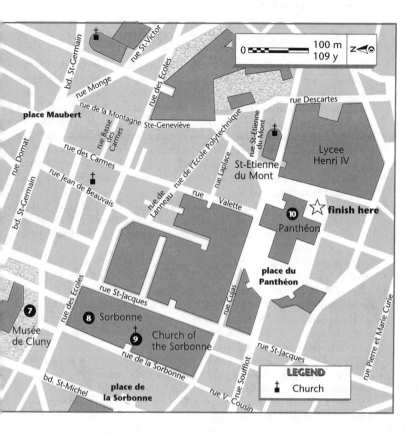

9. **Church of the Sorbonne,** built in 1635 by Le Mercier. It contains the marble tomb of Cardinal Richelieu, a work by Girardon based on a design by Le Brun. At his feet is the remarkable statue *Learning in Tears.*

From the church go south on rue Victor Cousin and turn left when you reach rue Soufflot. At street's end lies the place du Panthéon and the:

10. **Panthéon** (see chapter 6). Sitting atop Mont Ste-Geneviève, this nonreligious temple is the final resting place of such distinguished figures as Hugo, Zola, Rousseau, and Voltaire.

WALKING TOUR 3
The Marais

Start: Place de la Bastille

Finish: Place de la Bastille

Time: 4¹/₂ hours, with only cursory stops en route. The distance is about 2³/₄ miles.

Best Time: Monday to Saturday, when more buildings and shops are open. If interiors are closed, often you can walk into courtyards.

Worst Time: Toward dusk, when shops and museums are closed and it's too dark to admire the architectural details.

Begin your walking tour at the site that spawned one of the most celebrated and abhorred revolutions in human history, the:

1. **Place de la Bastille.** Here, on July 14, 1789, a mob of people attacked the Bastille—so began the French Revolution. Now nothing of this symbol of despotism remains. Built in 1369, its eight 100-foot towers once loomed over Paris. Within them, many prisoners, some sentenced by Louis XIV for "witchcraft," were kept, the best known being "The Man in the Iron Mask." And yet, when the revolutionary mob stormed the fortress, only seven prisoners were discovered. (The Marquis de Sade had been shipped to the madhouse 10 days earlier.) The authorities had discussed razing it anyway, so in itself, the attack meant nothing. But what it symbolized and what it started will never be forgotten. Bastille Day is celebrated with great festivity each July 14.

Since the late 1980s, what had been scorned as a once dull and grimy-looking traffic circle has become an artistic focal point of Europe, thanks to the construction of the Bastille Opéra, which occupies its eastern edge. (For details on the Opéra, see chapter 9).

It was probably easier to storm the Bastille in 1789 than it is to slip by today's speeding cars to the center of the square for a close-up view of the:

2. **Colonne de Juillet (July Column).** The July Column does not commemorate the Revolution. Instead, it honors the victims of the July Revolution of 1830, which put Louis-Philippe on the throne after the heady but wrenching victories and defeats of Napoléon Bonaparte. The tower is crowned by the winged and nude God of Liberty, whose forehead bears an emerging star.

From place de la Bastille, walk west along the rue St-Antoine for about a block. Turn right, and walk north along the rue des Tournelles, noting the:

3. **Statue of Beaumarchais.** Erected in 1895, it honors the 18th-century author of *The Barber of Seville* and *The Marriage of Figaro,* which Rossini and Mozart respectively (and brilliantly) set to music. Continue north for a long block along rue des Tournelles, then turn left at the colorful, medieval-looking rue Pas-de-la-Mule ("Footsteps of the Mule"), which will open suddenly onto the northeastern corner of the enchanting:

4. **Place des Vosges,** which is the oldest square in Paris and was once the most fashionable. Right in the heart of the Marais, it was called the Palais Royal in the days of Henri IV. The king planned to live here, but his assassin, Ravaillac, had other plans in mind. Henry II was killed while jousting on the square in 1559, in the shadow of the Hôtel des Tournelles. Afterwards his widow, Catherine de Médicis, had the place torn down.

Place des Vosges, once the major dueling ground of Europe, was one of the first planned squares on the continent. Its *grand-siècle* rosy-red brick houses are ornamented with white stone. Covered arcades allowed people to shop at all times, even in the rain—at the time, this was quite an innovation. In the 18th century, chestnut trees were added, sparking a continuing controversy: Critics say the trees spoil the perspective.

Over the years fame often passed this way: In place des Vosges lived Descartes, Pascal, Cardinal Richelieu, the courtesan Marion Delorme, Gautier, Daudet, and the most famous letter writer of all time, Madame de Sévigné. But its best-known occupant was Victor Hugo (his home, now a museum, is the only house that can be visited without a private invitation). The great writer could be seen rushing under the arcades of the square to an assignation with his mistress. In the center of the square is a statue of Louis XIII on horseback.

The Marais

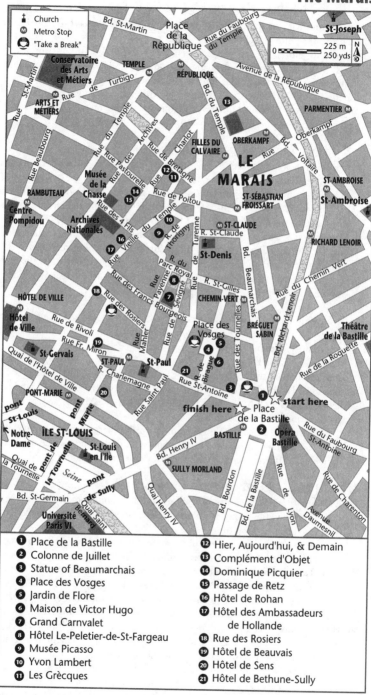

Church
Metro Stop
"Take a Break"

Bd. St-Martin
Place de la République
Rue du Faubourg du Temple
St-Joseph
Avenue de la République
0   225 m
    250 yds

Conservatoire des Arts et Métiers
TEMPLE
RÉPUBLIQUE
Rue de Turbigo
Bd. du Temple
PARMENTIER
Oberkampf
Bd. Voltaire

ARTS ET MÉTIERS
Rue Beaubourg
Rue St-Martin
Rue du Temple
Archives
Rue de Bretagne
Charlot
FILLES DU CALVAIRE
OBERKAMPF
LE MARAIS
ST-AMBROISE
St-Ambroise

RAMBUTEAU
Rue Pastourelle
Musée de la Chasse
Rue de Poitou
ST-SÉBASTIEN FROISSART

Centre Pompidou
Archives Nationales
Rue des 4 Fils
Rue Vieille du Temple
Rue de Thorigny
R. du Parc Royal
R. St-Claude
ST-CLAUDE
St-Denis
Rue de Turenne
RICHARD LENOIR
Rue du Chemin Vert

HÔTEL DE VILLE
Rue des Francs Bourgeois
Rue des Rosiers
R. de Sévigné
R. St-Gilles
CHEMIN-VERT
Bd. Beaumarchais
Bd. Richard Lenoir

Hôtel de Ville
Rue de Rivoli
Rue Mahler
Rue de Turenne
Place des Vosges
BRÉGUET SABIN
Théâtre de la Bastille
Rue de la Roquette

St-Gervais
Rue Fr. Miron
Quai de l'Hôtel de Ville
ST-PAUL
St-Paul
R. Charlemagne
Rue Saint Paul
R. de Birague
Rue St-Antoine

PONT-MARIE
pont Marie
pont St-Louis
Notre-Dame
ÎLE ST-LOUIS
Pont de la Tournelle
St-Louis en l'Île
Seine
pont de Sully
Bd. St-Germain
Université Paris VI
Quai Saint Bernard
Quai de la Tournelle
Quai Henry IV
Bd. Henry IV
BASTILLE
SULLY MORLAND
Bd. Bourdon
Bd. de la Bastille
finish here
start here
Place de la Bastille
Opéra Bastille
Rue du Faubourg St-Antoine
Rue de Lyon
Avenue Daumesnil
Rue de Charenton

❶ Place de la Bastille
❷ Colonne de Juillet
❸ Statue of Beaumarchais
❹ Place des Vosges
❺ Jardin de Flore
❻ Maison de Victor Hugo
❼ Grand Carnvalet
❽ Hôtel Le-Peletier-de-St-Fargeau
❾ Musée Picasso
❿ Yvon Lambert
⓫ Les Grècques

⓬ Hier, Aujourd'hui, & Demain
⓭ Complément d'Objet
⓮ Dominique Picquier
⓯ Passage de Retz
⓰ Hôtel de Rohan
⓱ Hôtel des Ambassadeurs
   de Hollande
⓲ Rue des Rosiers
⓳ Hôtel de Beauvais
⓴ Hôtel de Sens
㉑ Hôtel de Bethune-Sully

To an increasing degree, the Place des Vosges has become the centerpiece of many unusual, charming, and/or funky shops. One of the best of these lies very close to the point you entered the square:

5. **Jardin de Flore,** 24 Place des Vosges (☎ **01-42-77-61-90**). Purveyor of copies of 17th-century maps and engravings, this store seems like a neighborhood guardian. Look for stately reproductions of globes used by long-ago mariners and monarchs, examples of which were selected by Mitterrand to adorn his offices in the Élysée Palace. Established in 1977, the store has thrived on sales of objects that in all but a few cases begin at 300F ($60).

☕ TAKE A BREAK   Two separate cafes, each with loyal clients who have definite opinions about their relative merits, hold court from opposite sides of the Place des Vosges. Both serve café au lait, glasses of wine and *eaux de vie*, sandwiches, pastries, and steaming pots of midafternoon tea. They are **Ma Bourgogne,** 19 Place des Vosges (☎ **01-42-78-44-64**), on the western edge, and its east-side competitor, **La Chope des Vosges,** 22 Place des Vosges (☎ **01-42-72-64-04**). Ma Bourgogne gets so crowded at lunchtime that getting a table is well-nigh impossible. But La Chope gets more direct sunlight (something cherished by Parisians in midwinter) and is a bit less touristy. The debate is bitter and the caliber is even, but after circumnavigating the square, you'll be able to judge a winner for yourself.

Near the square's southeastern corner, commemorating the life and times of a writer whose works were read with something approaching passion throughout the 19th century, is the:

6. **Maison de Victor Hugo,** 6 place des Vosges (☎ **01-42-72-10-16**). Now a museum and literary shrine that can be visited by the public, Hugo lived here from 1832 until 1848, when he went into voluntary exile on the Channel Islands after the rise to power of the despotic Napoléon III. The "Le Marais" section of chapter 6 describes the museum in full.

Exit from the Place des Vosges from its northwestern corner (a point directly opposite the Maison de Victor Hugo), and walk west along the rue des Francs-Bourgeois. At the intersection with rue de Sévigné, take a right turn. At no. 23 is the:

7. **Grand Carnavalet** (☎ **01-42-72-21-13;** for a full description, see "Le Marais" in chapter 6), a 16th-century mansion that is now a museum devoted to the history of Paris and the French Revolution. Here, you can see a model of the Bastille as it looked before it was torn down.

Continue to a point near the northern terminus of the rue de Sévigné, noting no. 29 (now part of the Carnavalet Museum). This is the:

8. **Hotel Le-Peletier-de-St-Fargeau,** which bears the name of its former occupant, who was considered responsible for the death sentence of Louis XVI. At the end of the street, you reach rue du Parc-Royal. Take a left onto this lovely street lined with 17th-century mansions. The street leads to Place de Thorigny, where the:

9. **Musée Picasso** is at number 5 in the Hôtel Salé, originally built by a salt-tax collector (see "The Top Museums" in chapter 6 for a detailed description). You can visit the museum either now or after the end of the rest of this tour.

Next, walk northeast along the rue Thorigny, and turn left onto the rue Debelleyme. After a block, near the corner of the rue Vieille-du-Temple, is a worthwhile art gallery among the dozens in this neighborhood that feed on energy from the nearby Picasso Museum and the Centre Pompidou:

10. **Yvon Lambert,** 108 rue Vieille du Temple (☎ **01-42-71-09-33**). This gallery specializes in contemporary and sometimes radically avant-garde art from a spectrum of international artists that includes lots of cutting-edge Americans. Art is displayed in a cavernous main showroom, spilling over into an "annex" room on the side. An excellent primer for the local arts scene, it contrasts worthily to the evidence of the 17th century all around you.

Continue north for 2 short blocks along the rue Debelleyme until you reach the rue de Bretagne. Here, anyone who appreciates rummaging through the stocks of any really good deli will appreciate:

11. **Les Grècques,** 14 rue de Bretagne (☎ **01-42-71-00-56**). This is the most popular of the ethnic take-out restaurants in the neighborhood, a perfect starting point for anyone picnicking by the nearby Musée Picasso, the Square du Temple (just up rue de Bretagne), or the Place des Vosges, all within 400 yards. You'll find flavorful Greek cuisine, including moussaka, stuffed eggplant, stuffed vine leaves, several varieties of olives, tarama—a savory paste made from fish roe—and both meatballs and vegetarian balls. Les Grècques is open daily from 10am to 1:30pm, and Monday to Saturday from 4:30 to 8:30pm.

12. **Hier, Aujourd'hui, and Demain,** at the same address (☎ **01-42-77-69-02**), is where France's great love affair with 1930s art deco can really be appreciated. Michel, the shop's alert owner, provides a tempting array of *bibelots* and fashionable art objects. Select from one of the widest arrays of colored glass in town, knowing in advance that works by such late 19th-century glassmakers as Daum, Lalique, Gallé, and Legras are avidly collected by enthusiasts around the world. Some items require special packing and great care in transport; others (many amusing) can be packed with a suitcase and carted home as a souvenir of your walk through the Marais.

From here, if you feel energetic, you can opt for a 4-block hike northeast along rue de Saintonge for a view of what's been called the most inspired bric-a-brac, high-camp junk shop in Paris:

13. **Complément d'Objet,** 11 rue Jean-Pierre Timbaud, 11e. (☎ **01-43-57-09-28**). Looking for props seemingly out of *Sunset Boulevard,* or a gilded statue of a horse's head from a World War I–era horse meat shop? This place will have it, along with plastic and chrome souvenirs that were de rigueur around the time of France's loss of its Algerian and Indochina colonies. It's one of the most whimsical stores in the neighborhood, with an eclectic array of merchandise unified only by the taste and humor of its owner, Patrice Rotenstein. You're likely to find every conceivable kind of lamp inside, even a retro-chic *Sputnik*-era mass of plastic. Also for sale are brass shelves once affixed inside French railway cars and an alarming collection of chandeliers.

Retrace your steps to the previously visited Hier, Aujourd'hui, and Demain. Then, walk southeast along the rue Charlot, to the corner of the rue Pastourelle. Here, you'll be tempted by the fabrics of:

14. **Dominique Picquier,** 10 rue Charlot (☎ **01-42-72-39-14**). Looking to redo your favorite settee in the best decorative traditions of France? This 4-year-old shop sells a wide roster of fabric (50% cotton, 50% linen) that stands up to rugged use while maintaining stylish botanical themes. Virtually every pattern is based on some botanical inspiration, including ginko leaves, vanilla pods and vines, and magnolia branches. Everything inside costs the same: 380F ($76) per meter, 346F ($69) per yard, proof that the good life has come to the Marais.

Nearby, adjacent to the corner of rue Charlot and the rue du Perche, is the Marais's largest and most experimental art gallery:

15. **Passage de Retz,** 9 rue Charlot (☎ **01-48-04-37-99**). Established in 1994 in the heart of the Marais, this aggressively avant-garde gallery has about 2,100 square feet of floor space to show off its highly amusing exhibitions. The gallery has exhibited Japanese textiles, paintings by American abstract expressionists, modern Venetian glass, and an occasional exposition of contemporary Haitian paintings. Past exhibitions have even featured risqué brassieres presented more as works of sculpture than as high fashion.

From here, walk one block further along rue Charlot, turn left for a block onto the rue des 4 Fils, then go right on the rue Vieille-du-Temple, where you'll come across Delamair's:

16. **Hôtel de Rohan,** 87 rue Vieille-du-Temple, which was once occupied by the fourth Cardinal Rohan, the larcenous cardinal of the "diamond necklace scandal," which led to a flood of destructive publicity for the doomed Marie Antoinette. The first occupant of the hotel, was reputed to be the son of Louis XVI. The interior is usually closed to the public, except during an occasional exhibition. In some cases, the courtyard can be visited.

Along the same street at no. 47, is the:

17. **Hotel des Ambassadeurs de Hollande,** where Beaumarchais wrote *The Marriage of Figaro*. It is one of the most splendid mansions in Le Marais, and despite its name was never actually occupied by the Dutch embassy. It's not open to the public. Continue walking south along rue Vieille-du-Temple until you reach the:

18. **Rue des Rosiers** (Street of the Rosebushes), and turn left. It's one of the most colorful and typical streets remaining from Paris's old Jewish quarter, and you'll find an intriguing blend of living memorials to Ashkenazi and Sephardic traditions. The Star of David shines from some of the shop windows; Hebrew letters appear, sometimes in neon; couscous is sold from shops run by Moroccan, Tunisian, or Algerian Jews; restaurants serve strictly kosher food, and signs appeal for Jewish liberation. You'll come across many delicacies you might have read about but have never seen, such as savory sausage stuffed in a goose neck, roots of black horseradish, and pickled lemons.

☕ **TAKE A BREAK** The street offers a cornucopia of ethnic eateries, but two in particular remain especially steadfast to their central European, Ashkenazi origins. They include **Chez Jo Goldenberg,** 4 rue des Rosiers, (☎ **01-48-87-20-16**), where there's plenty of room to sit down and eat. (See chapter 5 for more details). A few steps away, there's a smaller and less formal take-away delicatessen, **Finkelsztajn,** 27 rue des Rosiers (☎ **01-42-72-78-91**), with delicious one-of-a-kind salty specialties, and room for only four sit-down diners at a time. Established in 1851 by Alsatian Jews, and owned since 1946 by members of the Finkelsztajn family, it specializes in the sale of figs, dates, dried prunes, pastries, grain products, and such creative dishes as eggplant caviar, taramasalata, savory mixtures of sheep cheese with pulverized peppers, and a seafood pâté (they call it *croisière jaune*) that combines smoked fish and curry powder into delectable sandwiches.

Head down the rue des Rosiers to the rue Pavée. (Its name, incidentally, derives from the fact that it was the first in Paris, sometime during the 1300s, to benefit from a sheathing of cobblestones that replaced what had until then been an open sewer.) At this "Paved Street," turn right and walk south until you reach the St-Paul Métro stop.

At that point, make a right turn along rue François-Miron. Although the facade at the 17th-century:

19. **Hôtel de Beauvais,** 68 rue François-Miron, was badly damaged in the French Revolution, it remains one of the most charming in Paris. A plaque announces that, in 1763, Mozart lived here and played to the court of Versailles. (He was all of 7 years at the time.) Louis XIV presented the masion to Catherine Belier, wife of Pierre de Beauvais, who reportedly had the honor of introducing Louis, then 16, to the facts of life. To visit the inside, apply any afternoon to the Association du Paris Historique, on the ground floor.

Continue your walk along rue François-Miron until you come to a crossroads. At that point, take a sharp left along rue de Jouy. Continue along the street, cross rue Fourcy, and turn onto rue du Figuier. The:

20. **Hôtel de Sens,** a Paris landmark at 1 rue de Figuier, was built between the 1470s and 1519 for the archbishops of Sens. Along with the Cluny on the Left Bank, it is the only domestic architecture remaining from the 15th century. Long after the archbishops had departed in 1605, it was occupied by the scandalous Queen Margot, wife of Henri IV. Her new lover, "younger and more virile," slew the discarded one as she looked on in great amusement. The restoration of the Hôtel de Sens, as usual, was the subject of great controversy; nonetheless, today it houses the Bibliothèque Forney (☎ **01-42-78-14-60**). Leaded windows and turrets characterize the facade; you can go into the courtyard to see more of the ornate stone decoration—the gate is open Tuesday through Saturday from 1:30 to 8pm.

Retrace your steps to rue Fourcy, turn right, and walk up the street until you reach the St-Paul Métro stop again. Turn right onto rue St-Antoine, the street where Henri II was fatally wounded in a jousting tournament in 1559. Walk along this street until you reach the:

21. **Hôtel de Bethune-Sully,** 62 rue St-Antoine. Work began on this mansion in 1625, on the order of Jean Androuet de Cerceau. In 1634 it was acquired by the duc de Sully, who had been Henri IV's minister of finance before the king was assassinated in 1610. After a straitlaced life as "the accountant of France," Sully broke loose in his declining years, adorning himself with diamonds and garish rings—and a young bride, who is said to have had a preference for very young men, whom she openly invited into their home.

Hôtel de Sully was acquired by the French government just after World War II. It is now the seat of the National Office of Historical Monuments and Sites. Recently restored, the relief-studded facade is especially appealing. You can visit the interior of the hotel with a guide, on either Saturday or Sunday at 3pm, depending on the program. There is daily admittance to the courtyard and the garden that opens onto place des Vosges. Frequent concerts of chamber music are staged here. In the building there's an information center and a bookshop.

Continue walking along the street until you come to place de la Bastille and the Métro stop. If you feel like winding down with a meal, continue east along the Rue St-Antoine, turning left onto the rue des Tournelles a block before the Place de la Bastille, and then taking a quick right onto the rue de la Bastille.

☕ **WINDING DOWN**   Dating from 1864, **Bofinger,** 5-7 rue de la Bastille (☎ **01-42-72-87-82**), is a French/Alsatian brasserie, the most famous in Paris. (See chapter 5 for more details.) Legend claims it was the first in Paris to pour draught beer. Go here for nostalgia, sauerkraut, and wines from the Côtes-du-Rhône.

8 Shopping

Shopping is the local pastime of the Parisians; some would even say it reflects the city's soul. The City of Light is one of the rare places in the world where you don't go anywhere to shop—shopping surrounds you instead. Each walk you take immerses you in uniquely French styles. The windows, stores, people (yes, and even their dogs), brim with energy, creativity, and a sense of visual expression found in few other cities.

You don't have to buy anything to appreciate shopping in Paris—just soak up the art form the French have made of rampant consumerism. Peer in the *vitrines* (display windows), absorb cutting-edge ideas, witness new trends, and take home with you a whole new education in style.

1 The Shopping Scene

When you walk into a French store, it's traditional to greet the owner or sales clerk with a direct address, not a fey smile or even a weak *bonjour*. Only *"Bonjour, madame"* (or monsieur) will do.

BEST BUYS

Perfumes, Makeup & Beauty Treatments   A flat discount of 20% to 30% makes these items a great buy; qualify for a detaxé refund (see below) and you'll save 40% to 45% off the Paris retail price, allowing you to bring home goods at half the U.S. price. *Note:* Duty-free shops abound in Paris and are always less expensive than the ones at the airport.

For bargain cosmetics, try out French dime store and drug store brands such as **Bourjois** (made in the Chanel factories), **Lierac**, and **Galenic. Vichy,** famous for its water, has a complete skin care and makeup line. The newest retail trend in Paris is the *parapharmacie*, a type of discount drug store loaded with inexpensive brands, health cures, French beauty regimes, and diet plans. These usually offer a 20% discount.

Foodstuff   Nothing makes a better souvenir than a product of France brought home to savor later. Supermarkets are located in prime tourist neighborhoods; stock up on coffee, designer chocolates, mustards (try Maille brand), and for the kids, perhaps American products in French packages.

Fun Fashion Sure you can splurge for couture or prêt but French teens and trendsetters have their own stores where the latest looks are affordable. Even the dime stores in Paris sell designer copies and hotshot styles.

In the stalls in front of the department stores on bd. Haussmann you'll find some of the latest fashion contraptions, guaranteed for a week's worth of small talk once you get home.

VALUE-ADDED TAX (VAT) REFUNDS

French tax is now a hefty 20.6%, but you can get most of that back if you spend 1,200F ($240) or more in any store that participates in the VAT refund program (see chapter 3, "Fast Facts: Paris"). Most stores participate, although discount perfume shops usually peg the minimum at 1,200F ($240) *net,* which is 1,600F ($320) or 1,700F ($340).

This can get particularly confusing when you are buying perfume and makeup, among the best buys Paris has to offer, because some of the stores list their discounted price, which means all you need to do is run the bill up to 1,200F. Other stores list the regular price and then take off 25% on the spot, so that you can watch the discount being applied to your bill. In this case, you need to get the bill to 1,600F or 1,700F, which becomes 1,200F when the price is recalculated.

Once you meet your required minimum purchase amount, you qualify for a tax refund. The amount of the refund varies with the way the refund is handled and the fact that some stores charge you a fee for processing it. So the refund amount at a department store may be 13%, whereas at a small shop it will be 15% or even 18%.

You will receive detaxé papers in the shop; some stores, like Hermès, have their own, others provide a government form. Fill in the forms before you arrive at the airport, and expect to stand in line at the customs desk for as long as half an hour. You are required by law to show the goods at the airport, so have them on you or visit the customs office before you check your luggage. Once the papers have been mailed to the authorities, a credit will appear, often months later, on your credit-card bill.

All refunds are processed at the final point of departure from the European Union (EU), so if you are going to another EU country, don't apply for the refund in France.

Be sure to mark the paperwork to request that your refund be applied to your credit card so you aren't stuck with a check in francs that is hard to cash. This also ensures the best rate of exchange. In some airports you are offered the opportunity to get your refund back in cash, which is tempting. If you accept cash in any currency other than francs, you will be losing money on the conversion rate. You'll do far better with a credit-card conversion.

AIRPORT DUTY-FREE BOUTIQUES

Both airports have shopping galore, but prices are often equal or better in Paris. Charles De Gaulle Airport has a virtual shopping mall with crystal, cutlery, chocolates, luggage, wine, whisky, pipes and lighters, lingerie, silk scarves, perfume, knitwear, jewelry, cameras and equipment, cheeses, and even antiques. Both airports have a small branch of Virgin Megastore.

Best bets at the airport are goods from the deluxe French houses that cost less than 1,200F (total) so that while you forfeit the detaxé refund, you at least get a break on the actual VAT.

BUSINESS HOURS

Shops are *usually* open Monday through Saturday from 10am to 7pm, but the hours vary greatly and Monday mornings in Paris do not run at full throttle. Small shops sometimes take a 2-hour lunch break and may not open until after lunch on Mondays. Thursday is the best day for late night shopping, with stores open until 9 or 10pm.

Sunday shopping is currently limited to tourist areas and flea markets, although there is growing demand for full-scale Sunday hours, à la the United States and the United Kingdom. The big department stores are now open for the five Sundays before Christmas, but other than that, most Parisian stores are dead on *dimanche*. **Carrousel du Louvre,** a mall adjacent to the Louvre, is open and hopping on Sundays, but closed on Mondays. The tourist shops that line the rue Rivoli across from the Louvre are all open on Sundays. The antiques villages are all open as are assorted flea markets and specialty events. There are several good food markets in the streets on Sundays. Virgin Megastore on the Champs-Elysées pays a fine to stay open on Sunday. It's *the* teen hangout.

U.S. CUSTOMS

You're allowed to bring overseas purchases with a retail value of $400 back into the United States, providing you have been out of the country at least 48 hours, and have claimed no similar exemptions within 30 days. After your duty-free $400 is exceeded, a tax of 10% is levied on the next $1,000 worth of items purchased abroad.

You pay no duty on antiques or art if such items are 100 years old or more, even if they cost $4 million or more. In addition, you're allowed to send one gift a day to family or friends back home, providing its value does not exceed $50.

SHIPPING IT HOME

Shipping charges will possibly double your cost on goods; you will also pay U.S. duties on the items if they are valued at more than $50. The good news: Detaxé is automatically applied to any item shipped to an American; no need to worry about the 1,200F minimum. Some stores have a $100 minimum for shipping. You can also walk into any PT&T (post office) and mail home a jiffy bag or small box of goodies. French do-it-yourself boxes cannot be reopened once closed, so pack carefully. The clerk at the post office will help you build the box (it's tricky), seal it, and send it off.

GREAT SHOPPING NEIGHBORHOODS

Paris neighborhoods are designated by the arrondissement (see chapter 3). When you are planning a day of combined sightseeing and shopping, check a map to see how the arrondissements connect so that you can maximize your efforts. Whereas the core of Paris is made up of 20 arrondissements, only a handful of them are prime real estate in terms of shopping.

The best of the shopping arrondissements include:

1st & 8th Arrondissements These two *quartiers* adjoin each other (invisibly) and form the heart of Paris's best Right Bank shopping strip—together they're just one big hunting ground. This area includes the famed rue du Faubourg-St-Honoré, where the big designer houses are, and the Champs-Elysées, where the mass market and teen scene are hot. At one end of the 1er is the **Palais-Royal,** one of the best shopping secrets in Paris, where an arcade of boutiques flanks each side of the garden of the former palace.

The 1er also contains the **avenue Montaigne,** the most glamorous shopping street in Paris, boasting 2 blocks of the fanciest shops in the world, where you simply float from big name to big name and in a few hours can see everything from **Louis Vuitton** to **Ines de la Fressange,** the model turned retailer. The avenue Montaigne is also the address of **Joseph,** a British design firm, and **Porthault,** makers of the fanciest sheets in the world.

2nd Arrondissement   Right behind the Palais Royal is the **Garment District** (Sentier), as well as a few very sophisticated shopping secrets such as **place des Victoires.** This area also hosts a few old-fashioned *passages,* alleys filled with tiny stores, such as **Galerie Vivienne,** on rue Vivienne.

3rd & 4th Arrondissements   The difference between these two arrondissements gets fuzzy, especially around the **place des Vosges,** center stage of the **Marais.** No matter. The districts offer several dramatically different shopping experiences.

On the surface, the shopping includes the "real people stretch" (where all the nonmillionaires shop) of the rue Rivoli and rue St-Antoine, featuring everything from **The Gap** and a branch of **Marks and Spencer,** to local discount stores and mass merchants. Two "real people" department stores are in this area, **Samaritane** and **BHV;** there's also **Les Halles** and the **Beaubourg,** which is anchored by the Centre Georges Pompidou.

Meanwhile, hidden away in the Marais is a medieval warren of twisting tiny streets all chockablock with cutting-edge designers and up-to-the-minute fashions and trends. Start by walking around the place des Vosges for art galleries, designer shops, and special little finds, then dive in and simply get lost in the area leading to the Picasso Museum.

Finally, the 4e is also the home of the Bastille, an up-and-coming area for artists and galleries where the newest entry on the retail scene, **Viaduc Des Arts** (which actually stretches into the 12e), is situated.

6th & 7th Arrondissements   Whereas the 6e is one of the most famous shopping districts in Paris—it is the soul of the **Left Bank**—a lot of the really good stuff is hidden in the zone that becomes the wealthy residential district of the seventh. **Rue du Bac,** stretching from the 6e to the 7e in a few blocks, stands for all that wealth and glamour can buy.

8th Arrondissement   See above, "1st & 8th Arrondissements."

9th Arrondissement   To add to the fun of shopping the Right Bank, 9e sneaks in behind 1er so that if you choose not to walk toward the Champs-Elysées and the 8e, you can instead head to the city's big department stores, all built in a row along **bd. Haussmann** in the 9e. Department stores here include not only the two big French icons, **Au Printemps** and **Galeries Lafayette,** but a large branch of Britain's **Marks and Spencer** and a branch of the Dutch answer to K-mart, the low-priced **C&A.**

2 Shopping A to Z

ANTIQUES

Le Louvre des Antiquaires. 2 place du Palais-Royal, 1er. ☎ **01-42-97-27-00.** Tues–Sun 11am–7pm. Closed Sun in July and Aug. Métro: Palais-Royal.

Located directly across from the Louvre, with three levels of fancy knickknacks, many of them dripping with gilt, Le Louvre des Antiquaires is just the place if you're looking for 30 Baccarat crystal matching champagne flutes from the 1930s, Sèvres tea service dated 1773, or maybe a small signed Jean Fouquet pin of gold and diamonds. Too stuffy? No problem. There's always the 1940 Rolex with the aubergine crocodile strap.

Prices can be high, but a few reasonable items are hidden here. What's more, the Sunday scene is fabulous, and there's a cafe with a variety of lunch menus beginning around 100F. Pick up a free map and brochure of the premises from the information desk.

Mlinaric, Henry, and Zervudachi. 54 Galerie de Montpensier, Palais-Royal, 1er. ☎ 01-42-96-08-62. Tues–Sat 11am–7pm. Métro: Palais-Royal.

David Mlinaric, one of the three musketeers here, is the British interior designer who recreated Spencer House—Princess Diana's ancestral manse in London—as well as all of Lord Jacob Rothschild's private residences. Tino Zervudachi is considered one of the hot young turks in Paris design. Hugh Henry, like Mlinaric, is English. Together they are considered the chicest antique dealers on the Right Bank. They specialize in museum-quality 18th-century items.

Village St. Paul. 23–27 rue St-Paul, 4e. No phone. 11am–7pm. Closed Tues–Wed. Métro: St-Paul.

This isn't an antiques center but a cluster of individual dealers in their own hole-in-the-wall hideout; the rest of the street, stretching from the river to the Marais, is lined with dealers, but most of them aren't open on Sunday. The Village St. Paul *is* open on Sunday, and hopping. Bring your camera, because inside the courtyards and alleys are every dreamer's visions of hidden Paris: Many dealers in a courtyard selling furniture and other decorative items in French country and formal styles.

ART

Carnavalette. 2 rue des Francs-Bourgeois, 3e. ☎ 01-42-72-91-92. Daily 10:30am–6:30pm. Métro: St-Paul.

Set adjacent to place des Vosges in the Marais, this historic shop sells unusual, one-of-a-kind engravings, plus a large collection of satirical 19th-century magazines and newspapers.

✪ **Galerie Adrien Maeght.** 42 and 46 rue du Bac, 7e. ☎ 01-45-48-45-15. Tues–Sat, 9:30am–1pm; 2pm–7pm. Métro: Bac.

This art house is among the most famous names in galleries, selling contemporary art on a very fancy Left Bank street that's far more chic and fashionable than the bohemian Left Bank Picasso knew.

Galerie 27. 27 rue de Seine, 6e. ☎ 01-43-54-78-54. Tues–Sat 10am–1pm and 2:30–7pm. Métro: St-Germain-des-Prés.

This tiny closet of a store sells lithographs by some of the most famous artists of the early 20th century, including Picasso, Coll, Miró, and Léger.

Viaduc des Arts. 9-147 av. Daumensil, 12e. ☎ 01-43-40-80-80. Tues–Sat 11am–7pm. Métro: Bastille, Ledru-Rollin, Reuilly-Diderot, or Gare de Lyon.

This newly renovated establishment occupies a long, 2-block stretch from the Bastille Opera to the Gare de Lyon, and features art galleries and artisans in individual boutiques created within the arches of an old train viaduct. As you can tell from the number of Métro stops that serve the address, you can start at one end and work your way to the other, or start in the middle. It's nothing spectacular, but it makes for interesting shopping.

BOOKS

Brentano's. 37 av. de l'Opéra, 2e. ☎ 01-42-61-52-50. Mon–Sat 10am–7pm. Métro: Opéra.

Brentano's is a large English-language bookstore selling guides, maps, novels, and nonfiction as well as greeting cards, postcards, holiday items, and gifts. It's conveniently located 1 block from Garnier Opera.

Galignani. 224 rue de Rivoli, 1er. ☎ **01-42-60-76-07.** Métro: Tuileries.

Sprawling over a very large street level, and supplemented with a mezzanine, this venerable, wood-paneled bookstore has thrived in this location since its establishment in 1810. Enormous numbers of books are available in both French and English, with special emphasis on French classics, modern fiction, sociology, and hundreds that discuss the art works of virtually every epoch and every country in the world. Looking for English-language translations of works by Balzac, Flaubert, Zola, or Colette? Most of them are here; if not, they can be ordered.

Tea and Tattered Pages. 24 rue Mayet, 6e. ☎ **01-40-65-94-35.** Daily 11am–7pm. Métro: Duroc.

At this cute, cozy, adorable bookshop, you can take a break from browsing amongst the shelves to have tea at a little table. Though the shop's slightly out of the way, its extra dose of charm makes it worth the trip.

The Village Voice. 6 rue Princesse, 6e. ☎ **01-46-33-36-47.** Mon 2–8pm, Tues–Sat 11am–8pm. Métro: Mabillon.

On a side street in the heart of the best Left Bank shopping district, this is a favorite venue for expatriate Yankees. The location is in the vicinity of some of the Left Bank gathering places described in Gertrude Stein's *The Autobiography of Alice B. Toklas.* The shop is a hangout for the literati of Paris.

W.H. Smith and Son. 248 rue de Rivoli, 1er. ☎ **01-44-77-88-99.** Mon–Sat 9:30am–7pm, Sun 1pm–6pm. Métro: Concorde.

This bookstore provides books, magazines, and newspapers published in English (most titles are from Britain). You can get the *Times* of London, of course, and the Sunday *New York Times* is available every Monday. There's a fine selection of maps and travel guides, and a special children's section that includes comics.

CHILDREN: FASHION, SHOES & ASSORTED KID STUFF

Au Nain Bleu. 406 rue St-Honoré, 8e. ☎ **01-42-60-39-01.** Mon–Sat 9:45am–6:30pm. Métro: Concorde.

This is the largest, oldest, and most centrally located toy store in all of Paris. More importantly, it is probably the fanciest toy store in the world. But don't panic; in addition to the elaborate and expensive fancy stuff, there are rows of cheaper items (like penny candy) in jars on the first floor.

Bonpoint. 15 rue Royale, 8e. ☎ **01-47-42-52-63.** Mon–Sat 10am–7pm. Métro: Concorde.

Grandparent alert! Bonpoint is part of a well-known *almost* haute couture chain. Clothing is well tailored, traditional—and extremely expensive. The shop sells clothes for boys and girls aged a day to 16 years. Drool over formal party and confirmation dresses, and the long and elegant baptismal robes, embroidered in France and edged in lace—and if you have the means, outfit your child or grandchild in the most sophisticated fashions.

Dipaki. 18 rue Vignon, 9e. ☎ **01-42-66-24-74.** Mon–Sat 10am–7pm. Métro: Madeleine.

If you prefer clothes that have hip, hot style and color but are wearable, washable, and affordable, forget Bonpoint and try this small shop—it's a representative of a truly sensational French line of clothes for toddlers. And it's only a block from the place Madeleine.

Natalys. 92 av. des Champs-Elysées, 8e. ☎ **01-43-59-17-65.** Mon–Sat 10am–7pm. Métro: F. D. Roosevelt.

This store is part of a French chain with a dozen stores in Paris and many elsewhere. They are upscale mass marketers of children's wear, children's needs (layette, stroller), and maternity wear. Just enough French panache without going over the top in design or price.

Nature et Decouvertes. Carrousel du Louvre, 99 rue Rivoli, 1er. ☎ **01-47-03-47-43.** Tues–Sun 10am–8pm. Métro: Palais-Royal.

This French version of the Nature Company also has other addresses in Paris that are convenient for tourists. It doesn't matter where you go, but it is worth visiting a Nature et Decouvertes to find a gift for the kids, or to bring the kids to browse and buy. A small frog *cliquet* (a little toy noisemaker) for $3 is all it takes.

Pom D'Api. 28 rue du Four, 4e. ☎ **01-45-48-39-31.** Mon–Sat 10:15am–7pm. Métro: St-Germain-des-Prés.

This adorable chain of kiddie shoes stores has other locations in Paris and all over France; it carries tiny gold woven sandals, patent leather high tops, and much more.

CHINA & CRYSTAL

✪ **Baccarat.** Factory: 11 place de la Madeleine, 8e. ☎ **01-42-65-36-26.** Tues–Fri 9:30am–6:30pm; Mon, Sat 10am–6:30pm. Métro: Madeleine. Showroom: 30 bis rue de Paradis, 10e. ☎ 01-47-70-64-30. Mon–Fri 10am–6:30pm, Sat 10am–5pm. Métro: Gare de l'Est.

Purveyor to kings and presidents of France since 1764, Baccarat produces world-renowned full-lead crystal in dinnerware, jewelry, chandeliers, and even statuary. The rue Paradis address is the factory cum museum and store, but this is no discount factory shop. The showroom at Madeleine is fancy, but the factory is incredible. Do it once in your lifetime. (See "More Museums" in chapter 6 for the Musée de Baccarat.)

Lalique. 11 rue Royale, 8e. ☎ **01-42-65-33-70.** Mon–Sat 9:30am–6:30pm. Métro: Concorde.

Lalique is known around the world for its smoky frosted glass sculpture, Art Deco crystal, and unique perfume bottles. The shop sells a wide range of merchandise including gorgeous silk scarves meant to compete with Hermès and leather belts with Lalique buckles. There's also a tiny boutique in the Carrousel du Louvre.

✪ **Limoges-Unic.** 12 & 58 rue de Paradis, 10e. ☎ **01-47-70-54-49** or 01-47-70-61-49. Mon–Sat 10am–6:30pm. Métro: Gare de l'Est.

Housed within two shops of more or less equal size, each within a 5-minute walk of the other, this store is crammed with Limoges china brands such as Céralène, Haviland, and Bernardaud, as well as other table items: glass and crystal, silver, whatever your heart desires. They will ship your purchases, but it will severely cut into your savings.

CHOCOLATE

Christian Constant. 26 rue du Bac, 7e. ☎ **01-47-03-30-00.** Mon–Sat 8am–9pm. Métro: Rue du Bac.

Chef of the Les Ambassadeurs restaurant, where he holds three Michelin stars, Constant is a chocolatier in his heart—of Paris's chocolate dealers, he is most often named tops in town. The little shop is unprepossessing; the chocolates are not. Figure to spend $100 a kilo ($45 per pound).

Debauve et Gallais. 30 rue Saints Pères, 7e. ☎ **01-45-48-54-67.** Mon–Sat 10am–7pm. Métro: Sèvres-Babylone.

Lose yourself in deep dark wood, deep dark chocolate, and one of Paris's best-known status brands. Note that the counters are lined by gentlemen who are doing the buying; there are few women who will sacrifice for the luxury.

Jadis et Gourmande. 27 rue Boissy d'Anglas, 8e. ☎ **01-42-65-23-23.** Mon–Sat 10am–1pm, 2pm–7pm. Métro: Madeleine

This small chain of Parisian chocolatiers have a less lofty rep than Christian Constant and much more reasonable prices. They are best known for their alphabetical chocolate blocks, which allow you to spell out any message you want, in any language. *Merci* comes prepackaged.

La Maison du Chocolat. 225 rue du Faubourg St-Honoré, 8e. ☎ **01-42-27-39-44.** Mon–Sat 9:30am–7pm. Métro: Ternes.

This chocolate shop has five other Paris locations. At each, racks and racks of chocolates are priced individually or by the kilo, although it costs near or over $100 for a kilo. It is similar to Hermès when it comes to wrap, ribbon, and prices. These stores offer a variety of chocolate-based products, including chocolate pastries, which are usually more affordable than the candy, and even chocolate milk!

DEPARTMENT & DIME STORES

✪ **Au Printemps.** 64 bd. Haussmann, 9e. ☎ **01-42-82-50-00.** Mon–Wed, Fri, Sat 9:35am–7pm; Thurs 9:35am–10pm. Métro: Havre-Caumartin. RER: Auber.

Before you even enter this landmark store, stand outside and take a look at the facade: They just don't make 'em like that any more. When you've thoroughly appreciated the building's superb architecture, head for the stores that occupy the structure: Au Printemps, the famous department store, and an affiliated housing ware shop, Maison. Don't be alarmed by the fragrances on Maison's first floor—upstairs you'll find floors and floors of wares devoted to the home.

Au Printemps, which competes with its neighbor, Galeries Lafayette (see below), by selling every designer and brand available in France, is next door. Note that Au Printemps feels more modern and American in style than Galeries Lafayette, especially now that the first floor of the main store has been renovated to match Maison.

Don't write off this store as too American: Check out the magnificent stained-glass dome, built in 1923, through which turquoise-colored light cascades into **Café Flo** on the 6th floor, where you can have a coffee or a full meal. While Galeries Lafayette also has a dome, you can't eat under theirs! Complete menus are available, with dishes and appetizers beginning around 60F; the menu is composed of pictures, so you needn't worry about your French accent.

Behind the two main stores, there's **Brummell,** Au Printemps's men's clothing store, as well as a branch of **Prisunic,** the dime store owned by Au Printemps which competes with Monoprix. This Prisunic also has a grocery store in it upstairs. It's not as special as Galeries Lafayette but it's worth a look.

Interpreters stationed at the Welcome Service in the basement will help you claim your detaxé, find departments, and so on. Au Printemps also has a discount card for tourists offering a flat 10% discount.

Bon Marché. 22 rue de Sèvres, 7e. ☎ **01-44-39-80-00.** Mon–Sat 9:30am–7pm. Métro: Sèvres-Babylone.

Another two-part department store, this one is on the Left Bank in the midst of all the cutie-pie boutiques. One building houses a gourmet grocery store with a small flea market upstairs; the other building is a source for all your general shopping needs.

Galeries Lafayette. 40 bd. Haussmann, 9e. ☎ **01-42-82-34-56.** Mon–Wed, Fri–Sat 9:30am–6:45pm; Thurs 9:30am–9pm. Métro: Chaussée d'Antin or Opéra. RER: Auber.

Built in 1912, Galeries Lafayette, an almost legendary Paris department store, is now divided into several subdivisions: **Galfa** (which specializes in men's clothing),

Lafayette Sports (sporting goods), and two other general merchandise stores, both known just as "GL," though the larger one is often called *"le magasin principal"* (the main store).

Typically, the Galeries complements its vast selection with world-class service: There's a welcome desk, multilingual help, and a free shopping tote if you turn in receipts totaling 200F ($40) or more. Be sure to pick up a tourist's discount card from your travel agent before you leave home, or from your hotel or the store itself after you arrive in Paris; the card provides a flat 10% discount for tourist shoppers that has nothing to do with the VAT detaxé program.

Galeries Lafayette and its neighbor, Au Printemps, have been competing for Parisian shoppers for nearly a century; you'll find France firmly divided into GL types and Printemps types, although the differences between the two stores fades with global trends and international imports.

Right now, Galeries Lafayette is more old-fashioned in the way it does business and therefore feels a little more staid, and French.

Next door to GL there's a branch of the dime store **Monoprix,** which the chain also owns. This isn't the best Monoprix in town, but it's convenient and can give you a taste of French dime store magic.

Above Monoprix is another affiliated store, **Gourmet Lafayette,** one of the fanciest grocery stores in Paris with prices half of those offered at the famous Fauchon, Paris's "supermarket for millionaires" (see below). This store has its own entrance next to Monoprix, and has extended hours.

FASHION
CUTTING-EDGE CHIC

Azzadine Alaia. 7 rue de Moussy, 2e. ☎ **01-42-72-19-19.** Mon–Sat 10am–7pm. Métro: Hôtel de Ville.

Alaia, who became the darling of French fashion in the 1970s, is the man who brought body consciousness back to put the oh la la in Paris chic. If you can't afford the current collection, try the stock shop around the corner, where last year's leftovers are sold at serious discounts: 18 rue de Verrerie (☎ 01-40-27-85-58).

Claude Montana. 31 rue de Grenelle, 7e. ☎ **01-45-49-13-02.** Mon–Sat 10:15am–7pm. Métro: Sèvres-Babylone.

The State of Claude Montana he calls it, making a lame pun and stunning you into wondering just what state that could be. Confusion? Undress? Or merely deconstructed chic? For rock and roll stars and wanna-bes, Montana's is the place.

Courrèges. 40 rue François, 1er, 8e. ☎ **01-47-20-70-44.** Mon–Fri 9:45am–6:45pm; Sat 9:45am–1pm, 2pm–6:45pm. Métro: Franklin Roosevelt.

Don't look now: André Courrèges is not only back in style, he's considered hot. Even those little white vinyl go-go boots are back. In Courrèges's collection, humor meets '70s retro with bold color, plastic, and fun. There's another branch of his store in the

Impressions

We worship not the Graces, nor the Parcæ, but Fashion. She spins and weaves and cuts with full authority. The head monkey at Paris puts on a traveller's cap, and all the monkeys in America do the same.

—Henry David Thoreau, *Walden,* 1854.

Carrousel du Louvre mall, and a discount shop as well, upstairs at 7 rue Turbigo (☎ 01-42-33-03-57; Métro: Etienne-Marcel).

Elle. 30 rue St. Sulpice, 6e. ☎ **01-43-26-46-10.** Mon–Sat 10am–7pm. Métro: Odeon.

Elle magazine runs its own boutique that sells specific items as featured in the magazine, most of them hot, hip, and affordable. The store carries both housewares and clothing items.

Hervé Leger. 29 rue du Faubourg-St-Honoré, 8e. ☎ **01-44-51-57-17.** Mon–Sat 10am–7pm. Métro: Concorde.

This creator of the Band Aid Dress, a tightly wrapped concoction of stretch materials and color, has opened his own shop for those with curves to flaunt and cash to burn.

Jean-Charles de Castelbajac. 6 place St-Sulpice, 6e. ☎ **01-46-33-83-32.** Mon–Sat 11am–7pm. Métro: Odeon or St-Sulpice.

Castelbajac is the bad boy of French fashion, known for flamboyant and amusing gear in primary colors, often with big bold sayings scribbled across the clothes. His store is located in a cluster of designer shops that's great for gawking.

Jean Paul Gaultier. 6 rue Vivienne, 2e. ☎ **01-42-86-05-05.** Tues–Sat 10am–7pm; Mon 11am–7pm. Métro: Bourse or Palais-Royal.

Hidden in one of Paris's most famous *passages,* this large boutique features Gaultier's street fashion made high fashion, the typical fare of this master punk turned tailor.

Lolita Lempicka. 14 rue du Faubourg-St-Honoré, 8e. ☎ **01-49-24-94-01.** Mon–Sat 10am–7pm. Métro: Concorde.

Lolita, formerly of the hidden Marais and the underground fashion scene, has gone mainstream with her own shop, tiny but quite visible, on the street of streets. The clothes continue to be inventive and creative, and, despite her new location, are hardly mainstream.

Thierry-Mugler. 10 place des Victories, 2e. ☎ **01-42-60-06-37.** Tues–Sat 10am–1pm, 2pm–7pm; Mon 11am–1pm, 2pm–7pm. Métro: Palais-Royal or Bourse.

Thierry-Mugler is most famous for body-hugging suits whose almost space-age construction makes for a "power look" that combines a serious fashion statement with whimsy and imagination. This closet-sized boutique designed by André Putnam is part of the whole shopping thrill of the place des Victoires, and even though there's another Thierry-Mugler shop at 49 av. Montaigne, stick with this one for the authentic Parisian shopping experience.

DISCOUNT & RESALE

Anna Lowe. 35 av. Matignon, 8e. ☎ **01-43-59-96-61.** Mon–Sat 10:30am–7pm. Métro: Miromesnil.

Anna Lowe is one of the premier boutiques in Paris for the discriminating woman who wishes to purchase a little Chanel, or perhaps a Versace, at discount. Many clothes are runway samples; some have been gently worn. The boutique is only half a block from rue du Faubourg-St-Honoré, where haute couture is much more expensive.

Mendès. 65 rue Montmartre, 2e. ☎ **01-42-36-83-32.** Mon–Thurs 10am–6pm, Fri, Sat 10am–5pm. Métro: Les Halles.

In the center of the French garment district, nowhere near Montmartre (don't let the street address throw you), this store mainly sells Yves Saint Laurent leftovers. The

Variations line is downstairs; Rive Gauche, upstairs. Prices, though discounted, can be quite steep and you have to get lucky to find anything worth sighing over.

Réciproque. 89–123 rue de la Pompe, 16e. ☎ **01-47-04-30-28.** Tues–Sat 10:30am–7pm. Métro: Pompe.

Forget about serious bargains but celebrate what could be your only opportunity to own designer clothing of this caliber; every major big name is carried here along with shoes, accessories, menswear, and wedding gifts. Everything has been worn, but some items only on runways or during photography shoots.

FASHION FLAGSHIPS

✪ **Chanel.** 31 rue Cambon, 1er. ☎ **01-42-86-28-00.** Mon–Fri 9:30am–6:30pm, Sat 10am–6:30pm. Métro: Concorde or Tuileries.

If you can't have the sun, the moon, and the stars, at least buy something with Coco Chanel's initials on it, either a serious fashion statement (drop-dead chic) or something fun and playful (tongue in chic). Karl Lagerfeld's Chanel designs come in all different flavors and have him laughing all the way to the bank.

This store is adjacent to the Chanel couture house and behind The Ritz, where Mademoiselle Chanel once lived. Check out the beautiful staircase of the maison before you shop the two-floor boutique—it's well worth a peek.

Christian Dior. 26–32 av. Montaigne, 8e. ☎ **01-40-73-54-44.** Mon–Fri 9:30am–6:30pm, Sat 10am–6:30pm. Métro: F.D. Roosevelt.

This famous couture house is set up like a small department store, selling men's, women's, and children's clothing, as well as affordable gift items, makeup and perfume on the first floor as you enter. Unlike some of the other big-name fashion houses, Dior is very approachable.

✪ **Hermès.** 24 rue du Faubourg-St-Honoré, 8e. ☎ **01-40-17-47-17.** Mon–Sat 10am–6:30pm. Closed Mon and Sat 1–2:15pm. Métro: Concorde.

The single most important status item in France is a scarf or tie from Hermès. But the choices don't stop there; this large flagship store has beach towels and accessories, dinner plates, clothing for men and women, a large collection of Hermès fragrances, and even a saddle shop; a package of postcards is the least expensive item sold.

Ask to see the private museum upstairs. Once back outside, do note the horseman on the roof with his scarf-flag flying.

✪ **Louis Vuitton.** 6 place St-Germain-des-Prés, 6e. ☎ **01-45-49-62-32.** Tues–Sat 10am–7pm. Métro: St-Germain-des-Prés.

This Left Bank store is so gorgeous to look at that the famed merchandise becomes secondary. Not content to cover the world with little LV's (Vuitton's designs are typically covered with the "LV" logo), Vuitton has branched into assorted colored leather goods, writing instruments, various travel products, and even publishing. Their *Carnet du Voyage,* a do-it-yourself scrapbook graced with watercolors and space in which to jot down your own memories, is a souvenir worth saving for and handing down in your family.

Don't just consider this a swanky overpriced store or an icon in which you have no interest: This store is a museum. Check it out; you might learn something.

INTERNATIONAL DESIGNER BOUTIQUES

There are two primary fields of dreams in Paris when it comes to showcases for the international big names in design: the **rue du Faubourg-St-Honoré** and the **avenue**

The Scent of a Parisian

If there's one thing that international shoppers come to Paris for, it's cosmetics—after all, the City of Light is the world capital of fragrances and beauty supplies. These are a few of my favorite perfume and makeup shops.

While you can buy **Caron** scents in any duty-free or discount parfumerie, it's worth visiting the source of some of the world's most famous perfumes. The store is located at 34 av. Montaigne, 8e (☎ 01-47-23-40-82; Métro: F.D. Roosevelt), and is a tiny shop with old-fashioned glass beakers filled with fragrances and a hint of yesteryear. *Fleur de Rocaille*, a Caron scent, was the featured perfume in the movie *Scent of a Woman*. Store hours are Monday to Saturday from 10am to 6:30pm.

While there are other branches of **Annick Goutal** (☎ 01-42-60-52-82; Métro: Concorde) in Paris—and while you can swipe Goutal bath amenities from any Concorde Hotel—the mosaic tile on the sidewalk at the 14 rue Castiglione store in the 1st arrondissement, and its unique and unearthly scents, make it a must-see. Try "Hadrien" for a unisex splash of citrus and summer. The shop is conveniently located near other fragrance landmarks including **Guerlain** and **Catherine,** a duty-free shop. Store hours are Monday to Saturday from 10am to 7pm.

Off a small courtyard halfway between the place Madeleine and the Champs-Elysées, **Makeup Forever,** 5 rue de la Boetie, 8e (☎ 01-42-65-48-57; Métro: Saint Augustin), is known as *the* makeup resource for French models and actors. Aside from their theatrical products, they have fashion shades at reasonable prices. The purse-sized makeup zipper case, about $15, is a must-have for status seekers. Store hours are Tuesday to Saturday from 10am to 7pm, and Monday from 2 to 7pm.

If you think you've seen and heard every perfume and aromatherapy gimmick known to man (and woman), this one will still impress you: At **Octée,** 53 rue Bonaparte, 6e (☎ 01-46-33-18-77; Métro: St-Germain-des-Prés or St. Sulpice), the collection of fragrances is color coded to match your personality, skin type, and mood. There's perfume, sprays, soaps, and body lotion, and you test everything on colored ribbons. Store hours are Monday to Saturday from 10am to 7pm.

Salons du Palais Royal Shiseido, 142 Galerie de Valois, Palais Royal, 1er (☎ 01-49-27-09-09; Métro: Palais Royal). Shiseido, the fourth-largest maker of cosmetics and skin-care goods in the world, has become more prominent thanks to the merchandising efforts of this store, one of the most beautiful in Paris. In addition to an awesome array of skin-care products and makeup, it stocks at least a dozen fragrances created by the company's artistic director, Serge Lutens. These are sold exclusively from the premises of this store. Don't be afraid to wander in and ask for some scent strips.

Sephora, 50 rue Passy, 16e (☎ 01-45-20-03-15; Métro: Passy), is a chain of makeup stores that do not offer discounts, but do offer an enormous selection of big name fragrance and makeup brands, their own brand of bath products, and a great assortment of hair accessories. You've simply never seen so much stuff that you want in your life. Their bath products, including shampoo, conditioner, and foaming bath gel, come in tiny travel sizes. Store hours are Monday to Saturday from 10am to 7pm.

Montaigne. While the Left Bank is gaining in designer status with recent additions, including Christian Dior, Giorgio Armani, and Louis Vuitton, the heart of the international designer parade is on the Right Bank.

The rue du Faubourg-St-Honoré is so famously fancy that it is simply known as "the Faubourg"; it was *the* traditional miracle mile until recent years, when the really exclusive shops shunned it for the wider and even more deluxe avenue Montaigne at the other end of the arrondissement. (It's a long but pleasant walk from one fashion strip to the other.)

While the avenue Montaigne is filled with almost unspeakably fancy shops, a few of them have affordable cafes (try **Joseph** at no. 14) and sales help is almost always cordial to the well dressed. You needn't be decked in fur to play the game: a good handbag and pair of shoes are all that matter. Leave *les baskets* (running shoes) at home, *s'il vous plaît.*

The mix is quite international—**Joseph** is British; **Jil Sander** is German, while **Krizia** is Italian. **Chanel, Christian Lacroix, Porthault, Nina Ricci, Christian Dior,** and **Ungaro** are just a few of the French big names; also check out some of the lesser known creative powers that be: the whimsical boutique run by **Ines de la Fressange,** former Chanel model, is a knockout. And don't miss a visit to **Caron.** Most of the designer shops sell men's and women's clothing.

The Faubourg hosts other traditional favorites: **Hermès, Lanvin, Jaeger, Sonia Rykiel,** and the upstart **Façonnable,** which sells preppy men's clothing in the United States through a business deal with Nordstroms. Note that Lanvin has its own men's shop (**Lanvin Homme**), which has a cafe downstairs—perfect for a light (and affordable) lunch; a bowl of designer pasta at Cafe Bleu is about $10.

MENSWEAR

Charvet. 28 place Vendôme, 8e. ☎ **01-42-60-30-70.** Mon–Sat 9:45am–6:30pm. Métro: Opéra.

The Duke of Windsor made Charvet famous, but Frenchmen of distinction have been buying their shirts here for years. The store offers ties, pocket squares, underwear, and pajamas as well, and women's shirts are also available, all custom-tailored or straight off the peg.

Favourbrook. Le Village Royal, 25 rue Royale, 8e. ☎ **01-40-17-06-72.** Mon–Sat 10am–7pm. Métro: Concorde or Madeleine.

This store is actually an English firm exploiting a French trend in a prime location that caters to visitors in search of cutesy souvenirs. The new rue Royale has been re-created to resemble an old-fashioned French village street—each boutique is cuter than the last. Favourbrook sells brocade vests and ties that would have made Louis XIV a happy man.

Alain Figaret. 21 rue de la Paix, 2e. ☎ **01-42-65-04-99.** Mon–Sat 10am–7pm. Métro: Opéra.

Alain Figaret is one of France's foremost designers for men's shirts and women's blouses. Although this store has a broad range of fabrics, 100% cotton is its specialty. Also check out the silk neckties, which come in distinctively designed prints that can be quickly identified by the educated eye. (Figaret is half a block from Charvet, if you are comparison shopping.)

FOOD

✪ **Fauchon.** Place de la Madeleine, 8e. ☎ **01-47-42-60-11.** Mon–Sat 9:40am–7pm. A "Mini-Fauchon" is open Mon–Sat 7–9pm. Métro: Madeleine.

At the place de la Madeleine stands one of the most popular sights in the city—not the church, but Fauchon, now a three-part shop crammed with gastronomical goodies. One shop sells dry goods; one sells candy, pastry, and bread; and one sells fresh fruits and veggies. A cafeteria and coffee bar (Brasserie Fauchon) are nestled in the basement of one shop, and a full restaurant, Le 30, is located above (see chapter 5).

Even though prices are steep, it's easier than ever to pay for your goods, because the store now employs its own electronic debit card. You are given the card when you first enter the store; when you finish shopping, head for the *caisse* (cash register), surrender the debit card, and pay the tally. Then return to the counters to pick up your groceries.

Hediard. 21 place de la Madeleine, 8e. ☎ **01-43-12-88-77.** Mon–Sat 9:30am–7:30pm. Métro: Madeleine.

Although this temple to haute gastonomie opened in 1850, it has recently been completely renovated, perhaps to woo tourists away from Fauchon. The decor is now a series of salons filled with almost Disneyesque displays meant to give the store the look of a turn-of-the-century spice emporium. Upstairs, you can eat at the Restaurant de l'Epicerie.

Maison de la Truffe. 19 place de la Madeleine, 8e. ☎ **01-42-65-53-22.** Mon–Sat 10am–7pm. Métro: Madeleine.

This tiny shop resembles a New York deli more than a Parisienne boutique. This is your source not only for truffles but foie gras, caviar, and other gourmet foodstuff. Gift food baskets are a house specialty. There's also a few tables and chairs so you can grab a quick bite.

La Maison du Miel. 24 rue Vignon, 9e. ☎ **01-47-42-26-70.** Tues–Sat 11am–7pm. Métro: Madeleine.

"The House of Honey" has been a family tradition since before World War I. The entire store is devoted to products made from honey: honey oil, honey soap, and certainly various honeys to eat, including one made from heather. This store owes a tremendous debt to the busy bee.

Marks and Spencer. 35 bd. Haussmann, 9e. ☎ **01-47-42-42-91.** Mon–Sat 9:30am–7pm. Métro: Chausée-d'Antin.

OK, so it's a British department store. But the entire first floor is a giant supermarket devoted to the St. Michael's brand of English foodstuff, and includes prepared foods for picnics.

Albert Menes. 41 bd. Malesherbes, 8e. ☎ **01-42-66-95-63.** Tues–Sat 10am–7pm; Mon 2pm–7pm. Métro: St-Augustin or Madeleine.

About 2 blocks from the big-time food dealers, this small shop serves the Parisian upper crust with jams, confiture, sugared almonds, honey, and assorted packed gourmet foodstuff, many from the provinces. Not only is this a chi-chi place for locals, but the owner is renowned in the French food industry for having rescued many regional specialties, packaging and distributing them to markets in order to carry on specific gourmet traditions. A specialty food basket for the holidays (and saints days) is a status treat.

JEWELRY

Cartier. 7 place Vendôme, 1er. ☎ **01-40-15-03-51.** Mon–Sat 10am–6pm. Métro: Opéra or Tuileries.

Definitely one of the most famous jewelers in the world, Cartier has the prohibitive prices to go with its glamorous image. Go to gawk, and if your pockets are deep enough, pick up an expensive trinket.

Chaumet. 12 place Vendôme, 1er. ☎ **01-44-77-24-00.** Mon–Sat 10am–6:30pm. Métro: Opéra or Tuileries.

This decidedly French establishment has long catered to old money. It's the kind of place where old respected *monsieurs* buy jewels for their wives and mistresses and no one bats an eye.

✪ **Van Cleef and Arpels.** 22 place Vendôme, 1er. ☎ **01-42-61-58-58.** Mon–Fri 10am–6:30pm. Métro: Opéra or Tuileries.

This place markets the jewels of the rich and famous.

KITCHENWARE

Dehillerin. 18 rue Coquellière, 1er. ☎ **01-42-36-53-13.** Tues–Sat 8am–6pm; Mon 8am–12:30pm, 2–6pm. Métro: Les Halles.

Dehillerin is the most famous cookware shop in Paris, located in the "kitchen corridor," alongside A. Simon and several other kitchenware stores. The shop has more of a professional feel to it than the beginner-friendly A. Simon, but don't be intimidated. Equipped with the right tools from Dehillerin, you too can learn to cook like a master chef.

A. Simon. 48 rue Montmarte, 2e. ☎ **01-42-33-71-65.** Tues–Sat 10am–7pm; Mon 2:30–7pm; Métro: Etienne Marcel.

This large kitchenware shop, not in Montmartre but near the Forum Les Halles mall (half a block from Mendès, the Yves Saint Laurent outlet), supplies restaurants and professional kitchens. But it will also cover your table with everything from menu cards and wine tags to knives, copper pots, and pans. It also stocks white paper doilies and those funny little paper things they put on top of the tablecloth at bistros.

LEATHER GOODS

Didier Lamarthe. 219 rue St. Honoré, 1er. ☎ **01-42-96-09-90.** Tues–Sat 11am–7pm; Mon 12pm–7pm. Métro: Tuileries.

A cult hero in France yet virtually unknown elsewhere, this designer is famous for his handbags and small leather goods in funky fashion shades like melon or mint. Sure, he does more conservative colors like navy and black, but if you want the world to know you've been to Paris and that you're totally *branché* (plugged in), spring for a risqué shade.

Didier Lavilla. 15 rue Cherche-Midi, 6e. ☎ **01-45-48-35-90.** Mon–Sat 10am–7pm. Métro: Sèvres-Babylone.

This darling of the French fashion press made his debut not in leather but in nylon—now he's branched into leather and suede. The look is color and texture in a tote bag–style handbag that smells of Paris and style and usually costs less than $100.

Longchamp. 390 rue St-Honoré, 1er. ☎ **01-42-60-00-00.** Mon–Sat 10am–7pm. Métro: Concorde.

Longchamp is a French brand known for high-quality leather and strong everyday durables that come in basics as well as fashion shades. Check out their pale pink patent leather for a touch of Paris. Their best bet is a series of nylon handbags attached to leather handles that fold for storage or travel and unfold for shopping. Items are priced according to size but begin around $40.

Morabito. 1 place Vendôme, 1er. ☎ **01-42-60-30-76.** Mon–Sat 9:45am–6:45pm. Métro: Tuileries.

While Hermès has the international rep, Morabito is the secret insider's source for chicer-than-thou handbags that begin at $1,000 and go up quickly.

LINGERIE

Cadolle. 14 rue Cambon, 1er. ☎ **01-42-60-94-94.** Mon–Sat 9:30am–1pm, 2–6:30pm. Métro: Concorde.

Herminie Cadolle invented the brassiere in 1889. Today the store she founded is managed by her family and they still make the specialty brassieres for the Crazy Horse Saloon. This is the place to go if you want made-to-order items or if you're hard to fit.

Marie-Claude Fremau. 16 rue de la Paix, 2e. ☎ **01-42-61-61-91.** Mon–Sat 10am–7pm. Métro: Opéra.

The French are big on shops that sell towels and bathrobes, as well as underwear. Naturally, French bathroom wear has characteristic flair and style—we're talking about a yellow silk bathrobe with ruffled collar for about $300.

Koba. Marché Saint Germain, 14 rue Lobineau, 6e. ☎ **01-46-33-91-17.** Mon–Sat 11am–7pm. Métro: Odeon.

This small chain of lingerie shops is for people who want French and fancy, but also frugal. Koba has Chiffon garter belts with ruffled edges for $100, but it also has simpler (and cheaper) items: pantyhose, tights, and white cotton and plain lace panties.

Sabbia Rosa. 73 rue des Sts-Pères, 6e. ☎ **01-45-48-88-37.** Mon–Sat 10am–7pm. Métro: Sévres-Babylone.

Madonna shops here for $400 silk panties. Doesn't everyone?

MALLS

Forum des Halles. 1–7 rue Pierre-Lescot, 1er. No general phone. Mon–Sat 10am–7:30pm. Métro: Etienne-Marcel, Les Halles, or Châtelet.

Once the site of Paris's great produce market, Les Halles is now a vast crater of modern metal with layers of boutiques built around a courtyard. There's one of everything here but the feel is very sterile, without a hint of the famous French joie de vivre.

Le Carrousel du Louvre. 99 rue de Rivoli, 1er. No general phone. Tues–Sun 10am–8pm. Métro: Palais-Royal or Musée du Louvre.

If you want to combine an accessible location, a fun food court, handy boutiques, and plenty of museum gift shops with a touch of culture, don't miss Le Carrousel for the world. Always mobbed with locals and visitors, this is one of the few venues allowed to open on Sundays. There's a Virgin Megastore, branch of the Body Shop, and several other terrific stores. Check out Diane Claire for the fanciest souvenirs of Paris you've ever seen.

Marché Saint Germain. 14 rue Lobineau, 6e. No phone. Mon–Sat 11am–7pm. Métro: Odeon.

Marché Saint Germain used to be an open-air food market until it was transformed into a modern shopping mall. Now only a few food and vegetable stalls remain in one corner—the rest of the market is dominated by low ceilings, neon lights, and chain stores from mostly the United States and the United Kingdom. Yep, there's a Gap here.

Montparnasse Shopping Centre. Between rue de l'Arrivée and 22 rue de Départ, 14e. No phone. Mon–Sat 8:30am–10pm. Métro: Montparnasse-Bienvenue.

This shopping center is sort of a quick fix minimall in a business center and hotel (Le Meredien) complex with a small branch of **Galeries Lafayette** and some inexpensive boutiques. Visiting it is really only worthwhile if you also take a trip across the street to **Inno**, a dime store division of Monoprix with a deluxe supermarket in the basement. You may want to play with the automatic train track for shopping carts.

Palais des Congrès de Paris Boutiques. 2 place de la Porte-Maillot, 17e. Mon–Sat 10am–7pm. Métro: Porte Maillot.

A shopping center for convention goers, located inside the Palais des Congrès building, this mall offers some 70 shops, including branch stores of many French big names. You'll also find a Japanese department store and hairdresser.

Les Trois Quartiers. 23 bd. de la Madeleine, 8e. No phone. Mon–Sat 10am–7pm. Métro: Madeleine.

This is a conveniently located modern mall with branch stores of many upscale designers and a large *parfumerie*, Silver Moon.

MARKETS

Marché aux Fleurs. Place Louis-Lépine, Ile-de-la-Cité, 4e. Daily 8am–4pm. Métro: Cité.

Artists and photographers love to capture the Flower Market on canvas or film. The stalls are ablaze with color, and each is a showcase of flowers, most of which escaped the perfume factories of Grasse in the French Riviera. The Flower Market is along the Seine, behind the Tribunal de Commerce. On Sundays, this is a bird market.

Marché aux Livres. Square Georges Brancion, 15e. Sat and Sun 10am–4pm in winter, 10am–6pm in summer. Métro: Porte de Vanves.

This charming two building market for used books, old books, rare books, and some ephemera, is slightly in the middle of nowhere but nonetheless thronged by serious collectors. The market is covered but open, and doesn't close on a rainy day—the really valuable texts are draped in plastic.

✪ **Marché aux Puces de Clignancourt.** Av. de la Porte de Clignancourt, 18e. Sat–Mon 9am–6pm. Métro: Porte de Clignancourt; from there, turn left and cross bd. Ney, then walk north on av. de la Porte de Clignancourt. Bus: 56.

The most famous flea market in Paris is actually a grouping of more than a dozen different flea markets. This is a complex of 2,500 to 3,000 open stalls and shops on the fringe of Paris, selling everything from antiques to junk, from new to vintage clothing.

The first clues showing you're there will be the stalls of cheap clothing along avenue de la Porte de Clignancourt. As you proceed, various streets will tempt you. Hold on until you get to the rue des Rosiers, then turn left. Vendors start bringing out their offerings around 9am and start taking them in around 6pm. Hours are a tad flexible depending on weather and crowds.

Monday is traditionally the best day for bargain seekers, as there is smaller attendance at the market and a greater desire on the part of the merchants to sell.

First-timers at the flea market always want to know two things: "Will I get any real bargains?" and "Will I get fleeced?" Actually, it's all comparative. Obviously, the best buys have been skimmed by dealers (who often have a prearrangement to have items held for them). And it's true that the same merchandise displayed here will sell for less in the provinces of France. But from the point of view of the visitor who has only a few days to spend in Paris—and only half a day for shopping—the flea market is worth the experience. Vintage French postcards, old buttons, and bistro ware are quite affordable; each market has its own personality and an aura of Parisian glamour that can't be found elsewhere.

Dress casually; show your knowledge if you are a collector. The dealers in most of the markets are serious and only get into the spirit of things if you speak French or make it clear that you know what you are doing and have some expertise in their field. The longer you stay, the more you chat, the more you show your respect for the goods, the more room for negotiating the price.

Most of the markets have toilets; some have a central office to arrange shipping. There are cafes, pizza joints, and even a few real restaurants scattered throughout. Beware of pickpockets and teenage troublemakers.

Marché aux Puces de la Porte de Vanves. Av. Georges-Lafenestre, 14e. Sat, Sun 6:30am–4:30pm. Métro: Porte de Vanves.

More of a giant yard sale than anything serious, this weekend event sprawls along two streets and is actually the best flea market in Paris; dealers swear by it. There's little in terms of formal antiques, and few large pieces of furniture. You'll do better if you collect old linens, used Hermès scarves, toys, ephemera, costume jewelry, perfume bottles, and bad art. Asking prices tend to be high as dealers prefer to sell to nontourists. On Sundays, there's a food market one street over.

Marché aux Timbres. Av. Matignon, off the Champs-Elysées at Rond-Point, 8e. Generally Thurs–Sun 10am–7pm. Métro: F.D. Roosevelt or Champs-Elysées–Clemenceau.

This is where Audrey Hepburn figured it out in *Charade*, remember? At this stamp collector's paradise, nearly two dozen stalls are set up on a permanent basis under shady trees on the eastern edge of the Rond-Point. The variety of stamps is almost unlimited—some common, some quite rare.

Marché Buci. Rue de Buci, 6e. Daily 9am–7pm. Métro: St-Germain-des-Prés.

This traditional French food market is held at the intersection of two streets and is only 1 block long, but what a block it is! Seasonal fruits and vegetables dance across table tops while chickens spin on the rotisserie. One stall is entirely devoted to big bouquets of fresh flowers. Monday mornings are light.

MUSEUM SHOPS

Boutique du Musée des Arts Decoratifs. 107 rue de Rivoli, 1er. ☎ **01-42-61-04-02.** Daily 10:30am–6:30pm. Métro: Palais-Royal or Tuileries.

This two-part boutique is divided by the entryway to the museum—on the right is a fabulous bookstore. On the left is a boutique selling reproductions of museum items: gifts, knickknacks, and even a custom-made Hermès scarf.

La Boutique de la Comédie Française. 2 rue de Richelieu, 1er. ☎ **01-44-58-14-30.** Daily 11am–8:30pm. Métro: Palais-Royal.

This is the official gift and souvenir shop of the most historic and prestigious theater in France. The plays commemorated inside have elicited in the French as much emotion and loyalty as Shakespeare has in the British. Look for plates and cups depicting 18th-century misers, maidens, and faithful servants, as well as scarves, pens, drinking glasses, and napkins honoring the French theater. You might appreciate the beer mugs (*les chopes*) emblazoned with the frontispiece of Molière's original folio for *Le Bourgeois Gentilhomme*. While the theater itself is closed in August, the gift shop is not.

Musée de la Monnaie. 11 quai de Conti, 6e. ☎ **01-40-46-58-92.** Tues–Sun, 1–6pm. Métro: Pont Neuf or St-Germain-des-Prés.

Cute jewelry made from coins is sold in the museum gift shop, in addition to other souvenirs, including medals, reproductions of antique coins, and other gift items.

Musée et Compaigne. 49 rue Etienne-Marcel, 1er. ☎ **01-40-13-49-12.** Daily 10am–7:30pm. Métro: Etienne-Marcel.

The museum shop features fancy reproductions of museum items, ranging from a vase pictured in a painting by Manet to jewelry from the 13th century.

MUSIC

FNAC. 136 rue de Rennes, 6e. ☎ **01-49-54-30-00.** Tues–Fri 10am–7pm; Mon 2–7pm; Sat 10am–1pm, 2pm–7pm. Métro: St-Placide.

This chain of large (by French standards) music and book stores is known for its wide selection and discounted prices. There are eight other locations in Paris.

Virgin Megastore. 52–60 av. des Champs-Elysées, 8e. ☎ **01-49-53-50-00.** Mon–Thurs 10am–midnight; Fri and Sat 10am–1am; Sun noon–midnight. Métro: F.D. Roosevelt. Branch stores: Carrousel du Louvre; both airports.

This is the largest music store in Paris, built into a landmark building that helped rejuvenate the Champs-Elysées. There's also a bookstore and cafe downstairs. It's a worthwhile store to visit, if only to stare at the other customers.

PERFUME & MAKEUP (DISCOUNT)

Catherine. 5 rue Castiglione, 1er. ☎ **01-42-61-02-89.** Mon–Sat 9:30am–7pm. Métro: Concorde.

This tiny shop has the best detaxé plan in Paris. In most stores, you pay the final amount and wait for a detaxé refund; here, you are given the discount up front. At Catherine, you sign two credit-card notes—one for the final price of your purchases with all discounts applied, and one for the detaxé. When your detaxé papers clear, the second note is destroyed. If you don't file for the refund, you are, of course, charged the value-added tax (VAT).

Even if you don't qualify for detaxé, you get a 30% discount on most brands of makeup and perfume, and a 20% discount on Chanel and Christian Dior. Spend 1,600F ($320) to qualify for detaxé. You can also order items, tax-free, by mail, with a $100 minimum order.

Parfumerie de La Madeleine. 9 place de la Madeleine, 8e. ☎ **01-42-66-52-20.** Mon–Sat 10am–7pm. Métro: Madeleine.

This shop offers good discounts, but the amount of the discount given varies with the brand—10% on Chanel, but 30% on Sisley. There's tons of fragrances and a few designer accessories in this light, bright, modern, chic shop. Prices are marked with the discount already applied, so it's hard to figure out which percent discount has been applied to which products and to comparison shop, but you get the detaxé refund when your total hits 1,200F ($240).

Michel Swiss. 16 rue de la Paix, 2e. ☎ **01-42-61-61-11.** Mon–Sat 9am–6:30pm. Métro: Opéra.

This is tricky for a first timer: You enter a courtyard and take an elevator to get upstairs to the shop. But once you get inside (there's no storefront window), you'll see the major brands of luxury perfumes, cosmetics, leather bags, pens, neckties, fashion accessories, and gifts. All items are discounted by varying degrees, plus an additional tax discount if you qualify for detaxé. In summer, don't be surprised if there is a line of people waiting to use the elevator. The minimum for detaxé refund is 1,700F ($340), which is 1,200F ($240) net.

SHOES

Maud Frizon. 81–83 rue des Sts-Pères, 7e. ☎ **01-45-49-20-59.** Mon–Sat 10:30am–7pm; Métro: Sèvres-Babylone.

The collection of shoes here is among the most inventive in the city. If prices are too high, go to the Maud Frizon Club next door where shoes are machine-made and go for about one-third of the price.

Stéphane Kélian. 23 bd. de la Madeleine, 1er. ☎ **01-42-96-01-84.** Mon–Sat 10am–7pm. Métro: Bourse.

Acclaimed as one of the most creative designers of women's shoes in Paris, Kélian attracts formidably chic and fashionable women from all over the city. A selection of men's shoes is also available.

SOUVENIRS & GIFTS

Galerie Architecture Miniature Gault. 206 rue de Rivoli, 1er. ☎ **01-42-60-51-17.** Mon–Sat 10am–7pm; Sun 11am–7pm. Métro: Tuileries.

This store features lilliputian town models complete with pint-sized houses, stores, and fountains—miniature versions of French country villages and Parisian neighborhoods, all built to scale. Collectors visit the Galerie to buy models and kits for their own villages and towns.

Hotel de Crillon Gift Shop. 10 place de la Concorde, 8e. ☎ **01-49-24-00-52.** Daily 9am–10pm. Métro: Concorde.

Now you don't have to steal the silverware and bathrobes when you stop by the most famous hotel in Paris; the hotel's dishes, napkin rings, linen, and a whole lot more are now on sale in two specialty boutiques. For an affordable but high-status gift, consider the tasseled silk napkins. The shop is located inside the hotel lobby and is open on Sundays. It's the perfect opportunity to gawk and shop.

Au Nom de la Rose. 46 rue du Bac, 6e. ☎ **01-42-22-22-12.** Mon–Sat 10am–7:30pm. Métro: rue du Bac.

This theme store, which sells cute and kitschy gift items, has narrowly missed becoming a Disney cliché—each item sold is in some way related to roses, be it rose soap or rose colored glasses. Nonetheless, the store radiates *charme.* Part of its glory is the fact that it's on one of the best streets in town for cute little shops.

La Tuile à Loup. 35 rue Daubenton, 5e. ☎ **01-47-07-28-90.** Tues–Sat 10:30am–7pm. Métro: Censier-Daubenton.

One of the few regional handicrafts stores in Paris worth going out of your way to find, La Tuile à Loup carries beautiful pottery and faience, and has all sorts of decorative notions and gift items. Drop by after visiting the Ile St-Louis or the student quarter in the Left Bank.

STATIONERY

✪ **Cassegrain.** 422 rue St-Honoré, 8e. ☎ **01-42-60-20-08.** Mon–Sat 10am–7pm. Métro: Concorde.

Nothing says elegance more than thick French stationery and note cards. Cassegrain offers beautifully engraved stationery, most often in traditional patterns; businesspeople can also get their business cards engraved to order. Several other items for the desk, many suitable for gifts, are for sale as well; there are even affordable pencils and small desktop accessories.

Cassegrain also has a shop at 81 rue des Sts-Pères, 6e (☎ 01-42-22-04-76; Métro: Sèvres-Babylone).

TABLEWARE

Au Bain Marie. 10 rue Boissy d'Anglas, 8e. ☎ **01-42-66-59-74.** Mon–Sat 10am–7pm. Métro: Concorde.

> These two floors of merchandise include tableware of many different styles, inspired by many different eras. There's also a collection of books relating to food and wine, and a good selection of bathroom towels. Even if you don't buy anything, it's glorious just to look, and it's conveniently located right off the rue du Faubourg-St-Honoré.

The Conran Shop. 117 rue du Bac, 6e. ☎ **01-42-84-10-01.** Tues–Sat 10am–7pm; Mon 12pm–7pm. Métro: Sèvres-Babylone.

> Do not get The Conran Shop and Habitat confused even though they look similar and were once associated with the same man. There are Habitat shops in Paris and they are OK, but The Conran Shop is a small piece of heaven, filled with color and style and all sorts of things to touch and take home—most of them for your home decorating needs. What's so shocking is how very French this British resource has become. It's situated next door to Bon Marché and at the top of a marvelous shopping street, so that from it, all the world is within your grasp.

Geneviève Lethu. 95 rue de Rennes, 6e. ☎ **01-45-44-40-35.** Mon–Sat 10am–7pm. Métro: St-Germain-des-Prés.

> This Provençale designer has shops all over France, with several others in Paris, all selling her clever and colorful designs that seem to reflect what happens when Pottery Barn style goes French Mediterranean. Prices are moderate. Her goods, filled with energy, style, and charm, are also sold in the major department stores.

Paris After Dark

9

After a long sleep, Paris nightlife has awakened. Late-night bars fill like gaudy aquariums, and rap has flourished as a kind of tincture of British, American, and North African influences. In this chapter we describe after-dark diversions that range from cafe-concerts to "where the boys are."

Parisians start the serious part of their evenings just as Anglos stretch, yawn, and announce it's time for bed. Once a Paris workday is over, people go straight to the cafe to meet up with friends; after a time, they proceed to a restaurant, bar, or theater, and much later, they grace a nightclub or late-night bar.

For the cafe scene, see chapter 5.

1 The Performing Arts

Announcements of shows, concerts, and operas are plastered on kiosks all over town. Listings can be found in *Pariscope*, a weekly entertainment guide, or the English-language *Boulevard*, a bimonthly magazine. Performances start later in Paris than in London or New York City—anywhere from 8 to 9pm—and Parisians tend to dine after the theater. You may not want to do the same since many of the less-expensive restaurants close as early as 9pm.

A STATESIDE TICKET AGENCY　For tickets and information to just about any show and entertainment in Paris (also Dijon, Lyon, and Nice), **Edwards and Edwards** has a New York office if you'd like to arrange your schedule before you go. It's at 1270 Avenue of the Americas, Suite 2414, New York, NY 10020 (☎ **800/223-6108** or 914/328-2150). They also have an office in Paris for assistance while you are there: 19 rue des Mathurins, 9e (☎ **01-42-65-39-21;** Métro: Hauvre-Caum). A personal visit isn't necessary. Edwards and Edwards will mail tickets to your home, fax confirmation, or leave tickets at the box office in Paris. There is a markup of 10% to 20% (excluding opera and ballet) over box office price plus a U.S. handling charge of $8. Hotel/theater packages are also available.

DISCOUNTS　Several agencies sell tickets for cultural events and plays at discounts of up to 50%. One is the **Kiosque Théâtre,** 15 place de la Madeleine, 8e (no phone; Métro: Madeleine), offering leftover tickets for about half price on the day of performance.

Finding Tickets

There are many ticket agencies in Paris, but most are found near the Right Bank hotels. *Avoid them if possible.* The cheapest tickets can be purchased at the box office of the theater itself. Remember to tip the usher who shows you to your seat in a theater or movie house 3F (60¢).

Tickets for evening performances are sold Tuesday to Friday from 12:30 to 8pm and Saturday from 2 to 8pm. If you'd like to attend a matinee, buy your ticket Saturday from 12:30 to 2pm or Sunday from 12:30 to 4pm.

For discounts of 20% to 40% on tickets for festivals, concerts, and the theater, try one of two locations of the **FNAC** department store chain: 136 rue de Rennes, 6e (☎ **01-49-54-30-00**; Métro: Montparnasse-Bienvenue), or in the Forum des Halles, 1–7 rue Pierre-Lescot, 1er (☎ **01-40-41-40-00**; Métro: Châtelet-Les-Halles).

THEATER

Comédie-Française. 2 rue de Richelieu, 1er. ☎ **01-44-58-15-15.** Tickets 30–210F ($6–$42). Métro: Palais-Royal or Musée-du-Louvre.

Those with a modest understanding of French can still delight in a sparkling production of Molière at this national theater, established to keep the classics alive and promote the most important contemporary authors. Nowhere else will you see the works of Molière and Racine so beautifully staged. The box office is open daily from 11am to 6pm, but the hall is dark from July 21 to September 5. In 1993, a Left Bank annex was launched, **Comédie Française-Théâtre du Vieux Colombier,** 21 rue du Vieux-Colombier, 4e (☎ **01-44-39-87-00**). Although its repertoire can vary, it's known for presenting some of the most serious French dramas in town.

OPERA, DANCE & CLASSICAL CONCERTS

Cité de la Musique. 221 av. Jean-Jaurès, 19e. ☎ **01-44-84-45-00,** or 01-44-84-44-84 for tickets and information. Tickets 60–100F ($12–$20) for 4:30pm concerts, 100–160F ($20–$32) for 8pm concerts.

Of the half-dozen *grands travaux* conceived by the Mitterrand administration, this testimony to the power of music has been the most widely applauded, the least criticized, and the most innovative. At the city's northeastern edge in what used to be a run-down and depressing neighborhood few Parisians ever thought much about, the $120 million stone and glass structure incorporates a network of concert halls, a library and research center for the study of all kinds of music from around the world, and a museum, described fully in chapter 6. The complex hosts a rich variety of concerts, ranging from Renaissance through the 19th and 20th centuries, including jazz and traditional music from different nations around the world.

✪ **Opéra Bastille.** Opéra National de Paris. Place de la Bastille, 120 rue de Lyon, 75012 Paris. ☎ **01-43-43-96-96.** Tickets 60–635F ($12–$127) opera, 50–395F ($10–$79) dance. Métro: Bastille.

The controversial building—it's been called a "beached whale"—was designed by Canadian architect Carlos Ott, with curtains created by Japanese fashion designer Issey Miyake. The showplace was inaugurated in July 1989 (for the French Revolution's bicentennial), and on March 17, 1990, the curtain rose on Hector Berlioz's *Les Troyens.* Since its much-publicized opening, the opera house has presented masterworks like Mozart's *Marriage of Figaro* and Tchaikovsky's *Queen of Spades.* The main hall is the largest of any French opera house, with 2,700 seats, but music critics have lambasted the acoustics. The building contains two additional concert halls, including an intimate 250-seat room that usually hosts chamber music. Both traditional opera performances and symphony concerts are presented here.

Several concerts are given for free in honor of certain French holidays. Write ahead for tickets.

Opéra-Comique. 5 rue Favart, 2e. ☎ **01-42-44-45-45.** Tickets 50–490F ($10–$98). Métro: Richelieu-Drouot.

For light opera, try the Opéra-Comique, which was founded by the duke of Choiseul in 1782. If possible, make arrangements 2 weeks before the performance. The box office is open Monday to Saturday from 11am to 6pm; the house closes in July and August.

✪ **Opéra Garnier (Palais Garnier).** Place de l'Opéra, 9e. ☎ **01-40-01-17-89.** Tickets 60–635F ($12–$127) opera, 50–395F ($10–$79) dance. Métro: Opéra.

Opéra Garnier is the premier stage for dance and once again for opera. Because of the competition from the Opéra Bastille, the original opera has made great efforts to present more up-to-date works, including choreography by Jerome Robbins, Twyla Tharp, Agnes de Mille, and George Balanchine. This rococo wonder was designed as a contest entry by young architect Charles Garnier at the heyday of the empire. The facade is adorned with marble and sculpture, including *The Dance* by Carpeaux. The world's great orchestral, operatic, and ballet companies have performed here. Now months of painstaking restorations have burnished the Garnier's former glory: In mid-1995 it reopened grandly with Mozart's *Così fan tutte*, its boxes and walls lined with flowing red and blue damask, gilt gleaming abundantly, its ceiling, painted by Marc Chagall, cleaned, and air-conditioning added. The box office is open Monday through Saturday from 11am to 6:30pm.

Maision de Radio France. 116 av. Président-Kennedy, 16e. ☎ **01-42-30-15-16.** Tickets 50–190F ($10–$38) for Orchestre National de France, 120F ($24) for Orchestre Philharmonique. Métro: Passy-Ranelagh.

For the best orchestra in Paris, try this hall, which offers top-notch concerts with guest conductors. It is the home of Orchestre Philharmonique de Radio France and Orchestre National de France. The box office is open Monday to Saturday from 11am to 6pm.

Théâtre des Champs-Elysées. 15 av. Montaigne, 8e. ☎ **01-49-52-50-00.** Tickets 90–750F ($18–$150). Métro: Alma-Marceau.

This Art Deco theater, which attracts the haute couture crowd, hosts both national and international orchestras as well as opera and ballet. If Brooke Astor were your date, you'd take her here, perhaps to a performance of the visiting Vienna Philharmonic. The box office is open Monday to Saturday from 11am to 6pm. Events are held year-round, except in August.

Théâtre Musical de Paris (Théâtre du Châtelet). 1 place du Châtelet, 1er. ☎ **01-40-28-28-40.** Tickets 80–580F ($16–$116) opera, 80–300F ($16–$60) concerts, 80–200F ($16–$40) ballet. Métro: Châtelet.

Théâtre Musical de Paris, whose prices are usually lower than those of other theaters, occupies a neoclassical building near the City Hall. Built in 1862 on the site of an ancient Roman stadium, it's largely subsidized by the government of Paris and known for its superb acoustics. Opera, classical music, and occasional dance recitals are performed here. Closed in July and August.

Théâtre National de Chaillot. 1 place du Trocadéro, 16e. ☎ **01-47-27-81-15.** Tickets: 80–750F ($16–$150) opera, 80–350F ($16–$70) concert, 50–190F ($10–$38) ballet. Métro: Trocadéro.

Designed as part of the architectural complex facing the Eiffel Tower, this is one of the city's largest concert halls, hosting a variety of cultural events that are announced on billboards in front. Sometimes dance is staged here, or else you might see a brilliantly performed play by the great Marguerite Duras. The box office is open Monday to Saturday from 11am to 7pm and Sunday from 11am to 5pm.

2 The Club & Music Scene

Paris is still a mecca of the night, though some of the once-unique attractions now glut the market. The fame of Parisian nights was established in those distant days of innocence when Anglo-Americans still gasped at the sight of a bare bosom in a chorus line. The fact is that contemporary Paris has less nudity than London, less vice than Hamburg, and less drunkenness than San Francisco.

Nevertheless, both the quantity and the variety of Paris nightlife still exceed all other metropoli. Nowhere else will you find such a huge and mixed array of nightclubs, bars, dance clubs, cabarets, jazz dives, music halls, and honky-tonks.

MUSIC HALLS

Le Bataclan. 50 bd. Voltaire, 11e. ☎ **01-47-00-39-12.** Tickets 120–150F ($24–$30). Métro: Oberkampf.

Few other night spots in Paris have been reconfigured so drastically into a amalgam of old and new. Set in a working-class area far from the beaten path, it was built as a music hall in the mid–19th century and later flourished during the reign of Napoléon III. Today, it retains wrought-iron and ornate plaster, reproductions of the works of Toulouse-Lautrec, and nostalgia for *La Belle Époque,* despite the fact that almost every night it echoes with blues, jazz, and electronica from around the world. (Emmylou Harris performed here during our most recent visit.) Concerts usually begin around 8pm and end before 11pm.

Following the concert, the place becomes one of the most culturally neutral discos in Paris, welcoming gay and straight dance enthusiasts from France and around the world. Disco hours extend from 11:30pm till whenever the party winds down, usually within a breath of dawn. The disco cover is 100F ($20), and includes one drink.

Olympia. 28 bd. des Capucines, 9e. ☎ **01-47-42-25-49.** Tickets 150–300F ($30–$60). Métro: Opéra.

Charles Aznavour and other big names make frequent appearances in this cavernous hall. The late Yves Montand appeared once, and the performance was sold out 4 months in advance. Today you are more likely to catch Gloria Estefan. A typical lineup might include an English rock group, showy Italian acrobats, a well-known French singer, a dance troupe, juggling American comedians (doing much of their work in English), plus the featured star. A witty emcee and an on-stage band provide a smooth transition. Performances usually begin at 8:30pm Tuesday to Sunday; Saturday matinees start at 5pm.

CHANSONNIERS

The *chansonniers* (literally "songwriters") provide a bombastic musical satire of the day's events. This combination of parody and burlesque is a time-honored Gallic amusement and a Parisian institution. Songs are often created on the spot, inspired by the "disaster of the day."

Au Caveau de la Bolée. 25 rue de l'Hirondelle, 6e. ☎ **01-43-54-62-20.** Fixed-price dinner 260F ($52) Mon–Fri; 300F ($60) Sat. Cover 100F ($20) Mon–Sat if you don't order dinner. Drinks 30–65F ($6–$13) each. Métro: St-Michel.

To enter this bawdy boîte, you descend into the catacombs of the early–14th century Abbey of St-André, once a famous cafe that attracted such personages as Verlaine and Oscar Wilde, who slowly snuffed out his life in absinthe here. The singing is loud and smutty, just the way the predominantly student audience likes it. Occasionally the audience sings along. Frankly, you'll enjoy this place a lot more if you can follow the thread of the French-language jokes and satire, but even if you don't, there are enough visuals (magic acts and performances by singers) to amuse.

A fixed-price dinner, which is served Monday through Saturday at 8:30pm, is followed by a series of at least four entertainers, usually comedians. The cabaret starts at 10:30pm, and in lieu of paying admission, you can order dinner. If you've already had dinner, you can just order a drink.

✪ Au Lapin Agile. 22 rue des Saules, 18e. ☎ **01-46-06-85-87.** Cover (including the first drink) 110F ($22). Métro: Lamarck.

Picasso and Utrillo patronized this little cottage near the top of Montmartre, then known as the Cabaret des Assassins. It has been painted by numerous artists, including Utrillo. For many decades the heart of French folk music has beat here. You'll sit at carved wooden tables in a dimly lit room with walls covered by bohemian memorabilia and listen to French folk tunes, love ballads, army songs, sea chanteys, and music-hall ditties. You're encouraged to sing along, even if it's only the "*oui, oui, oui—non, non, non*" refrain of "Les Chevaliers de la Table Ronde." The best sing-alongs are on weeknights after tourist season ends. Open Tuesday to Sunday from 9pm to 2am. No meals are served; drinks cost 25F to 30F ($5 to $6).

Théâtre des Deux Anes. 100 bd. de Clichy, 18e. ☎ **01-46-06-10-26.** Tickets 210F ($42). Performances Tues–Sat at 9pm; Sun matinee 3:30pm. Métro: Blance.

Since around 1920, this theater has staged humorous satires of the foibles, excesses, and stupidities of various French governments. Favorite targets include Pres. Jacques Chirac and other mandarins and kingmakers of the *héxagone française*. Cultural icons, French and foreign, receive a grilling that is very funny and sometimes harshly caustic. Don't expect the setup of a nightclub: The place considers itself more of a theater than a cabaret, and does not serve drinks or refreshments. The 2½-hour show is conducted entirely in rapid-fire French slang, so if your syntax isn't up to par, you won't appreciate its charms.

NIGHTCLUBS & CABARETS

Decidedly expensive, these places give you your money's worth by providing some of the most lavishly spectacular floor shows anywhere.

L'Ane Rouge. 3 rue Laugier, 17e. ☎ **01-47-64-45-77.** Dinner and show 250F ($50). Métro: Ternes.

Established shortly after World War II, this red-and-black minitheater has been a showcase for French satire and humor ever since. You'll enjoy an earthy, well-flavored dinner of conservative French specialties, followed by a 2-hour medley of (French-language) stand-up comedy, ribald stories, and sometimes politicized jokes. If your knowledge of French is zero, you probably won't enjoy this place, and if you hate being singled out by a comedian in front of a crowd, you'll flee in horror. But if you're an advanced amateur with an appreciation of eternally earthy themes (the cuckolded husband, the lecherous priest, the incompetent bureaucrat), you'll find the place a rollicking insight into another culture's humor. Dinner begins nightly at 8pm, the show is conducted nightly from 10pm to midnight. Reservations are recommended.

Le Canotier du Pied de la Butte. 62 bd. Rochechouart, 18e. ☎ **01-46-06-02-86.** Cover 190F ($38) includes the first drink. Closed mid-Jan to mid-Feb. Métro: Anvers.

The worst thing said about this place is that it's touristy, but if that's the case, the visitors who show up share a genuine appreciation of the nuances, lyricism, and poetry of popular French songs. Each performance includes appearances by two men and two women, who interact on stage with their own versions of the hits made famous by Edith Piaf, Yves Montand, Jacques Brel, and, among others, Maurice Chevalier. The byword is nostalgia, unleashed by the bucketful within a cozy red, black, and white theater with room for no more than 70 occupants. *Warning:* Advance reservations are essential here, as the place closes whenever the outlook for profitable bookings is bleak. Otherwise, performances begin anytime from 7:30 to 10:30pm.

Chez Michou. 80 rue des Martyrs, 18e. ☎ **01-46-06-16-04.** Cover including dinner, aperitif, wine, and coffee 550F ($110). Nightly 10:30pm–1am. Métro: Pigalle.

The setting is blue, the emcee wears blue, and the spotlights shining on the stage bathe performers in yet another shade of blue. The creative force behind the color-coordination and a hearty dollop of cross-genderism is Michou, veteran impresario whose 20-odd cross-dressing belles bear names like Hortensia and DuDuche, and who lip-synch in costumes from haute couture to haute concierge, reviving songs by anatomically accurate songstresses. Look for tributes to such American stars as Mlles Houston, Diana Ross, and Tina Turner, and such French luminaries as Mireille Mathieu, Sylvie Vartan, "Dorothée," and the immortal Brigitte Bardot. If you want to avoid dinner, you'll have to stand at the bar, paying a compulsory 200F ($40) for the first drink. Reservations are necessary for diners, but not for the bar flies.

✪ **Crazy Horse Saloon.** 12 av. George V, 8e. ☎ **01-47-23-32-32.** Cover (including two drinks) 450–560F ($90–$112); dinner spectacle 750F ($150). Sun–Fri at 8:30 and 11pm, Sat at 8pm, 10:35pm, and 12:50am. Métro: George V or Alma-Marceau.

Le Crazy has been hailed as the best nude revue in the universe. Founded in 1951, it's a French parody of a Western saloon, which became the first emporium in France where the strippers tossed their G-strings to the winds, throwing up their hands for the big "revelation." The management invites you to "Be cool! Do it yourself! We dig English like crazy!" and indeed the place fills with their beloved Anglos. Drinks run 100F ($20) and up. Between the acts, vaudeville skits are performed.

✪ **Folies-Bergère.** 32 rue Richer, 9e. ☎ **01-44-79-98-98.** Cover 150–300F ($30–$60); dinner and show 645–700F ($129–$140). Tues–Sat at 9pm, Sun at 3pm. Métro: Rue-Montmartre or Cadet.

The Folies-Bergère is a Paris institution. Since 1886 foreigners have flocked here for excitement. Josephine Baker, the nude African-American singer who used to throw bananas into the audience, became "the toast of Paris" at the Folies-Bergère. According to legend, the first GI to reach Paris at the 1944 Liberation asked for directions to the club.

Don't expect the naughty and slyly permissive skin-and-glitter revue that used to be the trademark of this place. In 1993, all of that ended with a radical restoration of the theater, and a reopening under new management. Today, the site is configured as a conventional 1,600-seat theater that focuses on musical revues permeated with a sense of nostalgia for old Paris. You're likely to witness an intriguing, often charming, but not-all-that-erotic repertoire of mostly French but sometimes English songs, interspersed with the banter of a master/mistress of ceremonies. After the opening curtain, latecomers are not admitted inside. An unexciting restaurant serves bland set-price dinners in an anteroom to the theater.

✪ **Lido de Paris.** 116 bis av. des Champs-Elysées, 8e. ☎ **800/227-4884** or 01-40-76-56-10. Cover (including a half bottle of champagne) for 10pm or midnight show 540F ($108); or 8pm dinner-dance (including a half bottle of champagne) and 10pm show 770–990F ($154–$198). Métro: George V.

As it heads for the millennium, the Lido has changed its feathers and modernized. Its $15 million current production, *C'est Magique,* reflects a dramatic reworking of the classic Parisian cabaret show, with eye-popping special effects, including costumes and sets seemingly made of laser projects, water technology using more than 60,000 gallons of water per minute, and bold new themes, both nostalgic and contemporary, even an acrobatic aerial ballet. The show, the most expensive ever produced in Europe, uses 70 performers, $4 million in costumes, and a $2 million lighting design with lasers. There's even an ice rink and swimming pool which magically appear and disappear. The 45 Bluebell Girls, those legendary sensual showgirls, are still here, however.

✪ **Moulin Rouge.** Place Blanche, 18e. ☎ **01-46-06-00-19.** Cover (including champagne) 510F ($102); or dinner and show 750F ($150). Shows run nightly at 8:30 and 11pm. Métro: Blanche.

Toulouse-Lautrec, who put this establishment on the map about a century ago, wouldn't recognize it today. The windmill is still here and so is the cancan. But the rest has become a superslick, gimmick-ridden variety show with a heavy emphasis on the undraped female form. You'll see young women in swings and on stairs, young women naked except for a satirical take on the bewigged grandeur of 18th-century Versailles, who cavort amid a handful of (fully clothed) men. Up to 60 artists participate in shows that include animal acts, comic jugglers, and singing trios. These are just a smattering of the acts usually found on the daily bill of fare—it's all expertly staged, but any connection with the old, notorious Moulin-Rouge is purely coincidental.

Le Paradis Latin. 28 rue Cardinal-Lemoine, 5e. ☎ **01-43-25-28-28.** Cover (including a half bottle of champagne) 465F ($93); or dinner and show 680–1,250F ($136–$250). Wed–Mon, dinner 8:30pm, revue 9:45pm. Métro: Jussieu or Cardinal-Lemoine.

Built by Alexandre-Gustave Eiffel with the same metallic skeleton as his famous tower, Le Paradis Latin represents the architect's only venture into theater design. The theater itself is credited with introducing vaudeville and musical theater to Paris. In 1903 the building functioned as a warehouse. In the 1970s, however, it was transformed into an amazingly successful cabaret. The master of ceremonies speaks in French and English.

Villa d'Este. 4 rue Arsène-Houssaye, 8e. ☎ **01-42-56-14-65.** Cover (including the first drink) 150F ($30); or dinner (including wine) and show 340–720F ($68–$144). Métro: Charles de Gaulle–Etoile.

In the past this club booked Amalia Rodrigues, Portugal's leading *fadista,* and French chanteuse Juliette Greco. Today you're more likely to hear French singer François de Guelte or other top talent from Europe and America. The Villa d'Este has been around for a long time and the quality of its offerings remains high. You'll probably

After-Dark Diversions: Dives, Drag & More

On a Paris night the cheapest entertainment, especially if you are young, is "the show" staged at the extreme southeasterly tip of the Ile de la Cité, behind the Notre-Dame. Equivalent in many ways to a Gallic version of the Sundowner Festival in Key West, Florida, it spontaneously attracts just about everyone who ever wanted to try their hand at performance art. Entertainment is strictly spontaneous, and usually includes magicians, fire-eaters, jugglers, mimes, and musicmakers from all over the world, performing against the backdrop of the illuminated cathedral. Completely unchoreographed, the venue provides one of the greatest places in Paris to meet other young people in a sometimes moderately euphoric setting.

What's the least formal way to quench the thirst you'll develop during your participation in the be-in? Wander over to the **Café-Brasserie St-Regis**, 6 rue Jean du Bellay, 4e (☎ **01-43-54-59-41**), for a take-out drink. It's on the Ile St-Louis, across the street from Pont St-Louis. If you want to linger inside, you can order a *plat du jour*, priced at around 57F ($11.40) or a coffee at the bar. But if you're looking for maximum mobility, do as the Parisians do, and order beer to go (*une bière à emporter*) in a plastic cup, priced at 12F ($2.40), and take it with you on a stroll around Ile St-Louis, wandering more or less aimlessly in the balmy air of a Parisian summer. The little cafe is open daily from 7am to 11:30pm. Métro: Musée-du-Louvre.

Want a dive to hang out in until the Métro starts running again at 5am? Try **Sous-Bock Tavern**, 49 rue St-Honoré, 1er (☎ **01-40-26-46-61**; Métro: Pont-Neuf), at the corner of rue du Pont-Neuf. A crowd of young drinkers gathers here to sample some 400 varieties of beer. If you want a shot of whisky to accompany your brew, you face a choice of 180 varieties. The tavern is open Monday to Saturday from 11am to 5am and Sunday from 3pm to 5am. The dish to order here is a platter of mussels—curried, with white wine, or with cream sauce. They go well with the brasserie-style french fries.

When it's time to check out some of the best drag in Paris far afield from the tourist circuit, head for **Le Piano Show**, 20 rue de la Verrerie, 4e (☎ **01-42-72-23-81**; Métro: Hôtel-de-Ville), modeled on the cabarets that bloomed between the wars in Berlin. Only four *artistes* perform in this somewhat bedraggled cabaret that attracts a crowd that's as gay as the day is long: All are stylish and fetchingly attired (with décolletage for miles)—and male. Variety acts change monthly, but

hear some of the greatest hits of such beloved French performers as Piaf, Aznavour, Brassens, and Brel. The doors open at 8pm, the orchestra plays from 8:30pm, the show begins at 9:30pm, and there's dancing after the show until 2am.

LE COOL JAZZ

The great jazz revival that long ago swept America is still going strong here, with Dixieland or Chicago rhythms being pounded out in dozens of jazz cellars, mostly called *caveaux*. Most clubs are between rue Bonaparte and rue St-Jacques on the Left Bank, which makes things easy for seekers of syncopation.

L'Arbuci. 25–27 rue de Buci, 6e. ☎ **01-44-32-16-00.** Cover: none after 11pm. Dinner 200–250F ($40–$50) per person. Wed–Sat, dinner 8pm, live music at 10:30pm. Métro: Mabillon.

The artists who perform are likely to be lesser-known jazz players, sometimes from Southeast Asia or the Philippines, and although it's rare that a really big name will appear, you can at least admire photos and wood sculptures of jazz legends on the

impersonations of those dear to the French include Edith Piaf and Melina Mercouri, but also the obligatory Streisand and Minnelli acts. The spectacle is preceded by a mandatory 200F ($40) dinner; after that, drinks cost 85F ($17). Open Thursday to Tuesday, with dinner beginning at 8:30pm and the show at 10:30pm.

Remember Marlon Brando in *Last Tango in Paris?* Relive it at **Le Tango,** 13 rue au Maire, 3e (☎ **01-42-72-17-78;** Métro: Arts-et-Métiers). Memories of Evita and Argentina live on in this dive with bordello decor. You get not only the tango but also salsa and zouk music ranging from the French Caribbean to Africa. The club attracts those in their 20s and 30s. The cover ranges from 50F to 60F ($10 to $12). Open Thursday to Saturday from 11pm to 4am and Sunday from 2 to 7pm.

Experience the best Brazilian samba and African music in Paris at **Chez Félix,** 23 rue Mouffetard, 5e (☎ **01-47-07-68-78;** Métro: Monge). Sometimes people-watching here is even more fun than dancing. The club features a cutting-edge blend of music from Cuba, Brazil, and the Antilles, and is often filled with Paris's late-night hard-core Latin party crowd. A cover and a first drink cost 100F ($20). Chez Félix is open Tuesday to Saturday from 11pm to 5am.

What's one of the most fun and trendy things to do in Paris today? Put on your red dancing shoes and head for **La Guinguette Pirate,** Quai de la Gare, 13e (☎ **01-44-24-89-89;** Métro: Quai de la Gare), a Chinese junk moored off the banks of the Seine. This is the latest '90s version of the fabled *guinguette* or river-bordering cafe. Some of the best jazz, zouk, and live salsa are waiting to enthrall you. Much hipper than that is **What's Up?,** 15 rue Daval, 11e (☎ **01-48-05-88-33;** Métro: Brég-Sabin), where budding *existentialistes* or would-be Jean-Paul Sartres or Simone de Beauvoirs flock. The later you go, the more fashionable you are. *Tout Paris* shuns the place, but some of the city's aspirant artists, writers, and painters, along with designers and models, show up.

What's so hot, hot, hot it will burn your flesh is the **Silver Factory,** 30 av. George V, 8e (☎ **01-40-70-07-05;** Métro: George V), for those who desire a touch of old-fashioned Parisian glamour. This megaspace, with its hard cement floors, exposed pipes, and anthracite walls, is, in its owners' words, a tribute to Andy Warhol. There's a fashionable bar and restaurant here. Don your finest gay apparel: Even if you're not gay, dress like you are anyway.

walls. The venue is cozy, subterranean, smoky, and intimate, and the music and ambience are often more appealing than the entrance suggests. Clients who opt not to have dinner pay no cover charge, but pay from 60F ($12) each per drink.

Le Bilboquet/Club St-Germain. 13 rue St-Benoît, 6e. ☎ **01-45-48-81-84.** No cover. Le Bilboquet open nightly 8pm–2:45am, jazz music 10:45pm–2:45am. Club St-Germain open Tues–Sun 11pm–5am. Métro: St-Germain-des-Prés.

This restaurant/jazz club/piano bar offers some of the best music in Paris. The film *Paris Blues* was shot here. Jazz is played on the upper level in the restaurant Le Bilboquet, a wood-paneled room with a copper ceiling, brass-trimmed sunken bar, and Victorian candelabra. The menu is limited but classic French, specializing in *carré d'agneau* (lamb), fish, and beef. Dinner costs 250F to 300F ($50 to $60).

Under separate management is the downstairs Club St-Germain disco, where entrance is free but drinks cost 100F ($20). You can walk from one club to the other but have to buy a new drink each time you change venues.

Caveau de la Huchette. 5 rue de la Huchette, 5e. ☎ **01-43-26-65-05.** Cover 60F ($12) Sun–Thurs, 70F ($14) Fri–Sat; students, 50F ($10) Sun–Thurs, 60F ($12) Fri–Sat. Sun–Thurs 9:30pm–2:30am, Fri–Sat and holidays 9:30pm–4am. Métro and RER: St-Michel.

This celebrated jazz *caveau*, reached by a winding staircase, draws a young crowd, mostly students, who dance to the music of well-known jazz combos. In prejazz days Robespierre and Marat frequented the place. Drinks go for 22F to 33F ($4.40 to $6.60).

La Chapelle des Lombards. 19 rue de Lappe, 11e. ☎ **01-43-57-24-24.** Cover 80–125F ($16–$25) includes first drink. Women enter free on Thursday. Thurs–Sat 10:30pm–dawn. Métro: Bastille.

Its nearness to the Opéra Bastille seems incongruous, considering the radically experimental African/Caribbean jazz that's the norm here. It's a magnet for South American and African expatriates, who feel at home with the rhythms and fire of a music that propels everyone onto the floor to dance, dance, dance.

Au Duc des Lombards. 42 rue des Lombards, 1er. ☎ **01-42-33-22-88.** Cover 80–100F ($16–$20). Tues–Sun 10pm–3am. Métro: Châtelet.

Popular, comfortable, and appealing, this jazz club replaced an earlier club 8 years ago, and has thrived in a low-key way ever since. Artists begin playing at 10pm and continue (with breaks) for 5 hours, touching on repertoires that include everything from "free jazz" to more traditional forms such as "hard bop." Unlike many of its competitors, tables can be reserved here, and will usually be held until 10:30pm. Getting hungry? A restaurant upstairs, Le Piano sur le Toit, serves meals throughout opening hours that average around 140F ($28) each, without wine.

Jazz Club La Villa. In the Hôtel La Villa, 29 rue Jacob, 6e. ☎ **01-43-26-60-00.** Cover (including the first drink) 120–150F ($24–$30). Mon–Sat 10:30pm–2am. Closed in August. Métro: St-Germain-des-Prés.

This club is unusual because it lies in the red-velour cellar of a small but chic four-star hotel in the Latin Quarter. Don't expect backpackers or a scattering of impoverished artists. It's more elegant than many other jazz clubs, and has a reputation for bringing in famous artists to please hard-core aficionados of styles from bebop to modern jazz. Artists rotate once a week. The venue includes a predictable array of tiny tables, banquettes, armchairs, and a stage that has welcomed such artists as Joe Lovano, Hank Jones, and Shirley Horn.

Jazz Club Lionel Hampton. In the Hôtel Meridien, 81 bd. Gouvion-St-Cyr, 17e. ☎ **01-40-68-30-42.** Cover (including the first drink) 140F ($28). Nightly 10:30pm–2am or later, depending on business. Métro: Porte-Maillot.

Some of the world's jazz greats, including Lionel Hampton, have performed in the Hôtel Méridien's central courtyard. The hotel is near the Champs-Elysées and the Arc de Triomphe.

New Morning. 7–9 rue des Petites-Ecuries, 10e. ☎ **01-45-23-51-41.** Cover 120–180F ($24–$36). Call ahead, but expect the hours to be 10pm–1:30am. Métro: Château-d'Eau.

Jazz maniacs come here to drink, talk, and dance at this long-enduring club, which is now in the same league as the Village Vanguard in New York's Greenwich Village. The club remains on the see-and-be-seen circuit, as exemplified by recent guests: Spike Lee and the artist formerly known as Prince. The high-ceilinged loft, formerly a newspaper office, was turned into a nightclub in 1981. Many styles of music are played and performed, except disco. The place is especially popular with jazz groups from Central and South Africa. If a well-known performer can be booked on a

Sunday, the place is open on Sunday. A phone call will let you know what's going on the night you plan to visit. No food is served.

Le Petit Opportun. 15 rue des Lavandières-Ste-Opportune, 1er. ☎ **01-42-36-01-36.** Cover 70F ($14). Tues–Sat noon–5am; live music 10:45pm–2am. Métro: Châtelet.

Cramped and convivial, with a lingering sense of the 13th-century masons who built the solid cellar around you, this is a jazz club seating no more than 45 patrons, many of whom are regular clients. Its specialty is the traditional, back-to-basics "*Hard Bop*" that avoids the dissonance and irregular rhythms of "free jazz." Artists drive mostly from Europe and North America, and perform for 3-hour sessions. During the remainder of the time, the place functions as an arts-conscious cafe and pub.

Slow Club. 130 rue de Rivoli, 1er. ☎ **01-42-33-84-30.** Cover 60F ($12) Tues–Thurs, 75F ($15) Fri–Sat and holidays. Tues–Thurs 10pm–3am, Fri–Sat and holidays 10pm–4am. Métro: Châtelet.

One of the most famous jazz cellars in Europe, the Slow Club features the well-known French jazz band of Claude Luter, who played 10 years with the late Sidney Bechet. The hip crowd tends to be in their 30s.

Le Sunset. 60 rue des Lombards, 1er. ☎ **01-40-26-21-25.** Cover 50–100F ($10–$20). Nightly 10:30pm–3am; Bar 7:30pm–3am. Métro: Châtelet.

Since 1976, this club has flourished within a two-story setting that includes a street-level restaurant, where set menus range from 78F to 128F ($16 to $26). The artistic centerpiece of the place, however, is within its smoky cellar, where gloss-white tiles emulate a workaday Métro station, and whose hard surfaces reverberate the music in ways that clients and musicians groove to. Its laissez-faire and often bemused staff presents a roster of Italian, French, and American jazz artists, who play in sets until 3 or 4am, depending on the crowd.

DANCE CLUBS

The nightspots below are among hundreds of places where people go chiefly to dance—distinct from others where the main attraction is the music. The area around the Eglise St-Germain-des-Prés is full of dance clubs. They come and go so quickly that you could arrive in your club-clothes to find a hardware store in the place of last year's Disco Inferno—but, like all things in nature, the new springs up to take the place of the old. Check out *Time Out: Paris* or *Pariscope* to get a sense of current trends; gays and lesbians may want to consult Gai Pied's *Guide Gai,* available at kiosks for 69F ($13.80), *Lesbia* (25F/$5), *Pariscope*'s regularly featured English-language section, "A Week of Gay Outings," or the magazines *Exit* and *3 Keller,* available free at many gay bars and clubs.

Les Bains. 7 rue du Bourg-l'Abbé, 3e. ☎ **01-48-87-01-80.** Cover (including the first drink) 100F ($20). Nightly midnight–6am. Métro: Réaumur.

This chic enclave has been pronounced "in" and "out," but lately it's very "in," attracting some of the better-looking Parisians and growing a bit gay. Customers dress more for show than for comfort. The name Les Bains comes from the place's old function as a Turkish bath attracting gay clients, none more notable than Marcel Proust. It may be hard to get in if the bouncer doesn't like your looks. A restaurant has been added to the venue.

La Balajo. 9 rue de Lappe, 11e. ☎ **01-47-00-07-87.** Cover (including the first drink) 50F ($10) Sun afternoon, 100F ($20) evenings. Thurs–Sat 11:30pm–5:30am, Sun 3–7pm. Métro: Bastille.

Established in 1936, this dance club is best remembered as the venue where Edith Piaf first won the hearts of thousands of Parisian music lovers. Today, Le Balajo is hardly as fashionable, although it continues its big-band tradition on Sunday afternoons when a group of patrons aged 45 and up dance to World War II–era swing and bebop. Thursday to Saturday nights they bring out the disco ball, and to a lesser degree play reggae, salsa, rock 'n' roll, and rap.

Club Zed. 2 rue des Anglais, 5e. ☎ **01-43-54-93-78.** Cover (including the first drink) 50–100F ($10–$20). Wed–Thurs 10:30pm–3am, Fri–Sat 10:30pm–5am. Métro: Maubert-Mutualité.

This popular nightspot in a former bakery may surprise you with its mix of musical offerings: samba from Rio, rock, 1960s pop, or jazz.

Les Coulisses/La Bohème. 5 rue du Mont-Cenis, 18e. ☎ **01-42-62-89-99.** Cover 100F ($20) Fri–Sat only, but free for patrons of either restaurant. Restaurants Wed–Sat 8pm–1am; disco 11pm–5am. Métro: Abbesses.

Its premises combine a cellar-level disco with two restaurants (La Bohème and Les Coulisses) on the street level and first floor. Amid a decor that mates a feudal château with a scene from the Italian *Commedia dell'Arte,* you can dance, dine, drink, and flirt like teenagers. The set menu in one of the restaurants is 160F ($32); otherwise, traditional items cost 70F to 100F ($14 to $20). Downstairs, ages range from 20 to around 45.

La Coupole. 102 bd. Montparnasse, 14e. ☎ **01-43-20-14-20.** Ballroom cover 60F ($12), Sat matinee 60F ($12), Sun matinee 80F ($16), Tues–Sat nights 95F ($19). Tues–Fri 9:30pm–4am, Sat 3:30–7:30pm and 9:30pm–4am, and Sun 5:30–9pm. Métro: Vavin.

This landmark cafe has a basement ballroom that's a popular place to waltz and tango to orchestra music as well as bump and grind to "disco retro" (the best disco tunes of the 1960s, 1970s, and 1980s). The upstairs cafe is covered in chapter 5's "The Top Cafes."

Rex Club. 5 bd. Poissonière, 2e. ☎ **01-42-36-83-98.** Cover (including the first drink) 50–80F ($10–$16). Tea dance Tues and Thurs–Sat 1:45–9pm; club Thurs–Sat 11:30pm–6am. Métro: Bonne-Nouvelle.

During its "tea dance" sessions, the place attracts clients aged 40 to 65 with its emphasis on recorded versions of tangos, waltzes, and occasional forays into 1970s disco music. A bizarre sideshow, however, begins after 11pm on the 4 nights a week it's open. Then, the echoing blue-and-orange space emulates the techno-grunge clubs of London, complete with an international, mood-altered clientele enjoying the kind of music only someone aged 18 to 28 could love. A revolving host of DJs is on hand, including regular appearances from a local techno-circuit celeb, Laurent Garnier, who from a tangerine-hued control booth orchestrates musical ambience.

Le New Riverside. 7 rue Grégoire-de-Tours, 6e. ☎ **01-43-54-46-33.** Cover (including first drink) of 90F ($18) imposed on men all the time, but on women only after 11:30pm on Fri–Sat. Daily 11pm–6am. Métro: St-Michel or Odéon.

This battered Left Bank cellar club attracts droves of jaded veterans, who appreciate the indestructible premises and a nostalgic approach to musical taste. You'll hear a K-Tel-ish range of 1970s electronic rock and pop, especially The Doors, whose music plays so much you think the CD's skipping. Expect a crowd from 25 to 40 in which women, especially when unaccompanied, are almost always admitted free. If thoughts of Woodstock fill you with love and nostalgia, and if you want to meet French people who feel the same, this is the place for you.

Le Saint. 7 rue St-Severin, 5e. ☎ **01-43-25-50-04.** Cover 60–90F ($12–$18), includes the first drink. Métro: St-Michel.

Set within three medieval cellars deep within Paris's densest concentration of university facilities, this place lures 20-somethings and 30-somethings who dance and drink and generally feel happy to be in a Left Bank student dive. The music melds New York, Los Angeles, and Europe, and often leads to episodes of "Young Love Beside the Seine" that many visitors remember in a kind of shameful glory for months afterward.

ROCK & ROLL

Bus Palladium. 6 rue Fontaine, 9e. ☎ **01-53-21-07-33.** Cover 100F ($20) for men Tues, Fri, and Sat. Cover 100F ($20) for women Fri–Sat. Tues–Sat 11pm–6am. Métro: Blanche or Pigalle.

Set in a single room with a very long bar, this rock and roll temple has varnished hardwoods and fabric-covered walls that barely absorb the reverberations of nonstop recorded music. You won't find techno, punk-rock, jazz, blues, or soul here. It's rock 'n' roll and nothing but rock 'n' roll, so help us God, for hard-core predatory breeders aged 25 to 35. Alcoholic drinks of any kind cost 80F ($16), except for women on Tuesdays, when they drink as much as they want for free.

SALSA

Les Étoiles. 61 rue du Château d'Eau, 10e. ☎ **01-47-70-60-56.** Cover charge, with dinner included, 120F ($24). Métro: Château d'Eau.

Since 1856, this red-swabbed old-fashioned music hall has shaken with the sound of performers at work and patrons at play. The newest manifestation of its good times rolling is a restaurant discotheque where the music is exclusively *salsa* and the food *Cubano*. Expect simple but hearty portions of fried fish, shredded pork or beef, white rice, beans, and *flan* as bands from Venezuela play salsa to a crowd who already know or quickly learn how to dance to South American rhythms.

3 Bars, Pubs & Clubs

WINE BARS

Many Parisians now prefer the wine bar to the traditional cafe or bistro. The food is often better and the ambience more inviting. For cafes, see "The Best Cafes" in chapter 5.

✪ **Au Sauvignon.** 80 rue des Sts-Pères, 7e. ☎ **01-45-48-49-02.** Mon–Sat 8:30am–10:30pm. Closed in Aug. Métro: Sèvres-Babylone.

This tiny place has tables overflowing onto a covered terrace where wines range from the cheapest Beaujolais to the most expensive Puligny-Montrachet. A glass of wine is 17F to 30F ($3.40 to $6), and it costs an additional 2F (40¢) to consume it at a table. To go with your wine, choose an Auvergne specialty, including goat cheese and terrines. The fresh Poilane bread is ideal with ham, pâté, or goat cheese. The place is decorated with old ceramic tiles and frescoes done by Left Bank artists.

Aux Négociants. 27 rue Lambert, 18e. ☎ **01-46-06-15-11.** Mon and Fri noon–8pm, Tues–Thurs noon–10:30pm. Métro: Lamarck-Caulincourt or Château-Rouge.

Ten minutes downhill from the north facade of Sacré-Coeur, this *bistro à vins* has flourished since it was founded in 1980 as an outlet for most of the wines produced in the Loire Valley. Artists, street vendors, and office workers all come here, linked only by an appreciation of wine and, in some cases, the allure of one of the simple but hearty *plats du jour* produced for 60F to 70F ($12 to $14) in the establishment's cramped kitchen. The place is hearty and unpretentious, the kind of place you'd have expected in the countryside. Wines range from 14F to 42F ($2.80 to $8.40) per glass.

Juveniles. 47 rue de Richelieu, 1er. ☎ **01-42-97-46-49.** Mon–Sat noon–11pm. Métro: Palais-Royal.

This is a spin-off of one of Paris's most successful wine bars, Willi's, which lies a short distance away. Louder, less formal, less restrained, and, at least to wine-lovers, more provocative than its older sibling, it prides itself on experimenting with a wide roster of wines from "everywhere." There's virtually no oenophilic chauvinism, and no automatic allegiance to prestigious Bordeaux or high-profile Burgundies at this British-owned spot, where high-quality but less well known wines from Spain, France, California, and Australia decant for between 14F and 42F ($2.80 and $8.40) a glass. Anything you like, including bottles of the "wine of the week," can be hauled away uncorked from a wine boutique on the premises. And if perchance hunger intrudes, Juveniles will sate you with an assortment of tapas-inspired platters for 30F to 40F ($6 to $8) each. Examples include roasted quail wings, marinated squid, tortillas (omelettes) with a tapenade of olives, various *charcuteries,* and assorted cheeses.

La Tartine. 24 rue de Rivoli, 4e. ☎ **01-42-72-76-85.** Thurs–Monday 8:30am–10pm and Wed noon–10pm. Closed 2 weeks in Aug. Métro: St-Paul.

Mirrors, brass detail, and frosted-globe chandeliers make La Tartine look like a movie set of Old Paris. At least 60 wines are offered at reasonable prices, including seven kinds of Beaujolais and a large selection of Bordeaux served by the glass. Glasses of wine cost 9F to 18F ($1.80 to $3.60), sandwiches 14F to 41F ($2.80 to $8.20), and the charcuterie platter is 46F ($9.20). We recommend the light wine Sancerre and goat cheese from the Loire Valley.

Le Sancerre. 22 av. Rapp, 7e. ☎ **01-45-51-75-91.** Mon–Sat 8am–9pm. Métro: Alma Marceau.

Very few of the bars of Paris have allied themselves as closely to the wine of an individual region the way this place has linked itself to Sancerre. Produced in the Loire Valley in red, rosé, and the best-known version of all, white, Sancerre is known for its not-too-dry fruity aroma and legions of fans who believe it should be more celebrated than it already is. Don't even think of asking for a wine from more celebrated, and more expensive, wine-producing regions. Glasses of this aromatic wine cost 24F ($4.80) each, derive from several different producers within the Sancerre district, and are consumed within a trio of rooms outfitted with wood paneling that's evocative of an *auberge Sancerrois.* Simple platters of food—chitterling sausages, and omelettes studded with potatoes and chives, or with country ham—are the most popular noshing items, and cost 41F to 71F ($8.20 to $14.20).

Les Bacchantes. 21 rue Caumartin, 9e. ☎ **01-42-65-25-35.** Mon–Sat noon–midnight. Métro: Havre-Caumartin.

It prides itself on offering more wines by the glass (at least 50) than any other wine bar in Paris. It also does a hefty restaurant trade, so much so that it's hard to define it as a bistro specializing in wine, or a wine bar with a particular penchant for well-prepared *cuisine bourgeoisie.* Amid massive exposed beams, old belle epoque posters, and old-fashioned paneling, blackboards announce a great list of vintages and platters. Bacchantes attracts dozens of theater-goers before and after performances at the nearby Olympia Theatre, as well as anyone interested in esoteric and carefully chosen vintages from small-scale winemakers. The wines, which cost 13F to 30F ($2.60 to $6) per glass, are mainly French, though a number come from neighboring countries. Platters of food are 60F to 95F ($12 to $19).

Willi's Wine Bar. 13 rue des Petits-Champs, 1er. ☎ **01-42-61-05-09.** Mon–Sat noon–2:30pm and 7–11pm. Métro: Bourse, Louvre, or Palais-Royal.

Journalists and stockbrokers patronize this increasingly popular wine bar in the center of the financial district, run by an Englishman, Mark Williamson. About 250 kinds of wine are offered, including a dozen wine specials you can taste by the glass for 26F to 30F ($5.20 to $6). Lunch is the busiest time—on quiet evenings you can better enjoy the warm ambience and 16th-century beams. Daily specials are likely to include lamb brochette with cumin or lyonnaise sausage in truffled vinaigrette, plus spectacular desserts such as chocolate terrine. The fixed-price menu is 155F ($31).

BARS & PUBS

These "imported" establishments try to imitate American cocktail bars or masquerade as British pubs—most strike an alien chord. But that doesn't prevent fashionable Parisians from bar-hopping (not to be confused with cafe-sitting). In general, bars and pubs are open daily between 11am and 1:30am, though of course there are exceptions to the rule.

L'Académie de la Bière. 88 bis bd. du Port-Royal, 5e. ☎ **01-43-54-66-65.** Métro: Port-Royal.

The decor is paneled, woodsy, and rustic, an appropriate foil for an "academy" whose curriculum includes access to more than 150 kinds of beer, each from a microbrewery. Stella Artois, the best-selling beer in Belgium, isn't available, although more than half of the dozen on tap are from small-scale, not-particularly famous breweries in Belgium that deserve to be better known. Mugs or bottles cost from 20F to 65F ($4 to $13) each, depending on how esoteric they are. Getting hungry? Snack-style food is available, including platters of mussels, assorted cheeses, and sausages with mustard.

Bar Anglais. In the Plaza Athénée, 25 av. Montaigne, 8e. ☎ **01-53-67-66-65.** Métro: Alma-Marceau.

As its name implies, this aggressively upscale bar, located in one of Paris's most opulent hotels, has a woodsy, leathery, and vintage Anglo-Saxon decor with splashes of French service and international drinks. Every evening from 11pm to 1:30am a pianist and singer entertain a prosperous clientele in a medley of languages.

Bar du Crillon. In the Hôtel de Crillon, 10 place de la Concorde, 8e. ☎ **01-44-71-15-00.** Métro: Concorde.

Although some visitors consider the Bar du Crillon too stiff and self-consciously elegant to ever allow anyone to have a good time, the social and literary history of this bar is remarkable. Hemingway set a climactic scene of *The Sun Also Rises* here, and over the years it has attracted practically every upper-level staff member of the nearby American embassy, including the recently deceased U.S. ambassador to France and *femme formidable*, Pamela Harriman, as well as a gaggle of visiting heiresses, stars, starlets, and wannabes. Under its new owner, the Concorde Group, the bar has been redecorated by Sonia Rykiel and no longer basks in the 1950s glow so favored by past clients such as Janet Flanner (legendary Paris correspondent of *The New Yorker*). If this particular bar doesn't appeal to you, there's another option just down the hall, the Edwardian-style **Jardin d'Hiver.** Here, amid potted palms and very upscale accessories, you can order tea, cocktails, or coffee.

Le Bar de l'Hôtel. In L'Hôtel, 13 rue des Beaux-Arts, 6e. ☎ **01-43-25-27-22.** Métro: St-Germain-des-Prés.

This is the hyper-artsy and theatrically overdecorated bar of a hotel that has wooed film-industry types who want to avoid the more mainstream luxury of Paris's palatial hotels. The rose-filter cheeriness is deceptive: This is the hotel where Oscar Wilde died, disgraced and impoverished, after his self-imposed exile from England. Don't expect a setting that's the least bourgeois—if the staff wasn't so consciously straitlaced, you'd expect a campy musical comedy to break out at any moment.

Bar Le 64. 64 rue de Charenton, 12e. ☎ **01-44-75-39-55.** Métro: Bastille or Ledru-Rollin.

The decor of this Bastille dive might remind you of a local pub in the English countryside, with wood paneling, rustic furniture, a dartboard, and some pool tables. It's enough off the beaten track to attract a neighborhood clientele when music isn't playing, and whenever the music begins (usually after 10pm), outsiders begin to gather. There's no cover charge, and music ranges from blues to jazz to 1970s rock 'n' roll. Preferred drinks include exotic coffees, usually with shots of cognac, beers (there are six kinds on tap), glasses of wine, and mint tea.

The China Club. 50 rue de Charenton, 12e. ☎ **01-43-43-82-02.** Métro: Bastille.

Designed to recall France's 19th-century colonies in Asia (on the ground floor) and England's empire-building zeal in India (upstairs), the China Club will allow you to chitchat or flirt with the singles who crowd into the street-level bar, and then escape to calmer, more contemplative climes upstairs. You'll see regulars from Paris' worlds of fashion and the arts, along with a pack of post-show celebrants from the nearby Opéra de la Bastille. There's a Chinese restaurant on the street level, a scattering of books, newspapers, and chess boards upstairs, and a more animated (and occasionally raucous) bar in the cellar.

Le Forum. 4 bd. Malesherbes, 8e. ☎ **01-42-65-37-86.** Métro: Madeleine.

Its clients, who include frequent business travelers to Paris from around the world, compare this place to a private club in London. Part of that derives from the carefully polished oak paneling and ornate stucco, and part from the fact that its store of single malt whiskies is among the most comprehensive in town. Cocktails? You can try 150 different libations, including many that haven't been in popular circulation since the jazz age. Champagne by the glass is common, as is that high-octane social lubricant, the martini.

George V Bar. In the Hôtel George V, 31 av. George V, 8e. ☎ **01-47-23-54-00.** Métro: George V.

If there's someone you're trying to avoid amid the tapestries and Regency antiques of the main lobby, this very *laissez-faire* watering hole provides a convenient hideaway.

Pub St-Germain-des-Prés. 17 rue de l'Ancienne-Comédie, 6e. ☎ **01-43-29-38-70.** Métro: Odéon.

With 9 different rooms and 650 seats, this is the largest pub in France, offering 500 brands of beer, 26 of which are on draft. The deliberately tacky decor, which has seen a lot of beer swilled and spilled since its installation, consists of faded gilt-framed mirrors, hanging lamps, and a stuffed parrot in a gilded cage. Leather booths render drinking discreet in an atmosphere that is usually quiet, relaxed, posh, and, crucially, open day and night. Featured beers change frequently, but usually include Amstel, many different Belgian brews (including both *blonde* and *brune* versions of Belforth), Whitbread, and Pimm's No. 1. If frat houses turn you on, it gets *really* fun between 10:30pm and 4am, when above the chatter of live rock everything becomes loud, raucous, and sudsy.

The Ritz Bars. In the Hôtel Ritz, 15 place Vendôme, 1er. ☎ **01-43-16-30-30.** Métro: Opéra.

In 1944 during the liberation of Paris, Ernest Hemingway made political and literary history by ordering a drink at the Ritz Bar while gunfire from retreating Nazi soldiers still rang in the streets outside. The Ritz commemorates this event with book-ish memorabilia, rows of newspapers, and stiff drinks served within a setting equivalent to that of a woodsy English Club. Look for its entrance, and homage to such other writers as Proust, close to the Ruen Cambon entrance to this hotel. If you get thirsty during the daytime, when the Hemingway Bar isn't open, head for the hotel's Bar Vendôme instead, which is near the hotel's main (Place Vendôme) entrance. The setting is equally cozy and woodsy, albeit a bit more grand.

4 Gay & Lesbian Clubs

Gay life is centered around Les Halles and Le Marais, with the greatest concentration of gay and lesbian clubs, restaurants, bars, and shops between the Hôtel-de-Ville and Rambuteau Métro stops. Gay dance clubs come and go so fast that even the magazines devoted somewhat to their pursuit—*3 Keller* and *Exit,* both distributed free in the gay bars and bookstores—have a hard time keeping up. *Lesbia,* a monthly national lesbian magazine, focuses on women's issues.

Amnesia. 42 rue Vieille-du-Temple, 4e. ☎ **01-42-72-16-94.** Métro: Hôtel-de-Ville.

Its function and clientele changes throughout the course of the day, despite the constant presence of a local cadre of gay men. Combining aspects of a cafe, tea room, bistro, and bar, it includes two beige bar and dining areas, a mezzanine, and a cellar-level bar that opens later in the evening. Beer and cocktails are the drinks of choice, with a specialty coffee (*café amnesia*) that combines caffeine with cognac and Chantilly cream. Deep armchairs and soft pillows combine with 1930s accents here, creating an ambience that's conducive to talk and a cheerfulness that's not always apparent in the more sexually charged bars nearby. *Plats du jour* cost 60F to 75F ($12 to $15) each and include surprisingly conservative food like Basque chicken and beef bourguignon.

Banana Café. 13 rue de la Ferronerie, 1er. ☎ **01-42-33-35-31.** Métro: Châtelet or Les-Halles.

It's the most popular gay bar in the Marais, a ritualized stopover for European homosexuals (mostly male) visiting or doing business in Paris. Occupying two floors of a 19th-century building, it has walls the color of an overripe banana, dim lighting, and a well-publicized policy of raising the price of drinks after 10pm, after things become really interesting. On theme nights such as Valentine's Day, expect the entire premises to be plastered with pink crepe paper. There's a street-level bar and a dance floor in the cellar that features a live pianist and recorded music—there, depending on the mood, clients sometimes dance. On many nights, go-go dancers from all over perform from spotlit platforms in the cellar.

Le Bar. 5 rue de la Ferronerie, 1er. ☎ **01-40-41-00-10.** Métro: Châtelet.

Covering the street level and the cellar of a sprawling building within a neighborhood long known for an availability of commercial sex, this is the largest gay bar in Paris. You'll find three bars on the premises, a mostly blue decor that incorporates lots of sinuous lines, and an ambience that's more sexually charged and explicit in the cellar than on the street level. The average age of most clients here is around 32, and the majority are gay and male.

Le Bar Central. 33 rue Vieille-du-Temple, 4e. ☎ **01-48-87-99-33.** Métro: Hôtel-de-Ville.

Le Bar Central is one of the leading bars for men in the Hôtel-de-Ville area. The club has opened a small hotel upstairs (see "Gay-Friendly Hotels" in chapter 4). Both the

Note

Also see the box "After-Dark Diversions: Dives, Drag & More," earlier in this chapter.

---

bar and its hotel are in a 300-year-old building in the heart of the Marais. The hotel caters mostly to gay men, less frequently to lesbians.

La Champmeslé. 4 rue Chabanais, 2e. ☎ **01-42-96-85-20.** Métro: Pyramides or Bourse.

With dim lighting, background music, and comfortable banquettes, La Champmeslé offers a cozy meeting place for women, and to a much, much lesser extent (around 5%) for "well-behaved" men. It is, in fact, the leading women's bar of Paris. The club is housed in a 300-year-old building heavy on exposed stone and ceiling beams, with retro 1950s-style furnishings. Every Thursday night one of the premier lesbian events of Paris, a cabaret, begins at 10pm (but the price of cover and drinks doesn't rise); and every month there is a well-attended exhibition of paintings by mostly lesbian artists. Josy is your accommodating and sophisticated hostess. Why did she pick this name for her bar? It's in honor of a celebrated 17th-century actress, La Champmeslé, who was instrumental in interpreting the then-fledging dramatic efforts of the celebrated playwright Racine.

Cox Café. 15 rue des Archives, 4e. ☎ **01-42-72-08-00.** Métro: Hôtel de Ville.

This is a bar for mature gay men of the Marais who appreciate a laugh and the proximity of other men. There's a long teakwood bar, early 20th-century stone walls, and copious amounts of beer that sell for around 16F ($3.20) a glass. Heineken, a Belgian brew named Adèle Scott, and several pale versions of wheat beer are all on tap. Although the place is open daily 1am to 2am, it's busiest from 6 to 11pm.

L'Entr'acte. 25 bd. Poissonnière, 2e. ☎ **01-40-26-01-93.** Métro: Rue Montmartre.

This is one of the most visible and popular lesbian discos in Paris. Outfitted like a burgundy-colored 19th-century French music hall, it welcomes gay women of every conceivable age within its premises. A new management has made its seedy past a distant memory. Today it's fun, trendy, and chic. It's best to show up here before midnight. The venue, as the French like to say, is very cool, with all types of cutting-edge music played within a setting that just happens to discourage the presence of men. What to do if you're gay and male and want to hang out with the girls? Head for the establishment's side entrance, where a "separate but equal facility" (Le Scorpion, same address) welcomes *les mecs gais* (gay guys) into a roughly equivalent format that, alas, never manages to be as much fun as such other gay male bastions as Le Queen. Both L'Entr'acte and Le Scorpion are open Tuesday to Sunday from 11:45pm till at least 5am. Entrance is free.

Madame Arthur. 75 bis rue des Martyrs, 18e. ☎ **01-42-54-40-21.** Cover (including the first drink) 165F ($33); or dinner and show 295F ($59). Métro: Abbesses or Pigalle.

This is the best-established and longest-running transvestite show in Paris, attracting both straight and gay people who find the revue funnier, and more tasteful, than they might have expected. The creative force behind the affair is Madame Arthur, who is no lady, and whose stage name during her shticks as mistress of ceremonies is Chantaline. How long has this place been here? Pigalle lore claims that it used to welcome the invading armies of Julius Caesar, and that they loved the show. But despite its detractors (and very few people don't like the *ooh-la-là's* that are every-night occurrences at Madame Arthur's) it's still going strong, thanks to between 9 and 11 *artistes* whose vampy and campy personae bear names like Vungala, Lady Lune, and Miss Badabou. You can visit just to drink, or you can dine from an uncomplicated fixed-price menu. Reservations are strongly advised. The club is open daily from 9 to 10:30pm for dinner, with the spectacle beginning at 10:30pm. Additional shows, according to demand, are on Friday and Saturday at 7:30pm, with dinner beginning at 6pm.

Le Piano Zinc. 49 rue des Blancs-Manteaux, 4e. ☎ **01-42-74-32-42.** No cover; one-drink minimum Fri–Sat. Métro: Rambuteau or Hôtel-de-Ville.

This ever-popular place is unusual. Founded 15 years ago by a German-born francophile named Jürgen, it's a piano bar/cabaret, filled with singing patrons who belt out old French *chansons* with humor and gusto. It defines itself as a gay bar, "but you can happily bring your *grandmère*, as some of our clients do," the management assures us. The place is on three floors of a building, with the cabaret presented in the basement nightly at 10pm for no charge.

Le Queen. 102 av. des Champs-Elysées, 8e. ☎ **01-53-89-08-90.** Cover 50F ($10) Mon, 100F ($20) Fri–Sat. Métro: F.D. Roosevelt.

Should you miss gay life *à la* New York, follow the flashing purple sign on the "main street" of Paris, near the corner of avenue George-V. The place is often mobbed, primarily with gay men and, to a much lesser degree, chic women (*photomannequins* and the like) who work in the fashion and film industries. Look for drag shows, muscle shows, strip tease from *danseurs* who gyrate atop the bars, and everything from 1970s-style disco nights (Monday) to Tuesday-night foam parties (only in summer), when cascades of mousse descend onto the dance floor. Go very, very late, as the place is open daily from midnight to 6 or 7am.

5 Literary Haunts

La Closerie des Lilas. 171 bd. du Montparnasse, 6e. ☎ **01-40-51-34-50.** Métro: Pont-Royal.

Hemingway, Picasso, Gershwin, and Modigliani all loved the Closerie, and ever since, Parisians and foreigners, literary or not, have been attracted to its premises. Even though the lilacs that gave the place its name bloom in spring from pots in front, management strews bouquets of them throughout the bar all year long. Don't expect a hush and reverence—on some nights the place is as energetic as a New York singles bar. Look for the brass nameplate of your favorite Lost Generation artist along the banquettes or at the bar.

✪ Harry's New York Bar. 5 rue Daunou, 2e. ☎ **01-42-61-71-14.** Métro: Opéra or Pyramides.

Sank roo doe Noo, as the ads tell you to instruct your cab driver, is the most famous bar in Europe—quite possibly in the world. Opened Thanksgiving Day 1911, by a bearded Hemingway precursor by the name of MacElhone, it's sacred to Papa disciples as the spot where members of ambulance corps during World War I drank themselves silly, and as the master's favorite place to snuff brain cells in Paris. The site is legendary for other reasons: White Lady and Sidecar cocktails were invented in 1919 and 1931, respectively. Also, it is the alleged birthplace of the Bloody Mary and the headquarters of a loosely organized fraternity of drinkers known as the International Bar Flies (IBF). Harry's New York Bar has stayed in the family: Duncan, MacElhone's bilingual grandson, now owns and runs it.

The place's core is the street-level bar, where CEOs and office workers loosen their neckties on more or less equal footing. Daytime crowds draw from the neighborhood's insurance, banking, and travel industries; evening crowds include pre- and post-theater groupies and night owls who aren't bothered by the gritty setting and deliberately unflattering lighting. In other words, Fitzgerald, Faulkner, Steinbeck, Ford Madox Ford, and Ring Lardner are long gone. A softer, somewhat less macho ambience reigns in the cellar, where a pianist provides highly drinkable music every night from 10pm to 2am, accompanied by whatever patron feels uninhibited enough to join in.

Rosebud. 11 bis rue Delambre, 14e. ☎ **01-43-35-38-54.** Métro: Vavin.

The popularity of this place known for a bemused and indulgent attitude toward anyone looking for a drink and some talk hasn't diminished since the 1950s, when it attained its fame. The name refers to the beloved sled of Orson Welles's greatest film, *Citizen Kane.* Just around the corner from Montparnasse's famous cafes, and thick in associations with Jean-Paul Sartre and Simone de Beauvoir, Eugene Ionesco, and Marguerite Duras, Rosebud draws clients aged 35 to 65, though the staff has recently remarked upon the appearance of, gasp!, students. Drop in at night for a glass of wine, a shot of whisky, or a bite to eat, maybe a hamburger or chili con carne.

Side Trips from Paris

10

Paris, the city that began on an island, is itself the center of a curious landlocked island known as the Ile de France.

Shaped roughly like a saucer, it lies encircled by a thin ribbon of rivers: the Epte, Aisne, Marne, and Yonne. Fringing these rivers are mighty forests with famous names—Rambouillet, St-Germain, Compiègne, and Fontainebleau. These forests are said to be responsible for Paris's clear, gentle air, and the unusual length of its spring and fall. This may be a debatable point, but there's no argument that they provide the capital with a fine series of excursions, all within easy reach.

The forests were the domain of kings and the ruling aristocracy, and they're still sprinkled with the magnificent châteaux (palaces) of their former masters. Together with ancient villages, glorious cathedrals, and little country inns, they turn Ile de France into a traveler's paradise. On a definite contrast, Disneyland Paris attracts visitors from all over. Because Paris is comparatively small, almost everything is on your doorstep.

The difficult question is where to go. What we're offering in this chapter is merely a handful of the dozens of possibilities for one-day jaunts. For a more extensive list of excursions in the Ile de France, consult *Frommer's France '98*.

1 Versailles

13 miles SW of Paris, 44 miles NE of Chartres

For centuries, the name of this Parisian suburb resounded through the consciousness of every aristocratic family in Europe. The palace at Versailles outdistanced and outdazzled every other kingly residence in Europe; it was a horrendously expensive scandal and a symbol to later generations of a regime obsessed with prestige above all else.

Back in the *grande siécle*, all you needed to enter was a sword, a hat, and a bribe for the guard at the gate. Providing you didn't look as if you had smallpox, you'd be admitted to the precincts of the Château de Versailles, here to stroll through salon after glittering salon—to watch the Sun King at his banqueting table, to dance or flirt or even do something far more personal. Louis XIV was accorded the privacy of a waiting room in a bus station.

Impressions

When Louis XIV had finished the Grand Trianon, he told [Mme de] Maintenon he had created a paradise for her, and asked if she could think of anything now to wish for . . . She said she could think of but one thing—it was summer, and it was balmy France—yet she would like well to sleigh ride in the leafy avenues of Versailles! The next morning found miles and miles of grassy avenues spread thick with snowy salt and sugar, and a procession of those quaint sleighs waiting to receive the chief concubine of the gaiest and most unprincipled court that France has ever seen!
                    —Mark Twain, *The Innocents Abroad* (1869)

ESSENTIALS

GETTING THERE   Seeing Versailles should take an entire day. To go to Versailles **by train,** catch the Réseau Express Régional (RER) at the Gare d'Austerlitz, St-Michel, Musée d'Orsay, Invalides, Pont de l'Alma, Champ-de-Mars, or Javel station, and take it to the Versailles-Rive-Gauche station, where you can catch a shuttle bus to the château. The 35F ($7) trip takes about half an hour. Eurailpass holders travel free. A regular train also leaves from the Gare Montparnasse to the Versailles-Rive-Gauche RER station.

   By Métro, get off at Pont de Sèvres and transfer to bus 171. The trip takes 15 minutes. To get here from Paris, it's cheaper to pay with three Métro tickets from a *carnet* (a 10-ticket packet). You'll be let off near the gates of the palace.

   By car, take the N10 highway. Park on place d'Armes in front of the palace.

ORIENTATION   The palace dominates the town. Three main avenues radiate from place d'Armes in front of the palace. The **tourist office** is at 7 rue des Réservoirs (☎ 01-39-50-36-22).

THE PALACE

The kings of France built a glittering private world for themselves, far from the grime and noise and bustle of Paris: the **Château de Versailles,** place d'Armes (☎ 01-30-84-74-00). Seeing all of the palace's rooms would take up an entire morning and leave you exhausted, so you should probably skip some of them and save your energy for the park, which is the ultimate in French landscaping. Its makers disciplined every tree, shrub, flower, and hedge into a frozen ballet pattern and spread them among soaring fountains, sparkling pools, grandiose stairways, and hundreds of marble statues. It's like a colossal stage setting—even the view of the blue horizon seems like a ornately embroidered backdrop. The garden is an Eden for puppet people, a place where you expect the birds to sing coloratura soprano.

   Inside, the **Grand Apartments,** the **Royal Chapel,** and the **Hall of Mirrors** (where the Treaty of Versailles was signed) can be visited without a guide Tuesday through Sunday between 9:45am and 5pm (it's closed on holidays). Admission costs 45F ($9) for adults; 35F ($7) adults after 3:30pm and those 18 to 25; and free to those under 18 and those over 60. Other sections of the château may be visited only at specific hours or on special days. Some sections are temporarily closed as they undergo restoration.

   Try to save time to visit the **Grand Trianon,** which is a good walk across the park. In pink-and-white marble, it was designed by Hardouin-Mansart for Louis XIV in 1687. The Trianon is mostly furnished with Empire pieces. You can also visit the **Petit Trianon,** built by Gabriel in 1768. This was the favorite residence of Marie

Paris & the Ile de France

Chantilly **5**
Château de Thoiry **2**
Chartres **8**
Disneyland Paris **12**
Fontainebleau **10**
Giverny **1**
Illiers–Combray **9**
Malmaison **4**
St-Germain-en-Laye **3**
Rambouillet **7**
Vaux–le–Vicomte **11**
Versailles **6**

Peaches & Peas Fit for a King

Between 1682 and 1789, the Versailles palace housed a royal entourage whose population, except for 8 years during the minority of Louis XV, remained constant at 3,000. To feed them, the sprawling kitchens employed a permanent staff of 2,000. Without benefit of running water or electricity, they labored over the banquets that became day-to-day rituals at the most glorious court since the collapse of ancient Rome.

The fruits and vegetables that appeared on the royal tables were produced on-site, in *Les Potagers du Roi* (the King's Kitchen Garden). Surprisingly, the gardens have survived and can be found a 10-minute walk south of the château's main entrance, at 6 rue du Hardy, behind an industrial-looking gate. Twenty-three acres of fertile earth are arranged into parterres and terraces as formal as the legendary showcases devoted to flowers, fountains, and statuary during the royal tenure.

Meals at Versailles were quite a ritual. The king almost always dined in state, alone at a table visible to hundreds of observers and, in some cases, other diners, who sat in order of rank. Fortunately for gastronomic historians, there are many detailed accounts about what Louis XIV enjoyed and how much he consumed: He was addicted to salads and ate prodigious amounts of basil, purslane, mint, and wood sorrel. He loved melons, figs, and pears. With him apples were not particularly popular, but he found peaches so desirable that he rarely waited to cut and peel them, preferring to let the juices flow liberally down his royal chin. The culinary rage, however, was peas imported from Genoa for the first time in 1660. According to Mme de Maintenon, Louis XIV's second wife, the entire court was obsessed with "impatience to eat them."

Today, *Les Potagers du Roi* are maintained by about half a dozen gardeners under the direction of the École Nationale du Paysage. It manages to intersperse the fruits and vegetables once favored by the monarchs with experimental breeds and hundreds of splendidly espaliered fruit trees.

Antoinette, who could escape the rigors of court here, and a retreat for Louis XV and his mistress, Madame du Barry. Both Grand and Petit Trianon are open Tuesday through Sunday from 10am to 5pm. Admission to the Grand Trianon costs 25F ($5) for adults, 15F ($3) for adults after 3:30pm and those 18 to 25, and is free for those under 18 and over 60. Admission to the Petit Trianon is 15F ($3) for adults, 10F ($2) for adults over 3:30pm and those under 18 and over 60. Admission to both Trianons is 30F ($6) for adults, 20F ($4) is the reduced rate.

EVENING SPECTACLES The tourist office in Versailles (see above) offers a program of evening fireworks and illuminated fountains on several occasions throughout the summer. These spectacles are announced a full season in advance. The dates usually fall on Saturday night, although the schedules change from year to year. Spectators sit on bleachers clustered at the boulevard de la Reine entrance to the Basin of Neptune. The most desirable seats cost 250F ($50), and standing room sells for 70F ($14); it's free for children under 10. Gates that admit you to the Grande Fête de Nuit de Versailles open 1¹/₂ hours before show time.

Tickets can be purchased in advance at the tourist office in Versailles—inquire by phone, fax, or mail. In Paris, **Agence Perroissier,** 6 place de la Madeleine, 8e (☎ 01-42-60-58-31), and **Agence des Théâtres,** 78 av. des Champs-Elysées, 8e

Versailles

To Paris

To St-Germain

To Rambouillet & Chartres

0   500 m
     550 y

N

Gare Rive Droite

Gare Rive Gauche

rue Berthier

bd. de la Reine

rue de la Paroisse

rue Carnot

av. de St-Cloud

av. de Paris

av. des Sceaux

rue de l'Orangerie

rue d'Anjou

rue Hardy

bd. du Roi

rue des Réservoirs

Place d'Armes

St-Cyr

petite av. de St-Antoine

rue de l'Ermitage

av. de St-Antoine

av. de Trianon

allée de Rendez-vous

allée du Hal

allée des Hal

allée des Matelots

allée de Bailly

Garden of Versailles

Grand Canal

Petit Canal

allée des Filles d'Honneur

allée de la Reine

allée des paons

route de

St-Cyr

LEGEND

✝ Church
✉ Post Office

Carriage Museum ⑧
Cathédrale St-Louis ⑤
Château ⑤
Grand Trianon ③
Hamlet (Hameau) ①
Lambinet Museum ⑥
Library ⑩
Notre-Dame ⑦
Petit Trianon ②
Royal Stables ⑧
Tourist Information ④
Town Hall (Hôtel de Ville) ⑨

PARIS

Versailles

3-0166

(☎ 01-43-59-24-60), also sell tickets. If you've just arrived in Versailles from Paris, you can take your chances and purchase tickets an hour ahead of show time at boulevard de la Reine. The show lasts 1¹/₂ hours.

From May until mid-October, a less elaborate spectacle is staged each Sunday. Called *Les Grandes Eaux Musicales*, it is a display of fountains in the park and costs only 25F ($5). Classical music is also played.

WHERE TO DINE

e Potager du Roy. 1 rue du Maréchal Joffre. ☎ 01-39-50-35-34. Reservations required. Main courses 80–190F ($16–$38); fixed-price menu 169F ($34). AE, MC, V. Tues–Sat noon–:30pm and 7:30–10:30pm. FRENCH.

Philippe Letourneur has emerged as a formidably talented chef in his own right. After spending years perfecting a distinctive cuisine, he now adds breaths of novelty to Versailles's jaded and world-weary dining scene. His attractive restaurant occupies an 18th-century building within a neighborhood that was known during the days of the French monarchs as the Parc des Cerfs ("Stag Park"). Here any courtier bored with rituals at the nearby palace, could find paid companionship with B- and C-list courtesans whose domain never attained the status of such A-list persons as the mistresses to the kings. The skillfully prepared menu items the chef serves within his trio of modern dining rooms are rotated, or reinvented, with the seasons. Examples include foie gras served with a vegetable-flavored vinaigrette, a ragout of macaroni with a *persillade* of snails; and roasted codfish served with creamed spinach and creamy croutons. Looking for something earthy and unusual? Try the *fondant* of pork jowls with a confit of fresh vegetables. One of our favorite less esoteric dishes is the supreme of turbot braised with fresh endive and herbs. Note that this restaurant derives its name from the nearby King's Kitchen Gardens (Les Potagers du Roi; see the box "Peaches & Peas Fit for a King," above).

✪ **Le Quai No. 1.** 1 av. de St-Cloud. ☎ 01-39-50-42-26. Reservations required. Main courses 80–150F ($16–$30); fixed-price menu 120–168F ($24–$34). MC, V. Tues–Sun noon–2pm; Tues–Sat 7:30–10:30pm. FRENCH.

Megachef Gérard Vié, along with his on-site manager, Dominique de Ravel, serve an elegant cuisine at this mostly seafood restaurant overlooking the château's western facade. Lithographs and wood paneling spangle the dining room, and outside there's a terrace. Though the cuisine isn't as opulent, esoteric, or expensive as what's served within Vié's main restaurant, the above-recommended Les Trois Marchés, it's charming, very French, and dependable in presentation. The fixed-price menus make Le Quai a dining bargain in high-priced Versailles. Specialties include seafood sauerkraut, seafood paella, bouillabaisse, and home-smoked salmon. The chef recommends the seafood platter. Care and imagination go into the cuisine, and the service is both professional and polite. Devourers of the earth and air appreciate the trio of meat-based main courses, two of the best of which include a magret of duckling dressed with aged vinegar, and a navarin of lamb.

Les Trois Marchés. In the Hôtel Trianon Palace, 1 bd. de la Reine. ☎ 01-30-84-38-40. Reservations required. Main courses 220–350F ($44–$70); set menus 300F ($60) (available only at lunch Tues–Fri) and 500–700F ($100–$140). AE, DC, MC, V. Tues–Sat noon–2pm and 7:30–10pm. FRENCH.

For lunch, you can dine regally at the Trianon Palace Hotel. Situated in a 5-acre garden, the hotel became world-famous in 1919 when it served as headquarters for signatories to the Treaty of Versailles. The dining room still retains an old-world splendor in its crystal chandeliers and fluted columns. The chef, Gérard Vié, is the most talented and creative chef in Versailles these days. He attracts a discerning clientele who don't mind paying the high prices. His *cuisine moderne* is subtle, often daringly conceived and inventive, the service smooth. Begin with a lobster salad flavored with fresh herbs and served with an onion soufflé, or perhaps the citrus-flavored bisque of scallops. You'll realize the chef is a great innovator when you taste his main courses, especially his pigeon roasted and flavored with rosé and accompanied by celeriac and truffles. Another favorite is the filet of sea bass with a "cake" of eggplant. The best dessert? It's impossible to decide, so opt for the signature assortment.

2 Fontainebleau

37 miles S of Paris, 46 miles NE of Orléans

Set within the vestiges of a forest (*Forêt de Fontainebleau*) that bear its name, this suburb of Paris has offered refuge to French monarchs throughout the tides of French history. Kings from the Renaissance valued it because of its nearness to rich hunting grounds and its distance from the slums and smells of contemporary Paris, and Napoléon referred to the Palais de Fontainebleau, which he re-embellished with his distinctive monogram and decorative style, as "the house of the centuries." Many pivotal or decisive events have occurred inside, perhaps no moment more memorable than when Napoléon stood on the horseshoe-shaped exterior stairway and bade farewell to his shattered army before departing to Elba. The scene of his exile has been the subject of seemingly countless paintings, including Vernet's *Les Adieux.*

ESSENTIALS

GETTING THERE   If you stay for lunch, a trip to Fontainebleau should last a half day. **Trains** to Fontainebleau depart from the Gare de Lyon in Paris; the trip takes from 35 minutes to an hour. The Fontainebleau station is just outside the town in Avon. The town bus makes the 2-mile trip to the château every 10 to 15 minutes Monday to Saturday (every 30 minutes on Sunday). A one-way ticket costs 8.70F ($1.75).

By car, take A6 south from Paris, exit onto N191, and follow the signs.

ORIENTATION   Dominated by its château, the town is surrounded by the dense Forêt de Fontainebleau. The main squares are place du Général-de-Gaulle and place d'Armes. The **Office de Tourisme** is at Avon 4, rue Royale (☎ **01-60-74-99-99**).

✪ THE PALACE

Napoléon's affection for Fontainebleau was understandable. He was following the pattern of a succession of French kings in the pre-Versailles days who used Fontainebleau as a resort and hunted in its magnificent forests. François I, who tried to turn the hunting lodge into a royal palace in the Italian Renaissance style, brought along several artists, including Benvenuto Cellini, to work for him.

Under this patronage, the School of Fontainebleau gained prestige, led by the painters Rosso Fiorentino and Primaticcio. The artists adorned the 210-foot long **Gallery of François I.** Stucco-framed panels depict such scenes as *The Rape of Europa,* and the monarch holding a pomegranate, a symbol of unity. The salamander, the symbol of the Chevalier King, is everywhere.

Sometimes called the Gallery of Henri II, the **Ballroom** displays the interlaced initials h&d, referring to Henri and his mistress, Diane de Poitiers. Competing with this illicit tandem are the initials h&c, symbolizing Henri and his ho-hum wife, Catherine de Médicis. At one end of the room is a monumental fireplace supported by two bronze satyrs, made in 1966 (the originals were melted down during the French

Revolution). At the other side is the balcony of the musicians, with sculptured garlands. The ceiling displays octagonal coffering adorned with rosettes. Above the wainscoting is a series of frescoes, painted between 1550 and 1558, which depict such mythological subjects as *The Feast of Bacchus.*

An architectural curiosity is the richly and elegantly adorned **Louis XV Staircase.** The room above it was originally decorated by Primaticcio for the bedroom of the duchesse d'Etampes, but when an architect was designing the stairway, he simply ripped out her floor. Of the Italian frescoes that were preserved, one depicts the queen of the Amazons climbing into Alexander the Great's bed.

When Louis XIV ascended to the throne, he neglected Fontainebleau because of his preoccupation with Versailles. However, he wasn't opposed to using the palace for houseguests, specifically such unwanted ones as Queen Christina, who had abdicated the throne of Sweden in a fit of religious fervor. Under the assumption that she still had "divine right," she ordered the brutal murder of her companion Monaldeschi, who had ceased to please her.

Louis XV, and later, Marie Antoinette, also took an interest in Fontainebleau.

The château found renewed glory under Napoléon. You can wander around much of the palace on your own, visiting sites that evoke his 19th-century imperial heyday. They include the throne room, the room where he abdicated his rulership of France, his offices, his monumental bedroom, and his bathroom. Some of the smaller **Napoleonic Rooms,** especially those containing his personal mementos and artifacts, are accessible by guided tour only.

After your long trek through the palace, visit the gardens and, especially, the carp pond; the gardens, however, are only a prelude to the Forest of Fontainebleau.

The **interior** (☎ **01-60-71-50-70**) is open Wednesday through Monday from 9:30am to 12:30pm and from 2 to 5pm. In July and August, it's open Wednesday through Monday from 9:30am to 6pm. A combination ticket allowing visitors to the *grands appartements,* the Napoleonic Rooms, and the Chinese Museum costs 35F ($7) for adults and 23F ($4.60) for students 18 to 25; children under 18 are admitted free. A ticket allowing access to the *petits appartements* goes for 16F ($3.20) for adults; 12F ($2.40) for students 18 to 25. Children under 18 are admitted free.

WHERE TO STAY & DINE

Le Beauharnais. In the Grand Hôtel de l'Aigle Noir, 27 place Napoléon-Bonaparte. ☎ **01-60-74-60-00.** Fax 01-60-74-60-01. Reservations required. Main courses 140–280F ($28–$56); fixed-price menus 180–450F ($36–$90). AE, DC, MC, V. Daily noon–2pm and 7:30–9:30pm. Closed Dec 25 to Jan 1. FRENCH.

This is the town's leading restaurant, which, although it's been completely renovated, still retains its old charm. Opposite the château, the building was once the home of the Cardinal dé Retz. It dates from the 16th century and was converted into a hotel in 1720. The restaurant was installed in a former courtyard. The beautiful interior is filled with Empire furniture and potted palms. The food has greatly improved in recent years, and the only establishment to give it serious competition is **François 1er** at 3 rue Royale. The refreshing menu includes such classics as Rouen roast duckling, but also dishes with more flair and subtlety, including sweetbreads with foie gras. The perfectly prepared grilled pigeon with pistachio nuts evokes Morocco. There is a changing variety of dishes, depending upon seasonal availability.

The hotel has 51 bedrooms and 6 suites, all with private baths and TVs, radios, minibars, direct-dial phones, double windows, and electric heating. The hotel also boasts a swimming pool, sauna, and fitness center. Each is individually decorated, often with antiques and pleasantly tasteful colors. Doubles range in price from 790F to 1,050F ($158 to $210) suites from 1,200F ($240).

Fontainebleau

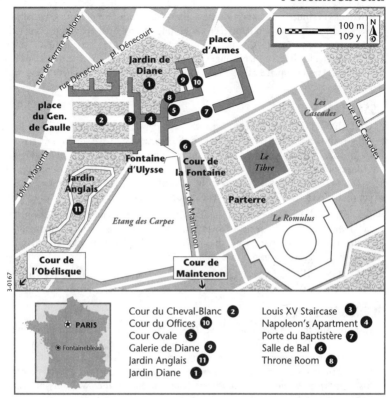

Cour du Cheval-Blanc **2**
Cour du Offices **10**
Cour Ovale **5**
Galerie de Diane **9**
Jardin Anglais **11**
Jardin Diane **1**

Louis XV Staircase **3**
Napoleon's Apartment **4**
Porte du Baptistère **7**
Salle de Bal **6**
Throne Room **8**

★ PARIS

● Fontainebleau

Le Caveau des Ducs. 24 rue de Ferrare. ☎ **01-64-22-05-05.** Reservations recommended. Main courses 90–125F ($18–$25); fixed-price menus 105–240F ($21–$48). AE, MC, V. Daily noon–2pm and 7–10pm. FRENCH.

Deep underground, beneath a series of 17th-century stone vaults built by the same masons who laid the cobblestones of the rue de Ferrare upstairs, is this reasonably priced restaurant occupying what once was a storage cellar for the nearby château. Wood and flickering candles preserve the illusion. The restaurant isn't in the same league as the grand cuisine leaders like Le Beauharnais: Its helpful staff offers simpler food in a more dramatic setting. Competently prepared, each dish could stand in a museum of French food of the 1950s: snails in garlic butter, roast leg of lamb with garlic-and-rosemary sauce, and virtually everything that can be done with the body of a duck. The fillet of rump steak is quite tasty, especially when served in a brie sauce, as are the platter of sole, crayfish tails, and salmon on a bed of pasta.

3 Saint-Germain-en-Laye

13 miles NW of Paris

Saint-Germain-en-Laye served as the seat of the royal court for centuries, and was even home to Louis XIV until he decided to build that little place in Versailles. Over the years, people have traditionally fled Paris for Saint-Germain-en-Laye during the hot summer months in hopes of cooling off, even though it is only 13 miles away. Today, this *très riche* bedroom community with its fancy boutiques and rural environs continues to maintain a certain allure for the citizens of Paris, especially on weekends. Part of its popularity centers around the forested areas that border the town. It is the perfect environment to carry on *en plein aire,* doing healthful things like walking, jogging, or picnicking. Of course, St-Germain-en-Laye is perhaps best known as the birthplace of béarnaise sauce, which was invented here along with pommes soufflés in 1447.

ESSENTIALS

GETTING THERE   Expect to spend a half day seeing Saint-Germain-en-Laye. RER **trains** from Paris leave regularly for St-Germain-en-Laye. From the very center of Paris, the trip takes about 30 minutes; a one-way ticket costs 20F ($4). The St-Germain-en-Laye station is located just across the street from the château.

By car, either take the N13 west out of Paris (direction St-Germain-en-Laye) or get on the A13 traveling west and take the St-Germain-en-Laye exit.

ORIENTATION   The town sits on the left bank of the Seine river. The large Parc St. Germaine is near the center of town and is bordered on its left side by the Château Vieux. Just across the street from the château is the RER station, and pedestrian and shopping streets then fan out to the south and east.

VISITOR INFORMATION   The **Office de Tourisme** is at 38 rue Au-Pain (☎ 01-34-51-05-12).

SEEING THE SIGHTS

Just opposite the St-Germain-en-Laye RER station stands the **Château Vieux,** place du Château (☎ 01-34-51-53-65), a brick and stone castle built by François I on a promontory overlooking the Seine in the 12th century. It served as a court in exile to the Stuart king of England, James II, who stayed here in the expectation that his supporters would wrest the throne from the Protestants William and Mary. (They never did.) Later Napoléon III ordered that the château be turned into a museum to display France's rich history beginning with the cave dwellers from the last ice age through to the Carolingian era. His orders were carried out to the letter and, today, two floors of the château are devoted to the **French Museum of National Antiquities,** where visitors can view displays of stone and metal tools, weapons, and jewelry used or worn by the early settlers of Gaul. **La Chapelle** is the oldest part of the château and was built by St. Louis in the 1230s. Although not actually part of the château proper, visitors can still walk through **Le Nôtre's Gardens** next door and admire the planned form of traditional French landscape design. The building is open Wednesday through Monday from 9am to 5:15pm; the gardens open daily from 7am to 8pm. Admission is 25F ($5) for adults, children under 18 are free.

Built in 1678 by the marquise de Montespan, a paramour of Louis XIV, the building that houses **Le Musée Départmental Maurice Denis "Le Prieuré,"** 2 bis rue Maurice-Denis (☎ 01-39-73-77-87), was lived in by the painter Maurice Denis from World War I until his death in 1943. It was here that he befriended a group of artists, known as "Nabis," including Paul Serusier. The museum has collections of works by Nabis masters such as Bonnard and Vuillard, along with members of the Pont-Avon group, including Gauguin and Emile Bernard. Works by other artists, including Toulouse-Lautrec, are exhibited as well. You can also visit La Chapelle St-Louis, a chapel decorated by Denis, as well as his workshop. The museum is open Wednesday through Friday from 10am to 5:30pm and Saturday to Sunday from 10am to 6:30pm. Admission is 25F ($5) for adults, 15F ($3) for students and seniors, and free for children under 12.

WHERE TO STAY & DINE

Cazaudehore. In the Hôtel La Forestière, 1 av. du Président-Kennedy. ☎ **01-39-10-38-38.** Fax 01-39-73-73-88. Reservations required. Main courses 110–170F ($22–$34); fixed-price menu 360F ($72) on Sat–Sun; fixed-price lunch 260F ($52) on Mon–Fri. AE, MC, V. Tues–Sun 12:30pm–2:30pm and 7:30–10:30pm. FRENCH.

Since its opening in 1982 by Jean-Baptiste Cazaudehore and his wife, Liliane, this restaurant has offered guests an unpretentious tradition of refined quality. The dining rooms, with their large fireplaces, are filled with a unique collection of furniture and paintings from the past, creating a warm and inviting atmosphere. In the summer months, guests can dine in the English garden that surrounds the restaurant. The menu changes with the seasons and tends to have characteristic undertones from southwestern France. Typical main courses may include roasted lamb filet served with orange polenta, truffled duck with braised new potatoes, and escalope of fresh foie gras with gingerbread and corn galette.

In addition to taking over the restaurant, the Cazaudehore's son, Pierre, has transformed the family's country house into an auberge-style hotel, La Forestière, with 25 rooms and 5 suites. The bedrooms range from small to large, and furnishings range from a classic Louis XIV style to a modern, contemporary look. Some rooms have a private balcony; others offer private terraces. A double costs 980F ($196) and suites start at 1,050F ($210). All rooms have minibar, TV, and telephone.

Le Pavillon Henri IV. 21 rue Thiers, 78100 St-Germain-en-Laye. ☎ **01-39-10-15-15.** Fax 01-39-73-93-73. TV TEL. 1,000–1,300F ($200–$260) double. AE, DC, MC, V.

This luxurious hotel dates from the 1500s when Henri IV, possibly the most promiscuous French king of a very randy bunch, built the Château Neuf as a terraced hideaway for his illegitimate children. It was later bequeathed to the comte d'Artois, the brother of Louis XVI, who had it slated for demolition. Thanks to a little affair known today as the French revolution, the château remained intact. Partially rebuilt in 1836, it now houses Le Pavillon Henri IV, where Dumas wrote *The Three Musketeers.* Standing at the edge of the belvedere gardens, originally laid out during the Renaissance, it is still elegantly old-fashioned. A corner room has been set aside in remembrance of where the Sun King romped with Madame de Montespan. A chapel in one of the wings has beautifully preserved painted ceilings. The handsome guest rooms vary in size but are all classically outfitted with antiques from Louis XIV to Louis XVI; many rooms have a panoramic view of the Seine valley.

The refined atmosphere of the hotel carries through to its restaurant which fills with sunlight on fair-weather days. The restaurant specializes in traditional French dishes like *rognon de veau* (veal kidney) *dijonnaise, carré d'agneau rôti* (roast lamb), and *pommes soufflés* (boiled and mashed potatoes dropped into hot oil—the result is an airy, crispy form resembling a french fried potato, but much lighter), which were invented here in 1447 along with sauce béarnaise, which is just the thing to top your chateaubriand. Most à la carte lunches and dinners cost between 300F and 400F ($60 and $80) without wine; and the fixed-price lunch is available Monday through Friday for 240F ($48).

4 Chantilly

26 miles N of Paris, 31 miles SE of Beauvais

This is a resort town for Parisians who want a quick getaway for *le weekend.* Known for its frothy whipped cream and black lace, it also draws visitors for its racetrack and château. The first two Sundays in June are the highlight of the turf season, bringing out an exceedingly fashionable crowd.

ESSENTIALS

GETTING THERE Seeing the major sights in Chantilly takes about 4 hours. **Trains** depart frequently for Chantilly from the Gare du Nord in Paris; the ride takes about an hour. By **car,** take the N-16 north, which runs directly to Chantilly.

VISITOR INFORMATION The **Office de Tourisme** is at 60 av. du Maréchal-Joffre (☎ **03-44-57-08-58**). Call ☎ **01-49-10-20-30** for horse racing information.

SEEING THE SIGHTS

Once the seat of the Condé, **Château de Chantilly** (☎ **03-44-62-62-62**) and **Musée Condé** are on an artificial carp-stocked lake. You approach via the same forested drive that Louis XIV, along with hundreds of guests, rode along for a banquet prepared by Vatel, one of the best-known French chefs. One day when the fish didn't arrive on time, Vatel committed suicide. The château is French Renaissance, with gabled and domed towers, but bears evidence of a substantial 19th-century rebuilding. It's skirted by a forest once filled with stag and boar.

In 1886 the château's owner, the duc d'Aumale, bequeathed the park and palace to the Institut de France, along with his fabulous art collection and library. The château boasts sumptuous furnishings as well as works by artists like Memling, van Dyck, Botticelli, Poussin, Watteau, Ingres, Delacroix, Corot, Rubens, and Vernet. See especially Raphael's *Madonna of Lorette, Virgin of the House d'Orléans,* and *Three Graces* (sometimes called the *Three Ages of Woman*). The foremost French painter of the 15th century, Jean Fouquet, is represented here by a series of about 40 miniatures. A copy of the rose diamond that received worldwide attention when it was stolen in 1926 is on display in the jewel collection. One of the most celebrated Condé library acquisitions is *Les Très riches heures du duc de Berri,* a 15th-century manuscript that used gold leaf and azure inks to illuminate prayers and meditations appropriate to a season, month, day, or hour. This book of hours, executed by the goldsmiths Pol, Jan, and Herman Limbourg, is thought to be the finest in existence.

The château was built about 1560 by Jean Bullant for one of the members of the Montmorency family. The stables (see below), a hallmark of French 18th-century architecture, were constructed to house 240 horses with adjacent kennels for 500 hounds. If you have time, take a walk in the garden laid out by Le Nôtre. A hamlet of rustic cottages and the Maison de Sylvie, a graceful building constructed in 1604 and rebuilt by Maria-Felice Orsini, are in the park.

The château is open March to October, Wednesday to Monday from 10am to 6pm; November to February, Wednesday to Monday from 10:30am to 12:45pm and 2 to 5pm. Admission is 39F ($7.80) for adults, 34F ($6.80) for children 12 to 18, and 12F ($2.40) for children 3 to 11.

Musée Vivant du Cheval, rue du Connétable (☎ **03-44-57-40-40**), occupies the restored Grandes Ecuries, the stables built between 1719 and 1735 for Louis-Henri, prince de Bourbon and prince de Condé, who occupied the château. Besides being fond of horses, he believed in reincarnation and expected to come back as a horse in his next life; therefore he built stables fit for a king.

The stables and an adjoining kennel fell into ruins over a couple of centuries, but they've now been restored as a museum of the living horse, with thoroughbreds housed alongside old breeds of draft horses, Arabs and Hispano-Arabs, and farm horses. Yves Bienaimé, the certified riding instructor who established the museum, presents exhibitions tracing the horse's association with humans, as well as a blacksmith shop and displays of saddles, equipment for the care of horses, and racing memorabilia. In April, September, and October, it's open Wednesday to Monday from 10:30am to 5:30pm; in May and June, daily from 10:30am to 5:30pm; in July and August, Wednesday to Monday from 10:30am to 5:30pm and Tuesday from 2 to 5:30pm; and November to March, Wednesday to Monday from 2 to 5pm. There are three equestrian displays per day: April to October at 11:30am, 3:30pm, and 5:15pm; the rest of the year there's one display, at 3:30pm. These last about half an hour and explain how the horse is ridden and trained. The first weekend of each month equestrian shows are presented. A restaurant on the premises, **Le caroussel Gourmand** (☎ 03-44-57-19-77), features the specialties of Picardy, and does so exceedingly well.

Two of the great horse races of France, **Le Prix du Jockey Club** (June 1 at 2pm) and the **Prix Diane-Hermès** (June 8 at 2pm), take place at the Hippodrome de Chantilly. Thoroughbreds from as far away as Kentucky and Brunei, as well as mounts sponsored by the old and new fortunes of Europe compete in a very civil format that's broadcast around France and talked about in horsey circles around the world. On race days, as many as 30 trains depart from Paris's Gare du Nord for Chantilly, where they are met with free shuttle buses to the track. Alternatively, buses depart on race days from Place de la République and Porte de St-Cloud, on a schedule that coincides with the beginning and end of the races. Call ☎ 01-49-10-20-30 for more information.

WHERE TO DINE

Le Relais Condé. 42 av. du Maréchal-Joffre. ☎ **03-44-57-05-75.** Reservations recommended. Main courses 95–140F ($19–$28); fixed-price menus Wed–Fri only 120–163F ($24–$33). AE, MC, V. Thurs–Mon noon–2:30pm and Wed–Mon 7–10pm. FRENCH.

The once-Anglican chapel that contains this restaurant was built during the 19th century for the many English horse owners who used to race at the nearby race track. This building was expanded to serve the gourmet demands of today's horse-loving patrons—many of whom inhabit villas in the surrounding countryside—and the tourists who come here to visit the château. The owner has provided a somber setting for traditional dishes that include appetizers like duckling foie gras, cassoulet of snails Burgundy style, and gratin of crayfish. Main dishes include grilled fillet of beef with béarnaise sauce and roasted scallops doused with whisky for extra flavor. The chef prepares a perfect duck and offers such seasonal favorites as veal kidneys and lamb cutlets. For dessert, try the black-chocolate mousse. Note that some dishes may come with too much cream for modern tastes. The unremarkable wine list includes some vintages from throughout France. A garden provides outdoor dining.

5 Malmaison

10 miles W of Paris, 3 miles NW of St-Cloud

In the 9th century the Normans landed in this area and devastated the countryside, hence the name of this suburb of Paris, which translates to "bad house."

ESSENTIALS

GETTING THERE It takes about 3 hours to get to Malmaison and to see the chateau. **By train,** take the RER A-1 line from place Charles-de-Gaulle–Etoile to La Défense. Transfer to bus no. 258 for the 6-mile ride to the chateau (stop Rueil-Malmaison). **By car,** take the N-13 west to Rueil-Malmaison.

SEEING THE CHÂTEAU

Construction on the **Château de Malmaison,** avenue du Château (☎ **01-41-29-05-55**), which was used as a country retreat far removed from the Tuileries or Compiègne, began in 1622. It was purchased in 1799 by Joséphine Bonaparte,

Napoléon's wife, who had it restored and fashionably decorated as a "love nest." She then enlarged the estate (but not the château). Popular references to Malmaison as having been a lepers' sanitarium are unfounded.

Today Malmaison is filled with mementos from Napoléon's euphoric early days as a general shortly after the Revolution, and during his rise to power as First Consul of France. The veranda and council room were obviously inspired by the tent Napoléon occupied on his military campaigns, and filled with Empire-style furnishings. His study and desk are exhibited in the library. Marie-Louise, his second wife, took Napoléon's books with her when she left France; however, these books were purchased by an English couple who presented them to the museum here. Most of the furnishings are original; some came from the Tuileries and St-Cloud. Napoléon always had a sentimental attachment to Malmaison, and he spent a week here before his departure for St. Helena.

Napoléon's court artists were no fools: In their portraits and sculpture they made a god of the little emperor—see, for example, David's equestrian portrait of Napoléon and Gérard's flattering portrait of Joséphine.

In 1809, following her divorce because she couldn't bear Napoléon an heir, Joséphine retired here and was passionately devoted to her roses until her death in 1814 at the age of 51. The roses in the garden today are a fitting memorial. The bed in which Joséphine died is exhibited, as is her toilette kit, including her toothbrush.

Also here is the small **Château de Bois-Préau** (follow the signs through the park, a 5-minute walk from the main building). Originally built in 1700, and acquired (some say "annexed") by Joséphine in 1810, it's smaller, darker, and sadder, and less architecturally distinguished than Malmaison itself. The château (actually, more of a villa since its reconstruction in 1854, 30 years after Joséphine's death) is a museum/shrine to the emperor's exile on the isolated Atlantic outpost of St. Helena, after his fall from grace. (In case you're interested, all is revealed here: Napoléon preferred boxers to briefs.) Coverage of the years between his rise to power (as exhibited at Malmaison) and his disgrace and death on St. Helena can best be viewed in the Napoleonic museum in the Château of Fontainebleau (see above).

Admission to Malmaison, which includes entrance to Bois Préau, if it's open, costs 30F ($6) Monday and Wednesday to Saturday and 20F ($4) on Sunday; children 17 and under and students enter free. Between May and October, Malmaison is open Monday and Wednesday through Friday from 9:30am to noon and 1:30 to 5pm, and Saturday and Sunday from 10am to 5:30pm. During the period, Bois Préau is open only from Thursday through Sunday from 12:30 to 6pm. From November to April both châteaux close a half hour earlier.

6 Vaux-le-Vicomte

29 miles SE of Paris, 12 miles NE of Fontainebleau

ESSENTIALS

GETTING THERE Despite its nearness to Paris, Vaux-le-Vicomte is inconvenient to reach if you lack an automobile. Once you get there, allow 2 hours to see the château. **By car,** take the N-6 southeast from Paris to Melun, which is 3³/₄ miles west of the château. **By train,** you'll need to take the 45-minute ride from Gare de Lyon to Melun first, then take one of the taxis lining up at the railway station for the jaunt to Vaux-le-Vicomte.

✪ SEEING THE CHÂTEAU

Château de Vaux-le-Vicomte, 77950 Maincy (**01-64-14-41-90**), was built in 1656 for Nicolas Fouquet, Louis XIV's ill-fated finance minister. Louis wasn't at all pleased that Fouquet was able to live so extravagantly at Vaux-le-Vicomte, hosting banquets that rivaled the king's. Then Louis discovered that Fouquet had embezzled funds from the country's treasury—the king was not amused. After Fouquet's swift arrest, Louis hired the same artists and architects who had built Vaux-le-Vicomte to begin the grand task of creating Versailles. If you visit both you'll see the striking similarities between the two monuments to the *grand siècle.*

The view of the château from the main gate will reveal the splendor of 17th-century France. On the south side, a majestic staircase sweeps toward the formal gardens, designed by Le Nôtre. The grand canal, flanked by waterfalls, divides the lush greenery. The château's interior, now a private residence, is completely furnished and decorated with 17th-century pieces. The great entrance hall leads to 12 state rooms, including the oval rotunda. Many of the rooms are hung with Gobelin tapestries and decorated with painted ceiling and wall panels by Le Brun, with sculpture by Girardon. A tour of the interior includes Fouquet's personal suite, the huge basement with its wine cellar, the servants' dining room, and the copper-filled kitchen.

A **carriage museum** is housed in the stables. The carriages are of three types—country, town, and sports and hunting. Some 25 perfectly restored 18th- and 19th-century carriages are on exhibit, with mannequin horses and people. Hours are the same as that of the château itself, and entrance is included in the price of admission to the château.

From May to mid-October, **candlelight evenings** are held every Saturday from 8:30 to 11pm, when you can visit the château under the light of more than a thousand candles. On those evenings, the Ecureuil cafeteria (below) and carriage museum stay open until midnight. On the second and last Saturday of each month the fountains of the 13 main pools bubble from 3 to 6pm.

Admission is 56F ($11.20) for adults, 46F ($9.20) for children 6 to 15, and free for children 5 and under. The château is open only from April to October, daily from 10am to 6pm. Additionally, on a schedule that varies with whatever school holidays happen to be in effect at the time, the château is open during most of March and from November 1 to 11, daily from 11am to 5pm.

WHERE TO DINE

Restaurant l'Ecureuil. At the Château de Vaux-le-Vicomte. ☎ **01-60-66-95-66.** Main dish of the day 45–55F ($9–$11); children's menu 49F ($9.80). AE, V. Sun–Fri 11am–6pm, Sat 11:30am–11pm. Open Apr–Oct. FRENCH.

The only place to eat in the village is this dull self-service eatery near the château's entrance, in what was once the stables. You can order suprême of chicken in white-wine sauce, steak in red-wine sauce with gratinéed potatoes, and fillet of sole with butter-and-parsley sauce. For more formal meals, try the nearby town of Melun.

Although there are many grand and expensive restaurants in and around Melun, your best bet in town is **La Melunoise,** 5 rue Gatinais (☎ **01-64-39-68-27**), known for its superb French viands. The chef brings out the best in fine, sometimes luxurious, ingredients, and meals cost from 135F ($27). Closed August, Sunday and Monday nights, and Saturday.

7 Rambouillet

34 miles SW of Paris, 26 miles NE of Chartres

Once known as La Foret d'Yveline, the Forest of Rambouillet is one of the loveliest woods in France. More than 47,000 acres of greenery stretch from the valley of the Eure to the high valley of Chevreuse, the latter rich in medieval and royal abbeys. The lakes, copses of hiding deer, and even wild boar are some of the attractions of this "green lung."

ESSENTIALS

GETTING THERE It takes 2 hours to see the chateau at Rambouillet. **Trains** depart from Paris's Gare Montparnasse every 20 minutes throughout the day. One-way passage costs 41F ($8.20) for a ride of about 35 minutes. Information and **train schedules** can be obtained by contacting La Gare de Rambouillet, place Prud'homme (☎ 01-53-90-20-20). By **car,** take the N-10 southwest from Paris, passing Versailles along the way.

VISITOR INFORMATION The **tourist office** is at the Hôtel de Ville, place de la Libération (☎ 01-34-83-21-21).

SEEING THE SIGHTS

George Pompidou used to visit the château here, as did Louis XVI and Charles de Gaulle. Dating from 1375, the **Château de Rambouillet,** Parc du Château (☎ 01-34-83-00-25) is surrounded by a park in one of the most famous forests in France. Before the château became a royal residence, the marquise de Rambouillet kept house here; it is said she taught the cultured ladies and gentlemen of Paris how to talk, introducing them to a long gaudy string of poets and painters.

François I, the Chevalier King, died of a fever at Rambouillet in 1547 at the age of 52. When the château was later occupied by the comte de Toulouse, Rambouillet was often visited by Louis XV, who was amused (in more ways than one) by the comte's witty and high-spirited wife. Louis XVI acquired the château, but his wife, Marie Antoinette, was bored with the place and called it "the toad." In his surprisingly modest boudoir are four panels representing the continents.

In 1814, Napoléon's second wife, Marie-Louise (daughter of Francis II, emperor of Austria), met at Rambouillet with her father, who convinced her to abandon Napoléon and France itself after her husband's humiliating defeats at Moscow and Leipzig. Afterwards, she fled to her original home, the royal court in Vienna, with Napoléon's 3-year-old son, François-Charles-Joseph Bonaparte (also known as l'Aiglon, the young eagle, and, at least in title, the King of Rome). Later, before his death in Vienna at the age of 21, his claim on the Napoleonic legacy would be rejected by France's enemies, despite the fact that his father had had a special annex to the château at Rambouillet built especially for his use.

A year later, before his final exile to the remote island of St. Helena, a British colony in the south Atlantic, Napoléon insisted on spending one final night in the château of Rambouillet, where he secluded himself, according to witnesses, with his meditations and memories.

In 1830, the elderly Charles X, Louis XVI's brother, abdicated the throne of France at Rambouillet as a Parisian mob marched on the château, and his troops began to desert him. From Rambouillet, he embarked for a safe, but politically controversial, haven in England.

Following that, Rambouillet became privately owned. At one time it was a fashionable restaurant, attracting Parisians, who could also go for rides in gondolas.

Napoléon III, however, returned it to the Crown. In 1897 it was designated as a residence for the presidents of the Republic. In 1944, Charles de Gaulle lived here briefly before giving the order for the remnants of the French army to join the Americans in liberating Paris.

Superb woodwork is used throughout, and the walls are adorned with tapestries, many dating from the era of Louis XV.

The château is open Wednesday to Monday: April 1 to September 30 from 10 to 11:30am and 2 to 5:30pm, and October 1 to the end of March from 10am to 11:30am and 2 to 4:30pm. Admission is 30F ($6) for adults and 18F ($3.60) for children 11 and under.

WHERE TO DINE

La Poste. 101 av. du Général-de-Gaulle. ☎ **01-34-83-03-01.** Reservations recommended Sat–Sun. Main courses 70–120F ($14–$24); fixed-price menu 74F ($15; Mon–Fri only), and 103–190F ($21–$38). AE, MC, V. Tues–Sun noon–2pm and Tues–Sat 7–10pm. FRENCH.

Set on a street corner in the town's historic center, across from the Sous-Préfecture de Police, this restaurant has been serving food since the mid–19th century, when it provided meals and shelter for the region's mail carriers. The two dining rooms are outfitted with rustic beams and old-fashioned accents that complement the flavorful, old-fashioned food that has been a staple here since the beginning. Good-tasting menu items include homemade terrines of foie gras and freshly made pastries. Main courses of note include fricassée of chicken with crayfish and noisettes of lamb prepared "in the style of roebuck" with copious amounts of red wine and herbs. A particularly flavorful, two-fisted dish that appeals to beef-lovers is a fillet of beef served with a Perigueux sauce composed of Madeira wine and foie gras.

8 Disneyland Paris

20 miles E of Paris

After evoking some of the most enthusiastic and controversial reactions in recent French history, the multimillion-dollar Euro Disney Resort opened in 1992 as one of the most lavish theme parks in the world. In 1994, it unofficially changed its name to "Disneyland Paris." Because the park was conceived on a scale rivaling that of Versailles, the earliest days of the project were not particularly happy. European journalists delighted in belittling it and accusing it of everything from cultural imperialism to sounding the death knell of French culture. But after financial jitters, and goodly amounts of public relations and financial juggling, the resort is on track, welcoming visitors at prices that have been reduced by around 20% from those at the resort's initial opening. In 1996 profits rose 77% as a record 11.7 million visited. But all is not rosy in the future. Beginning in 1999, Paris's Disney will have to start paying royalties and management fees to the Walt Disney folks in California.

Situated on a 5,000-acre site (about one-fifth the size of Paris) in the suburb of Marne-la-Vallée, the park incorporates the most successful elements of its Disney predecessors, but with a European flair. Allow a full day to see Disneyland Paris.

GETTING THERE

BY TRAIN The resort is linked to the RER commuter express rail network (Line A), which maintains a stop within walking distance of the theme park. Board the RER at such inner-city Paris stops as Charles de Gaulle–Etoile, Châtelet-Les Halles, or Nation. Get off at Line A's last stop, Marne-la-Vallée/Chessy, 45 minutes from central Paris. The round-trip fare from central Paris is 75F ($15). Trains run every 10 to 20 minutes, depending on the time of day.

BY BUS   Each of the hotels in the resort connects by shuttle bus to both Orly Airport and Roissy–Charles de Gaulle. Buses depart from both airports at intervals of between 30 and 45 minutes, depending on the time of day and day of the year. One-way transportation to the park from either of the airports costs 75F ($15) per person.

BY CAR   Take the A-4 highway east from Paris, getting off at Exit 14 where it's marked PARC EURO DISNEYLAND. Guest parking at any of the thousands of parking spaces costs 40F ($8) per day. An interconnected series of moving sidewalks speeds up pedestrian transit from the parking areas to the theme park's entrance. Parking for guests at any of the hotels within the resort is free.

ESSENTIALS

INFORMATION   All hotels listed below provide general information about the theme park, but for specific theme park information in all languages, contact the Disneyland Paris Guest Relations office, located in City Hall on Main Street, U.S.A. (☎ 01-64-74-30-00).

FAST FACTS   Coin-operated lockers can be rented for 10F ($2) per use, and larger bags can also be stored for 15F ($3) per day. Children's strollers and wheelchairs can be rented for 30F ($6) per day, with a 20F ($4) deposit. Baby-sitting is available at any of the resort's hotels if 24-hour advance notice is given.

SEEING THE SIGHTS

The resort was designed as a total vacation package; included within one enormous unit are the Disneyland Park with its five different entertainment "lands," six large hotels, a campground, an entertainment center (Village Disney), a 27-hole golf course, and dozens of restaurants, shows, and shops.

One of the attractions, **Main Street, U.S.A.,** features horse-drawn carriages and street-corner barbershop quartets. From the "Main Street Station," steam-powered railway cars leave for a trip through a Grand Canyon Diorama to Frontierland, with paddle-wheel steamers reminiscent of the Mississippi Valley Mark Twain described.

The park's steam trains chug past **Adventureland**—with swashbuckling 18th-century pirates, the tree house of the Swiss Family Robinson, and reenacted legends from the *Arabian Nights*—to **Fantasyland.** Here, one can see the symbol of the theme park, the Sleeping Beauty Castle (*Le Château de la Belle au Bois Dormant*), whose soaring pinnacles and turrets are an idealized (and spectacular) interpretation of the châteaux of France.

Visions of the future are displayed at **Discoveryland,** whose tributes to human invention and imagination are drawn from the works of Leonardo da Vinci, Jules Verne, H.G. Wells, the modern masters of science fiction, and the *Star Wars* series. Of all the areas, Discoveryland has proven among the most popular, and is one of the few that was enlarged (in 1995) after the park's original inauguration.

As Disney continues to churn out animated blockbusters, look for all its newest stars to appear in the theme park. The fact that the characters from such films as *Aladdin, The Lion King,* and *Pocahontas* are actually made of celluloid, like the rest, hasn't kept them from the Ice Capades and it certainly won't keep them from Disneyland Paris. Also joining the ranks are characters from *Toy Story.*

Disney also maintains an entertainment center, **Village Disney,** whose indoor/outdoor layout resembles the whelp of a California mall and the Coney Island boardwalk. Scattered on either side of a pedestrian walkway, illuminated by an overhead grid of spotlights, it's set just outside the boundaries of the fenced-in acreage containing the bulk of Disneyland's attractions. The complex accommodates dance clubs, snack bars, restaurants, souvenir shops, and bars for adults who want to escape from the children for a while. Unlike the rest of the park, admission to Festival Disney is free, and consequently attracts night owls from Paris and its suburbs who wouldn't otherwise be particularly interested in the park itself.

Admission to the park for 1 day, depending on the season, costs 150F to 195F ($30 to $39) for adults, and 120F to 150F ($24 to $30) for children 3 to 12. Admission to the park for 2 days ranges from 290F to 375F ($58 to $75) for adults, and from 230F to 290F ($46 to $58) for children. Children 2 and under are always admitted free. Peak season is from mid-June to mid-September, as well as Christmas and Easter weeks. Entrance to Village Disney, is free, although there's usually a cover charge for the dance clubs.

Disneyland Paris is open July and August daily from 9am to 11pm; September to June 11, Monday to Friday from 10am to 6pm; and Saturday and Sunday from 9am to 8pm. Opening and closing hours, however, vary with the weather and the season. It's usually a good idea to phone the information office (see above).

Guided tours can be arranged for 50F ($10) for adults and 35F ($7) for children ages 3 to 11. Lasting 3^{1}/2 hours and including 20 or more people, the tours offer an opportunity for a complete visit. In view of the well-marked paths leading through the park, and the availability of ample printed information in virtually any language once you get there, guided tours are not a particularly viable idea, and are not recommended.

WHERE TO STAY

The resort has six theme hotels that share a common reservation service. For more information call ☎ **407/W-DISNEY (934-7639)** in North America, or 0171/753-2900 in London. For information or reservations in France, contact the **Central Reservations Office,** Euro Disney Resort, S.C.A., B.P. 105, F-77777 Marne-la-Vallée Cedex 4 (☎ **01-60-30-60-30**).

EXPENSIVE

Disneyland Hotel. Disneyland Paris, B.P. 105, F-77777 Marne-la-Vallée Cedex 4. ☎ **01-60-45-65-00.** Fax 01-60-45-65-33. 479 rms, 21 suites. A/C MINIBAR TV TEL. 1,350–2,050F ($270–$410) for one to four persons; from 3,850F ($770) suite. AE, DC, DISC, MC, V.

Located at the entrance to the park, this flagship hotel is Victorian in style, with red-tile turrets and jutting balconies; some observers have likened it to the town hall of a major European city. The bedrooms are plushly and conservatively furnished. On the "Castle Club" floor, there are free newspapers, all-day beverages, and access to a well-equipped private lounge.

Dining/Entertainment: Three restaurants (the California Grill is recommended separately; see "Where to Dine," below) and two bars.

Facilities: Health club with indoor/outdoor pool, whirlpool, sauna, private dining and banqueting rooms.

Services: Room service, laundry, baby-sitting.

Hotel New York. Disneyland Paris, B.P. 100, F-77777 Marne-la-Vallée Cedex 4. ☎ **01-60-45-73-00.** Fax 01-60-45-73-33. 538 rms, 31 suites. A/C MINIBAR TV TEL. 750–1,200F ($150–$240) for one to four persons; from 2,200F ($440) suite. AE, DC, DISC, MC, V.

Inspired by the Big Apple at its best, this hotel was designed around a nine-story central "skyscraper" flanked by the Gramercy Park Wing and the Brownstones Wing. (The exteriors of both of these wings resemble row houses.) The bedrooms are comfortably appointed with art deco accessories and New York–inspired memorabilia.

Dining/Entertainment: The hotel has a diner, one restaurant, a cocktail and wine bar, and an art deco bar.

Services: Room service, laundry, baby-sitting.

Facilities: Indoor/outdoor pool, two outdoor tennis courts, health club.

MODERATE

Newport Bay Club. Disneyland Paris, B.P. 105, F-77777 Marne-la-Vallée Cedex 4. ☎ **01-60-45-55-00.** Fax 01-60-45-55-33. 1,083 rms, 15 suites. A/C MINIBAR TV TEL. 675–950F ($135–$190) for one to four persons; from 1,600F ($320) suite. AE, DC, DISC, MC, V.

This hotel was designed with a central cupola, jutting balconies, and a blue-and-cream color scheme, reminiscent of a harbor-front New England hotel. Each nautically decorated bedroom offers closed-circuit TV information and movies. The upscale Yacht Club and the less formal Cape Cod restaurants are the dining choices. Facilities include a lakeside promenade, a glassed-in pool pavilion, an outdoor pool, and a health club.

Sequoia Lodge. Disneyland Paris, B.P. 114, F-77777 Marne-la-Vallée Cedex 4. ☎ **01-60-45-51-00.** Fax 01-60-45-51-33. 997 rms, 14 suites. A/C MINIBAR TV TEL. 525–1,035F ($105–$207) for one to four persons; from 1,500F ($300) suite. AE, DC, DISC, MC, V.

Built of gray stone and roughly textured planking, and capped with a gently sloping green copper roof, this hotel resembles a rough-hewn, comfortable and very large lodge in a remote section of the Rocky Mountains. The hotel consists of a large central building with five additional chalets (each housing 100 bedrooms) nearby. The rooms are comfortably rustic. The Hunter's Grill serves spit-roasted meats carved directly on your plate. Less formal is the Beaver Creek Tavern. Facilities include an indoor pool and health club.

INEXPENSIVE

Hotel Cheyenne and Hotel Santa Fé. Disneyland Paris, B.P. 115, F-77777 Marne-la-Vallée Cedex 4. ☎ **01-60-45-62-00** (Cheyenne) or 01-60-45-78-00 (Santa Fé). Fax 01-60-45-62-33 (Cheyenne) or 01-60-45-78-33 (Santa Fé). 2,000 rms. TV TEL. Hotel Cheyenne 400–815F ($80–$163) for one to four persons. Hotel Santa Fé 350–615F ($70–$123) for one to four persons. AE, DC, DISC, MC, V.

Located next door to one another, these are the least expensive hotels at the resort. Both are situated near a re-creation of Texas's Rio Grande and evoke different aspects of the Old West. The Cheyenne accommodates visitors within 14 two-story buildings along "Desperado Street," whereas the Santa Fé, sporting a desert theme, encompasses four different "nature trails" winding among 42 adobe-style pueblos. Both have bare-boned accommodations. Their only disadvantage, according to some parents with children, is the lack of a swimming pool.

Tex-Mex specialties are offered at La Cantina (Hotel Santa Fé), and barbecue and smokehouse specialties predominate at the Chuck Wagon Café (Hotel Cheyenne).

WHERE TO DINE

Within the resort, there are at least 45 different restaurants and snack bars, each trying hard to please millions of European and North American palates. Here are a few recommendations:

Auberge de Cendrillon. Fantasyland. ☎ **01-64-74-31-86.** Reservations recommended. Main courses 80–105F ($16–$21); fixed-price menus 115–195F ($23–$39). AE, DC, MC, V. Thurs–Mon 11:30am to 90 minutes before closing of the park. FRENCH.

This is a fairy-tale version of Cinderella's sumptuous country inn, with a glass couch in the center. It is the major French restaurant at the resort. A master of ceremonies, in a plumed tricorne hat and wearing an embroidered tunic and lace ruffles, welcomes you. For an appetizer, try the warm goat cheese salad with lardons or the smoked salmon platter. If you don't choose one of the good fixed-price meals, you can order from the limited but excellent à la carte menu. Perhaps you'll settle happily for poultry in a pocket (puff pastry), loin of lamb roasted with mustard, or sautéed medallions (medallion-shaped pieces) of veal. The only drawback to this restaurant is its location within the theme park. This limits its accessibility, as it follows the park's seasonal schedules. As such, lunches are usually easier to arrange than dinners.

The California Grill. In the Disneyland Hotel. ☎ **01-60-45-65-00.** Reservations required. Main courses 67–205F ($13.40–$41); fixed-price menu 175–260F ($35–$52). AE, DC, MC, V. Sun–Fri 7–11pm; Sat 6–11pm. CALIFORNIAN.

Focusing on the lighter recipes for which the Golden State is famous, this airy and elegant restaurant features specialties like poached oysters with leeks and salmon, grilled tuna with white beans and soy sauce, and grilled shrimp with spicy rice. Main courses are likely to include cheese tortellini with bacon-cream sauce, grilled veal chops with morel-flavored cream sauce; and glazed veal loin with asparagus and fresh chives. Some items are conceived for two, such as a very savory version of a roasted rib of beef with traditional rib-sticking garnishes. The Napa Feast, the more elegant of the two fixed-price menus, begins with home-cured smoked salmon, follows with roast rack of lamb scented with fresh thyme, and ends with crème brûlée. Goodly numbers of the items (especially the pastas or any of "Mickie's Pizzas") are conceived specifically for children. Children (one per adult) dine free every Saturday between 6 and 7pm when accompanied by an adult guardian. Note: If you're looking for a quiet, mostly adult venue, go here as late as your hunger pangs will allow.

DISNEYLAND AFTER DARK

Buffalo Bill's Wild West Show. In the Festival Disney Building. ☎ **01-60-45-71-00.** Two shows are staged nightly, at 6:30 and 9:30pm, costing (with dinner included) 295F ($59) for adults, 195F ($39) for children ages 3–11.

This is the premier theatrical venue of Disneyland Paris, a twice-per-night stampede of entertainment that recalls the show that once traveled the West with Buffalo Bill and Annie Oakley. You'll dine at tables that ring, amphitheater-style, a dirt-floored riding rink where sharpshooters, runaway stage coaches, and dozens of horses and Indians ride very fast and perform some alarmingly realistic acrobatics. A Texas-style barbecue, served assembly line style by waiters in ten-gallon hats, is part of the experience. Despite its cornpone elements, it's not without its charm and an almost mournful nostalgia for a way of life of another continent and another century. Wild Bill himself is dignified, and the Indians suitably brave.

9 Chartres

60 miles SW of Paris, 47 miles NW of Orléans

Many observers feel that the architectural aspirations of the Middle Ages reached their highest expression in the Cathedral at Chartres. Come to see its soaring architecture, highly wrought sculpture, and, above all, its stained glass, which gave the world a new color, Chartres blue.

ESSENTIALS

GETTING THERE It takes a full day to see Chartres. From Paris's Gare Montparnasse, **trains** run directly to Chartres, taking less than an hour and passing through a sea of wheat fields. By **car,** take A10/A11 southwest from the *périphérique* and follow the signs to Le Mans and Chartres (the Chartres exit is clearly marked).

VISITOR INFORMATION   The **Office de Tourisme** is on place de la Cathédrale
(☎ 02-37-21-50-00).

SEEING THE SIGHTS

✪ **Cathédrale Notre-Dame de Chartres.** 16 Cloître Notre-Dame. ☎ **02-37-21-56-33.**

Reportedly, Rodin once sat for hours on the edge of the sidewalk, admiring this cathedral's Romanesque sculpture. His opinion: Chartres is the French Acropolis. When it began to rain, a kind soul offered him an umbrella, which he declined, so transfixed was he by the magic of this place.

The cathedral's origins are uncertain; some have suggested it grew up over an ancient Druid site that had later become a Roman temple. It is known that as early as the 4th century there was a Christian basilica here. A fire in 1194 destroyed most of what had then become a Romanesque cathedral, but spared the western facade and crypt. The cathedral you see today dates principally from the 13th century, when it was rebuilt with the efforts and contributions of kings, princes, churchmen, and pilgrims from all over Europe. One of the world's greatest High Gothic cathedrals, it was the first to use flying buttresses to support the soaring dimensions within.

French sculpture in the 12th century broke into full bloom when the Royal Portal was added. A landmark in Romanesque art, the sculptured bodies are elongated, often formalized beyond reality, in their long flowing robes. But the faces are amazingly (for the time) lifelike, occasionally winking or smiling. In the central tympanum, Christ is shown at the Second Coming, with his descent depicted on the right, his ascent on the left. Before entering, stop to admire the Royal Portal and then walk around to both the north and south portals, each dating from the 13th century. They depict such biblical scenes as the expulsion of Adam and Eve from the Garden of Eden.

Inside is a celebrated choir screen; work on it began in the 16th century and lasted until 1714. The niches, 40 in all, contain statues illustrating scenes from the life of the Madonna and Christ—everything from the Massacre of the Innocents to the Coronation of the Virgin.

But few rushed visitors ever notice the screen: They're too transfixed by the light from the stained glass. Covering an expanse of more than 3,000 square yards, the glass is without peer in the world and is truly mystical. It was spared in both World Wars because of a decision to remove it painstakingly piece by piece. Most of the stained glass dates from the 12th and 13th centuries.

See the windows in the morning, at noon, in the afternoon, at sunset—as often as you can. Like the petals of a kaleidoscope, they constantly change. It's difficult to single out a panel or window of special merit; however, an exceptional one is the 12th-century *Vierge de la belle verrière* (Our Lady of the Beautiful Window) on the south side. Of course, there are three fiery rose windows, but you couldn't miss those if you tried.

The nave, the widest in France, still contains its ancient floor-maze, which formed a mobile channel of contemplation for monks. The wooden *Virgin of the Pillar*, to

---

Impressions

I am entirely absorbed by these plains of wheat on a vast expanse of hills like an ocean of tender yellow, pale green, and soft mauve, with a piece of worked (farmed) land dotted with clusters of potato vines in bloom, and all this under a blue sky tinted with shades of white, pink, and violet.

—Vincent van Gogh (1890)

Notre-Dame de Chartres

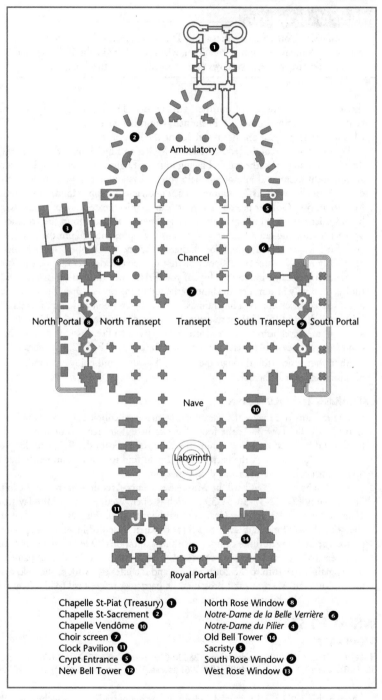

Ambulatory

Chancel

North Portal North Transept Transept South Transept South Portal

Nave

Labyrinth

Royal Portal

Chapelle St-Piat (Treasury) ❶
Chapelle St-Sacrement ❷
Chapelle Vendôme ❿
Choir screen ❼
Clock Pavilion ⓫
Crypt Entrance ❺
New Bell Tower ⓬

North Rose Window ❽
Notre-Dame de la Belle Verrière ❻
Notre-Dame du Pilier ❹
Old Bell Tower ⓮
Sacristy ❸
South Rose Window ❾
West Rose Window ⓭

313

Music of the Spheres

Are you visiting on a Sunday afternoon? The church features free 1-hour organ concerts every Sunday beginning at 4:45pm, when the filtered light of the Ile de France sunset makes the western windows of the cathedral come thrillingly alive.

the left of the choir, dates from the 14th century. The crypt was built over two centuries, beginning in the 9th. Enshrined within is *Our Lady of the Crypt,* a 1976 Madonna that replaced one destroyed during the Revolution.

Try to get a tour conducted by Malcolm Miller, an Englishman who has spent 3 decades studying the cathedral and giving tours in English. His rare blend of scholarship, enthusiasm, and humor will help you understand and appreciate the cathedral. He usually conducts 75-minute tours at noon and 2:45pm Monday to Saturday for a fee of 30F ($6) per person. Tours are canceled in the event of pilgrimages, religious celebrations, and large-scale funerals. French-language tours are conducted between Easter and late October at 10:30am and 3pm, and at 2pm the rest of the year, for a fee of 28F ($5.60). From Easter to the end of October, the cathedral is open daily from 7:30am to 7:30pm. The rest of the year, daily closings are at 7pm. Entrance to the cathedral itself is free. If you feel fit enough, don't miss the opportunity, especially in summer, to climb to the top of the tower. Open the same hours as the cathedral, except for a lunchtime closing between noon and 2pm, it costs 25F ($5) for adults, and 15F ($3) for students. The crypt, gloomy and somber, but rich with a sense of medieval history, can be visited only as part of a French-speaking tour that's conducted whenever there's enough demand. The cost is 11F ($2.20) per person.

After your visit, stroll through the episcopal gardens and enjoy yet another view of this remarkable cathedral.

EXPLORING THE OLD TOWN

If time remains you may want to explore the medieval cobbled streets of the **Vieux Quartiers** (Old Town). At the foot of the cathedral are lanes containing gabled houses and humped bridges spanning the Eure River. From the Boùju Bridge, you can see the lofty spires in the background. Try to find rue Chantault, which boasts houses with colorful facades, one 8 centuries old.

A highlight of your visit will be **Musée des Beaux-Arts de Chartres,** 29 Cloître Notre-Dame (☎ **02-37-36-41-39**), which is open Wednesday to Monday from 10am to noon and 2 to 5pm. Next door to the cathedral, this museum of fine arts charges 10F ($2) for adults and 5F ($1) for children. Installed in a former episcopal palace, the building at times competes with its exhibitions. One part dates from the 15th century and encompasses a courtyard. The permanent collection of paintings covers mainly the 16th to the 20th century, and includes the work of such old masters as Zurbarán, Watteau, and Brosamer. Of particular interest is David Ténier's *Le Concert.* Special exhibitions are often mounted.

WHERE TO STAY
MODERATE

Hôtel Châtlet. 6–8 av. Jehan-de-Beauce, 28000 Chartres. ☎ **02-37-21-78-00.** Fax 02-37-36-23-01. 48 rms. TV TEL. 420–480F ($84–$96) double. Third person 60F ($12) extra. AE, DC, MC, V.

Though this 1982 hotel is part of a chain, it has many traditional touches, and the rooms are inviting, with reproductions of Louis XV and Louis XVI furniture. Most rooms face a garden and many windows open to a panoramic cathedral view. In chilly weather guests gather around the log fire. Breakfast is the only meal served, but there are numerous restaurants nearby.

Le Grand Monarque Best Western. 22 place des Epars, 28005 Chartres. ☎ **800/528-1234** in the U.S., or 02-37-21-00-72. Fax 02-37-36-34-18. 49 rms, 5 suites. MINIBAR TV TEL. 585–700F ($117–$140) double; 1,160F ($232) suite. Rates include continental breakfast. AE, DC, MC, V. Parking 45F ($9).

The leading hotel of Chartres is housed in a classical building enclosing a courtyard. Functioning as an inn almost since its original construction, and greatly expanded over the centuries, it still attracts guests who enjoy its old-world charm, such as art nouveau stained glass and Louis XV chairs in the dining room. The rooms are decorated with reproductions of antiques; most have sitting areas. The hotel also has an anachronistic restaurant. One local critic found the kitchen trapped in an "*ancien régime* time warp."

INEXPENSIVE

Hôtel de la Poste. 3 rue du Général-Koenig, 28003 Chartres. ☎ **02-37-21-04-27.** Fax 02-37-36-42-17. 58 rms. TV TEL. 290–310F ($58–$62) double. AE, DC, MC, V. Parking 39F ($7.80).

This modest hotel offers one of the best values in Chartres even though it's short on charm. It's in the center of town, across from the main post office. The rooms are soundproof and comfortably furnished and have wall-to-wall carpeting. The surprise here is the good food served at affordable prices, everything backed up by one of the town's finest wine cellars. The curse of the hotel is bookings by group tours. There's also an in-house garage.

WHERE TO EAT

Le Buisson Ardent. 10 rue au Lait. ☎ **02-37-34-04-66.** Reservations recommended. Main courses 98–122F ($20–$24); fixed-price menus 128F, 168F, 228F ($26, $34, $46). MC, V. Mon–Sat 12:30–2pm and 7:30–9:30pm, Sun 12:30–2pm. FRENCH.

In a charming 300-year-old house in the most historic section of town, this restaurant is one floor above street level in the shadow of the cathedral. From its location you might expect it to be a tourist trap, but it isn't, although it steadfastly refuses to follow many of the fads that sometimes sweep through big-city restaurants in nearby Paris. The composition of the set-price menus change with the seasons, and, like the à la carte dishes, are based on fresh meats, produce, and fish. Best-sellers include an escalope of warm foie gras prepared with apples and Calvados, or an émincée of roasted pigeon with lemon juice and a galette of potatoes and fresh vegetables. Other dishes are simpler, the kind you might have noticed in bistros: stuffed mushrooms with garlic butter, and codfish flavored with coriander and served with parsley flan as a main course is an especially good choice. A dessert specialty is crispy hot apples with sorbet and Calvados-flavored butter sauce.

10 Château de Thoiry

25 miles W of Paris

The Château et Parc Zoologique de Thoiry is a major attraction that in a year draws more visitors than the Louvre or Versailles.

GETTING THERE

It's so awkward to reach this place by public transportation that the château doesn't recommend the attempt. Isolated as it is, it's really a destination to visit by car. Take

To Taste a Madeleine

And suddenly the memory returns. The taste was that of the little crumb of madeleine which on Sunday mornings at Combray (because on those mornings I did not go out before church-time), when I went to say good day to her in her bedroom, my aunt Léonie used to give me, dipping it first in her own cup of real or of lime-flower tea.
　　　　　　　　　　　　　　—Marcel Proust, *Remembrance of Things Past*

　　Illiers-Combray, a small town 54 miles southwest of Paris and 15 miles southwest of Chartres, was once known simply as Illiers. Then Proust groupies started to come and signs were posted: ILLIERS, LE COMBRAY DE MARCEL PROUST. Illiers was and is a real town, but Marcel Proust in his masterpiece, *A la recherche du temps perdu* (*Remembrance of Things Past*), made it so famous as Combray that Life acknowledged Fiction and the town came to be known as Illiers-Combray.

　　It was the taste of a luscious little madeleine that launched Proust on his immortal recollection. To this day hundreds of his readers from all over the world flock to the pastry shops in Illiers-Combray to eat a madeleine or two dipped in lime-flower tea. Following the Proustian labyrinth, you can explore the gardens, streets, and houses he frequently visited until he was 13 and wrote about so richly later on. The town's pivot is the **Eglise St-Jacques,** where Proust as a boy placed hawthorn on the altar.

　　Some members of Proust's family have lived in Illiers for centuries. His grandfather, François, was born here on rue du Cheval-Blanc. At 11 place du Marché, just opposite the church, he ran a small candle shop. His daughter, Elisabeth, married Jules Amiot, who ran a shop a few doors away. Down from Paris, young Marcel would visit his aunt at 4 rue du St-Esprit, which has been renamed rue du Docteur-Proust, honoring Marcel's grandfather.

　　The **Maison de Tante Léonie,** 4 rue du Docteur-Proust (☎ 02-37-24-30-97), is a museum, charging 30F ($6) for admission. In the novel this was Aunt Léonie's home; filled with antimacassars, it's typical of the solid bourgeois comfort of its day. Upstairs you can visit the bedroom where the young Marcel slept; today it contains souvenirs of key episodes in the novel. The house can be visited Tuesday to Sunday for tours conducted at 2:30 and 4pm.

　　In the center of town, a sign will guide you to further Proustian sights.

---

the Autoroute de l'Ouest (A13) toward Dreux, exiting at Bois-d'Arcy. Then get on N12, following the signs on D11 to Thoiry. Most visitors budget a full day to visit the Chateau de Thoiry.

THE CHÂTEAU

The 16th-century Château de Thoiry, 78770 Thoiry-en-Yvelines (☎ **01-34-87-52-25**), owned by the vicomte de La Panouse family (now run by son Paul and his wife, Annabelle), displays two unpublished Chopin waltzes, antique furniture, more than 343 handwritten letters of French or European kings, as well as the original financial records of France from 1745 to 1750. But these are not as much a draw as the game reserve.

　　The château's grounds have been turned into a game reserve with elephants, giraffes, zebras, monkeys, rhinoceroses, alligators, lions, tigers, kangaroos, bears, and wolves—more than 1,000 animals and birds roam at liberty. The reserve and park cover 300 acres, though the estate is on 1,200 acres.

In the French gardens you can see llamas, Asian deer and sheep, and many types of birds, including flamingos and cranes. In the tiger park a promenade stretches above the tigers. In addition, in the basement of the château is a vivarium (a terrarium used especially for small animals). Paul and Annabelle are also restoring the 300 acres of 17th-, 18th-, and 19th-century gardens as well as creating new ones.

To see the animal farm you can drive your own car, providing it isn't a convertible, which if you know monkeys, isn't really a sane vehicle to bring. Anticipating troubles, the farm owners carry thousands of francs' worth of insurance.

The park is most crowded on weekends, but if you want to avoid the crush, visit on Saturday or Sunday morning. The park is open from April to October, Monday to Saturday from 10am to 6pm and Sunday from 10am to 6:30pm; November to March, daily from 10am to 5pm. The cost for the reserve and gardens is 100F ($20) for adults and 79F ($15.80) for children 3 to 12; 2 and under free. The château is open April to October, daily from 2 to 6pm; off-season, daily from 2 to 5pm. Admission is 30F ($6) for adults and 20F ($4) for children 3 to 12; 2 and under free.

WHERE TO STAY & DINE

Hôtel de l'Etoile. 78770 Thoiry. ☎ **01-34-87-40-21.** Fax 01-34-87-49-57. 12 rms. TEL. 315F ($63) double. AE, DC, MC, V.

Built centuries ago, this rustic three-story inn has a stone-and-timber garden sitting room for guests. The guest rooms are comfortably furnished and well maintained. A dolphin fountain decorates one of the walls, and the pleasant restaurant has masonry trim. Meals consist of fairly routine homemade French dishes. Expect to pay 115F to 165F ($23 to $33) for a fixed-price meal.

11 Giverny—In the Footsteps of Claude Monet

50 miles NW of Paris

On the border between Normandy and the Ile de France, Giverny is home to the Claude Monet Foundation, the house where Claude Monet lived for 43 years. The restored house and its gardens are open to the public.

ESSENTIALS

GETTING THERE   It takes a full morning to get to Giverny and to see its sights. Take the Paris-Rouen **train** from Paris–St-Lazare to the Vernon station. A taxi can take you the 3 miles to Giverny. In addition, **bus tours** are operated from Paris by **American Express,** 11 rue Scribe, 9e (☎ 01-47-77-70-00; Métro: Opéra), and **Cityrama,** 147–149 rue Saint-Honoré, 1er (☎ 01-44-55-61-30; Métro: Palais-Royal). If you're driving, take the Autoroute de l'Ouest (Port de St-Cloud) toward Rouen. Leave the autoroute at Bonnières, then cross the Seine on the Bonnières Bridge. From here, a direct road with signs will bring you to Giverny. Expect about an hour of driving and try to avoid weekends.

Another way to get to Giverny is to leave the highway at the Bonnières exit and go toward Vernon. Once in Vernon, cross the bridge over the Seine and follow the signs to Giverny or Gasny (Giverny is before Gasny). This is easier than going through Bonnières, where there aren't many signs.

SEEING THE SIGHTS

✪ **Claude Monet Foundation.** rue Claude-Monet. ☎ **01-32-51-28-21.**

The French painter Claude Monet was a spiritualist of light, brilliantly translating its effects at different times of the day. In fact, some critics claim that he "invented light." His series of paintings of the cathedral at Rouen and of the water lilies, which one critic called "vertical interpretations of horizontal lines," are just a few of his masterpieces.

Monet came to Giverny in 1883, at the age of 43. While taking a small railway linking Vetheuil to Vernon, he discovered the village at a point where the Epte stream joined the Seine. Many of his friends used to visit him here at Le Pressoir, including Clemenceau, Cézanne, Rodin, Renoir, Degas, and Sisley. When Monet died in 1926, his son, Michel, inherited the house but left it abandoned until it decayed into ruins. The gardens became almost a jungle, inhabited by river rats. In 1966 Michel died and left it to the Académie des Beaux-Arts. It wasn't until 1977 that Gerald van der Kemp, who restored Versailles, decided to work on Giverny. A large part of it was restored with gifts from American benefactors, especially the late Lila Acheson Wallace, former head of *Reader's Digest*, who contributed $1 million.

You can stroll through the garden and view the thousands of flowers, including the *nymphéas*. The Japanese bridge, hung with wisteria, leads to a dreamy setting of weeping willows and rhododendrons. Monet's studio barge was installed on the pond.

The foundation is open only late March to late November, Tuesday to Sunday from 10am to 6pm, charging 35F ($7) for adults and 25F ($5) for children. You can visit just the gardens for 25F ($5). Reservations are a must.

WHERE TO DINE

Auberge du Vieux Moulin. 21 rue de la Falaise. ☎ **02-32-51-46-15.** Main courses 70–110F ($14–$22); fixed-price menus 98–178F ($19.60–$35.60). MC, V. Tues–Sun noon–3pm and 7:30–10pm. Closed Jan. FRENCH.

Set within a stone-sided building that was originally built as a farmhouse in 1935, this is a convenient lunch stop for visitors at the Monet house. The Boudeau family maintains a series of cozy dining rooms filled with original Impressionist paintings. Since you can walk here from the museum in about 5 minutes, leave your car in the museum lot. Specialties include appetizers like snails in puff pastry with garlic-flavored butter sauce; guinea fowl braised in cider, escalope of salmon with sorrel sauce, and auiguillettes of duckling with peaches. Dessert might be a *tarte Normande* prepared with apple slices and Calvados. The kitchen doesn't pretend the food is any more than it is: good, hearty country fare with panache. The charm of the staff helps a lot, too. The stone building is ringed with lawns and has a pair of flowering terraces.

Appendix

A Glossary of Useful Terms

A well-known character is the American or lapsed Canadian who returns from a trip to Paris and denounces the ever-so-rude French. "I asked for directions and he glowered at me, muttered inaudibly, and turned his back." "She threw her baguette at me!" While Parisians often seem to carry upon their backs a burden of misery, that they famously dole out to immigrants and foreigners, it is often amazing how a word or two of halting French will change their dispositions, and if not bring out the sun, at least put an end to the Gallic thunder and rain. At the very least, try to learn a few numbers, basic greetings, and—above all—the life-raft, *"Parlez-vous anglais?"* ("Do you speak English?"). As it turns out, many Parisians do speak a passable English, and will use it liberally, *if* you demonstate the basic courtesy of greeting them in their language. Go out, try our glossary on, and don't be bashful. *Bonne chance!*

ENGLISH	FRENCH	PRONUNCIATION
Basics		
Yes/No	Oui/Non	wee/nohn
OK	D'accord	dah-*core*
Please	S'il vous plaît	seel voo *play*
Thank you	Merci	mair-*see*
You're welcome	De rien	duh ree-*ehn*
Hello (during day-light hours)	Bonjour	bohn-*jhoor*
Good evening	Bonsoir	bohn-*swahr*
Good-bye	Au revoir	o ruh-*vwahr*
What's your name?	Comment vous appellez-vous?	ko-mahn-voo za-pell-ay-*voo?*
My name is	Je m'appelle	jhuh ma-*pell*
Happy to meet you	Enchanté(e)	ohn-shahn-*tay*
Miss	Mademoiselle	mad mwa-*zel*
Mr.	Monsieur	muh-*syuh*
Mrs.	Madame	ma-*dam*
How are you?	Comment allez-vous	kuh-mahn-tahl-ay-*voo?*
Fine, thank you, and you?	Très bien, merci, et vous?	tray bee-ehn, mare-ci, ay *voo?*
Very well, thank you	Très bien, merci	tray bee-ehn, mair-*see*

So-so	Comme ci, comme ça	kum-*see*, kum-*sah*
I'm sorry/excuse me	Pardon	pahr-*dohn*
I'm so very sorry	Désolé(e)	day-zoh-*lay*
That's all right	Il n'y a pas de quoi	eel nee ah pah duh *kwah*

Getting Around/Street Smarts

Do you speak English?	Parlez-vous anglais?	par-lay-voo-ahn-*glay?*
I don't speak French	Je ne parle pas français	jhuh ne parl pah frahn-*say*
I don't understand	Je ne comprends pas	jhuh ne kohm-*prahn* pas
Could you speak more loudly/more slowly?	Pouvez-vous parler un peu plus fort/plus lentement?	Poo-*vay* voo par-*lay* un puh ploo for/plus lan-te-*ment?*
Could you repeat that?	Répetez, s'il vous plaît	ray-pay-*tay,* seel voo *play*
What is it?	Qu'est-ce que c'est?	kess-kuh-*say?*
What time is it?	Qu'elle heure est-il?	kel uhr eh-*teel?*
What?	Quoi?	kwah?
How? or What did you say?	Comment?	ko-*mahn?*
When?	Quand?	kahn?
Where is?	Où est?	ooh-eh?
Who?	Qui?	kee?
Why?	Pourquoi?	poor-*kwah?*
Here/there	ici/là	ee-*see*/ lah
Left/right	à gauche/à droite	a goash/a drwaht
Straight ahead	tout droit	too-drwah
I'm American/Canadian/ British	Je suis américain(e), canadien(e), anglais(e)	jhe sweez a-may-ree-*kehn*/ can-ah-dee-*en*/ahn-glay(glaise)
Fill the tank (of a car), please	Le plein, s'il vous plaît	luh plan, seel-voo-*play*
I'm going to	Je vais à	jhe vay ah
I want to get off at	Je voudrais descendre à	jhe voo-*dray* day-son drah-ah
I'm sick	Je suis malade	jhuh swee mal-*ahd*
airport	l'aéroport	lair-o-*por*
bank	la banque	lah bahnk
bridge	pont	pohn
bus station	la gare routière	lah gar roo-tee-*air*
bus stop	l'arrêt de bus	lah-*ray* duh boohss
by means of a bicycle	en vélo/par bicyclette	uh *vay*-low, par bee-see-*clet*
by means of a car	en voiture	ahn vwa-*toor*
cashier	la caisse	lah *kess*
cathedral	cathédral	ka-tay-*dral*
church	église	ay-*gleez*
dead end	une impasse	ewn am-*pass*
driver's license	permis de conduire	per-*mee* duh con-*dweer*
elevator	l'ascenseur	lah sahn *seuhr*
entrance (to a building or a city)	une porte	ewn port
exit (from a building or a freeway)	une sortie	ewn sor-*tee*

fortified castle or palace	château	sha-*tow*
garden	jardin	jhar-*dehn*
gasoline	du pétrol/de l'essence	duh pay-*trol*/de lay-*sahns*
ground floor	rez-de-chausée	ray-de-show-*say*
highway to	la route pour	la root por
hospital	l'hôpital	low-pee-*tahl*
insurance	les assurances	lez ah-sur-*ahns*
luggage storage	consigne	kohn-*seen*-yuh
museum	le musée	luh mew-*zay*
no entry	sens interdit	sehns ahn-ter-*dee*
no smoking	défense de fumer	day-*fahns* de fu-may
on foot	à pied	ah pee-*ay*
one-day pass	ticket journalier	tee-kay jhoor-nall-ee-*ay*
one-way ticket	aller simple	ah-*lay sam*-pluh
police	la police	lah po-*lees*
rented car	voiture de location	vwa-*toor* de low-ka-see-*on*
round-trip ticket	aller-retour	ah-*lay* re-*toor*
second floor	premier étage	prem-ee-*ehr* ay-*taj*
slow down	ralentir	rah-lahn-*teer*
store	le magazin	luh ma-ga-*zehn*
street	rue	roo
suburb	banlieu, environs	bahn-*lieu,* en-veer-*ohns*
subway	le métro	le may-tro
telephone	le téléphone	luh tay-lay-*phone*
ticket	un billet	uh *bee*-yay
ticket office	vente de billets	vahnt duh bee-*yay*
toilets	les toilettes/les WC	lay twa-*lets*/les vay-*say*
tower	tour	toor

Necessities

I'd like	je voudrais	jhe voo-*dray*
a room	une chambre	ewn *shahm*-bruh
the key	la clé (la clef)	la clay
I'd like to buy	Je voudrais acheter	jhe voo-dray ahsh-*tay*
aspirin	des aspirines/des aspros	deyz ahs-peer-*eens*/deyz ahs-*prohs*
cigarettes	des cigarettes	day see-ga-*ret*
condoms	des préservatifs	day pray-ser-va-*teefs*
dictionary	un dictionnaire	uh deek-see-oh-*nare*
dress	une robe	ewn robe
envelopes	des envelopes	days ahn-veh-*lope*
gift (for someone)	un cadeau	uh kah-*doe*
handbag	un sac	uh sahk
hat	un chapeau	uh shah-*poh*
magazine	une revue	ewn reh-*vu*
map of the city	un plan de ville	unh plahn de *veel*
matches	des allumettes	dayz a-loo-*met*
necktie	une cravate	uh cra-*vaht*
newspaper	un journal	uh zhoor-*nahl*
phone-card	une carte téléphonique	uh cart tay-lay-fone-*eek*
postcard	une carte postale	ewn carte pos-*tahl*
road map	une carte routière	ewn cart roo-tee-*air*

shirt	une chemise	ewn che-*meez*
shoes	des chaussures	day show-*suhr*
skirt	une jupe	ewn jhoop
soap	du savon	dew sah-*vohn*
socks	des chaussettes	day show-*set*
stamp	un timbre	uh *tam*-bruh
trousers	un pantalon	uh pan-tah-*lohn*
writing paper	du papier à lettres	dew pap-pee-*ay* a *let*-ruh
How much does it cost?	C'est combien?/ Ça coûte combien?	say comb-bee-*ehn*?/ sah coot comb-bee-*ehn*?
That's expensive	C'est cher/chère	say share
That's inexpensive	C'est raisonnable/ C'est bon marché	say ray-son-*ahb*-bluh/say bohn mar-*shay*
Do you take credit cards?	Est-ce que vous acceptez les cartes de credit?	es-kuh voo zaksep-*tay* lay kart duh creh-*dee*

In Your Hotel

Are taxes included?	Est-ce que les taxes sont comprises?	ess-keh lay taks son com-*preez*
balcony	un balcon	uh bahl-cohn
bathtub	une baignoire	ewn bayn-*nwar*
bedroom	une chambre	oon shahm-bruh
for two occupants	pour deux personnes	poor duh pair-*sunn*
hot and cold water	l'eau chaude et froide	low showed ay fwad
Is breakfast included?	Petit déjeuner inclus?	peh-*tee* day-jheun-*ay* ehn-*klu*?
room	une chambre	ewn *shawm*-bruh
shower	une douche	ewn dooch
sink	un lavabo	uh la-va-*bow*
suite	une suite	ewn sweet
We're staying for . . . days	On reste pour . . . days	ohn rest poor . . . jhoor
with	avec	ah-*vek*
with air-conditioning	avec climatization	ah-*vek* clee-mah-tee-zah-ion
without	sans	sahn
youth hostel	une auberge de jeunesse	oon oh-bayrge-duh-jhe-*ness*

In the Restaurant

I would like	Je voudrais	jhe voo-*dray*
to eat	manger	mahn-*jhay*
to order	commander	ko-mahn-*day*
Please give me	Donnez-moi, s'il vous plaît	doe-nay-*mwah*, seel voo play
a bottle of	une bouteille de	ewn boo-*tay* duh
a cup of	une tasse de	ewn tass duh
a glass of	un verre de	uh vair duh
a plate of	une assiette de	ewn ass-ee-*et* duh
an ashtray	un cendrier	uh sahn-dree-*ay*
bread	du pain	dew pan
breakfast	le petit-déjeuner	luh puh-*tee* day-zhuh-*nay*
butter	du beurre	dew burr

check/bill	l'addition/ la note	la-dee-see-*ohn*/ la noat
Cheers!	À votre santé!	ah vo-truh sahn-*tay*!
Can I buy you a drink?	Puis-je vous acheter un verre?	*pwee*-jhe voo *zahsh*-tay uh *vaihr*
cocktail	un apéritif	uh ah-pay-ree-*teef*
coffee	du café	dew ka-*fay*
coffee, black	un café noir	uh ka-*fay* nwahr
coffee, with cream	un café-crème	uh ka-*fay* krem
coffee, with milk	un café au lait	uh ka-*fay* o *lay*
coffee, decaf	un café décaféiné	uh ka-*fay* day-kah-fay-*nay*
coffee, espresso	un café express	uh ka-*fay* ek-*sprehss*
dinner	le dîner	luh dee-*nay*
fixed-price menu	un menu	uh may-*new*
fork	une fourchette	ewn four-*shet*
Is the tip/service included?	Est-ce que le service est compris?	ess-ke luh ser-*vees* eh com-*pree*?
knife	un couteau	uh koo-*toe*
napkin	une serviette	ewn sair-vee-*et*
pepper	du poivre	dew *pwah*-vruh
platter of the day	un plat du jour	uh plah dew jhoor
salt	du sel	dew sell
soup	une soupe/un potage	ewn soop/uh poh-*tahj*
spoon	une cuillère	ewn kwee-*air*
sugar	du sucre	dew *sook*-ruh
tea	un thé	uh tay
tea, with lemon	un thé au citron	un tay o see-*tron*
tea, herbal	une tisane	ewn tee-*zahn*
Waiter!/ Waitress!	Monsieur!/Mademoiselle!	mun-*syuh*/mad-mwa-*zel*
wine list	une carte des vins	ewn cart day van
appetizer	une entrée	ewn en-*tray*
main course	un plat principal	uh plah pran-see-*pahl*
tip included	service compris	sehr-*vees* cohm-*pree*
wide-ranging sampling of the chef's best efforts	menu dégustation	may-*new* day-gus-ta-see-*on*
drinks not included	boissons non comprises	bwa-*sons* no com-*pree*
cheese tray	plâteau de fromage	plah-*tow* de fro-*mahj*

Shopping

antique store	un magasin d'antiquités	uh maga-*zan* d'on-tee-kee-*tay*
bakery	une boulangerie	ewn boo-lon-zhur-*ree*
bank	une banque	ewn bonk
bookstore	une librairie	ewn lee-brehr-*ree*
butcher	une boucherie	ewn boo-shehr-*ree*
cheese shop	une fromagerie	ewn fro-mazh-*ree*
dairy shop	une crémerie	ewn krem-*ree*
delicatessen	une charcuterie	ewn shar-koot-*ree*
department store	une grande magasin	ewn gronde maga-*zan*
drugstore	une pharmacie	ewn far-mah-*see*
fishmonger shop	une poissonerie	ewn pwas-son-*ree*
gift shop	un magasin de cadeaux	uh maga-*zan* duh ka-*doh*

greengrocer	un marchand de légumes	uh mar-*shon* duh lay-*goom*
hairdresser	un coiffeur	uh kwa-*fuhr*
market	un marché	uh mar-*shay*
pastry shop	une pâtisserie	ewn pa-tee-*sree*
supermarket	un supermarché	uh soo-pehr-mar-*shay*
tobacconist	un tabac	uh ta-*bah*
travel agency	une agencie de voyages	ewn azh-on-*see* duh vwa-*yazh*

Colors, Shapes, Sizes, Attributes

black	noir	nwahr
blue	blue	bleuh
brown	marron/brun	mar-*rohn*/bruhn
green	vert	vaihr
orange	orange	o-*rahnj*
pink	rose	rose
purple	violette	vee-o-*let*
red	rouge	rooj
white	blanc	blahnk
yellow	jaune	jhone
bad	mauvais(e)	moh-*veh*
big	grand(e)	gron/gronde
closed	fermé(e)	fer-*meh*
down	en bas	on *bah*
early	de bonne heure	duh bon *urr*
enough	assez	as-*say*
far	loin	lwan
free, unoccupied	libre	*lee*-bruh
free, without charge	gratuit(e)	grah-*twee*/grah-*tweet*
good	bon (bonne)	boa/bun
hot	chaud(e)	show/shoad
near	près	preh
open (as in "museum")	ouvert(e)	oo-*ver*
small	petit(e)	puh-*tee*/puh-*teet*
up	en haut	on *oh*
well	bien	byehn

Numbers & Ordinals

zero	zéro	*zare*-oh
one	un	uh
two	deux	duh
three	trois	twah
four	quatre	*kaht*-ruh
five	cinq	sank
six	six	seess
seven	sept	set
eight	huit	wheat
nine	neuf	nuf
ten	dix	deess
eleven	onze	ohnz
twelve	douze	dooz

thirteen	treize	trehz
fourteen	quatorze	kah-*torz*
fifteen	quinze	kanz
sixteen	seize	sez
seventeen	dix-sept	deez-*set*
eighteen	dix-huit	deez-*wheat*
nineteen	dix-neuf	deez-*nuf*
twenty	vingt	vehn
twenty-one	vingt-et-un	vehnt-ay-*uh*
twenty-two	vingt-deux	vehnt-*duh*
thirty	trente	trahnt
forty	quarante	ka-*rahnt*
fifty	cinquante	sang-*kahnt*
sixty	soixante	swa-*sahnt*
sixty-one	soixante-et-un	swa-*sahnt*-et-*uh*
seventy	soixante-dix	swa-sahnt-*deess*
seventy-one	soixante-et-onze	swa-sahnt-et-*ohnze*
eighty	quatre-vingts	kaht-ruh-*vehn*
eighty-one	quatre-vingt-un	kaht-ruh-vehn-*uh*
ninety	quatre-vingt-dix	kaht-ruh-venh-*deess*
ninety-one	quatre-vingt-onze	kaht-ruh-venh-*ohnze*
one-hundred	cent	sahn
one-thousand	mille	meel
one-hundred-thousand	cent mille	sahn meel
first	premier	*preh*-mee-ay
second	deuxième	*duhz*-zee-em
third	troisième	*twa*-zee-em
fourth	quatrième	*kaht*-ree-em
fifth	cinquième	*sank*-ee-em
sixth	sixième	*sees*-ee-em
seventh	septième	*set*-ee-em
eighth	huitième	*wheat*-ee-em
ninth	neuvième	*neuv*-ee-em
tenth	dixième	*dees*-ee-em
eleventh	onzième	*ohnz*-ee-em
twelfth	douzième	*dooz*-ee-em
thirteenth	treizième	*trehz*-ee-em
fourteenth	quatorzième	kah-*torz*-ee-em
twentieth	vingtième	*vehnt*-ee-em
thirtieth	trentième	*trahnt*-ee-em
one-hundredth	centième	*sant*-ee-em

The Calendar

January	janvier	jhan-vee-*ay*
February	février	feh-vree-*ay*
March	mars	marce
April	avril	a-*vreel*
May	mai	meh
June	juin	jhwehn

July	juillet	jhwee-*ay*
August	août	oot
September	septembre	sep-*tahm*-bruh
October	octobre	awk-*toe*-bruh
November	novembre	no-*vahm*-bruh
December	decembre	day-*sahm*-bruh
Sunday	dimanche	dee-*mahnsh*
Monday	lundi	luhn-*dee*
Tuesday	mardi	mahr-*dee*
Wednesday	mercredi	mair-kruh-*dee*
Thursday	jeudi	jheu-*dee*
Friday	vendredi	vawn-druh-*dee*
Saturday	samedi	sahm-*dee*
Yesterday	hier	ee-*air*
Today	aujourd'hui	o-jhord-*dwee*
This morning/this afternoon	ce matin/cet après-midi	suh ma-*tan*/ set ah-preh mee-*dee*
Tonight	ce soir	suh *swahr*
Tomorrow	demain	de-*man*

Index

See also separate Accommodations, Restaurant, and Cafe indexes, below.

GENERAL INDEX

RESTAURANTS

WHEREVER YOU TRAVEL, *H*ELP IS NEVER FAR AWAY.

From planning your trip to providing travel assistance along the way, American Express® Travel Service Offices are always there to help you do more.

Paris

American Express Bureau de Change
14 Bd. de la Madeleine
1/53 30 50 94

American Express Bureau de Change
26 Avenue de L'Opéra
1/53 29 40 39

American Express TFS Bureau de Change
5 rue St. Eleuthère
1/42 23 93 52

American Express Travel Service
11 rue Scribe
1/47 77 77 07

Travel

http://www.americanexpress.com/travel

American Express Travel Service Offices are found in central locations throughout France.